HALLUCINATIONS

HALLUCINATIONS

BEHAVIOR, EXPERIENCE, AND THEORY

EDITED BY
R.K. Siegel and L.J. West
University of California, Los Angeles

A WILEY BIOMEDICAL PUBLICATION
WITH 21 COLOR ILLUSTRATIONS

JOHN WILEY & SONS, New York • London • Sydney • Toronto

Library of Congress Cataloging in Publication Data:
  Main entry under title:

  Hallucinations: behavior, experience, and theory.

    (A Wiley biomedical publication)
    Includes bibliographies and index.
    1. Hallucinations and illusions.   I. Siegel,
Ronald K.   II. West, Louis Jolyon. [DNLM: 1. Halluci-
nations. WM200 H193]
RC534.H34   153.7'4   75-12670
ISBN 0-471-79096-6

AUTHORS

Roland Fischer, Ph.D. Research Coordinator, Maryland Psychiatric Research Center, Baltimore; Lecturer, The Johns Hopkins University School of Medicine, Department of Psychiatry and Behavioral Sciences, Baltimore; Associate Professor of Pharmacology, The Ohio State University, College of Medicine, Department of Pharmacology, Columbus; Clinical Professor of Psychiatry, Georgetown University Medical School, Washington, D.C.; on the teaching staff of the Washington School of Psychiatry.

Ernest Hartmann, M.D. Director, Sleep and Dream Laboratory, Boston State Hospital; Associate Professor of Psychiatry, Tufts University School of Medicine, Boston; Medical Director, Sleep Research Foundation, Boston.

Mardi J. Horowitz, M.D. Associate Professor of Psychiatry, University of California, San Francisco; Faculty, San Francisco Psychoanalytic Institute.

Murray E. Jarvik, M.D., Ph.D. Professor of Psychiatry and Pharmacology, University of California, Los Angeles; Chief, Psychopharmacology Research Unit, Brentwood Veterans Administration Hospital.

Joseph B. Juhasz, Ph.D. Visiting Assistant Professor of Psychology, University of California, Santa Cruz; Assistant Professor of Psychology, Bucknell University, Philadelphia.

Weston La Barre, Ph.D. James B. Duke Professor of Anthropology, Duke University, Durham, North Carolina.

Theodore R. Sarbin, Ph.D. Professor of Psychology and Criminology, University of California, Santa Cruz.

C. Wade Savage, Ph.D. Associate Professor of Philosophy, Department of Philosophy, Minnesota Center for Philosophy of Science, University of Minnesota, Minneapolis.

Ronald K. Siegel, Ph.D. Assistant Research Psychologist, Department of Psychiatry, University of California, Los Angeles; Lecturer, Department of Psychology, University of California, Los Angeles. (Present address: Department of Pharmacology, University of California, Los Angeles.)

Louis Jolyon West, M.D. Professor and Chairman of Psychiatry, The Neuropsychiatric Institute, University of California, Los Angeles.

Wallace D. Winters, M.D., Ph.D. Professor of Pharmacology and Family Practice, University of California, San Diego.

ARTISTS

David Sheridan.   Dave Sheridan was born in Cleveland in 1943 and studied at the Cleveland Institute of Art. In 1972–1973 he served as art director for the *Rip-Off Review of Western Culture*. His cartoons and graphic illustrations have appeared in several national magazines, including *Ramparts* and *Playboy*. Among the many "underground" comic book titles to his credit are the *Mother's Oats* series, which has received widespread critical acclaim for illustrations of hallucinations and altered states of consciousness. Sheridan lives in Fairfax, California, where his company, The Overland Vegetable Stagecoach, is now producing animated films.

Yando (Hildebrando de Rios).   Yando was born in the Peruvian Amazonian city of Pucallpa in 1940. He studied at the National School of Fine Arts in Lima from 1962–1965. In 1966 he executed murals in Pucallpa. Now a resident of California, Yando has shown widely in Peru. As a consultant for the Smithsonian Institution in 1970, while preparing for an exhibit on man's use of drugs, he was commissioned by the Smithsonian to do a mural on altered states of consciousness. The Lang Art Gallery of Scripps College in Claremont, California, hosted a one-man show in 1971. Since 1973 Yando has taught art at Pitzer College of the Claremont Colleges.

In the infancy of a science generalizations are rarely true beyond narrow and too often undefined limits. The important contributions to psychology are not the classifications which confuse the issues, the explanations which overlook the problems, and the neologisms which disguise our ignorance but the tracing of relations through the intricate web of dependent processes which is mind. Always the question, How? punctures the bubble of theory, and the answer is to be sought in analysis and ever more analysis.

K. S. LASHLEY, 1933

PREFACE

When I began my career in psychiatry as a resident at Payne Whitney Clinic of the New York Hospital 25 years ago, it was with a great sense of adventure. Psychiatry was a specialty just beginning to fulfill its enormous potentialities. The information explosion in both biomedical and behavioral sciences had begun; the magnitude of that explosion, although beyond comprehension, could already be felt in a young scholar's bones. Surely numerous mysteries of human nature, of sanity and madness, of prevention and cure, would shortly yield to the onslaughts of modern science and ultramodern technology! Alas, many mysteries have not yet yielded; but after all, the joy lies in the search. *Felix qui potuit rerum cognoscere causas.*

As an eager novice, reading the history of medicine with an academic career in mind, I thought it would be good to devise a master plan for my own research. The early formulation of a long-range strategy might define a line of inquiry that could, with luck, prove fruitful for a lifetime. But what should such a strategy encompass in 1949? And what would serve as its model?

It seemed to me then that psychiatry could profit by following the example provided by the field of infectious disease, which to my mind was the aspect of medicine that had made the most dramatic progress in the previous 100 years. What was it that underlay such a fabulous eruption of new knowledge? Microscopy, microbiology, immunology, epidemiology, to be sure. But there had been strategy behind the great modern thrust of this work. There had been Robert Koch's famous postulates. There had been the grand design of experimental pathology from Louis Pasteur to René Dubos.

What we needed for a great leap forward in psychiatry was the development of an experimental psychopathology.

Of course by then other scientists had clearly seen the necessity for experimental work on animal models of abnormal behavior. Jules Masserman was already publishing important studies of experimentally induced maladaptive states (e.g., the production of "alcoholism" and self-mutilitating behavior in cats). His work seemed to follow naturally from the earlier research of such pioneers as I. P. Pavlov and Howard Lidell, and it blended into the subsequent experimental production of disturbed animal behavior by major investigators like Harry Harlow, Neal Miller, Kurt Richter, and Joseph V. Brady. When I shared my early notions with a senior visionary, Lawrence S. Kubie, he greatly flattered me by publishing a formal call for the utilization of a set of "Koch's postulates" for research in psychiatry. In fact, with the rise of modern psychopharmacology and behavioral biochemistry, something very much like Koch's postulates is now in common use in biobehavioral research, as reflected by the publications of psychiatrist-scientists George Aghajanian, Arnold Friedhoff, Solomon Snyder, and a number of others.

But the extrapolation of results obtained from research on animals—even nonhuman primates—to man is much more difficult to make in the field of psychiatry than in the field of infectious disease. Does an animal have a "psyche" or even a "personality"? A *human* experimental psychopathology was what I had in mind. This would not be easy to develop—even as a beginner I knew that; subsequent experience has confirmed the knowledge. However, in retrospect I do not at all regret the model that I chose for this purpose 25 years ago: the hallucinatory experience in the human subject.

Consider the benefits of studying hallucinations in human experimental psychopathology back in 1949. There was a century of fascinating literature to review, starting with the great French clinical investigators of the 1840s and progressing through various German, Viennese, and English contributions, right up to the elegant and inspiring writings of the (then) contemporary Heinrich Klüver. To read the literature on hallucinations was—and in truth remains—to gain great insight into the evolution of modern psychiatry.

Furthermore, the hallucination provided a peculiarly human model. Hallucinations in other animals, if they occur, are very difficult to ascertain and evaluate. But many important human experiences (such as the dreams and visions of biblical prophets and the creative imagery of great artists) are not only related to hallucinations, but also deeply bound into the history and cultural experience of mankind.

Moreover, although not all psychotic persons hallucinate, and hallucinations are not necessarily pathognomonic of mental illness, even a first-year resident in 1949 knew that there was a well-established association between certain types of hallucinosis and psychiatric disease. At the same time, there were the much-studied (at least by psychoanalysts, for content) normal hallucinations called dreams.

What remained was to define more precisely the pathogenesis and psychophysiology of those hallucinations which are symptomatic of mental illness, and to compare these with the genesis and psychophysiology of dreams, (which in 1949 had scarcely been investigated from that point of view). Simultaneously, in the tradition of Koch, one could proceed to generate hallucinations (or waking dreams) in normal subjects under laboratory conditions or at least in an experimental context.

As I first began to think along these lines, the two most studied experimental hallucinatory maneuvers were hypnosis and the administration of hallucinatory drugs (especially mescaline). However, during the 1950s there occurred an extraordinary flowering of important new work highly relevant to hallucinations and related phenomena.

Nathaniel Kleitman and his students—particularly William Dement —developed new and powerful methods to study and measure dreaming (REM sleep). Different sleep-related studies (by myself, Harold Williams, and others) documented the way in which prolonged sleep *deprivation* produced hallucinatory experiences. Donald Hebb and his followers were able to produce hallucinations by reducing and depatterning environmental stimuli; thus sensory isolation (or sensory deprivation) studies began. Meanwhile, J. G. Miller was producing some similar effects by *increasing* stimuli from the environment, a maneuver sometimes called information input overload or sensory bombardment.

Also during the 1950s there was a tremendous increase of interest in hallucinogenic chemicals, sparked by the fascinating phenomenology of LSD. Simultaneously, advances in clinical neurophysiology led to great refinements in neurological surgery, permitting considerable progress in cortical stimulation studies (including those inducing hallucinations in predisposed epileptics) of awake and communicating human subjects.

The excitement of my first decade in psychiatry, with its enormous significance for research on hallucinations, stimulated me to organize a conference on the subject sponsored jointly by the American Psychiatric Association's Committee on Research and by the American Association for the Advancement of Science. This event took place in December 1958. A volume containing its substance appeared after some delay.* The topic continued to attract much new interest and attention, which has continued up to the present time. A second symposium, sponsored by the Eastern Psychiatric Research Association in November 1969, was published less than five years ago.†

The present volume differs from its two recent predecessors in several respects. It does not undertake to pull together a century of progress in the field and somehow integrate it into a meaningful whole, as I tried to do in 1958. Nor does it attempt to offer a comprehensive cross section of one decade's progress in research on hallucinations, as Keup defined his intention in 1969.

Instead, this collection of essays represents current ideas about the *meaning* of recent findings, in the perspective both of the new knowledge itself (including some observations presented here for the first time) and of a reconsideration of what has gone before. The contributors were chosen for their long-standing interest and experience in the study of hallucinations, and for their special knowledge rather than for their availability to take part in a conference. Their theories and conclusions are highly individual. Yet each may shed new light on the others; it is the editors' hope that the whole will prove to be brighter than the sum of the parts.

The true progenitor and organizer of this book is Dr. Ronald K. Siegel, who personally solicited and reviewed each chapter and also provided the energy necessary to bring it to publication. Any credit deriving from its conceptual originality and editorial quality is his alone. Special thanks must be expressed to Dr. Barnett Addis for his masterful photography, to Mrs. Evelyn Stone who provided outstanding executive editorial assistance, and to Mrs. Marsha Addis for her superb help in preparing the manuscript.

LOUIS JOLYON WEST, M.D.

Los Angeles, California
February 1975

---

*West L. J. (Ed.), *Hallucinations*. New York: Grune & Stratton, 1962.
†Keup W. (Ed.), *Origin and mechanisms of hallucinations*. New York-London: Plenum Press, 1970.

ACKNOWLEDGMENTS

We thank the following for numerous helpful services: Evelyn Stone, for editorial assistance; Joan M. Brewster and Cheryll A. Johnson, for research assistance; Oscar Janiger, M.D., Stanley Krippner, Ph.D., and Thelma Moss, Ph.D., for illustrations; Barnett Addis, Ph.D., John A. Christner, Philip Condit, and Bruno Nardizzi, for photography; Florence Comes, for assistance in preparing the index; Barbara Cookler and Sarah Richland, for proofreading; and Ruth Marx for typing. We are indebted to the following for advice and criticism given at various stages in the development of this book: Carlos Castaneda, Ph.D.; William C. Dement, M.D., Ph.D.; Marlene Dobkin de Rios, Ph.D.; Peter Furst, Ph.D.; Donald O. Hebb, Ph.D.; Reese Jones, M.D.; John G. Kennedy, Ph.D.; Heinrich Klüver; Susan Price; C. Wade Savage, Ph.D.; Samuel I. Stone, Ph.D.; Seymour Weingarten; and Wallace D. Winters, M.D., Ph.D.

We also thank Drs. Sarbin and Juhasz for permission to use part of a larger manuscript entitled "The Social Psychology of Hallucinations" being prepared for a forthcoming book on the psychology of imagination. (The larger manuscript, which will include sections on lexicographic definitions of hallucinations and case examples, is available from the authors.)

R.K.S.

CONTENTS

Introduction   Ronald K. Siegel   1

**1 Anthropological Perspectives on Hallucination and
Hallucinogens**   9

Weston La Barre

2 The Continuum of CNS Excitatory States and Hallucinosis   53

Wallace D. Winters

**3 Dreams and Other Hallucinations:
An Approach to the Underlying Mechanism**   71

Ernest Hartmann

4 Drug-Induced Hallucinations in Animals and Man   81

Ronald K. Siegel and Murray E. Jarvik

5 Hallucinations: An Information-Processing Approach   163

Mardi J. Horowitz

6 Cartography of Inner Space   197

Roland Fischer

7 The Social Context of Hallucinations   241

Theodore R. Sarbin and Joseph B. Juhasz

8 The Continuity of Perceptual and Cognitive Experiences   257

C. Wade Savage

**9 A Clinical and Theoretical Overview of Hallucinatory
Phenomena**   287

Louis Jolyon West

Index   313

INTRODUCTION

RONALD K. SIEGEL, Ph.D.

Man's study of hallucination has been both plagued and blessed by the phenomena of perception. Perception is that process which enables man to acquire information about his environments. While perception limits man's knowledge to information obtained from the sensory modalities such as vision and audition, it challenges him to utilize other processes such as thinking and problem-solving to increase the scope and accuracy of his sensory apparatus. Man has risen admirably to the challenge with the wheel, the microscope, the telescope, the stethoscope, the submarine, and the spaceship. He has juxtaposed his sensory apparatus with his environments and has refined his tools for measuring stimulus events. He has evolved an objective science for drawing valid inferences from such information.

Through such measurements and inferences man is able to construct a map of his physical environment, including his own body. When the map is accurate, perception is considered normal and veridical. When the map is inaccurate, preception may be false, as in the case of a visual illusion. True and false perceptions both involve objects that are really there or really not there. Psychologist William James characterized such perceptions by the presence of "objective reality." Conversely, James defined an hallucination as having no "objective reality"—simply a false perception having no objective stimulus but bearing various degrees of apparent objectivity. James cites the following illustrative account from a friend working late at night in his room:

About eleven o'clock, as I sat there buried in sines, cosines, tangents, cotangents, secants, and cosecants, I felt very distinctly upon my left shoulder a touch, and a slight shake, as if somebody had tried to attract my attention by other means and had failed. Without rising I turned my head, and there between me and the door stood my wife, dressed exactly as I last saw her, some five weeks before. As I turned she said: "It is a little Herman; he has come." Something more was said, but this is the only sentence I can recall. To make sure that I was not asleep and dreaming, I rose from the chair, pinched myself and walked toward the figure, which disappeared immediately as I rose. I can give no information as to the length of time occupied by this episode, but I know I was awake, in my usual good health. The touch was very distinct, the figure was absolutely perfect, stood about three feet from the door, which was closed, and had not been opened during the evening. The sound of the voice was unmistakable, and I should have recognized it as my wife's voice even if I had not turned and had not seen the figure at all. The tone was conversational, just as if she would have said the same words had she been actually standing there (James, 1890, p. 119).

Throughout the ages philosophers have enjoyed a running commentary on such experiences. When man's perception focuses on physical objects such as the open door in the case just given, there is little disagreement over the character of the entity perceived. The descriptions of such perceptions can be communicated and shared by several observers. They can be subjected to the processes of consensual validation, and the validity of "public events" or the external world can thus be established. In a manner of speaking, one's perceptions can be "seen" by another. But in a strictly logical sense, one cannot dream another's dreams, have another's twinges, or see another's images (cf. Ryle, 1949, p. 199). Indeed, as scientist-philosopher Sir John Eccles notes, such observations of the so-called objective world depend

on an experience which is just as private as the so-called subjective experiences. The public status of an observation is given by symbolic communication between observers in particular through the medium of language. By means of this same method of communication, our inner or subjective experiences can likewise achieve a public status (Eccles, 1970, p. 53).

Thus when man's perception focuses on more private events, such as the husband's perception of his wife's disappearing image, our initial discomfort and confusion over what is meant is itself illusory. When we describe that mental image or hallucination, we are not describing our perception or even observing the operation of the mind in the perceiving process. Rather, we are describing the object—the hallucination per se—that is perceived. From the descriptions one may then draw inferences about the nature of the perceptual process. In this sense, the description of a private event such as an hallucination is a valid and legitimate unit for objective scientific study.

Man's study of hallucinations is highly dependent on the words, pictures, and other symbols used in description. Many symbols have sensory qualities and describe properties such as sights, sounds, tastes, and smells. Long-distance truck drivers, driving alone on monotonous highways, often experience visions of "cars" that are not there or "jackrabbits big enough to step over their cars" (Hebb, 1969). Amputees frequently report feeling a "phantom limb" immediately following amputation of an arm, leg, or breast:

The phantom limb is usually described as having a tingling feeling and a definite shape that resembles the real limb before amputation. It is reported to move through space in much the same way as the normal limb would move when the person walks, sits down, or stretches out on a bed (Melzack, 1973, p. 50).

Terminal patients often experience unbidden memory images of long-forgotten childhood events. These hallucinatory images arise with such startling vividness that they often prompt the patient to react by speaking with the image or moving toward it (cf. Maudsley, 1939). Some children have imaginary playmates or companions that are as vivid and real to them as real playmates would be, complete with visual and auditory properties (Harvey, 1918).

Maudsley (1939) described such hallucinations as "mental representation so intense as to become mental presentation" (p. 98) and equated this ability to that of certain artists—William Blake, for example. Indeed, in style, content, and intention, many artists are unmistakably concerned with the sensory qualities of hallucinatory experiences, particularly hallucinogen-induced hallucinations (Masters and Houston, 1968). Many artists—like Sheridan and Yando, whose works are presented in this volume—attempt to portray these elements.

Man's descriptions of hallucinations have also used symbols with affective and evaluative qualities. Ancient man regarded hallucinations as having "supernatural" significance and believed that some deity or demon was at work in them. The vivid visions and voices that often accompany epileptic seizures were once thought to be so mysterious that the sufferer believed "he really saw or heard an angel from heaven, or had a visit from the Holy Ghost, or was carried up into heaven or down into hell" (Maudsley, 1939, p. 89). Man's inevitable ecological encounters with plant hallucinogens gave rise to other descriptions based on religious, magical, and superstitious thinking. The periodic outbreaks of ergotism during the Middle Ages, and even in this century, were commonly thought to be "supernatural" happenings and were described as "Saint Anthony's Fire." The Huichol Indians of Mexico describe their peyote-induced hallucinations as communications with their gods, and they interpret the visions as a totally separate and valid reality (Benzi, 1972). Man's cultures have employed a multitude of terms to describe these hallucinatory phenomena. As Weston La Barre points out in his chapter on anthropological perspectives, the etymology of such terms is itself an exercise in cross-cultural ideology. Whether dream, vision, trance, REM state, sensory deprivation, or hysteric possession, La Barre believes that there is no "supernatural" psychic event in tribal life that cannot be better understood as a dissociated state or an hallucinatory activity of the brain. His scholarly study of the effects of hallucinogens in their ethnographic contexts reveals that only the comparative cultural contexts differ, not the processes themselves. He argues that the hallucinatory processes are not "supernatural"; rather, they are psychodynamic states related to animistic superstitions.

Traditionally, man has held a tacit belief that these hallucinatory processes are initiated by nervous excitement, since hallucinations are conspicuous in descriptions of epileptic convulsions, fever delirium, hunger and thirst, intense cold, monotonous stimulation, severe pain, and drug intoxications. In 1918 Harvey hypothesized that hallucinations, like imaginary playmates, are sensory "ideas" that become as vivid as real percepts when accompanied by stimulation or excitation:

It is accompanied by a centrally initiated impulse, that is, one which starts in the eye, or the ear, as a percept would be. The centrally initiated impulse that accompanies the experience of the imaginary playmate, traverses the same brain centers that would be traversed by the peripherally initiated impulse, if it were a real child, or other object that is seen. The principal distinction between the idea which is projected as the imaginary playmate, and other ideas, is found in the unusual strength of the centrally initiated impulse which accompanies the process (p. 23).

Harvey believed that any condition that induced an unusual strength of a centrally initiated impulse in the brain was likely to be favorable to hallucinations. Accordingly, he argued that children generate a great amount of nervous energy and consequently are more susceptible to phenomena such as imaginary playmates. Although the latter notion is only speculative, it is known that the ability to form eidetic imagery decreases with age and that hallucinatory phenomena like "night terrors" and hypnagogic imagery are frequent in childhood (Egdell and Kolvin, 1972).

Similarly, Moreau (1845) believed that hallucinations resulted from cerebral excitement that enabled imaginary thoughts and memories to become transformed into sensory impressions. Based on phenomenological observations, Moreau proposed the classic argument that hallucinations of hashish and mental illness were essentially the same and were derived from underlying excitation. In the present volume, Wallace Winters presents supporting evidence that the disorganization of sensory systems and the perceptual abnormalities in hallucinosis result from states of hyperexcitation. On the basis of several neurophysiological studies with various pharmacological agents, he demonstrates a continuum of central nervous system excitation coupled with characteristic changes in EEG and behavioral patterns. In the cat, agents such as LSD, mescaline, and nitrous oxide induce desynchronization and then hypersynchrony, which is associated with the bizarre postures and inappropriate behaviors labeled "hallucinatory." As the excitation continues and induces a functional disorganization of the reticular formation modulating system, an augmentation of sensory information occurs, and there are multisensory aberrations, manifested in man by sensory distortions.

The possibility of another continuum, one between hallucinations and dream states, has been suggested both by phenomenological and experimental studies. Hallucinations have often been described and defined as waking dreams. Moreau (1845) believed that hallucinations were so similar to dream states ("one dreams while awake") that he preferred the term "hallucinatory state." Consider his description of that state as induced by hashish:

Gradually, under the influence of hashish, the psychic factor I have just indicated [excitement] grows; a profound change takes place in the thinking process. Outside of one's awareness and in spite of all efforts to remain aware, there occurs a state of dream, but of sleepless dream, where sleep and the waking state are mingled and confused. The clearest, most alert consciousness cannot distinguish between these two states, nor between the mental operations that characterize either one (Moreau, 1845, p. 19).

The similarity between dreams and hashish hallucinations was also stressed by Ludlow (1857), who made the critical observation that his sleep was completely dreamless during periods of chronic hashish intoxication. Since his sleep was normally rich with dreams, Ludlow concluded that "the visions of the drug entirely supplanted those of nature." Interestingly, there has been some recent evidence that marihuana suppresses REM (dream) sleep and withdrawal after chronic usage results in a moderate REM rebound (Kales et al., 1971).

The visions induced by other drugs have also been referred to as dreams. The opium visions of De Quincey, Poe, Crabbe, Coleridge, Thompson, and others provide many examples of the similarity of dreams and hallucinations (cf. Harper, 1970). Indeed, De Quincey (1856) himself thought that opium facilitated and intensified the dreaming faculty and that such dreams crystallized memories and feelings into "involutes" or symbolic patterns:

. . . a sympathy seemed to arise between the waking and the dreaming states of the brain in one point—that whatsoever I happened to call up and to trace by a voluntary act upon the darkness was very apt to transfer itself to my dreams . . . so whatsoever things capable of being visually represented I did but think of in the darkness, immediately shaped themselves into phantoms for the eye; and, by a process apparently no less inevitable, when thus once traced in faint and visionary colours, like writings in sympathetic ink, they were drawn out by the fierce chemistry of my dreams, into insufferable splendour that fretted my heart. . . . Buildings, landscapes, etc., were exhibited in proportions so vast as the bodily eye is not fitted to receive. Space swelled, and was amplified to an extent of unutterable and self-repeating infinity. . . . The minutest incidents of childhood, or forgotten scenes of later years, were often revived. . . . I recognized them instantaeously. . . . I feel assured, that there is no such thing as ultimate forgetting; traces once impressed upon the memory are indestructible . . . (pp. 233–235).

The hallucinations in alcohol withdrawal share a similar relationship with dreams. The Iroquois Indians, who used alcohol to stimulate dreaming as part of their "vision quest," regarded the intoxicated state as indistinguishable from the dream state. Recently investigators have suggested that alcohol induces REM suppression followed by a REM rebound and intrusion into the waking state. This phenomenon could be expressed behaviorally as waking dreams or hallucinosis. Wolin and Mello (1972) have postulated the existence of a continuum that extends during alcohol withdrawal from dreams, through frightening hypnagogic phenomena, and finally progresses to hallucinosis.

If dreams and hallucinations do indeed lie on a continuum, what prevents us from hallucinating (or dreaming) during waking states? Ernest Hartmann approaches this question from the point of view that an inhibitory factor, present in normal waking mental activity, is removed, thus allowing for the emergence of hallucinations and dreams. This factor is psychologically related to functions of "reality testing" and physiologically mediated by ascending norepinephrine systems to the cortex.

Once this continuum is activated, either by central nervous system excitation or disinhibition, certain responses emerge. The phenomenology of these responses is illustrated by Siegel and Jarvik in their chapter on drug-induced hallucinations. The authors adopt a neo-behaviorist view that hallucinations are stimulus events of which organisms become aware and to which they subsequently respond. But we can never really know what another organism perceives (although Von Uexküll made a classic and daring attempt in 1908 to draw pictures through a fly's eye). Therefore, the extent to which such responses support the notion of animals (including man) having hallucinations depends on what one is willing to infer about the behavior. Based on an extensive review of observations and studies on the reactions of infrahuman species to drugs that produce reports of hallucinations in man, Siegel and Jarvik conclude that some animals do indeed hallucinate. They then present a series of human experiments designed as an objective and quantitative approach to hallucinations, which they find are characterized by imagery constants.

Mardi Horowitz extends these findings in his chapter, which describes this continuum in terms of an information-processing model. The author views the prototypic hallucination as a nonvolitional and intense image of internal origin that is erroneously regarded as a perception by the observer. He discusses each property and determinant of the hallucinatory experience in terms of an image system of representation that derives input from internal and external sources of information. Evidence from experimental studies of perception and imagining, as well as clinical observations of illusion and hallucination, are offered to support the argument that hallucinations are a final common pathway entered because of various determinants in the information-processing system.

Experiences along this continuum are described in the chapter by cartographer Roland Fischer as a circular journey through perceptual, hallucinatory, and meditative states. Voyages on the continuum can be marked by noradrenergic hyperarousal, serotonergic hypoarousal, a shift of information processing to the right or nondominant hemisphere, an increase in interoceptive imagery, a decrease in willed motor activity, and a decrease in the variability of the EEG amplitude. According to Fischer, man interprets these activities as normal, creative, hyperphrenic, ecstatic, mystical, or meditative experiences.

But the interpretation of these voyages by someone other than the experiencer is often influenced by the social context in which the events occur. For example, in modern Western psychiatric diagnosis the reports of experiences along the continuum are generally considered to be discrete and discontinuous states:

The notion of the discreteness of these symptoms encourages the conception of psychosis and schizophrenia as states that are also discrete and discontinuous and the further conception that patients with these diagnoses are somehow different from other people (Strauss, 1969, p. 581).

Since "symptoms" such as hallucinations are key diagnostic criteria of the psychoses, especially schizophrenia, Strauss (1969) emphasizes the importance of evaluating and interpreting them as points on continua of perceptual and ideational functions. In their chapter, Sarbin and Juhasz discuss the social psychology of this type of evaluation and interpretation. They note that the term "hallucination" as traditionally defined and employed by Western psychiatry represents a role relation in which one actor reports imaginings and another actor declares an evaluation on the report. The evaluation can be positive or negative depending on the status of the imaginer, and the authors argue that the usual psychiatric application of hallucination is pejorative.

Man's introspective reports of his voyages along the continuum suggest that the experiences are capable of evolving one into the other. Examing such reports from a philosophical perspective, C. Wade Savage proposes that sensations, perceptions, hallucinations, dreams, fantasies, and thoughts are not sharply distinguishable from one another. He argues that hallucinations may appear to be similar to perceptions, but the criteria of vivacity, coherence, voluntariness, concreteness, veridicality, and causality do not divide up the continuum of experiences into separable stages. Savage goes on to offer a criticism of empiricist theories of hallucinations and to suggest that any general theory of hallucinations must also be a general theory of cognition.

In the concluding chapter, L. Jolyon West summarizes some of the preceding material in the book and attempts to formulate a comprehensive theory of hallucinations. He argues that fantasies, illusions, visions, dreams, and hallucinations occur when percepts or memory traces are released from within the brain. Under normal waking conditions, there is a sufficient amount and variety of sensory input to inhibit the emergence of this stored material. When effective sensory input decreases below a critical point, these previously recorded perceptions may be released into awareness. The greater the arousal of these perceptions, the more vivid the hallucinations.

Taken together, the chapters in this book view hallucinations as points on a continuum involving neurochemical, neurophysiological, behavioral, imaginal, experiential, and cognitive systems. But all of nature presents itself to man primarily as a continuum. In perceiving this continuum, man recognizes groups of phenomena that share many cohesive features, in contrast to other events displaying less stability and persistence of pattern. As Weiss (1969) points out, the "success of science over the ages has validated the abstraction involved in our dealing with such reasonably constant entities as if they had an autonomous existence of their own" (p. 32). Hallucination is such an abstraction, and its continua of behavior, experience, and theory are the subject of this book.

REFERENCES

Benzi, M. *Les derniers adorateurs du peyotl*. Paris: Gallimard, 1972.

De Quincey, T. (1856) *The confessions of an English opium-eater*. New York: Dutton, 1967.

Eccles, J. *Facing reality*. New York: Springer-Verlag, 1970.

Egdell, H. G., and Kolvin, I. Childhood hallucinations. *Journal of Child Psychology and Psychiatry and Allied Disciplines*, 1972, **13**, 279–287.

Harvey, N. A. *Imaginary playmates and other mental phenomena of children*. Ypsilanti, Mich.: State Normal College, 1918.

Hayer, A. *Opium and the romantic imagination*. Berkeley: University of California Press, 1970.

Hebb, D. O. The mind's eye. *Psychology Today*, 1969, **2**, 55–57, 67–68.

James, W. *The principles of psychology*, Vol. 1. New York: Henry Holt, 1890.

Kales, A., Hanley, J., Rickles, W., Kanas, N., Baker, M., and Goring, P. Effects of marijuana administration and withdrawal in chronic users and naïve subjects. Paper presented at the First International Congress of the Association for the Psychophysiological Study of Sleep, Bruges, Belgium, June 1971.

Ludlow, F. *The hasheesh eater*. New York: Harper and Brothers, 1857.

Masters, R. E. L., and Houston, J. *Psychedelic art*. New York: Grove Press, 1968.

Maudsley, H. *Natural causes and supernatural seemings*. London: Watts & Co., 1939.

Melzack, R. *The puzzle of pain*. Ringwood, Australia: Penguin, 1973.

Moreau (de Tours), J. J. (1845) *Hashish and mental illness*. New York: Raven Press, 1973.

Ryle, G. *The concept of mind*. London: Hutchinson, 1949.

Strauss, J. S. Hallucinations and delusions as points on continua function. *Archives of General Psychiatry*, 1969, **21**, 581–586.

v. Uexküll J. Die Libellen. In C. Voit (Ed.), *Zeitschrift für Biologie*. Munich: Druck und Verlag von P. Oldenbourg, 1908.

Weiss, P. A. The living system: Determinism stratified. In A. Koestler and J. R. Symthies (Eds.), *Beyond reductionism*. Boston: Beacon Press, 1969.

Wolin, S. J., and Mello, N. K. The dream hallucinations continuum: Behavioral and EEG data. Paper presented at the 10th Annual Meeting of the American College of Neuropsychopharmacology, Las Vegas, January 18–21, 1972.

ANTHROPOLOGICAL PERSPECTIVES ON HALLUCINATION AND HALLUCINOGENS

WESTON LA BARRE, Ph.D.

IDENTIFICATION AND DEFINITION OF DATA

Because of great cultural variety in concepts and social contexts regarding certain mental states which, moreover, are easily confused with one another, it is important to delimit the phenomena we seek to discuss. The etymology of terms, it is presently seen, is already an exercise in cross-cultural ideology.

"Illusion" is a false mental appearance made by some actual external cause acting on the senses but capable of conceptual correction. Thus mistaking a tree in the dark for a man is an illusion, of which the subject may be disabused by various forms of reality testing; emphasis is on the ready correctability of an illusion. "Delusion" is a fixed false concept occasioned by external stimuli; but these stimuli are so consistently misconstrued that delusion remains largely insusceptible to correction. Thus a strongly held belief that one's food is "poisoned," based on some imagined taste or appearance, is a delusion. Both illusion and delusion are based on the Latin *ludere*, "to play." Illusion implies the innocent subjective misinterpretation and exists only in the form of a noun state. But to delude, as a transitive verb, means sometimes intentionally to befool the mind or judgment, to make sport of, beguile, or mislead. "Delusion" falls easily into a demonological view of causality, as of some ill-intentioned external *anima* or spirit actively deceiving the subject—a view rejected by modern psychology, which sees the subject "projecting" demons as a way of disclaiming psychic responsibility for his own thought productions. In this sense one is always self-deluded. Illusion and delusion vary along a vector of increasing psychological intensity, subjective needfulness, and relative incorrectability. These features are dynamically important, both psychiatrically and cross-culturally.

"Hallucination" derives from the Latin deponent or half-passive verb *alucinari*, "to wander in mind"—again dependent on archaic animistic notions to which modern psychology does not subscribe. In careful present-day usage, hallucination indicates a false appearance, in sensory form, hence seemingly external, but occasioned by an internal condition of the mind, the central suggestion of the term being its subjectivity and groundlessness. Hallucinations can occur in any sensory modality, whether visual, auditory, olfactory, gustatory, tactile, or kinesthetic, and they may sometimes be synesthetic—that is, input in one sensory modality is perceived in terms of another, as when a peyotist hears the sun come up with a roar, or when ritual drumming lifts the hearer up into the air. Since all men are accustomed to believe their senses, it is the *sensory* form of its presentation that gives hallucination its psychic conviction.

Two other terms must be examined before we travel cross-culturally: possession and trance. "Possession" implies the now wholly inadmissible demonological notion that the body in such a state is possessed or held by an invading alien spirit. "Trance" derives from Latin *transitus*, "a passage," in turn from *transire*, "to pass over," namely, to go into another psychic state, to swoon half-dead, to undergo rapture (being taken away) or ecstasy (the soul's standing outside the body). The word again is entangled with false animistic notions now discarded, but in medicine "trance" is still used to designate a cataleptic or hypnotic state of partial consciousness and high suggestibility.

These etymologies already descry comparative ethnography along a time line within a Western tradition. But to use any of these terms uncritically is to be victim of archaic thought categories. It is therefore scholastic fecklessness and confusion further to divide "possession" into supposed subtypes, as some students have done, when we no longer espouse the ideology of possession itself. The notion of an ec-static or body-separable soul (brainless mind or organismless life) that can wander in space and time has long since been banished from psychology, and all the supposed attributes of the soul can be better explained in terms of the sciences (La Barre, 1954, pp. 267–302; La Barre, 1972a, pp. 367–374).

Similarly, with such ethnographic complexes as shamanism, ancient and near-universal in the world, we should note that the only valid subdivisions of shaman (black and white, bird and reindeer) are those provided by natives themselves. To label shamans genuine or false is to foment bogus problems, since we do not accede to shamanistic suppositions themselves. For us properly to perceive diverse ethnographic phenomena all the way from Haitian *vodūn* to Amerindian vision quest requires conceptual clarity and awareness of our own cognitive maps. It is better to use our own experiment-derived terms to maintain self-critical control of theory and implication.

A few other terms that disclose ethnography may be examined. "Revelation" refers to a supposed human contact with a "supernatural" world, whether this contact is through trance, vision, possession, or whatever. In this sense of course all religions are "revealed," and all our alleged information about the supernatural is only the statements made about this realm by self-designated authorities: shamans and visionaries, prophets and priests, and other "seers." A "vision" is a seen hallucination, and since sight is the predominant sense in primates, both dreams and hallucinations are ordinarily visual. Prophecy is to "speak forth" with the voice of the god or spirit, whose "medium" or mere *porteparole* the inspired ("breathed into") enthusiast ("god-inside-belabored") may temporarily be. "Divination" makes statements of supposed fact in past, present, or future time through the aid of spirit-helpers. "Prognostication" is spirit-given "foreknowledge" of events or alleged precognition. "Clairvoyance" is to "see clearly" beyond the range in space and time of the workaday mind and eye. All these alleged phenomena can be subsumed under subsequent scientific description and, accepted as fantasies, can serve psychiatric understanding.

SCIENTIFIC CONSIDERATIONS

It is evident that any sound cross-cultural understanding has awaited the discernment of an authentic and verifiably cross-cultural phenomenon. This necessary psychological tool is afforded by new understanding of the dream. The dream is not only a pan-human psychic state (Lincoln, 1935; La Barre, 1958, p. 316, fn. 55; Eggan, 1949; Eggan, 1961, pp. 551–557); it occurs in all the warm-blooded mammals and birds so far investigated. We are far from a complete knowledge of the physiological and psychological functions of the dream. Nonetheless, present understanding of the dream profoundly illuminates a whole universe of human beliefs and social institutions; such understanding embraces both the revolutionary psychiatric insights of Freud and the new experimental psychology of REM states (Aserinsky and Kleitman, 1953; Dement, 1954; Fisher, 1956; Dement and Kleitman, 1957a, 1957b; Dement, 1960; Kleitman, 1961, 1963; Fisher and Dement, 1963; Dement and Fisher, 1963; Dement, 1965a, 1965b; Dement and Greenberg, 1966; Dement el al., 1966; Roffwarg et al., 1966; Hartmann, 1973).

As a first rough approximation, the human mind can be said to exist in two relatively distinct and differing states of being: wakefulness and sleep. The major difference between them is that the waking mind ordinarily has full access to sensory input, hence is adaptively environment-oriented. It is highly significant that in experimental "sensory deprivation" (Bexton et al., 1954; Lilly, 1956; Solomon, 1958; Vernon et al., 1958; Goldberger and Holt, 1958; Wexler et al., 1958; Cohen et al., 1959; Wheaton, 1959; Freedman and Greenblatt, 1960; Freedman et al., 1961; Silverman et al., 1961; Solomon et al., 1961; Solomon and Mendelson, 1962; Brownfield, 1965; Zubek, 1969)—as in a subject suspended in a tank of body-warm water as isolated and shielded from all sensory stimuli as possible, thus deprived of customary complex information from the outside world—the wakeful mind promptly begins to project its own contents onto the blank screen of consciousness. In a word, the individual hallucinates.

In ordinary sleep the mind is by some neural process normally cut off from sensory input. Mental activity continues in ordinary sleep, with a momentum still fairly realistic and matter of fact, although thoughts are somewhat apocopated and fragmentary. But in the REM state of "paradoxical sleep" there erupts an extraordinary discontinuity with the waking state and even with ordinary sleep. Objectively, and visibly to the observer, the sleeper displays a curious rapid eye movement (hence the acronym REM), a restless skittering of the eyeballs behind closed lids—as if, psychologically, a "seer" were seeing without sight. Subjectively, the sleeper "dreams," as can easily be ascertained by awakening him during the REM state. By EEG measurements and other psychophysical signs the brain is more furiously active in the REM state than it ever is when the subject is awake.

Paradoxical sleep is paradoxical indeed. In the REM state the mind seems to "be in business for itself"—and the outside real world takes the hindmost. Aristotle long ago observed that dreams lack the element of critical judgment *(to epikrīnon)*

(La Barre, 1972a, pp. 55–60). Deprived of edifying restraint and editing by environing reality, in this state too, as in simple sensory deprivation, the central nervous system hallucinates. REM sleep is a "spree of the id"—a freewheeling of the central nervous system in a kind of "primary process thinking" otherwise most visible in dereistic schizophrenic fantasy. Indeed, Kant suggested that "the lunatic is a wakeful dreamer," and Schopenhauer that "a dream is a short-lasting psychosis, and a psychosis is a long-lasting dream" (Moreau de Tours, 1845; Rosenzweig, 1959, pp. 326–329; Katan, 1960; Kleitman, 1963, p. 106; La Barre, 1972a, pp. 67–68; Fisher, in Kleitman, 1973, p. 50).

Subjects who are REM-deprived over protracted periods (by being awakened each time the eyes or EEGs indicate dreaming) appear to build up a proportionate need, which they indulge by prolonged dreaming, roughly proportionate to the amount of deprivation, at the next opportunity for sleep. It is as though waking thought produced some serotonin-like toxin or metabolic product that only REM activity could neutralize. In fact, the cerebrospinal fluid of a REM-deprived cat, when injected into another cat, produces abnormally high REM activity in the second animal. Ethanol tends to repress REM dreaming, thus giving rise to the provocative suggestion that delirium tremens in chronic alcoholics is an explosive return to hallucination out of deferred REM-need. Given at bedtime, d-amphetamine sulfate considerably reduces the amount of REM activity during sleep. Can the paranoid hallucinations of chronic "speed freaks" be owing to a similar frustrated REM-need? By contrast, LSD seems to exert a specifically stimulating effect on the REM mechanism (Dement, 1954, p. 587; Greenberg and Pearlman, 1964; Roffwarg et al., 1966, p. 614).

All these differential psychopharmacological facts should be carefully attended to, for their possible bearing on varied ethnographic behaviors. Mescaline and psilocybin both induce wakefulness but seem to provide either a simulacrum of REM or an hallucinatory REM substitute, for their use may be followed ultimately by a deep, dreamless sleep. The fomenting of REM or REM-like activity may account in part for the subjectively "therapeutic" effects of the use of these drugs, much as in intentionally induced "sleep therapy" in psychiatry. The residual gentle happiness that may last for weeks after psilocybin is clearly such a *psychological* phenomenon, for it persists long after any possible pharmacological effect or immediate euphoric action on the pleasure center of the brain. And some hallucinogens appear to release deep affectively toned memories, but these are for a more leisurely conscious contemplation of "inner space" than haphazard or unremembered dreams afford, since the effect that follows is the same as that which normally comes after refreshingly well-dreamt sleep. Of course the same release of "primary process" material that cannot be handled may cause severe upset or even psychosis of varying length in other individuals. In this context, the experimentally little-known *Amanita* intoxication appears first to produce a two-hour "sleep"—during which, however, the subject is conscious of every sensory occurrence; afterward he "awakens" to hallucinate actively for eight to ten hours.

Psilocybin, peyote, and perhaps other hallucinogens produce a curious double consciousness such that without diminishing the convincingness of an open-eyed visual hallucination, "another part of the mind" can be firmly aware that "I am hallucinating." The suggestion is that these drugs may differentially affect sensory and cognitive brain regions or brain functions. In some subjects, visual hallucinations promptly and regularly recur some minutes after ingestion of psilocybin, with auditory hallucinations being at their peak some two hours later, whereas tactile, kinesthetic, olfactory, or gustatory hallucinations occur only sporadically and in no discernible time sequence. Some subjects hallucinate realistic though distorted persons and scenery; others see only complex geometric patterns and forms. Still others report that they "never" have visual hallucinations under psilocybin, except for the "ec-static" seeing of their own bodies from outside.

Some hallucinogens produce specific response to sound, as to shamanic drumming and singing, which may have ethnographic relevance. Some, as noted later, evoke peculiarly red or yellow or "painted" hallucinations; others macropsia, and still others micropsia, which may affect the shaping of myths about giants or "little folk." Bufotenin (5-OH-dimethyltryptamine), an hallucinogen present in toadskins as well as in the Amazonian–Antillean narcotic snuff (Anadenanthera peregrina) and in some higher plants and animals, seems specifically to promote a feeling of flying through the air—a factor to be taken into account in reports of shamanistic "journeys" among Palaeo-Siberians, and in witches' flights in late medieval Europe. Any similar cross-cultural psychophysiological constants in the hallucinatory process (as opposed to symbolic content) will increase our confidence in inferences based on such psychic uniformitarianism.

Hallucinogens evidently produce pharmacodynamic variants of the normally occurring dream state. Several other phenomena give dimension to our understanding of REM states. Some individuals are afflicted with the curious ailment of narcolepsy, once thought to be merely overpowering attacks of daytime sleep but now regarded as persistent occurrences of specifically REM states; significantly, the eyeballs skitter in narcolepsy too. Again, experimenters have taped subjects' eyelids open and have demonstrated that REM dreaming can occur with the eyes wide open. The dreamer gives the uncanny impression of being wide awake, although judging from the EEGs he is undoubtedly asleep. Normal reverie (literally "dreaming") or ruminative woolgathering sometimes partake of this catatonic-schizophrenic quality of wideawake daydreaming. Clinical experience shows that a catatonic may be hallucinating at the very moment he is talking with another person. Again, a late-night reader may suddenly become aware that what he is reading is outrageously inapposite to what went before and indeed preposterous in itself. He finds that his eyes are closed: he has been dreaming.

Experiments in sensory deprivation demonstrate how very much waking sanity depends on constant wavelets of sensory experience lapping on the shore of consciousness, so to speak, defining the body image and conscious ego. Even the absence of one sensory modality, such as hearing, may induce pathology. A familiar instance is that of the deaf person; deprived of the chief means of social intercourse—language—the person who cannot hear commonly has mildly paranoid delusions. Again, a guilt-laden and self-preoccupied college student walking across the campus may have delusions of reference when other students, too far away for him to hear their speech, suddenly laugh. Both projective phenomena in deaf man and student are dynamically akin to the paranoiac's hallucination of hearing accusatory voices. The same phenomenon is evidently the case in primitives' hallucinations.

So important is language for social communication that occasionally clinics receive acute cases of psychotic "culture shock." A soldier has brought home an alien wife, perhaps to a small and isolated town where she has no culturally similar others, and after perhaps a very short time the alien wife has a psychotic episode, usually with depression and hallucinatory experiences of a mild to severe paranoid-persecutory nature. Cases of culture-shock suicide have even occurred in privileged diplomatic circles where no literal social deprivation exists. And self-perceptively honest anthropologists know the depressive-paranoid stage that comes early in fieldwork and is another form of culture shock: much of the self is socially mirrored and must be continuously reaffirmed (La Barre, 1972a, pp. 51–54).

Even the most hardened sociopath can become "stir crazy"—often from the social and indeed massive sensory deprivation in prolonged solitary confinement (Burney, 1952), sometimes in pitch dark; habits of compensatory hallucination may continue long after this cruel but not unusual punishment has ceased. The lonely child, deprived even of a dog, may invent a truly hallucinatory "imaginary companion" (Vostrovsky, 1895; Harvey, 1919; Hurlock and Burnstein, 1932; Svendsen, 1934). A sufficiently normal Admiral Byrd in the South Pole hut described in *Alone,* and other individuals isolated from people for long periods, especially in featureless landscapes, have had hallucinatory experiences of this nature. A famous case is that of Captain Joshua Slocum. This hardy man sailed around the world alone at the turn of the century and once in a North Atlantic gale hallucinated a bearded man taking the wheel as Slocum himself was forced below by sickness. At first Slocum thought the intruder was a pirate, but he later told Slocum he was the pilot of Columbus' *Pinta* and would return whenever needed. Despite the vividness and obviously reassuring function of the experience, the tough-minded captain knew it was an hallucination. An imaginary presence also haunted Sir Ernest Shackleton and his companions in the Antarctic. Stypulkowski, a Russian confined in Lubyanka Prison, experienced such hallucinations, as did Christiana Ritter during her long winter isolation, and Jan Baalsrud, a wounded Norwegian resistance fighter, who spent 27 days before rescue alone on a mountain plateau (Slocum, 1900; Shackleton, 1920, p. 209; Byrd, 1938; Gibson, 1954; Ritter, 1954; Lindemann, 1958, pp. 19, 128, 144, 152, 157–159, 161, 171; Solomon et al., 1961; La Barre, 1972a, pp. 53–54).

These well-attested hallucinatory experiences of psychiatrically normal men and women may be invoked for an understanding of similar phenomena among preliterate peoples. For example, prominent in both Americas and indeed among many Palaeo-Siberian tribes is the ancient supernatural "vision quest" (Benedict, 1922, 1923). Usually about the time of puberty, the individual goes alone to some remote place where he fasts and struggles to stay awake for four days and four nights. During this time he may receive an hallucinatory "vision" that gives him great medicine-power, embodied in his medicine bundle, collected on the same vigil. So important is this vision that it may give direction, normal or pathological, for the rest of his life (La Barre, 1938a, pp. 93–104; La Barre, 1972a, p. 140). The shamanic vision quest is so ubiquitous and ancient in Eurasia and the Americas that it is evidently of at least Mesolithic cultural horizons. It is suggested here that the intentionally sought supernatural vision is either a sensory-deprivation hallucination in a lonely place or a literal REM dream fomented by ritual sleeplessness.

Hallucination would appear to be implicated in such "ethnic psychoses" as *kayakangst, windigo,* and "Arctic hysteria." Kayakangst (Gussow, 1963; Taylor and Laughlin, 1963) comes to the hunter out alone in his kayak in the featureless sea; there is a trancelike lowering of consciousness from a kind of hypnotic fixing (?of foveal vision), along with curious kinesthetic shifts of body image and body ego. This disoriented and disorganizing experience can be deeply frightening, and panic ensues, together with acute phobic and conversion-hysteric symptoms. Kayakangst may be related to the "windigo psychosis" (Barnouw, 1955, pp. 73–75, 211–223, 341–355; Parker, 1960; Fogelson, 1965, pp. 74–99; Cooper, 1968, pp. 288–292; La Barre, 1972a, p. 66) that seizes lonely hunters in winter among high-latitude Algonquin Indians in the northern United States and Canada. Windigo is culturally stylized, for the hunter is believed to be possessed by the spirit of a cannibal giant whose bones are made of ice, and when the windigo-possessed hunter returns without game he attempts to bite chunks out of the flesh of his campmates. One thinks here of the initiate's possession by the Cannibal Spirit in the main winter dance of the Kwakiutl (Boas, 1897, pp. 436–462, 500–544; Benedict, 1934a, pp. 173–222); the ritually psychotic initiate must be lured back from the woods with corpse flesh, to be tamed into cannibal society membership. One wonders what tragic horrors of Hyperborean forced cannibalism may lie behind these violent ritual exorcisms. In Tungusic "olonism" in Siberia (Shirokogoroff, 1935; La Barre, 1972a, pp. 171–175), the brooding adolescent also runs off into the woods and becomes entangled in a bush or tree, whence he must be brought back and exorcised of his demonic spirit-hallucinations (and here again one thinks of Odin, bound on his shamanic initiate's ordeal-tree). In Tibetan *chöd* (Schnier, 1957), the candidate for shamanic vision goes to a wild and lonely spot, preferably to a place where violent death has occurred; in Malayan *mejapi* (literally "to hide onself"), flight to a lonely spot in the forest is also the pattern (Van der Kroef, 1962, pp. 80–121).

The motif of loneliness and social deprivation seems to be constant in these fantasies. Many Arab folktales tell of encounters with evil *jinn* in lonely places in the featureless desert; Jacob, when alone, seems to have wrestled with one of these Semitic demons at the ford of the Jabbok river. His experience seems to be similar to the phenomenon described by Hippocrates (Dodds, 1951, p. 117) of a man, traveling in a wild and lonely place, who was seized by terror on seeing an apparition—for is not "panic" the possession by Pan, the god of lonely places? In all these events, hallucination appears to be interpreted as spirit encounters. But a demon is no more real than the phobic projection to the outside of one's own psychic processes, experienced now as hallucination.

A near-universal explanation of disease is that it is possession by an evil spirit, perhaps sent by an enemy or god (Kali, Apollo). The cure, naturally, is to exorcise, literally "to curse out," the malevolent spirit. An example might be taken from the Devil Dance of the Sinhalese. Here the shaman takes the appropriate one of a set of 19 masks—say, the black mask with lolling tongue, bulging eyes, and fearsome fangs at the corners of the mouth, representing the cholera spirit—and frightens the disease spirit from its victim by a dramatic, knee-spread shamanic dance. The Navaho night chanter uses a ground painting into which to cast the disease spirit, and afterward the painting is destroyed. Aymara Indians project disease spirits into objects they leave at a path crossing, there to be caught and carried out of the vicinity by the next passerby (La Barre, 1948, p. 221). Jesus used magic verbal formulas to cast evil spirits out of a man into the Gadarene swine. Self-referent narcissistic man believes that everything in nature, even disease, is caused by the omnipotent acts of manlike entities. Spirits and demons are hallucinated everywhere to account for all happenings in nature; but demons and spirits are manlike because they have been made of men's own psychic stuff. In fact, a surprisingly good case could be made that much of culture is hallucination: the concerted "seeing" of mind-tailored clothes on the emperor, nature.

HYSTERIA, HYPNOSIS, AND DISSOCIATED STATES

Repeated fieldwork on many continents produces the conviction that all the defense mechanisms described by Freud occur universally among all men as psychic processes, quite apart from wide differences in symbolic content and cultural context. By far the most common defense of all seems to be simple denial, the shutting off of manifest unwelcome facts, perhaps because that is what all men habitually do in dreams and visions, as well as in the dereistic crisis-cult religions based on such revelations. Self-aware or psychiatrically sophisticated anthropologists may come to conclude that the simpler peoples, or for that matter most simple unpsychological-minded people anywhere, are chronic hysterics. That is, denial of unwelcome fact and hallucination of wish are conspicuous in the species.

The intense suggestibility of a subject under hypnosis is well known. The subject will act out all manner of absurd suggestions made by the hypnotist, yet later retain no memory of his acts. Or, at a covert cue from the hypnotist, the subject who has just come out of a hypnotic trance will perform some act quite compulsively and have no idea why he was "compelled" to do it. The persistent naïveté of the hysteric personality is quite astonishing. Indeed, Freud gained his first major insights from the famous case of Dora (Freud, 1925, **III,** 13–146), who naïvely laid out her transparent psychodynamics with no insight into them whatever. Although hypnosis was marvelously useful in research (cf. Agogino, 1965), Freud later abandoned it as a therapeutic technique because it involved neither the conscious ego of the patient nor democratically shared insight. But many a facile montebank, lacking Freud's integrity, still obtains symptomatic cure without insight or personality change, through his thus cheaply omniscient insight and easily omnipotent suggestion to hysteric patients. Easy insight and simple suggestion are the stock in trade of primitive witch doctors and other tribal therapists (La Barre, 1958, fn. 95, pp. 325–326; Galdston, 1963; Kiev, 1964). Similarly, any psychotropic effect on the patient of his medicines can be rationalized as proof of his power.

Both phobic and conversion hysterics use the defense of projection. The phobic projects some unwanted evil aspect of the psyche into an as-if-outside person or spirit—a true "dissociation" of psychic components normally integrated in the healthy personality. Similarly, the conversion hysteric projects and transforms psychic anxiety into as-if-physical pain. The Greeks divined the symbolic erotization of organs through displacement, by theorizing a wandering womb *(hysteron),* reappearing now here, now there, as a cause of symptoms in conversion hysteria. The primitive medicine man meets the dissimulation of hysterics by shamanic histrionics of his own: he obliges fantasy by sucking out some foreign body, a stick or stone or feather that had been "causing" the sickness (to psychiatrists the symbolic nature of the "foreign body" is plain, both in hysteria and paranoia). But the earnest general physician, who can honestly find no physical evidence of illness, in exasperation finally pronounces the pain as "here, there, everywhere, but mostly in the neck." Since psychic pain has been banished from the hysteric's consciousness, the "belle indifference" of the patient leaves the doctor unconvinced of any pain as she gives the endless long organ recital of her illnesses, any handful of which, if real, would long since have left her a corpse. (How difficult it is to see that mental illness is mental!) Rejected in her self-diagnosis, the hysteric then shops around from surgeon to surgeon to remove each successively erotized naughty organ in turn. The conversion hysteric denies and projects (somatizes) anxiety: she *hallucinates* pain. In fact, after literal hysterectomy, with no more sinful body parts that can be spared to punish or extirpate, the hysteric commonly becomes psychotic, for all the surgery has not removed the psychic cause, and her pscyhic defense by conversion fails.

The gambit of hallucination in hysteroids is clear. The phobic hysteric can be deliciously, moreover morally, preoccupied with the fictitious man under the bed she wishes were really in it, but she can be blissfully unaware of her denial, dissociation, and projection. She fears her own disclaimed inner wish as though it were outside; she excretes the unbearable noxiousness from her conscious psyche by dissociation and projective denial. Similarly, conversion allows one to hallucinate the "attack" of illness as though the organ inside were wicked, not the guilty wish. Surely devils and demons everywhere, inside or out, are projective hallucinations!

Habitual hysteroid denial and projection sometimes result in the dramatic "multiple personality."* In this dissociative state, two or more distinct, indeed contrastive, personalities seem alternately to "take possession" of the conscious mind. The availability of this phenomenon for demonological interpretation is manifest. But from a psychiatric point of view it is, rather, just another instance of the dissociative states to which the hysteroid is susceptible (for multiple personality is a hysteroid, not schizoid phenomenon). Psychodynamically, we would suggest, "possession" is not so much invasion by an alien psyche as it is the overwhelming of conscious ego function by ego-alien primary process mentation, a sort of stylized REM-hallucinosis or auto-suggestion to which poorly integrated hysterics are prone in the service of unconscious wish.

SACRED AND SECULAR

Anthropologists have long noted that most societies divide their culture into the "holy" and the "profane," either conceptually or in their behavior, or both. The secular is the realm of mundane workaday technology, of ego control, of relatively low emotional charge, and of constantly evolving adaptation to the environment.

*Lay notions of psychiatric syndromes are often grotesque. Of a piece with the superstition that "hysteria" is a kind of screeching mania, instantly cured by a slap on the face ("Thanks, I needed that"), is the cliché that the schizophrenic has a "split personality." On the contrary, schizoids are notably in close contact with "primary process" id material; hysteroids just as notably are not. Meanwhile *consciousness of conflict* is no evidence for "split personality" but is rather a hallmark of normality.

By contrast, the sacred is a realm of adaptation to anxieties, of high emotional potential, of positions the more heatedly defended the less defensible by common sense. Sacred knowledge is commonly traceable, even by natives themselves, to an origin in revelation given to the ancestors or to some similarly charismatic individual, such as a shaman, visionary prophet, or other culture hero believed to have been able to tap the unseen world of the "supernatural."

In actual fact, all men live alternately in two psychological states of being, that of waking life and that of REM hallucination or dream. It is here contended that the two realms of sacred and secular are at least as "real" as man's two psychic worlds. The secular tends to maintain sensory-enforced loyalty to the Reality Principle, to the animal environment. But the sacred insistently maintains a warmly nurturant attitude toward subjective and arbitrary organic need, thus primarily indulging the Pleasure Principle. For most men, the dream is the only escape from their often unwilling imprisonment in obdurate waking space and time. If one world seems to be remolded nearer to the heart's desire, it is no wonder we balk at attributing reality only to the vexatious waking world. And all men dream. It is not a matter for invidious contumely, but simple recognition of the way things are. As a matter of fact, this process in a big-brained, symbol-using, social, and culture-innovating animal may serve the cognitive speciation that is its chief adaptation, largely alternative to the random genetic mutation of other animals.

But since man is a thinking and self-perceptive animal as well, the discrimination between waking and hallucinatory dream-knowledge of his "inner space" remains a persistent problem in epistemology. Revelatory dreams are close to myth, which is the dream-thinking of a society, much as the dream is the mythology of the individual. Dreams and myths are thus similar if only because much of mythology originates in the dreams of individuals. Australian Bushmen themselves equate dream-time with the eternal myth-time that is mysteriously brought back in ritual: "alcheringa-time" is as timeless as the unconscious mind, just as half-forgotten childhood is the eternal private myth-time still at work beneath the conscious mind of the adult. Timelessness, of course, is also experienced with some hallucinogens.

It is the delectability of dream wish that makes it desirable. But it is only a lowered critical threshold that gives dreams their more intense "deeper reality." The fact that he dreams first forces on man the need to epistemologize. But dreaming is as inescapable and inevitable as the fact that one brings his whole learned self to acts of friendship and love. If religion is the poetry in which we believe, cult is also a way men have of carrying one another's emotional burdens. The schizoid seer doubtless knows his id-self far better than do we normals. But what advantage is it to gain one's soul in eternal dream, yet lose the whole waking world? There is no need to be reactively antirational just because rational critique often demonstrates that men are sometimes disenchantingly nonrational. Let no one denigrate the dream. But let everyone be epistemologically tidy about the location of these various realities: the supernatural is wholly housed in the subconscious.

RITUAL AND ALTERED STATES OF CONSCIOUSNESS

Ritual is a technique groups have of magically pretending what is not true: that at christening a soul is saved from eternal hellfire by a few apotropaic drops of tap water; at baptism, human sin is undone and washed away by a more massive ablution; at communion, eating the god's flesh and drinking his blood (magically transsubstantiated of course from ordinary foodstuffs) negates metazoan death entirely; at a puberty ritual there emerges an adult man; blood-brother rites make blood kin of men who are not; at marriage two persons are spiritually united forever; a sheepskin and long speeches create a learned man, and so on. Individuals evidently participate in rituals with varying degrees of critical loss of ego function, depending in part perhaps on whether one is the *pièce de résistance* in the ritual or merely a jaded onlooker. And yet the whole intent and function of ritual appears to be coercive group wish to hallucinate reality.

Heated objection to these statements about ritual—calling cynical what is merely cool, case-hardened objectivity—only demonstrates that there are varying degrees of conviction in the efficacy of acting out various magic wishes, which is the only point we wish to make here. Likewise, calling an officiant shaman or pseudoshaman is a statement only of relative belief within the observer, not a discrimination of objective difference in psychic function for the ritual participants. No man can criticize, since he cannot experience, another's hallucination. What ritual *does* for the participant is the critical psychological issue.

Dark night, with a flickering fire, is the best time for ritual. The long ecstatic drumming and singing of the Siberian shaman, his uncanny replication of the bird calls of his attendant spirits, ventriloquism of voice against the reverberant taut cone of the skin tent,* magic shaking of the tent itself, loss of sleep, shamanic calls, and repetitive response by participants—all these induce an empathic half-hypnosis of the whole group. It has been suggested (Nadel, 1950; cf. LaBarre, 1972a, pp. 121–122) that music itself began in the singing of shamans, who wanted a special language other than speech with which to address the supernaturals. Music is the *sine qua non* of ritual: rhythm, song, and other contrived appeals to the senses seduce belief. Since much humanly configurated sound is customarily in the form of semantic speech, music is the perfect Rorschach stimulus for pseudocommunication of meaning in reverie: we hallucinate meanings that are evoked only in the mind. Pronounced rhythm in song and dance, especially in crowd situations, may constitute sensory overload, hence induce an altered state of consciousness.† Dancing by ritual participants kinesthetically "confirms" the reality of myth: compulsive act coerces obsessive belief. That belief is the wished-for, and that others join in mutual support of belief, together make ritual a hypnotic-hallucinatory social substitute for reality.

It is now evident that the earlier designation of REM and waking states as only

---

*The most compelling shamanistic performance known to this writer is the chanting of Tantric rituals by Tibetan abbots, recorded in 1968 by Huston Smith of the Massachusetts Institute of Technology. The style of singing is said to be possible only to lamas of the Gyume and Gyäto monasteries of Lhasa. The singing, to invoke fearsome cosmic demons, is in incredibly virtuoso male coloratura, on the single syllable Om, in prodigiously *basso profundo sostenuto* two octaves below middle C and lower—against which the soloist cantillates or "double-sings," evidently by opening and closing resonance chambers in the skull, producing timbre change in high-frequency harmonics of remarkable amplitude *simultaneously with* the deep bass tone. Part-singing by a single voice is multidimensional "monotone" indeed, illustrating with so much in a single note the *multum in parvo* doctrine of Tantric Buddhism. The experience is so unbelievable to one conversant with the physics of sound as to seem hallucinatory.

† Neher (1962) has argued that primitive drumming (and other rhythmic sensory stimuli synergistic with physiological rhythms) induces trance. But Kane (1975) considers trance in the Appalachian snakehandling religion a complexly over-determined phenomenon not adequately explained by this *simpliste* and reductionist physiological view.

contingently polar and constrastive states of mind was a necessary caution. Hypnosis, hysteria, and hallucination in dream, vision, delusion, and trance show manifestly infinite gradations in altered states of consciousness, with respect to their relative proportions of dereistic REM versus sense-nourished contact with "reality." It is often diffucult to assess accurately the relative proportion of these factors in exotic ritual and ritual curing, since our own cognitive maps, reality testing, and level of ego functioning all intervene to distort judgment. But since our minds operate variously between the poles of deep dreaming and wakened consciousness, we may safely suspect that so also do the minds of our ethnographic subjects.

THE PROBLEM OF CROSS-CULTURAL "NORMALITY"

The ease with which individuals designated as abnormal in our society may function in other societies is well known to anthropologists. In India, for example, the mildly to severely schizoid individual is preadapted, so to speak, to a *saddhu* role of holy man, whereas in extroverted Western societies schizoid trends are highly visible socially. Yet among us, hypomania and even markedly sociopathic behaviors either pass unnoticed or are highly esteemed in business and political circles, much as obsessive traits are admired in academe. Again, in classic China, normal occidental male aggressiveness is obtrusively painful, upsetting, and contemned.

As Ruth Benedict has noted in her celebrated essay *Anthropology and the Abnormal* (Benedict, 1934a; cf. Devereux, 1956, pp. 3–32), homosexuality in our society exposes the individual to conflicts we tend to identify with neurotic disposition,

. . . but these consequences are obviously local and cultural. Homosexuals in many societies are not incompetent, but they may be such if the culture asks adjustments of them that would strain any man's vitality. Wherever homosexuality has been given an honorable place in any society, those to whom it is congenial have filled adequately the honorable roles society assigns to them. (p. 64).

Benedict cites the classic Greeks, among whom homosexuality was presented "as one of the major means to the good life," as "the most convincing statement of such a reading of homosexuality." In the same vein but somewhat differently, transvestism in Indian *berdaches* of both Americas was regarded as evidence of marked supernatural status (La Barre, 1972a, pp. 139–141, 156–157).

Cultural relativity of judgment extends to other psychic states. For example, epilepsy is a fear-shadowed and tabooed state in modern industrial societies. Yet in the classical world and in the ancient orient it was a blessed sign of visitation by a god. In many Moslem societies an epileptic habitus is necessary to authenticate the holy man—so much so that the ambitious aspirant must be able to produce at least the protective coloration of epilepsy if he is not so gifted naturally. It is the *dissimulation* of such states that leads outsiders to judge fraudulence in some shamans, which is no proof that the dissociative state itself is not the authentic *fons et origo* of the institution. Meanwhile, conviction in the shaman's clientele is the only significant matter functionally. The Shasta Indian shamaness is chosen by her constitutional liability to trance states. Cataleptic skill is essential to Siberian shamans, and in Zulu candidates a stylized neurosis is needed for medicineman-ship. Benedict notes that a "culture may value and make socially available even highly unstable human types [which] force upon us the fact that normality is culturally defined . . . [and] every culture besides its abnormals of conflict has presumably its abnormals of extreme fulfillment of the cultural type" (1934, p. 64).

In the all-important function of intermediary with the sacred supernatural world in any society, a tendency to hallucination in vision or trance is indispens-able. A most convincing study of shamanism is by the Korean psychiatrist Kwang-iel Kim (1972). In Korea, despite modernization and acculturation to Con-fucianism, Buddhism, and Christianity in turn, the ancient "shamanistic passion remains without any change among the masses." An estimated 100,000 shamans in South Korea alone means one shaman for every 314 persons. The priestly shaman is hereditary, but the "charismatic shaman" must suffer *sin-byung* ("dis-ease of god") or possession by an ancestral spirit, which Dr. Kim regards psychiat-rically as a "depersonalization syndrome." This depersonalization resolves "inces-tuous fantasy with symbolic marriage to ancestral gods whose image is parental . . . compensating their inferiority feeling with elevation of their status from the humble to the higher" one of spousehood with the god. Psychiatric significance is also evident in the twenty-four-hour-long curing ritual *goot,* with shamanic danc-ing, trance, and oracular pronouncements by the god. "Catharsis, abreaction, suggestion and hypnotism, as well as transference to [the] shaman are the main mechanisms of [the] shaman's psychotherapeutic approach . . . other essences [of which] are the trance state of participants during group dancing," adding group psychotherapy to the shaman's empathized compassion. Dr. Kim considers that "the vicious cycle of projection" in the shamanic worldview reinforces a paranoid tendency already present in the ethos of the people; moreover "the weakening of the ego function" by dependency on suggestion by the shaman prevents any gaining of insight. Anthropologists, he notes, tend to emphasize "the positive function of shamanism as a culturally integrated system," but as a psychiatrist he deplores the enhancement of "a paranoid cultural system" (Kim, 1972, pp. 127–129; see also Lewis, 1971).

CROSS-CULTURAL STUDIES OF DISSOCIATIVE STATES

In a half-century-old classic, *Possession, Demoniacal and Other among Primitive Races, in Antiquity, the Middle Ages, and Modern Times,* T. K. Oesterreich (1922) is at pains to argue "the constant nature of possession throughout the ages." In the "som-nambulistic form," normal individuality is replaced by another, but with no memory in the subject; in the "lucid form" the subject does not lose consciousness. Oesterreich also discusses the relation of possession and obsession (in Europe the latter rubric includes compulsive acts as well), and "artificial and voluntary posses-sion amongst primitive peoples, so-called shamanism." Although differing de-grees of conscious ego participation are alluded to, the only cross-cultural con-stant would be REM-like hallucination of possession demons, no doubt of phobic- or conversion-hysteric nature.

Erika Bourguignon has edited an anthology (Bourguignon, 1972a; see also

Bourguignon, 1965, 1968a, 1972b; cf. Wallace, 1972) concerning the relation of social change to religious beliefs and institutions in which altered states of consciousness are exploited.

Bourguignon uses two systems of classification: (1) that of Roland Fischer (Fischer, 1970, pp. 303–332; cf. Van der Walde, 1968, pp. 57–68), who examines states of consciousness varying on a continuum with respect to degree of central nervous system arousal, thus a neurophysiological model; and (2) that of Arnold Ludwig (1968), who presents a classification based on modes of inducing modification in CNS activity, thus a psychobiological model.

In spite of the great variety of states included in his classification, Ludwig finds that they share a series of 10 general characteristics: alterations in thinking, disturbed time sense, loss of control, change in emotional expression, change in body image, perceptual distortion, change in meaning or significance (that is, the attributing of heightened significance to subjective experiences, ideas, or perceptions in this state), sense of the ineffable, feelings of rejuvenation, and hypersuggestibility (Bourguignon, 1972a, p. 7).

Bourguignon classifies altered states culturally into two categories, which she calls "possession trance" (belief in spirit invasion) tending toward public and ritual manifestation, and "trance" (typically hallucinatory, with visions), which may be private. Both, she maintains, involve learning to greater or lesser but always significant degrees; and, statistically, each type is associated with different degrees of complexity in society, as well as clustering in ethnographic region, thus suggesting both historical diffusion and ecological factors.

La Barre (1972a, index) has noted that all religions begin in the hallucinatory revelation (vision, trance, or dream) of an individual, who is accounted "charismatic" to the degree that his message coincides with the unconscious wishes of his clientele; and that every established religion began as a "crisis cult," when contemporary secular culture failed to provide resolution of overwhelming anxieties. Crisis cults, derived from the stress of massive acculturation, have arisen in great numbers throughout the postcolonial world. But more fundamentally, the propensity to magic cults and religions derives, he believes, from the psychobiological neoteny (La Barre, 1954, pp. 303–304, 357) of the human animal, since each individual has passed through a magical (patterned on talking and walking) and a religious (nuclear-familial) stage of ego-differentiation to which, under stress, he may regress. Worldview is thus a function of ego differentiation and consequent psychosexual maturation. Similarly, cultural institutions roughly manifest *degrees of hallucinosis* in their epistemological grounds.

COMPARATIVE ETHNOGRAPHY OF DISSOCIATED STATES

Since compendious volumes have been written on hallucinatory trance and possession states—notably by Oesterreich, Prince, and Bourguignon—we attempt here only a representative sampling of more recent studies, in roughly areal sequence, to indicate their range and scope. By the fifth edition of his *Lehrbuch* in 1896, Emil Kraepelin (Zilboorg and Henry, 1941), the great taxonomist of modern psychiatry, had already included an appendix on such anomalous ethnic syndromes as "Arctic hysteria," *amok,* and *latah,* and in 1925 Freud (**IV,** pp.

436–472) published "A Neurosis of Demoniacal Possession in the Seventeenth Century"—thus giving rise to what might be termed "comparative psychiatry," subsequently developed by the culture-and-personality school of anthropology stemming from the work of Edward Sapir (La Barre, 1958, pp. 279–280, 309–311, 318–326). An influential report by F. E. Williams (1923; 1934, pp. 369–379) on the New Guinea "Vailala Madness" (which included hysteroid hallucination) and another by James Mooney (1896) on the Ghost Dance (which began in shamanic visions) drew attention to the frequent origin of cults in individual trance experiences. A considerable anthropological interest in crisis cults ensued, and La Barre (1971) has provided an extensive bibliography.

Raymond Prince (1968, pp. 157–165) has discussed possession cults in relation to "social cybernetics"; Bourguignon (1968b, pp. 3–34), the world distribution and patterns of possession and trance states; Davidson (1965), the psychiatric significance of trance cults; the Mischels (Mischel and Mischel, 1958), psychological aspects of spirit possession; Akstein (1966), kinetic trances and therapeutic ritual dancing; Lee (1966), the complex sociology of trance performances; and Harper (1962), spirit possession and social structure.

Regionally, we have the ethnopsychiatry of hallucinations among Chicano populations by Schepers (1972), and Henney (1972, pp. 219–263) on the Shakers of St. Vincent, whose cult hallucinations are induced by ritual sensory deprivation. One of many such acculturational rites with possession and glossolalia, the Apostolics of Yucatan, has been studied by Goodman (1972, pp. 178–218). For the Caribbean, *vodūn* trance in Haiti has been much studied by a number of scholars (Simpson, 1960; Kiev, 1961; Mars, 1962; Ravenscroft, 1962; Wittkower, 1963, 1964; Douyou, 1965) and is perhaps best understood as therapeutic acting-out by low-status persons under the guise of possession by cult spirits, some having African origins. Similar cults include *Umbanda* and others in Brazil, reported on by Ribeiro (1960), Pressel (1972, pp. 264–318), and Willems (1974, pp. 452–468).

For Africa, Greenbaum (1972a, pp. 58–87) has given a descriptive analysis of possession trance, with valuable ethnographic references, in 14 Negro tribes, also analyzing their societal correlates (Greenbaum, 1972b, pp. 39–57). Bourguignon (1968c) has summarized divination, trance, and spirit possession in sub-Saharan Africa; Collomb et al. (1964, pp. 136–137) have discussed the sociotherapeutic aspects of the *n'doep* initiation into the possession society of the Wolof and Lebou of Senegal; Gerlach (1965) related possession hysteria among the Digo of Kenya to the changing roles of men and women in a new market economy; and Giel et al. (1968), studied spirit possession and faith healing among the Ghion of Ethiopia. The sociopsychological implications of spirit possession among the Sidamo of southwest Ethiopia were investigated by John and Irene Hamer (1966); and Gussler (1972, pp. 88–126) reported on social change, ecology, and spirit possession among the South African Nguni. Lee (1950, 1970) notes the relevance of Zulu concepts of psychogenic disorder; Lombard (1967) treats possession cults in Black Africa, especially among the Hausa; Sangree (1968) relates spirit possession to marriage stability in Irigwe, and Wintrob (1967) relates sexual guilt to culturally sanctioned delusions in West Africa and discusses psychosis in association with possession by genii in Liberia (1966). Since the foregoing is only a sampling of the rich materials available from Africa, it is useful to have Zaretsky's (ca. 1970) bibliography on spirit possession and mediumship in Africa.

In north India, spirit possession is in the cultural context of illness, according to the Freeds (1964). Obeyesekere (1970) sees possession in Ceylon as the cultural idiom of mental illness. The same appears true of the whole Indic area, in which ritual exorcism of demons is the traditional cure. In Bali (Belo, 1960), trance dancing is a highly stylized drama in which, suddenly grasping his snaky *kris* dagger, the dancer attempts to assault the masked witch Rangda—but, gorgonized by a gesture from her, he falls senseless, and the bumbling, kindly male figure Barong aids him to a slow recovery. Scholars regard Balinese trance dancing as an abreaction of violent rage against the teasing and rejecting mother of the child displaced by the birth of a younger sibling.

In Oceania, hallucination as an experience of the supernatural is the idiom of cultural cognition among Filipino peasants, according to Jocano (1971). Leonard (1972, pp. 129–177) notes transformations of the traditional spirit mediums in Palau. Langness (1965, 1967, 1969a, 1969b) sees possession in the New Guinea highlands as an ethnic psychosis; Salisbury (1966, 1967, 1969), however, regards it somewhat differently among the Siane of New Guinea. The psychiatry of highland New Guinea is in any case a complex matter. The mysteriously localized endemic *kuru* seems now to be firmly established by the Gajdusek group (Gajdusek and Zigas, 1959) as a virus disease of the central nervous system, spread by endocannibalism of insufficiently cooked brains; but the "mushroom madness" of some highland groups has been thought (Heim and Wasson, 1964, 1965; Reay, 1960, 1965; Emboden, 1972a, pp. 25–26) to come from the eating of *nonda*, various hallucinogenic *Boletus* species of mushrooms.* "Wild man" behavior, on the other hand, appears to be an institutionalized means of violent abreaction of culturally imposed tensions, according to Newman (1964).

THE ETHNOGRAPHY OF PSYCHOTROPIC DRUGS

There appears to be no human society so simple in material culture as to lack some sort of mood-altering drug as an escape from the workaday world. Even the primitive Australians used *pituri (Duboisea hopwoodii)* as a narcotic; in larger amounts, they put the same drug into waterholes to stupefy emus, permitting hunters to run them down and club them for food. And the Bantu hallucinogen *iboga (Iboga tabernenthes)* of West African cults in the Gabon and Congo appears to have been borrowed from more primitive Pygmy hunters (Fernandez, 1965a, 1965b; Pope, 1969; Emboden, 1972a, pp. 12–13; Fernandez, 1972, pp. 237–260; Schultes and Hofmann, 1973, pp. 139–141). The *kanna (Mesembranthemum* spp.) euphoriant and hallucinogen of South Africa was chewed, and later smoked, by the Hottentot (Schultes and Hofmann, 1973, pp. 206–207). Botswana Bushmen use *kwashi* bulbs *(Pancratium trianthum)* as an hallucinogen (Schultes and Hofmann, 1973, pp. 201–202; Emboden, 1972, pp. 29–30, 49). There is even a narcotic bamboo grub in Amazonia, to match the hallucinogenic "dream fish" *(Kyphosus fuseus)* caught off Norfolk Island by native Melanesians.

*The rhizome of *Kaempferia galanga* is used in New Guinea as the hallucinogen *maraba;* and the Papuans use the leaves and bark of *Galbulimima belgraveana* (sometimes mixed with *Homalomena ereriba* leaves as *agara,* which intoxicates with spectacular visions and later a dreamlike somnolence. It contains several isoquinoline alkaloids (Emboden, 1972a, pp. 25–26).

Many stimulants have long been in customary secular use. *Coffea arabica* (Abyssinian coffee), *Camellia sinensis* (Himalayan tea), *Cola acuminata* (African cola nut), *Paullinia yoco* and *P. cupana* (Orinocan and Amazonian *pasta guarana*), *Ilex guayusa* (used by Indians of the eastern slope of the Ecuadorean Andes), *Ilex paraguayensis* (Paraguayan *maté*), and *Theobroma cacao* (Mayan cocoa or "food of the gods") all contain caffeine or caffeinelike alkaloids, but all are ignored here as being neither hallucinogens nor in ritual religious use. Kava *(Piper methyisticum)* is a narcotic and mild hallucinogen, but it is used solely in a social-status ritual in Polynesia. Betel *(Areca catechu)* is widely used in the Indic cultural sphere, both mainland and insular, but for secular enjoyment only. Nutmeg *(Myristica fragrans, M. malabarica)* from the seed, and mace, from the aril of the same plants, are violently hallucinogenic in sufficient quantities and have been used in the medicine *made shaunda* since Ayurvedic times; otherwise these have served as condiments only since Arabic introduction to the West in the early centuries of Christianity and never with certainty as an hallucinogen (Weiss, 1960; Weil, 1965; West, 1966; Weil, 1967, pp. 202–214; Schultes, 1967, pp. 185–201, 215–229; Schultes and Hofmann, 1973, pp. 66–70), doubtless because of their toxicity.

Christian Europe has been traditionally hostile to the consumption of hallucinogens. A possible factor is the survival of the practice of using a number of the most powerful ones—for example, belladonna *(Atropa belladonna)*, mandrake *(Mandragora officinarum)*, and henbane *(Hyoscyamus niger)*—from pagan times into European witchcraft. Belladonna has been used as a potent poison since early classical times. Renaissance ladies are said to have used it to produce enlargement of the pupils, which men found attractive; hence it is indirectly an aphrodisiac, provoking un-Christian lust. Mandrake, despite its toxicity, was a panacea in medieval folk medicine, used as a sedative and hypnotic agent in treating nervous conditions and acute pain. A magic plant in folklore, Greek and Hebraic alike, mandragora was surrounded with many legends and greatly feared. The forked root was named *Alraune, Erdmännchen,* and *Erdweibchen* from the fancied resemblance of the "Hexenkraut" to the human figure, and was used as an amulet and in all kinds of profane medieval European magic. An animal was employed to drag out the dangerous root, yet even so the man-plant's screams at deracination would drive a person mad. Mandragora was used as an analgesic in surgery, but it also had a wide reputation as an aphrodisiac. Belladonna, mandrake, and henbane were all reputedly used in witches' brews (Harner, 1973a, pp. 125–150; Schultes and Hofmann, 1973, pp. 161–163, 181–182, 185–187), and therefore were sinfully connected with the Evil One. All contain hyoscyamine, a powerful hallucinogen, which gives the sensation of flying through the air, as on a witches' broom or on a shamanic journey, among other effects. The use of toads in witches' brews is interesting, since the skin of some toads contains bufotenin, a hydroxytryptamine that is highly hallucinogenic. The virtually panic fear of "toadstools" by some Europeans may also derive from pagan times, since the use of hallucinogenic *Amanita* mushrooms antedated (and culturally influenced) the Greek and other Indo-European gods originating in northern Eurasia, *Amanita* being thought to be born of divine thunderbolts (Wasson, 1956, pp. 605–612).

But the European fear of psychotropics, and even of new foods such as potatoes, sometimes passed all reason. King James I of England was as much exercised over tobacco as he was over witchcraft: tracts of his time allege that smokers' brains, after their early death, would be found to be blackened with soot. Again, early in the present century, children were forcefully adjured not to eat even a single berry of the much-cultivated ornamental vine called "love apple," for it would surely kill them, probably within the hour, since it was botanically related to "the deadly nightshade." Children nevertheless persisted in eating the fruit, and no child ever died of eating love apples: bred to larger and tastier varieties, tomatoes are an even better source of vitamin C than the ritual orange juice, being both cheaper and more stable to oxidation and cooking. Meanwhile, after an interim of worldwide approbation and even praise of tobacco (by now thoroughly entrenched in the economic and political establishment), medical scientists have come to agree with King James, though with better evidence, on the dangers of smoking.

But—to the credit of European morality—municipal councils and national governments were deluged with petitions against the opening of the new coffeehouses or cafés in seventeenth-century Europe. Savants averred that coffee was a strong poison and that on Judgment Day all coffee drinkers would arise from their graves "as black as coffee grounds." But King Gustavus Adolphus of Sweden took twin brothers, both murderers, and condemned them to death, the one by drinking "fatal" doses of coffee, the other of tea, and appointed a medical commission to watch and report on their condition. The brother criminals both developed palpitations from the enormous doses given them, but both outlived their doctors, until the tea drinker died—at the age of 83. Voltaire, a passionate coffee drinker himself, remarked that "Coffee is a deadly poison, but it acts slowly"; he proved this by dying at the age of 84. The consumption of coffee has since spread insidiously over half the world, although the downfall of civilization is no longer blamed exclusively on its use.

Coffee is otherwise edifying to the anthropologist, accustomed as he is to detached awareness of cultural contexts. Originally, the sugar-containing coffeeberry of Christian Abyssinia had been fermented into an alcoholic drink, of a sort that later Moslem religion fanatically prohibited. But religious prohibition never stopped the coffeeberry. By dry roasting, Moslems converted some of its substances into a complex of chemical stimulants that are even now not exhaustively known to science; and in this new form, sometimes with added sugar, coffee drinking spread over the Arabic world (coffee, sugar, and alcohol are all Arabic words), and with Christian contact in the late medieval crusades, into Europe. Here, as we have seen, coffee became so widely established, even among otherwise respectable folk, that they ignore the psychotropic properties of the drug—a related *Rubiacea* of the tropical rain forest of Puerto Rico is even hallucinogenic—and most hardened drinkers freely and shamelessly admit psychological dependency.

Cross-cultural paradoxes are as instructive as cross-generational ones. Despite their much-proved danger, we accept alcohol and tobacco blandly but rabidly reject marihuana for its as yet unproved danger, since unknown euphoriants must surely be more dangerous than known ones. By contrast, Moslems rigidly forbid the drinking of alcohol, although drugs, even dangerous ones, are acceptable to them. In fact, all the Moghul emperors of India were addicted to opium, a habit they acquired from fellow Moslems in Persia (Kritikos and Papadaki, 1967), and the use of hashish is well-established among Moslems of Africa and Asia. On this matter we are capable of a certain ethnocentric smugness and blindness. We consider the Near-Eastern custom of giving opium to children while the mother is absent from the home to be quite outrageous. However, the last generation in America admired the parental concern and care represented by giving paregoric in "soothing syrup" to babies and laudanum to teethers—yet both substances are opium derivatives, such as were used by degenerate literary men like De Quincey and Baudelaire.* And many people are aware that a popular and now worldwide proprietary—still called a "tonic" in New England—once contained both cocaine and cola drugs, from Andean and African natives, respectively.

Again, among American Indians, hallucinogens are in the hands of the social and religious establishment and are administered to adolescents to give proper awe for the sacred institutions of their cultural mentors—a somewhat different context from drug use by our adolescents with contracultural intent. Yet at the end of the last century it was the pinnacle of the establishment—ladies—who were widely the unwitting addicts of successive derivatives of opium in their elixirs (Sonnedecker, 1962, 1963). The staunch pillar of the Women's Christian Temperance Union might combat female troubles with a "vegetable compound," the alcoholic content of which varied in different periods up to 19%, while her beleaguered husband got, at best, only 10% in his beer. The final irony, however, rests in today's worthy taxpayer settling down to his beer, enjoying the manly bite of the hops while righteously railing at the bearded "pot-smoking freak" he has the misfortune to call son. But hops *(Humulus lupulus)* and marihuana *(Cannabis sativa)* are the only members of the dioecious family Cannabaceae (Schultes and Hofmann, 1973, pp. 53–59; *Century Dictionary,* 1914, p. 2880), the female of which produces the resins cannabinol and lupulin, both mild narcotics suspected of producing psychological dependency. High moral dudgeon has here only a dubious basis: hop drinker and hippie smoker are biogenetically brothers under the skin.

OLD WORLD HALLUCINOGENS

Indeed, the European plant hops may be only a late additive to Levantine-originated beer (the *Oxford English Dictionary* gives 1440 for its first appearance in English, and the drug was introduced from Flanders between 1520 and 1524), whereas hemp is certainly one of the oldest cultigens of man. All Indo-European languages from Polish *konop,* Old Bulgarian and Russian *konoplya,* Lithuanian *kanapes,* Greek *kannabis,* Latin *cannabis,* Persian *kanab,* Sanskrit *ṣana,* French *chanvre,* and English *hemp,* to Irish *canaib,* manifest dialectic equivalents of the same word, and this constitutes the solidest possible evidence for the antiquity of the plant's use, since the undivided Indo-Europeans began to migrate and break up dialectically only in the early Bronze Age. Cannabis of course grows wild in north-central Eurasia, whence the Indo-Europeans came.

Care must be taken to discriminate in sources the textile use of the plant

---

*The Victorian poets Francis Thompson and Samuel Taylor Coleridge were also addicted to opium. The classicist Jevons (1965) has shown that the neo-Platonist philosopher Plotinus, on his own evidence and that of his students, was an opium addict, as were the celebrated physicians Avicenna and Paracelsus. In distinction from these, Hugo, Gauthier, and Mallarmé were members of *Le Club des Hachichins* in Paris (Rice, 1876, 1877). The herb known to Rabelais as "pantagruelion" has been alleged to be cannabis by N. Marty-Laveaux and also by Faye (1854).

("canvas" is a term cognate with cannabis) from its use as a drug. But the drug use
is very old. An archaeological find of 1896, in a Bronze Age urn field at Wilmers-
dorf in Germany, contained fragments of the leaves and fruit scales of hemp,
which strongly suggests narcotic use because these parts contain cannabinol,
whereas the textile fibers are in the larger stems. Thus independent linguistic
evidence of the plant's antiquity is confirmed. The Chinese valued hemp since the
middle of the Seventh Millennium B.C.; in the Emperor Shen Nung's phar-
macopocia of 2737 B.C., cannabis was described as an important medicine. As-
syrians burned it as an incense in the sixth century B.C. Hindu Ayurvedic medicine
has used it from the ninth century A.D. onward, although hemp itself was known in
India perhaps as early as the fourth century B.C. The *Avesta,* perhaps our oldest
textual authority for the drug, first mentioned the intoxicating resin in 600 B.C. In
480 B.C., Herodotus referred to the use of hemp as a narcotic by the Scythians of
southern Russia, who threw the seeds on heated rocks in their sweat baths and
shouted with joy on inhaling the steamy smoke. The Thebans made a drink of it
that was reputed to have opiumlike properties. The Hellenistic physician Galen
recorded general use in cakes which, if eaten to excess, were intoxicating. And in
thirteenth-century Asia Minor, the *hashishen* (whence our words "assassin" and
"hashish") were politicoreligious murderers, given the drug by the terrorist leader
Al-Hasan ibn-al-Sabbah, the "Old Man of the Mountains," for assassination of
Christian leaders of the crusades.

Since early times, cannabis has been used in other religious cults, most notably
in India but also, later, in Africa. The ancient sacred book of the Aryans, the
Atharva Veda, called it a "liberator from sin" and "heavenly guide," and the plant is
still accounted sacred in many temples, where it is grown in gardens. In India,
cannabis is largely drunk as *bhang,* an infusion of the dried leaves in water or milk.
Candies called *majun* are made of cannabis with sugar and spices, sometimes with
added datura and opium.* *Ganja,* made of the dried pistillate tops from cannabis
"races" rich in resin, is usually smoked, probably a post-Columbian practice. The
eating of *ganja* and *charas* (the resin that under certain climatic conditions occurs
spontaneously on leaves and stems) is more prevalent among Hindus, whereas the
smoking of *charas* is more usual among Moslems; but *charas* may also be eaten,
sometimes mixed with opium. Sometimes an aqueous solution or an alcoholic
tincture is drunk. And sometimes various fats, used to absorb the cannabinol
gums but contaminated with chlorophyll, are the greenish paste base from which
highly spiced honeyed sweetmeats are made; references to these are common in
Persia and north Africa. The poor in India use cannabis leaves as a folk medicine
and reputed aphrodisiac (Bouquet, 1950, 1951; Chopra and Chopra, 1957a;
Mikuriya, 1969; Emboden, 1972b, pp. 214–236; Mechoulam, 1973).

Cannabis taxonomy has been much debated, and until recently cannabis has

*S. and Ved Prakash Vatuk have reported on *Chatorpan* in Uttar Pradesh, India, as a culturally
conditioned form of addiction to certain sweetmeats and salty-spicy snacks, which have social consequences quite like those found in alcoholism and drug addiction. "The *chatora* acquires an urge for these
expensive delicacies, gradually neglects other foods and spends considerable cash on them. Eventually
he resorts to sale of jewelry, land and other possessions and even illegal activities to support his habit,
precipitating his own and family's economic and social decline." Folk stories and beliefs, and even
Hindu fiction all testify to the reality of *chatorpan* addiction, and yet the substances involved are alleged
to be only highly pleasant foods. But Emboden (1972a, p. 14) reports that cannabis is made into the
candy *dwamsec,* and there is reasonable question whether *chatora* is simply a food.

been accepted as a monotypic but highly polymorphous genus. However, recent cytological work by Schultes (Wolstenholme and Knight, 1965; Schultes and Hofmann, 1973, pp. 53–65) and his colleagues distinguishes *Cannabis sativa, C. indica,* and *C. ruderalis,* although there are many polymorphous ecotypes and cultivated "races." Oriental hemps are ordinarily richer in hashish (the gum proper) than Western ones. It is probable that Arabic merchants early brought cannabis to Africa, where it is known as *kif* in Morocco and North Africa (Benabud, 1951; Soueif, 1967). In 1888 Kalambe-Mukenge, chief of the Baluba, brought cannabis into the conquered parts of the Congo to unite the people in a new cult of the Bena-Riamba, "Sons of Cannabis." As *dagga,* in sub-Saharan regions, cannabis has an important role in magic and religion (Watt, 1961; Asuni, 1964). Perhaps brought from Africa by slaves, cannabis is known as *maconha* in Brazil (Cordeiro de Farias, 1955).

Since prehistoric times, hemp was used for clothing in Europe, but gradually it was displaced by other very old textile fibers such as linen *(Linum usitatissimum)* and Near-Eastern cotton *(Gossypium herbaceum,* originally from India, *G. barbadensis* being the independently discovered indigenous New World cotton). Because of its high tensile strength, hemp has been widely used in making rope and canvas. The need for large amounts of rope to hoist and furl canvas on sailing ships greatly increased hemp production during the days of exploration and trade in sailing ships. At one time, early American farmers were forced under penalty of fine to grow hemp; it is said that British prohibition of local growing in favor of their own trade monopoly was a major economic cause of the Revolution. With the coming of the steamship, naval need for rope and canvas greatly diminished. But hemp, which readily reproduces itself as a weed that takes kindly to waste places in both temperate and hot, dry climates, escaped from cultivation and now grows wild in many parts of the world, including much of the United States.

In both Americas, European hemp seems originally to have been grown only commercially for its fiber. But in port cities of Brazil, possibly under stimulus from Oriental or African sailors, *maconha* (the dried flowering tops and leaves) has long been smoked, often mixed with tobacco, in cigarettes. In Mexico, although Indians might easily have taken to the new drug to add to their many others, the alleged tribal or ritual use of cannabis is geographically limited. The modern use of *ganja* in the Jamaican Ras Tafari cult was probably taken directly from emigrants from India, since this is the word invariably used by cultists. *"Marihuana"* is of Mexican origin, though the etymology is obscure; the term "Mary Warner" was early Anglicized from this. Equally obscure, the Caribbean term *grifos* (from Spanish "kinky"?), was brought to Harlem by Puerto Ricans and Anglicized in New York as "reefers." In the 1920s and early 1930s, the demimonde of jazz musicians knew "muggies," "joints," and "Mary Jane," as did Bohemians and a few visiting college students in Greenwich Village. Transients among musicians, originally from the international port city of New Orleans, spread knowledge of muggies to large cities like Chicago and San Francisco, along with the new proletarian music, jazz, but little public stir was created. Only in the 1950s, with the rise of the so-called counterculture of disaffected Beatniks in San Francisco, did the use of "pot," "tea," or "grass" become widespread and widely publicized among middle-class college students; the Vietnam war spread the use of hashish and heroin from nearby oriental sources among all classes of the young (Winick,

1959–1960; Marcovitz and Myers, 1964; McGlothlin and Cohen, 1965; Winick, 1965, pp. 19–35; Carey, 1968; Emboden, 1972b, pp. 214–236, 229–232). Because of the ready availability of marihuana growing wild, many signs point to a growing and perhaps ultimately uncontrollable use of the drug (Gamage and Zerkin, 1965; Kalant, 1968), and some thoughtful citizens, including prominent anthropologists, have suggested legalizing cannabis because of the unenforceability of any prohibition law (Kline, 1967, pp. xvii–xix, 1–2).

Opium (Greek *opos*, "juice" from the milky sap of the lightly cut partly ripened seed capsule) is known only from the opium poppy, *Papaver somniferum*, a flowering annual not known in the wild state, hence perhaps an ancient cultigen of *P. setigerum*, which is indigenous in the Mediterranean region. The main ingredient is morphia (Morpheus, the Roman god of sleep), usually employed in medicine as various morphine salts, but two dozen other alkaloids have been found in opium. Mediterranean use is far older than the Odyssey episode, in which a compassionate older woman gave Telemachus opium to lessen grief at the supposed death of his father. The Ebers Papyrus (ca. 1500 B.C.) copied references to opium from a source at least a thousand years earlier; indeed, the earliest Sumerian cuneiform tablets mention its use. But opium is still older; remains of poppy capsules were recently excavated in prehistoric camp sites in the Rigi Mountains of Switzerland, and both seeds and capsules have been found in Stone Age lake dwellings. Representations of the poppy capsule are also archaeologically ancient in religious iconography of Mycenaean and Minoan date; for example, the body of an early Greek bronze vase is shaped like a poppy capsule, and a terracotta head from Knossos bears a headdress of incised capsules (Emboden, 1972, Figs. 1 and 2).

Opium was well known from classical times through the Middle Ages. Paracelsus carried opium in the pommel of his sword and named the alcoholic tincture *laudanum*, (that which is to be praised); another physician-addict, Avicenna, died of opium poisoning in Persia in 1037. Opium was probably brought to India in the Arab invasion of the eighth century. European traders took opium to China, but for long afterward none was grown in China. The British East India Company forced poppy cultivation in China in the eighteenth century, eventuating in the Opium Wars of 1840 and 1861. As late as 1923, two-thirds of the arable land in Yunnan province grew opium; in the capital city, Kunming, 90% of the men and 60% of the women were said to be addicts. In Shensi and Kansu provinces, opium was the principal crop that could be sold at a distance for a profit. In the nineteenth century, cultivation returned massively to the Near East, notably Turkey, with the French Mediterranean port of Marseilles the chief processing center into heroin (diacetyl morphia) for the world trade. Opium and its derivatives constitute the main indisputably addictive drugs. But except for ancient references to the "Lotus Eaters" and perhaps Circean witchcraft, opium, despite its known hallucinogenic effects, appears never to have been used ritually but only medically as an anodyne, and so on, and secularly as a euphoriant—doubtless because it is a true narcotic, promoting sleep, which would not lend it to ritual use, whereas in the form of heroin it constitutes the chief "hard drug" of illicit commerce (Rice, 1876, 1877; Anon., 1950a; Anon., 1953; Chopra and Chopra, 1957b; Kritikos and Papadaki, 1967). In southeast Asia, especially in Bangkok and Singapore, *Mitragyna speciosa,* a rubiaceous (coffee family) plant is sold as *kratom* (leaves) or *mambog* (syrupy distillate), either as an opium substitute or withdrawal agent (Emboden, 1972a, pp. 13–14).

In vivid contrast to opium, the long mysterious "soma" of the *Rig Veda* was without question the major religious hallucinogen of ancient Eurasia and one, moreover, that has exerted an incalculable influence on later religions. In their oral form, the earliest Vedic hymns date from about 1800 B.C.; but once the Aryans entered India around 1500 B.C., the identity of the plant, which does not grow south of the Himalayas, was lost and never rediscovered in Hinduism, despite much discussion in the endless Brahmanas or priestly commentaries. In the *Rig Veda* only priests drank ritually prepared soma, which conferred divinity on the Brahmanic "living gods" much as in Greek legend the gods, originally shamans too (La Barre, 1972a, pp. 159, 435; La Barre, 1972b, pp. 261–278), obtained immortality by imbibing odorous "ambrosia" with "nectar" (the latter probably pan-Indo-European mead, traces of which use reach even as far back as Mesolithic wall engravings).

Ever since Sanskrit was discovered by eighteenth-century Europeans, soma has been the apparently insoluble riddle lying at the heart of Vedic studies. The French Vedist Renou thought the whole of *Rig Veda* religion was present *in nuce* in the ecstatic hymns to soma; and the Sanskritist O'Flaherty states that all Indic practice of mysticism, from the *Upanishads* to the more mechanical methods of *yoga*, were merely attempts to replace the visions granted by the lost soma. And mysticism is indubitably the core and foundation of Indian religion. Soma, a suspected plant hallucinogen, is thus at the root of visionary Vedantism. In 1968, with only the word "soma" and the *Rig Veda* hymns to proceed on (the Brahmanas were manifestly useless), R. Gordon Wasson solved the riddle, with overwhelming evidence that illuminates much of ancient Eurasiatic religion, in one of the most admirable triumphs of modern scholarship (Wasson, 1968).

First of all, "soma" is linguistically cognate with the slightly later Avestan "haoma," but the plant identified as haoma did not correspond with Vedic descriptions. Moreover, the word is only Indo-Iranian, not pan-Indo-European, and it is Greek "ambrosia" that is cognate with Sanskrit "amrita," an equally unknown sacred substance that appeared at the cosmogonic "churning of the ocean"; however, most scholars think that amrita is merely an exalted alternative term for soma. But if, on these hints, the soma-ambrosia complex came from Indo-European haunts of northern Eurasia, another interesting clue emerges from the Vedic equating of soma with the god Agni, Fire (Latin *ignis*). The associations are complex, but mutually supporting at all points: fire emerges from the mysterious striking of Promethean sparks from "thunderstones" (flints) into punk tinder; and a very old European tinder was *Fomes fomentarius*, a punk fungus discovered in quantities in the Mesolithic (Maglemosian) camp at Star Carr in Yorkshire, where many objects used in hunting magic were manufactured. And fire (along with lightning, the heavenly fire of the sun and other celestial bodies, and the mysterious soul fire of the living body) is one aspect of the original high god of the Indo-Europeans, **diw* ("the shining one") in linguistic reconstruction—whence *deus, theos, Ze*-us, *Ju*-piter, *Di*-onysus, *Di*-ana, *div*-ine, and so on, of later languages. In European folklore, the sky god hurls thunderbolts, long equated with the mysterious flint hand axes we now know were Palaeolithic human tools; the very old temple of Zeus Feretrius at Rome had as a cult object a *silex*, "flint" thunderstone. Also old in European folklore is the notion that toadstools (French *crapaudin,* from *crapaud,* "toad") are engendered by bolts of lightning, since both toads and toadstools commonly appear after rain. Leaving aside the hallucinogen bufotenin in toadskins, let us return to the word fungus itself. The Indo-European root for the fungus-spunk-punk-sphongos-sponge group of words is **panx,* a root so very old that it is shared with Uralic, the otherwise unrelated language family of northern Eurasia. Since all the regular sound changes have occurred in both sets of daughter dialects, it is impossible to ascertain whether the loan word was from the Uralic to Indo-European, or vice versa. For example, the Ob-Ugric *pong* is the Ostyak [*tul*]-*panx* ("fool's punk"; cf. Magyar "fool's mushroom," whence German "mad-mushroom") and also the Ob-Ugric *ponx* (cf. the Siberian Chukchi *pong*). The starred form **panx* was proto-Uralic, which ceased to be spoken about 6000 B.C. But in Uralic dialects of Asiatic Siberia, *panx*-words referred specifically to *Amanita muscaria,* a fiery red mushroom still in use among Paleo-Siberian tribes when first studied by eighteenth-century European ethnographers. Could this Vedic "Agni" be a thing god-engendered by lightning bolt, or fire-life itself, immortality, a toadstool fungus?

Most impressively, all the supposedly extravagant *Rig Veda* metaphors for soma turn out to be exact botanical descriptions of *Amanita muscaria.* The fly agaric emerges from its underground mycelium looking like a little cottonwool ball. With growth, the enveloping white veil splits and breaks up into patches adhering to the flaming scarlet skin beneath, although sometimes these wash off in rain. After gathering, or when old, it loses luster, and one phase is a dull, tawny chestnut color. Wasson adduces color photographs for each one of these phases in the Vedic descriptions: "He makes of milk his vesture-of-grand-occasion" (the early stage of milky white flocculence); "he sloughs off the asurian [demonic] color that is his, he abandons his envelope" (the scarlet pileus splits the veil in such fashion that only fragments of it remain); "the vesture of *hari,* the vault of heaven clothed in storm cloud" (the fiery canopy flecked with bits of the integument); "the hide of the bull, the dress of sheep" (the envelope adhering in fragments to the red skin); "by day the color of fire, by night silvery white: (Wasson shows two color photographs, by day and night, of the recognizably same three plants, to which one might add remarks on the physiology of color vision with respect to seeing red at night); "the single eye" (the veil-free red ball); Surya the Sun (a larger fire-shining red sphere); the tawny yellow *pávamāna* (in its opened-parasol mature golden form); "the mainstay of the sky" (a long stem supporting a white-flecked canopy); "with his thousand knobs" (a neatly polka-dotted form with studs like the cudgel of Indra); "tongue of the Way" (a long-stemmed glans-headed specimen), and so on. By ancient criteria, even the Brahmanas sought a reddish, small, leafless, and fleshy-stalked plant—which all the suggested substitutes (e.g., *Ephedra* spp.) fail to meet.

If all this interlocking evidence holds (Wasson, 1958; Wasson, 1972a, pp. 185–200; Wasson, 1972b, pp. 201–213), then the hallucinogenic mushroom *Amanita* was being invoked as a divine inebriant in northern Eurasia long before the Indo-Europeans left their home, in the Chalcolithic or early Bronze Age, to scatter from Ireland to Ceylon. It is a common fallacy of historians to suppose, just because Christianity became officially the religion of the mainline great tradition, that the suppressed Old Religion disappeared without a trace. On the contrary, throughout the Middle Ages and into contemporary England there has survived the witches' coven, an old fertility cult of women centering around an ancient horned god, now the cloven-hooved and horned Evil One (which may trace back to the Palaeolithic "Cogul dance" and a tradition unbroken in France from the Trois Frères Dancing Sorcerer down to the Celto-Roman horned god Cernunnus) (Murray, 1921; Wasson and Wasson, 1957, Vol. I, pp. 117, 190–191; Murray, 1960; La Barre, 1972a, pp. 257, 410–416; Harner, 1973a, pp. 125–150). Similarly, apart from the classic Greek gods' imbibing of ambrosia and Brahman priests' use of soma, there are other unmistakable traces of the survival of the *Amanita* cult of the Old Religion. St. Augustine (354–430 A.D.) still bitterly censured the heretic Manichaeans for their fungus-eating, and Manichaeism was a powerful though repressed religious force, active from Spain to China, that influenced Eurasia for at least 12 centuries. Indeed, the Chinese, in a twelfth century text, refer to Manichaeans who *eat red mushrooms*. And the indigenous Taoist religion still remembered the mysterious *ling-chih*, "mushroom of immortality," which even the great emperor Shih-huang searched for in vain.

Although nectar and ambrosia of the "immortals" survived in the legends of the classic Olympian sky gods of state religion, still another tradition was strong in chthonic folk religion from eighth century B.C. Orphism to the Hellenistic mystery cults that shaped early Christianity. The core of the Dionysian Mysteries was eating the flesh (as a bull god) and drinking the blood (as a wine god) to obtain Orphic immortality, the same promised in the central Christian sacrament, the Eucharist. The sacramental meal has a hoary antiquity both in Palaeolithic Europe and Neolithic Asia Minor. But the present writer finds it difficult to believe that maddened Maenads were driven to wild night dancing on mountain tops from simple eating of a cereal wafer in the Eleusinian Mysteries—unless the "bearded one" were some such ancient ritual grain as spelt *(Tricitum spelta)* that was subject to a fungus infection like the LSD-producing smut *Claviceps purpurea* on rye (La Barre, 1972a, pp. 468, 470–471). The whole thrust of Indo-European religion may well be (among religions at large) the rather specialized goal of obtaining immortality—through eating and drinking substances, some of which are undoubtedly ancient hallucinogens. And behind all these later religious traditions, Indic and European, looms the very old Eurasiatic soma.

At one time alcoholic mead was a sacred substance, giving immortality to Greek gods. As the blood of the wine god Dionysus, alcohol was sacred well into the Hellenistic period, and so it remained in the Christian Eucharist. Otherwise, in the Mediterranean world of Europe and Africa, alcohol became secularized, whereas in the Asiatic and African Moslem world "alcohol" became rigorously forbidden by religion, though the potentially hallucinatory *qat (Catha edulis)* might be used even before prayer.*

---

*Qat is a minor hallucinogen of East African and South Arabian habitat, brought by Yemenites to Israel. It contains three alkaloids—cathenine, cathedine, and cathine—the last its main ingredient, the same as in *Ephedra vulgaris,* which produces euphoria, loquacity, diminished hunger, and finally, sleepiness. The aftereffects include apathy, anorexia, and depression; the side effects, palpitation, sweating, and thirst. Occasionally it produces psychosis, with incoherence, excitation, and schizo-preniform visual and auditory hallucinations, much like amphetamine psychosis; these effects, too, subside a few days after stopping intake (Hes, 1970).

NEW WORLD HALLUCINOGENS

By contrast, in the native American world, aboriginal beers and wines (La Barre, 1938a, p. 21, fn. 51, p. 137; La Barre, 1938b; Bunzel, 1940; Carpenter, 1959; Madsen and Madsen, 1965; Dailey, 1968; Washburne, 1968; Driver, 1970, pp. 109–111; La Barre, 1972a, pp. 145–146) were used ritually from the American Southwest, southward through Middle America and the Antilles, to Andean and Amazonian South America. In the Americas, *all psychotropics were sacred* in the peculiar American Indian sense of being "medicine," which implies a quasi-supernatural *power* (Algonkian *manitou,* Iroquoian *orenda,* Siouan *wakan,* etc.) inherent in some plants, as in many animals. These terms are somewhat misleadingly translated as "great spirit" but really mean a vast indeterminate and impersonal reservoir of magic power in the world that can be tapped by man. Thus a man's "medicine bundle" can be imbued with this power in the vision quest (Benedict, 1922), physically imbibed by a person in a plant "medicine" (La Barre, 1972a, pp. 131–138) or even transferred to a younger in intercourse with an older man's wife (Kehoe, 1970). The "medicine man" (shaman) presides over both curing and ritual, which are really the same in Indian thought; and, especially with hallucinogens like peyote *(Lophophora williamsii),* medical attention to an ailing individual is indistinguishable from cult ritual.

Indeed, since the drug produces perceptible psychotropic effect, tobacco itself was never used secularly by American Indians (Harrington, 1932, pp. 225–233) but only as a supernatural "medicine" to sanction solemn peace pipe agreements, in prayer, and in religious ritual. It should be noted that many varieties of tobacco *(Nicotiana rustica, N. bigelovii, N. attenuata, N. trigonophylla,* etc.) often contain far larger amounts of nicotine than the familiar *N. tabacum,* and among the Warao of Venezuela, and elsewhere in South America, the *bahanarotu* shamans used tobacco in truly hallucinogenic amounts to travel in trance states to the bahana-spirit realms in the eastern cosmic vault, and to feed with smoke the *kanabo* (ancestral spirits) and the *hoarotu* (spirits of dead shamans), or to initiate new *hoarotu* into shamanhood (Wilbert, 1972, pp. 55–83). The native American tobaccos, wild or cultivated, were used wherever *Nicotiana* species will grow—which is to say from southern Canada to northern Patagonia—in cylindrical or elbow pipes, in cigarettes and cigars, or snuffed, chewed with lime, or drunk in infusion (Wissler, 1922, p. 26, Fig. 6; Driver, 1970, Map 10). As typical examples: Amazonian post-adolescents dipped a spatula into a thick tobacco syrup and licked it off to sanction adherence (under supernatural penalty) to conventionally "unanimous" tribal vote; and an Iroquois meeting a "tobacco-begging spirit" in the woods, after suitable gifts of tobacco, would carve the face of the supernatural on a living basswood tree and use the power-laden mask later in long house "False Face Society" ceremonies. (Masks of course, everywhere in the world, promote a sense of identification with, or possession by, gods and spirits.)

The entire aboriginal Southeast, including the northern half of Florida, the Arawakan Greater and the Cariban Lesser Antilles, and the Gulf Coast used *Ilex vomitoria (I. cassine* and *I. yaupon),* which Indians brewed into a heroically strong stimulant and emetic Black Drink. Virginia and Carolina tribes used it in the "huskinaw" or ritual puberty initiation of boys; and Creek mixed tobacco with their Black Drink for purification before important councils and sacred rites like the corn harvest busk (Hale, 1891; Wissler, 1922, pp. 195, 239; La Barre, 1938a, pp. 26, 39, 55, 96, 131, 133, fn. 14; Lawson, 1951, pp. 253–254; Driver, 1970 pp. 107, 115, 304, Map 14). It is probable that the botanically related *Ilex paraguayensis* in South America was also aboriginally used in ritual, before becoming the widespread South American secular stimulant maté.

The violently hallucinatory and toxic *Daturas* were so widespread and so deeply entrenched in aboriginal American ritual use as to provide an exemplary overview in more detail of the various ways in which psychotropics and hallucinogens in general were used in the New World. In Virginia, the "Jamestown"* or jimson weed was used as "wysoccan" (probably *D. stramonium*) in the puberty ordeals for boys. Confined for long periods, they were given "no other substance but the infusion or decoction of some poisonous, intoxicating roots [and] they became stark, staring mad, in which raving condition they were kept eighteen or twenty days [and were said to] unlive their former lives" and begin manhood by losing all memory of ever having been boys (Safford, 1922, pp. 557–558). Algonkian and other Eastern Woodlands tribes also may have used the thorn apple as an hallucinogen in initiatory rites (Schultes and Hofmann, 1973, p. 167).

In the Southwest, the ancient Aztec *toloache* (*D. inoxia* = *D. meteloides* of older sources, but *D. discolor* and *D. wrightii* were also valued hallucinogens), was also used by the Cocopa, Havasupai, Hopi, Navaho, Pima, Walapai, Yuma, and Zuñi of the Southwest; again, in California, by the Akwa'ala, Cahuilla, Chumash, Diegueño, Gabrieleno, Luiseño, Miwok, Mohave, Mono, Salinan, Serrano, and Yokuts. The distribution of datura use is continuous with that in northwestern Mexico among the Cora, Opata, Tepecano, and Tepehuane; and it extends southward into Andean and Amazonian South America. Zuñi rain priests and the heads of two medicine societies were exclusively allowed to gather *D. inoxia;* to commune with bird spirits at night, they put the powdered root into their eyes; the rain priests chewed the roots to ask ancestral spirits to intercede for rain. Besides use as an hallucinogen, Zuñi valued *aneglakya* as an anesthetic and analgesic for broken bones and serious wounds; medicine men also gave it to clients to discover robbers by divination. Besides employment in puberty ceremonials (the typical Californian use), tribes of the Yuman stock used datura to induce dreams for predicting the future. Yokuts usually took the seeds only once in a lifetime, but shamans had to undergo yearly intoxication to keep in practice. Navaho eat the root for divination and prophecy, but the Hopi used it in doctoring. In southern California, the Akwa'ala, Yuma, and Eastern Mono ate datura for luck in gambling; Central Miwok do not eat it but think a dream about datura brings luck in gambling. "Of the remaining tribes of the area who used it ceremonially, some features were held in common: (1) datura was not taken before puberty, (2) it was usually administered to a group, and (3) a supernatural helper, sometimes an animal, was sought" (La Barre, 1938a, p. 135). In southwestern California, datura use was strongly ritualized in the Chungichnich cult of the Luiseño, Diegueño,

---

*The name "Jamestown" or jimson weed did not arise from the Virginian native tribal use of *wysoccan*. Rather, it comes from the behavior of soldiers, sent to Jamestown in 1676 to put down Bacon's Rebellion, who ate young shoots of datura as a pot green and became for several days amusingly intoxicated. In 38–37 B.C., during a retreat, Antony's legion had a similar experience with a European datura (Beverly, 1722). The use of daturas since prehistoric times in the Old World is documented in Schultes and Hofmann (1973, pp. 166–167).

Cahuilla, and tribes of the San Joaquin basin and Sierra Nevada, in a male puberty rite that Kroeber (1923, pp. 309–311) thinks overlay older nonritual uses in a wider area (Kroeber, 1925, pp. 462, 589, 593, 605, 614). White Mountain Apache and Tarahumare added datura to their *tesguino* (maize beer). Tepehuano used it instead of peyote; indeed, the aboriginal areas of datura and peyote use are mutually exclusive (La Barre, 1938a, pp. 136–137; Driver, 1970, p. 113, Maps 13 and 14). But Tepecano prayers implicate *toloache* with maize and the sun, much as in Mexican peyotism, and the Pima had a jimson weed deerhunting song, as in Huichol peyotism.

In South America, the arborescent *Datura* species (*D. candida*, *D. sanguinarea* of the Andean highlands of Colombia southward to Chile, and *D. suaveolens* of the warmer lowlands) are never found wild, and all are evidently ancient cultigens, given their chromosomal aberrancy and extreme variation into several hundred cultivars or "races." The Chibcha, Choco, Ingano, Kamsá, Siona, and Kofan of Colombia, the Quechua of Ecuador, Peru, and Bolivia, the Mapuche-Huilliche of Chile, the Canelo, Piojo, Omagua, Jivaro, and Zoparo of eastern Ecuador—all use datura hallucinogens in daily life, the Mapuche as a correctional medicine for unruly children, the Jivaro to bring ancestral spirits to admonish recalcitrant youth in datura hallucinations. Chibchans mixed daturas (including perhaps *D. aurea* as well as their other two) with maize chicha beer, giving it to wives and slaves of chiefs and warriors to induce stupor before burial alive with husband or master. Indians at Sogamoza, Colombia, used *D. sanguinea* in sacred rituals at the Temple of the Sun, as did Quechuans to communicate with ancestors and the spirit world, and in Matucanas (Peru) to reveal treasures in *huaca* (tombs). Initial intoxication on the scopolamine and other tropane alkaloids in daturas is so violent that physical restraint is needed before users pass into hallucinatory sleep, with dreams that are interpreted by shamans to diagnose disease, identify thieves, and prognosticate events of tribal concern (Schultes and Hofmann, 1973, pp. 168–179). Beyond botanical evidence, the antiquity of datura use is proven by remains of the drug in a Tiahuanacoid shaman's tomb in Peru (Wassén, 1972).

The *earliest-known* Amerindian hallucinogen was of course *Anadenanthera* [formerly *Piptadenia*] *peregrina*, an Antillean narcotic snuff of the Caribbean Taino, *cohoba*, used for spirit communication, mentioned in a letter of Columbus in 1496. The main area of use, however, is that of Orinocan *yopo*, von Humboldt's *niopo?* (Altschul, 1972), the indoles of which initially cause unconsciousness; then, as the limbs and head droop, users may see the world "upside-down and men walking with their heads downwards," according to a colonial observer (Schultes and Hofmann, 1973, pp. 84–93). However, the highly narcotic *parica* snuffs are made of the blood-red sap of *Virola* species trees, Puinave *yaki*, and Kuripako *yato*; these are taken by shamans for diagnosis and treatment of disease, divination, and prognostication, among the Burasana, Makuna, Kabuyari, and others of the Vaupés drainage. In the headwaters of the Orinoco and north of the Rio Negro, the Waiká groups (Kirishaná, Shirianó, Karauetari, Karimé, Parahuri, Surará, Pakidái, Yanömamö (Chagon et al., 1971) and others use *Virola* snuffs they variously call *epena*, *ebene*, or *nyakwana*, "in excessive—even frightening-—amounts" in daily use as an hallucinogen (Schultes, 1967).

South American snuffs are still somewhat confused in the botanical and anthropological literature (Schultes, 1955; Zerries, 1960; Wassén, 1965; Seitz, 1967, pp. 315–338; Wassén, 1967, pp. 233–289; Schultes and Holmstedt, 1968; Schultes, 1969a, 1969b; Prance, 1970; Schultes, 1970; Schultes and Hofmann, 1973, pp. 70–83), but Peruvian *vilca* and *cébil* in northern Argentina may be *A. colubrina. Cytisus (Genistus) canariensis,* the Old World "genistus" of florists, is a minor hallucinogen apparently employed only by Yaqui shamans in Mexico- —suggesting, as with Mazatec *Salvia divinorum* and perhaps Tepehuano *Cannabis sativa,* an Indian readiness to use newly available hallucinogens. Despite its restricted area of modern use, only recently discovered, *S. divinorum* nevertheless may be the psychotomimetic *pipilsintzintli* of the Aztec, a mint, like *Nepeta cataria* (catnip) (Jackson and Reed, 1969).

If cohoba snuff was the earliest known, the oldest presently known Indian narcotic is the newly discovered Texas buckeye *Ungnadia speciosa,* found in northeast Mexican and trans-Pecos caves in association with Folsom points and stratigraphically below abundant Red Bean *(Sophora secundiflora)* specimens in ritual context, and dated by C_{14} at 8500 B.C. But the buckeye is so highly toxic that later and successively less toxic hallucinogens like the Red Bean, peyote, and psilocybe mushrooms in turn may have been gradually substituted in ritual use (Adovasio and Fry, 1972). Archaeologically, the buckeye is dated to 8500 B.C., the Red Bean to the range 8440–8120 B.C., peyote as yet only to A.D. 810–1070, but mushroom stones indicating ritual use in highland Guatemala conservatively to 1000 B.C. The Red Bean was used by the Tarahumare and other Mexican tribes, the Southwestern Apache, and the Texan Tonkawa in historic times, and in the Plains also by Comanche, Delaware-Caddo, Iowa, Kansa, Omaha, Osage, Pawnee, Ponca, and Wichita (La Barre, 1938a, pp. 105–109; Schultes and Hofmann, 1973, pp. 96–101). The Iowa had a Red Bean dance in the spring in which initiates bought membership into a medicine society; but the Pawnee were their source for the cult (Skinner, 1915, pp. 718–719). The Pawnee initiates painted themselves and danced to the music of musical bows and gourd rattles.

During the ceremonies the singers seated themselves in four different places at the side of the lodge, corresponding to the four directions, and sang in each one the verses prescribed by tradition, the order being: east, south, west, and north. The dance is said to have consisted of peculiar jumping movements (Skinner, 1926, pp. 245–247).

A large number of beans were "killed" by pounding and boiling in a pot with herbs said to make the decoction milder in action; a cup or two of it stupefied and caused everything to look red. Heavy taboos were laid on the red-medicine-bundle owners. Numerous similarities led La Barre to postulate that a "Red Bean Cult" had preceded and influenced the later peyote cult (La Barre, 1957; Howard, 1957), a supposition later confirmed archaeologically and botanically (Campbell, 1958; Troike, 1962; Adovasio and Fry, 1972; Schultes, 1972, pp. 31–32). Peyotism, of course, is too well known to need more than mention here (Shonle, 1925; La Barre, 1938a; Slotkin, 1956; Driver, 1970, Map 13).

Likewise the universal Andean ritual use of coca *(Erythroxylon coca),* the source of cocaine, is well documented in Americanist sources (Wissler, 1922, Fig. 6, p. 26; Anon., 1950b; Buck et al., 1968; Guerra, 1971, p. 47). The widespread Amazonian use of the "vine of the spirits," *Banisteriopsis caapi,* earlier only poorly known ethnographically, has been abundantly documented by Harner and his associates in *Hallucinogens and Shamanism* (Dobkin de Rios, 1972, 1973, pp. 67–85; Harner,

1973b, pp. 15–27; Kensinger, 1973, pp. 9–14; Naranjo, 1973, pp. 176–190; Siskind, 1973, pp. 29–39; Weiss, 1973, pp. 40–47) and by others (Morton, 1931; Reichel-Dolmatoff, 1972, pp. 84–113; Schultes and Hofmann, 1973, pp. 114–118).

Since the interested reader may now be referred to easily accessible monographs on some American hallucinogens, attention is focused on lesser known and newly discovered ones. For example, a mescaline-containing Peruvian cactus, "San Pedro" or *cimora (Trichocereus pachanoi)*, is used in folk healing (Gutierrez-Noriega and Sanchez, 1947; Gutierrez-Noriega, 1950; Huerta, 1960; Dobkin de Rios, 1968, 1969a, 1969b; Sharon, 1972, pp. 114–135). According to seventeenth-century Jesuit sources, the Yurimagua of Peruvian Amazonia had a potent beverage made from a "tree fungus," possibly *Psilocybe yungensis* (Schultes and Hofmann, 1973, pp. 39, 41, 51). The Guegue, Acroa, Pimenteira, and Atanayé of eastern Brazil formerly made "a miraculous drink," *ajuca* or *vinho de jurema*, from *Mimosa hostilis*, which gave "glorious visions of the spirit land," used especially before going to war (Schultes and Hofmann, 1973, pp. 94–96). *Brunfelsia* species were apparently used in psychotomimetic drinks by the Kachinahua of Brazilian Amazonia; but the Kofan and Jivaro of Colombia and Ecuador employed them only as additives to their basically *Banisteriopsis yaje* or *natemä* drink (Schultes and Hofmann, 1973, pp. 163–166)—a general Amazonian custom that makes botanical identification of hallucinogens very difficult. The spiny shrub *latué* or *árbol de los brujos (Latua pubiflora*, which contains hyoscyamine and scopolamine) was used in central montane Chile to produce delirium, hallucinations, and, sometimes, permanent insanity; it is said that shamans could produce madness of any chosen duration, according to the dose (Schultes and Hofmann, 1973, pp. 182–185). Schultes discovered an anomalous monotypic genus *Methysticodendron amesianum*, known only in clones and called *culebra borrachera*, in the Sibundoy valley of Colombia, which he considered allied to the tree daturas (Schultes, 1955b; Schultes and Hofmann, 1973, pp. 186–191). The Kofan and Kashinahua of Amazonia use two *Psychotria* species (coffee family) they call *nai-kawa* and *matsi-kawa*, elsewhere sometimes added to ayahuasca (Schultes and Hofmann, 1973, pp. 194–196). Schultes, the ranking ethnobotanical authority, believes there are 80 to 100 psychotropics and hallucinogens in the New World alone. Even in more easily accessible North America, there are some little-known but interesting plant "medicines." The Cree and other Canadian Indians chew flag root or sweet calomel *(Acorus calamus)* to lessen fatigue on long journeys; the plant contains asarones similar in structure to mescaline, and larger doses produce an LSD-like experience (Schultes and Hofmann, 1973, pp. 200–201). Northwest Indians chewed *Lycopodium selago* fern for its narcotic effects, three stems intoxicating, and eight rendering a man unconscious; the Calpella considered their "sleeproot," red larkspur *(Delphinium nudicaule)*, a powerful soporific (Weiner, 1972, pp. 101—102).

Of all regions in the world, perhaps the Nahuatl culture area of Mexico had the largest number of psychotropic plants in native use. The Aztec had pre-Columbian *chocolatl (Theobroma cacao*, originally from Amazonia) (Emboden, 1972a, p. 87) and *ololiuqui* (the seeds of *coatlxoxouhqui, Rivea corymbosa*, containing d-lysergic acid amide or ergine): "when the priests wanted to commune with their gods and to receive a message from them, they ate [ololiuqui] to induce a delirium,

during which a thousand visions and satanic hallucinations appeared to them"
(Hernandez, 1651; Schultes and Hofmann, 1973, pp. 144–145). They also had
peyotl (Lophophora williamsii, but the Aztec term referred also to other cacti and
noncacti) (La Barre, 1938a, pp. 124–125); *picietl* (probably *Nicotiana rustica*)
(Driver, 1970, Map 10); *pipiltzantzantli* (the hallucinogenic mint *Salvia divinorum*)
(Schultes and Hofmann, 1973, pp. 158–159); pulque (a beer made from mescal,
Agave mexicana, sap), *sinicuichi (Heimia salicifolia,* a little-known narcotic from
highland Mexico, producing especially auditory hallucinations that "help to remember events that took place many years earlier . . . even prenatal events," and
giving a yellow cast to everything seen (Emboden, 1972, p. 54; Schultes and
Hofmann, 1973, pp. 135–137); *teonanacatl* [the famous "flesh of the gods," a
group of *Conocybe, Panaeolus, Psilocybe* and *Stropharia* species (Borhegyi, 1961;
Schultes and Hofmann, 1973, pp. 36–52)] some of which Wasson discovered still
in use by the Mazatec (Wasson, 1962); *teyhuinti* (narcotic mushrooms "that cause
not death, but madness that on occasion is lasting . . . with night-long vigils are
they sought, awesome and terrifying" (Hernandez, 1651; Schultes and Hofmann,
1973, p. 38); *tlitliltzin* (the seeds of *Ipomoea violacea,* a morning-glory yielding
LSD-like alkaloids) (Schultes and Hofmann, 1973, pp. 147–153); *toloatzin* (Mexican toloache, *Datura inoxia*) (Schultes and Hofmann, 1973, p. 168); and *yauhtli*
("Rosa maria" or marihuana)—but all these leave unidentified Sahagun's
aquiztli, atlepatli, mixitl, quimichpatli, tenxoxoli, tlapatl, tochtetepi, and *tzintzinlapatl.*
Nor do these exhaust the Mexican list. For example, the Chontal of Oaxaca used
the leaves of the sacred *thle-pelakano (Calea zacatechichi)* as a hallucinatory narcotic,
and more doubtless remain to be discovered.

So numerous, in fact, are Amerindian hallucinogens that a decade ago La Barre
(1964) postulated a "New World narcotic complex" extending from a mid-United
States latitude southward to include most of the Andean and Amazonian regions
of South America, of Mesolithic time-depth (La Barre, 1972a, pp. xiv–xv,
124–135, 154, 160, 363, 468), and inextricably bound to Indian shamanism (La
Barre, 1972a, pp. 133, 161; La Barre, 1972b, 261–268; Furst, 1972, p. viii;
Wilbert, 1972, p. 83). In 1963 and again in 1966, Schultes (1963a,.1963b, p. 147;
1965, 1966) raised the pertinent question: why, since hallucinogens are found in
alkaloids, glucosides, resins, and essential oils, in Fungi and cacti and in the
seeds, leaves, barks, stems, flowers, roots, and saps of many angiosperm species
distributed with botanical indiscrimination in both hemispheres, should New
World natives have many scores of psychotropic plants, whereas the Old World
knew scarcely a half-dozen? Since the question could not be resolved on any
rational botanical grounds, La Barre then suggested (1970) that given their
ancient vision quest and universal shamanism, perhaps Indians are *culturally
programmed* to value, seek for, remember, and use any available psychotropic
plants, since these provided a manifest experience of the supernatural world.
Epistemologically, the life-guiding and decision-making authority for American
Indians is the *individually experienced* supernatural "power" they find in many
plants—quite as much as the European authority for belief since the days of
Heraclitus and the pre-Socratic nature-philosophers, has been found in the common *koine* world of group-validated *intersubjective experience,* as opposed to the
private world of the vision or dream. These are quite different cognitive maps.
And yet we should remember that if our vested interest in rational establishment

controls vision, nevertheless vision bursts the cognitive establishment, even in the history of science (Kuhn, 1962). The wisdom of knowing he might be wrong distinguishes the scientist from the tribalist.

SUMMARY

In the social sciences, in which men study themselves, the *motive* for our researches may well determine what we find. The true believer will encounter only a *consensus gentium* for such sacred superstitions as the belief in animism. But the detached skeptic may find shocking though edifying new information, from an unanticipated quarter, about his own tendentious psyche and social self.

Comparative ethnography can be a potent ally in helping us delimit and calibrate our own more exotic experiences—that is, if we maintain a firmly scientific, benevolent skepticism toward ethnic data (including our own), instead of indulging a voraciously gullible appetite for miracle. What we then accumulate from ethnology is not additional occasion for slackjawed awe, but only soberly empirical confirmation of perhaps unwelcomely-learned pathologies of mental behavior in the species.

The present study has attempted a wholly secular approach to the often spectacular "mysteries" in religion and cult. We are confident there is no "supernatural" psychic event in tribal life anywhere that may not be better understood as a dissociated state—whether endogenous dream, vision, trance, REM state, sensory deprivation, hysteric "possession"—or as an hallucinatory activity of the brain, under the influence of exogenous psychotropic substances.

Supposedly "divine revelation" of some spirit land is merely tapping the id-stream of primary process thinking, and it should be approached not as a cosmological but as a psychiatric phenomenon. What we seem to experience as an external "supernatural" *mysterium tremendum et fascinosum* appears to be external and objective only because it is presented in sensory-hallucinatory form, since our senses are the customary conduit of information from the outside environment. Furthermore, we see ghosts dance because of specific *universal experiences of development* in the individual human animal. That is, we bring from each individual past a mode of response to the supposed Stimulus, the nature of the Unknown being projected, not perceived. Technically, supernatural information is misapprehended information about the mind itself. The Mystery is in fact only our own brains and minds, often in an altered state of consciousness; experiencing the "supernatural" is only a functionally differing *state of mind*. Only for the naïve and psychologically nonself-perceptive person does hallucination appear to embody an epistemological problem. We trust our personalities because we have honestly learned them; but evidently we have not examined them. For part of the mind is learned defenses against self-knowledge. The authoritarian personality is doubly confused: sacred defense mechanisms shape his "knowledge" of nature, and he looks to the authority of his charismatic fellows for knowledge which only a fresh assessment of nature can properly provide; and both he and his authority rely on unexamined wish fantasy for "knowledge" of themselves. What the authoritarian personality is actually seeking is not comprehension of self and world, but group-confirmed fantasies. Therefore we should not expect other tribes, however multiplied, to provide grounds for belief, when all they can provide are data on believers for our skeptical scrutiny.

Every individual, presumably, is aware of his own psychic subjectivity. And gradually he discovers, no doubt accurately, many other such subjectivities crowding all about him. But he often overextrapolates this discovery of mind, and he projects it into nonliving objects that only appear to have volition or will, because they also move or seemingly evidence other attributes of mind. For the child, other persons are often primarily alien wills; thus the frustrations abundantly provided both by people and by things are perceived by the child as willed frustrations of his willful self. Nevertheless, the psychic is always a function of material entities. The most absurd and most punished error in the history of *sapiens* is the triple paradox of animism: that all things can think; that thinking can be disembodied from any thing; and that thinking (soul, spirit) is a thing, whereas mind is only (and always) a function of a thing, the brain.

With this critique of animism, the logic and developmental sequence of the present study now emerge with some clarity. We attempted first of all a psychodynamic understanding of pathological states—illusion, delusion, and hallucination—in their relation to animistic superstitions. When "objectified," these are disassociative projection of the subject's disclaimed psychic components. Psychodynamically, "possession" is not so much invasion by an alien psyche as it is the *overwhelming of conscious ego functions* by ego-alien primary-process mentation, a sort of stylized dream hallucinosis or autohypnosis to which poorly integrated hysterics are prone, in the service of id-wish. Ego function is "possessed" (overrun or displaced) by ego-alien process: we are literally self-seduced. The neurotic gain of such "possession" in *vodún* and other cults is plain, even on cursory examination: the one who is sacredly possessed does justifiably what he wants to do and cannot do in his secular state.

Revelation, vision, divination are mere "supernormal" functions of the *sub*conscious, when the critical threshold of the more canny conscious mind is lowered in dissociative states. The dream, paradoxical (REM) sleep, narcolepsy, sensory deprivation—all leave the person subject to primary process thinking, unedited by sensory input. The relation of REM process to alcohol, amphetamines, and LSD has also been briefly discussed. The ubiquitous dichotomy by natives of their world into the sacred and the secular is now understandable: they are both as "real" as sleeping and waking. The ubiquity of the "supernatural" is the human ubiquity of the REM state: as *process* it is everywhere humanly identical, and only in symbolic *content* is there cultural variation.

With these understandings we then embarked on a study of the effects of hallucinogens in their ethnographic contexts. There are cross-cultural constants: hallucination in occidental "normals" and in vision-questing Indians; kayakangst, windigo, and Arctic hysteria are related to cultural institutions, especially to ritual-religious ones, as dreams are related to myths. Hysteric projection and suggestibility, when ego function is variously in abeyance, are everywhere the same: the hallucination of pain in conversion hysteria and the projection of anxiety in phobic hysteria. Only the comparative *cultural* contexts of psychiatric pathologies differ, not the processes themselves. And just as hallucinosis "confirms" whatever is subjectively present, so also ritual acts and accompanying sensory input operate to "confirm" religious beliefs. The "charisma" seemingly streaming from the supernaturally endowed individual, like a compelling animal magnetism, is no more than the psychic delectability of his message for each wishful communicant; his supernatural "rightness" is *déjà vu* in each compelling id-wish. If he tells us we are eternal, we already secretly knew it before.

The historically changing attitudes toward now familiar and accepted psychotropic substances in European tradition, the violent rejection of others, and the varying Hindu and Moslem attitudes toward both—all these provide an ironic commentary and critique of current fanaticisms. Hashish but no ethanol for Arabs, soma but no mead for Vedantists, hops but no pot for America. Continuities from soma to Host are evident ethnographically: secularization to prohibition of once-sacred alcohol, terror at toadstools but mass acceptance of nicotine, a specific poison to each tissue in the body. Rationality plays no part in our attitudes toward psychotropics and hallucinogens.

The many uses of toxic *Daturas* in both hemispheres, from witchcraft to witch-doctoring, were next detailed, to illustrate the wide range of the magic and ritual contexts of one drug. And, in the New World, so numerous are the substances used that we have suggested an aboriginal narcotic complex and "cultural programming" to account for ethnobotanic statistical discrepancies in hemispheric distribution of plant hallucinogens. Individuals and groups may differ in their attitudes toward hallucinogens and psychotropic drugs. But in the alternate inhabiting of two psychic worlds, all mankind is kin. In hallucinosis, cultural or chemical, we need postulate no fatuous "separate reality," for it is always our selfsame selves, but in varying psychic states.

REFERENCES

Adovasio, J. M., and Fry, G. F. Prehistoric psychotropic drug use in Northeastern Mexico and trans-Pecos Texas. Paper presented at the 71st Annual Meeting of the American Anthropological Association, Toronto, 1972.

Agogino, G. A. The use of hypnotism as an ethnologic research technique. *Plains Anthropologist*, 1965, **10** (27), 31–36.

Akstein, D. Kinetic trances and their application in the treatment and prophylaxis of psychoneuroses and psychomatic diseases. Paper presented at the Fourth World Congress of Psychiatry, Madrid, September 1966. (Reviewed in *Transcultural Psychiatry Research Review*, 1968, **5**, 74–75.)

Akstein, D. Terpischoretrancetherapy: A form of group psychotherapy based on ritual possession. *Transcultural Psychiatry Research Review*, 1968, **5**, 74–75.

Altschul, S. R. *The genus Anadenanthera in Amerindian cultures*. Cambridge, Mass.: Harvard Botanical Museum, 1972.

Anon. The cultivation of the opium poppy in Turkey. *Bulletin on Narcotics*, 1950, **2** (1), 13–25. (a)

Anon. Coca chewing, geography and nutrition. *Bulletin on Narcotics*, 1950, **2** (4), 2–13. (b)

Anon. History of heroin. *Bulletin on Narcotics*, 1953, **5** (2), 3–16. (c)

Aserinsky, E., and Kleitman, N. Regularly recurring periods of eye motility and concomitant phenomena during sleep. *Science*, 1953, **118**, 273–274.

Asuni, T. Socio-psychiatric problems of cannabis in Nigeria. *Bulletin on Narcotics*, 1964, **16** (2), 17–28.

Barnouw, V. A psychological interpretation of a Chippewa origin legend. *Journal of American Folklore*, 1955, **68** (267–269), 73–85, 211–223, 341–355.

Belo, J. *Trance in Bali*. New York: Columbia University Press, 1960.

Benabud, A. Psycho-pathological aspects of the cannabis situation in Morocco. *Bulletin on Narcotics*, 1951, **9** (4), 1–16.

Benedict, R. The vision in Plains culture. *American Anthropologist,* 1922, **24,** 1–23.

Benedict, R. *The concept of the guardian spirit in North America.* Menasha, Wisc.: American Anthropological Association, 1923, Memoir 29.

Benedict, R. *Patterns of culture.* Boston: Houghton Mifflin, 1934. (a)

Benedict, R. Anthropology and the abnormal. *Journal of General Psychology,* 1934, **10,** 59–82. (b)

Bennett, A. M. H. Sensory deprivation in aviation. In P. Solomon, P. E. Kubzansky, P. H. Leiderman, J. H. Mendelson, R. Trumbell, and D. Wexler (Eds.), *Sensory deprivation.* Cambridge, Mass.: Harvard University Press, 1961.

Beverly, R. History of Virginia, by a native and inhabitant of the place, 2nd ed. London: B. and S. Tooke, 1722. (Cited by M. C. Stevenson, *Ethnobotany of the Zuni Indians.* Washington, D.C.: Bureau of American Ethnology, Annual Report, 1915, **30,** 31–102.)

Bexton, W. H., Heron, W., and Scott, T. H. Effects of decreased variation in the sensory environment. *Canadian Journal of Psychology,* 1954, **8,** 70–76.

Boas, F. *The social organization and secret societies of the Kwakiutl Indians.* Washington, D.C.: Report of the U.S. National Museum for 1895, 1897, 311–738.

Borhegyi, S. A. Minature mushroom stones from Guatemala. *American Antiquity,* 1961, **26,** 498–504.

Bouquet, R. J. Cannabis. *Bulletin on Narcotics,* 1950, **2** (4), 14–30; 1951, **3** (1), 22–43.

Bourguignon, E. The self, the behavioral environment and the theory of spirit possession. In M. E. Spiro (Ed.), *Context and meaning in cultural anthropology.* New York: Free Press, 1965.

Bourguignon, E. *A cross-cultural study of dissociational states.* Columbus: Ohio State University Research Foundation, 1968. (a)

Bourguignon, E. World distribution and patterns of possession states. In R. Prince (Ed.), *Trance and possession states.* Montreal: R. M. Bucke Memorial Society, 1968. (b)

Bourguignon, E. Divination, transe et possession en Afrique transsaharienne. In A. Caquot and M. Leibovici (Eds.), *La divination.* Paris: Presses Universitaires de France, 1968. (c)

Bourguignon, E. *Religion, altered states of consciousness, and social change.* Columbus: Ohio State University Press, 1972. (a)

Bourguignon, E. Dreams and altered states of consciousness in anthropological research. In F. L. K. Hsu (Ed.), *Psychological anthropology.* Cambridge, Mass.: Schenkman, 1972. (b)

Brownfield, C. A. *Isolation: clinical and experimental approaches.* New York: Random House, 1965.

Buck, A. A., Sasaki, T. T., Hewitt, J. J., and Macrae, A. A. Coca chewing and health, an epidemiological study among residents of a Peruvian village. *Journal of Epidemiology,* 1968, **88,** 159–177.

Burney, C. *Solitary confinement.* London: Clerke and Cockeran, 1952.

Bunzel, R. The role of alcoholism in two Central American cultures. *Psychiatry,* 1940, **3,** 361–387.

Byrd, R. *Alone.* New York: Putnam, 1938.

Campbell, T. N. Origin of the mescal bean cult. *American Anthropologist,* 1958, **60,** 156–160.

Carey, J. T. Marihuana use among the new Bohemians. *Journal of Psychedelic Drugs,* 1968, **2,** 79–92.

Carpenter, E.S. Alcohol in the Iroquois dream quest. *American Journal of Psychiatry,* 1959, **116,** 148–151.

Century Dictionary. New York: Century, 1914.

Chagnon, N. A., LeQuesne, P., and Cook, J. M. Yanömamö hallucinogens, anthropological, botanical, and chemifindings. *Current Anthropology,* 1971, **12,** 72–74.

Chopra, I. C., and Chopra, N. R. The use of the cannabis drugs in India. *Bulletin on Narcotics,* 1957, **9** (1), 4–29. (a)

Chopra, I. C., and Chopra, N. R. The abolition of opium smoking in India. *Bulletin on Narcotics,* 1957, **9** (3), 1–7. (b)

Cohen, B. D., Rosenbaum, G., Dobie, S. I., and Gottlieb, J. S. Sensory isolation: Hallucinogenic effects of a brief exposure. *Journal of Nervous and Mental Disease,* 1959, **129,** 486–491.

Collomb, H., Zempleni, A., and Sow, D. Aspects socio-thérapeutiques du "N'doep" cérémonie d'initiation à la société des possédés chez les Lebou et les Wolof du Senegal. *Neuro-Psychiatrie* [Université de Dakar], 14–16. (Reviewed in *Transcultural Psychiatry Research Review,* 1964, **1,** 136–137.)

Cooper, J. M. The Cree witiko psychosis. In A. Dundes (Ed.), *Every man his way*. Englewood Cliffs, N.J.: Prentice-Hall, 1968.

Cordeiro de Farias, R. Use of maconha (*Cannabis sativa*, L.) in Brazil. *Bulletin on Narcotics*, 1955, **7** (2), 5–19.

Dailey, R. C. The role of alcohol among North American Indians as reported in the Jesuit relations. *Anthropologica*, 1968, **10**, 45–49.

Davidson, W. D. Psychiatric significance of trance cults. Paper presented at the 118th Annual Meeting of the American Psychiatric Association, New York, 1965. (Reviewed in *Transcultural Psychiatry Research Review*, 1966, **3**, 45–47.)

Dement, W. Studies on the function of rapid eye movement (paradoxical) sleep in human subjects. In M. Jouvet (Ed.), *Aspects anatomo-fonctionnels de la physiologie du sommeil*. Paris: Centre de la Recherche Scientifique, 1954.

Dement, W., and Kleitman, N. Cyclic variations in EEG during sleep and their relation to eye movements, body motility, and dreams. *Electroencephalography and Clinical Neurophysiology*, 1957, **9**, 673–690. (a)

Dement, W., and Kleitman, N. The relation of eye movements during sleep to dream activity: An objective method for the study of dreaming. *Journal of Experimental Psychology*, 1957, **53**, 339–346. (b)

Dement, W. The effect of dream deprivation. *Science*, 1960, **131**, 1705–1707.

Dement, W., and Fisher, C. Experimental interference with the sleep cycle. *Canadian Psychiatric Association Journal*, 1963, **8**, 400–405.

Dement, W. Dreaming: A biologic state. *Modern Medicine*, July 5, 1965, 184–206. (a)

Dement, W. Recent studies on the biological role of rapid eye movement sleep. *American Journal of Psychiatry*, 1965, **122**, 404–408. (b)

Dement, W., and Greenberg, S. Changes in total amount of stage four sleep as a function of partial sleep deprivation. *Electroencephalography and Clinical Neurophysiology*, 1966, **20**, 523–526.

Dement, W., Rechtschaffen, A., and Gulevish, G. The nature of the narcoleptic sleep attack. *Neurology*, 1966, **16**, 18–33.

Devereux, G. Normal and abnormal: The key problem of psychiatric anthropology. In J. B. Casagrande and T. Gladwin (Eds.), *Some uses of anthropology: Theoretical and applied*. Washington, D.C.: Anthropological Society of Washington, 1956.

Dobkin de Rios, M. *Trichocereus pachnoi:* A mescaline cactus used in folk healing in Peru. *Economic Botany*, 1968, **22**, 191–194.

Dobkin de Rios, M. Folk healing with a psychedelic cactus in north coastal Peru. *International Journal of Social Psychiatry*, 1969, **15**, 23–32. (a)

Dobkin de Rios, M. Fortune's malice: Divination, psychotherapy, and folk medicine in Peru. *Journal of American Folklore*, 1969, **82** (324), 132–141. (b)

Dobkin de Rios, M. *Visionary vine. Psychedelic healing in the Peruvian Amazon*. San Francisco: Chandler, 1972.

Dobkin de Rios, M. Curing with Ayahuasca in an urban slum. In M. J. Harner (Ed.), *Hallucinogens and shamanism*. New York: Oxford University Press, 1973.

Dodds, E. R. *The Greeks and the irrational*. Berkeley: University of California Press, 1951.

Douyou, E. *La crise de possession dans le vaudou Haïtien*. Unpublished thesis, Université de Montréal, 1965. (Reviewed in *Transcultural Psychiatry Research Review*, 1965, **2**, 155–159.)

Driver, H. E. *Indians of North America*, 2nd ed. Chicago: University of Chicago Press, 1970.

Eggan, D. The significance of dreams for anthropological research. *American Anthropologist*, 1949, **51**, 177–198.

Eggan, D. Dream analysis. In B. Kaplan (Ed.), *Studying personality cross-culturally*. Evanston, Ill.: Row, Peterson, 1961.

Emboden, W. A. *Narcotic plants*. New York: Macmillan, 1972. (a)

Emboden, W. A. Ritual use of *Cannabis sativa* L.: A historicoethnographic study. In P. T. Furst (Ed.), *Flesh of the gods. The ritual use of hallucinogens*. New York: Praeger, 1972. (b)

Faye, L. *Rabelais botaniste*. Angers: Cosnier et Lachèse, 1854.

Fernandez, J. W. Politics and prophecy: African religious movements. *Practical Anthropology*, 1965, **12**, 71–75. (a)

Fernandez, J. W. Symbolic consensus in a Fang religious movement. *American Anthropologist*, 1965, **67**, 902–909. (b)

Fernandez, J. W. *Tabernanthe iboga*: Narcotic ecstasies and the work of the ancestors. In P. T. Furst (Ed.), *Flesh of the gods. The ritual use of hallucinogens*. New York: Praeger, 1972.

Fischer, R. Prediction and measurement of perceptual-behavioral change in drug-induced hallucination. In W. Keup (Ed.), *Origin and mechanisms of hallucinations*. New York: Plenum Press, 1970.

Fisher, C. Dreams, images and perception: A study of unconscious–preconscious relationships. *Journal of the American Psychoanalytic Association*, 1956, **4**, 5–48.

Fisher, C., and Dement, W. Studies in the psychopathology of sleep and dreams. *American Journal of Psychiatry*, 1963, **119**, 1160–1168.

Fogelson, R. Psychological theories of windigo "psychosis" and a preliminary model approach. In M. E. Spiro (Ed.), *Context and meaning in cultural anthropology*. New York: Free Press, 1965.

Freed, S. A., and Freed, R. S. Spirit possession as illness in a North Indian village. *Ethnology*, 1964, **3**, 152–171.

Freedman, S. J., and Greenblatt, M. Studies in human isolation. *U.S. Armed Forces Medical Journal*, 1960, **11**, 1330–1497.

Freedman, S. J., Gruenbaum, H., and Greenblatt, M. Perceptual and cognitive changes in sensory deprivation. *Journal of Nervous and Mental Disease*, 1961, **132**, 17–21.

Freud, S. *Collected papers*. London: Hogarth Press, 1924–1925.

Furst, P. T. Introduction. In P. T. Furst (Ed.), *Flesh of the gods. The ritual use of hallucinogens*. New York: Praeger, 1972.

Gajdusek, D. C., and Zigas, V. Kuru: Clinical, pathological and epidemiological study of an acute progressive disease of the central nervous system among natives of the Eastern Highlands of New Guinea. *American Journal of Medicine*, 1959, **26**, 442–469.

Galdston, I. (Ed.) *Man's image in medicine and anthropology*. New York: International Universities Press, 1963.

Gamage, J. R., and Zerkin, E. L. *A comprehensive guide to the English-language literature on cannabis (Marihuana)*. Beloit, Wisc.: Stash Press, 1965.

Gerlach, L. P. Possession hysteria among the Digo of Kenya. Paper presented at the 64th Annual Meeting, American Anthropological Association, Philadelphia, 1965. (Abstracts, p. 23.)

Gibson, W. *The boat*. Boston: Houghton Mifflin, 1954.

Giel, R., Gezahegn, Y., and van Luijk, J. N. Faith healing and spirit-possession in Ghion, Ethiopia. *Transcultural Research Review*, 1968, **5**, 64–67.

Goldberger, L., and Holt, R. R. Experimental interference with reality contact. *Journal of Nervous and Mental Disease*, 1958, **127**, 99–112.

Gonzales Huerta, I. Identificacion de la mescalina contenida en el *Trichocereus pachanoi* (San Pedro). *Revista del Viernes Medico* [Lima] 1960, **11**, 133–137.

Goodman, F. D. Apostolics of Yucatan: A case study of a religious movement. In E. Bourguignon (Ed.), *Religion, altered states of consciousness, and social change*. Columbus: Ohio State University Press, 1972.

Greenbaum, L. Possession trance in sub-Saharan Africa: A descriptive analysis of fourteen societies. In E. Bourguignon (Ed.), *Religion, altered states of consciousness, and social change*. Columbus: Ohio State University Press, 1972. (a)

Greenbaum, L. Societal correlates of possession trances in sub-Saharan Africa. In E. Bourguignon (Ed.), *Religion, altered states of consciousness, and social change*. Columbus: Ohio State University Press, 1972. (b)

Greenberg, R., and Pearlman, C. *Delirium tremens and dream privation*. Washington, D.C.: Association for the Psychophysiological Study of Sleep, 1964.

Guerra, F. *The pre-Columbian mind: A study into the aberrant nature of sexual drives, drugs affecting behavior, and the attitude towards life and death, with a survey of psychotherapy in pre-Columbian America*. London: Seminar Press, 1971.

Gussler, J. Social change, ecology, and spirit possession among the South African Nguni. In E. Bourguignon (Ed.), *Religion, altered states of consciousness, and social change.* Columbus: Ohio State University Press, 1972.

Gussow, Z. A preliminary report of "kayakangst" among the Eskimo of West Greenland: A study of sensory deprivation. *International Journal of Social Psychiatry,* 1963, **9,** 18–26.

Gutiérrez-Noriega, C., and Sanchez, G. C. Alteraciones mentales producidas por la *Opuntia cylindrica. Revista de Neuropsiquiatria* [Lima], 1947, **10,** 422ff.

Gutiérrez-Noriega, C. Area de mescalinismo en el Peru. *America Indigena,* 1950, **10,** 215.

Hale, E. M. Ilex cassine, the aboriginal North American tea. Washington, D.C.: Department of Agriculture, Bulletin 14, 1891.

Hamer, J., and Hamer, I. Spirit possession and its socio-psychological implications among the Sidamo of Southwest Ethiopia. *Ethnology,* 1966, **5,** 392–408.

Harner, M. J. The role of hallucinogenic plants in European witchcraft. In M. J. Harner (Ed.), *Hallucinogens and shamanism.* New York: Oxford University Press, 1973. (a)

Harner, M. J. The sound of rushing water. In M. J. Harner (Ed.) *Hallucinogens and shamanism.* New York: Oxford University Press, 1973. (b)

Harper, E. B. Spirit possession and social structure. In B. Ratman (Ed.), *Anthropology on the march.* Madras: Thompson and Co., 1962. (Reviewed in *Transcultural Psychiatry Research Review,* 1964, **1,** 107–108.)

Harrington, J. P. Tobacco among the Karuk Indians of California. Washington, D.C.: *Bureau of American Ethnology,* 1932, Bulletin 94, 1–284.

Hartmann, E. L. *The functions of sleep.* New Haven, Conn.: Yale University Press, 1973.

Harvey, N. A. *Imaginary playmates and other mental phenomena.* Ypsilanti, Mich.: State Normal College, 1919.

Heim, R., and Wasson, R. G. La folie des Kuma. *Cahiers du Pacifique,* 1964, **6,** 3–27.

Heim, R., and Wasson, R. G. The "mushroom madness" of the Kuma. [Harvard] *Botanical Museum Leaflets,* 1965, **21** (1), 1–36.

Henney, J. H. The Shakers of St. Vincent: A stable religion. In E. Bourguignon (Ed.), *Religion, altered states of consciousness, and social change.* Columbus: Ohio State University Press, 1972.

Hernandez, F. *Nova plantarum, animalium et mineralium Mexicanorum historia.* Rome: B. Deuersini e Z. Masotti, 1651. In R. E. Schultes and A. Hofmann. *The botany and chemistry of hallucinogens.* Springfield, Ill.: Charles C Thomas, 1973.

Hes, J. P. On the use of *Catha edulis* among Yemenite Jews. *Journal of the Israel Medical Association,* March 1970, **78** (6), 283–284. (Reviewed in *Transcultural Psychiatry Research Review,* 1971, **8,** 62.)

Howard, J. H. The mescal bean cult of the Central and Southern Plains: An ancestor of the peyote cult. *American Anthropologist,* 1957, **59,** 75–87.

Hurlock, E. B., and Burnstein, M. The imaginary playmate: A questionnaire study. *Journal of Genetic Psychology,* 1932, **41,** 380–392.

Jackson, B., and Reed, A. Catnip and the alteration of consciousness. *Journal of the American Medical Association,* 1969, **207,** 1349–1350.

Jevons, F. R. Was Plotinus influenced by opium? *Medical History,* 1965, **9,** 374–380.

Jocano, F. L. Varieties of supernatural experiences among Filipino peasants: Hallucination or idiom of cultural cognition. Paper presented at the 123rd Annual Meeting of the American Psychiatric Association, San Francisco, 1970. (Reviewed in *Transcultural Psychiatry Review,* 1971, **8,** 43–45.)

Kalant, O. J. *The cannabis (Marihuana) literature.* Toronto: Addiction Research Foundation Bibliographic Series No. 2, 1968.

Kane, S. M. Ritual possession in a Southern Appalachian religious sect. *Journal of American Folklore* (in press, Jan.-Feb. 1975).

Katan, M. Dream and psychosis: Their relationship to the hallucinating processes. *International Journal of Psycho-analysis,* 1960, **41,** 341–351.

Kehoe, A. B. The function of ceremonial sexual intercourse among the northern Plains Indians. *Plains Anthropologist,* 1970, **15** (48), 99–103.

Kensinger, K. M. *Banisteriopsis* usage among the Peruvian Cashinahua. In M. J. Harner (Ed..), *Hallucinogens and shamanism.* New York: Oxford University Press, 1973.

Kiev, A. Spirit possession in Haiti. *American Journal of Psychiatry,* 1961, **118,** 133–138.

Kiev, A. (Ed.) *Magic, faith, and healing.* New York: Free Press, 1964.

Kim, K. Psychoanalytic consideration of Korean shamanism. [Journal of the] *Korean Neuropsychiatric Association,* 1972, **11** (2), 121–129.

Kleitman, N. The nature of dreaming. In G. E. W. Wolstenholm and M. O'Connor (Eds.), *The nature of sleep.* Boston: Little, Brown, 1961.

Kleitman, N. *Sleep and wakefulness.* Chicago: University of Chicago Press, 1963.

Kleitman, N. Patterns of dreaming. In T. J. Teyler (Ed.), *Altered states of awareness.* San Francisco: Freeman, 1973.

Kline, N. S. Introduction. The psychology, philosophy, morality, and legislative control of drug uses. In D. Efron, B. Holmstedt, and N. S. Kline (Eds.), *Ethnopharmacologic search for psychoactive drugs.* Washington, D.C.: Public Health Service Publication No. 1645, 1967.

Kritikos, P. G., and Papadaki, S. P. The history of the poppy and of opium and their expansion in antiquity in the Eastern Mediterranean area. *Bulletin on Narcotics,* 1967, **19** (3), 17–38; 1967, **19** (4), 5–10.

Kroeber, A. L. *Anthropology.* New York: Harcourt Brace, 1923.

Kroeber, A. L. *Handbook of the Indians of California.* Washington, D.C.: Bureau of American Ethnology, Bulletin 78, 1925.

Kuhn, T. S. The structure of scientific revolutions. Chicago: University of Chicago Press, 1962.

La Barre, W. *The peyote cult.* New Haven, Conn.: Yale University Publications in Anthropology, 1938, **19,** 93–104. (a)

La Barre, W. Native American beers. *American Anthropologist,* 1938, **40,** 224–234. (b) (Mapped in H. E. Driver, *Indians of North America,* 2nd ed. Chicago: University of Chicago Press, 1970, Map 12.)

La Barre, W. *The Aymara Indians of the Lake Titicaca Plateau, Bolivia.* American Anthropological Association, 1948, Memoir 68.

La Barre, W. *The human animal.* Chicago: University of Chicago Press, 1954.

La Barre, W. Mescalism and peyotism. *American Anthropologist,* 1957, **59,** 708–711.

La Barre, W. The influence of Freud on anthropology. *American Imago,* 1958, **15,** 275–328.

La Barre, W. The narcotic complex of the New World. *Diogenes,* 1964, **48,** 125–138.

La Barre, W. Old and new world narcotics: A statistical question and an ethnological reply. *Economic Botany,* 1970, **24,** 73–80. (a)

La Barre, W. Review of R. G. Wasson, "Soma." *American Anthropologist,* 1970, **72,** 368–373. (b)

La Barre, W. Materials for a history of studies of crisis cults: A bibliographic essay. *Current Anthropology,* 1971, **12** (1), 3–44.

La Barre, W. *The ghost dance: Origins of religion,* rev. ed. New York: Delta Books, 1972. (a)

La Barre, W. Hallucinogens and the shamanic origins of religion. In P. T. Furst (Ed.), *Flesh of the gods. The ritual use of hallucinogens.* New York: Praeger, 1972. (b)

Langness, L. L. Hysterical psychosis in the New Guinea Highlands: A Bena Bena example. *Psychiatry,* 1965, **28,** 258–277.

Langness, L. L. Rejoinder to R. Salisbury regarding his articles "On possession in the New Guinea Highlands, review of the literature" and "Possession among the Siana (New Guinea)". *Transcultural Psychiatry Research Review,* 1967, **4,** 125–130.

Langness, L. L. Possession and ethnic psychosis—A cross-cultural view. Paper presented at the Second International Congress of Social Psychiatry, London, 1969. (a)

Langness, L. L. On possession in the New Guinea Highlands. *Transcultural Psychiatry Research Review,* 1969, **6,** 95–100. (b)

Lawson, J. *History of North Carolina.* Richmond, Va.: Garrett and Massie, 1951.

Lee, R. B. The sociology of Bushman trance performances. Paper presented at the Second Annual Conference of the R. M. Bucke Memorial Society on Possession States in Primitive Societies, Montreal, March 4–6, 1966.

Lee, S. G. Some Zulu concepts of psychogenic disorder. *Journal for Social Research,* 1950, **1,** 9–18.

Lee, S. G. Spirit possession among the Zulu. In J. Beattie and J. Middleton (Eds.), *African mediumship and society.* New York: Africana Publishing, 1970.

Leonard, A. P. Spirit mediums in Palau: Transformations in a transitional system. In E. Bourguignon (Ed.), *Religion, altered states of consciousness, and social change.* Columbus: Ohio State University Press, 1972.

Lewis, I. M. *Ecstatic religion: An anthropological study of spirit possession and shamanism.* Middlesex, England: Penguin Books, 1971.

Lilly, J. C. Illustrative strategies for research on psychopathology in mental health. *Group for the Advancement of Psychiatry* (GAP), 1956, Symposium No. 2, 13–20. (a)

Lilly, J. C. Mental effects of ordinary levels of physical stimuli on intact, healthy persons. *Psychiatric Research Reports, American Psychiatric Association,* 1956, **5,** 1–28. (b)

Lincoln, J. S. *The dream in primitive cultures.* Baltimore: Williams & Wilkins, 1935.

Lindemann, H. *Alone at sea.* New York: Random House, 1958.

Lombard, J. Les cultes de possession en Afrique noir et le Bori Hausa. *Psychopathologie Africaine,* 1967, **3,** 419–439. (Reviewed in *Transcultural Psychiatry Research Review,* 1969, **6,** 65–69.)

Ludwig, A. Altered states of consciousness. In R. Prince (Ed.), *Trance and possession states.* Montreal: R. M. Bucke Memorial Society, 1968.

Madsen, W., and Madsen, C. The cultural structure of Mexican drinking behavior. In D. B. Heath and R. N. Adams (Eds.), *Contemporary cultures and societies of Latin America.* New York: Random House, 1965.

Marcovitz, E., and Myers, H. J. The marihuana addict in the army. *War Psychiatry,* 1964, **6,** 382–391.

Mars, L. La crise de possession et la personalité humaine en Haïti. *Revue de Psychologie des Peuples,* 1962, **17,** 6–22.

Mayor's Committee on Marihuana. *The marihuana problem in the City of New York.* New York: Random House, 1944.

Mechoulam, R. (Ed.) *Marihuana: Chemistry, pharmacology, metabolism and clinical effects.* New York: Academic Press, 1973.

Mikuriya, T. H. Marihuana in medicine: Past, present and future. *California Medicine,* January 1969, **110,** 3–40.

Mischel, W., and Mischel, F. Psychological aspects of spirit possession. *American Anthropologist,* 1958, **60,** 249–260.

Mooney, J. *The ghost dance religion and the Sioux outbreak of 1890.* Washington, D.C.: 14th Annual Report, Bureau of American Ethnology, Part 2, 1896, 641–1136.

Moreau (de Tours), J. *Du hachiche et de l'alienation mentale.* Paris: Fortin, Massin, 1845.

Morton, C. V. Notes on yajé, a drug plant of Southeastern Colombia. *Journal of the Washington Academy of Sciences,* 1931, **21,** 485–488.

Murray, M. A. *Witch cults in Western Europe.* London: Oxford University Press, 1921.

Murray, M. A. *The god of the witches.* New York: Doubleday-Anchor, 1960.

McGlothlin, W. H., and Cohen, S. The use of hallucinogenic drugs among college students. *American Journal of Psychiatry,* 1965, **122,** 572–574.

Nadel, S. F. The origins of music. *Musical Quarterly,* 1950, **16,** 538–542.

Naranjo, C. Psychological aspects of the Yagé experience in an experimental setting. In M. J. Harner (Ed.), *Hallucinogens and shamanism.* New York: Oxford University Press, 1973.

Neher, A. A physiological explanation of unusual behavior in ceremonies involving drums. *Human Biology,* 1962, **34,** 151–160.

Newman, P. L. "Wild man" behavior in a New Guinea Highlands community. *American Anthropologist,* 1964, **66,** 1–19.

Obeyesekere, G. The idiom of demonic possession. *Social Science and Medicine,* 1970, **4,** 97–111.

Oesterreich, T. K. *Die Bessessenheit.* Halle: Wendt und Klauwell, 1922. (Translated as *Possession, demoniacal and other, among primitive races, in antiquity, the middle ages, and modern times.* New York: Richard R. Smith, 1930; University Books, 1966.

Parker, S. The windigo psychosis in the context of Ojibwa culture and personality. *American Anthropologist,* 1960, **62,** 603–624.

Pope, H. G., Jr. *Tabernanthe iboga*—An African narcotic plant of social importance. *Economic Botany,* 1969, **23,** 174–184.

Prance, G. T. Notes on the use of plant hallucinogens. *Economic Botany*, 1970, **24**, 62–68.

Pressel, E. Umbanda in São Paulo: Religious innovation in a developing society. In E. Bourguignon (Ed.), *Religion, altered states of consciousness, and social change.* Columbus: Ohio State University Press, 1972.

Prince, R. Possession cults and social cybernetics. In R. Prince (Ed.), *Trance and possession states.* Montreal: R. M. Bucke Memorial Society, 1968.

Ravenscroft, K. *Spirit possession in Haiti: A tentative theoretical analysis.* Unpublished thesis, Yale University. (Reviewed in *Transcultural Psychiatry Research Review*, 1963, **14**, 51–52.)

Reay, M. Mushroom madness in the New Guinea Highlands. *Oceania*, 1960, **31**, 135–139.

Reay, M. Mushrooms and collective hysteria. *Australian Territories*, 1965, **5**, 18–21.

Reichel-Dolmatoff, G. The cultural context of an aboriginal hallucinogen: *Banisteriopsis caapi.* In P. T. Furst (Ed.), *Flesh of the gods. The ritual use of hallucinogens.* New York: Praeger, 1972.

Ribeiro, R. Possessão: Problema de etnopsicologia. *Boletim do Instituto Joaquin Nabuco de Pesquisas Socials*, 1960, **5**, 2–44.

R[ice], Ch. Historical notes on opium. *New Remedies*, August 1876, **5**, 229–232; May 1877, **6**, 144–145; July 1877, **6**, 194–195.

Ritter, C. E. A woman in the polar night. New York: Dutton, 1954.

Roffwarg, H. P., Muzio, J. N., and Dement, W. C. Ontogenetic development of the human sleep-dream cycle. *Science*, 1966, **152**, 604–619.

Rosenzweig, N. Sensory deprivation and schizophrenia: Some clinical and theoretical similarities. *American Journal of Psychiatry*, 1959, **116**, 326–329.

Safford, W. E. *Daturas of the Old World and New: an account of their narcotic properties and their use in oracular and initiatory ceremonies.* Washington, D.C.: Smithsonian Institution Annual Report for 1920, 537–567, 1922.

Sangree, W. H. Spirit possession and marriage stability in Irigwe, Nigeria. Paper presented at the 67th Annual Meeting, American Anthropological Association, Seattle, Wash., 1968.

Salisbury, R. Possession among the Siana (New Guinea). *Transcultural Psychiatry Research Review*, 1966, **3**, 108–116.

Salisbury, R. R. Salisbury replies. *Transcultural Psychiatry Research Review*, 1967, **4**, 130–134.

Salisbury, R. On possession in the New Guinea Highlands. *Transcultural Psychiatry Research Review*, 1969, **6**, 100–102.

Schepers, E. Psychiatry and folk evaluations of hallucinations and other psychiatric symptoms among Chicano populations. Paper presented at 71st Annual Meeting, American Anthropological Association, Toronto, 1972. (Abstracts, p. 105.)

Schnier, J. The Tibetan Lamaist ritual: Chöd. *International Journal of Psycho-analysis*, 1957, **38**, 402–440.

Schultes, R. E. A new narcotic snuff from the Northwest Amazon. [Harvard] *Botanical Museum Leaflets*, 1954, **16**, 241–260.

Schultes, R. E. A new narcotic genus from the Amazon slope of the Columbian Andes. [Harvard] *Botanical Museum Leaflets*, 1955, **17**, 1–11.

Schultes, R. E. Native narcotics of the New World. *Texas Journal of Pharmacology*, 1961, **2**, 141–167.

Schultes, R. E. Hallucinogenic plants of the New World. *Harvard Review*, 1963, **1**, 18–32. (a)

Schultes, R. E. Botanical sources of New World narcotics. *Psychedelic Review*, 1963, **1**, 145–166. (b)

Schultes, R. E. Ein halbes Jahrhundert ethnobotanik amerikanscher Hallucinogene. *Planta Medica*, 1965, **13**, 125–157.

Schultes, R. E. The search for new natural hallucinogens. *Lloydia*, 1966, **26**, 293–308.

Schultes, R. E. The botanical origins of South American snuffs. In D. Efron, B. Holmstedt, and N. S. Kline (Eds.), *Ethnopharmacologic search for psychoactive drugs.* Washington, D.C.: Public Health Service Publication No. 1645, 1967.

Schultes, R. E., and Holmstedt, B. The vegetal ingredients of the myristicaceous snuffs of the Northwest Amazon. *Rhodora*, 1968, **70**, 113–160.

Schultes, R. E. Virola as an orally administered hallucinogen. [Harvard] *Botanical Museum Leaflets*, 1969, **22**, 133–164. (a)

Schultes, R. E. The plant kingdom and hallucinogens. *Bulletin on Narcotics,* 1969, **21** (3), 3–13; 1969, **21** (4), 15–27; 1970, **22** (1), 25–53. (b)

Schultes, R. E. The New World Indians and their hallucinogenic plants. *Bulletin of the Morris Arboretum,* 1970, **21,** 3–14.

Schultes, R. E. An overview of hallucinogens in the Western Hemisphere. In P. T. Furst (Ed.), *Flesh of the gods. The ritual use of hallucinogens.* New York: Praeger, 1972.

Schultes, R. E., and Hofmann, A. *The botany and chemistry of hallucinogens.* Springfield, Ill.: Charles C Thomas, 1973.

Seitz, G. Epena, the intoxicating snuff powder of the Waiká Indians and the Tucano medicine man, Agostino. In D. Efron, B. Holmstedt, and N. S. Kline (Eds.), *Ethnopharmacologic search for psychoactive drugs.* Washington, D.C.: Public Health Service Publication No. 1645, 1967.

Shackleton, E. *South: The story of Shackleton's last expedition, 1914–17.* New York: Macmillan, 1920.

Sharon, D. The San Pedro cactus in Peruvian folk healing. In P. T. Furst (Ed.) *Flesh of the gods. The ritual use of hallucinogens.* New York: Praeger, 1972.

Shirokogoroff, S. M. *Psychomental complex of the Tungus.* London: Kegan Paul, Trench, Trübner, 1935.

Shonle, R. Peyote: The giver of visions. *American Anthropologist,* 1925, **27,** 53–75.

Silverman, A. J., Cohen, S. I., Schmavonian, B. M., and Greenberg, G. Psychophysiological investigations in sensory deprivation. *Psychosomatic Medicine,* 1961, **23,** 48–60.

Simpson, G. E. The acculturative process in Jamaican revivalism. In A. F. C. Wallace (ed.), *Men and cultures.* Philadelphia: University of Pennsylvania Press, 1960.

Siskind, J. Visions and cures among the Sharanahua. In M. J. Harner (Ed.), *Hallucinogens and shamanism.* New York: Oxford University Press, 1973.

Skinner, A. Societies of the Iowa, Kansa, and Ponca Indians. *American Museum of Natural History, Anthropological Papers,* 1915, **11,** 679–740.

Skinner, A. Ethnology of the Iowa Indians. *Public Museum of the City of Milwaukee Bulletin,* 1926, **5,** 181–354.

Slocum, J. *Sailing alone around the world.* New York: Century, 1900.

Slotkin, J. S. *The peyote religion.* New York: Free Press, 1956.

Solomon, P., Kubzansky, P. E., Leiderman, P. H., Mendelson, J. H., Trumbull, R., and Wexler, D. (Eds.), *Sensory deprivation.* Cambridge, Mass.: Harvard University Press, 1961.

Solomon, P., and Mendelson, J. Hallucinations in sensory deprivation. In L. J. West (Ed.), *Hallucinations.* New York: Grune & Stratton, 1962.

Sonnedecker, G. Emergence of the concept of opiate addiction. *Journal Mondial de Pharmacie,* 1962, **3,** 275–290; 1963, **4,** 27–43.

Soueif, M. I. Hashish consumption in Egypt, with special reference to psychosocial aspects. *Bulletin on Narcotics,* 1967, **19** (2), 1–12.

Svendsen, M. Children's imaginary companions. *Archives of Neurology and Psychiatry,* 1934, **32,** 985–999.

Taylor, K. I., and Laughlin, W. S. Sub-Arctic commitment and "kayak fear." Paper presented at the 62nd Annual Meeting of the American Anthropological Association, San Francisco, 1963.

Teyler, T. J. (Ed.) *Altered states of awareness.* San Francisco: Freeman, 1973.

Troike, R. C. The origin of Plains mescalism. *American Anthropologist,* 1962, **64,** 946–963.

Van der Kroef, J. Messianic movements in the Celebes, Sumatra, and Borneo. In S. L. Thrupp (Ed.), *Millenial dreams in action: Essays in comparative study.* The Hague: Mouton, 1962.

Van der Walde, P. H. Trance states and ego psychology. In R. Prince (Ed.), *Trance and possession states.* Montreal: R. M. Bucke Memorial Society, 1968.

Vernon, J. A., McGill, T. E., and Schiffman, H. Visual hallucinations during perceptual isolation. *Canadian Journal of Psychology,* 1958, **12,** 31–34.

Vostrovsky, C. A study of imaginary companions. *Education,* 1895, **15,** 393–398.

Wallace, A. F. C. Mental illness, biology and culture. In F. L. K. Hsu (Ed.), *Psychological anthropology.* Cambridge, Mass.: Schenkman, 1972.

Washburne, C. Primitive religions and alcohol. *International Journal of Comparative Sociology*, 1968, **9,** 97–105.

Wassén, S. H. The use of some specific kinds of South American Indian snuff and related paraphernalia. *Etnologiska Studier*, 1965, **28,** 1–116.

Wassén, S. H. Anthropological survey of the use of South American snuffs. In D. Efron, B. Holmstedt, and N. S. Kline (Eds.), *Ethnopharmacologic search for psychoactive drugs*. Washington, D.C.: Public Health Service Publication No. 1645, 1967.

Wassén, S. H. Ethnobotanical follow-up of Bolivian Tiahuanacoid tomb material and of Peruvian shamanism, psychotropic plant constituents, and espingo seeds. *Göteborgs Etnografiska Museum Årstryck 1972*, 1973, 35–52.

Wasson, R. G. Lightning-bolt and mushrooms: An essay in early cultural exploration. In *To honor Roman Jakobson*. The Hague: Mouton, 1956.

Wasson, R. G., and Wasson, V. P. *Mushrooms, Russia and history*. New York: Pantheon, 1957.

Wasson, R. G. The divine mushroom: Primitive religion and hallucinatory agents. *Proceedings of the American Philosophical Society*, 1958, **102** (3) 221–223.

Wasson, R. G. The hallucinogenic mushrooms of Mexico and psilocybin: A bibliography. [Harvard] *Botanical Museum Leaflets*, 1962, **20,** 25–73.

Wasson, R. G. *Soma, divine mushroom of immortality*. New York: Harcourt Brace Jovanovich, 1968.

Wasson, R. G. The divine mushroom of immortality. In P. T. Furst (Ed.), *Flesh of the gods. The ritual use of hallucinogens*. New York: Praeger, 1972. (a)

Wasson, R. G. What was the soma of the Aryans? In P. T. Furst (Ed.), *Flesh of the gods. The ritual use of hallucinogens*. New York: Praeger, 1972. (b)

Watt, J. M. Dagga in South Africa. *Bulletin on Narcotics*, 1961, **13** (3), 9–14.

Weil, A. T. Nutmeg as a narcotic. *Economic Botany*, 1965, **19,** 194–217.

Weil, A. T. Nutmeg as a psychoactive drug. In D. Efron, B. Holmstedt, and N. S. Kline (Ed.), *Ethnopharmacologic search for psychoactive drugs*. Washington, D.C.: Public Health Service Publication No. 1645, 1967.

Weiner, M. A. *Earth medicine—earth foods: Plant remedies, drugs, and natural foods of the North American Indians*. New York: Macmillan, 1972.

Weiss, G. Hallucinogenic and narcotic-like effects of powdered myristica (nutmeg). *Psychiatric Quarterly*, 1960, **34,** 346–356.

Weiss, G. Shamanism and priesthood in light of the Campa *Ayahuasca* ceremony. In M. J. Harner (Ed.) *Hallucinogens and shamanism*. New York: Oxford University Press, 1973.

West, A. T. The use of nutmeg as a psychotropic agent. *Bulletin on Narcotics*, 1966, **18** (4), 15–23.

Wexler, D., Mendelson, J. H., Leiderman, H., and Solomon, P. Perceptual isolation, A technique for studying psychiatric aspects of stress. *AMA Archives of Neurology and Psychiatry*, 1958, **79,** 225–233.

Wheaton, J. L. Fact and fancy in sensory deprivation. *Aeromedical Review*, 1959, **5.**

Wilbert, J. Tobacco and shamanistic ecstasy among the Warao Indians of Venezuela. In P. T. Furst (Ed.), *Flesh of the gods. The ritual use of hallucinogens*. New York: Praeger, 1972.

Willems, E. Religious mass movements and social change in Brazil. In D. B. Heath (Ed.), *Contemporary cultures and societies of Latin America*, 2nd ed. New York: Random House, 1974.

Williams, F. E. The Vailala madness and the destruction of native ceremonies in the Gulf Division, Port Moresby. *Territory of Papua: Anthropological Reports*, 1923, **4.**

Williams, F. E. The Vailala madness in retrospect. In E. E. Evans-Pritchard, R. Firth, B. Malinowski, and I. Schapera (Eds.), *Essays presented to C. G. Seligman*. London: Kegan Paul, Trench, Trübner, 1934.

Winick, C. The use of drugs by jazz musicians. *Social Problems*, Winter 1959–1960, **3,** 240–253.

Winick, C. Marihuana use by young people. In E. Harms (Ed.), *Drug addiction in youth*. New York: Pergamon Press, 1965.

Wintrob, R. M. Psychosis in association with possession by Genii in Liberia. *Psychopathologie Africaine*, 1966, **2,** 249–258. (Reviewed in *Transcultural Psychiatry Research Review*, 1968, **5,** 55–59).

Wintrob, R. M. Sexual guilt and culturally sanctioned delusions in West Africa. Paper presented at the 123rd Annual Meeting, American Psychiatric Association, Detroit, 1967 (Reviewed in *Transcultural Psychiatry Research Review*, 1967, **4**, 149–152).

Wissler, C. *The American Indian*, 2nd ed. New York: Oxford University Press, 1922.

Wittkower, E. D. Spirit possession in Haitian vodun ceremonies. *Transcultural Psychiatry Review*, 1963, **14**, 53–55.

Wittkower, E. D. Spirit possession in Haitian vodun ceremonies. *Acta Psychotherapeutica* (Basel), 1964, **12**, 72–80.

Wolstenholme, G. E. W., and Knight, J. (Eds.) *Hashish: Its chemistry and pharmacology*. Boston: Little, Brown, 1965.

Zaretsky, I. I. *Bibliography on spirit possession and spirit mediumship*. Berkeley: Department of Anthropology, mimeographed copy, ca. 1970.

Zerries, O. Medizinmannwesen und Geisterglaube der Waika-Indianer des oberen Orinoko. *Ethnologica*, 1960, **2**, 485–507.

Zilboorg, G., and Henry, G. W. *A history of medical psychology*. New York: Norton, 1941.

Zubek, J. P. (Ed.) *Sensory deprivation: Fifteen years of research*. New York: Appleton-Century-Crofts, 1969.

CHAPTER TWO

THE CONTINUUM OF CNS EXCITATORY STATES AND HALLUCINOSIS

WALLACE D. WINTERS, M.D., Ph.D.

Rarely is it possible for scientists to express the results of their investigations and to synthesize them with other data into an unifying concept. It is with this approach in mind that we embarked on the present chapter, which presents a continuum of central nervous system (CNS) excitatory states and the relationship of hallucinations to this continuum, to the symptomatology of schizophrenia, and to the development of inappropriate ideation. The possible etiology of the hallucinatory states is also discussed.

An hallucination may be defined as a state whereby a subject experiences perceptual changes in his environment which appear inappropriate to an observer. At least four causes of hallucinations can be described: the hallucination of sensory deprivation, the hallucination of dreams during rapid eye movement (REM) sleep, the hallucination induced by psychotomimetic drugs, and the hallucinations that occur during schizophrenia. In sensory deprivation and dream hallucinosis, the underlying mechanism appears to be related to a reduction in environmental sensory cues, resulting in a reduction of sensory stimulation that induces an endogenously triggered perceptual distortion. The hallucinations following treatment with psychotomimetic agents or during a schizophrenic episode appear to be characterized by sensory input overload from environmental sensory cues. We discuss the hallucinosis induced by psychotomimetic agents and the possible relation between this phenomenon and the schizophrenic hallucinatory state.

The first question one must deal with in a discussion of drug-induced hallucinatory states is whether there is a relation between these induced states and schizophrenia. The advent of phenothiazine therapy for schizophrenia and the concomitant indications of a possible neurochemical basis for the psychotic states set the groundwork for the idea that schizophrenia results from subtle changes in the endogenous metabolic activity of the CNS. Although much of this work is still theoretical, it does form the framework for establishing an experimental approach to the examination of the physiological and biochemical basis of the schizophrenic state.

It is highly desirable to evaluate disease states by inducing a comparable condition in experimental animals under rigid laboratory conditions. At present, there are no surgical procedures capable of inducing a state comparable to that of schizophrenia in man. However, pharmacological agents have been used to induce animal syndromes similar to schizophrenic syndromes (Hollister, 1968). Much enthusiasm was initially generated by the demonstration of the hallucinatory properties of lysergic acid diethylamide (LSD), and it was proposed as a chemical model for psychosis (Giberti and Gregoretti, 1955; Rinkel, 1955). Unfortunately, this has not been well accepted, since LSD induces predominantly visual hallucinations (Stoll, 1949; Forrer and Goldner, 1951), whereas schizophrenia usually elicits a greater degree of auditory and other sensory hallucinatory behaviors. In addition, the problem of bizarre and abnormal ideation was not significantly observed with LSD (Hollister, 1968). Shortly after the early research, it was demonstrated that individuals using high dosages of amphetamines did manifest profound symptoms of paranoid delusions and other abnormal ideation similar to the schizophrenic state, but they rarely hallucinated (Connell, 1958). Although use of amphetamines and LSD results in some of the symptomatology of schizophrenic syndromes, neither is totally adequate as a model for those states.

The majority of LSD users do not generally end up as overt schizophrenics. Therefore we looked at other agents that induce hallucinatory behavior to determine whether it was possible to demonstrate symptomatology more closely resembling the schizophrenic syndrome. The goal was to demonstrate drugs that have the ability to facilitate auditory and other sensory input, as well as visual input. If the schizophrenic state is induced by a biochemical change within the central nervous system, it is essential to show that suspected endogenous substances, as well as exogenous psychotomimetic agents, could induce this mixed sensory hallucinatory behavior.

The technique chosen involved an assessment of gross behavior and brain activity. Cortical and subcortical electroencephalograms (EEGs), averaged evoked responses to auditory and visual stimuli, and multiple-unit activity from the midbrain reticular formation were recorded. Studies were performed on cats in which chronic brain electrodes were implanted (Winters et al., 1967a; Mori et al., 1968; Winters et al., 1972). With these techniques, characteristic changes were noted for each control state. Such changes included wakefulness, slow-wave sleep, and rhombencephalic sleep (RPS or paradoxical sleep). After acquisition of suitable control data, a drug was administered and the drug-induced states were examined (Winters, 1964; Winters et al., 1967a; Mori et al., 1968).

CONTINUUM OF CNS STATES

On the basis of studies with various CNS excitatory and depressant agents, a biphasic continuum of CNS excitation or depression was demonstrated (Winters et al., 1967b; Mori et al., 1968). This schema (Fig. 1) states that anesthetics and CNS excitants induce an initial excitation (Stage I) characterized by increased movement—initially searching, then purposeless—followed by ataxia. Some anesthetics then induce surgical anesthesia (Stage III) characterized by a loss of responsiveness to painful stimuli, slow, regular respiration, a loss of the righting

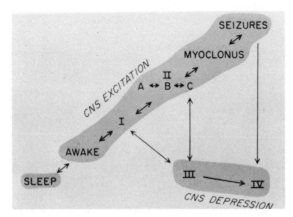

Figure 1 Schema of reversible progression of states of CNS excitation and depression.

reflex, and CNS depression. Other anesthetics induce Stage II prior to Stage III. Stage II (Fig. 2) is characterized by bizarre postures and hallucinatory (A,B) movements, such as appearing to visually track objects in space, then fixate on unseen objects. Cataleptoid (C) behavior is characterized by a loss of the righting reflex, unresponsiveness to noxious stimuli, and bizarre, fixed postures with eyes opened. Many anesthetics do not induce Stage III following II but either induce only Stage II or progress to heightened levels of CNS excitation (i.e., a cataleptoid posture with spontaneous or induced myoclonic jerking of the face, limbs, or entire body, followed by generalized grand mal type, clonic–tonic seizures). Further CNS depression during Stage III will progress to Stage IV (medullary paralysis), with depressed respiration and/or cardiovascular function, terminating in death. The progression is reversible provided the subject does not die either during the convulsions or during Stage IV depression.

There are characteristic patterns of behavior and EEG during the various stages and levels of CNS excitability (Figs. 2 and 3). The EEG during Stage I is characterized by an activated pattern with high-frequency, low-voltage activity (desynchronizations). During Stage II, the initial phase (A) is characterized by intermittent bursts of high-amplitude, 2.5-Hz waves (hypersynchrony) associated with the hallucinoid behavior previously described. During Stage II B, the hypersynchronous waves are continuous, and the bizarre actions of the cats are more intense. During Stage II C, the animals lose the righting reflex and maintain bizarre cataleptoid postures; the EEG pattern changes to 1.5-Hz slow waves with occasional spiking. More profound CNS excitation is accompanied by myoclonic jerks and the EEG patterns of spike bursts followed by increasingly prolonged periods of relative electrical silence. This phase can continue for prolonged periods or can culminate in a generalized tonic–clonic seizure with a high-frequency, high-voltage EEG discharge in all leads, lasting up to one minute. During Stage III, there is a progressive reduction in the amplitude of the EEG (Fig. 3), and the general EEG pattern is not as stereotyped as it is for the general group of CNS excitants. All the preceding EEG patterns reappear during emergence, but they are not as clear-cut as during induction.

Neuronal activity of the reticular formation during these various phases of

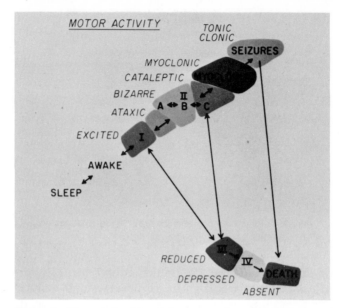

Figure 2 The relationship of the progression of CNS states and motor activity.

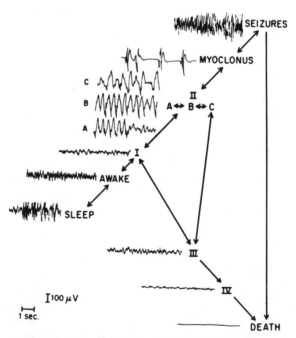

Figure 3 The relationship of the progression of CNS states and corresponding EEG patterns.

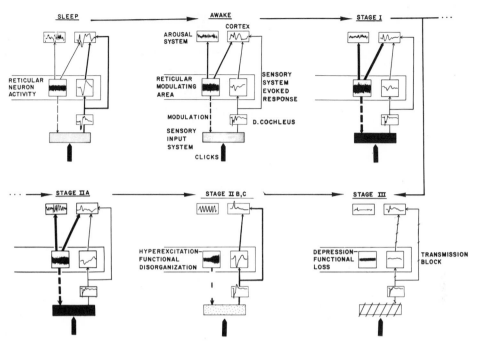

Figure 4 Diagrammatic representation of modulation control of sensory input and arousal systems by the reticular modulating area; representation of effect of this modulation and the transmission of an AER at the level of the dorsal cochlear, midbrain reticular formation, and cortex. The left-side box in reticular area denotes the envelope of reticular multiple-unit activity; the upper left box, the cortical EEG; the right side boxes, the auditory responses. The darker the box denoting the sensory input system, the greater the degree of modulation; during Stage III, there is no modulation. The thickness of the lines indicates a qualitative difference in degree of effect (i.e., the thicker the line, the greater the effect). Absence of lines denotes complete loss of the transmission, and cross marks on lines represent markedly reduced transmission.

excitation and depression correlates with the EEG and behavior (Fig. 4). During Stage I, the degree of tonic activity and phasic excitability of reticular units is equal to or slightly elevated over the awake control levels. During the initial phases of Stage II (i.e., A and B), the tonic level of the units is equal to or slightly less than Stage I, and during C it is lower than Stage I; however, the phasic excitability is increased. This degree of phasic excitability is greater during myoclonus (spiking), and during generalized seizures the neuronal excitability is markedly increased. Those agents inducing Stage III clearly demonstrate a marked fall in both the tonic and phasic levels of unit activity, indicating a marked reduction in unit excitability.

All the agents examined have the same general initial EEG and behavioral patterns, differing only in the degree of progression of CNS excitation or depression. The least active CNS excitant agents induce only the initial phases of the progression (Fig. 5). For example, 2 to 8 mg/kg of d-amphetamine induces only the initial desynchronization and motor excitability; 50 to 100 μg/kg of LSD-25 induces desynchronization followed by intermittent hypersynchrony. Mescaline (25 mg/kg) and 80 to 90% nitrous oxide (N_2O) induce desynchronization, intermittent and then continuous hypersynchrony associated with bizarre postures,

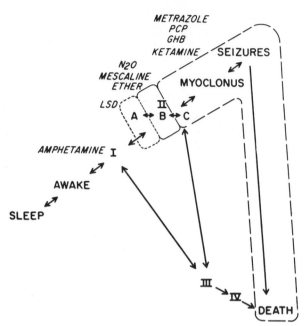

Figure 5 Schema of the progression CNS states induced by various CNS active agents.

and inappropriate behavior. Similarly, 10 to 15% diethyl ether induces the initial progression up to continuous hypersynchrony, followed by the characteristic EEG and behavioral patterns of CNS depression. In addition, 2 to 8 mg/kg of phency-clidine, 500 to 800 mg/kg of gamma-hydroxybutyrate (GHB), and 20 mg/kg of pentylenetetrazol transcend the initial phases and induce the total progression to generalized seizure.

Although the initial state of CNS excitation (Fig. 6) is clearly a behavioral and electrical psychomotor stimulation, the next three induced states are less clearly defined. These states are characterized by inappropriate behavior coupled with abnormal postures indicative of "hallucinatory" behavior. We cannot be certain that this induced state in cats is an hallucinatory phenomenon similar to that which occurs in man; however, the behavior is pronounced in the cat following treatment with agents such as LSD, mescaline, and psilocybin, all of which induce profound hallucinatory actions in man. In addition to the induction of hallucinatory behavior in man, these agents induce 2.5- to 3-Hz hypersynchronous EEG wave patterns during the hallucinatory state in our cats as well as in man (Heath and Mickle, 1960). Adey and his co-workers (1962) demonstrated that LSD induced an apparent intermittent loss of contact with the environment at the same time that the hypersynchronous 3-Hz EEG waves appeared in the EEG of cats performing in a T-maze. Thus there is strong presumptive evidence that the induced state of intermittent and continuous hypersynchrony, coupled with inappropriate postures, represents an hallucinoid state in the cat. We refer to these states as hallucinoid with the clear realization that this is speculation about the cat's behavior.

The human subject is usually conscious of the experience of hallucinations

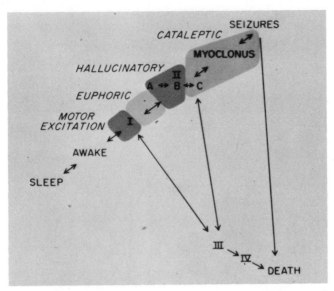

Figure 6 The relationship of the progression of CNS states and behavioral responses.

induced by LSD. Since the EEG (Figs. 3 and 5) is characterized by intermittent bursts of hypersynchronous activity during the LSD-induced state, the periodic episodes of desynchronization between hypersynchrony suggest that the subject returns intermittently to an excited, nonhallucinating, aware state. He thus has a reference point to aid his consciousness of the experience. This EEG pattern is also quite labile, since arousal stimuli, such as a rat placed in the box with the cat, will block the hallucinatory behavior and intermittent hypersynchrony. The cat orients to the rat. When the rat is removed, the pattern and behavior return to an hallucinatory state. We refer to this state as Hallucinatory A (Fig. 7).

The next EEG pattern induced by mescaline, nitrous oxide, ether, ketamine, or phencyclidine (Figs. 3 and 5) is one of continuous hypersynchrony (Mori et al., 1968). Anecdotally, subjects hallucinating following these agents are not conscious that they are hallucinating at the time but later usually have recall of the event. This state is called Hallucinatory B (Fig. 7). It is postulated that the unawareness of subjects during Hallucinatory B is a manifestation of the induced continuous hypersynchrony, with no return to the desynchronized EEG patterns, as was characteristic of Hallucinatory A.

During the EEG pattern of reduced-frequency hypersynchrony induced by ketamine, phencyclidine, GHB, diethyl ether, or pentylenetetrazol, the subjects apparently are unaware that they are hallucinatory, are not rousable, and have no recall. This state is referred to as Hallucinatory C (Fig. 7). Of interest is the finding that the Hallucinatory C phase is utilized in anesthesiology as a state of general anesthesia. For example, ketamine, phencyclidine, and GHB have been reported to be anesthetic agents (Winters et al., 1967b; Winters et al., 1972). Apparently then, these agents meet the major requirements of an anesthetic agent (i.e., loss of responsiveness, and amnesia). Many of these agents such as GHB, ethrane, etoxidrol, and phencyclidine traverse the continuum and induce generalized

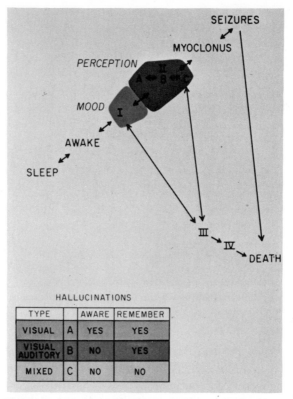

Figure 7 The relationship of the progression of CNS states with mood and perception; and a table of the relationship between the hallucinogenic states, consciousness and recall.

seizures (Winters and Spooner, 1965a, 1965b; Winters et al., 1967b) in a manner similar to the progression induced by pentylenetetrazol. The hallucinoid activity preceding the generalized seizure activity induced by these convulsant agents may be the same as the aura noted clinically prior to pentylenetetrazol or spontaneous grand-mal seizures. The major difference between these agents is based on the differences in potency and speed of onset of each stage of the continuum, 40-mg/kg pentylenetetrazol crossing the continuum rapidly within three minutes, and 800 mg/kg GHB taking four hours. Thus it is easier to achieve an hallucinatory stage with GHB because the substance is less potent and has a longer latency to each stage, and because the duration of each stage is prolonged. For example, an hallucinatory dose of pentylenetetrazole is 20 mg/kg, and the duration 5 to 10 minutes. On the other hand, an hallucinatory dose of GHB is 300 to 400 mg/kg, which lasts 20 to 90 minutes (Winters and Spooner, 1965a).

CONTROL OF SENSORY SYSTEMS

A neuropharmacological approach to the study of the basic etiology of schizophrenia would be to select drugs that induce a state identical with the clinical disease. Thus far, the search for suitable drugs has been deemed unsuccessful because, as noted previously, hallucinogenic agents like LSD induce mainly visual aberrations, whereas psychotic episodes usually involve auditory or multisensory hallucinations (Hollister, 1968).

In an attempt to develop a working hypothesis of the etiology and the development of schizophrenia, the relationship between the auditory and visual system during acute drug-induced states of "hallucinatory" activity was examined.

Our continuum model focuses mainly on the intermediate states of excitation characterized by hallucinoid activity.

Modulation of Sensory Systems.   To clarify the dichotomy between drug-induced hallucinatory states and those found in psychotic patients, the modulation control of various sensory inputs was examined during spontaneous and drug-induced states, and a model was postulated (Winters and Spooner, 1965a, 1965b; Winters et al., 1967b; Mori et al., 1968; Winters, 1969; Winters and Wallach, 1970). The model is based on the assumptions that sensory inputs are directly controlled by a subcortical modulating system located in the midbrain reticular formation, and that the reticular system varies the level of modulation in accordance with the regulation of the state of arousal. The existence in the reticular formation of an inhibitory system acting on the first synaptic relays within each of the classic afferent systems, has been postulated previously. Killam and Killam (1958) suggest that this inhibitory system filters incoming information to control its priority level. Scheibel and Scheibel (1962) have demonstrated that reticular neurons bifurcate and send ascending branches into the diencephalon and cortex and descending branches caudally as far as the spinal cord and receptors. Therefore, there appears to be some anatomic evidence for the proposed modulatory system.

Auditory System.   Comparison of the auditory evoked response (AER) during the natural states of wakefulness and sleep demonstrates that the potential recorded at the dorsal cochlear nucleus, the midbrain reticular formation, and the association cortex is largest during slow-wave sleep (SWS), smaller when the animal is awake, and smallest during RPS. A comparison of the reticular unit activity with these findings indicates an inverse correlation (i.e., the level of unit activity is lowest during a slow-wave sleep and highest during RPS). Since the level of reticular neuronal activity is directly correlated with the level of arousability (i.e., wakefulness and sleep), it appears likely that this level of neuronal activity is likewise related to the degree of modulation exerted by the reticular system on the auditory sensory input system (Winters et al., 1967a). The model states that when reticular unit activity is reduced there is less modulation exerted at the peripheral input system; therefore the transmitted sensory signal is larger, making the evoked response larger. Conversely, when the animal is highly alert, reticular unit activity is elevated, modulating activity is elevated, the transmitted sensory input signal is reduced, and the evoked response is smaller (Fig. 4).

Drugs that induce desynchronization, intermittent hypersynchrony, and early continuous hypersynchrony also induce a slight fall in the amplitude of the evoked responses as compared with the awake control. During this activity the reticular unit activity is high, the animals are markedly aroused, and sensory modulation is increased; thus there is an apparent reduction in the amplitude of the sensory input, and evoked responses are reduced.

During the later phase of the hypersynchronous activity, the animal does not arouse either electrically or behaviorally, the evoked potentials are slightly larger than controls, and the basal level of unit activity begins to fall, but the units appear to fire in synchronous bursts. Since the arousal response disappears at the same time that this intermittent bursting of units occurs, it appears that the reticular unit activity has undergone a partial functional disorganization (Schlag and Balvin, 1963; Winters and Spooner, 1966), and although highly excitable, the reticular units exert a reduced control over the level of arousal and sensory modulation. As this functional disorganization becomes more profound, the EEG pattern changes to the spiking phase, and the bursting pattern of unit activity becomes more pronounced. At this time there is a more profound loss of reticular modulation, the sensory input becomes markedly elevated, and the evoked response in all brain areas is enlarged (Figs. 4 and 8).

Reviewing the action of agents on the auditory system during the hallucinatory phase of action, it appears that drugs that induce only intermittent hypersynchrony (i.e., LSD) reduce the auditory evoked response, whereas agents that induce a progression of action to continuous 2.5- to 1.5-Hz hypersynchrony (i.e., mescaline, nitrous oxide, ether, phencyclidine, and GHB) can induce an augmen-

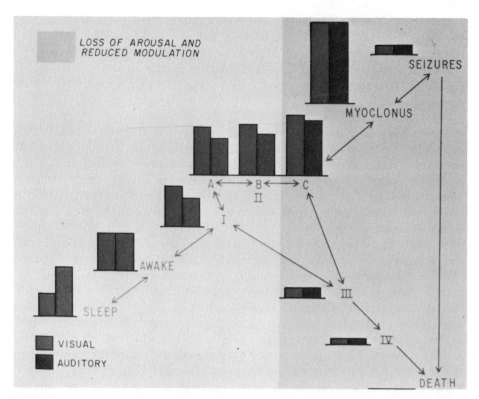

Figure 8 The relationship of the progression of CNS states and auditory or visual evoked responses. Loss of reticular arousal and modulation appears between Hallucinatory B and C and Stages I and III.

tation of the auditory evoked response. This augmentation appears when the modulation of auditory input is reduced because of functional disorganization of the reticular system (Figs. 4 and 8). Thus it appears that agents inducing 2.5- to 1.5-Hz hypersynchronous activity may be useful tools for investigating states of auditory aberration more closely associated with the clinical symptoms of the psychotic hallucination.

Visual System.   To understand better the role of LSD action on the visual system, studies paralleling those described for the auditory system were performed. Apter and Pfeiffer (1957) reported that the visual system activity induced by LSD starts in the retina and travels through visual pathways up to the visual cortex. They also describe clinical studies indicating that LSD does not induce hallucinations when administered to patients whose optic nerves had been severed.

Visual hallucinations can be postulated to result from an abnormally large number of visual stimuli entering the CNS; these overload the visual system, resulting in bizarre sensory manifestations. Evidence in favor of this premise is noted by the studies of Purpura (1956a, 1965b) that demonstrated an increase in the visual evoked response (VER) in both lateral geniculate and cortex following LSD, at the same time that the AER was reduced.

Studies in our laboratory demonstrate that the VER is largest during wakefulness, smaller during SWS, and smallest during RPS. These findings are in agreement with Granit (1955), who demonstrated that reticular activation induces facilitated responsiveness of retinal cells. Thus the cat appears to show both an inverse relationship between the level of reticular neuron activity and that of the auditory system activity and a direct relationship between the visual system and the reticular system level of activity. The exception to this is noted during RPS, when both auditory and visual responses are reduced. It appears that the cat is an "auditory animal" during sleep and a "visual animal" when awake (Fig. 8). During RPS, both auditory and visual inputs are markedly reduced, and the cat is a "sensory-deprived animal."

Following amphetamine, and during the initial desynchronous activity induced by the more potent CNS excitant agents (i.e., LSD, mescaline, nitrous oxide, ether, phencyclidine, GHB, and pentylenetetrazol), the visual evoked response increases in size over the awake control. During the intermittent hypersynchronous activity (Hallucinatory A), the VER is further enhanced, apparently so much that abnormal amounts of visual information are transmitted within the CNS, resulting in the visual hallucinations. This state is characterized by an enlarged evoked response, elevated reticular unit activity, and intermittent 2.5-Hz hypersynchronous EEG bursts. Mescaline, nitrous oxide, ether, phencyclidine, and GHB produce a progression of increasing reticular functional disorganization (i.e., 2.5–1.5-Hz hypersynchrony, Hallucinatory C) to spikes with electrical silence. During the progression, there is an increase in the VER, reaching markedly enlarged response amplitudes during the latter phases.

It appears that the visual system, which has a high functional priority during the awake state, can be excessively activated to the point of disruption by overloading the input system during states of increased excitation induced by LSD. As the CNS excitation continues to the point of inducing a functional disorganization of the reticular formation modulation system, other sensory systems, such as the auditory system, lose reticular modulation. As a result, there is an augmentation of sensory information through these systems (Fig. 8) and multisensory aberrations appear, manifested, in man, by sensory distortions.

All the data presented in this chapter are based on neurophysiological responses in the implanted cat preparation. Unfortunately, these phenomena are not easily observed in cortical recordings in human subjects. Heath and Mickle (1960) have found that hypersynchronous epileptoid EEG patterns do appear in subcortical brain areas of implanted human subjects following treatment with psychotomimetic agents and during schizophrenic episodes. However, the cortical manifestation of these phenomena is an activated, desynchronized cortical pattern. Goldstein and co-workers (1965) showed that this pattern could be differentiated from normal awake EEG patterns by a reduction in variability. This indicates an increased level of CNS excitation during the psychotic states. The cortical manifestation of hyperexcitation is compatible with the concept of a CNS continuum of excitability, resulting in a loss of reticular modulating control in the schizophrenic state.

Three points are relevant regarding the relation of visual and auditory systems to reticular formation modulation of input signals (Fig. 8): (1) as evidenced by the amplitude of the evoked response, the asleep cat is an auditory animal and the awake cat is a visual animal; (2) as one progresses through the continuum, the AER is reduced and the VER is progressively increased through Hallucinatory A and B; and (3) during Hallucinatory C, the animal is no longer arousable, the AER begins to enlarge, and both AER and VER are markedly enlarged during the pattern of spiking with electrical silence. The increase in size of the AER during Hallucinatory B and C and the loss of the arousal response correlate with the progressive increase in the pattern of reticular neuronal activity. There is an initial loss of functional organization during Hallucinatory B, and during Hallucinatory C there is complete functional disorganization. Thus sensory inputs are no longer modulated, and the evoked responses to all sensory stimuli are increased.

Since the schizophrenic hallucination involves more than one modality (i.e., auditory, visual, somatosensory, etc.), an abnormality in the general modulation system in the reticular formation appears to exist during this disease. The psychotic hallucination may be triggered by abnormally large numbers of sensory stimuli entering the CNS, which would normally be inhibited at the peripheral sense organ. In psychosis or after hallucinogenic agents, these stimuli can enter the CNS and overload one or more sensory systems, resulting in altered sensory experiences.

SYNTHESIS

In our operational definition, schizophrenia is a syndrome that develops over time in response to alternating states of perceptual imbalance, resulting in superstitious and inferred inappropriate behavior and ideation. The schizophrenic state appears to fall in the general range of Hallucinatory B to C. As the modulatory control of the prepsychotic becomes increasingly more disrupted, perception of the patient's total environment becomes more and more bizarre. Thus lack of a clear symptomatology in schizophrenic states may be a function of the patient's individuality, past experiences, and rate of change in sensory control.

Our continuum theory leads to the expectation that the schizophrenic patient will have a predominance of visual hallucinatory experiences rather than auditory and other sensory aberrations. Small et al. (1966) have reported that 66% of the hallucinations of schizophrenic patients were auditory, 42% were bodily, 38% were olfactory, and only 30% were visual. Our interpretation of this finding is based on the knowledge that man is a visual animal. He has learned to rationalize and accept visual inputs even though they are distorted, reversed, or unreal (e.g., mirror images, depth sensation, afterimages, dreams). Visual aberrations are less threatening to him than other sensations, such as auditory disturbances, that have no rational basis. Man does not show concern about visual perceptual disturbances but does when auditory and/or somatosensory symptoms occur. Perhaps the 30% incidence of visual hallucinations is more indicative of the percentage of visual imagery that was of great concern to subjects rather than the actual percent of occurrence. Chapman (1966), studying early childhood symptoms of patients who became schizophrenic, noted a high incidence of visual perceptual disturbances prior to disturbances of other modalities, long before the patient sought medical help.

Anecdotal descriptions of schizophrenic hallucinations further indicate the validity of a failure of a modulation system. For example, McGhie and Chapman (1961) described disturbances of the process of perception in schizophrenic patients:

Patient 11. It's as if I am too wide awake—very, very alert, I can't relax at all, everything seems to go through me, I just can't shut things out.

Patient 25. I can't concentrate on television because I can't watch the screen and listen to what is being said at the same time. I can't seem to take in two things like this at the same time especially when one of them means watching and the other means listening. On the other hand I seem to be always taking in too much at one time and then I can't handle it and can't make sense of it.

Patient 2. During the last while back I have noticed that noises all seem to be louder to me than they were before. It's as if someone had turned up the volume . . . . I notice it most with background noises—you know what I mean, noises that are always around but you don't notice them. Now they seem to be just as loud and sometimes louder than the main noises that are going on . . . . It's a bit alarming at times because it makes it difficult to keep your mind on something when there's so much going on that you can't help listening to.

Patient 17. Colors seem to be brighter now, almost as if they are luminous. When I look around me it's like a luminous painting. I'm not sure if things are solid until I touch them.

Patient 10. Have you ever had wax in your ears for a while and then had them syringed? That's what it's like now as if I had been deaf before. Everything is much noisier and excites me (pp. 104–105).

The conclusions drawn by McGhie and Chapman (1966) are as follows:

The first type of perceptual change recorded by the patients appears as a heightening sensory vividness which is experienced particularly in the auditory and visual fields. These subjective experiences might be interpreted as a further extension of the loss in the selective functioning of attention. In normal perception we are aware of only a small but significant sector of the total field of sensory stimulation. The reports here indicate that the patients find themselves attending in an involuntary fashion to features of their perceptual field which have hitherto occupied their background position. This widening of the range of conscious perception tends to disturb the constancy and stability of the perceptual matrix, thus causing a changing sense of subjective reality (pp. 106–107).

DRUG-INDUCED SCHIZOPHRENIA

Since we have demonstrated that pharmacological agents have the potential of inducing multisensory perceptual aberrations following acute administration, we now must attempt to differentiate between the drug-induced psychotic state and the state of the schizophrenic patient. Users of LSD and/or other CNS stimulants, such as phencyclidine, do not experience prolonged psychotic episodes because they are aware of the cause-and-effect relation between the administration of the drug and the ensuing bizarre behavior. In other words, the set is critical. Visualize what would happen if a subject received increasingly larger doses of a psychotomimetic agent like phencyclidine over a period of months or years, without ever being told that he was receiving this agent. The intermittent occurrence of bizarre sensory perception would not be related to a known cause. As the bizarre perceptual experiences became more and more profound, the subject would lose the ability to distinguish reality from unreality. If the initial dose were low, only visual perceptual changes would be noted. As the dose was increased, the symptoms would become more profound, progressing to frequent episodes of multisensory perceptual changes. As a result, the subject would lose his concepts of reality based on sensory cues. His basic personality structure would change to such a degree that he would manifest delusional ideation relating to his environment. This would progress until a symptom complex characteristic of the schizophrenic state ensued (Fig. 9). Thus it should be possible to induce a state of

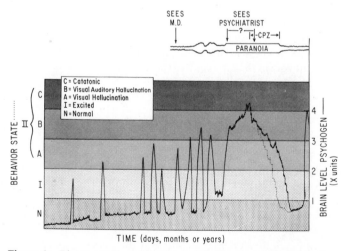

Figure 9 Diagrammatic representation of the concept of the development of a schizophrenic syndrome due to the development of increasingly higher levels of an endogenous psychotogen inducing varying levels of the progression of CNS excitation.

schizophrenia in man under the proper time and dose regimen by putting increasing amounts of a CNS excitant in his diet without his knowledge, thereby removing his ability to rationalize the altered state of his perception on a cause-and-effect basis.

ENDOGENOUS PSYCHOTOMIMETIC SUBSTANCES

At present there is no evidence that endogenous substances induce schizophrenia. However, it is possible that schizophrenics, during periods of stress, have induction of enzymes (Mandell and Mandell, 1969) capable of forming abnormal psychotomimetic substances in sufficient amounts to produce a progression of CNS excitation. In addition, endogenous substances have the ability to produce the type of CNS continuum that results in perceptual aberrations. One of these substances could be present intermittently at varying time intervals, leading to the development of the schizophrenic symptom complex.

The endogenous psychotomimetic agents can be divided into two groups (Fig. 10). The first are normally present within the body, and in sufficient amounts they can produce the symptom complex of the continuum: for example, insulin; short-chain free fatty acids; 11-deoxycortisol; dehydroepiandrosterone; GHB; imidazole acidic acid (Heuser, 1967; Marcus et al., 1967; Marcus et al., 1971). The second group are postulated psychotomimetics that could be formed by enzyme induction or some alternate metabolic pathway. Indole or catechole compounds that may form methylated or oxidized substitutions include bufotenin, dimethyltryptamine, 3,4-dimethoxyphenylethylamine, mescaline, methoxyharmalan, 6-hydroxydopamine, or adrenochrome (Fig. 10). Methylation of serotonin could

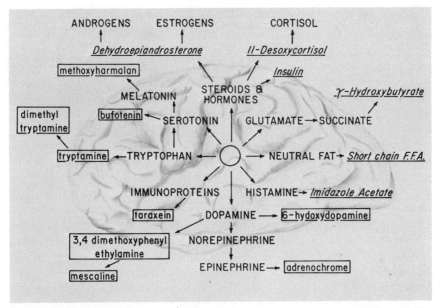

Figure 10 Representation of normal endogenous substances (labels in capital letters), that may be metabolized to psychotogens during normal metabolism (italic and underlined labels) or abnormal metabolism (boxed labels).

occur as a result of sudden increases in endogenous biogenic amines, resulting in an overload of the monoamine oxidase system, which in turn causes a switch to the alternate pathway of N-methylation. Some potentially active substances such as adrenochrome (Hoffer and Kenyon, 1957) or 6-hydroxydopamine (Stein and Wise, 1971) have been postulated as endogenous psychotogens. Recently our laboratory demonstrated that the pineal gland may influence the action of the psychotomimetic agent ketamine (Winters et al., 1973). The role of the pineal and other brain areas in affecting brain metabolism and the formation of psychotomimetic agents has yet to be adequately explored.

Neurochemical Theory of Action.   We have described the possibility that the development of endogenous psychotomimetic agents results in the schizophrenic syndrome. How might these substances alter perception in terms of an underlying nonspecific biochemical mechanism? Our approach to answering this question is based on the previously described continuum of the excitatory states. We presented evidence for the concept that progressive CNS excitation results in progressive changes in motor function, mood, perception, and arousability. This progressive change in CNS excitability is induced by substances that are capable of interfering with the utilization of glucose, high-energy phosphate, or cyclic adenosine-3′,5′ monophosphate. Progressive interference with the metabolic process at any level, from glucose degradation, through the Krebs cycle, to the maintenance of levels of cyclic AMP within neurons, results in progressive CNS hyperexcitability. Most of the compounds we have been discussing have the ability to induce some degree of metabolic inhibition. The degree of metabolic inhibition relates to the degree of CNS excitability of the neurons. As demonstrated with convulsive agents such as pentylenetetrazol, the continuum of CNS excitation is paralleled by a continuum of increasing CNS depolarization of the mammalian cortical cellular membrane (Matsumoto, 1964; Creutzfeldt et al., 1966). Van Harreveld and Schade (1962) demonstrated that anoxia or subconvulsant levels of pentylenetetrazol result in an increase in sodium, water, and chloride penetration into CNS cells and a reduction in extracellular conductance. This implies that varying degrees of metabolic inhibition of neuronal activity result in interference with the sodium metabolic pump, causing progressive depolarization of the membrane. As depolarization progresses, the neuronal membrane approaches the critical firing threshold; thus the neuromembrane becomes increasingly more excitable and fires at a lower and lower threshold.

It is our contention that the varying levels of CNS excitation from Stage I through Stage II to myoclonus then to generalized seizures represent varying degrees of this metabolic inhibition, resulting in the varying degrees of behavioral excitation noted in the continuum. In addition, it is our assumption that the schizophrenic state is the result of the development of endogenous substances that have the ability to produce a degree of metabolic inhibition of the sodium metabolic pump, resulting in a depolarization of the membrane and a subsequent increase in excitability. Thus the schizophrenic state is one in which the CNS is hyperexcited. The degree of CNS excitation resulting in the development of this schizophrenic syndrome implies so great a reduction in the modulating control of the integrative areas of the CNS, specifically the reticular formation, that modulatory control of sensory input systems is disorganized. This results in the perceptual abnormalities of schizophrenia.

This theoretical approach to hallucinosis and schizophrenia is only a hypothesis based on neuropharmacological data filtered through the bias of one neuropharmacologist. How much of the theory is true? Time will tell. The theory represents a model of brain function that can be tested at the chemical, cellular, organ, and clinical levels in an organized manner. It is a target to shoot at and work with to fulfill our ultimate goal, the definition of the basic mechanisms involved in drug-induced and spontaneous CNS pathologic states.

REFERENCES

Adey, F. R., Bell, R. R., and Dennis, B. J. Effects of LSD-25, psilocybin, and psilocin on termporal lobe EEG patterns and learned behavior in the cat. *Neurology,* 1962, **12**, 591–602.

Apter, J. T., and Pfeiffer, C. C. The effect of the hallucinogenic drugs LSD-25 and mescaline on the electroretinogram. *Annals of the New York Academy of Sciences,* 1957, **66**, 508–514.

Chapman, J. The early symptoms of schizophrenia. *British Journal of Psychiatry,* 1966, **112**, 225–251.

Connell, P. H. Amphetamine psychoses. *Maudsley Monographs,* No. 5., 1958.

Creutzfeldt, O. D., Watanabe, S., and Lux, H. D. Relations between EEG phenomena and potentials of single cortical cells. II. Spontaneous and convulsoid activity. *Electroencephalography and Clinical Neurophysiology,* 1966, **20**, 19–37.

Forrer, G. R., and Goldner, R. D. Experimental physiological studies with lysergic acid diethylamide (LSD-25). *AMA Archives of Neurology and Psychiatry,* 1951, **65**, 581–588.

Giberti, F., and Gregoretti, L. Prime esperienze di antagonismo psicofarmacologica. *Sistema Nervoso,* 1955, **7**, 301–310.

Granit, R. Centrifugal and antidromic effects on ganglion cells of retina. *Journal of Neurophysiology,* 1955, **18**, 388–411.

Goldstein, L., Sugarman, A. A., Stolberg, H., Murphree, H. B., and Pfeiffer, C. C. Electro-cerebral activity in schizophrenics and non-psychotic subjects: Quantitative EEG amplitude analysis. *Electroencephalography and Clinical Neurophysiology,* 1965, **19**, 350–361.

Heath, R. G., and Mickle, W. A. Evaluation of seven years' experience with depth electrode studies in human patients. In E. R. Ramey and D. S. O'Doherty (Eds.), *Electrical studies on the unanesthetized brain.* New York: Hoeber, 1960.

Heuser, G. Induction of anesthesia, seizures and sleep. *Anesthesiology,* 1967, **28**, 173–183.

Hoffer, A., and Kenyon, M. Conversion of adrenaline to adrenolutin in human blood serum. *Archives of Neurology and Psychiatry,* 1957, **77**, 437–438.

Hollister, L. E. *Chemical psychoses—LSD and related drugs.* Springfield, Ill.: Charles C Thomas, 1968.

Killam, K. F., and Killam, E. K. Drug action on pathways involving the reticular formation. In H. H. Jasper, L. D. Procter, R. S. Knighton, W. D. Noshay, and R. T. Costello (Eds.), *Reticular formation of the brain.* Boston: Little, Brown, 1958.

Mandell, A. J., and Mandell, M. P. *Psychochemical research in man: methods, strategy, and theory.* New York: Academic Press, 1969.

Marcus, R. J., Winters, W. D., Mori, K., and Spooner, C. EEG and behavioral comparison of the effects of gamma-hydroxybutyrate, gamma-butyrolacton, and short-chain fatty acids in the rat. *International Journal of Neuropharmacology,* 1967, **6**, 175–185.

Marcus, R. J., Winters, W. D., Roberts, E., and Simonsen, D. G. Neuropharmacological studies of imidazole-4-acetic acid actions in the mouse and rat. *Neuropharmacology,* 1971, **10**, 203–215.

Matsumoto, H. Intracellular events during the activation of cortical epileptiform discharges. *Electroencephalography and Clinical Neurophysiology,* 1964, **17**, 294–307.

McGhie, A., and Chapman, J. Disorders of attention and perception in early schizophrenia. *British Journal of Medical Psychology,* 1961, **34**, 103–117.

Mori, K., Winters, W. D., and Spooner, C. E. Comparison of reticular and cochlear multiple unit activity with auditory evoked response during various stages induced by anesthetic agents. II. *Electroencephalography and Clinical Neurophysiology,* 1968, **24**, 242–248.

Purpura, D. P. Electrophysiological analysis of psychotogenic drug action. I. Effect of LSD on specific afferent systems in the cat. *Archives of Neurology and Psychiatry,* 1956, **75**, 122–131. (a)

Purpura, D. P. Electrophysiological analyses of psychotogenic drug action. II. General nature of lysergic acid diethylamide (LSD) action on central synapses. *Archives of Neurology and Psychiatry,* 1956, **75**, 132–141. (b)

Rinkel, M. Experimentally induced psychoses in man. In H. A. Abramson (Ed.), *Neuropharmacology.* Madison, N.J.: Madison Printing, 1955.

Scheibel, M. E., and Scheibel, A. B. Hallucinations and the brain stem reticular core. In L. J. West (Ed.), *Hallucinations.* New York: Grune & Stratton, 1962.

Schlag, J., and Balvin, R. Background activity in the cerebral cortex and reticular formation in relation with the electroencephalogram. *Experimental Neurology,* 1963, **8**, 203–219.

Small, I. F., Small, J. G., and Andersen, J. M. Clinical characteristics of hallucinations of schizophrenia. *Diseases of the Nervous System,* 1966, **27**, 349–353.

Stein, L., and Wise, C. D. Possible etiology of schizophrenia: Progressive damage to noradrenergic reward system by 6-hydroxydopamine. *Science,* 1971, **171**, 1032–1036.

Stoll, W. A. Ein neues, in sehr kleinen Mengen wirksames Phantastikum, *Schweizer Archiv für Neurologie und Psychiatrie,* 1949, **64**, 483–486.

Van Harraveld, A., and Schade, J. P. Changes in the electrical conductivity of cerebral cortex during seizure activity. *Experimental Neurology,* 1962, **5**, 383–400.

Winters, W. D. Comparison of the average cortical and subcortical evoked response to clicks during various stages of wakefulness, slow wave sleep, and rhombencephalic sleep. *Electroencephalography and Clinical Neurophysiology,* 1964, **17**, 234–245.

Winters, W. D., and Spooner, C. E. A neurophysiological comparison of gamma-hydroxybutyrate with pentobarbital in cats. *Electroencephalography and Clinical Neurophysiology,* 1965, **18**, 287–296. (a)

Winters, W. D., and Spooner, C. E. Various seizure activities following gamma-hydroxybutyrate in cats. *International Journal of Neuropharmacology,* 1965, **4**, 197–200. (b)

Winters, W. D., and Spooner, C. E. A neurophysiological comparison of gamma-hydroxybutyrate and alpha-chloralose in cats. *Electroencephalography and Clinical Neurophysiology,* 1966, **20**, 83–90.

Winters, W. D., Mori, K., Spooner, C. E., and Kado, R. T. Correlation of reticular and cochlear multiple unit activity with evoked responses during wakefulness and sleep. I. *Electroencephalography and Clinical Neurophysiology,* 1967, **23**, 539–545. (a)

Winters, W. D., Mori, K., Spooner, C. E., and Bauer, R. O. The neurophysiology of anesthesia. *Anesthesiology,* 1967, **28**, 65–80. (b)

Winters, W. D. A neuropharmacological theory of psychosis. In A. J. Mandell and M. P. Mandell (Eds.), *Methods on a theory in psychochemical research.* New York: Academic Press, 1969.

Winters, W. D., and Wallach, M. B. Drug-induced states of CNS excitation: A theory of hallucinosis. In D. H. Efron (Ed.), *Psychotomimetic drugs.* New York: Raven Press, 1970.

Winters, W. D., Ferrar-Allado, T., Guzman-Flores, C., and Alcarez, M. The cataleptic state induced by ketamine: A review of the neuropharmacology of anesthesia. *Neuropharmacology,* 1972, **11**, 303–316.

Winters, W. D., Alcaraz, M., Cervantes, M. Y., and Guzman-Flores, C. The synergistic effect of reduced visual input on ketamine action: The possible role of the pineal gland. *Neuropharmacology,* 1973, **12**, 407–416.

CHAPTER THREE

DREAMS AND OTHER HALLUCINATIONS: AN APPROACH TO THE UNDERLYING MECHANISM

ERNEST HARTMANN, M.D.

Hallucination is an ubiquitous "capacity." The significant question is not "what makes us hallucinate at certain times?" but rather "what keeps us from hallucinating during most of our normal waking existence?" There is an important inhibitory factor to be studied. This chapter attempts to identify this factor in psychological, neurophysiological, and neurochemical terms.

WIDESPREAD OCCURRENCE OF HALLUCINATIONS

Actual hallucinatory activity is extremely common, and the ability to hallucinate is probably ubiquitous. If hallucination is defined, as it sometimes is, merely as seeing, hearing, or otherwise sensing the presence of something that is not present, without necessarily believing in its reality, it becomes obvious that hallucination is truly ubiquitous; in fact, one could be said to hallucinate almost every time one closes one's eyes. Even accepting the stricter and more usual definition of hallucination, which includes the sensing of something that is not there and imposes the additional criterion that one must believe in its existence, hallucinations are still immensely widespread.

First of all, the dream meets the definition of hallucination in every respect and most of us, according to a large body of recent physiological data, spend from one to two hours dreaming every night. Hallucinations occur at times during schizophrenia and other psychiatric illnesses, and in a variety of specific neurological conditions; they also appear to be quite frequent in nonspecific deteriorative conditions such as senile or presenile dementia. Hallucinations can be brought on by a large number of chemical stimuli—not only LSD, mescaline, and other such well known "hallucinogens," but also by most anticholinergic drugs if taken to excess; anesthetics at certain stages of their action; alcohol, and sometimes barbiturates, during withdrawal; and others. It is well known that hallucinations can sometimes be induced by sleep deprivation, sensory deprivation, starvation, and other extreme stresses.

In addition, hallucinations are frequent when one is somewhat confused (i.e., just before falling asleep or just after waking up). Such experiences are frequently described as hypnagogic or hypnopompic hallucinations. Again, hallucinations at times of "sensory uncertainty" are not uncommon. Many people have occasionally heard their names called or a sentence uttered while in the shower or some similar place surrounded by "white noise" and, on turning off the shower or source of noise, have discovered that no one was there, that no such event had actually occurred.

Finally, it is not impossible that young children do a great deal of hallucinating. Certainly they do not distinguish dreams, fantasies, and their normal waking perception as adults later learn to do. Rapaport (1951, pp. 689–730) suggests that wish-fulfilling fantasy, or hallucination, is a common mode of thought in the young child.

Thus we are dealing with an almost ubiquitous mental and neural phenomenon, including instances when hallucination is perfectly normal and an accepted part of mental activity. For the present, we are not concerned with schizophrenic hallucinations or frightening, disturbing hallucinations, although these often come to mind when the word is used. Such conditions generally involve hallucination plus a simultaneous determination to hold on to the remainder of reality; thus the hallucination is seen as alien and disturbing, as something to be warded off. Psychodynamically, the latter situation is of course fascinating and important. But it would be confusing to consider these unusual and complex forms of hallucination when trying to understand the basic mechanism underlying all such phenomena.

POSITIVE AND NEGATIVE (EXCITATORY AND INHIBITORY) FACTORS

As a broad general framework, we can attempt to understand the emergence of hallucinations, as indeed of many other mental phenomena and central nervous system phenomena, as occasions when the balance between positive forces tending to produce hallucinations and negative (inhibitory) forces is appropriately shifted—in the direction of greater positive forces and/or less inhibition. There is obviously a positive determinant, a pressure of some kind leading toward hallucinations, and a negative or inhibiting determinant that must be removed or reduced to allow hallucinations to emerge. The positive side can occasionally be identified as an overwhelming wish or need, as when a starving man or a very hungry child hallucinates food. In other situations, the positive pressure can be seen in terms of specific dynamic conflict, unacceptable as such, or as a wish or feeling that cannot be acknowledged as internal and is projected onto the outside world. Dynamically, the hallucination often represents a restitution, an attempt to make better or more acceptable sense of a confusing or painful internal and external reality. This new situation, including the externalization of something internal—the hallucination—feels better than the previous situation; in this sense one can say that the hallucination, like the dream, is the fulfillment of a wish. Often, however, the pressure toward hallucination can only be identified as a generally high level of arousal—for example, anxiety or terror in some individuals left alone in the dark or in a situation of sensory isolation. Here one is more likely to see transient and less well-defined hallucinations—for example, a whole sequence of frightening objects hallucinated by a child in the dark or in another frightening, isolated situation. No one of these objects is as dynamically over-determined as the typical firmly held hallucinations of a chronic schizophrenic. In other cases, especially after certain drugs, the subject's individual dynamics play little part; they may determine the exact form or content of the hallucination, but the fact of hallucination is apparently produced by the state of the brain, usually described as general arousal. There may even be a sort of higher central nervous system continuum in which hallucination occurs when overall excitation reaches a certain (very high) level.

There is maximum probability of hallucinations occurring when such a positive "arousal" or "need for projection" factor coincides with the weakening of an inhibitory factor. Frequently, however, the latter determinant (weakening of an inhibitory factor) appears to be sufficient for the development of hallucinatory states. In many of the neurological conditions, and in dreaming, there is no need at all for any specific positive factor or pressure. Thus it may be especially relevant to identify the factor or factors present in "normal nonhallucinatory waking" that are absent in hallucinatory states and whose absence is necessary to allow hallucinations to emerge.

In other words, if we look at the wide variety of situations in which hallucinations occur (one could almost say that hallucinations occur in all situations except clear-headed wakefulness), we can now turn around the usual question and ask, not what produces hallucination or why do we hallucinate, but rather, why do we not hallucinate all the time? What prevents us from hallucinating during clear-headed wakefulness? We can think of hallucinating or at least the "hallucinating ability" as something that is always present, but inhibited, prevented from manifesting itself under certain conditions. Speaking in neurophysiological terms, we can think of hallucination as a phenomenon of disinhibition, or a phenomenon at a "lower level" that is released when a "higher level" inhibitory influence is removed.

THE PSYCHOLOGY OF THE INHIBITORY FACTOR

What is the nature of the posited inhibitory factor? West (1962) and others have suggested a lack of sensory input as a principal influence producing hallucination, so that the ratio of arousal level to sensory input determines the likelihood of hallucinating. In this scheme, adequate sensory input would be the inhibiting factor. However, sensory input is only one aspect of a more general condition. Certainly an acute schizophrenic can hardly be said to be deprived of external stimuli; in fact, some claim that his deficit is precisely an overwhelming amount of input and an inability to keep it out or to sort it properly. But possibly something in the realm of ability to pattern sensory input or interact with it may be involved in the "inhibitory factor" (see below).

Let us attempt an _empirical_ approach to hallucinations, based on defining the inhibitory factor, or "higher influence," whose absence allows hallucinatory phenomena to appear in certain known situations. It may be useful to begin by examining the dream, which is widespread, available for study, and usually uncontaminated by secondary anxiety or other types of reaction to the hallucination. The dream can be used as a prototype for other hallucinations, since the state during which typical dreaming occurs (the "D-state" or "REM-state") has recently been so extensively studied. We can ask what attributes found in "clear-headed waking thought" are definitely *absent* in dreams; we can then attempt to see whether the same attributes are lacking in other forms of hallucination; and we can try to describe this waking function, absent in dreams and other hallucinations, not only in psychological but also in physiological and chemical terms.

What is not present in the dream and hallucination? The question of what waking functions are lacking or almost totally lacking during dreaming has been considered elsewhere (Hartmann, 1973). First of all, the ability to have sensory experience, in all modalities, is definitely present in the dream; although there is generally a shift toward visual modalities, it is clear that nothing is lacking in terms of pure sensory experience. Likewise, emotion clearly occurs during dreams; although there is no simple defect here, there do appear to be certain differences between feelings in dreams and in waking life. For instance, simple and more primitive emotions such as anger, joy, and anxiety definitely occur in dreams, whereas softer or subtler more adult emotions are less prominent. Especially lacking is any modulated emotion that depends on feedback and interaction between the dreamer and others, the dreamer and his environment, and so on. Abrupt shifts in emotion may occur during a dream. The shifts frequently do not correspond to the action of the dream in the way the dreamer would respond to such action during waking life. Thus in terms of emotions, feedback and continuity are in some sense lacking. The sense of being free, the feeling of free will, so characteristic of ordinary waking life, is reduced under certain stressful or pathological situations and is almost totally absent during dreaming (Hartmann, 1966, pp. 521–536).

Cognitive processes also are altered, even though thinking definitely does occur in dreams. The dreamer seldom concentrates for a long period on a single task while pushing away other distracting influences, although this is certainly a common aspect of normal waking life. One cannot shift attention flexibly among several objects as one can in normal waking. Certain kinds of long-term planning thought or comprehensive synthetic thought are not present in dreams. And again, thought that is patterned and develops over time in terms of feedback and relationship with other thoughts hardly exists at all in dreaming. This may in part be rephrasing Freud's statement that there is more primary and less secondary process in dreams, but the lack of flexibility and feedback is especially worth stressing.

Related to this is a very striking characteristic of dreams—so obvious that it often escapes mention: the dreamer accepts bizarre, unusual events in his dreams without evincing any surprise or disturbance at what is happening. The dreamer does not relate the event before him to the rest of his life and experience; he does not say "wait a second; this isn't right," as he would were he awake.* This we can see as the lack of "reality testing" or "judgment," a function that, again, may

---

* The exception is the occasional experience of persons who can "stop" a dream and say "wait, let me try that again a different way" or "it's okay because this is only a dream," and then go on. My impression is that such events are not typical parts of dreaming thought, but rather brief partial arousals from dreams.

depend on feedback interaction and modulation. Perhaps all this is somewhat tautological: obviously, reality testing and patterning of the environment are not present, since one is not "living in reality" or interacting with one's environment. Nonetheless, the lack of reality testing and of feedback interaction may be worth noting, and we can inquire whether other forms of hallucination resemble the dream in this respect.

Certainly lack of reality testing is characteristic of hallucinations; in fact, it is present by definition, if we adhere to the strict definition that the subject not only sees, hears, or otherwise senses something that is not there, but believes that it is actually present. However, the situation is somewhat complicated because we must consider a whole range of hallucinatory situations. One extreme is the patient with an acute drug-induced hallucinatory delirium; his entire world is hallucinatory, and there is obviously little testing of reality and feedback functioning, at least for a time. The other extreme is the chronic paranoid schizophrenic, who may be capable of fairly good reality testing and feedback functioning in dealing with his environment, except for one encapsulated area in which he may have delusions and hear voices.

Thus other hallucinatory situations we have mentioned are quite similar to the dream if we consider those in which the subject is completely involved in his hallucination. This occurs with certain drugs, temporarily in the hypnagogic and hypnopompic situations, and certainly in many of the neurological conditions. The situation is less clear in the frightening psychiatric hallucinations, since here the subject is often attempting to maintain his nonhallucinatory reality, side by side with the hallucinations. And in the chronic paranoid schizophrenic, these functions may be lacking for only a small portion of the world; but this is the same portion we are calling hallucinatory.

PHYSIOLOGY OF THE INHIBITORY FACTOR

Can we characterize hallucinatory situations in (neuro)physiological terms? Perhaps to a small extent we can. We can at least try to identify a positive, and a more pervasive negative (inhibitory) determinant to the emergence of hallucinations. On the positive side, hallucinations can be "produced" by direct cortical and subcortical brain stimulation. It is well known that direct stimulation of the visual cortex produces sensations such as flashes of light, whereas stimulation in surrounding areas—visual association areas—can produce more completely formed hallucinations with a varying sense of reality. The same is probably true of other sensory modalities, although the evidence is less certain.

The hallucinatory state produced by various drugs and the hallucinatory state of dreaming are accompanied by a general widespread cortical excitation or arousal (Feinberg, 1962, pp. 64–76; Gross et al., 1966; Feinberg and Evarts, 1969, pp. 334–393). This is presumably secondary to activation of the brain stem. Again, D-sleep has been the most carefully studied such state: the fact that almost all mammals show such similar and almost certainly homologous patterns during D-sleep makes this an especially accessible situation for studying the brain during one hallucinatory state. D-sleep is characterized by activation of the cortex, accompanied by activated patterns in most of the limbic system and much of the autonomic nervous system, but with inhibition of the skeletal muscle system. All this is probably secondary to activity in certain brain-stem areas, prominent among which are the nuclei reticularis pontis oralis or caudalis (Jouvet, 1969; Pompeiano, 1970), the locus coeruleus (Jouvet and Delorme, 1965), and the gigantocellular tegmental fields (McCarley and Hobson, 1971). The latter may play a unique role in initiating D-periods. All these areas include some neurons with ascending axons and a widespread distribution to the forebrain, including the entire cerebral cortex. Thus arousal is present and could easily lead to internal stimulation of the cortex in, for example, the visual association area. Along with this arousal, D-sleep is associated with widespread depression of waking inhibitory paths, and it has been called a state of extreme disinhibition (Feinberg and Evarts, 1969, pp. 334–393).

These studies include results at many levels of the brain, but I believe that images and thoughts are probably formed in the cerebral cortex; thus it is a different "environment" at the cortex that produces dreaming rather than waking-thinking. This altered environment apparently includes powerful sporadic stimulation from the brain stem* (Bizzi and Brooks, 1963), combined with the lack of an inhibitory influence. I am not certain we can now better define this inhibitory influence present in "clear-headed waking" and absent in dreaming, except that it presumably focuses on the cortex and is widespread. Here then, arousal, perhaps involving specific sensitive cortical association areas, plus widespread disinhibition, constitute an hallucinatory state.

CHEMISTRY OF THE INHIBITORY FACTOR

Can we not go on to make a guess at the chemistry of the inhibitory factor—that is, the chemistry of reality-testing and feedback patterning, which may also turn out to be the chemistry of our postulated neurophysiological inhibitor at the cortex?

There are possible hints. Some evidence indicates that brain catecholamines, especially norepinephrine, may be involved in maintaining attention functions and patterning functions during waking (Hartmann, 1970, 1973). Indeed, norepinephrine (NE) has often been considered to be an inhibitory neurotransmitter. A system such as the ascending dorsal NE bundle with widespread terminations in the cortex (Dahlstrom and Fuxe, 1965; Auden et al., 1966) might be a likely candidate for an essentially inhibitory system, accounting for such functions as focused attention, and perhaps more broadly, patterning and reality-testing. It has been suggested elsewhere (Hartmann, 1973) that this system may wear out during a day of wakefulness and even more during a period of sleep deprivation, since some of the functions listed are exactly those which are diminished by fatigue and sleep deprivation. Furthermore, the norepinephrine system may be in a process of restoration during sleep, and dreaming may allow us to examine the

*During D-sleep the cortex is bombarded by irregular impulses originating in the pontine brain stem, which are known as "pontogeniculooccipital (PGO) spikes." It has been suggested that these spikes themselves may produce waking hallucinations when they occur during waking rather than during D-sleep (Dement et al., 1970, pp. 775–811).

functioning of the cortex without this inhibitory norepinephrine-mediated influence, which is prevalent during normal waking (Hartmann, 1973). And the dream is, above all, a series of hallucinations; therefore if these hypotheses are correct, the absence of norepinephrine influence on the cortex allows the emergence of at least one form of hallucination.

Perhaps once more the dream can be considered prototypical, and we can consider whether other hallucinatory states may be characterized by some defect in this norepinephrine-mediated system. The state of fatigue or sleep deprivation, as well as the state of D-sleep, as mentioned, may be characterized by poor functioning of these norepinephrine systems, and indeed these are times when one is prone to hallucinations.

Neurological studies might be expected to give an answer, but unfortunately the ascending norepinephrine bundles are not prominent or easy to localize in man, although very prominent and easily identified by fluorescence studies in the rat and cat (Dahlstrom and Fuxe, 1965; Auden et al., 1966). Thus it is not easy to say whether localized or diffuse lesions in these systems in man might produce hallucinations.

Drug studies should be helpful. I would postulate that a drug specifically interfering with the ascending norepinephrine system of release of norepinephrine at the cortex should be associated with a tendency toward lack of reality-testing, thus with hallucination. A major problem is that drugs that interfere with the synthesis, storage, or release of norepinephrine, such as reserpine and alpha-methyl paratyrosine, interfere with dopamine as well as with norepinephrine activity. It is not easy to produce differential effects on these two amines, at least with drugs that can be used in man. And dopamine systems may have quite different effects: the phenothiazine antipsychotic drugs are now thought to act on dopamine receptor-blockers, and there is considerable evidence suggesting that schizophrenia may be associated with overactivity of dopamine systems (reviewed in Matthysse, 1974). Thus interfering with brain dopamine might be expected to have very different effects from interfering with brain norepinephrine systems. In fact, the reserpine group of drugs and alpha-methyl paratyrosine clinically produce lethargy and a tendency to depression.

If indeed brain dopamine is involved in the pathophysiology of schizophrenia, excessive dopamine might lead toward pathology and perhaps hallucinations, whereas the norepinephrine system functions in an opposite, inhibitory direction. Hence, it would be especially important to look at drugs that separate the two amines, by blocking or otherwise altering the functioning of the enzyme dopamine beta hydroxylase. For instance, an enzyme that blocks the activity of dopamine beta hydroxylase would be expected to exaggerate dopamine effects and minimize norepinephrine effects.

Drugs which inhibit dopamine beta hydroxylase tend to be nonspecific and quite toxic. The drug disulfiram, used (as Antabuse) as an adjunct in the treatment of alcoholism, is a dopamine beta hydroxylase inhibitor and does occasionally produce toxic psychosis, including hallucinations, especially in a patient also taking monoamine oxidase inhibitors. However, this is only one of many symptoms found occasionally after these drugs. Unpublished recent studies show that another inhibitor, fusaric acid, exacerbates psychosis in some manic and schizophrenic patients. The drug is considered somewhat dangerous and has not been tested on a large scale. The effects are in the direction we would predict on the basis of increasing dopamine and decreasing norepinephrine activity, but the effects appear to be on psychotic thinking in general, including but not limited to hallucinations. It could be tentatively suggested that the chemistry of our "inhibitory factor" involves the integrity of ascending brain norepinephrine systems and perhaps especially the normal functioning of the enzyme dopamine beta hydroxylase.

CONCLUSIONS

The problem of hallucinations has been considered chiefly from the point of view of the negative as inhibitory factor—something present during nonhallucinating waking mental activity, whose removal allows hallucinations (including dreams) to emerge.

Psychologically this inhibiting factor can be related to the functions of "reality-testing" or "feedback interaction." (The process is assisted by positive factors including confusing or unpatterned input, and general activation, anxiety, etc.) Physiologically and chemically, I suggest that the inhibitory influence is mediated especially by ascending norepinephrine systems to the cortex; thus normal nonhallucinatory waking thought requires the integrity of these norepinephrine systems and the integrity of function of the enzyme dopamine beta hydroxylase.

Obviously this line of thought has implications beyond defining the factors allowing hallucinations to emerge. We are approaching a position of being able to define the "chemistry of the mind"—the physiological and chemical substructure of functions such as reality-testing, which previously have been described only in psychological terms.

REFERENCES

Auden, N. E., Dahlstrom, A., Fuxe, K., Larsson, D., Olson, L., and Ungerstedt, U. Ascending monoamine neurons to the telencephalon and diencephalon. *Acta Physiologica Scandinavica,* 1966, **67**, 313–326.

Bizzi, E., and Brooks, D. Functional connections between pontine reticular formation and lateral geniculate nucleus during deep sleep. *Archivio Italiano Biologia,* 1963, **101**, 666–680.

Dahlstrom, A., and Fuxe, K. Evidence for the existence of monoamine-containing neurons in the central nervous system. I. Demonstration of monoamines in the cell bodies of brain stem neurons. *Acta Physiologica Scandinavica (Supplementum* **232**), 1965, **62**, 1–55.

Dement, W. C., Zarcone, V., Ferguson, J., Cohen, H., Pivik, T., and Barchas, J. Some parallel findings in schizophrenic patients and serotonin-depleted cats. In D. B. S. Sankar (Ed.), *Schizophrenia. Current concepts and research.* Hicksville, N.Y.: PJD Publications, 1970.

Feinberg, I. A comparison of the visual hallucinations in schizophrenia with those induced by mescaline and LSD-25. In L. J. West (Ed.), *Hallucinations.* New York: Grune & Stratton, 1962.

Feinberg, I., and Evarts, E. V. Some implications of sleep research for psychiatry. In I. Zubin and C. Shograss (Eds.), *Neurobiological aspects of psychopathology.* New York: Grune & Stratton, 1969.

Gross, M. M., Goodenough, D., Tobin, M., Halpert, E., Lepore, D., Pearlstein, A., Sirota, M., Dibianco, J., Fuller, M., and Kishner, I. Sleep disturbances and hallucinations in the acute alcoholic psychoses. *Journal of Nervous and Mental Disease,* 1966, **142**, 493–514.

Hartmann, E. The psychophysiology of free will. In R. Lowenstein, L. Newman, M. Schur, and A. Solnit (Eds.), *Psychoanalysis, a general psychology.* New York: International Universities Press, 1966.

Hartmann, E. The D-state and norepinephrine-dependent systems. In E. Hartmann (Ed.), *Sleep and dreaming.* Boston: Little, Brown, 1970.

Hartmann, E. *The functions of sleep.* New Haven, Conn.: Yale University Press, 1973.

Jouvet, M. Recherches sur les structures nerveuses et les mecanismes responsables des differentes phases du sommeil physiologique. *Archivio Italiano Biologia,* 1962, **100**, 125–206.

Jouvet, M., and Delorme, F. Locus coeruleus et sommeil paradoxal. *Compte Rendu de la Société de Biologie (Paris),* 1965, **159**, 895–899.

Matthysse, S. Schizophrenia: Relation to dopamine transmission, motor control, and feature extraction. In F. O. Schmitt and F. G. Worden (Eds.), *The neurosciences third study program.* Cambridge, Mass.: MIT Press, 1974.

McCarley, R. W., and Hobson, J. A. Single neuron activity in cat giganto-cellular tegmental field: Selectivity of discharge in desynchronized sleep. *Science,* 1971, **174**, 1250–1255.

Pompeiano, O. Mechanisms of sensorimotor integration during sleep. In E. Stellar and J. M. Spraque (Eds.), *Progress in physiological psychology,* Vol. 3. New York: Academic Press, 1970.

Rapaport, D. Toward a theory of thinking. In D. Rapaport (Ed.), *Organization and pathology of thought.* New York: Columbia University Press, 1951.

West, L. J. (Ed.) *Hallucinations.* New York: Grune & Stratton, 1962.

CHAPTER
FOUR

DRUG-INDUCED HALLUCINATIONS
IN ANIMALS AND MAN

RONALD K. SIEGEL, Ph.D.

MURRAY E. JARVIK, M.D., Ph.D.

The behavior of organisms is rich in examples of reactions to the pharmacological agents known as hallucinogens. Mice frequently exhibit head twitches that remind a human observer of someone trying to shake off some pesty insect or unpleasant feeling. Pigeons adopt a characteristic posture designating fear or else peck wildly at the air and retreat from what our human observer might describe as imaginary aggressors. Cats exhibit stereotypic approach and avoidance behaviors or play with what our observer might infer are imaginary mice or butterflies. The eye movements of monkeys seem to track imaginary insects, or the animals adopt a crouched posture with their head on their hands, a posture our human observer (by now running the risk of being labeled hallucinatory himself) finds vaguely reminiscent of Rodin's "Thinker" (Grunfeld and Edery, 1969). Men adopt similar behavioral postures or utilize verbal and other behaviors to describe their imaginary happenings.

Experiences with hallucinogens have puzzled and intrigued man for centuries. They have given him "sights" to see, "voices" to listen to, "thoughts" to ponder, and "altered states of consciousness" to explore. They have generated conditions that can only be described by such global and imprecise terms as ecstasy or madness. Some men feel closer to an understanding of themselves. Others feel closer to each other. Some feel a unity with all in their environment. Still others feel one with a universal being and might remark, like Baudelaire (1857) in "Poem of Hashish," "It will amaze no one that one last supreme thought comes bursting from the dreamers brain! 'I have become God!'" (p. 76). But each man finds himself alone. For when man perceives an hallucination he does so alone, in the privacy of his body.

Traditionally, man has attempted to understand hallucinations by analysis of overt verbal behaviors. Thus private (covert) experiences can achieve public status and can be subjected to the processes of consensual validation. Descriptive symbols such as words or pictures can be precisely defined, and their controlled use can be shared by others. In a sense, an individual's hallucination can be "seen" by others. However, the task of analyzing such symbolic communication as language is not unlike the problem of analyzing the mouse's head twitches, the pigeon's pecks, or the monkey's eye movements. All these behaviors involve responses to perceived stimuli in the internal or external environment. Even though there are no objective stimuli in the case of hallucinations, we are still dealing with a valid type of inquiry into the behaviors of perceptual systems (cf. Hebb, 1968; Richardson, 1969; Bugelski, 1970; Horowitz, 1970).

This chapter attempts to describe such behaviors and to outline the methods used in their experimental analysis. Part I discusses the behavioral responses of infrahuman species to hallucinogens; it includes observations in the field and laboratory as well as experimental paradigms that have been modestly successful in understanding hallucinogen-induced changes in animal perception. Part II treats the nature of drug-induced visual imagery in man; it includes sections on the definition and phenomenology of drug-induced hallucinations as well as the history of experimentation in this area. In addition, a series of studies on drug-induced visual imagery in man is presented. A theoretical model to account for the findings of these studies is developed in Part III.

Since the title of this chapter raises a variety of empirical questions, it is appropriate to define the limits of the present discussion. Not only are hallucinations responses to pharmacological stimuli, they may also be considered stimulus events of which organisms become "aware" and to which they subsequently respond. In this chapter, however, we are primarily concerned with hallucinations functioning as stimulus events, not with pharmacological stimuli or their mechanisms of action (see reviews by Weil-Malherbe and Szara, 1971; Brawley and Duffield, 1972).

It should also be noted that the chapter does not address itself to the variety of sensory modalities in which hallucinations may occur. Since man's behavior is primarily visually mediated, we have chosen the visual modality for study. The responses to the visual imagery of hallucinations can be surprisingly realistic. Many of our subjects under the influence of *Cannabis* would have thought that they were watching a motion picture if they had not known they were in a completely dark chamber. Equally remarkable reactions occur to the nonvisual imagery of hallucinations (e.g., auditory, olfactory, or kinesthetic imagery). Imagery often occurs simultaneously in two or more modalities and is referred to as synesthesia. One mescaline-treated subject reported a visual-algesic synesthesia in response to being pricked with a sharp instrument: "I've got concentric circles like round the top of a radio mast. If you touch me, jagged things shoot up; little-sort-of-jagged things, from the centre" (McKellar, 1957, p. 63). Taken together, these responses can constitute the "psychedelic" or "consciousness-expanding" experiences commonly associated with drug-induced hallucinations. The present chapter does not attempt to comment on these phenomena. However, the possibility of complex multimodal hallucinations existing in the drug state can temper an initial excitement and perplexity about reactions in the single modality of vision.

PART I: ANIMALS

It is well known that *Homo sapiens* voluntarily learns to self-administer psychoactive drugs, and among the many drugs used in this way by man are the hallucinogens. Indeed, it is a traditional, albeit tacit, assumption of psychophar-macological thinking that *Homo sapiens* is the only species that will self-administer hallucinogens without additional reinforcement. It is often further assumed that the human use of hallucinogens is both a necessary and sufficient condition to determine whether a given drug produces hallucinations and thus can be classified as a true hallucinogen. Such assumptions have led investigators to restrict the use of infrahuman species to the formulation of biochemical and physiological models of hallucinogen action since, a priori, these animals neither self-administer hallucinogens nor report private events such as hallucinations. The recent increases in the nonmedical use of these drugs in Western societies, together with the interest in hallucinatory experiences as reflected in current literature, have made these assumptions more explicit, leading to a myriad of studies and analyses of hallucinogen-induced behavior in man. The resulting research has generated a number of hypotheses regarding hallucinations pro-duced by drugs, but these are not always practically, morally, or legally verifiable by systematic empirical study. The urgent need for a firmly grounded theory of hallucinogens and hallucinations prompts a reevaluation of the basic assumptions just stated.

This part of the chapter examines these assumptions in light of recent ethologi-cal and laboratory findings, encompassing field and laboratory observations and studies. The discussion is guided by existing observations and data and is fostered by some speculation and inference. The observations, however crude and uncon-trolled, provide valuable information on animal reactions to hallucinogens. Some allowance for speculation and inference must be made, since the search for infrahuman reactions to hallucinogens may uncover new areas and models for the study of hallucinations in man. Such infrahuman models would have the advan-tage over others of greater experimental control without the addition of "untesta-ble mentalistic constructs" (Schuster and Thompson, 1969).

FIELD OBSERVATIONS OF HALLUCINOGEN-INDUCED BEHAVIOR

We have few reliable ethological reports of animal reactions to psychoactive drugs in general, and hallucinogens in particular, since many of the observations are based on mythology and folklore (Siegel, 1973a). For example, many an-thropologists believe that primitive people may have learned the rudiments of medicine by observing which plants were used by animals suffering from wounds, fever, or infection. In India, folklore maintains that the mongoose, when bitten by a cobra, retires to the jungle to look for a plant known as mungo root *(Ophiorrhiza mungos)*, which it eats as an antidote to the venom. Mongooses have also been reported to pretreat themselves by rubbing the root over the parts of the body that the snake is likely to attack. This treatment usually results in a "drugged sleep" from which the animal quickly recovers (Hinton and Dunn, 1967). Although the mungo root naturally enough evolved as a native charm against snake bites, and infusion teas of the root were later used for treatment of gonorrhea and scabies, there has been no evidence to indicate that it is effective against snake venom. Many anthropologists also believe that early man learned about drugs by observ-ing the effects of accidental self-administrations in animals. The legendary dis-covery of coffee purportedly occurred around 900 A.D. An Abyssinian tending his herd of goats noticed that his animals became abnormally frisky after eating the bright red fruit of a tree: the substance was later isolated and identified as coffee (Taylor, 1965). Similarly, Pope (1969) suggests that *Tabernanthe iboga,* an hallucinogenic plant containing ibogaine, may have been discovered by boars, porcupines, and gorillas in the jungles of Gabon and the Northern Congo in Africa: "Several accounts mention that the natives saw boars dig up and eat the roots of the plant, only to go into a wild frenzy, jumping around and perhaps fleeing from frightening visions" (p. 174). The folklore of several other peoples is replete with equally intriguing and speculative notions. In Czechoslovakia, peasant stories tell that man learned of the stimulant properties of *Cannabis* by observing the abnormally high jumps of grasshoppers that fed on local varieties of this plant. Some Indian groups in Central Mexico abstain from *Cannabis* use because of a long-held belief it is "food fit only for animals," since local monkeys continually raid and feed on the young plants.

There are other reports in which it is only speculated that animals that regularly ingest toxins that cause hallucinations in man show the same psychoactive effects. For example, it is claimed that domesticated horses and cattle develop "cravings" for and "addictions" to a variety of poisonous plants, many of which cause psychoactive effects in man (Forsyth, 1954). Domesticated dogs, which help herd cows in the Hawaiian Islands, have been observed to become abnormally playful after ingesting the psilocybin mushrooms that grow in the pastures (Siegel, unpublished observation). Some mongooses in the West Indies and the Hawaiian Islands ingest mostly *Bufo marinus* toads, which contain the hallucinogen bufotenine. This phenomenon is something of a mystery, since other toads as well as other natural prey are more abundant in these regions. Although it is not known whether there are psychoactive effects resulting from such ingestions, the mongoose is considered by some natives to be a drug addict. It goes out of its way to ingest a variety of psychoactive compounds and poisons, including the poison bulb of scorpions and the sting, "which it seems to consider a *bonne bouche*" (Hinton and Dunn, 1967, p. 20). Birds in the Hawaiian Islands have been observed to feed on San Pedro cactus *(Trichocereus pachanoi)*—which contains mescaline—and local people claim that this affects the birds' disposition and flight patterns (Siegel, unpublished observation). Bees are naturally attracted to male *Cannabis* plants, and their honey, when collected and assayed, has been shown to contain traces of tetrahydrocannabinol (THC) (Mendell, 1969). Some writers in the "underground press" have enjoyed speculating about "stoned bees"; however, there are no studies of individual bees showing psychoactive effects or repeating that particular pattern of behavior. The insect *Oxythris canabensis* is a natural enemy of *Cannabis* plants in Rumania but, again, there are no behavioral studies on the effect of this relationship. Similarly, it is rumored that the natural predators of the South Pacific goatfish may become intoxicated after eating their prey. Such stories are probably based on the "fantastic nightmares" and hallucinations produced in man by ingestion of this fish (Halstead, 1965).

Many field reports, like some just cited, are based on single accidental administrations of the drugs and lack the support of controlled observational or laboratory studies. There are occasional journalistic reports of animals self-administering hallucinogens, as well as several studies of accidental *Cannabis* poisoning in grazing horses and mules and in domesticated dogs (e.g., Clarke et al., 1971). Even when such accidental ingestion does not result in death, there is only scant evidence that the animals are "intoxicated" and no firm evidence that the behavior is "hallucinatory." The most common instance of such accidents is found in the etiology of locoweed disease, which affects cattle, horses, and sheep on the Great Plains of the western United States and is caused by ingestion of locoweed (*Astragulus*). Locoweed (which literally means cracked brain) contains selenium, which is absorbed from the surrounding soil, and the disease resulting from its ingestion is characterized by paresis, ataxia, dullness, and a tendency of the animals to isolate themselves from social groupings.

Although alcohol is not classified as an hallucinogen, there are a number of reports illustrating the hallucinosis that results from chronic alcohol ingestion and/or subsequent delirium tremens (e.g., Clarke, 1878; Brinkmann, 1972). Both Carrington (1959) and Sikes (1971) review evidence suggesting that African elephants, like man, have a "passion" for alcohol. The usually graceful movements of these animals are marked by awkward and inappropriate behaviors after ingestion of this substance. Drummond (1875) described this phenomenon:

> They [the elephants] frequent, as I have mentioned, the country from the Pongolo northward, during the summer season, retiring to their fortresses in the interior at the approach of winter. The time of their arrival is simultaneous with the ripening of the umganu-tree, of which they are passionately fond, and doubtless come in search of. This fruit is capable of being made into a strong intoxicating drink, and the elephants after eating it become quite tipsy, staggering about, playing huge antics, screaming so as to be heard miles off, and not seldom having tremendous fights (in Carrington, 1959, p. 68).

Several members of the cat family repeatedly self-administer catnip (*Nepeta cataria*). Catnip, a member of the mint family, has been used by man as an hallucinogen with effects similar to those of *Cannabis* (Jackson and Reed, 1969), probably caused by the nepetalactone oils in the plant. In cats, the reponse is characterized by sniffing, licking, chewing with head shaking, chin and cheek rubbing, and headover and body rolls accompanied by some salivation (Todd, 1963). Hatch (1972) described frequent signs of apparent hallucinations such as "phantom butterflies" above the cat and "phantom mice" in the cat's cage as inferred from the observed behavior.

The reindeer of the Asian forest and tundra regions are frequently afflicted by insects in their nostrils. These states are marked by wild and frenzied behaviors, and the reindeer run aimlessly away from the herd. The reindeer and the native Chukchki people ingest *Amanita muscaria* mushrooms, which contain the hallucinogens muscimol and ibotenic acid. The people's behavior is characterized by elation, sedation, colored visions, and hallucinations. Wasson (1968) summarizes observational evidence suggesting that the reindeer may also be "hallucinating" since their behavior is described as "drunk," "intoxicated," "noisy," abnormally agressive, and similar in many ways to the insect-induced state.

Hempseeds (*Cannabis sativa*) and avians have enjoyed a long historical association. Many birds, including the pigeon (*Columba livia*), eat hempseeds, which until recently were available in commercial bird feeds. The pigeon has a marked behavioral preference for these seeds, and it has been reported that wild mourning doves and pheasants in areas of Illinois and Iowa also eat them. Hempseeds can contain small quantities of cannabinoids, including tetrahydrocannabinol. In addition, they nearly always contain some green gummy calyx, which probably contains additional amounts of cannabinoids. Levi (1957) discusses the historical uses of hempseed as a source of pigeon food and summarizes evidence from breeders, who refer to the seed as "pigeon candy" and use it as a delicacy and a stimulant for their birds. The following account illustrates the behavioral effects:

[Hempseed] feeding has a decided beneficial psychological effect upon the bird's happiness. Pigeons fed sparingly with a little hemp in the middle of the day during the moulting season take a new interest in life which is almost inconceivable. In general, scattering any feed upon the ground of the flypen is dangerous because of possible contamination and infection. An exception to this rule is the feeding of hempseed in such fashion. When some hemp is fed out on the dry ground of the flypen, every bird comes out for its share. The avidity with which the seed is devoured has to be seen to be believed. Even after the portion of hemp has been consumed, many of the birds may be seen for hours diligently searching for a possible addititional grain. . . . It [hempseed] is of great assistance in taming birds and in training them for shows, as all fears seem to be set aside when they know that hempseed is being offered (p. 499).

All these observations must be accepted with caution since, as a rule, infrahuman species do not readily self-administer hallucinogens in natural states. Even under laboratory conditions, only a handful of investigators have been successful in training animals to self-administer hallucinogens, and then only to obtain additional food or water reward (e.g., Zimmerberg et al., 1971). Recently, however, Pickens and Thompson (1972) have reported that one monkey in their laboratory self-administered hashish on an operant schedule without additional reinforcement.

One explanation for these findings that hallucinogens are not readily self-administered by animals is that such treatment involves a punishing or negative reinforcing component. Indeed, conditioned taste aversion tests in rats have shown that high doses of mescaline and tetrahydrocannabinol are unpleasant and serve as a punishment in this situation. The classic paradigm of this test involves a novel taste, such as sodium saccharin, that is paired with novel gustatory cues associated with noxious internal states, such as produced by emetic agents like lithium chloride or X-irradiation (Garcia and Ervin, 1968). Usually, aversion to the novel gustatory cues becomes associated with (or conditioned to) the novel taste, and animals will subsequently avoid instances of the taste alone. Corcoran (1973) paired saccharin with intraperitoneal injections of hashish extract in rats. Subsequently, the novel saccharin taste was avoided by water-deprived rats offered a solution with that taste. One could object to Corcoran's conclusion that this indicates hashish was unpleasant and punishing for the rat on the grounds that such drug experiences can be aversive for pharmacologically naïve animals, as they often are for humans. These animals might experience unpleasant disorientation produced by the very novelty of the drug state itself. Repeated drug treatments might have the effect of decreasing novelty and reducing aversion. Corcoran's demonstration that three saccharin-hashish pairings did not significantly affect the strength of the aversions may not have been sufficient treatment to allow the animal to become pharmacologically experienced or tolerant. More recently, however, Corcoran and Amit (1974) have shown that rats are generally reluctant to self-administer hashish orally. This reluctance is not affected by several experimental procedures that can increase their intake of other drugs.

Nevertheless, hallucinogen-induced aversive effects have been compared with drug-induced "illness" or "sickness" (Elsmore and Fletcher, 1972). It has even been argued that such aversiveness supports the notion that the naturally occurring plant hallucinogens are evolutionarily justified in terms of the maladaptive effects they could have on herbivores (Eisner and Halpern, 1971). For example, the plant henbane (*Hyoscyamus niger*) contains the active principles hyoscyamine, hyoscine, and atropine, and it causes hallucinations in man. In addition, henbane has a strong nauseating odor and taste that animals and men actively avoid, ingesting the plant only by accident.

LABORATORY OBSERVATIONS OF HALLUCINOGEN-INDUCED BEHAVIOR

The behavioral consequences of hallucinogen treatment in animals can vary with a number of interactions between behavioral and pharmacological systems (see reviews by Brown, 1967; Weckowicz, 1967). The description of these interactions requires information about concomitant variations between the parameters of the behaviors and of the drugs. Information about the behaviors should be specific with respect to species variability, type of behavior, past behavioral history, and other factors. Information about the drugs should be specific with respect to dose, time, dose order, route of administration, localization of the site of drug action, absorption and distribution in the body, and biological fate, to name just a few items. Such variables can be further modified by environmental set and setting. The resultant behavior cannot be fully understood unless all these underlying variables are so specified. Furthermore, recent advances in neurochemistry suggest that many drug effects on behavior are mediated by neurochemical events and that these relationships are reciprocal in that changes in one may affect the state of the other. If all these possible combinations and permutations appear to be hopelessly confounded, it should simply caution us in making any generalizations about hallucinogen-induced behavior in animals. A full understanding of these interactions is restricted by the limits of present empirical data, but the presence of such intricacies should make us suspicious of studies that simplify the behaviors with terms such as "hallucinatory." For example, Klüver (1933) reported that mescaline produced in monkeys a characteristic "oral syndrome" that was marked by lip, tongue, and jaw movements coupled with licking and chewing. The syndrome was frequently accompanied by the monkey's wiping, touching, and scratching various parts of its own body. The presence of a similar mescaline-induced oral syndrome in man prompted Klüver (1966) to suggest the possibility of somatosensory hallucinations, although he cautioned that observations of such behaviors do not permit reliable inferences about their sensory concomitants. Similarly, Dement and his co-workers (1970) have argued that the demonstration of drug-induced hallucinations in an animal depends entirely on what one is willing to infer from the associated behavior of that animal. Indeed, these authors note that "it is also obvious that the behavior alone can be somewhat misleading. For example, the response of a decerebrate cat to pinching the tail invariably convinces at least one student that [the animal] is in great pain" (p. 346).

Nonetheless, there is a certain utility in discussing broad areas of behavior and the ways in which drugs may affect them. Such an analysis permits us to focus on

categories directly relevant to man's hallucinatory behavior. Behavior is usually
defined as activity of an organism observable by the organism itself or other
organisms. Thus one of the first approaches that might be valuable to man is the
observation of hallucinogen-induced behavior in other species under laboratory
conditions.

Mice. Several uncontrolled studies have noted interesting patterns of
hallucinogen-induced behavior in mice. Woolley (1955) reported that mice injected with LSD (100 mg/kg, i.p.) exhibited headshaking, piloerection, and behavioral postures consisting of spread forelegs and backward locomotion. This
author compared the latter behavior with that of mice resisting movement down
an inclined plane and hastily concluded that the LSD-treated animals were hallucinating sliding down an inclined surface or resisting and backing away from an
uncertain situation. Grainer-Doyeux (1956) gave mice and rats Nopo powder
prepared from the seeds of *Anadenanthera peregrina,* an hallucinogen used by
Guahibo Indians. The mice exhibited increased grooming behavior, head twitching, and nasal scratching, and appeared to be "drunk" and "hallucinatory" as
inferred from their locomotor activity and visual orienting responses. Fellows and
Cook (1957) noted that mescaline (20–100 mg/kg) given orally to mice increased
the frequency of scratching and grooming postures and cited such behavior as
evidence for cutaneous paresthesias (hallucinations). Haley (1957) found that
intracerebral injections of LSD (5 mg) in mice produced hyperexcitability to visual
and auditory stimuli as well as direct aggressive attacks on any object placed in
front of the animals. Intracerebral injection of mescaline (10 mg) produced
similar effects, coupled with paroxysmal ear scratching. Several other investigators have noticed similar hallucinogen-induced responses in mice, and these
always include head twitching (e.g., Corne and Pickering, 1967; Siegel and Poole,
1969; Siegel and Jarvik, 1971; Kulkarni, 1973).

The drug-induced head twitch in mice has been described as resembling a
strong pinna reflex involving lateral movement of the entire head without observable tactile stimulation (Corne and Pickering, 1967). In subjective terms, the
animal is shaking its head as if to escape from an "apparently" aversive stimulus.
As already noted, the concomitant increases in both frequency and duration of
grooming postures, such as paroxysmal ear scratching, have even been cited as
evidence for "cutaneous hallucinations." A device recently developed to record
and measure these twitches (Siegel et al., 1972) consists of a magnetic head unit,
worn chronically by the mice and allowing for free movement in the cage. When a
mouse twitched its head, lateral movement of the unit produced a change in its
adjacent magnetic field which was amplified and channeled to digital and analog
recorders. Treatment with hallucinogens induced significant changes in head-
twitch rates when compared with predrug periods or treatment with nonhal-
lucinogens. In one series of experiments, Siegel and Jarvik (1972) attempted to
rank and compare various hallucinogens by determining the minimum effective
dose necessary to induce head twitches in at least 50% of the population
(MED-50). These MED-50s, determined in groups of 15 to 20 mice, were found to
be 15 mg/kg for bufotenine, 0.05 mg/kg for LSD, 25 mg/kg for mescaline, and 10
mg/kg for ketamine. Figure 1 shows mean head-twitch rates during pre- and
postdrug periods for various mescaline doses. In Fig. 2 the hallucinogens

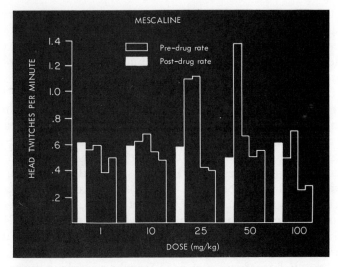

Figure 1 Mean head-twitch rates per minute for groups of mice in mescaline conditions. Predrug rates calculated from the 30-minute baseline recording before drug treatment; postdrug rates calculated in consecutive blocks (represented by steps on the histograms) of 30-minutes from the two-hour recording following treatment. Each dose level represents a group of 20 animals.

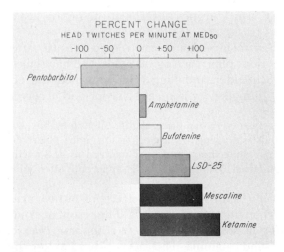

Figure 2 Mean percent change in head-twitch rates per minute at MED-50 levels for each drug. Each histogram represents separate groups of 20 mice each.

bufotenine, LSD, mescaline, and ketamine are arranged in ascending order; interestingly, this continuum is virtually identical to that depicting the degree of central nervous system excitation induced by the same agents in cat brain (see Winters, this volume). As expected, pentobarbital suppressed head twitches as well as general activity, and d-amphetamine induced maximal twitching at 5 mg/kg (but this change was not significant). Although we still do not know whether these head twitches represent hallucinations, the dosages necessary to induce them are highly correlated with doses that produce reports of hallucinations in man (Corne and Pickering, 1967). In addition, prolonged solitary confinement produces identical head-twitch responses in mice (Keller and Umbreit, 1956) as well as hallucinations in man (Zuckerman and Cohen, 1964).

Recently Boulton and Handley (1973) have demonstrated that the head twitch is highly dependent on sensory input from the pinna. These investigators infiltrated the local anesthetic lignocaine around the base of mice's ears, and this was highly effective in antagonizing both the head-twitch response and the pinna reflex. Increasing sensory input from the pinna with the irritant xylene increased a drug-induced head-twitch response. In these studies, the authors induced head twitching with 5-hydroxytryptophan (5-HTP). This compound has not been shown to be hallucinogenic in man, but Corne et al. (1963) have argued that this is simply because a large enough dose has not yet been administered. Nonetheless, 5-HTP-induced head twitching has been correlated with rises in 5-hydroxytryptamine (5-HT) levels in the brain stem. Furthermore, it has been hypothesized that hallucinogens such as LSD act by mimicking the central actions of 5-HT (Aghajanian, 1972), which may result in abolition of the sensory filtering mechanisms in the reticular formation (Bradley and Key, 1958). Boulton and Handley's study shows that the 5-HTP head twitch is highly dependent on sensory input from the pinna and that "this response could be due to the perception of previously subliminal stimuli from the pinna region" (p. 213) if not hallucinations per se. These authors also found that isolation greatly diminished the head-twitch response to 5-HTP, which argues in favor of the notion just advanced.

Cats and Dogs.   Several investigators have noted unusual patterns of behavior in cats treated with various pharmacological agents and have labeled such behaviors "hallucinatory." Schneider and Sigg (1957) studied the effects of ibogaine hydrochloride (2–10 mg/kg, i.v.) on cat behavior and observed that:

Usually the animal remained in one place, slightly shivering, the tail out-stretched, while making hissing sounds as if trying to scare off an imaginary object. Often the cat tried to move toward a corner, hide there, and bury its head in it. Sometimes the animal approached a corner and tried to climb up the walls, apparently attempting an escape (p. 766).

Sturtevant and Drill (1956) studied the effects of intraventricular injections of mescaline (1–3 mg) on the behavior of cats. The resultant syndrome consisted of continuous yowling noises as well as severe autonomic reactions including mydriasis, tachypnea, and catatonia. The cats appeared to lose their aggressiveness toward mice, "fondling" them instead of attacking. Conversely, Norton and Tamburro (1958) found that LSD increased aggression and hostility in cats and decreased their "sociability."

In another study, cats treated with LSD (25–100 mg) exhibited head shaking and staring while adopting a "kangaroo" posture consisting of sprawled legs with claws and tail extended (Adey et al., 1962). Similar abnormal postures and inappropriate behaviors have been observed in cats following treatment with LSD, mescaline, nitrous oxide, diethyl ether, ketamine, tiletamine hydrochloride, and a diazepone derivative (Winters and Wallach, 1970; Winters et al., 1972; Massopust et al., 1973). The "kangaroo" posture is also seen in dogs treated with ibogaine

(Lambert and Heckel, 1901) or mescaline (Hardman et al., 1973). In addition, the dogs assume other bizarre postures and manifest convulsions with apparent hallucinations:

The convulsive episodes are preceded and followed by barking, yelping, and apparent hallucinations. The dog usually exhibits marked mydriasis and runs wildly about the room bumping into walls and furniture. The dog also appears to be apprehensive, frightened and disoriented; barking or snarling at inanimate objects is noted frequently. The 7 analogs of mescaline produce similar qualitative effects in the dog with adequate doses (Hardman et al., 1973, p. 304).

Harmine and diethyltryptamine (DET) also induce apparent hallucinations in dogs (Sai-Halász and Endröczy, 1959; Gershon and Lang, 1962):

The whole behaviour was similar to that observed in humans in a hallucinatory state: the dog was staring at a point in front of it, suddenly jumped back, then went on staring again, etc. (Sai-Halász and Endröczy, 1959, p. 405).

Sudilovsky et al. (in press) described amphetamine-induced stereotypy in cats as including minutia-searching patterns involving head and neck movements and a "fly-catching movement" comprised of a sudden swing of the head with rapid extrusion of the tongue. They observed "alternating flexion and extension of the paw as if the cat were attempting to shake something off of it," as well as signs of hallucinations such as "striking at nonexistent objects in the air, retreating movements or eluding jumps." And even though the cats often were frozen in catatonic postures following chronic amphetamine intoxication, abrupt orienting movements "towards a real or 'hallucinated' stimulus were often observed . . . not infrequently a cat would jump back and turn vigorously to one side in response to a nonexistent apparently hallucinatory stimulus" (Ellinwood et al., 1973, pp. 1089–1090). It is interesting to note that severe psychogenic shock can produce similar behavior. Mitchell (1953) noted that after serious flooding of a coastal area of Britain, six out of ten cats examined exhibited continuous and repeated attempts to catch imaginary objects on the ground and in the air.

The effects of hallucinogenic amphetamines on cat behavior as compared with the behavior of other species were examined by Florio et al. (1972). These investigators found that 2, 5-dimethoxy-4-methyl-amphetamine (DOM or STP) induced EEG excitation in rats, as well as backward locomotion, head nodding, and a stereotypic pattern of behavior known as the "wet dog syndrome" (a shaking of the body, like a wet dog trying to dry itself). Such excitation and wet dog shakes were also induced in rats by $d, 1$-3-4-5 methylendioxy-methoxy-amphetamine (MMDA). DOM produced searching and exploration in rabbits, alternating with periods of stupor and catatonia. Another hallucinogenic amphetamine, $d, 1$-4-methoxyamphetamine (PMA) produced excitation and backward locomotion in rabbits. As the authors tested animals further up the phylogenetic scale, these amphetamine-induced behavioral changes appeared even more purposeful. In cats, DOM (0.25 mg/kg) "gave rise to characteristic changes in behavior which we have designated as 'hallucinatory': striking at imaginary objects in the air, sometimes exhibiting bizarre postures, staring intently at a corner of the cage, and shaking the head" (Florio et al., 1972, p. 406).

Analyzing videotape records of cats, Dement et al. (1970) found that they responded to internally generated brain excitation (pontine-geniculo-occipital or PGO spikes) with orienting responses including head and eye searching movements. These behaviors are similar to those seen in cats treated with para-chlorophenylalanine (PCPA), a selective depletor of brain serotonin (Dement et al., 1969). It is tempting to label behaviors in both cases "hallucinatory," since the animals "looked around" for no apparent reason, but Dement and his colleagues present one of the most reasoned and cautious interpretations of these phenomena in the literature:

> Our current feeling is that the PGO spike activity does not instigate fullblown hallucina-tions (waking dream images) in the cat. In the first place, the behavior is *not* ordinarily accompanied by signs of emotion—anger, fear, or affection. In the second place, the animals rarely exhibit visual fixation—rather, the behavior more properly suggests alert-ing, searching, and/or expectancy. The best inference is that a burst of PGO spikes in the waking state is perceived by the cat as a barrage of simple stimuli, like knocking on a door or flashing a light. Occasionally, the cat does respond to waking spike bursts with behavior that could be termed hallucinatory. However, we are willing to stipulate that although PGO spikes may be a necessary ingredient in the production of hallucinations, they are not sufficient, and that the ability to respond to their occurrence with the elaboration of complex imagery might require more brain than the cat possesses (Dement et al., 1969, pp. 793–794).

Monkeys.   Although Dement and his colleagues were appropriately cautious about labeling PCPA-treated cats "hallucinatory," the dramatic effects of PCPA treatment in two rhesus monkeys convinced them that the resultant behavior was indeed hallucinatory:

> In other words, both monkeys appeared to be experiencing and responding to internally generated visual imagery projected into the outer world. A specific example involved the complex threat behavior executed by monkeys when human observers approached too near the cages, consisting essentially of teeth baring and sudden jumps at the intruder. When the PCPA effect developed, this behavior was often emitted (videotape) when no one was in the vicinity (Dement et al., 1970, p. 352).

Monkeys treated with PCPA have displayed numerous other behaviors that have been cited as evidence of apparent perceptual distortions, if not hallucinations themselves. In one study reviewed by Boelkins (1973), a monkey was observed to make an oriented and focused visual search of his environment without apparent stimulus targets. In addition, there was an increase in a stereotyped vocalization pattern that functions as an alerting and warning bark "with no external stimula-tion visible or audible to the observer." Evidence of such perceptual disturbances induced by PCPA has also been offered by Whalen and Luttge (1970), who found that PCPA treatment in rats facilitates homosexual mountings but not heterosex-ual interactions. They argue that the drug works "not by enhancing sexual motivation, but rather by altering the male's ability to adequately distinguish appropriate sexual partners" (p. 1001).

Scheckel et al. (1968) found that the general behavioral changes in squirrel monkeys given THC were more relevant to the question of hallucinations than changes in operant responding. Low doses of THC (4 or 8 mg/kg) caused the monkey to sit quietly near the operant levers and look down at the lower part of the chamber. Higher doses seemed to induce apparent hallucinations that

.. excited the monkeys and caused them to walk about the box, apparently looking at something the experimenters did not see, or crouch and move their heads from side to side and up and down as if watching some moving object. Some animals had a blank expression and gazed into space. We assumed that the animals had visual hallucinations. . . . In all monkeys given 32 or 64 mg/kg, this apparent hallucinatory reaction was more obvious. Monkeys moved quickly about the box, looked above and behind themselves, seemed to be in a state of panic, and appeared to fight with imaginary objects; their arms would swing rapidly through the air and they would attempt to grasp objects that were not there (Scheckel et al., 1968, p. 1467).

Similar behaviors have been reported with marihuana by McIsaac et al. (1971) and with inhalation of volatile solvents by Yanagita et al. (1970). Lagutina et al. (1964) observed that baboons injected with LSD (10–40 μg/kg) exhibited orienting responses, hyperexcitability, and periodic catatonia. In addition, the animals grasped at objects in the air, jumped about the cage, and tried to escape "as if they had hallucinations." Similar reactions were observed in a chimpanzee treated with LSD (800 μg, p.o.) who struck at the air in front and above him, screamed, and displayed fear reactions without apparent stimuli:

He began to look at his right hand, which he extended about 8 in. before his eyes. Suddenly he screamed, beat the air before him with his right hand, and defecated. Then he lashed the air before his face with both hands, grimaced, leaped upwards, and screamed. He landed in a sitting position and covered his eyes with his hands. As he sat he continued to salivate and he began to whimper. He screamed once more and ran backward, beating at the air before him with both hands. He stopped, stared at the roof, and then looked quickly to his right. Once again he struck at the air over his head and screamed. Then he began to run about the floor, alternately screaming and whimpering . . . (Baldwin et al., 1957, pp. 46–47).

Interestingly, Baldwin and his co-workers compared this drug-induced behavior with that induced in chimpanzees by sensory isolation, concluding that both treatments produce identical behavioral syndromes. In another study, Evarts (1958) found that LSD (1 mg/kg) failed to impair the accuracy of monkeys' performance on a variety of learned responses but did produce a syndrome characterized by ataxia and loss of responsiveness to normal visual stimuli. Similar syndromes have been produced in monkeys exposed to conflict situations (Masserman, 1959). At feeding time, Masserman presented monkeys with a toy rubber snake in the food box or with unavoidable electric shock. These conflict procedures produced "experimental neuroses" coupled with hallucinatory behaviors:

Some monkeys also showed deep anachronistic regressions, extreme or bizarre affectivity and evidence of hallucinatory and delusional behavior such as unremitting searching and exploration or the recurrent seeking, chewing and swallowing of imaginary food while refusing real food immediately available (p. 100).

During cocaine self-administration studies in rhesus monkeys, Deneau et al. (1969) constantly observed "behavior consistent with visual hallucinations (staring and grasping at the wall) and tactile hallucinations (continued scratching and biting of the extremities, to the point of producing extensive wounds and even amputation of the digits)" (p. 41). Of course, the tactile hallucinatory behavior may have been the result of local irritation; but the description closely resembles the human reports of "cocaine bugs." The latter, perhaps the most common hallucinations in cocaine users, consist of sensations of live insects or animals crawling on or under the skin. In man and monkey, such tactile sensations can lead to skin abrasions, chronic sores, and even local wounds (Woods and Downs, 1973).

Recently an attempt was made to develop an objective behavioral profile that could be used to distinguish the effects of hallucinogens from those of other drugs (Siegel et al., 1974). Saline, bromo-lysergic acid diethylamide (BOL), LSD, dimethyltryptamine, chlorpromazine, and d-amphetamine were administered to solitary adolescent rhesus monkeys whose behavior was observed, videotaped, and scored by blind observers in a number of categories. Hallucinogens could be distinguished from the other drugs by the increased frequency of unusual behaviors such as spasms, stereotypy, and inappropriate behavior. Hallucinogens also produced qualitative changes in behavior such as convulsive body jerks, grooming with hand covering face, walking around the cage with eyes closed, and ataxic locomotion. These investigators did not find significant hallucinogen-induced increases in behaviors (e.g., fear grimace, threat, tracking), which normally occur only in the presence of an appropriate stimulus; thus, they could not support the notion of "hallucinatory stimuli." Nonetheless, they did suggest that an hallucinogen-induced decrease in exploration time was due to a shift in attention toward internally generated stimuli.

Borenstein et al. (1969) found that LSD (100μg/kg) produced stereotypic behavior in *Macaca nemestria* monkeys. Such stereotypy was marked by reduced motor activity and incessant eyeball and head movements. The monkeys engaged in continuous exploration of their environments, and the authors identified this as "visual hallucinatory behavior." However, this conclusion would have been strengthened if the authors had tried to correlate the eye movement patterns with stimuli that may or may not have been fixated. Indeed, Cohen (1968) has stressed the need for this type of measure to identify the nature of hallucinatory behavior in monkeys, but to date no one has done so. However, several investigators have found that hallucinogens induce measurable changes in monkey brain activity which are correlated with changes in visual perception (e.g., Vuillon-Cacciuttolo and Balzamo, 1971). For example, Bermond and Bert (1969) reported that psilocybin (3 mg) enhanced the alertness of monkeys as estimated from EEG recordings, decreased spontaneous mobility, and increased the frequency of eye movements. The authors conclude that such behavioral patterns could be explained by alteration of visual perception (i.e., hallucinations). Recently Heath (1973) found that marihuana produces in the septal area of rhesus monkey brain an activation that could be associated with this observed heightened awareness as well as accompanying changes in emotional expressions.

LABORATORY STUDIES OF HALLUCINOGEN-INDUCED CHANGES IN PERCEPTION

The field and laboratory observations discussed previously emphasize the importance of considering the uniqueness of animal perception. The behavior of organisms is often guided by perceptions, and we can never really *know* the perceptions of other animals, including those of our own species. Von Uexküll (1921) used the word *umwelt* to emphasize that each species perceives the world uniquely, and this constitutes a further limitation to the understanding of what is perceived by others. Nonetheless, some examples of animal behavior do agree with an intuitive sense of what is reasonable to infer, as in the mescaline-treated cat's fondling of a mouse or the THC-treated monkey's orientation to imaginary stimuli. Other examples are less apparent and must make us cautious about a priori assumptions about what an animal does and does not perceive in a given situation.

The question of whether an hallucinogen-treated animal perceives an hallucination can be approached in several ways. Bridger (1973) suggested two such approaches:

> First is that in some way LSD and mescaline activate previously stored memory images independent of any external stimulus, and the animals show searching behavior, aggressive behavior, etc., without responding to a known external stimulus. The second approach assumes that an external signaling stimulus is necessary and that the animals have a decreased ability to differentiate this signaling from what is being signaled (p. 136).

Evidence supporting Bridger's first approach has already been discussed in terms of observations in the field and laboratory. Additional evidence might be found in studies that train animals to report perceptual events and then substitute hallucinogen treatment for the stimulus events themselves. Examples of such studies conducted with pigeons are discussed below. Bridger's second approach involves experiments in which we examine the effects of hallucinogens on externally signaled avoidance behavior in rats, and examples of these are also given below.

Pigeons. A number of studies on the perceptual effects of hallucinogens have been carried out in the pigeon because of that animal's visual acuity and proved ability to perform complex tasks. Typically, low doses of LSD ($20–300\mu g/kg$) improve the accuracy of some visual discriminations. For example, LSD causes an improvement in the accuracy of a brightness (Blough, 1957) and flicker discrimination (Becker et al., 1967), and little change in hue discrimination (Berryman et al., 1962). Higher doses usually lower the response rate, thus making it difficult to assess performance.

In the usual design of the experiments, pigeons are trained to respond (key peck) in the presence of one stimulus (S+) to gain access to a food reward (reinforcement), but responding in the presence of another stimulus (S−) is not reinforced. The two stimuli are presented on different trials, randomly alternated, and separated by blackout periods (intertrial intervals) during which stimuli are not presented and responses have no consequences. As the animal learns to discriminate between the two stimuli, responses in the presence of the nonreinforced stimulus and during the blackout period gradually disappear; that is, the animal learns that these do not earn rewards. However, in many studies with hallucinogens, the animals occasionally make inappropriate responses during the intertrial intervals. Since stimuli are not presented to the animal during these intervals, responses during that time are as inappropriate as responses on nonreinforced trials, and stimulus control is said to be disrupted. These responses are of great interest because they are, in effect, false reports (i.e., animals are responding as if stimuli were present).

Siegel (1969) attempted to investigate hallucinogen-induced "false reports" in pigeons. In one initial experiment, not previously reported, 12 pigeons were placed in a totally dark operant discrimination unit and trained to peck at a rear-illuminated response key for food reinforcement. The animals were then divided into three groups of four birds each. Group 1 was trained to peck at the response key whenever a rear-projected slide was shown on the key. The slides, which constantly varied from trial to trial, consisted of a wide variety of geometric forms, colors, complex objects, and scenes of landscapes, houses, cars, and people. Most of the slides were obtained from commercial "psychedelic" light-show companies and were representative of the types of visual imagery reported with hallucinogenic reactions in man. Many of the slides displayed scenes in distorted and exaggerated form, and most contained examples of hallucinogen-induced geometric form-constants (cf. Klüver, 1966; Horowitz, this volume). The rationale for this choice in stimulus material was independently suggested by research psychiatrist Frank Ervin:

The animal could be conditioned to the type of geometrical patterns commonly seen in these hallucinosis. Then one could see if the animal responded more with LSD than did a control. This would be getting closer to an animal model of hallucination (in Smythies, 1970, p. 85).

Subjects received 20 daily sessions of discrimination training, and each session consisted of 40 successively presented slides, 20 blank (white light) slides (S−) and 20 with the features previously described (S+). All slides presented during a session differed from one another, and different sets of slides were presented at each session. Thus animals in Group 1 could earn reinforcements for responses to a variety of stimuli but were not rewarded for responses made when these stimuli were absent and only white light was present. In effect, the animals were trained to respond to the "concept" of "slide on" or "stimulus present," and these responses could be considered equivalent to the verbal statement "is" (i.e., when slide is on, or when stimuli are present, reinforcement is available). Conversely, animals in Group 2 were trained on the opposite problem: responses to "slide off" or white light only were rewarded (S+), and responses to "slide on" were not rewarded (S−). In other words, contingencies in Group 2 were equivalent to the verbal statement "is not" (i.e., the animal must learn that when stimulus is not present, or is absent, reinforcement is available). Animals in Group 3 received differential training on the problem white light on (S+), white light off (S−). After 20 training sessions, animals in Groups 1 and 2 were emitting 80 to 90% of their responses during S+ trials. Subjects were then given a series of drug sessions in which they were treated with a variety of doses of LSD, pentobarbital, or saline. At high doses of LSD (300–500μg/kg, i. p.) pigeons in Group 1 made significantly more responses to blank trials when compared with predrug or saline sessions; pigeons in Group 2 maintained their discrimination ratios but did not respond to as many "slide off" (S+) trials as they did during predrug and saline sessions.

Although it could be argued that LSD treatment merely broke down stimulus control for Group 1, resulting in lower discrimination ratios, such an explanation does not account for the unimpaired performance of Group 2. Indeed, pentobarbital (2–10 mg/kg), which does break down stimulus control in some visual discrimination tasks for pigeons, only suppressed responding here: there were no concomitant changes in discrimination accuracy. Since animals in Group 3 showed no disruption of the simple white light on-off problem under the same doses of LSD, this stimulus control notion cannot be supported. Another explanation is that pigeons in Groups 1 and 2 were reporting perceptual events. Accordingly, the responses of pigeons in Group 1 to blank trials in LSD sessions may be interpreted as statements that stimuli were perceived to be present at these times. Similarly, the maintenance of discrimination ratios for Groups 2 and 3 in LSD sessions indicates that stimuli could still be accurately perceived and discriminated. Furthermore, the failure of pigeons in Group 2 to respond to some of the "slide off" trials in LSD sessions suggests that these animals may have been perceiving stimuli at these times. Since these effects were not observed in saline or pentobarbital sessions, it is possible that such results are a consequence of the LSD treatment, if not hallucinatory stimuli per se.

Another way of conceptualizing the verbal statements "is" and "is not" involves the discriminations of matching and oddity. When an animal matches stimuli, he chooses a response that in essence says what the stimulus "is." On the other hand, oddity or "nonmatching" involves choosing what the stimulus "is not." Several investigators have observed that matching and oddity performances in the pigeon are differentially affected by pentobarbital (Cumming and Berryman, 1965; Nevin and Liebold, 1966). Oddity performance is far less sensitive to this drug than matching performance, which is readily disrupted by low doses. Utilizing the more sensitive matching procedure, Siegel (1969) studied the effects of hallucinogens on the separate dimensions of form and color, dimensions along which humans report hallucinogenic disturbances (Hoffer and Osmond, 1967, pp. 111ff).

In the Siegel study, four pigeons were trained in an operant unit equipped with three response keys. During a 10-second intertrial interval, all response keys were dark. A trial started when the two side keys were illuminated with white light and the center key was illuminated with one of three groups of stimuli. The stimulus on the center key was either a white triangle (the standard) or another form or a color. The forms included squares, circles, rectangles, lines, dots, and crosses (Fig. 3). Colors included various changes in hue, saturation, or brightness. If the standard triangle appeared, the animal was required to respond to the center key to earn food reinforcement. If a color appeared, responses to the right key were reinforced, whereas if a form other than triangle appeared, responses to the left key were rewarded. The stimuli were constantly varied from trial to trial, and the animals, in effect, had to learn the concepts of "form change" and "color change" to select correctly when presented with a novel stimulus configuration.

After the animals had mastered this rather difficult discrimination, they were given a series of drug sessions. In general, most drug treatments did not disrupt accuracy of this performance. When given several doses of a *Cannabis* extract or LSD, pigeons suppressed responding for some minutes, but when they resumed, their performance remained relatively unchanged. Only the high dose of LSD (750μg/kg) significantly disrupted accuracy. Nonetheless, a very interesting effect emerged when the type of errors the animals did make (they usually performed between 80 and 90% accuracy on this problem) were analyzed. Table 1 shows the

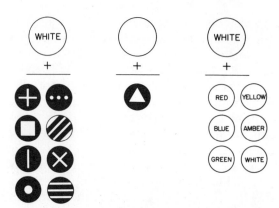

Figure 3 Response keys and sample stimuli used in pigeon discrimination study (Siegel, 1969). The two side keys were always illuminated with white light. Other stimuli were displayed on the center key. When a triangle was displayed, responses to the center key were reinforced (+). When other forms were displayed, responses to the left (white) key were reinforced (+). When colors were displayed, responses to the right (white) key were reinforced (+).

mean distribution of errors during all drug sessions. Errors were scored according to the following procedure. Responses to the color key when either a form or standard triangle was displayed were scored as color errors. Responses to the center key when either a form or color was displayed were scored as standard (triangle) errors. Similarly, responses to the form key when either a color or the standard was displayed were scored as form errors. As Table 1 indicates, during the pretest mean of 10 sessions, errors were relatively equally distributed between form and color keys. However, with 300μg/kg of LSD there was a significant increase in the number of color errors. This increase was also seen with the two other doses of LSD as well as with the *Cannabis* treatments. Equal doses of BOL, which is similar to LSD except for the psychological effects and EEG activation, produced no changes in error distribution.

Several interpretations of these findings suggest themselves. First, it may be argued that the hallucinogens used simply break down stimulus control. This notion may explain the decrement in performance under high doses of LSD, but it fails to account for the accuracy of performance under comparable doses of *Cannabis*. Indeed, a breakdown in stimulus control might also be expected to distribute errors more equally among the three keys. In addition, pentobarbital did produce some decrement in accuracy of the discrimination with no concomitant change in error distribution; thus the stimulus control interpretation must be regarded with caution. Alternatively, Siegel argues that "a particularly attractive but more speculative explanation is that animals were reporting perceptual events" (p. 8). Pigeons under LSD and *Cannabis* may have been reporting color changes when no color changes were occurring on the center key. Since color errors did not prevail under BOL, the results seem to be at least a consequence of the central nervous system effects of the drugs, if not the hallucinogenic properties themselves.

TABLE 1. MEAN PERCENT DISTRIBUTION OF PIGEON ERRORS DURING ALL DRUG SESSIONS[a] (N = 4)

Errors	Pretest	Saline	LSD 300 μg/kg	LSD 500 μg/kg	LSD 750 μg/kg	BOL 500 μg/kg	BOL 750 μg/kg	Cannabis 20 mg/kg	Cannabis 30 mg/kg	Pento- barbital 10 mg/kg
Form	53.3	52.5	33.3	7.1	11.9	63.2	55.8	8.7	3.3	60.6
Standard	2.4	6.4	3.7	5.2	4.8	1.1	2.3	5.0	2.1	3.2
Color	44.3	41.1	63.0	87.7	83.3	35.7	42.9	86.3	94.6	36.2

[a]Adapted from Siegel (1969).

Using a similar procedure with monkeys, Ferraro (1972) found that THC (1 mg/kg, p.o.) produced a significant decrease in correct responses to a delayed matching-to-sample problem. In this procedure, a time delay is introduced between the sample stimulus and the choice stimuli to which the animal will try to match the sample. As the delay grows longer, the problem becomes more difficult for the animal. THC produced no decrement at 0-second delay, thus demonstrating that the animal still had the motivation, attention, and motor responses necessary for correct responding. The same dose of THC, however, disrupted performance at delays of 5, 10, and 20 seconds, indicating some type of interaction between perception and short-term memory.

Rats.   Several studies with rats have demonstrated that hallucinogens selectively impair externally signaled behaviors. In the simple version of one of these procedures, the conditioned avoidance response, an animal is placed on an electric grid adjacent to a safe (nonshocked) area. A tone or light is presented to the animal, followed a few seconds later by a shock delivered to the grid. The animal soon learns to take the appropriate avoiding action and moves to the safe area as soon as the light or tone is presented. When treated with intermediate doses of LSD, psilocybin, dimethyltryptamine, or other hallucinogenic amphetamines, the reaction time is at first increased and then decreased (Smythies and Sykes, 1964). In other words, the animal takes longer to respond to the signal and avoid the shock. Only the hallucinogens seem to have this characteristic "biphasic" response, and so far it has not been induced by any other compound (Smythies et al., 1969).

That hallucinogens selectively impair an animal's discrimination of external signals is further illustrated by studies involving a free operant avoidance procedure (Bovet and Gatti, 1963; Beaton et al., 1969; Smythies et al., 1969; Webster et al., 1971). In this procedure, also referred to as Sidman avoidance, the animal can keep on postponing the shock by pressing a lever that continually resets a shock delivery circuit for a fixed time period. The onset of shock is preceded by a 10-second light, after which animals usually learn to press the lever and postpone the shock. In this way, the animal can avoid shock as long as he responds efficiently. Hallucinogens characteristically increase the proportion of inefficient responses—premature (made before the light comes on) and late (made too late to avoid shock)—and decreases the proportion of efficient responses. The reaction time (the time between onset of the light or the conditioned stimulus and the rat's response) shows a decrease with low doses and an increase with high doses.

OVERVIEW: DO ANIMALS HALLUCINATE?

The traditional assumption that *Homo sapiens* is the only species that uses hallucinogens is challenged by field observations on several other species that either by accident or design also self-administer these drugs. Many of the examples cited here need further controlled psychopharmacological study to identify the biological, pharmacological, and environmental variables. Nonetheless, it is clear that such self-administrations dramatically affect the animals' behavior.

The extent to which such behaviors support the notion of animals having hallucinations depends on what we are willing to infer about the behavior. Such inferences can be dangerously speculative in natural milieus, where pharmacological and behavioral controls are lacking. However, in more controlled laboratory studies there are abundant observations of hallucinogen-induced perceptual changes, if not hallucinations themselves. Mice treated with such drugs as LSD exhibit bizarre postures, aggression, fear, paroxysmal ear scratching, head twitching, and other behaviors. The descriptions of the mice's locomotion and exploration have included numerous reports of reactions to stimuli that were not present. This has prompted many investigators to speak of apparent hallucinatory behavior. At the very least, such drug-induced behaviors occur at doses correlated with human hallucinogenic doses. Cats treated with hallucinogens manifest similar bizarre postures, head shaking, and inappropriate approach and withdrawal behavior, as well as orienting responses to stimuli that are not present in the experimental situation. Monkeys treated with hallucinogens execute oriented and focused visual searching of their environments without apparent stimulus targets, exhibit oral syndromes described as somatosensory hallucinations, and frequently appear to fight with "imaginary" objects.

Taken together, these studies indicate that so-called drug-induced hallucinations appear clearer and more purposeful as observations are made higher up the phylogenetic scale. The comparatively limited behavioral repertoires of rodents and cats, and their basic "alien" nature, prevent human observers from agreeing on the interpretation of drug-induced changes. However, with infrahuman primates the range of behaviors is fuller and more familiar, the temptation to anthropomorphize is greater, and human observers find the reactions to hallucinogens more convincingly hallucinatory. If such observations were extended to hallucinogen-induced changes in *Homo sapiens,* it is doubtful whether any clearer examples of hallucinatory behavior could be found than those provided earlier. For in all organisms, this behavior is probably related to hallucinogen-induced states of central nervous system excitation and sympathetic nervous system arousal, marked by a behavioral "turning inward toward a mental dimension at the expense of the physical" (Fischer, 1971a, p. 897). Consequently, it is not surprising to find that the initial behavioral excitation and arousal induced by hallucinogens is often followed by quiescence and catatonia. Elsewhere, it has been shown that this contributes to the tendency of hallucinogen-treated animals to avoid further stimulation, thus to isolate themselves from social groups (Siegel, 1973a).

It is probably fortunate for the study of hallucinations that animals do not primarily react to hallucinogens with understandable verbal responses or "higher level cognitions," since that much more of their behavior is "outside" the organism and observable to others. Such behaviors are strikingly similar to those of preverbal children given the hallucinogenic anesthetic ketamine prior to surgical procedures (Siegel et al., 1971). The recovery behavior of these children is frequently marked by pointing, reaching, and grasping at the air; spontaneous head and eye orientations in the absence of apparent stimuli; and, in one case, a crawling away from an area of the bed which the child continued to strike at with his hands, screaming and crying.

Many of these studies have included the observation that hallucinogens increase stereotyped behavior (e.g., oral syndrome, grooming, head twitching). Stereotyped behavior is usually defined as "that which has little variation and might include a single activity performed continuously or a repertory of a few sequences which dominate behavior" (Ellinwood and Sudilovsky, 1973, p. 52). In most instances these stereotypies appear "nondistractable" and "driven" or performed in a rapid and repetitious manner, and they seem to evolve from motor components of investigatory and exploratory behaviors. Examples of hallucinogen-induced stereotyped behavior, which include increased head twitching, paroxysmal ear scratching, and grooming, have been observed in rats, rabbits, cats, monkeys, and man (Knoll et al., 1971; Randrup and Munkvad, 1971; Rylander, 1971). There even appear to be similarities between animals and man in operant behaviors under some of these drugs, such as amphetamines (Weiss and Laties, 1971).

Recently Ellinwood and Sudilovsky (1973) compared amphetamine-induced stereotypy across species and developed a model of how hallucinatory behavior might be generated from such a basis. These authors note that as one looks along the phylogenetic scale from rodents to primates, there appear more developed patterns of amphetamine-induced stereotypy: rats sniff, nose, and lick; cats orient and track; and primates use coordinated hand–eye movements directed toward external objects or their own bodies. Often distinctive body postures and activities accompany the development of such behavior. For example, in the cat such postures were characterized by hyperreactivity:

In the end stages of the chronic intoxication cycle, even though the animal might be in a frozen posture, sudden orienting movements toward a real or "hallucinated" stimulus were often observed. Many animals appeared to be increasingly aware of minor stimuli in their environment and acutely apprehensive about it . . . Not infrequently a cat would jump back and turn vigorously to one side in response to a nonexistent [apparently hallucinatory] stimulus (Ellinwood et al., 1973, pp. 1089–1090).

These findings can be compared with amphetamine-induced behaviors in primates, which include incessant examining, rubbing, and picking of the skin. Interestingly, both human and infrahuman primates use the forefinger probe and pincer grasp in executing these behaviors. Hallucinations may easily develop from such behaviors in man:

. . . many of the patients with "grooming responses" developed marked delusions of parasitosis and spent many hours examining their skin and digging out imagined encysted parasites. These delusions appeared to develop out of earlier sequences of skin sensations and repetitive "grooming responses" that evolved over time. . . . Other repetitive examining, searching, and sorting behaviors are directed towards the external environment and are often associated with an intense feeling of curiosity. . . . Amphetamine addicts frequently state that the scanning, prying, and probing behaviors subsequently evolve into what is at first a pleasurable sense of suspiciousness in the old meaning of suspiciousness: that is, looking beneath the surface for the truth or meaning (literally, to look from below). They describe looking for meaningful details and for relationships between details, or they often impart great meaning to trivial details. . . . Progressing from this stage, the previous suspiciousness flourished to a more paranoid form, and still later the patient was often fearful and not infrequently panic-stricken, agitated, and overreactive. At this point it is not unusual for patients to suddenly misinterpret stimuli and often have delusions and hallucinations (Ellinwood and Sudilovsky, 1973, pp. 52–53).

Can such hallucinations develop in animals? Let us examine this question in terms of the stages of the model proposed. First, there is the observed increase in stereotyped behaviors, and this stage is observed in both animals and man. Second, there is a "looking for meaningful details" or attributing great meaning to trivial details. The second stage can also be conceptualized in terms of attentional shifts. If an animal shifts his attention from relevant cues to irrelevant cues (e.g., inner sensations, "imagined stimuli"), we might predict an impairment in the performance of discriminations that require the animal to attend exclusively to relevant cues. Indeed, there appears to be substantial evidence that hallucinogens disrupt animal discrimination performance in specific ways consistent with this notion. For example, Sharpe et al. (1967) found that in squirrel monkeys simple discriminations were unaffected, and only fine or difficult size discriminations were impaired by LSD treatment (10–40 μg/kg). It is well known that in making difficult discriminations animals often shift their attention from the relevant dimensions to irrelevant stimuli. Thus the authors speculated that LSD may have facilitated such attentional shifts to irrelevant stimuli.

The third stage of the amphetamine model involves a state of fear, panic, and overreaction, sometimes manifested in the misinterpretation of stimuli. It is clear from the observational studies discussed that hallucinogen-treated animals display fear, panic, and hyperreactivity. The increase in aggressive postures, the severe autonomic reactions, and the tracking and grasping of imaginary objects all seem to argue in favor of Stage 3 in animals. Another example of Stage 3 fear and autonomic reactions was found in chimpanzees administered LSD (30μg/kg):

Suddenly, Sampson, the normal animal, stopped his play. His pupils dilated. He seemed to stare, and his mouth opened in a grimace as he began to salivate. His face flattened, and he began to hyperventilate. Then his hair stood on end, and he screamed and leaped backward. As he moved, he struck at the air before him with both hands (Baldwin et al., 1959, p. 473).

Furthermore, the hallucinogen-induced impairment of externally signaled avoidance behavior seems to support the notion that these animals were also misinterpreting stimuli. There is also some evidence that the fear in Stage 3 is an important determinant in both human and infrahuman reactions to hallucinogens. For example, human reaction to hallucinogens are often dependent on the degree of fear or anxiety present. Similarly, the effect of mescaline on rat behavior has been shown to be greatly potentiated when the rat is placed in a fear-producing situation where unavoidable shock is signaled (Smythies et al., 1969).

Thus far we have seen that the ingredients for the three stages of our developmental model of hallucinations are probably present for hallucinogen-treated animals. However, Ellinwood and Sudilovsky mention that delusions often accompany such hallucinations; and other writers have even stated this as a necessary condition for true hallucinations. In other words, true hallucinations involve the perception of stimuli that are not really there, concomitant with a delusion that they are indeed present (James, 1890). It could be argued that we have no way of knowing about an animal's delusions or false beliefs and, therefore, we can never know whether an animal is truly hallucinating. But animals might confirm the presence of hallucinations by responding to them, trying to grasp them, tracking them, avoiding them, or in some other way behaving as if "things" were actually there. The sheer abundance of the observational studies reporting such phenomena cannot be lightly dismissed. That animals are also capable of manifesting false beliefs in the perception of stimuli has been demonstrated in rat studies on the conditioned avoidance response. Here, in a sense, the animal acquires a true belief in the external signal and learns to avoid the incipient shock. The animal's avoidance behavior is true because it is conformable to a standard pattern. It is a belief because the animal's avoidance response is a deliberate habitual readiness to act in a certain manner under appropriate conditions. The hallucinogen-treated rat waits too long to avoid quickly and sometimes endures shock. His behavior is now indicative of a false belief: it is no longer conformable to a standard rule established by training. Similarly, the persistent errors made in the Sidman avoidance procedures (premature and late responses) have no basis in the physical reality of the situation, but the animal behaves as if the trust, confidence, or reliance placed in the external signal by training is no longer present. Simply stated, the animal behaves in accordance with the description that he is deluded. With all this in mind, we return to our initial question: can animals hallucinate? Yes, they can. Do animals hallucinate? Yes, they do. We all do.

PART II: MAN

True perceptions involve objects that are really there or really not there. Psychologist William James characterized such perceptions by the presence of "objective reality." Conversely, James defined an hallucination as having no objective stimulus at all:

They are often talked of as mental images projected outwards by mistake. But where an hallucination is complete, it is more than a mental image. An hallucination is a strictly sensational form of consciousness, as good and true as if there were a real object there. The object happens not to be there, that is all (James, 1890, p. 115).

True hallucinations are distinguished from pseudohallucinations, which lack the character of "objective reality." Both types, however, share the qualities of being vivid, minute, detailed, abrupt, and spontaneous. James described the hallucinations of opium, hashish, and belladonna as a mixture of pseudohallucination, true hallucination, and illusion. He cites the following account from a friend who ingested hashish:

Directly I lay down upon a sofa there appeared before my eyes several rows of human hands, which oscillated for a moment, revolved and then changed to spoons. The same motions were repeated, the objects changing to wheels, tin soldiers, lamp-posts, brooms, and countless other absurdities. . . . I saw at least a thousand different objects. These whirling images did not appear like the realities of life, but had the character of the secondary images seen in the eye after looking at some brightly-illuminated object. . . . I became aware of the fact that my pulse was beating rapidly. . . . I could feel each pulsation through my whole system. . . . There were moments of apparent lucidity, when it seemed as if I could see within myself, and watch the pumping of my heart. A strange fear came over me, a certainty that I should never recover from the effects. . . . Suddenly there was a roar and a blast of sound and the word "Ismaral". . . . I thought of a fox, and instantly I was transformed into that animal. I could distinctly feel myself a fox, could see my long ears and bushy tail, and by a sort of introversion felt that my complete anatomy was that of a fox. Suddenly, the point of vision changed. My eyes seemed to be located at the back of my mouth; I looked out between the parted lips, saw the two rows of pointed teeth, and, closing my mouth with a snap, saw—nothing . . . the whirling images appeared again. . . . It was an image of a double-faced doll, with a cylindrical body, running down to a point like a peg-top. It was always the same, having a sort of crown on its head, and painted in two colors, green and brown, on a background of blue (pp. 121–122).

It is clear from this account that the hashish experience generated visual, auditory, kinesthetic, as well as emotional reports. Despite the alleged distinctiveness of the experiences, it is doubtful whether the subject was ever convinced of the reality of his perceptions. Although James calls these events hallucinations, a true hallucination, one that "fools" the subject and appears "out there," is rare in drug-induced states. Such reports as the letter just quoted are more properly classified as pseudohallucinations, since the perceptions appear to lack the concomitant delusion that they really exist. Other researchers have labeled such phenomena as "reported visual sensations," "fantasies," "visions," "imagination," "inner events," "private events," and "conditioned sensations." Still others speak of the "imagery of hallucinations" by broadly defining hallucination to include any spontaneous imagery that might be taken for a perception, even if the subject knows that he is not perceiving (Hebb, 1968). It is in this latter sense that we speak of the visual imagery of drug-induced hallucinations in the following sections.

A number of studies have attempted to distinguish between normal mental imagery and the imagery of hallucinations. Most view mental imagery as "all those quasi-sensory or quasi-perceptual experiences of which we are self-consciously aware, and which exist for us in the absence of those stimulus conditions that are known to produce their genuine sensory or perceptual counterparts" (Richardson, 1969, pp. 2–3). Accordingly, hallucinations are referred to as exaggerated mental images (Roman and Landis, 1945; Pylsyshyn, 1973) or cognitive constructions elaborated on by expectancies and past experiences (Segal, 1971). Furthermore, hallucinations are considered to be more vivid and more real than normal mental images (Stockings, 1940; Seitz and Molholm, 1947; Aggernaes, 1972a, 1972b; Mintz and Alpert, 1972). When the imagery of hallucinations is drug-induced, it is readily distinguished from other forms of imagery in that the former has its own space in which the objects appear and the action unfolds (Masters and Houston, 1967). Some of our subjects who reported such imagery with eyes open have coined the phrase "intraspatials" to indicate that the space or locus of these events is interposed with real physical stimuli and does not interfere with them.

Analysis of the imagery of such drug-induced hallucinations is intimately dependent on the words and pictures used in their description. James's friend who ingested hashish tells us that literally a thousand things were seen; but he describes very few of them. Therefore it is not surprising that more than a few scientific investigators have suggested that the talent of a poet like Milton is needed to fully describe hashish-induced hallucinations (Robinson, 1930).

But poets and scientists have long argued over their respective abilities to describe and interpret such complex phenomena. The argument is best illustrated by the classic rivalry between Purkinje and Goethe, who visited and corresponded with each other in the early nineteenth century (cf. Kruta, 1968; Ratliff, 1971). Purkinje's scientific method was heautognosis, in which one observes and experiments on one's own body. Combining this method with an ethic of laborious research and analysis, Purkinje investigated the behavioral and hallucinogenic effects of digitalis, nutmeg, and opium. He treated the visual imagery and allied phenomena as something that could be accurately represented and could have an informative scientific relationship with the actual processes involved in their production. Purkinje's pioneering work with heautognosis in the study of entoptic phenomena and vertigo is testimony to the success of this method. Goethe disagreed with this approach and expressed his own ethic as a poet: ". . . the knowledge of the world is inborn in a true poet, that in no way does he need much experience or great empiricism for its depiction" (in Kruta, 1968, p. 24).

Goethe's inquiry into plant morphology (*Zur Morphologie und Naturwissenschaft*) presented numerous images of the form and structure of plant development. However, whereas Purkinje used the image as a *representation* that could only abstract from phenomena those aspects which conform to accepted systems of scientific explanation, Goethe used the image as an *illustration* that had to be elaborately abstracted from reality to convey the essential beauty of nature. His visual image of the ideal plant was beautiful and moving but lacked a scientifically meaningful relationship to the processes of plant growth it was intended to represent (Ritterbush, 1968). Nonetheless, the approach epitomized by Goethe has been as successful in depicting the experiential aspects of hallucinations as Purkinje's approach has been in conveying the sensory components. Therefore, it is not surprising that the literary world is replete with analyses of the imagery of hallucinations (cf. Abrams, 1970; Hayer, 1970) and that the scientific literature contains many artistic and literary excursions into drug-induced imagery. For example, numerous descriptions of drug-induced hallucinations can be found in poetry (e.g., Ginsberg, 1961; Leary, 1966a; Durr, 1970), essays (e.g., Huxley, 1959; Watts, 1962), novels (e.g., Larner, 1968), and art and film (Masters and Houston, 1968), as well as in other forms (e.g., Metzner, 1968; Wolfe, 1968). Indeed some poets have combined approaches as in Henri Michaux's (1963) drawings and essays on his mescaline experiences or Jean Cocteau's (1957) art and poetry of opium addiction. Similarly, in the sciences, researchers have often employed literary and artistic devices such as poetry (e.g., Leary, 1966a) and graphics (e.g., Szuman, 1930) to supplement their findings.

It is not the purpose of the present section to argue for or against the positions represented by Purkinje and Goethe. Both apporaches are immensely valuable in communicating aspects of the imagery of drug-induced hallucinations. Indeed, as Polish scientist and artist Szuman wrote concerning the imagery of mescaline-induced hallucinations: "It is easy to describe the content of *what* was seen as trees, jewelry, the sea, etc., but it is difficult to describe *how* it is seen and this can only be expressed in a drawing" (translated from original: Szuman, 1930, p. 159). Accordingly, we have chosen to include graphic representations and illustrations of drug-induced imagery as found in both our experiments as well as those of others.

HISTORICAL INTRODUCTION

In 1845 French psychiatrist Jacques Moreau published one of the first books on hashish, in which he developed the principle of "objective experimentation" (Purkinje's heautognosis) in the study of mental disorders such as hallucinations.

Moreau claimed that one should study mental illness by provoking it artificially through the ingestion of hashish, which possessed the characteristics of plunging one into an hallucinatory state while preserving the ability to observe and report events. Moreau described hallucinations as being similar to dreams wherein imagined visual, auditory, and tactile stimuli appear to be part of reality. He noted that the psychological phenomena of hallucinations were basically the same whether induced by nitrous oxide, opium, alcohol, thorny apple, belladonna, henbane, half-sleep or total sleep, dizziness, fevers, convulsive disorders, neuroses, hunger, thirst, or intense cold. With uncanny insight into what future neurophysiological research would reveal, Moreau believed that the hallucinatory state resulted from excitation of the brain which enabled imagined thoughts and memories to become transformed into the sensory impressions of visions and sounds:

... the hallucinating person hears his own thoughts as he sees, hears the creations of his imagination as he is moved by his memories ... and, what is even more extraordinary, certain combinations of thought are transformed into sensory impressions—that is to say, are endowed with the property of acting physically upon our senses in the manner of exterior stimuli (translated from original: Moreau, 1845, p. 168).

After experimenting on both himself and his patients, Moreau tried to persuade his colleagues at the Hôpital de Bicêtre to try hashish for themselves. His medical friends were hesitant to accept this idea of "objective experimentation," but the Bohemian artists and writers of nineteenth century Paris were more receptive. Among them was novelist Théophile Gautier, who became interested in the visual imagery of hashish hallucinations. Gautier described some of his imagery after eating the marihuana resin:

Little by little the salon was filled with extraordinary figures ... as if I were the king of the feast, each figure came up in turn into the luminous circle of which I was the center. ... A bluish haze, an Elysian day, a reflection of an azurine grotto, formed, in the room, an atmosphere where I could see uncertain shapes vaguely tremble; ... After some moments of contemplation and by a strange miracle, I myself melted into the objects I regarded; I became that very object (in Ebin, 1961, pp. 9–13).

Gautier went on to organize the Club des Haschichins, which included Honoré de Balzac, Charles Baudelaire, Alexander Dumas, and Victor Hugo. The members' writings emphasized various aspects of their hashish experiences, including the intense and rapid flow of images. Throughout their reports one can find frequent references to colorful and vivid images, often composed of such forms as wheels, whirlpools, spirals, and rainbows (see Ebin, 1961). However, the drug experience so overwhelmed these early writers that a detailed analysis seemed almost impossible. As Baudelaire wrote in "The Poem of Hashish" (1857):

... in the more common effect the images are so multiplied and superimposed that all harmony is lost; the brain fails to keep pace with its impressions, still less to codify and control them (in Regardie, 1968, p. 108).

Although reluctant to follow Moreau's advice and use hashish, P. Max Simon (1888) studied the imagery of schizophrenic hallucinations in his patients at Asile. He reported the consistent occurrence of spider webs, ropes, meshes, and balls in the visual imagery of his hallucinating patients. These images, like the images of hashish hallucinations, appeared suddenly and changed constantly from one form to another. Some years later, fellow countryman Dheur (1899) suggested that these visual images appeared to display consistent movement patterns as form changes occurred.

While these events were taking place in Europe, the American Fitzhugh Ludlow (1857) published a journalistic account of hashish experiences based on his self-experimentation. Ludlow was so impressed by the consistent and predictable nature of the visual imagery that he even attempted to formulate two "laws of hasheesh operation":

First, after the completion of any one fantasia has arrived, there almost invariably succeeds a shifting of the action to some other stage entirely different in its surroundings. In this transition the general character of the emotion may remain unchanged. . . . Second, after the full storm of a vision of intense sublimity has blown past the hasheesh eater, his next vision is generally of a quiet, relaxing, and recreating nature (pp. 36–37).

These "fantasias" were not unique to the hashish experience. Several other hallucinogens were reported to be equally capable of eliciting such imagery. Lewin (1924, 1931) noted that the smoking of marihuana frequently produced hallucinations such as "fireworks, rockets, and many-coloured stars." When mescaline was ingested and the subject closed his eyes or entered a dark room, forms and colors became even more vivid. The forms included "coloured arabesques," "carpets," "filigree lacework," "stars," "crystals," and "geometrical forms of all kinds." Lewin's account is remarkably similar to such other descriptions of mescaline-induced visual imagery as Beringer's (1927) report of colored arabesques, crystals, and crosses that appeared repeatedly during the latter investigator's experiences. Surprisingly similar imagery has been noted for alcohol delirium tremens (Clarke, 1878; Brinkmann, 1972), *Amanita muscaria* (Wasson and Wasson, 1957), antihistamines (Csillag and Landauer, 1973), various methoxy amphetamines (Shulgin, 1970), numerous anesthetics (Smith, 1972), *Banisteriopsis* (Harner, 1968; Dobkin de Rios, 1972), various forms of *Cannabis* (Kanner and Schilder, 1930; Bromberg, 1934; Lucena, 1950), carbon dioxide (Meduna, 1952), *Datura stramonium* (Boismont, 1853; Gowdy, 1972), harmala alkaloids (Naranjo, 1967), ketamine (Kreuscher, 1969; Collier, 1972), LSD (Bliss and Clarke, 1962; Masters and Houston, 1967), marihuana (Keeler, 1968; Keeler et al., 1971), mescaline (Zador, 1930), nitrous oxide (Davy, 1800; Müller, 1826; Steinberg, 1956; Sheldin and Wallace, 1972; Sheldin et al., 1973), peyote (Spindler, 1952; Masters and Houston, 1967), psilocybin mushrooms (Heim and Wasson, 1958), and tobacco (Lane, 1845; Shaw, 1849). In addition, visual imagery has been reported for a wide variety of classic hallucinogens including plant β-phenethylamines, ololiuqui, indole hallucinogens derived from tryptophan, cholinergic-blocking agents, and many other drugs (see reviews by Hoffer and Osmond, 1967; Jarvik, 1970). Also, undefined hallucinatory effects have been reported to be associated with alcoholic intoxication (Scott et al., 1969; Wolin, 1973; Wolin and Mello, 1973) and with chemotherapy involving amantadine, anticholinergic drugs, cortisol, cyclosersine, and digitalis (Shader, 1972; Harper and Knothe, 1973). However, it should be noted that the hallucinogenic effects of many drugs including some classified pharmacologically as hallucinogens (e.g., bufotenine) and some listed previously (e.g., tobacco) are still in dispute (cp. Fabing and Hawkins, 1956; Turner and Merlis, 1959; Janiger and Dobkin de Rios, 1973).

THE EXPERIMENTAL ANALYSIS OF DRUG-INDUCED IMAGERY

Despite the frequent reports of drug-induced visual imagery, it was not until the work of Heinrich Klüver (1926, 1928, 1942, 1966) that the analysis of this phenomenon began. Klüver reported that following the ingestion of mescaline, visual imagery could be observed with either closed or opened eyes and that in the latter case, it was "impossible to look at walls without seeing them covered with visionary phenomena." The images generated in his own mescaline experiments, coupled with data reported by other investigators, were meticulously analyzed and the consistencies became apparent:

So far the analysis of the records published has yielded a number of forms and form elements which must be considered typical for mescal visions. No matter how strong the inter- and intra-individual differences may be, the records are remarkably uniform as to the appearance of the above-described forms and configurations. We may call them form-constants, implying that a certain number of them appear in almost all mescal visions and that many "atypical" visions are upon close examination nothing but variations of these form-constants (Klüver, 1966, p. 22).

These form-constants included four types. One type was always referred to by terms such as grating, lattice, fretwork, filigree, honeycomb, or chessboard design; the second resembled cobweb figures; the third was described by terms such as tunnel, funnel, alley, cone, or vessel; and spiral figures were designated as the fourth type. The form-constants were further characterized by varied and saturated colors, intense brightness, and symmetrical configuration. The visions seemed to be localized at reading distance, varied greatly in apparent size, and, generally, could not be consciously influenced by "thoughts" or "will." Stein (1928) confirmed the presence of these hallucinatory form-constants in mescaline intoxications. Szuman (1930) also found evidence of these constants in the mescaline state when the eyes were closed. When the subject opened his eyes, the patterns would appear projected against the real world as "pictures painted before your imagination." Szuman found that the images were often a repetition of the same motif, but displayed in different arrangements and filling the entire visual field.

Klüver made the critical observation that the same form-constants appeared in hypnagogic hallucinations (just prior to falling asleep), in insulin hypoglycemia, and, occasionally, in fever deliriums. McKellar (1957) reviewed studies suggesting that these "regularities" appear in many forms of human visualization including visions produced by mescaline, hypnagogic states, psychotic states, measles, malaria, tonsilitis, and influenza. Hypnagogic images were described by the Marquis d'Hervey in an 1867 monograph entitled *Les Rêves et les Moyens de les Diriger* as "wheels of light, tiny revolving suns, colored bubbles rising and falling . . . bright lines that cross and interlace, that roll up and make circles, lozenges, and other geometric shapes" (cited in MacKenzie, 1965, p. 108). Fever delirium hallucinations reported by Kandinsky (1881) bear a close resemblance to the mescaline imagery reported above by Szuman:

These vivid visual pictures completely covered real objects. During a week I saw on one and the same wall, covered with smooth uniformly colored wallpaper, a series of large pictures set in wonderfully gilded frames, landscapes, views of the seashore, sometimes portraits, in which the colors were just as vivid as in the real pictures of an Italian artist. . . . Hallucinations occurred as often with open eyes as with closed ones. In the first case they were projected on the surfaces of the floor, the ceiling, or the wall, or they appear in space, covering the objects that lie behind them. In one case the real environment disappeared completely and was suddenly replaced by an entirely new one; I suddenly saw myself transported out of the room to the shore of a bay . . . with closed eyes the complicated hallucinations appeared in the form of corporeal objects surrounding me; the less complicated ones, like, e.g., pictures, microscopic preparations, or ornamental figures, were drawn on the dark ground of the visual field . . . (Kandinsky, 1881, pp. 459–460).

Form-constants and allied phenomena have also been observed by subjects in sensory deprivation situations (Zubek, 1969), following photostimulation (Smythies, 1960; Freedman and Marks, 1965), electrical current (Knoll et al., 1962), crystal gazing (McKellar, 1957; Garvin, 1973), while gazing at a light bulb (Prince, 1939), during migraine scintillating scotoma (Richards, 1971; Aring, 1972), and even during "swinging" or "pendulumlike" motion (Masters and Houston, unpublished manuscript). Many of the geometric forms and designs common to the form-constants were also observed entoptically by Ladd (1892), Purkinje (1918), and many others. Although many investigators have stressed the similarity of drug-induced form-constants and entoptic phenomena (Pokorny, 1969; Barber, 1970; Oster, 1970), there is some evidence that the two phenomena may be quite different (see section on entoptic phenomena). In general, drug-induced patterns appear to be more vivid, more colorful, more regular, and more ornate than those elicited by the other methods.

It has been shown that hallucinatory imagery associated with schizophrenia, epilepsy, and syphilis is somewhat similar to the form-constants of drug-induced states, but the supporting evidence is scant (Plaut, 1913; Leuner, 1962; Malitz et al., 1962). Even the artistic behavior of some schizophrenic patients reflects a "geometromania" in which geometric designs are distorted, exaggerated, and repeated in symmetrical arrangements similar to the designs of cubism (Anastasi and Foley, 1940). The latter cases reflect idiosyncratic content to a far greater extent than those of drug-induced imagery, but the structure of schizophrenic and epileptic imagery suggests many similarities. Indeed, compare the examples of drug-induced imagery already given with the following account of an epileptic seizure:

These were "cartoon-like figures," pictured in [the patient] mind's eye as if they were projected on a television screen in close proximity to him. The images were always in black and white, he could "see" them with his eyes open or closed, but he could neither conjure them nor dispel them. They were experienced by the patient as something apart from himself and out of his control (Sedman, 1966, pp. 46–47).

Thus drug-induced visual imagery appears to be similar in many aspects to imagery observed in a wide variety of situations. One might be surprised to find such similarities, but Keeler (1970) has noted that "there are fewer mechanisms than etiologies of hallucinations. There is thus no reason for surprise if different precipitants give wholly or partly similar hallucinatory experiences" (p. 208).

But the form-constants, characteristic of these similar experiences, are only the first stage of a two-stage process of drug-induced imagery. Unfortunately Klüver did not examine the development of imagery past the first stages of mescaline intoxication. Earlier observers (e.g., Knauer and Maloney, 1913; Rouhier, 1927) had noted that the simple geometrical forms give way to landscapes, faces, and familiar objects as the experience progresses to the second stage. Balestrieri (1964) examined drug-induced hallucinations in a group of 50 patients and reported that the elementary forms of the first stage seem to combine with "complex" images, which eventually may replace the forms in the second stage. He thought that such complex images were derived from the activation of images already recorded and retained in the brain. Interestingly, Balestrieri found no differences in the content of LSD-, mescaline-, and psilocybin-induced complex imagery, although it is unlikely that his techniques were sensitive enough to detect any such variation. In a review of more than 500 LSD-induced experiences, Butterworth (1967) noted that certain identical second-stage "symbols" or images recurred both within and between individual patients. Astonishingly, 79% of all the images reported were shared by all subjects. Moreover, between 62 and 72% of the subjects experienced the designs and images that Klüver referred to as form-constants. Of the many "complex" images shared, 49% of the subjects experienced images of small animals or human figures, usually friendly and often in human caricature, whereas 72% experienced religious imagery.

Since this work, there have been few attempts to extend the type of analysis pioneered by Klüver. No one has tried to study the sequential development of the form-constants in a drug experience. There have been no well-controlled investigations of dose–response or time–response relationships, nor any well-controlled studies of the contents of imagery that develops after the initial phase of form-constants. And no attempt has been made to examine other dimensions of visual imagery, such as movement patterns and colors, which may also manifest constancies. Indeed, Klüver had noted that the form-constants were frequently repeated, combined, or elaborated on in various designs, but no consistent patterns or directions of movement were seen. Nonetheless, rotational and left–right horizontal motion were frequently reported by subjects. La Barre (1969) reported that the motion of peyote-induced visual imagery is primarily one of pulsation. Leuner (1964) commented on this movement in LSD- and psilocybin-induced imagery:

On closing his eyes, [the subject] soon sees the brightly coloured whorls of the simple primary hallucinations so often described in the literature of hallucinogens: patches of colour-striped flashes appear; abstract patterns, at first geometrical but later brilliantly coloured, flow lackadaisically, move in myriads, spread in a shower of coloured sparks in a deceptive motion that may take the form of turbulent rushing (p. 2).

Most investigators like Klüver and Balestrieri referred to such movement, color, and second-stage forms as "complex" and did not describe them in detail. It is curiously paradoxical that earlier workers had used similar words in reference to the forms that Klüver himself later analyzed. Klüver attributed this attitude to the novelty of the visions and claimed that observers are often enticed by the color or brightness of the images and ignore the basic forms. They are often awed by the experience and surrender before it as something overwhelming and "indescribable," causing more than one researcher to use grandiose metaphors and to attribute religious significance and cosmic meaning to visual imagery. But, as Adler (1972) points out: "To attach cosmic meaning to these events is a presumption. We are more likely confronting here the projection of affect onto the outside world. The response that one thinks he recognizes is his own projected and reflected image" (p. 19). This "indescribableness" of the form imagery had challenged Klüver to describe it. The apparent complexity of other dimensions challenged us to attempt their description as well. We believed that the study of such phenomena might suggest a typological construct or some common visual imagery underlying drug-induced hallucinations, which could help us understand the etiology of these and related perceptions. It is in this spirit that we began the following experiments.

IMAGERY IN UNTRAINED OBSERVERS

A series of experiments was designed to investigate the phenomenology of marihuana- and THC-induced visual imagery in groups of untrained observers. Although several of the studies have been reported previously (Siegel, 1971a; Siegel et al., 1972; Miller et al., 1973; Siegel, 1973b), the most current data are presented in this volume.

In our preliminary work, 14 subjects were required to self-administer each of the following drugs in eight weekly sessions. Only one drug was administered in any given session, and the treatment orders were given according to a Latin square design. Each dosage was placed in a 400-mg cigarette, which subjects were required to smoke by inhaling for 5 seconds, holding for 20 seconds, resting for 20 seconds, and repeating the cycle until the cigarette was consumed. The drug treatments were: marihuana: 4.25, 9.41, and 40.0 μg delta-9-THC/lb., b.w.; delta-9-THC on alfalfa: 4.25, 9.41, and 40.0 μg/lb., b.w.; and alfalfa placebo. Each subject in each session gave a five-minute verbal report of his visual imagery at approximately 90 minutes (Trial 1) and 300 minutes (Trial 2) following drug treatment. Prior to the start of each trial, all subjects were dark-adapted and brought into a darkroom in which they sat in a straight-back chair with eyes closed. They were instructed to give a continuing verbal report or running commentary of any visual images or pictures they might see when their eyes were closed. They were asked to pay particular attention to and to report on forms, colors, and movements. The taped-recorded reports were typed and the transcripts analyzed according to the following procedure.

In the scoring procedure, two double-blind experimenters scored each transcript on dimensions of form, color, direction of movement, and action patterns. On each dimension, the frequency of occurrence of each of several categories of verbal responses was noted. The correlation between the two experimenters' sets of scores was $r = .92$, and means were used in the analysis of the data. The dimensions, their respective categories, and examples that define them are given below:

FORM DIMENSION

Random. Blobs, amorphous shapes, blurry patterns, watery patterns with no definite design, etc. (Any form that cannot be classified in the categories below.)

Line. Herringbone patterns, zig-zags, polygons, all angular figures without curves or rounded corners, crosses, etc.

Curve. Circles, ellipses, parabolas, hyperbolas, sine wave patterns, fingerprint whorls, spheres, balls, scribbling, etc.

Web. Spider webs, nets, unsymmetrical lattices and filigrees, veins, etc.

Lattice. Lattices, gratings, grids, screens, fretwork, checkerboard, honeycombs, etc.

Tunnel. Tunnels, funnels, alleys, cones, vessels, pits, corridors, etc.

Spiral. Spirals, pinwheels, springs, etc.

Kaleidoscope. Kaleidoscopes, mandalas, symmetrical snowflakes, lacework, mosaics, symmetrical flowerlike patterns, etc.

Complex. Any recognizable imagery such as faces, people, landscapes, panoramic vistas, animals, inanimate objects, cartoons, etc.

COLOR DIMENSION

Black, violet, blue, green, yellow, orange, red, brown, and white.

(Color responses were scored in the category nearest to the response on the spectrum. For example, maroon = red, tan = brown, purple = violet, blue-green = blue and green, etc.)

MOVEMENT DIMENSION

Aimless. Any movement without apparent direction, "things floating around," etc.

Vertical. Up or down.

Horizontal. Right or left.

Oblique. Any linear motion at an angle other than vertical (90°) or horizontal (180°) with respect to the observer's midline axis.

Explosive. Motion away from the center, outward from the center, etc.

Concentric. Motion toward the center.

Rotational. Circular motion, clockwise or counterclockwise, etc.

Pulsating. Flickering, pulsating, throbbing, twinkling, etc.

ACTION PATTERNS (applies only to complex imagery)

Complete image changes. Any complete change of the visual field with substitution of new material for old. This is not to be confused with the development of movement or embellishment of already existing visual imagery. A complete image change usually means a successive transformation from one complex form to another complex form (e.g., "a shark changing into a dolphin changing into a skin diver changing into a submarine" contains four distinct images and three distinct image changes).

Changes within a single image. This measure connotes changes within a single image rather than the preceding measure of changes between single images. This can include changes in size or perspective, color changes of the same object, movement changes of the same object, elaboration, etc. A change within a single image usually implies that the image is "doing something" (e.g., "a man is walking down the street and his head gradually swells in size and changes from pink to red, becomes a red balloon, and floats away").

Combining of images. Two forms combining to form one (e.g., "a horse and a man combining to form a centaur"). In this case, the horse and man images are not replaced by the centaur image but are "observed" by the subject to actually change or combine through gradual and successive approximations.

Repeating of images. This measure implies duplication or multiplication of form (e.g., "one toy soldier is duplicating and becoming a whole army of toy soldiers").

Overlaying of images. This measure implies two distinct forms overlaying one another but remaining separate and independent. In other words, there are two levels of imagery and two different sets of action occurring. For example, a football game is overlayed by a sky full of northern lights and exploding fireworks. Or, more commonly, the subject reports geometric forms overlaying complex imagery.

Some of the results are presented in Table 2 in terms of the total number of visual imagery reports for all subjects in each treatment condition. Note that the number of reports increased dramatically with the increase in dosage of marihuana and THC, although the absolute number of reports in THC sessions was usually higher. The distribution of these reports indicated that normal baseline (no drug) imagery was composed of aimlessly moving black and white random forms with some lines and curves. Only one of 14 subjects reported any complete changes of visual imagery during baseline conditions. Conversely, 6 of the 14 reported a total of 37 complete imagery changes during placebo sessions, marked by complex (58%), random (23%), or curve (14%) forms, which tended to be mostly black, white, yellow, or green. Although movement during placebo sessions was generally aimless (30%), small amounts of concentric, explosive, horizontal, and vertical movements were also reported. The distribution of imagery reports during marihuana and THC sessions showed less random forms than baseline or placebo sessions, as well as slight increases in all other simple forms as dosage increased. Color reports showed a decrease in black and an increase in colors near the red end of the spectrum as dosage increased. Concomitantly, slight decreases in aimless and pulsating movements were reported with increases in more organized motion, particularly explosive and concentric. The actual percentage distribution of complex forms did not change substantially with marihuana and THC sessions (usually approximately 50%), but dramatic changes in action patterns were associated with such imagery. Indeed, changes within a single complete image showed a linear increase with dose, and there were also increases in the combining, repeating, and overlay-

TABLE 2. TOTAL IMAGERY REPORTS FOR ALL Ss IN ALL TRIALS[a] (N = 14)

Dimension	Baseline	Placebo	M1	T1	M2	T2	M3	T3
Form	69	170	248	229	277	290	313	347
Color	94	246	248	291	296	317	327	340
Movement	17	33	67	68	72	77	84	83

[a]Adapted from Siegel (1973b). Abbreviations: M = marihuana; T = THC. The numbers 1, 2, and 3 indicate the dose: M1 and T1 = 4.25μg. Δ^9-THC/1b; M2 and T2 = 9.41μg. Δ^9-THC/1b; M3 and T3 = 40.00μg. Δ^9-THC/1b.

ing of images. Generally, the distribution in color, form, and movement reports was relatively the same for THC and marihuana sessions. However, the absolute number of reports for THC sessions was usually greater than marihuana sessions in Trial 2; this suggests a somewhat longer duration of action for the THC treatments. There were only minimal changes in the content of complex imagery as dosage increased. Perhaps the most interesting change reported was the small increase in cartoons and humans.

The most obvious aspect of the findings is that the amount of visual imagery was dose-dependent and increased linearly with increased doses of marihuana and THC. Changes in the distribution of specific forms paralleled changes previously reported for mescaline by Klüver in 1942. Furthermore, *Cannabis*-induced changes in color and movement of imagery suggest the presence of hallucinatory constants in these dimensions. The most apparent color constant was red, and the most apparent movement constant was explosive and concentric motion.

Phenomenology.   The previous analyses of form, color, and movement reports did not reflect the exact nature of all the hallucinogenic constancies. One reason appeared to be that most subjects experienced difficulty in verbally describing their visual imagery. Careful analysis of the transcripts revealed that *Cannabis*-induced visual imagery was reported to be like a movie or slide show projected in front of the subject's eyes. This finding is similar to hypnagogic imagery, which has also been described to be like "a series of images which pass across my field of vision from right to left as if projected from a magic lantern that is being rotated" (McKellar, 1957, p. 39). In companion studies we have determined that there were no significant differences between eyes-closed imagery and eyes-open imagery when the latter occurred in a dark and lightproof room. Although many of the subjects could not label simple forms, they frequently acknowledged "geometric forms of all kinds" to be present.

Such imagery was often characterized by a very bright light in the center of the visual field (Fig. 4) which obscured central details but permitted imagery on the periphery to be observed. The locus of this point of light probably created a tunnel-like perspective, and subjects reported viewing much of their imagery in this regard (Fig. 5). The tunnel perspective probably contributed to the reports that imagery tended to pulsate and move toward the center of the tunnel (concentric movement) or move away from the center light in the tunnel (explosive), or both. When imagery appeared colored, all colors of the spectrum were reported although the incidence of red increased with dosage. Figure 6 (see color section) illustrates a blue lattice-tunnel reported by many subjects during the first stages of marihuana or THC intoxication. As the experience progresses, this tunnel appears red. Complex forms tended to change rapidly and often in associative ways (Fig. 7). Indeed, so rapid was the flow of imagery that most subjects found it difficult to maintain a running commentary on these events. Nonetheless, such imagery reports of recognizable scenes, people, and objects reflected characteristic symmetry, often in caricature or cartoon form, with some degree of depth. Numerous examples of distinctive memories occurred, and these were projected onto the visual field, often overlaid by the form-constants. We have chosen to illustrate some of these properties with examples from studies with *Cannabis* derivatives, commonly considered weak hallucinogens, and from studies with

Figure 4   Bright light in center of the visual field reported during early stages of *Cannabis* intoxication. Drawing by Sheridan, pen and ink.

ketamine hydrochloride, recently recognized as a potent hallucinogen (Doenicke
et al., 1969; Rumpf et al., 1969; Reher, 1971; Collier, 1972). The *Cannabis* reports
are from the previously described study (Siegel, 1971a) and the ketamine reports
are from an identical companion study with that compound (Siegel, Lebowitz, and
Jarvik, unpublished data). All ketamine dosages were 1 to 2 mg/kg, i.v.

MOVIE OR SLIDE SHOW FORMAT WITH RAPID FLOW OF IMAGERY

Everything's changing really fast, like pictures in a film, or television, just right in front of
me. I am watching it happen right there. (ketamine)

In fact, the scenes in my head are very real. I mean if you get right into it it's as though you
are there sort like a movie or something. It looks in a way like a movie. They're surrounding
all around. (THC)

... people standing in the office, appearing like slides crossing my field of vision.
(marihuana)

TUNNEL PERSPECTIVE OF IMAGERY

I'm moving through some kind of train tunnel. There are all sorts of lights and colors,

Figure 5 Pulsating spiral-tunnel reported as *Cannabis*-induced imagery constant. Drawing by Sheridan, pen and ink.

mostly in the center, far, far away, way, far away, and little people and stuff running around the walks of the tube, like little cartoon nebishes, they're pretty close. (ketamine)

It's sort of like a tube, like I sort of feel—like sort of—that I'm at the bottom of a tube looking up. You can see the slides [imagery] converging with a point in the center. (THC)

It's better described as if I was traveling through the inside of a tube and the background faded towards the center of the tube and so that all of it seems to be going from behind, below, over, above me and down towards my feet again and just like a circular motion. . . . I am traveling into a tunnel and out into space. (marihuana)

SIMPLE GEOMETRIC FORMS IN IMAGERY

Checkers, changing red checkers. Oh, I'm getting pinwheels. It's like a horseshoe shape, now it's gone. Now it's got stripes. Two, there's two spots, oval shapes, they're outlined in white. (ketamine)

There's like a honeycomb in the background, like a real honeycomb. And it's kind of moving from me. (THC)

There are a lot of intense little geometric figures over a mess of coke. (marihuana)

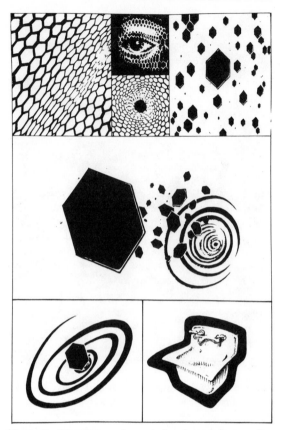

Figure 7   Illustration of associative changes in complex THC-induced imagery. Subject actually reported: "And then my eyes again, a hexagon, a little hexagon—whoa— —here comes a big hexagon! He is pushing those little hexagons aside because he doesn't fit. My God! He split up the whole, all the little hexagons are going out to the right, all out the funnel, they all disappeared, nothing left but a plastic sink." Drawing by Sheridan, pen and ink.

COMPLEX FORMS WITH RAPIDLY CHANGING ASSOCIATIONS IN IMAGERY

Now I see a woman's face and she's got real big eyes and I don't see part of her hair, and her hair is gold. And there's a grandfather clock, it's more like a toy not a real one. Now I see an old man and he's lying on his back, now he is bending down and he's picking something up. (ketamine)

There was some kind of insect which changed to a salamander which changed to an outline of a toad. Now, it's changing quickly and I don't know what it is. (THC)

Now I can see flowers. Now it's like a bird. Like a pretty ostrich, a white ostrich with a purple crown around his head, walking and flapping its wings and now it turned into a donkey carrying somebody on his back. At first it looks like Christ and then it looks like Indians riding around a horse. It's a horse now and it's getting closer and closer and breathing very heavily and riding very hard. (marihuana)

MEMORY IMAGERY

I can see a movie that I saw recently, *2001*. Hey, this is really groovy! Really groovy! It's like it's right there and I'm seeing it all over again. The spaceships, the space station, floating through space, it's all so vivid and real. (ketamine)

... the house, like inside a house and it's the house where I grew up and it's the stairs I used to go upstairs into the hall, and I can see it all. And there's the kitchen, and there's my mother. She's wearing her nursing uniform. She's sad cause she's so . . . doesn't seem strange . . . as if I'm back in the past, as if I never was in the house, as if I never belonged there, and it's like a summer day in Regina, very clear blue skies, just how things were when I was about 13 years old I guess. (THC)

I am living in the past, and now I'm at where I broke my two teeth swinging on some bars outside synagogue, in a synagogue where you hang up your clothes, and I thought the chair was underneath me, but my friend had taken the chair away to get up on it himself and I just fell down, fell, flat on my face and started yelling and screaming and everybody came out of the church, and I'm screaming. I mean out of the synagogue, out of the chapel, and like I was seeing them, you know, the cuddling and the—I don't know—and I am bawling my head off. I am so much in pain. (marihuana)

IMAGERY IN TRAINED OBSERVERS

A series of studies was designed to investigate the phenomenology of drug-induced imagery in trained and untrained observers. A preliminary report of some of these findings has appeared elsewhere (Siegel, 1973b), but some data are presented here for the first time.

Development of method.   Previous reports of drug-induced visual imagery suggest that these events were as dissimilar as they were similar. Subjects differed widely in their choice of words to describe phenomena. Form, movement, and color constants did emerge from these different reports, but the imagery was riddled with idiosyncratic experiences. For example, one subject continually experienced unbidden images involving sexual fantasies with the experimenter, and another subject reported recurring images of the hospital in which the experiment was conducted. Most subjects were unable to communicate various aspects of the imagery such as the precise geometric forms or directions of motion, and would comment: "I'm seeing things I can't describe" or "I don't know what they are and don't know how to explain them." In addition, the rapid flow of images interfered with verbal reporting for many subjects: "There's a lot happening. It's constantly changing all the time. It's very difficult to keep up with what's appearing and disappearing."

Similarly, McKellar (1957) observed that when his subjects tried to convey the nature of complex or novel experiences, such as mescaline-induced hallucinations, they often found it necessary to introduce many new words. McKellar referred to such words as experimentally produced neologisms, not sanctioned by literary or scientific canons. Since these words possess a purely private meaning, being understood by the subject and no one else, they are useless and misleading as vehicles for communication. For example, McKellar encountered neologisms such as "quadrupus," a newly coined word referring to some type of animal, and "pink"—a new use of this word to describe a bright red car.

One approach to overcoming this problem of inefficient and individualized reports would be to pretrain observers in a standard method for rapid imagery identification and reporting. Such an approach was indirectly advocated by Tart (1971), who maintained that consensual validation of internal phenomena (e.g., imagery) might be possible with trained observers. Indeed, Lilly (1970a) proposed that a new language be established for the sharing of and agreeing on the nature of such subjective experiences. This new language or code would have to satisfy several important requirements.

1. The code must utilize an operant response, the rate of which would not be impaired by the experience to be reported.
2. The code must be empirical and derived from the actual verbal reports of imagery rather than from a theory that is applied to the material (cf. Hall and Van de Castle, 1966).
3. The code must include physical standards to which observers can compare their reports.
4. The code must allow observers to anticipate novel stimulus events and classify them with confidence and reliability. Indeed, as B. F. Skinner (1971) cautioned ". . . even a carefully trained observer runs into trouble when he studies new private stimuli."

In meeting requirement (1) we were guided by the pilot studies conducted by Timothy Leary (1966b, 1966c) as well as the basic research of Ogden Lindsley and his co-workers (Lindsley, 1957; Lindsley et al., 1961; Lindsley and Contran, 1962). Throughout his many studies with hallucinogens, Leary noted that drug-induced imagery often "defies external metaphor." Instead of using objective physical standards, he recommended the use of experienced (trained) subjects who could compare phenomena between and within drug sessions. Leary used the operant key press as his report and equated it to the occurrence of a subjective state. For example, in the case of an hallucination, the verbal report of "I saw it" or "I heard it" was equated to a key press. This particular equation and procedure has been used by other investigators in the study of hallucinations (cf. Hefferline et al., 1973).

Indeed, Lindsley and his colleagues had already demonstrated that operant behavior provides a continuous and objective method for the study of gross behavior in such altered states of consciousness as anesthesia, coma, and sleep. However, a method for obtaining detailed information regarding subjective phenomena in these states had not been developed until Leary collaborated with Lindsley and developed the "experiential typewriter." This apparatus consisted of a 20-key typewriter connected to a recording instrument. The keys were used to code various subjective states including modes of perception, internal images, external images, eyes-closed and eyes-open experiences, hallucinations, and colors. The subjects were pretrained by simply having them memorize the experiential categories and their corresponding keys. When a subject felt a bodily sensation such as "pain," he would press a specific key to signify this event. Similarly, the experience of oscillating colors could be signified by pressing a different key. The locus of this particular hallucination in terms of eyes-open or eyes-closed imagery could be signified by simultaneously pressing yet another key. The device recorded the occurrence of these events as a function of time. In pre-liminary trials with LSD and DMT, Leary found that the ataxia associated with these drugs interfered with the simple motor task of depressing the type-writer keys, and continuous experiential reporting was not always possible. This problem might have been circumvented if minimal dosages had been employed. In addition, the key press could have been replaced by a verbal operant, since Leary found that this was the only useful technique for continuous reporting. Therefore we decided to develop a verbal code for the reporting of drug-induced hallucinations.

Requirement (2) was fulfilled by data derived from the previous study of imagery in untrained subjects. On the basis of this material it was possible to construct a list of eight forms (random, line, curve, web, lattice, tunnel, spiral, kaleidoscope), eight colors (black, violet, blue, green, yellow, orange, red, white), and eight movement patterns (aimless, vertical, horizontal, oblique, explosive, concentric, rotational, pulsating), which the subject could use in describing visual imagery.

Requirement (3) called for a matching of reported events to physical standards. This is a standard procedure employed in many perceptual and psychophysical experiments, and its application to imagery measurement has been advocated by Segal (1972):

... in both instances [perception and imagery] the observer reports on the phenomenolog-ical experience and the neural substrate is obscured. The main difference is that the perception is characterized by the presence of a clearly defined physical stimulus against which verbal report or other behavioral measures can be scaled, but no clearly relevant external stimulus characterized the images. However, if the image could also be matched against the objective standard of a physical stimulus, then it could be measured in much the same way (p. 204).

Both requirements (3) and (4) were fulfilled by pretraining subjects in concept-formation procedures whereby reports could be matched to previously learned categories, which were defined by physical standards but allowed for broad generalization within categories.

Human observers can learn to code complex stimuli or visual perceptions into categories, thus simplifying the environment to some degree. Many psychologists think of such learning as concept formation (cf. Bourne, 1966). Concept forma-tion allows man to code features into categories and to respond to all instances of the features in the same way; otherwise learning would be overwhelmingly com-plex, since the observer would be forced to deal with each individual perception as an unique event. Thus learning of categories to respond to restricts the number of response alternatives and facilitates the observer's reporting: He is said to "ab-stract" or to "generalize." The effect of controlling the learning of such generali-zations in the laboratory is to specify the precise accuracy with which they will be applied to new stimuli (i.e., drug-induced imagery) never before encountered by the subject.

In the type of concept-formation training used in the study of drug-induced imagery in trained observers (Siegel, 1973b), stimulus displays consisting of 35mm slide transparencies were presented to the subjects. Only one display was presented on any given trial. The displays differed from trial to trial, and the subject was required to make one response in the presence of one stimulus and another response in the presence of another stimulus. Usually, responses in the presence of positive stimuli can be rewarded, whereas negative stimuli are presented while extinction is in effect. This type of successive discrimination is often referred to as a go/no-go discrimination. However, in the conditional successive discrimination used by Siegel (cf. Siegel, 1970a), it is possible for a subject to make a correct response and obtain a reward (verbal statement of "correct" from experimenter) on each trial.

A notation for the application of these procedures to the Siegel study may be helpful. Consider the concept-formation paradigm where T represents a class of stimuli containing the distinctive form feature "tunnel." Since T features change from trial to trial, a suitable notation becomes $T_1 \ldots n$. In effect, the subject never encounters a constant or invariant T, and he must learn to abstract or to generalize to select correctly from among the many displays. In the actual training procedure, subjects were rewarded for verbal responses of "tunnel" to displays containing some instance of T but were never rewarded for responses of "tunnel" to displays with T features absent. However, there was always an appropriate response available to the subject for all displays seen. Thus when "tunnel" was judged inappropriate, the subject would be required to select another feature present in the displays, such as "spiral" or "lattice."

Twelve subjects, between the ages of 21 and 30, were used. Although all subjects had previous recreational experience with hallucinogens, three had never experienced drug-induced visual imagery prior to entering the experiment. Subjects were randomly assigned to three groups of four each (each group included one subject who had not had previous drug-imagery experiences). In Group A (trained subjects), subjects received daily sessions of concept-formation training on form, color, and movement dimensions.

Each training session consisted of 72 successively presented 35mm slides including three trials of each of the 24 categories (eight each of forms, colors, and movements), all randomly alternated. Examples of the training slides used in the form dimension are given in Fig. 8. Slide material for the color catergories was compiled from the 267 color name pockets of the Inter-Society Color Council and the National Bureau of Standards (ISCC–NBS) color-naming system, as well as numerous Kodak Wratten filters. Slide material for the movement patterns was constructed from rotary-polarized materials according to a previously described procedure (cf. Siegel, 1970b; Siegel, 1971b).

Briefly, the principle of rotary polarization allows apparent movement to be displayed in conventional 35mm slides and is similar to that used to achieve motion in animation techniques. For example, it is similar to techniques employed by many television meteorologists to depict rain or snow "moving" on local areas of weather maps. It is also similar to motion produced by the flicker of neon lights, such as "arrows" directing customers to a particular commercial establishment.

In the training sessions, subjects were required to identify each slide's category with a correct verbal response before they could advance to the next trial. Incorrect responses resulted in repeat of the trial until there was a correct response. The slides presented during a session all differed from one another, and different sets of slides were presented in each session. Trial length was gradually shortened from 15 seconds to 8 milliseconds, and the intertrial interval was reduced from an initial 10 seconds to 1 second, to simulate the rapid changes reported in the

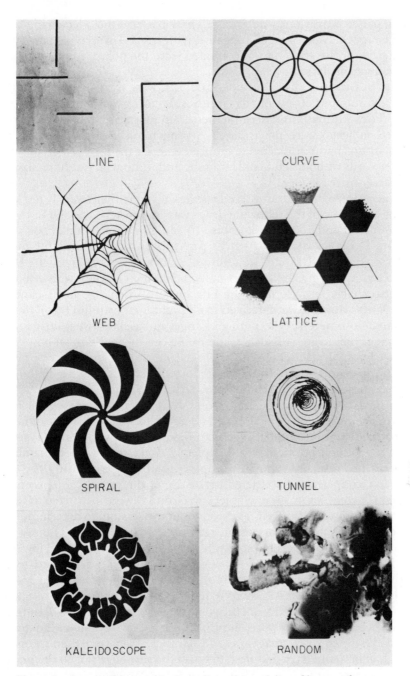

Figure 8   Sample slides used in form dimension training of human observers.

previous study with untrained observers. Subjects were trained until five successive sessions without error had been achieved; all subjects reached this criterion after 20 training sessions. To handle unique combinations of forms, colors, and movements that may not have been anticipated by the training procedure, subjects in Group A received five additional sessions of concept-formation training on the action patterns previously described. These patterns included changes within images, changes between images, repeating patterns and overlaying patterns. The slide material for this training was compiled from the polarized material used in the movement displays.

Subjects in Group B (pseudotrained subjects) were exposed to the same slide material and number of sessions as Group A, but they were instructed to simply view the slides without any discrimination training per se. Subjects in Group C (untrained subjects) were not trained. A companion group of two additional subjects (Group D) was instructed to simply memorize the form, color, movement, and action words without actual slide training and without any additional explanation of these words.

All subjects were then administered a series of single-blind weekly test sessions in each of which one of the following drugs was administered orally: LSD, 50 and 100μg; BOL, 50 and 100μg; psilocybin, 10 and 20 mg; mescaline, 200 and 300 mg; delta-9-THC, 10 and 20 mg; phenobarbital, 30 and 60 mg; and d-amphetamine, 5 and 15 mg. In addition, marihuana (2.8% delta-9-THC) was administered by having the subject smoke a 500 mg cigarette with a fixed time inhalation–exhalation cycle until the first onset of a change in baseline visual imagery. These dosages were derived from preliminary studies that determined the minimal dose necessary to induce changes in baseline visual imagery. Since high doses of hallucinogens such as mescaline can incapacitate an observer and impair psychophysical judgments (Karwoski, 1936), the doses here were necessarily low and had no known effects on sensory thresholds (Caldwell et al., 1969, 1970). Placebo trials were included for each drug listed, as well as an initial baseline (no drug) session. For subjects in Groups A, B, and D, regular training sessions or memorization drills intervened between weekly drug sessions.

After administration of the drug, each subject in Groups A, B, and C was placed alone in the supine position in a completely dark, soundproof chamber and instructed to continually report eyes-open visual imagery during the session. Subjects in Group A were restricted to the use of the verbal code except in the description of complex imagery. Subjects in Group D were instructed to recite the memorized list of verbal responses throughout the session, to determine what, if any, preferences subjects manifest in reciting the code words. The test session terminated at the subject's request or when verbal reporting reached low operant levels. The average session was six hours. All subjects were asked to give a subjective rating of their "high" on a 0 to 7 point scale at variable 15-minute intervals throughout the test session. When this rating indicated a peak subjective high, subjects were removed from the room and escorted to an outdoor botanical garden. There the subjects wore blindfold goggles, lay supine on the grass, and reported eyes-open visual imagery for 15 minutes. They were then taken back to the test chamber, and dark-adapted, to finish the session. Prior to reentering the chamber, subjects in Group A were tested for accuracy of performance in the concept-formation tasks with new concept slides never before seen.

Results and Phenomenology.   In experiments of this scope and magnitude it is always difficult to decide which of the copious data to discuss. Here we give results that support the use of trained observers as well as the results obtained from that group of subjects.

The distribution of simple form reports for each group of subjects throughout the first 120 minutes of the smoked marihuana sessions is presented in Fig. 9. The simple forms reported here represent 67% of the form reports for all subjects; the remaining 33% were complex imagery. The distribution of form reports during baseline sessions (in mean percentages) appears on the graphs in Fig. 9 at time 0. The distribution of form reports (in mean percentages) following treatment with marihuana appears ʾalong the postdrug axis in blocks of 15 minutes. The distribution of these reports for trained subjects indicates that there is a shift from baseline random and curve forms to lattices and tunnels within 15 minutes postdrug, with maximum change at 30 minutes. Interestingly, this change corresponds to the subjects' self-reports of a peak subjective high after 30 minutes. This distributional shift starts to reverse after 90 minutes and returns to near-baseline levels by 120 minutes. Concomitantly, there are small increases in reports of kaleidoscope forms, an example of which is presented in Fig. 10. Combinations of forms were frequently reported, and the most common of these—repeating curved lines in a tunnel-like arrangement—is illustrated in Fig. 11. Although it might be argued that extensive exposure to training slides influenced reports in this group of subjects, the concept-formation procedures provided for equal exposure to all eight form categories. Thus there would be no reason to expect this skewed distribution to occur during drug sessions. Indeed, subjects in the pseudotrained group received equal exposure to the training stimuli and they also manifested this shift, albeit smaller, to lattice-tunnel forms, as did the untrained subjects who did not view slide material (Fig. 9). Furthermore, subjects in Group D showed neither sequential dependencies with the code words nor preferences for any groups of words such as lattice-tunnel.

The curves for the trained subjects were based on significantly more reports than the other groups. For example, the average rate of imagery reports per minute (rpm) in the 120-minute marihuana sessions was: Group A, 20 rpm; Group B, 6 rpm; and Group C, 5 rpm. In addition, the inter-observer variance was high in all groups except Group A, which demonstrated the most significant shift to lattice-tunnel forms. The trained subjects, however, were not impaired in concept-formation ability during hallucinogen sessions, since only the 60 mg dose of phenobarbital significantly disrupted performance in both concept and color-naming tasks. The latter result is somewhat surprising, since doses of THC as low as 7.2 mg impair concept formation as measured by a category test (Konoff et al., 1973). Nonetheless, many trained subjects showed increased reaction times in performing concept tasks during hallucinogen sessions. This effect may be caused by momentary lapses of attention (Moskowitz et al., 1972) or changes in retrieval processes dealing with short-term memory (Darley et al., 1973).

Figure 12 shows the distribution of form, color, and movement reports for trained subjects, averaged over each six-hour high-dosage drug session, including a placebo session. In general, the low-dosage treatments resulted in similar distributions but with a greatly reduced number of imagery reports. From Fig. 12 it is clear that treatment with placebo, BOL, phenobarbital, or d-amphetamine did not significantly alter the normal baseline distribution of form imagery. Conversely, the hallucinogens THC, psilocybin, LSD, and mescaline induced a significant and dramatic shift to the lattice-tunnel forms, as seen in the earlier marihuana data (Fig. 9). The shift here occurred between 90 and 120 minutes after ingestion and

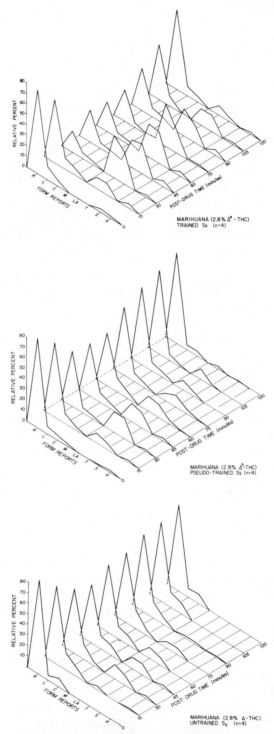

Figure 9 Percent distribution of form reports for each group of subjects for predrug baseline (0) and postdrug blocks of 15 minutes following inhalation of marihuana. R = random, L = line, C = curve, W = web, LA = lattice, T = tunnel, S = spiral, and K = kaleidoscope.

Figure 10   Kaleidoscopic form pattern reported during marihuana-induced imagery sessions. Drawing by Sheridan, pen and ink.

was probably related to the slower absorption of the drugs following the oral route of administration. The distribution of color reports in Fig. 12 shows a parallel shift from the black, violet, and white colors, which characterize baseline imagery, to red, orange, and yellow during hallucinogen sessions. The single exception was THC, which produced significantly more blue reports than the other drugs, and these may be related to the lowered oral temperature found in some subjects treated with THC (Hosko et al., 1973). However, Marshall (1937) noted that the shorter wavelengths of light, particularly blue, characterized the initial phase of mescaline-induced hallucinations. Indeed, early color reports by subjects in hallucinogen sessions indicated much blue, and this may be related to the hypothermia induced in animals by such drugs (Ladefoged, 1973). The distribution of movement reports in Fig. 12 indicates an hallucinogen-induced shift from the aimless and pulsating patterns of baseline sessions to more organized explosive and rotational motion. However, the subjects did note that the pulsating motion was characteristic of all imagery movement (e.g., "No matter what else the imagery is doing, no matter how it's moving, it's always pulsating, always flickering and this is the *basso continuo* of its motion.")

Complex imagery usually did not appear until well after the lattice-tunnel shift was reported. At that time, the complex forms constituted between 43 and 75% of the total form reports of trained subjects during hallucinogen sessions. Such images first appeared in the reports as overlaying the lattices and tunnels (Fig. 13,

Figure 11   Repeating curved lines in tunnel arrangement reported during marihuana-induced imagery sessions. Drawing by Sheridan, pen and ink.

see color section) and generally located in the periphery of these images (Fig. 14). Complex imagery was often duplicated and repeated, not infrequently involving symmetrical geometric arrays (Fig. 15).

Initially subjects reported that form imagery was like a slide show or movie located about two feet in front of their eyes. As the high-dosage hallucinogen sessions progressed, subjects frequently claimed that they became part of the imagery itself (Fig. 16), and reporting for all but the trained subjects was periodically suppressed. It was at these times that subjects stopped using similes in their imagery reports and started reporting that images were, in point of fact, really what they appeared to be. This is undoubtedly related to McKellar's (1957) finding that subjects in mescaline and nitrous oxide experiences intermittently lose insight into the difference between literal and analogous meanings. Thus normal undrugged individuals might describe an experience in terms of the similes "like," "as if," or "it is as though," but mescaline-treated subjects describe experiences as "it is so." McKellar describes this *"feeling into experience"* as a type of exaggerated empathy with thoughts and hallucinations, when the complex imagery almost totally replaced the simple geometric forms. The content of this imagery primarily included recognizable landscapes, scenes, people, and objects subjects could identify as memory images, but often presented in unique combinations and arrangements. Our subjects' best estimate is that at the peak of the drug experience such imagery was changing at the rate of 10 images per second,

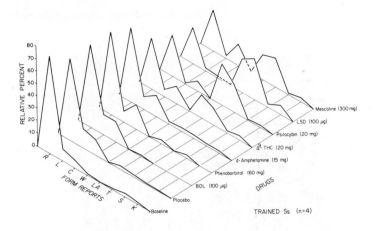

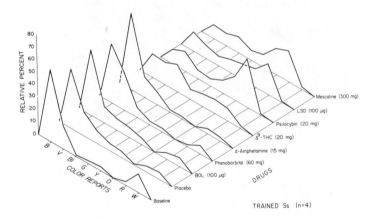

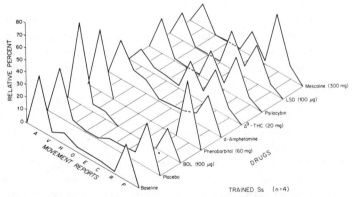

Figure 12 Mean percent distribution of form, color, and movement reports for trained subjects in each six-hour high-dose drug condition. Form reports: R = random, L = line, C = curve, W = web, LA = lattice, T = tunnel, S = spiral, K = kaleidoscope. Color reports: B = black, V = violet, Bl = blue, G = green, Y = yellow, O = orange, R = red, W = white. Movement reports: A = aimless, V = vertical, H = horizontal, O = oblique, E = explosive, C = concentric, R = rotational, P = pulsating.

Figure 14 Complex imagery located in periphery of visual field in early stages of hallucinogen intoxication. Drawing by Sheridan, pen and ink.

although they were not trained for making such judgments. One such sequence of complex imagery changes, illustrating how one image is associated with and influenced by another, is represented in Fig. 17.

McKellar (1957) describes a type of mescaline-induced thinking wherein the ability to inhibit and control irrelevant associations seems to diminish as the drug effect emerges. When one of his subjects was asked to explain the proverb "Those who live in glass houses shouldn't throw stones," she was able to reach the parable of the mote and beam by a purely associative chain of ideas: "glass house → glass → crystal → palace → castle → moat → mote → mote and beam parable" (p. 100). In the types of associative image changes illustrated in Fig. 17, we believe the subjects were simply experiencing drug-induced facilitation of this type of mental imagery projected into the visual modality. Typically, the memory imagery reported by subjects took on one of four characteristic perspectives (Fig. 18). During the outdoor sessions, there was a significant reduction in memory imagery and a concomitant increase in reports of birds, planes, trees, and other objects, often triggered by auditory and tactile cues in the outdoor garden setting. The latter finding is similar to Marinesco's (1933) report that mescaline-induced hallucinations were easily influenced by voice, sound, music, and smell. In one subject, for example, music induced moving visions of arabesques and murals spiraling about, while the smell of alcohol brought on images of a countryside. Also similar is

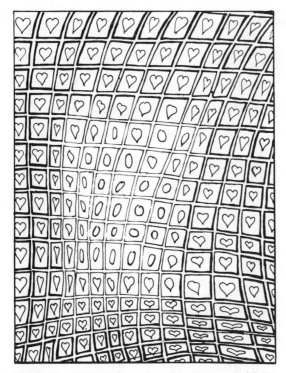

Figure 15 Multiplication of complex imagery involving symmetrical lattice imagery. Redrawn from original subject's drawing by Sheridan, pen and ink.

Figure 16 Illustration of subject becoming part of visual imagery in psilocybin session. From *Mother's Oats, No. 1,* by Dave Sheridan, pen and ink. Reprinted with permission of the artist.

Figure 17 Illustration of changes in complex imagery. Sequence shown here reported during mescaline session (200 mg). Subject reported: "I see pulsating stars outlining the shape of a dog overlaying a spiral-tunnel of lights, changing to a real dog which is barking with the words 'Arf, arf' coming out of his mouth, changing into a toy dog on wheels changing into a sports car on the same wheeled platform in the desert with the sun high in the sky, changing back into the toy dog still barking, changing back to the sports car with the Road-Runner and another cartoon character driving in the same desert scene." Drawing by Sheridan, pen and ink.

Singer's (1966) finding that extraneous stimuli can influence imagery, as in the case of the sound of feet running leading to the visual image of a child running.

FLASHBACK IMAGERY

A flashback is usually defined as the return of part of the drug experience after the acute effects of the drug have worn off. Such flashbacks occur months or even years after the initial experience (Irwin, 1970), and the major symptoms experienced as flashbacks include depersonalization, perceptual distortion, and visual hallucinations (Stern and Robbins, 1969). Horowitz (1970) reviewed the phenomenology of flashback visual imagery and found the content to be primarily composed of complex images of people, places, or objects. The complex imagery is often idiosyncratic but similar to the imagery seen under the acute effects of the drug (Cohen, 1970). Examples of patient's LSD flashbacks include skulls of familiar people moving around the room, motion on a TV screen when the set is off, and frightening animals crawling around the room (Cohen, 1970). The mechanism of action of these flashbacks is unknown, although explanations based on a breakdown in the filtering of irrelevant stimuli entering the brain (Freedman, 1970) or cerebral seizure activity (Thurlow and Girvin, 1971) have been proposed. Perhaps the most salient theory is that which views flashbacks as a special case of state-dependent learning whereby "statebound recall can be evoked not only by imagery, melodies, and other symbols of the *content* of an experience, but also by simply inducing that particular level of arousal which prevailed during the initial experience" (Fischer, 1971b, p. 32).

In a study of flashbacks following ketamine anesthesia (Siegel, Lebowitz, and Jarvik, unpublished data), six surgical patients were followed for 18 months after

Figure 18 Characteristic perspectives of memory imagery reported during hallucinogen sessions. Upper left: distant scene marked by abundant detail, often recognized as childhood event. Upper right: distant scene of landscape marked by detailed and recognizable image in foreground, often accompanied by emotional reports. Lower left: scene viewed as if subject were under water, looking up toward and through the surface. Lower right: aerial perspective, often accompanied by sensations of floating and flying. Drawing by Sheridan, pen and ink.

ketamine treatment (1–2 mg/kg, i.v.). Table 3 shows the total number of visual flashbacks reported for each patient in blocks of days following treatment. There was a total of 74 flashbacks reported by all patients over this period of time; 65 of these were complex images, and 9 (12%) were simple geometric patterns and colors composed of lattices, tunnels, and repeating lines and dots. All flashbacks were observed with open eyes, and most were characterized by immobility of the patient, as well as anxiety. Flashbacks lasted between a fraction of a second and five minutes. One patient required psychotherapy for a persistent anxiety reaction to these flashbacks. The vividness and clarity of this ketamine-induced flashback phenomenon was best illustrated by patient M.R.'s second flashback during the first week following treatment. The patient had a true hallucination of her physicians standing around her bed. Her surgeon advised her to take her bandages off, and the patient acted on this "suggestion" and removed her bandages, which contributed to the need of further corrective surgery. Patient A.M. reported the greatest number of flashbacks, which consisted primarily of either a geometric spiral pattern or one of three complex scenes as shown in Fig. 19. Taken together, these reported flashbacks support the view that flashbacks are largely composed of complex visual imagery with few if any hallucinogenic form-constants.

One particular case of LSD flashbacks, however, represents exclusive spiral-tunnel imagery. Patient R.S. entered the Neuropsychiatric Institute at UCLA with complaints about persistent LSD flashbacks. This patient reported a history of a dozen LSD experiences, but none within the last five years. During this period the patient was experiencing approximately two flashbacks per day. The incidents were marked by eyes-open visual imagery for about 15 minutes followed by acute panic and fear, which sometimes persisted for several hours. During observation in the hospital R.S. experienced two flashbacks while being tested in a dark, soundproof chamber. In both instances he reported that his imagery consisted exclusively of a spiral tunnel form with a bright center (Fig. 20). The form was always black and white, although he said that at other times "I've seen all kinds of colored lights and lines shooting out of it [the tunnel] at me." Interestingly, this patient's diagnosis was paranoid schizophrenic, and his flashback imagery was virtually identical to the persistent visual imagery reported by another paranoid schizophrenic studied at the UCLA Neuropsychiatric Institute (Fig. 21).

TABLE 3. DISTRIBUTION OF FLASHBACKS FOR KETAMINE PATIENTS

Patients	Blocks of Days								
	0–7	8–14	15–21	22–28	29–60	61–90	91–180	181–360	361–450
M.R.	8	3	0	0	3	1	0	1	0
A.M.	5	3	4	1	8	4	0	5	2
I.D.	2	0	1	0	0	0	0	0	0
E.G.	2	1	0	0	3	1	0	0	0
G.G.	6	0	0	0	2	0	0	0	0
P.L.	7	0	1	0	0	0	0	0	0

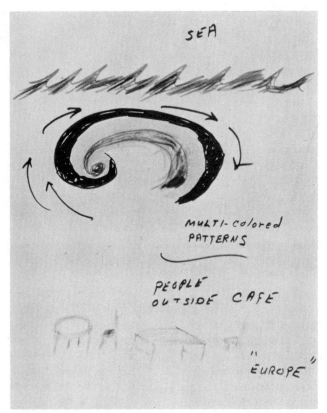

Figure 19   Three types of ketamine-induced flashback images reported and drawn by patient A.M.

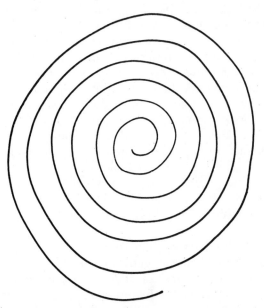

Figure 20   Spiral-tunnel LSD-induced flashback imagery reported and drawn by patient R.S.

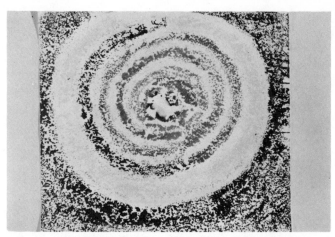

Figure 21 Persistent eyes-open visual imagery reported and drawn by schizophrenic patient.

CROSS-CULTURAL STUDIES

Visual imagery constants produced by a wide variety of treatments and in a wide variety of individuals lead us to consider their universality. The remarkable similarity of imagery induced by the centrally acting hallucinogens prompts speculation about common mechanisms of action in the central nervous system. In addition, the emergence of constants between and within subjects is strikingly similar to the construct of primordial images or archetypal forms, such as the mandala, which C. G. Jung (1969) claimed as part of man's collective unconscious. However, no matter how imperialistic we are in our theoretical desires, Freedman (1971) cautions that psychotropic drug experiences are very plastic and are formed by the cultural context in which they occur.

Indeed, Wallace (1959) notes that internalized cultural definitions of hallucinatory experience have a profound effect on an individual's responses, and he points out several prevailing contrasts in a comparison of white and Indian responses to mescaline intoxication. The white response is characterized by extremely variable mood changes, disinhibition, unwelcome feelings of depersonalization and dissociation, idiosyncratic hallucinations, and no permanent behavioral changes. Conversely, the Indian response is marked by a relatively stable mood, religious enthusiasm, maintenance of orderly and socially appropriate behavior, welcome feelings of contact with a new reality, hallucinations strongly patterned after some doctrine, and marked therapeutic benefits and behavioral changes. Finding such striking differences between the two peoples, Wallace argues for controls on cultural determinants in any research with hallucinogens.

The presence of cultural determinants of hallucinations is further illustrated by reactions to the aboriginal hallucinogen *Banisteriopsis* spp., also known as yagé or ayahuasca. The yagé experiences of Indians in the tropical forests of South America manifest several common themes, such as visions of jaguars, snakes, and other local predators, distant "cities," and recent crimes in the area (Harner, 1973). For example, consider the following account of ayahuasca visions:

Color visions, indefinite in form, began to evolve into immense vistas of enchanting beauty. . . . There was a tawny puma, several varieties of the smaller spotted ocelot, then a giant rosetta-spotted jaguar. . . . From a memory recess in my brain there emerged with the stimulation of the cats an experience from my past. On a trip to the Rio Putumayo a year before coming to the Jurua to cut *caucho,* I had come face to face on a forest path with a rare black jaguar. It had been a terrifying experience, but . . . we had gone our separate ways without violence. . . . This mighty animal now intruded on our visions and a shudder passed through us all. . . . Other animals, snakes, birds passed in review, each with some significant characteristic important to the Huni Kui [the tribe] in dominating the forest. . . . Then came scenes of combat with the hated enemy, the Guacamayos. . . . Scenes in the new village, where we now lived, gradually brought the visions to an end (Cordova-Rios and Lamb, 1971, pp. 157–158).

An example of such a rosetta-spotted jaguar, often reported in these visions, is provided in Fig. 22 (see color section). Nonetheless, despite the intrusion of such environmental stimuli into the visual imagery of yagé hallucinations, an equally common theme includes visions of geometric designs of bright colors and constantly changing shapes. Naranjo (1973) found tunnels and funnels to be particularly common elements in these yagé hallucinations:

The center can appear in the different visions as a source of motion or the region to which motion flows, a source of light or a perceiving eye, a geometric region such as a circular pond in the middle of Heaven or Hell, a being at the center of the earth, of the universe, the skull or inside the subject's body (p. 182).

The Tukano Indians in the Amazon region of Colombia frequently decorate their homes and pottery with large geometrical paintings of their yagé imagery (Reichel-Dolmatoff, 1972). Such motifs, derived from the initial stages of yagé intoxication, include curves, spirals, lattices, and the sun, as well as other forms remarkably similar to the Klüver constants. Interestingly, the Indians themselves claim that the hallucinations are a projection and that their order is fixed. Unsurprisingly, therefore, it has been hypothesized that the individual yagé user projects his cultural memory onto the waving screen of these geometric motifs (Reichel-Dolmatoff, 1972) and that these common themes "invite us to regard some shamanistic conceptions more as the expression of universal experiences than in terms of acculturation to local traditions" (Naranjo, 1973, p. 190). Indeed, Pokorny (1969) has compared the geometric designs on ornaments from several Neolithic artifacts with mescaline-induced form-constants and entoptic phenomena. He concluded that the similarity of all these reflects universal archetypes in man's history.

Common themes have also been noted in visual experiences associated with peyote *(Lophophora williamsii)* and San Pedro *(Trichocereus pachanoi),* both types of cacti that contain mescaline. Sharon (1972) reports that one Peruvian San Pedro vision consisted of "a whirlpool of red and yellow light spinning inward before my eyes and lightly printed on everything I looked at," as well as kaleidoscopic patterns and shapes. Lumholtz (1900, 1904) reported that Huichol Indians of Mexico represent the peyote cactus with traditional artistic designs consisting of concentric tunnel arrangements or spirals. Such designs may be based on the occurrence of hallucinogenic imagery constants for these people. Indeed, Schultes (1972) notes that peyote intoxication is often marked by "brilliantly colored visions in kaleidoscopic movement." Benzi (1969), however, argues that such visions, no matter how abstract and geometric, are never dissociated from the cultural context. For example, symmetrical crystal forms seen at the peak of peyote intoxication are often impregnated with divinity and godlike forms, pinpoints of light are described as gods, and visions generally follow the tribal beliefs. Thus, even beyond certain universal visual images, "there are powerful cultural factors at work that influence, if they do not actually determine, both content and interpretation of the drug experience" (Furst, 1972, pp. 182–183). In this regard, it is of interest that the peyote visions of the Menomini Indians of Wisconsin reflect a common theme of salvation through baptismal conversion, perhaps indicating the acculturation of the imagery by North American Christian society (cf. Spindler, 1955).

In May 1972, one of us (R.K.S.) joined an expedition to study a group of Huichol Indians in the high Sierra Madre range of Mexico. Initially, 11 male Huichols, 23 to 78 years of age, were interviewed at the Centro Coordinador para el Desarrollo de la Region Huichot in Tepic, Nayarit. The respondents were probed about their peyote-induced hallucinations both with open eyes and closed eyes. Only one respondent denied any visual experiences; the rest offered remarkably similar accounts of their visions. The reports contained frequent references to snakes, deer, the sun, the moon, rainbows, the birth of the world, eagles, oxen, and other images having significance in the mythology and history of these people (cf. Lumholtz, 1898; Simoni-Abbat, 1963; Furst, 1969). In addition, there were numerous reports of geometric patterns, spirals, lines, tunnels, and lattices. One vision was described as "a big spiral and I saw the *Tatewari* [deified fire god] in the center and rushing out towards me. I saw mostly repeating squares, reds and blues, against the sky and everywhere I looked into the night." Most respondents had difficulty in describing the geometric visual imagery, but all agreed that such imagery was virtually identical to the symmetrical and repeating patterns used in Huichol embroidery and weaving. With the cooperation of the Museo Regional de Nayarit, we arranged to have several Indian artists depict their eyes-closed peyote imagery in the form of traditional yarn paintings; the results appear in Figs. 23 to 26 (see color section). Figure 26 depicts an eyes open true hallucination of a tree. The subject reported that this tree actually appeared on the mesa before him, but when he turned to move toward it, the image disappeared. The two groups of concentric circles or tunnel arrangements in figure 26 were not "seen" by the subject but used as a traditional symbol labeling peyote visions. This vision was reported at the peak of peyote intoxication.

Next, a small study was conducted on a group of four male Huichols during a ritual peyote ceremony conducted at our request in the remote village of Banco de Calitice. Over a period of several hours, each Indian ingested the equivalent of approximately 200 mg of mescaline in the form of a suspension of ground peyote buttons in water (0.002% mescaline in 100 g of peyote). The ceremony was conducted outdoors at sunset with about 60 people in attendance. Approximately four hours after ingestion, each subject gave a five-minute verbal report of eyes-closed visual imagery. Baseline reports of nondrug visual imagery were obtained five days later in a separate group of subjects. The reports were translated and analyzed according to the previously described method of scoring form, color, movement, and action constants. The four subjects made a total of 95 imagery reports during the peyote session, compared with 7 imagery reports

TABLE 4.   DISTRIBUTION OF PEYOTE-INDUCED IMAGERY REPORTS FOR HUICHOL
INDIAN SUBJECTS (N = 4)

Form		Color		Movement		Complex	
Random	6	Black	2	Aimless	0	Cattle	1
Line	5	Violet	0	Vertical	0	Deer	4
Curve	8	Blue	9	Horizontal	3	Eagle	3
Web	0	Green	0	Oblique	0	Mountain	1
Lattice	13	Yellow	3	Explosive	11	People	3
Tunnel	15	Orange	1	Concentric	2	Peyote	1
Spiral	4	Red	6	Rotational	2	Snake	1
Kaleidoscope	7	White	1	Pulsating	3	Stars	1
						Sun-god	10
						World	2
Total	58	Total	22	Total	21	Total	27

during the nondrug session. During the peyote session, 68 reports referred to simple forms, colors, and movement patterns, and 27 reports referred to complex scenes. From Table 4, which shows the distribution of these reports across the respective dimensions, it is clear that the predominant form is lattice-tunnel, the major colors are blue and red, and the primary movement is explosive motion toward the subject. In addition, the distribution of complex forms indicates a predominance of natural objects found in the Indians' immediate environment (e.g., the sun, deer, eagles).

PART III: A THEORY OF DRUG–INDUCED HALLUCINATIONS

The most apparent aspect of our findings on drug-induced hallucinations in man is the presence of form, color, and movement constants in the visual imagery. These constants are primarily lattice-tunnel forms, red colors, and exploding and rotational movements. The imagery appears to the observer as a movie or slide show located in front of his eyes and is characterized by a bright light in the center of the visual field. Complex imagery, consisting of recognizable people and objects, can overlay and sometimes replace these constants as the drug experience progresses from an initial geometric and fragmentary quality to more formed memory images. These complex images share the properties of the simple constants and are often presented in consistent symmetrical and repeating arrangements.

This fundamental phenomenology is illustrated in Fig. 27. Here we can see the basic lattice-tunnel form of the visual imagery. The tunnel appears to spiral toward the center of the visual field, where pulsating bright lights obscure any detail that might be present. The periphery of the tunnel seen in the foreground is clearer and more detailed than in the center. The peripheral lattices appear here

Figure 27 Prototypic drug-induced visual imagery. From *Mother's Oats, No. 1,* Dave Sheridan, pen and ink. Reprinted with permission of the artist.

as small television sets containing distinctive complex images, which the subject reported as recognizable television scenes. He also reported that the imagery completely surrounded him, rotating about him on all sides. Subjects on high doses of hallucinogens typically report that the visual imagery surrounds them in this manner. For example, one subject in an LSD (100 μg) session reported:

> I see a visual image of the last movement of Berlioz's *Symphonie Fantastique*, which I listened to last night. All the goblins and witches are dancing around and teasing and tormenting me. The *idée fixe* is a cobra dancing around me, its tongue lashing out at my face, and now its body is encircling mine. Now Mickey Mouse and Donald Duck are in the circle shaking hands with me.

This particular account is uncannily similar to a *Datura stramonium* hallucination described by Boismont (1853): "[The subject] saw troops of men whirling [in] a circle before him, who endeavored to drag him into their vortex. All the characters in the ballet of *Gustavus*, in which he had been engaged during the evening, appeared to him making grimaces, and harassing him in every way" (p. 343). Boismont also describes a case of belladonna-induced hallucinations in which the subject found herself surrounded by small animals of various colors running on the ground.

The two basic phenomenological observations that emerge here are: (1) the form, color, and movement constants, and (2) the predominance of recognizable complex memory images. In the sections that follow, we consider explanations of these phenomena and attempt to develop a general theoretical model of hallucinations.

FORM, COLOR, AND MOVEMENT CONSTANTS

Similarity to Entoptic Phenomena.   Parish (1897) expressed one of the earliest opinions that visual hallucinations are the perception of entoptic events that arise from the visualization of certain structures within the eye through the appropriate arrangement of incident light. Since the work of Parish, numerous investigators have noted the similarity of drug-induced visual imagery to these entoptic phenomena. Marshall (1937) believed that mescaline may induce a "transient retroretinal illumination," enabling such phenomena to be observed:

The geometrical figures, in my opinion, are due to the compactness and small diameter and regular arrangement of the rods and cones and a light source behind, mainly pigment granules, producing diffraction-like figures (p. 293).

Marshall argued that the choriocapillary circulation was responsible for tapestry, ornamental, and floral designs; spirals; and for all the sinuous, circulatory, and multiplicated movements. He believed that the luminous points in this circulation were responsible for fireballs, crystals, diamonds, and kaleidoscopic objects, whereas the retinal pigment and arrangement of rods and cones were responsible for the mosaics, honeycombs, and related lattice patterns. He even claimed that the cone or funnel distortion (tunnel form-constant) could be explained in terms of entoptic events:

The purely geometric forms of squares, hexagons and the like probably arise . . . from the smallness and regularity of cross sections of the rods and cones producing diffraction-like effects. The perspective effect [tunnel] arises partly from the foveal cones and environing rods being smaller and more closely arranged than those of the periphery, and in consequence the geometrical figures perceived are likely to be smaller in the centre than at the periphery; and it is enhanced by the luminous points or areas which may be present in the region of the fovea (p. 300).

Maclay and Guttman (1941) found examples of these entoptic phenomena in artists' drawings of their mescaline-induced hallucinations. These authors also noted the similarity of "elementary visual sensations" to elaborated complex hallucinations, which they suggested were simply projections of mental imagery. They concluded that the formal character of mescaline hallucinations is so similar to physiological and pathological phenomena that the former can be assumed to be physiological, whereas the contents of the complex hallucinations are determined by individual psychological experience. Zador (1930) referred to the elementary visual sensations as "primitive" imagery and labeled the complex imagery "scenic." Zador, like Maclay and Guttman, believed that both types of imagery originated from the same geometric patterns and were subject to the same controlling variables. Such a controlling variable could be entoptic phenomena. Indeed, the hypothesis has been advanced that hallucinogens like LSD may lower the threshold for perception of these events (Barber, 1970, 1971).

Adler (1959) described various types of entoptic phenomena; some are the result of normal structures within the eye, and others arise from imperfections such as opacities in the ocular media (cells with opaque nuclei, which can cast an umbra on the retina and produce a positive scotoma). In either case, entoptic phenomena are usually not seen because the subject does not attend to them, because they adapt out as "stabilized images," or because the illumination conditions are not appropriate (Adler, 1959; Hall et al., 1970). Indeed, some light is necessary for the observation of most entoptic phenomena, as described by Adler (e.g., superficial horizontal bands due to folds in corneal epithelium that change with eyelid motion; a longitudinal strip due to lacrimal fluid that adheres to the upper-lid margin, central moving bright spots surrounded by a dark ring due to droplets of tear fluid and mucus on the cornea; diffraction of light by radial fibers of the lens; a black lacework seen against a red background due to retinal blood vessels, which cast a shadow on rods and cones; and pulsating figures due to excursions of distended blood vessels on underlying receptor cells). Adler also suggests that small dancing spots seen entoptically may be caused by red blood cells passing through retinal capillaries. During the passage of these cells, sometimes called "floaters," the hemoglobin in the cells absorbs blue light and casts a shadow on the underlying rods and cones. It could be speculated that this phenomenon is related to the blue colors reported by subjects during the early stages of hallucinogenic intoxication, particularly with THC (Part II). These subjects did not report the colors in motion as they were in the supine position, where the loose cells could settle in an aqueous pool in the foveal crater, thus stopping all movement (White and Levatin, 1962). However, the area around the fovea, corresponding to the center of the visual field, does not contain retinal blood vessels and fails to show these entoptic phenomena. This could be related to the bright light and loss of central detail observed in drug-induced visual imagery.

Light is necessary for most entoptic phenomena, but it is not required for a type known as *eigengrau* or phosphenes. Eigengrau or phosphene phenomena occur in the dark where a normal subject does not see black but rather [a sensation of] grayness (Adler, 1959); they are characterized by neuronal discharge activity in the retina, lateral geniculate, and visual cortex (R. Jung, 1972). Phosphenes may also include spots, disks, concentric arcs or circles, and even checkerboard patterns. Rapid eye movement causes "flick phosphenes" or a sensation of motion in these patterns. These patterns and effects can also be induced by light pressure on the closed eyelid. Oster (1970), whose illustrations of phosphenes include examples of lattices and spiral tunnels, claims that hallucinogens also produce these phenomena. Since the phosphene phenomena are partly due to pressure on the retina (Ladd-Franklin, 1927), and LSD raises intraocular pressure (Holliday and Sigurdson, 1965), Oster's suggestion of hallucinogen-induced phosphenes could be related to such reactions. The finding, recently contested by Adams and Flom (1972), that marihuana reduces intraocular pressure (Hepler and Frank, 1971), but induces identical imagery phenomena (Part II), casts doubt on such a mechanism of action. Nonetheless, phosphenes may account for many other subjective visual phenomena ordinarily labeled hallucinations:

Phosphenes may account for the "illuminations," the visions or the experience of "seeing the light" reported by religious mystics meditating in the dark; they are the "prisoners' cinema" experienced by people in dark dungeons; they may well constitute the fact behind reports of phantoms and ghosts. . . . Phosphenes are a hazard to the long-haul truck driver peering for hours into a snowstorm. Airplane pilots often experience phosphenes, especially when they are flying alone at high altitudes, where the sky is cloudless and empty of the usual depth cues (Oster, 1970, p. 83).

As appealing as such entoptic events are for explaining drug-induced constants, since some light is required for their visualization, they play a minimal role in the determination of visual imagery constants as found in our experiments conducted in total darkness (Part II). The presence of some LSD- or marihuana-induced visual imagery in totally blind subjects (Krill et al., 1963; Kirtley, 1971), as well as non-drug-induced complex hallucinations in recently blinded subjects (Fitzgerald, 1971), would seem to support this notion. However, adequately controlled studies with blind subjects have not been conducted, and the latter point must be accepted with caution (cp. Rosenthal, 1964). Moreover, recent neurophysiological studies in cats have found that hallucinogens like LSD and DMT "mimic" the effect of light on the retina (Heiss et al., 1973) or on EEG tracings (Marczynski, 1972), and such drugs "might be interpreted by the brain as light and this may contribute to the origin of abnormal reactions within brain structures which are also influenced, leading to hallucinations" (Heiss et al., 1973, p. 457). Additionally, we question the exclusive role of entoptic phenomena here because they are not as symmetrical or as well-organized as the drug-induced constants.

Many investigators have suggested that retinal blood vessels and capillaries contribute to drug-induced form-constants such as spirals (e.g., Marshall, 1937; Klüver, 1942), but others (e.g., Wise et al., 1971) have shown that the pattern and structure of retinal vessels (Fig. 28) are simply not as regular and geometrical as drug-induced visual imagery. It remains possible, however, that such entoptic

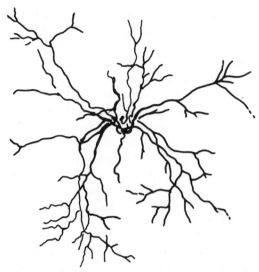

Figure 28   Retinal blood vessels. Drawing by Sheridan, pen and ink.

structures only provide the basic structural templates for the cognitive elaboration in higher centers to imagery constants (cf. Horowitz, 1972). Indeed, Barber (1970) reviews compelling evidence showing that phosphenelike phenomena may be induced at higher levels of the visual system than the retina itself.

Similarity to Migraine Hallucinations.   Similar phosphenelike phenomena have been observed in migraine hallucinations (Maclay and Guttman 1941; Oster, 1970). For example, Maclay and Guttman found instances of mescaline-induced zigzag lines, similar to the fortification patterns of migraine hallucinations, moving from the center of the visual field to the periphery. Richards (1971) described these classic fortification "illusions," which often precede or accompany the head pain:

It generally begins near the center of the visual field as a small, gray area with indefinite boundaries. . . . During the next few minutes the gray area slowly expands into a horsehoe, with bright zigzag lines appearing at the expanding outer edge. These lines are small at first and grow as the blind area expands and moves outward toward the periphery of the visual field (p. 89).

These patterns may show changes in color, line orientation, and in spacing between the lines. The arc may become a grid, and the colors may change from black and white to red, blue, and yellow. Often the basic patterns change into different geometric arrays. For example, one patient reported seeing "a bright red, central flickering spot composed of many smaller spots. The central scotoma quickly expands into concentric circles of multicolored spots that obscure whatever he looks at" (Hachinski et al., 1973, pp. 573–574). Migraine phenomena also include the development of fully formed hallucinations, including people and scenes, which often accompany these geometric displays. Distortions of body imagery (e.g., growing bigger or smaller) are also reported. Lewis Carroll wrote about such personal migraine attacks in his diary, and it has been suggested that some of *Alice's Adventures in Wonderland* may have originated in his migraine hallucinations (Lippman, 1952).

Although the mechanism underlying the production of these phenomena remains uncertain, Hachinski et al. (1973) believe that it is unlikely to be based on entoptic events. Alternatively, these authors favor Lashley's (1941) and Richards's (1971) argument that migraine visual images provide information on the arrangement of cells in the visual cortex, which are probably excited by a spreading wave of cortical depression. For example, the regular geometric nature of migraine fortification patterns, similar to drug-induced patterns in that respect, may represent the electrical output of organized groups of cells in the visual cortex. Somjen (1972) notes that the visual cortex is organized as a mosaic of detectors of contrast, with each element representing a defined orientation relative to the visual horizon and functioning in the detection and recognition of all shapes. Excitation of these elements by a smooth electrical wave traveling across the cortex from one individual discrete element to the next could create both geometric designs and the consistent patterns of movement. Indeed, Richards (1971) argues that line detectors are probably organized in the cortex in lattice arrangements, and excitation of these detectors could account for lattice forms in migraine as well as in other phenomena. This discrete cortical organization might be expected to give rise to only straight-line figures. But all outlines with curved or straight edges can be subdivided into sets of straight lines, since the direction of a curve at any point is defined by the orientation of its tangent. Thus excitation of cortical line and edge detectors can produce circular as well as straight figures.

COMPLEX MEMORY IMAGERY

Brain Excitation.   Thus far we have seen that excitation of the central nervous system with hallucinogens (Part II), by photostimulation (Symthies, 1960), by electrical current (Knoll et al., 1962), or in migraine, results in remarkably similar visual imagery constants. Even direct electrical stimulation of man's visual cortex or temporal lobes produces moving and stationary colored lights, geometric forms, stars, and lines (Penfield, 1958; Knoll et al., 1962). Several investigators have suggested that the central nervous system excitation induced by hallucinogens may be directly related to hallucinations (e.g., Winters and Wallach, 1970). For example, Wikler (1954) examined the EEG records of 12 subjects given mescaline (700 mg) and found that 6 displayed intermittent desynchronization concomitant with their verbal reports of hallucinations.

Hebb (1968) proposed a theoretical model to explain how hallucinations may develop from this excitation:

In normal waking hours there is a constant modulating influence of sensory input upon cortical activities, helping both to excite cortical neurons and to determine the organization of their firing. When this influence is defective for any reason—pathological processes, or habituation resulting from monotony or "sensory deprivation"—there is still cortical activity. . . . The activity may be unorganized. . . . But when by chance the spontaneous cortical firing falls into a "meaningful" pattern—when the active neurons include enough of those constituting a cell assembly to make the assembly active and so excite other assemblies in an organized pattern—S may find himself with bizarre thoughts or . . . with vivid detailed imagery (pp. 474–475).

This process can be initiated by treatment with hallucinogens, which would have the cortical disorganizing effect referred to by Hebb (Marrazzi, 1962). Indeed, Hernandez-Peon (1968) maintains that hallucinogens "act first by disinhibiting that part of the cortex which lies in the temporal lobes and corresponds to the recent memory system. Therefore, if that part of the cortex is removed (as in recent studies with chimpanzees), the drug cannot act, and thus there would be no hallucinations" (p. 190).

In the intact brain of man, the result of such excitation is the production of visual imagery. A number of investigators have described this phenomenon for various forms of excitation. Moreau (1845) wrote of the hashish-induced excitation of the brain which enabled thoughts and memories to be visualized. Timothy Leary and his co-workers (1964) claimed that hallucinogens like LSD enabled one to watch the contents and processes of the human mind. Lilly (1970b) described how imagery induced by sensory deprivation comes from "program storage" (memory) and internal body sources of excitation. The excitation causes visual displays to be projected onto a normally-blank screen in front of the eyes. The subject then

interprets the resultant filling of these perceptual spaces at first as if this excitation were coming from outside. In other words, the sources of the excitation are interpreted by the self as if coming from the real world. For certain kinds of persons and personalities this is a very disturbing experience in one sphere or another . . . (Lilly, 1970b, p. 29).

Penfield (1958, 1970) described excitation induced by cortical stimulation as memory "flashbacks" and *"experiential hallucinations"*:

These hallucinations are made up of elements from the indivudual's past experiences. They may seem to him so strange that he calls them dreams, but when they can be carefully analyzed it is evident that the hallucination is a shorter or longer sequence of past experience. The subject re-lives a period of the past although he is still aware of the present. Movement goes forward again as it did in that interval of time that has now been, by chance, revived and all of the elements of his previous consciousness seem to be there, sights, sounds, interpretations, emotions. The hallucination includes those things that were within the focus of his attention. The things he ignored then are missing now. Sometimes it would seem that even fancies reappear, as in the case of R.W., a little boy who saw "robbers with guns" such as he had seen pictured in his comic books (Penfield, 1958, p. 23).

Memory Retrieval.   The notion of hallucinations consisting of complex memory imagery is neither a radical nor a new idea. It is not radical because it appeals to an intuitive sense of what is reasonable to infer. When one hallucinates something that is not there, the stimuli being perceived (i.e., the image) must come from some source. It is not reasonable for normal man to infer that such stimuli, when auditory, are "voices talking to me," "radio waves from another planet," or clairvoyant communications with a deceased loved one. Nor is it always reasonable to infer that the stimuli, when visual, are real (e.g., "that little green man is really there") or self-contained in a recently administered drug (e.g., "God is in the LSD"). Rather, it is more reasonable to infer that such phenomena originate in stored information in the brain, that is, memories.

Figure 6. Blue lattice-tunnel reported in early stages of marihuana and THC intoxication. Synthesis of reports of 14 subjects. Drawing by Sheridan, pen and ink.

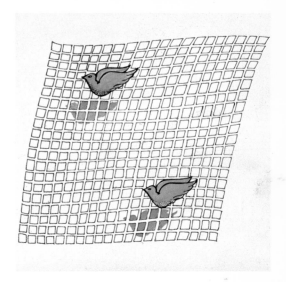

Figure 13. Illustration of complex imagery overlaying geometric lattice imagery in early stages of hallucinogen intoxication. Redrawn by Sheridan, pen and ink.

Figure 22. Depiction of an hallucinatory experience, by Yando, untitled, oil, 1971.

Figure 23. Huichol yarn painting depicting peyote-induced visual imagery of a peyote flower. Yarn on beeswax on wood.

Figure 26. Huichol yarn painting depicting eyes-open true hallucination of a tree. Yarn on beeswax on wood.

Figure 24. Huichol yarn painting depicting eyes-closed peyote-induced imagery. Subject reported bright light in center was the deified fire god. Deer heads were reported to be rotating over blue lattices. Vision during early stages of intoxication. Yarn on beeswax on wood. Painting by Martin de la Cruz.

Figure 25. Huichol yarn painting depicting eyes-closed peyote-induced imagery. The four red spiral tunnels were not actually "seen" by the subject but were used to indicate that this painting was a peyote vision. Interestingly, one of the traditional Huichol symbols for peyote is this spiral-tunnel design. Yarn on beeswax on wood. Painting by Martin de la Cruz.

Plate I Isaac Abrams, *Flying Leap*, oil, 1966. (By permission of Isaac Abrams, Stanley Krippner, and Grove Press.)

Plate II LSD-induced visual imagery (right and below). (By permission of Oscar Janiger.)

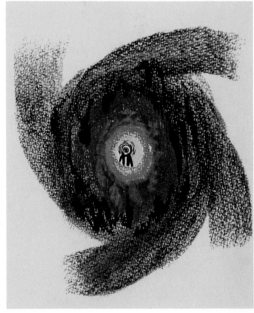

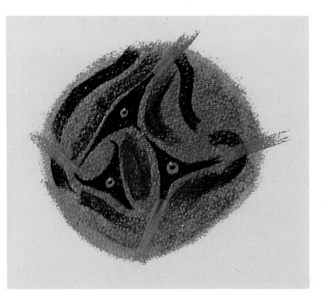

Plate III Depiction of an hallucinatory experience, by Yando, untitled, oil, 1970.

Plate IV Depiction of an hallucinatory experience, by Yando, untitled, oil, 1971–1972.

Plate V Depiction of an hallucinatory experience, by Yando, untitled, oil, 1970.

Plate VI Isaac Abrams, *Magician's Night,* oil. (Used with permission of Isaac Abrams and Stanley Krippner.)

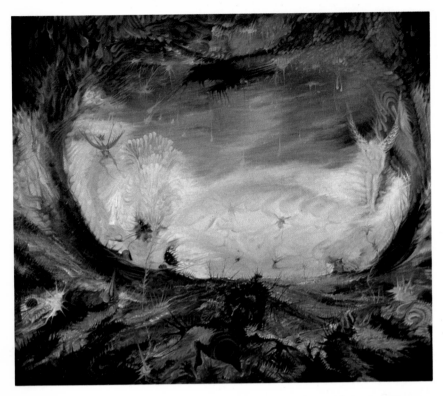

Plate VII   Depiction of an hallucinatory experience, by Yando, untitled, oil, 1971.

Plate VIII   Depiction of an hallucinatory experience, by Yando, untitled, oil, 1971–1974.

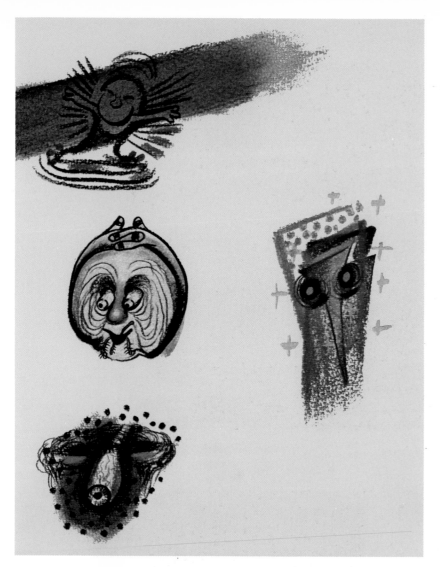

Plate IX LSD-induced visual imagery. (By permission of Oscar Janiger.)

Plate X Doorknob seen at two different times under LSD treatment. (By permission of Oscar Janiger.)

Plate XI (*right*) Dion Wright, example of LSD-induced visual imagery. (By permission of Stanley Krippner.)

Plate XII (*below*) Angelo Miranda, *Angel of Death*—dimethyltryptamine-induced visual image. (By permission of Angelo Miranda and Stanley Krippner.)

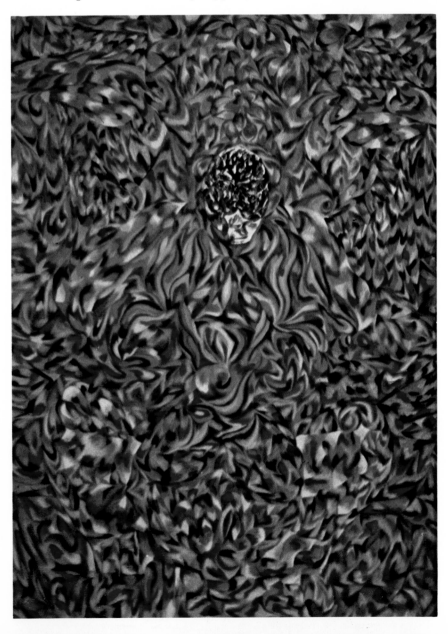

The idea is hardly original. In 1813 Ferriar wrote an essay on apparitions in which he claimed that formed hallucinations consisted of retrieved memory images:

From recalling images by an art of memory, the transition is direct to beholding spectral objects, which have been floating in the imagination. Yet, even in the most frantic assemblage of this nature, no novelty appears. The Spectre may be larger or smaller; it may be compounded of the parts of different animals; but it is always framed from the recollection of familiar though discordant images (p. 100).

According to Boismont (1853), "the involuntary exercise of memory and imagination" together with internal excitation of sensory systems and suspension of external impressions, results in the production of hallucinations. Similarly, Parish (1897) discussed hallucinations as strictly images of the memory and imagination:

The content of a fallacious perception [hallucination] depends primarily on the past experience of the individual. Only what has passed in at the portals of sense can be reproduced. The neural elements which attain to activity may indeed be associated in the most unfamiliar and bizarre combinations, but they can be called into play only in the way to which they have been predisposed by former sensory stimuli (p. 185).

Studying visual hallucinations occurring in association with tumors compressing the optic nerves and chiasm, Weinberger and Grant (1940) concluded that hallucinations can arise from excitation of any level of the visual system, but "they are the result of the total integrative activities of the mind, which fuse memory, affectural associations and previous visual experience with simple sensory presentations to create an image" (p. 198). Even the visual imagery of daydreams is considered to be chiefly memories and stored fantasy material, although memory sequences are regarded as the easiest to maintain and retrieve (Singer, 1966).

In discussing drug-induced hallucinations, Anstie (1865) described hashish, alcohol, chloroform, and opium as producing "involuntary reminiscence," a class of mental phenomena characterized by retrieved memories: "Alcohol, taken in poisonous doses, not infrequently recalls to the mind circumstances and ideas long since forgotten" (p. 174). In discussing hypnagogic and hypnopompic hallucinations, Ahlenstiel and Kauffmann (1953) described how geometric images (e.g., lines, cones, spirals) are *released* from the mind and lead to concrete complex images through direct projection of pictures onto the geometric structure. These authors claimed that mescaline, *Cannabis,* and morphine were effective agents in producing this phenomenon. Leuner (1962) wrote of a similar geometric screen in the visual field of subjects in mescaline and LSD states. He believed that psychodynamic principles caused certain images to be retrieved from a person's past and *released* onto the screen. More recently, Jarvik (1970) proposed that hallucinations are a memory defect characterized by uninhibited retrieval and that one way in which hallucinogens work is by impairing short-term memory and inducing "vicarious retrieval" of long-term memories.

Memory retrieval forms the central part of many theories of hallucinations. The perceptual release theory (Jackson, 1931; West, 1962) assumes that normal memories are suppressed by a mechanism that gates the flow of information from outside to inside the body. Input of new information inhibits the emergence and awareness of previous perceptions and processed information. If the input is decreased or impaired and internal arousal is sufficient to permit awareness, the *released* perceptions may be dynamically organized and experienced as hallucinations, dreams, or fantasies. Psychoanalytic theories (e.g., Savage, 1955; Leuner, 1962) postulate a general regression to primitive or childlike thinking, coupled with the emergence of repressed information and memories. Similarly, psychedelic theories (e.g., Leary et al., 1964; Osmond, 1957) postulate that hallucinogens release normally suppressed information and memories in the mind, bringing such components to our attention.

THE EXPERIENTIAL PROJECTOR MODEL OF HALLUCINATIONS

We propose the following model as a theoretical approach to hallucinations. The model views man as an information-processing system whose output can be described as projections of experience in the form of images, dreams, and hallucinations.

As an information-processing system, man is capable of executing several processes by which sensory input is transformed, reduced, elaborated, stored, retrieved, and used. These processes are generally defined as cognition (Neisser, 1967). That cognitive process by which man receives or extracts information about the internal and/or external environment is referred to as "perception." As information is acquired through experience and becomes part of one's storage of facts, learning occurs. When information is manipulated, as in remembering or problem-solving, the thinking process is said to take place.

In waking consciousness, thinking involves images or representations of a sensation or perception without adequate sensory input (Holt, 1964). Images may appear to represent a perception in any sensory modality and can be considered to be pictures to the extent that "they portray things located at a lower level of abstractness than they are themselves. They do their work by grasping and rendering some relevant qualities—shape, color, movement—of the objects or activities they depict" (Arnheim, 1969, p. 137). The picture metaphor is somewhat misleading, however, since images are more a description than a replica of information. Indeed, Pylyshyn (1973) has argued that these mental images are essentially conceptual and propositional rather than sensory or pictorial because they often contain abstract aspects that are the result of (not inputs to) perceptual processes. Moreover, image formation is generally considered to be a constructive process in that man not only retrieves stored information but carries out new activities such as forming new representations (Neisser, 1972). The propositional and constructive aspects of mental imagery can be illustrated by a simple exercise. Recall the last time you went swimming in the ocean. Now ask yourself if this memory includes a picture of yourself running along the beach or moving about in the water. Such a picture is entirely fictitious, but memory images often include fleeting pictures of oneself. Similarly, subjects in our drug experiments often reported such equally improbable elements in imagery as aerial perspectives and underwater views. It has not been experimentally established where such constructions occur, but contributions are probably made in the encoding, storage, and retrieval stages of the memory process (cf. Paivio, 1972).

When the sensory input that would normally give rise to perceptions is absent, man is either thinking, imagining, dreaming, or hallucinating. These quasi-perceptions are forms of mental imagery that lie on a continuum of intensity of vividness, thought images being the least vivid and images of hallucinations being the most vivid. The transition from one form of imagery to another along this continuum depends on the arousal state; when arousal is low, there is still a baseline amount of spontaneous firings by cortical cells in normal waking behavior. This activity is suppressed and inhibited from entering into conscious awareness whenever one is asleep or new information is being scanned and processed. However, some introspection or thinking can retrieve the results of these firings, and they are presented as baseline imagery data. The information is projected in the mind's eye (or mind's ear or some other sense organ) and reflects elements of physical structures (e.g., entoptic phenomena, symmetrical organization, and experiences (e.g., recent memories). With low arousal, such experiental projections are weak thought images. When arousal is increased, however, retrieval of information by this system is more successfully obtained (Goldstein and Nelsen, 1973). The information may now appear to be more vividly projected and may contain increasing amounts of complex imagination and fantasy imagery. When arousal is further increased, information may appear to be projected on a sensory field outside the body, especially if other sensory inputs are reduced (e.g., closed eyes, dim light, sensory deprivation). In our drug experiments, visual imagery appeared to be projected on a screen in front of the subject's eyes, and it was at this stage that the transition to hallucinations was achieved. Higher states of arousal may cause information to be projected on and overlaid with the actual stimulus environment, as in the case of hallucinations induced by sensory bombardment (Davenport and Winstead, 1972) or high doses of hallucinogens.

Thus hallucinations occur when imagery is projected outside the observer and is viewed as separate from the projector. The screen contributes very little to the imagery except to provide a locus for its projection; most if not all organization resides in the projector. The observer may feel detached from the projection, a state similar to the breakoff phenomenon experienced by solitary pilots and astronauts who find themselves observing their craft from the outside. The observer's experience of these projections—the sensory fields, emotions, thoughts, and images—make up consciousness.

This conceptualization of hallucinations as experiential projections began more than 130 years ago with Moreau's experiments on hashish. The subsequent inquiry into drug-induced hallucinations has helped to clarify the phenomenology and to suggest methods for further experimental analysis. The investigation of imagery constants suggests possible mechanisms of action, and the emergence of memory imagery reveals itself as man's projection of experiences. Perhaps the time has now come for investigation into even more dramatic aspects of hallucinations, such as the experience of the projector itself as it projects experiences. It will be none too soon, for as Moreau's fellow "hachischin" Baudelaire noted in 1857

"It is time to set aside all this jugglery, all those great marionettes, born of the dreams of childish minds. There are more serious things for us to speak of, are there not?—the changes that occur in human feelings, and, in a word, the 'morality' of hashish" (p. 63).

ACKNOWLEDGMENTS

Preparation of this chapter was supported by grant MH-23880 from the National Institute of Mental Health (NIMH). The animal and human research reported here were supported in part by grants MH-5319, MH-6418, and contract #4-976 from NIMH. Cross-cultural studies were supported in part by grant MH-17202 from NIMH. Human drug studies reported here were approved by the UCLA Clinical Research Committee for Human Study, the Subcommittee on Clinical Research for the Neuropsychiatric Institute, the State of California Research Advisory Panel, and the NIMH–FDA Psychotomimetic Agents Advisory Committee. Drugs were supplied by NIMH (BOL, LSD, marihuana, psilocybin, and THC), Aldrich Chemical Co. (mescaline hydrochloride), Bristol Laboratories (ketamine hydrochloride), and Parke, Davis and Co. (ketamine hydrochloride). The authors wish to thank T. Ball, J. Brewster, and V. Williams for invaluable technical assistance, and S. Beadenkopf, L. Ehrlich, A. Harlow, M. Schwartz, and E. Shafner for translation services. The cross-cultural studies were conducted with J. Amundson, E. Campos-Chavez, P. Collings, D. Dorrance, O. Janiger, and R. Teplitz.

REFERENCES

Abrams, M. H. *The milk of paradise. The effect of opium visions on the works of De Quincey, Crabbe, Francis Thompson, and Coleridge.* New York: Harper & Row, 1970.

Adams, A. J., and Flom, M. C. Influence of marijuana on intraocular pressure. *American Journal of Optometry and Archives of American Academy of Optometry,* 1972, **49,** 880. (Abstract)

Adey, W. R., Bell, F. R., and Dennis, B. J. Effects of LSD-25, psilocybin, and psilocin on temporal lobe EEG patterns and learned behavior in the cat. *Neurology,* 1962, **12,** 591–602.

Adler, F. H. *Physiology of the eye.* St. Louis: C. V. Mosby, 1959.

Adler, N. *The underground stream. New life styles and the antinomian personality.* New York: Harper & Row, 1972.

Aggernaes, A. The experienced reality of hallucinations and other psychological phenomena. *Acta Psychiatrica Scandinavica,* 1972, **48,** 220–228. (a)

Aggernaes, A. The difference between the experienced reality of hallucinations in young drug abusers and schizophrenic patients. *Acta Psychiatrica Scandinavica,* 1972, **48,** 287–299. (b)

Aghajanian, G. K. LSD and CNS transmission. *Annual Review of Pharmacology,* 1972, **12,** 157–168.

Ahlenstiel, H., and Kauffmann, R. Geometrisches Gestalten in optischen Halluzinationen. *Archiv für Psychiatrie und Zeitschrift Neurologie,* 1953, **190,** 503–529.

Anastasi, A., and Foley, J. P. A survey of the literature on artistic behavior in the abnormal: III. Spontaneous productions. *Psychological Monographs,* 1940, **52** (6), 1–71.

Anstie, F. E. *Stimulants and narcotics, their mutual relations.* Philadelphia: Lindsay and Blakiston, 1865.

Aring, C. D. The migrainous scintillating scotoma. *Journal of the American Medical Association,* 1972, **220,** 519–522.

Arnheim, R. *Visual thinking.* Los Angeles: University of California Press, 1969.

Baldwin, M., Lewis, S. A., and Frost, L. L. Perceptual interference after cerebral ablation. *Perceptual and Motor Skills,* 1957, **7,** 45–48.

Baldwin, M. Lewis, S. A., and Bach, S. A. The effects of lysergic acid after cerebral ablation. *Neurology,* 1959, **9,** 469–474.

Balestrieri, A. Hallucinatory mechanisms and the content of drug-induced hallucinations. In P. B. Bradley, F. Flugel, and P. H. Hoch (Eds.), *Neuro-psychopharmacology,* Vol. 3, New York: Elsevier, 1964.

Barber, T. X. *LSD, marihuana, yoga, and hypnosis.* Chicago: Aldine Press, 1970.

Barber, T. X. Imagery and hallucinations: Effects of LSD contrasted with the effects of "hypnotic suggestions." In S. J. Segal (Ed.), *Imagery. Current cognitive approaches.* New York: Academic Press, 1971.

Baudelaire, C. "The poem of hashish." Translated by A. Crowley. In I. Regardie, *Roll away the stone,* St. Paul, Minn.: Llewellyn Publications, 1968.

Baudelaire, C. (1857) *Artificial paradise.* Translated by E. Fox. New York: Herder and Herder, 1971.

Beaton, J. M., Smythies, J. R., Benington, F., and Morin, R. D. The behavioural effects of 2,5-dimethoxy-4-methyl-amphetamine (DOM) in rats. *Communications in Behavioral Biology,* Part A, 1969, **3,** 81–84.

Becker, D. I., Appel, J. B., and Freedman, D. X., Some effects of lysergic acid diethylamide on visual discrimination in pigeons. *Psychopharmacologia (Berl.),* 1967, **11,** 354–364.

Benzi, M. Visions des Huichols sous l'effet du peyotl. *L'Hygiene Mentale, Supplement de l'Encephale,* 1969, **58,** 61–97.

Beringer, K. Der Meskalinrausch. Seine Geshichte und Erscheinungsweise. *Mongraphien aus dem Gesamtgebiet der Neurologie und Psychiatrie,* 1927, **49,** 1–315.

Bermond, F., and Bert, J. The effect of psilocybin on the behavior of the Cercopithecinae Papiopapio. *Psychopharmacologia (Berl.),* 1969, **15,** 109–115.

Berryman, R., Jarvik, M..E., and Nevin, J. A. Effects of pentobarbital, lysergic acid diethylamide and chlorpromazine on matching behavior in the pigeon. *Psychopharmacologia (Berl.),* 1962, **3,** 60–65.

Bliss, E. L., and Clark, L. D. Visual hallucinations. In L. J. West (Ed.), *Hallucinations.* New York: Grune & Stratton, 1962.

Blough, D. S. Effects of drugs on visually controlled behavior in pigeons. In S. Garattini and V. Ghetti (Eds.), *Psychotropic drugs.* Amsterdam: Elsevier, 1957.

Boelkins, R. C. Effects of parachlorophenylalanine on the behaviors of monkeys. In J. Barchas and E. Usdin (Eds.), *Serotonin and behavior.* New York: Academic Press, 1973.

Boismont, A. Brierre de. *Hallucinations: Or, the rational history of apparitions, visions, dreams, ecstasy, magnetism, and somnambulism.* Philadelphia: Lindsay and Blakiston, 1853.

Borenstein, P., Chatelier, G., Cujo, P., and Gekiere, F. Behavior and neurophysiological study of the effect of LSD-25 in the monkey. *Semaine des hôitaux de Paris,* 1969, **45,** 1258–1270.

Bornstein, M. H. Color vision and color naming: A psychophysiological hypothesis of cultural difference. *Psychological Bulletin,* 1973, **80,** 257–285.

Boulton, C. S., and Handley, S. L. Factors modifying the head-twitch response to 5-hydroxytryptophan. *Psychopharmacologia (Berl.),* 1973, **31,** 205–214.

Bourne, L. E. *Human conceptual behavior.* Boston: Allyn & Bacon, 1966.

Bovet, D., and Gatti, G. L. Pharmacology of instrumental avoidance conditioning. *Proceedings of the Second International Pharmacology Meeting,* Prague, 1963, 75–89.

Bradley, P. G., and Key, B. J. The effect of drugs on arousal responses produced by electrical stimulation of the reticular formation of the brain. *Electroencephalography and Clinical Neurophysiology,* 1958, **10,** 97–110.

Brawley, P., and Duffield, J. C. The pharmacology of hallucinogens. *Pharmacological Reviews,* 1972, **24,** 31–66.

Bridger, W. H. Psychotomimetic drugs, animal behavior and human psychopathology. In J. O. Cole, A. M. Freedman, and A. J. Friedhoff (Eds.), *Psychopathology and psychopharmacology.* Baltimore: Johns Hopkins University Press, 1973.

Brinkmann, H. J. Das Alkoholdelir. *Therapiewoche,* 1972, **22,** 3134–3140.

Bromberg, W. Marihuana intoxication: A clinical study of *Cannabis sativa* intoxication. *American Journal of Psychiatry,* 1934, **91,** 303–330.

Brown, H. Behavioral studies of animal vision and drug action. *International Review of Neurobiology,* 1967, **10,** 277–322.

Bugelski, B. R. Words and things and images. *American Psychologist,* 1970, **25,** 1002–1012.

Butterworth, A. T. The psychotomimetic effect: A discussion of its unique nature and character. *Existential Psychiatry,* Winter 1967, 489–498.

Caldwell, D. F., Myers, S. A., Domino, E. F., and Merriman, P.E. Auditory and visual threshold effect of marihuana in man. *Perceptual and Motor Skills,* 1969, **29,** 755–759.

Caldwell, D. F., Myers, S. A., and Domino, E. F. Effects of marihuana smoking on sensory thresholds in man. In D. H. Efron (Ed.), *Psychotomimetic drugs.* New York: Raven Press, 1970.

Carrington, R. *Elephants*. New York: Basic Books, 1959.

Clarke, E. G. C., Greatorex, J. C., and Potter, R. Cannabis poisoning in the dog. *Veterinary Record,* 1971, **88,** 694.

Clarke, E. H. *Visions: A study of false sight*. Boston: Houghton, Osgood, 1878.

Cocteau, J. *Opium*. Knightsbridge: Icon Books, 1957.

Cohen, L. A. Drug-induced hallucinations in primates. In A. Herxheimer (Ed.), *Drugs and sensory functions*. Boston: Little, Brown, 1968.

Cohen, S. *Drugs of hallucination*. London: Paladin, 1970.

Collier, B. B. Ketamine and the conscious mind. *Anaesthesia,* 1972, **27,** 120–134.

Corcoran, M. E. Role of drug novelty and metabolism in the aversive effects of hashish injections in rats. *Life Sciences,* 1973, **12,** 63–72.

Corcoran, M. E., and Amit, Z. Reluctance of rats to drink hashish suspensions: Free-choice and forced consumption, and the effects of hypothalamic stimulation. *Psychopharmacologia (Berl.),* 1974, **35,** 129–147.

Córdova-Rios, M., and Lamb, F. B. *Wizard of the Upper Amazon*. New York: Atheneum, 1971.

Corne, S. J., and Pickering, R. W. A possible correlation between drug-induced hallucinations in man and a behavioral response in mice. *Psychopharmacologia (Berl.),* 1967, **11,** 65–78.

Corne, S. J., Pickering, R. W., and Warner, B. T. A method for assessing the effects of drugs on the central nervous actions of 5-hydroxytryptamine. *British Journal of Pharmacology,* 1963, **20,** 106–120.

Csillag, E. R., and Landauer, A. A. Alleged hallucinogenic effect of a toxic overdose of an antihistamine preparation. *The Medical Journal of Australia,* 1973, **1,** 653–654.

Cumming, W. W., and Berryman, R. The complex discriminated operant: Studies of matching-to-sample and related problems. In D. I. Mostofsky (Ed.), *Stimulus generalization*. Stanford, Calif.: Stanford University Press, 1965.

Darley, C. F., Tinklenberg, J. R., Hollister, L. E., and Atkinson, R. C. Marihuana and retrieval from short-term memory. *Psychopharmacologia (Berl.),* 1973, **29,** 231–238.

Davenport, D. M., and Winstead, C. L. The consequences of sensory bombardment. *Proceedings, Virginia Journal of Science,* 1972, **23,** 149.

Davy, H. *Researches, chemical and philosophical; chiefly concerning nitrous oxide*. London: J. Johnson, 1800.

Dement, W., Zarcone, V., Ferguson, J., Cohen, H., Pivik, T., and Barchas, J. Some parallel findings in schizophrenic patients and serotonin-depleted cats. In S. Sankar (Ed.), *Schizophrenia: Current concepts and research*. New York: PJD Publications, 1969.

Dement, W., Halper, C., Pivik, T., Ferguson, J., Cohen, H., Henriksen, S., McGarr, K., Gonda, W., Hoyt, G., Ryan, L., Mitchell, G., Barchas, J., and Zarcone, V. Hallucinations and dreaming. In D. Hamburg (Ed.), *Perception and its disorders*. Baltimore: Williams & Wilkins, 1970.

Deneau, G. A., Yanagita, T., and Seevers, M. H. Self-administration of psychoactive substances by the monkey. *Psychopharmacologia (Berl.),* 1969, **16,** 30–48.

Dheur, P. *Les hallucinations volontaires (l'état hallucinatoire)*. Paris: Société des Editions Scientifiques, 1899.

Dobkin de Rios, M. *Visionary vine*. San Francisco: Chandler, 1972.

Doenicke, A., Kugler, J., Emmert, M., Laub, M., and Kleinert, H. Ein Leistungsvergleich nach Ketamine und Methodhexital. In H. Kreuscher (Ed.), *Ketamine*. Berlin: Springer-Verlag, 1969.

Durr, R. A. *Poetic vision and the psychedelic experience*. Syracuse, N. Y.: Syracuse University Press, 1970.

Ebin, D. (Ed.) *The drug experience*. New York: Grove Press, 1961.

Eisner, T., and Halpern, B. P. Taste distortion and plant palatability. *Science,* 1971, **172,** 1362.

Ellinwood, E. H., and Sudilovsky, A. Chronic amphetamine intoxication: Behavioral model of psychoses. In J. O. Cole, A. M. Freedman, and A. J. Friedhoff (Eds.), *Psychopathology and psychopharmacology*. Baltimore: Johns Hopkins University Press, 1973.

Ellinwood, E. H., Sudilovsky, A., and Nelson, L. M. Evolving behavior in the clinical and experimental amphetamine (model) psychosis. *American Journal of Psychiatry,* 1973, **130,** 1088–1093.

Elsmore, T. F., and Fletcher, G. V. Delta-9-tetrahydrocannabinol: Adversive effects in rats at high doses. *Science,* 1972, **175,** 911–912.

Evarts, E. V. Neurophysiological correlates of pharmacologically induced behavioral disturbances. In

H. C. Solomon, S. Cobb, and W. Penfield (Eds.), *The brain and human behavior*. Baltimore: Williams & Wilkins, 1958.

Fabing, H. D., and Hawkins, J. R. Intravenous bufotenine injection in the human being. *Science*, 1956, **123**, 886–887.

Fellows, G. J., and Cook, L. The comparative pharmacology of a number of phenothiazine derivatives. In S. Garattini and V. Ghetti (Eds.), *Psychotropic drugs*. Amsterdam: Elsevier, 1957.

Ferraro, D. P. Effects of Δ^9-*trans*-tetrahydrocannabinol on simple and complex learned behavior in animals. In M. F. Lewis (Ed.), *Current research in marihuana*. New York: Academic Press, 1972.

Ferriar, J. *An essay towards a theory of apparitions*. London: Cadell and Davis, 1813.

Fischer, R. A cartography of the ecstatic and meditative states. *Science*, 1971, **174**, 897–904. (a)

Fischer, R. The "flashback": Arousal-statebound recall of experience. *Journal of Psychedelic Drugs*, 1971, **3**, 31–39. (b)

Fitzgerald, R. G. Visual phenomenology in recently blind adults. *American Journal of Psychiatry*, 1971, **127**, 1533–1539.

Florio, V., Fuentes, J. A., Ziegler, H., and Longo, V. G. EEG and behavioral effects in animals of some amphetamine derivatives with hallucinogenic properties. *Behavioral Biology*, 1972, **7**, 401–414.

Forsyth, A. A. *British poisonous plants*. Bulletin No. 161, Ministry of Agriculture and Fisheries. London: Her Majesty's Stationery Office, 1954.

Freedman, D. X. Problems and prospects of research with the hallucinogens. In J. R. Gamage and E. L. Zerkin (Eds.), *Hallucinogenic drug research: Impact on science and society*. Beloit, Wis.: Stash Press, 1970.

Freedman, D. X. Drugs and culture. *Triangle*, 1971, **10**, 109–112.

Freedman, S. J., and Marks, P. A. Visual imagery produced by rhythmic photic stimulation: Personality correlates and phenomenology. *British Journal of Psychology*, 1965, **56**, 95–112.

Furst, P. T. Myth in art: A Huichol depicts his reality. *Quarterly* (Los Angeles County Museum of Natural History), 1969, **7**, 16–25.

Furst, P. T. Peyote among the Huichol Indians of Mexico. In P. T. Furst (Ed.), *Flesh of the gods. The ritual use of hallucinogens*. New York: Praeger, 1972.

Garcia, J., and Ervin, F. R. Gustatory-visceral and telereceptor-cutaneous conditioning—Adaptation in internal and external milieus. *Communications in Behavioral Biology*, 1968, **1** (Part A), 389–415.

Garvin, R. M. *The crystal skull*. New York: Doubleday, 1973.

Gershon, S., and Lang, W. J. A psycho-pharmacological study of some indole alkaloids. *Archives Internationales de Pharmacodynamie et de Therapie*, 1962, **135**, 31–56.

Ginsberg, A. *Kaddish and other poems 1958–1960*. San Francisco: City Lights Books, 1961.

Goldstein, L., and Nelsen, J. M. Some views on the neurophysiological and neuropharmacological mechanisms of storage and retrieval of information. In H. P. Zippel (Ed.), *Memory and transfer of information*. New York: Plenum Press, 1973.

Gowdy, J. M. Stramonium intoxication. *Journal of the American Medical Association*, 1972, **221**, 585–587.

Granier-Doyeux, M. Una toxicomania indigena: El uso de la *Piptadenia peregrina*. *Revista Técnica*, 1956, **2** (8), 49–55. (Cited in S. von Reis Altschul, *The genus Anadenanthera in Amerindian cultures*. Cambridge, Mass.: Harvard University Botanical Museum Monograph, 1972.)

Grunfeld, Y., and Edery, N. Psychopharmacological activity of the active constituents of hashish and some related cannabinoids. *Psychopharmacologia (Berl.)*, 1969, **14**, 200–210.

Hachinski, V. C., Porchawka, J., and Steele, J. C. Visual symptoms in the migraine syndrome. *Neurology*, 1973, **23**, 570–579.

Haley, T. J. Intracerebral injection of psychotomimetic and psychotherapeutic drugs in conscious mice. *Acta Pharmacologica et Toxicologica*, 1957, **13**, 107–112.

Hall, C. S., and Van de Castle, R. L. *The content analysis of dreams*. New York: Appleton-Century-Crofts, 1966.

Hall, R. J., Karsh, R., and Wilsoncroft, W. E. The production and fading of entoptic images. *Behavior Research Methods and Instrumentation*, 1970, **2**, 22–23.

Halstead, B. W. *Poisonous and venomous marine animals of the world*. Washington, D.C. Government Printing Office, 1965.

Hardman, H. F., Haavik, C. O., and Seevers, M. H. Relationship of the structure of mescaline and seven analogs to toxicity and behavior in five species of laboratory animals. *Toxicology and Applied Pharmacology*, 1973, **25,** 299–309.

Harner, M. J. The sound of rushing water. *Natural History*, 1968, **77,** 23–33.

Harner, M. J. Common themes in South American Indian yagé experiences. In M. J. Harner (Ed.), *Hallucinogens and shamanism*. New York: Oxford University Press, 1973.

Harper, R. W., and Knothe, B. U. C. Coloured liliputian hallucinations with amantadine. *The Medical Journal of Australia*, 1973, **1,** 444–445.

Hatch, R. C. Effect of drugs on catnip *(Nepeta cataria)* induced pleasure behavior in cats. *American Journal of Veterinary Research*, 1972, **33,** 143–155.

Hayer, A. *Opium and the romantic imagination*. Berkeley: University of California Press, 1970.

Heath, R. G. Marihuana: Effects on deep and surface electroencephalograms of rhesus monkeys. *Neuropharmacology*, 1973, **12,** 1–14.

Hebb, D. O. Concerning imagery. *Psychological Review*, 1968, **75,** 466–477.

Hefferline, R. F., Bruno, L. J. J., and Camp, J. A. Hallucinations: An experimental approach. In F. J. McGuigan and R. A. Schoonover (Eds.), *The psychophysiology of thinking*. New York: Academic Press, 1973.

Heiss, W. D., Hoyer, J., and Poustka, F. Participation of retinal mechanisms in DMT hallucinations. *Experientia*, 1973, **29,** 455–457.

Heim, R. and Wasson, R. G. (Eds.) *Les champignons hallucinogènes du Mexique,* Archives du Muséum National d'Histoire Naturelle. Paris: Éditions du Muséum, 1958, Series 7, No. 6.

Hepler, R. S., and Frank, I. M. Marihuana smoking and intraocular pressure. *Journal of the American Medical Association*, 1971, **217,** 1392.

Hernandez-Peon, R. A unitary neurophysiological model of hypnosis, dreams, hallucinations, and ESP. In R. Cavanna and M. Ullman (Eds.), *Psi and altered states of consciousness*. New York: Parapsychology Foundation, 1968.

Hinton, H. G., and Dunn, A. M. S. *Mongooses*. London: Oliver and Boyd, 1967.

Hoffer, A., and Osmond, H. *The hallucinogens*. New York: Academic Press, 1967.

Holliday, A. R., and Sigurdson, T. The effects of lysergic acid diethylamide. II: Intraocular pressure. *Proceedings of the Western Pharmacology Society*, 1965, **8,** 51–54.

Holt, R. R. Imagery: The return of the ostracized. *American Psychologist*, 1964, **12,** 254–264.

Horowitz, M. J. *Image formation and cognition*. New York: Appleton-Century-Crofts, 1970.

Horowitz, M. Unbidden images: Implications for a model of image formation. In P. Sheehan (Ed.), *The nature and function of imagery*. New York: Academic Press, 1972.

Hosko, M. J., Kochar, M. S., and Wang, R. I. H. Effects of orally administered delta-9-tetrahydrocannabinol in man. *Clinical Pharmacology and Therapeutics*, 1973, **14,** 344–352.

Huxley, A. *The doors of perception. Heaven and hell*. Middlesex: Penguin Books, 1959.

Irwin, S. Potential dangers of the hallucinogens. In J. R. Gamage and E. L. Zerkin (Eds.), *Hallucinogenic drug research: Impact on science and society*. Beloit, Wis.: Stash Press, 1970.

Jackson, B., and Reed, A. Catnip and the alteration of consciousness. *Journal of the American Medical Association*, 1969, **207,** 1349–1350.

Jackson, J. H. *Selected writings*. London: Hodder and Stoughton, 1931.

James, W. *The principles of psychology*. Vol. 1. New York: Henry Holt, 1890.

Janiger, O., and Dobkin de Rios, M. Suggestive hallucinogenic properties of tobacco. *Medical Anthropology Newsletter*, 1973, **4,** 6–11.

Jarvik, M. Drugs, hallucinations and memory. In W. Keup (Ed.), *Origin and mechanisms of hallucinations*. New York: Plenum Press, 1970.

Jung, C. G. *The archetypes and the collective unconscious*. Princeton, N.J.: Princeton University Press, 1969.

Jung, R. Neurophysiological and psychophysical correlates in vision research. In A. C. Karczmar and J. C. Eccles (Eds.), *Brain and human behavior*. New York: Springer-Verlag, 1972.

Kandinsky, V. Zur Lehre von den Hallucinationen. *Archiv für Psychiatrie und Nervenkrankeiten*, 1881, **11,** 453–464.

Kanner, L., and Schilder, P. Movements in optic images and the optic imagination of movements. *Journal of Nervous and Mental Disease*, 1930, **72,** 489–517.

Karwoski, T. F. Psychophysics and mescal intoxication. *Journal of General Psychology*, 1936, **15,** 212–220.

Keeler, M. H. Marihuana-induced hallucinations. *Diseases of the Nervous System*, 1968, **29,** 314–315.

Keeler, M. H. Klüver's mechanisms of hallucinations as illustrated by the paintings of Max Ernst. In W. Keup (Ed.), *Origin and mechanisms of hallucinations*. New York: Plenum Press, 1970.

Keeler, M. H., Ewing, J. A., and Rouse, B. A. Hallucinogenic effects of marihuana as currently used. *American Journal of Psychiatry*, 1971, **128,** 213–216.

Keller, D. L., and Umbreit, W. W. "Permanent" alteration of behavior in mice by chemical and psychological means. *Science*, 1956, **124,** 723–724.

Kirtley, D. Effects of marijuana on the imagery of a blind subject. Paper presented at the California State Psychological Association Meeting, San Diego, April 1971.

Klonoff, H., Low, M., and Marcus, A. Neuropsychological effects of marijuana. *Canadian Medical Association Journal*, 1973, **108,** 150–156, 165.

Klüver, H. Mescal visions and eidetic vision. *American Journal of Psychology*, 1926, **37,** 502–515.

Klüver, H. *Mescal: The "divine" plant and its psychological effects*. London: Kegan Paul, Trench, Trübner, 1928.

Klüver, H. *Behavior mechanisms in monkeys*. Chicago: University of Chicago Press, 1933.

Klüver, H. Mechanisms of hallucinations. In Q. McNemar and M. A. Merrill (Eds.), *Studies in personality*. New York: McGraw-Hill, 1942.

Klüver, H. *Mescal and mechanisms of hallucinations*. Chicago: University of Chicago Press, 1966.

Knauer, A., and Maloney, W. J. M. A. A preliminary note on the psychic action of mescalin, with special reference to the mechanism of visual hallucinations. *Journal of Nervous and Mental Disease*, 1913, **40,** 425–436.

Knoll, J., Vizi, E. S., and Knoll, B. Development of tolerance to some substituted amphetamines in rats, cats and rabbits. In S. B. de C. Baker (Ed.), *The correlation of adverse effects in man with observations in animals. (Proceedings of the European Society for the Study of Drug Toxicity*, 1971, **12.**) Amsterdam: Exerpta Medica, 1971.

Knoll, M., Kugler, J., Echmeier, J., and Hofer, O. Note on the spectroscopy of subjective light patterns. *Journal of Analytical Psychology*, 1962, **7,** 55–69.

Kreuscher, H. (Ed.) *Ketamine*. Berlin: Springer-Verlag, 1969.

Krill, A. F., Alpert, H. J., and Ostfeld, A. M. Effects of a hallucinogenic agent in totally blind subjects. *Archives of Ophthalmology*, 1963, **69,** 180–185.

Kruta, V. (Ed.) *The poet and the scientist. Johann Wolfgang Goethe. Jan Evangelista Purkyně*. Prague: Academia (Czechoslovak Academy of Sciences), 1968.

Kulkarni, A. S. Scratching response induced in mice by mescaline and related amphetamine derivatives. *Biological Psychiatry*, 1973, **6,** 177–180.

La Barre, W. *The peyote cult*. New York: Schocken Books, 1969.

Ladd, G. T., (1892). Contributions to the psychology of visual dreams. *Mind*, **1.** Cited in P. McKellar, *Imagination and thinking*. New York: Basic Books, 1957, 81–82.

Ladd-Franklin, C. Visible radiation from excited nerve fiber: The reddish blue arcs and the reddish blue glow of the retina. *Science*, 1927, **66,** 239–241.

Ladefoged, O. The effects of LSD, psilocybin, harmaline and amphetamine on the body temperature of para-chlorophenylalanine pretreated rats. *Archives Internationales de Pharmacodynamie et de Thérapie*, 1973, **204,** 326–332.

Lagutina, N. I., Laricheva, K. A., Mil'stein, G. I., and Norkina, L. N. Effect of D-lysergic acid diethylamide on higher nervous activity in baboons. *Federation Proceedings*, 1964, **23,** T 737.

Lambert, M., and Heckel, M. Sur la racine d'iboga et l'ibogine. *Comptes Rendus Hebdomadaires des Séances de l'Académie des Sciences*, 1901, **133,** 1236–1238.

Lane, B. I. *The mysteries of tobacco*. New York: Wiley and Putnam, 1845.

Larner, J. *The answer*. New York: Macmillan, 1968.

Lashley, K. S. Patterns of cerebral integration indicated by the scotomas of migraine. *Archives of Neurology and Psychiatry*, 1941, **46,** 331–339.

Leary, T. *Psychedelic prayers*. Kerhonkson, N.Y.: Poets Press, 1966. (a)

Leary, T. The experiential typewriter. *Psychedelic Review,* 1966, **7,** 70–85. (b)

Leary, T. Programmed communication during experiences with DMT (dimethyltryptamine). *Psychedelic Review,* 1966, **8,** 83–95. (c)

Leary, T., Metzner, R., and Alpert, R. *The psychedelic experience.* New Hyde Park, N.Y.: University Books, 1964.

Leuner, H. *Die experimentelle Psychose.* Berlin: Springer-Verlag, 1962.

Leuner, H. *The interpretation of visual hallucinations.* Basel: S. Karger, 1964.

Levi, W. M. *The pigeon.* Sumter, S.C.: Levi, 1957.

Lewin, L. *Phantastica. Die betäubenden und erregenden Genussonittel.* Berlin, 1924.

Lewin, L. *Phantastica, narcotic and stimulating drugs; their use and abuse.* English translation of second German edition. London: Kegan Paul, Trench, Trübner, 1931.

Lilly, J. C. Solitude, isolation and confinement and the scientific method. In L. Madow and L. H. Snow (Eds.), *The psychodynamic implications of physiological studies on sensory deprivation.* Springfield, Ill.: Charles C Thomas, 1970. (a)

Lilly, J. C. *Programming and metaprogramming in the human biocomputer.* Menlo Park, Calif.: Portola Institute, 1970. (b)

Lindsley, O. Operant behavior during sleep: A measure of depth of sleep. *Science,* 1957, **126,** 1290–1291.

Lindsley, O. R., Hobika, J. H., and Etsten, B. E. Operant behavior during anesthesia recovery: A continuous and objective method. *Anesthesiology,* 1961, **22,** 937–946.

Lindsley, O. R., and Contran, P. Operant behavior during EST: A measure of depth of coma. *Diseases of the Nervous System,* 1962, **23,** 407–409.

Lippman, C. W. Certain hallucinations peculiar to migraine. *Journal of Nervous and Mental Disease,* 1952, **116,** 346–351.

Lucena, J. Maconhismo e allucinacoes. *Jornal Brasileiro de Psiquiatria,* 1950, **1,** 218–227.

Ludlow, F. *The hasheesh eater.* New York: Harper and Brothers, 1857.

Lumholtz, C. The Huichol Indians of Mexico. *Bulletin of the American Museum of Natural History,* 1898, **10,** 1–14.

Lumholtz, C. Symbolism of the Huichol Indians. *Memoirs of the American Museum of Natural History,* 1900, **3,** 1–228.

Lumholtz, C. Decorative art of the Huichol Indians. *Memoirs of the American Museum of Natural History,* 1904, **3,** 279–327.

MacKenzie, N. *Dreams and dreaming.* New York: Vanguard Press, 1965.

Maclay, W. S., and Guttman, E. Mescaline hallucinations in artists. *Archives of Neurology and Psychiatry,* 1941, **45,** 130–137.

Malitz, S., Wilkens, B., and Esecover, H. A comparison of drug-induced hallucinations with those seen in spontaneously occurring psychoses. In L. J. West (Ed.), *Hallucinations.* New York: Grune & Stratton, 1962.

Marczynski, T. J. Lysergic acid diethylamide (LSD-25) mimics the effect of diffuse light input on EEG correlates of conditioned operant behavior in cats. *Experimental Neurology,* 1972, **34,** 255–263.

Marinesco, M. G. Visions colorées produites par la mescaline. *La Presse Medicale,* 1933, **41,** 1864–1866.

Marrazzi, A. S. Pharmacodynamics of hallucination. In L. J. West (Ed.), *Hallucinations.* New York: Grune & Stratton, 1962.

Marshall, C. R. An enquiry into the cause of mescal visions. *The Journal of Neurology and Psychopathology,* 1937, **17,** 289–304.

Masserman, J. H. Behavioral pharmacology in animals. In P. B. Bradley, P. Deniker, and C. Radouco-Thomas (Eds.), *Neuro-psychopharmacology.* Amsterdam: Elsevier, 1959.

Massopust, L. C., Wolin, L. R., and Albin, M. S. The effects of a new phencyclidine derivative and diazepinone derivative on the electroencephalographic and behavioral responses in the cat. *T.I.T. Journal of Life Sciences,* 1973, **3,** 1–10.

Masters, R. E. L., and Houston, J. *The varieties of psychedelic experience.* New York: Dell, 1967.

Masters, R. E. L., and Houston, J. *Psychedelic art.* New York: Grove Press, 1968.

Masters, R. E. L., and Houston, J. The altered states of consciousness induction device: Some possible uses in research and psychotherapy. (Unpublished manuscript.)

McIsaac, W. M., Fritchie, G. E., Idanpaan-Heikkila, J. E., Ho, B. T., and Englert, L. F. Distribution of marihuana in monkey brain and concomitant behavioural effects. *Nature,* 1971, **230,** 593–594.

McKellar, P. *Imagination and thinking.* New York: Basic Books, 1957.

Meduna, L. J. The carbon dioxide treatment. In *The Biology of Mental Health and Disease.* The 27th annual conference of the Milbank Memorial Fund. New York: Hoeber, 1952.

Mendell, Y. Dr. Dorrenbos cuts grass; says marihuana dangerous. *Reflector* (Mississippi State University), 1969, **1,** 81.

Metzner, R. (Ed.) *The ecstatic adventure.* New York. Macmillan, 1968.

Michaux, H. *Miserable miracle.* San Francisco: City Lights Books, 1963.

Miller, R., Hansteen, R., Adamec, C., Brewster, J., Bijou, J., Dayken, S., Farmilo, C., Hamilton, D., Link, S., Siegel, R., Willinsky, M., Mechoulam, R., and Moiseiwitsch, C. A comparison of the effects of Δ^9-THC and marihuana in humans. Unpublished commission research project. Cited in *Final Report of the Commission of Inquiry into the Non-medical Use of Drugs.* Ottawa: Information Canada, 1973.

Mintz, S., and Alpert, M. Imagery vividness, reality testing, and schizophrenic hallucinations. *Journal of Abnormal Psychology,* 1972, **79,** 310–316.

Mitchell, J. R. A psychosis among cats. (correspondence) *The Veterinary Record,* 1953, **65,** 254.

Moreau (de Tours), J. *Du hachisch et de l'alienation mentale, études psychologiques.* Paris: Librairie de Fortin, Masson, 1845.

Moskowitz, H., Sharma, S., and Schapero, M. A comparison of the effects of marijuana and alcohol on visual functions. In M. F. Lewis (Ed.), *Current research in marijuana.* New York: Academic Press, 1972.

Müller, J. (1826). *Über die phantastischen Gesichtserscheinungen.* Reprinted by J. A. Barth: Leipzig, 1968.

Naranjo, C. Psychotropic properties of the harmala alkaloids. In D. H. Efron (Ed.), *Ethnopharmacologic search for psychoactive drugs.* Washington, D.C.: Government Printing Office, 1967.

Naranjo, C. Psychological aspects of the yagé experience in an experimental setting. In M. J. Harner (Ed.), *Hallucinogens and shamanism.* New York: Oxford University Press, 1973.

Neisser, U. *Cognitive psychology.* New York: Appleton-Century-Crofts, 1967.

Neisser, U. Changing conceptions of imagery. In P. W. Sheehan (Ed.), *The function and nature of imagery.* New York: Academic Press, 1972.

Nevin, J. A., and Liebold, K. Stimulus control of matching and oddity in a pigeon. *Psychonomic Science,* 1966, **5,** 351–352.

Norton, S., and Tamburro, J. Effects of hallucinogens on spontaneous behavior patterns of animals. *Journal of Pharmacology and Experimental Therapeutics,* 1958, **122,** 57A.

Osmond, H. A review of the clinical effects of psychotomimetic agents. *Annals of the New York Academy of Sciences,* 1957, **66,** 418–434.

Oster, G. Phosphenes. *Scientific American,* 1970, **222,** 83–87.

Paivio, A. The role of imagery in learning and memory. In P. W. Sheehan (Ed.), *The function and nature of imagery.* New York: Academic Press, 1972.

Parish, E. *Hallucinations and illusions.* London: Walter Scott, 1897.

Penfield, W. *The excitable cortex in conscious man.* Springfield, Ill.: Charles C Thomas, 1958.

Penfield, W. Memory and perception. In D. A. Hamburg, K. H. Pribram, and A. J. Stunkard (Eds.), *Perception and its disorders.* Baltimore: Williams & Wilkins, 1970.

Pickens, R., and Thompson, T. Simple schedules of drug self-administration in animals. In J. M. Singh, L. H. Miller, and H. Lal (Eds.), *Drug addiction,* Vol. 1. *Experimental pharmacology,* Mount Kisco, N.Y.: Futura, 1972.

Plaut, F. *Über Halluzinosen der Syphilitiker.* Monographien aus dem Gesamtgebiete der Neurologie und Psychiatrie No. 6. Berlin: Springer-Verlag, 1913.

Pokorný, A., Význam neolitické lineárni ornamentiky pro poznáni neolitických toxikomanii a magie. *Sborník Přírodovědeckého klubu při Západomor, muzeu v Třebíči,* 1969, **7,** 34–45.

Pope, H. G. *Tabernanthe iboga:* An African narcotic plant of social importance. *Economic Botany,* 1969, **23**, 174–184.

Prince, M. *Clinical and experimental studies in personality.* Cambridge, Mass.: Sci-Art Publishers, 1939.

Purkinje, J. E. *Opera omnia.* Prague: Society of Czech Physicians, 1918, **1**, 1–162.

Pylyshyn, Z. W. What the mind's eye tells the mind's brain: A critique of mental imagery. *Psychological Bulletin,* 1973, **80**, 1–24.

Randrup, A., and Munkvad, I. Behavioural toxicity of amphetamines studied in animal experiments. In S. B. de C. Baker (Ed.), *The correlation of adverse effects in man with observations in animals. (Proceedings of the European Society for the Study of Drug Toxicity,* 1971, **12**). Amsterdam: Excerpta Medica, 1971.

Ratliff, F. On the objective study of subjective phenomena: The Purkyne Tree. In V. Kruta (Ed.), *Jan Evangelista Purkyne, 1787–1869.* Brno Universita Jana Evangelisty Purkyne, 1971.

Reher, C. E. Ketamine—"Dissociative agent" or hallucinogen? Letter to the Editor, *The New England Journal of Medicine,* 1971, **284**, 791–792.

Reichel-Dolmatoff, G. The cultural context of an aboriginal hallucinogen: *Banisteriopsis caapi.* In P. T. Furst (Ed.), *Flesh of the gods. The ritual use of hallucinogens.* New York: Praeger, 1972.

Richards, W. The fortification illusions of migraines. *Scientific American,* 1971, **225**, 89–96.

Richardson, A. *Mental imagery.* New York: Springer-Verlag, 1969.

Ritterbush, P. C. *The art of organic forms.* Washington, D.C.: Smithsonian Institution Press, 1968.

Robinson, V. *An essay on hasheesh.* New York: Dingwall-Rock, 1930.

Roman, R., and Landis, C. Hallucinations and mental imagery. *Journal of Nervous and Mental Disease,* 1945, **102**, 327–331.

Rosenthal, S. H. Persistent hallucinosis following repeated administration of hallucinogenic drugs. *American Journal of Psychiatry,* 1964, **121**, 238–244.

Rouhier. A. *La plante qui fait les yeux émerveillés; le peyotl (Echinocactus williamsii* Lem.), Paris: Doin, 1927.

Rumpf, K., Dudeck, J., Teuteberg, H., Münchhoff, W., and Nolte, H. Traumähnliche Erlebnisse bei Kurznarkosen mit Ketamine, Thiopental und Propanidid. In H. Kreuscher (Ed.), *Ketamine.* Berlin: Springer-Verlag, 1969.

Rylander, G. Stereotype behaviour in man following amphetamine abuse. In S. B. de C. Baker (Ed.), *The correlation of adverse effects in man with observations in animals. (Proceedings of the European Society for the Study of Drug Toxicity,* 1971, **12**). Amsterdam: Excerpta Medica, 1971.

Sai-Halász, A., and Endröczy, E. The effect of tryptamine derivatives on the behaviour of dogs during brain-stem stimulation. In P. B. Bradley, P. Deniker, and C. Radouco-Thomas (Eds.), *Neuro-psychopharmacology.* Amsterdam: Elsevier, 1959.

Savage, C. Variations in ego feeling induced by d-lysergic acid diethylamide (LSD-25). *Psychoanalytic Review,* 1955, **43**, 1–16.

Scheckel, C. L., Boff, E., Dahlen, P., and Smart, T. Behavioral effects in monkeys of racemates of two biologically active marijuana constituents. *Science,* 1968, **160**, 1467–1469.

Schneider, J. A., and Sigg, E. B. Neuropharmacological studies on ibogaine, an indole alkaloid with central-stimulant properties. *Annals of the New York Academy of Sciences,* 1957, **66**, 765–776.

Schultes, R. E. Hallucinogens in the Western hemisphere. In P. T. Furst (Ed.), *Flesh of the gods. The ritual use of hallucinogens.* New York: Praeger, 1972.

Scott, D. F., Davies, D. L., and Malherbe, M. E. L. Alcoholic hallucinosis. *The International Journal of the Addictions,* 1969, **4**, 319–330.

Schuster, C. R., and Thompson, T. Self-administration of and behavioral dependence on drugs. *Annual Review of Pharmacology,* 1969, **9**, 483–502.

Sedman, G. A phenomenological study of pseudohallucinations and related experiences. *Acta Psychiatrica Scandinavica,* 1966, **42**, 35–70.

Segal, S. J. Processing of the stimulus in imagery and perception. In S. J. Segal (Ed.), *Imagery. Current cognitive approaches.* New York: Academic Press, 1971.

Segal, S. J. Assimilation of a stimulus in the construction of an image: The Perky effect revisited. In P. W. Sheehan (Ed.), *The function and nature of imagery.* New York: Academic Press, 1972.

Seitz, P. F. D., and Molholm, H. B. Relation of mental imagery to hallucinations. *Archives of Neurology and Psychiatry*, 1947, **57**, 469–480.

Shader, R. I. (Ed.) *Psychiatric complications of medical drugs.* New York: Raven Press, 1972.

Sharon, D. The San Pedro cactus in Peruvian folk healing. In P. T. Furst (Ed.), *Flesh of the gods. The ritual use of hallucinogens.* New York: Praeger, 1972.

Sharpe, L. G., Otis, L. S., and Schusterman, R. J. Disruption of size discrimination in squirrel monkeys *(Saimiri sciureus)* by LSD-25. *Psychonomic Science*, 1967, **7**, 103–104.

Sheldin, M., and Wallace, D. The East Bay Chemical Philosophy Symposium. Unpublished manuscript, 1972.

Sheldin, M., Wallechinsky, D., and Salyer, S. (Eds.) *Laughing gas (nitrous oxide).* San Francisco: And/Or Press, 1973.

Shaw, J. *Tobacco: Its history nature, and effects on the body and mind.* New York: Fowlers and Wells, 1849.

Shulgin, A. T. Some qualitative properties of the psychotomimetics. *Neurosciences Research Program Bulletin*, 1970, **8** (1), 72–78.

Siegel, R. K. Effects of *Cannabis sativa* and lysergic acid diethylamide on a visual discrimination task in pigeons. *Psychopharmacologia (Berl.)*, 1969, **15**, 1–8.

Siegel, R. K., and Poole, J. Psychedelic-induced social behavior in mice: A preliminary report. *Psychological Reports*, 1969, **25**, 704–706.

Siegel, R. K. Discrimination learning between and within complex displays. Unpublished doctoral dissertation, Dalhousie University, September, 1970. (a)

Siegel, R. K. Apparent movement detection in the pigeon. *Journal of the Experimental Analysis of Behavior*, 1970, **14**, 93–97. (b)

Siegel, R. K. Cannabis-induced visual imagery. A report prepared for the Commission of Inquiry into the Non-medical Use of Drugs, Ottawa, Canada, December, 1971. (a)

Siegel, R. K. Apparent movement and real movement detection in the pigeon: Stimulus generalization. *Journal of the Experimental Analysis of Behavior*, 1971, **16**, 189–192. (b)

Siegel, R. K., and Jarvik, M. E. Evidence for state-dependent learning with mescaline in a passive avoidance task. *Psychonomic Science*, 1971, **25**, 260–261.

Siegel, R. K., Lebowitz, M., and Jarvik, M. E. Ketamine-induced visual imagery in surgical and non-surgical patients. Unpublished study, 1971.

Siegel, R. K., Miller, R. D., and Hansteen, R. W. Cannabis-induced visual imagery. Unpublished Commission research project, 1971. Prepared for the Commission of Inquiry into the Non-medical Use of Drugs, Ottawa, Canada. Cited in *Cannabis*, Ottawa: Information Canada, 1972.

Siegel, R. K., and Jarvik, M. E. Hallucinogen-induced responses in mice: Measurement and analysis. Paper presented at the Fifth International Congress for Pharmacology, San Francisco, July 23–28, 1972.

Siegel, R. K., Lee, M. A., and Jarvik, M. E. A device for analyzing drug-induced responses in freely moving mice. *Journal of the Experimental Analysis of Behavior*, 1972, **18**, 415–418.

Siegel, R. K. An ethologic search for self-administration of hallucinogens. *The International Journal of the Addictions*, 1973, **8**, 373–393. (a)

Siegel, R. K. Visual imagery constants: Drug-induced changes in trained and untrained observers. *Proceedings, 81st Annual Convention, APA*, 1973, 1033–1034. (b)

Siegel, R. K., Brewster, J. M., and Jarvik, M. E. An observational study of hallucinogen-induced behavior in unrestrained *Macaca mulatta*. *Psychopharmacologia (Berl.)*, 1974, **40**, 211–223.

Sikes, S. K. *The natural history of the African elephant.* London, Weidenfeld and Nicolson, 1971.

Simon, P. M. *Le monde des Rêves.* Paris: Librairie J. B. Baillière, 1888.

Simoni-Abbat, M. *Collections Huichol.* Paris: Muséum National d'Histoire Naturelle, 1963.

Singer, J. L. *Daydreaming.* New York: Random House, 1966.

Skinner, B. F. *Beyond freedom and dignity.* New York: Knopf, 1971.

Smith, P. B. *Chemical glimpses of paradise.* Springfield, Ill.: Charles C Thomas, 1972.

Smythies, J. R. The stroboscopic patterns. III. Further experiments and discussion. *Journal of Psychology*, 1960, **51**, 247–255.

Smythies, J. R., and Sykes, E. A. The effect of mescaline upon the conditioned avoidance response in the rat. *Psychopharmacologia (Berl.)*, 1964, **6**, 163–172.

Smythies, J. R., Johnston, V. S., and Bradley, R. J. Behavioral models of psychoses. *British Journal of Psychiatry*, 1969, **115**, 55–68.

Smythies, J. R. The mode of action of psychotomimetic drugs. *Neurosciences Research Program Bulletin*, 1970, **8**.

Somjen, G. *Sensory coding in the mammalian nervous system*. New York: Appleton-Century-Crofts, 1972.

Spindler, G. D. Personality and peyotism in Menomini Indian acculturation. *Psychiatry*, 1952, **15**, 151–159.

Spindler, G. D. *Sociocultural and psychological processes in Menomini acculturation*. Berkeley: University of California Press, 1955.

Stein, J. Pathologie der Wahrnehmung. I. Über die Veränderung der Sinnesleistungen und die Entstehung von Trugauhrnehmungen. In O. Bumke (Ed.), *Handbuch der Geisteskrankheiten*. Berlin: Springer-Verlag, 1928.

Steinberg, H. "Abnormal behaviour" induced by nitrous oxide. *British Journal of Psychology*, 1956, **47**, 183–194.

Stern, M., and Robbins, E. S. Clinical diagnosis and treatment of psychiatric disorders subsequent to use of psychedelic drugs. In R. E. Hicks and P. J. Fink (Eds.), *Psychedelic drugs*. New York: Grune & Stratton, 1969.

Stockings, G. T. A clinical study of the mescaline psychosis, with special reference to the mechanism of the genesis of schizophrenic and other psychotic states. *Journal of Mental Science*, 1940, **86**, 29–47.

Sturtevant, F. M., and Drill, V. A. Effects of mescaline in laboratory animals and influence of ataraxics on mescaline-response. *Proceedings of the Society of Experimental Biology and Medicine*, 1956, **92**, 383–387.

Sudilovsky, A., Nelson, L., and Ellinwood, E. H. Amphetamine dyskinesia: A direct observational study in cats. In J. M. Singh and H. Lal (Eds.), *Drug addiction: Behavioral and clinico-toxicological aspects*, Vol. 3. Mount Kisco, N.Y.: Futura, in press.

Szuman, S. Analiza formalna 1 psychologiczna widzén meskainowych. *Kwartalnik Psychologiczny*, 1930, **1**, 156–212.

Tart, C. Scientific foundations for the study of altered states of consciousness. *The Journal of Transpersonal Psychology*, 1971, **3**, 93–124.

Taylor, N. *Plant drugs that changed the world*. New York: Dodd, Mead, 1965.

Thurlow, H. J., and Girvin, J. P. Use of anti-epileptic medication in treating "flashbacks" from hallucinogenic drugs. *Canadian Medical Association Journal*, 1971, **105**, 947–948.

Todd, N. B. The catnip response. Unpublished doctoral dissertation. Harvard University, 1963.

Turner, W. J., and Merlis, S. Effect of some indolealkylamines on man. *AMA Archives of Neurology and Psychiatry*, 1959, **81**, 121–129.

von Uexküll, J. *Umwelt und Imenwelt der Tiere*. Berlin: Springer-Verlag, 1921.

Vuillon-Cacciuttolo, G., and Balzamo, E. Effets de la psilocyne sur le comportement, la photosensibilité et l'EEG du singe *Papio papio*. *Compte Rendu de la Société de Biologie*, 1971, **165** (12), 2377–2379.

Wallace, A. F. C. Cultural determinants of response to hallucinatory experience. *AMA Archives of General Psychiatry*, 1959, **1**, 58–69.

Wasson, R. G. *Soma, divine mushroom of immortality*. New York: Harcourt Brace Jovanovich, 1968.

Wasson, V. P., and Wasson, R. G. *Mushrooms, Russia, and history*. Vols. I and II. New York: Pantheon, 1957.

Watts, A. W. *The joyous cosmology*. New York: Vintage, 1962.

Webster, C. D., Willinsky, M. D., Herring, B. S., and Walters, G. C. Effects of l-Δ^1-tetrahydrocannabinol on temporally spaced responding and discriminated Sidman avoidance behaviour in rats. *Nature*, 1971, **232**, 498–501.

Weckowicz, T. Animal studies of hallucinogenic drugs. In A. Hoffer and H. Osmond, *The hallucinogens*. New York: Academic Press, 1967.

Weil-Malherbe, H., and Szara, S. I. *The biochemistry of functional and experimental psychoses.* Springfield, Ill.: Charles C Thomas, 1971.

Weinberger, L. M., and Grant, F. C. Visual hallucinations and their neuro-optical correlates. *Ophthalmologic Reviews*, 1940, **23**, 166–199.

Weiss, B., and Laties, V. G. Reconciling the effects of amphetamine on human and animal behavior. In S. B. de C. Baker (Ed.), *The correlation of adverse effects in man with observations in animals. (Proceedings of the European Society for the Study of Drug Toxicity*, 1971, **12**). Amsterdam: Excerpta Medica, 1971.

West, L. J. A general theory of hallucinations and dreams. In L. J. West (Ed.), *Hallucinations,* New York: Grune & Stratton, 1962.

Whalen, R. E., and Luttge, W. G. *p*-Chlorophenylalanine methyl ester: An aphrodisiac. *Science,* 1970, **169**, 1000–1001.

White, H. E., and Levatin, P. "Floaters" in the eye. Scientific American, 1962, **206**, 119–127.

Wikler, A. Clinical and electroencephalographic studies on the effects of mescaline, *n*-allylnormorphine and morphine in man. *Journal of Nervous and Mental Disease,* 1954, **120**, 157–175.

Winters, W. D., and Wallach, M. B. Drug-induced states of CNS excitation: A theory of hallucinosis. In D. H. Efron (Ed.), *Psychotomimetic drugs.* New York: Raven Press, 1970.

Winters, W. D., Ferrar-Allado, T., Guzman-Flores, C., and Alcaraz, M. The cataleptic state induced by ketamine: A review of the neuropharmacology of anesthesia. *Neuropharmacology,* 1972, **11**, 303–315.

Wise, G. N., Dollery, C. T., and Henkind, P. *The retinal circulation.* New York: Harper & Row, 1971.

Wolfe, T. *The electric Kool-aid acid test.* New York: Farrar, Straus and Giroux, 1968.

Wolin, S. J. Hallucinations during experimental intoxication. In M. M. Gross (Ed.), *Alcohol intoxication and withdrawal. Experimental Studies. Advances in Experimental Medicine and Biology.* New York: Plenum Press, 1973, **35**, 305–319.

Wolin, S. J., and Mello, N. K. The effects of alcohol on dreams and hallucinations in alcohol addicts. In F. A. Seixas and S. Eggleston (Eds.), Alcoholism and the central nervous system. *Annals of the New York Academy of Sciences,* 1973, **215**, 266–302.

Woods, J. H., and Downs, D. A. The psychopharmacology of cocaine. In National Commission on Marihuana and Drug Abuse, *Drug use in America: Problem in perspective.* Appendix. Vol. 1: Patterns and consequences of drug use. Washington, D.C.: Government Printing Office, 1973.

Woolley, D. W. Production of abnormal (psychotic?) behavior in mice with lysergic acid diethylamide, and its partial prevention with cholinergic drugs and serotonin. *Proceedings of the National Academy of Sciences (U.S.),* 1955, **41**, 338–344.

Yanagita, T., Takahashi, S., Ishida, K., and Funamoto, H. Voluntary inhalation of volatile anesthetics and organic solvents by monkeys. *Japanese Journal of Clinical Pharmacology,* 1970, **1**, 13–16.

Zador, J. Meskalinwirkung bei Störungen des optischen Systems. *Zeitschrift für die gesamte Neurologie und Psychiatrie,* 1930, **127**, 30–107.

Zimmerberg, B., Glick, S. D., and Jarvik, M. E. Impairment of recent memory by marihuana and THC in rhesus monkeys. *Nature,* 1971, **233**, 343–345.

Zubek, J. P. (Ed.) *Sensory deprivation: Fifteen years of research.* New York: Appleton-Century-Crofts, 1969.

Zuckerman, M., and Cohen, N. Sources of reports of visual and auditory sensations in perceptual isolation experiments. *Psychological Bulletin,* 1964, **62**, 1–20.

CHAPTER FIVE

HALLUCINATIONS: AN INFORMATION– PROCESSING APPROACH

MARDI J. HOROWITZ, M.D.

At the heart of the riddle of hallucinations are four properties that are present in "ideal" or prototypical hallucinations and are used in defining these phenomena. A careful examination of each property may provide an explanation of hallucinations in terms of information-processing theory. These properties, which are discussed sequentially, are:

1. *Image representation.* The hallucinatory episode is a conscious awareness in which information is represented by means of imagery.

2. *Increased internal input.* The image representations are unusually intense derivations from the inner realm of information.

3. *Impaired information processing.* The representations are appraised incorrectly, as if they were derivatives of the immediately outer realm of information.

4. *Impaired control.* The episode occurs intrusively (without a sense of conscious intent, or a realization that one is thinking rather than perceiving).

These properties are modeled schematically in Fig. 1. Before discussing them we present their limitations, historical background, and definitions.

Focusing on the obvious definitional properties of hallucinations makes the hallucinatory experience seem less exciting or mysterious than it often is in observation or subjective episode. This dryness is acceptable because one aim of this chapter is the demystification of hallucinations without rejecting the existence of such phenomena. A second hazard: the editors have licensed authors to speculate. The following text contains speculative assertions; the examples given are illustrations, not proof. Similarly, references are not extensive. (Review of the relevant literature and meager "proofs" are published elsewhere [Horowitz, 1970].) Because of the author's interest in visual events, visual hallucinations provide the focus and prescribe the limitations. Many remarks, however, are pertinent to other modalities.

The information-processing approach has been advocated as a general

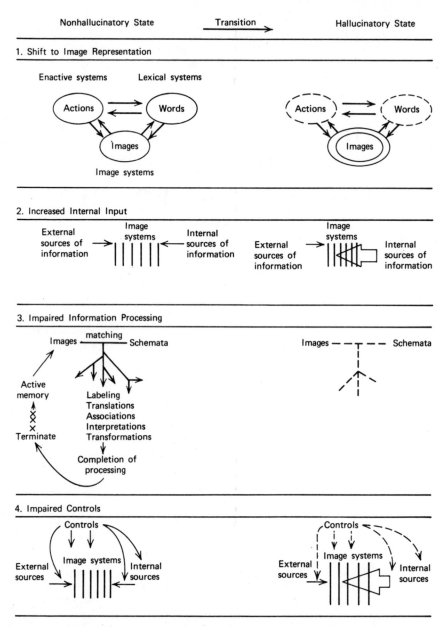

Figure 1   Schematization of the four properties of prototypical hallucinations.

paradigm for the behavioral sciences and psychodynamics by Miller et al. (1960), Neisser (1967), Klein (1967), and Peterfreund (1971). This approach does not contradict other explanatory systems. A starving man hallucinates a turkey dinner and we interpret it as a wish fulfillment. An electrode stimulates the temporal lobe of an epileptic patient and he reports the hallucination of a park scene. This event is caused by an alteration in brain electrochemistry. These familiar explanations are not conflictual: the turkey hallucination may have biological determinants, such as hypoglycemia; the park scene may have psychological determinants in that it might fulfill a wish to be elsewhere than in surgery. The information-processing approach does not conflict with biological or motivational explanations. It focuses on where the information about the turkey and the park comes from and how it is encoded, transformed, and interpreted.

Background. With the development of psychoanalytic theory, a strong effort was directed toward explaining the meaning of hallucinatory content. Meaning was found in the memory sources of the image, in the drive motivation for hallucination, in the psychodynamics of the process, and in reactions to the episode. As a result, the symbolic basis of hallucinatory and dream images has been reported in a large psychoanalytic literature by followers of both Jung and Freud.

More recently, the development of neuroscience has encouraged a focus on the electrical and physiochemical conditions that may prevail in association with the subjective experience of hallucinatory states. Such studies may one day lead to predictive knowledge about *when* hallucinations will occur. But the day they will lead to knowledge about *what* will be hallucinated seems to be much farther off—farther off, indeed, than suggested by the initial hopes of such investigators as Penfield (1958) that memory "engrams" might be localized at a particular anatomical area. If localization were precise, "engrams" could be activated into hallucinations by some kind of stimulation, just as a phonograph needle set on a given groove might lead to a particular sound. Contrary to some popular belief, experimental evidence, including that of Penfield (Penfield, 1966; Penfield and Rassmussen, 1950) and others (Horowitz et al., 1968) does *not* support that view. The *what* of hallucinations will be harder to predict than the *when* on the basis of evidence from electrochemical data.

Whatever the meaning of the content, and whatever the material substrates of a conscious episode, there are the experiential qualities that determine what label will be attached to the event, whether "percept," "thought," or "hallucination," by whoever is interpreting the experience (self or other). First, we define the label "hallucination," as it is used in this chapter; then we consider the relevant experiential qualities.

Definitions. Discussion is not limited to the strict, standard definition of hallucination because hallucinatory experiences are one among many forms of image thinking. The varieties blend together without clear distinction except in extreme instances. Table 1 explains this further by categorizing visual events as suggested elsewhere, since analogous categorizations could be assumed for events in other sensory modes (Horowitz, 1970).

Hallucinations are images based on immediately internal sources of information, which are appraised as if they came from immediately external sources of information. A close relative of the hallucinatory experience is the pseudohallucination, an image phenomenon in which the representations, based on internal information, are uncommonly vivid yet lack the sense of reality found in "ideal" hallucinatory experiences. An alternate definition of pseudohallucination is that the person responds emotionally as if the image were real, although in terms of cognitive appraisal, he knows it is not. *Note that these two definitions are only points*

TABLE 1.   CATEGORIES AND TYPES OF IMAGES

A.   Images Categorized by Vividness
    1.   Hallucination
    2.   Pseudohallucination
    3.   Thought image
    4.   Unconscious image
B.   Images Categorized by Context
    1.   Hypnagogic or hypnopompic image
    2.   Dream image; nightmare
    3.   Psychedelic image
    4.   Flashbacks
    5.   Dream scintillations
C.   Images Categorized by Interaction with Perceptions
    1.   Illusion
    2.   Perceptual distortion
    3.   Synesthesia
    4.   Déjà vu
    5.   Negative hallucination
    6.   Afterimage
D.   Images Categorized by Content
    1.   Memory image; eidetic image
    2.   Imaginary image
    3.   Entoptic image
    4.   Body image; body schema experience
    5.   Phantom limb
    6.   Paranormal hallucination
    7.   Imaginary companion
    8.   Number and diagram forms

along a dimension of experience, a dimension that is itself a composite including attributes of representational modality, vividness, intensity, appraisal, emotional reaction, and volitional control. For brevity, this can be called the "vividness" dimension. Other points on the vividness dimension are thought images and unconscious images.

Dimensions other than vividness include the degree of interaction with perception, the type of content, and the general context in which the experience occurs. "Degree of interaction with perception" refers to the extent to which an image experience is independent of or interactive with information derived from the external environment. The other conventional labels of image experiences that might fit in the "interaction with perception" dimension, include perceptual distortions, synesthesia, *déjà vu,* negative hallucinations, and afterimages. The "ideal" hallucination, according to Esquirol's (1838) strict definition, is independent of immediate external information except as external information is "negatively hallucinated" to allow conceptual "space" for (the externalized) information of internal origin. But clinicians do not adhere to this strict definition, and many experiences labeled as hallucinations would be called illusions or pseudohallucinations with stricter labeling.

The third dimension includes common labels of image experience based on types of content. For example, when someone reports seeing a ghost, he is said to have had a "paranormal hallucination." If he reports seeing himself entire, an "impossible" direct perception without mirrors or graphic tools, he is said to have experienced an "autoscopic phenomenon."

These labels of content interact with typologies on the "vividness" dimension forming composite terms, such as autoscopic thought images, autoscopic pseudohallucinations, or autoscopic hallucinations. But, as it actually happens in clinical judgments, the more unusual the content of experience reported, the more likely the label "hallucination" will be applied. For example, if a man smells of alcohol, says "I see pink elephants," and does not add details, he is likely to be labeled "hallucinatory," perhaps erroneously, without much ado about "thought images" or "pseudohallucinations."

The "smell of alcohol" leads into the fourth dimension, context of experience. A given mental event will mean different things to a person, depending on when it occurs. An hallucination of a monster, for example, may be unsettling to a pilot while he is alert and landing an airplane in the fog. The "identical" experience (same content, same vividness, same degree of interaction with perception) during dreaming sleep may mean little to him. Similarly, the "monster" experience while going to sleep, waking up, intoxicated, delirious, meditating, or after a horror movie has quite different implications. Some of the conventional labels that are based on context include "psychedelic" images, dreams, hypnagogic or hypnopompic events, and flashback images or hallucinations.

To repeat and summarize, an "ideal hallucination" is an image experience in which there is a discrepancy between subjective experience and actual reality. The information is entirely from internal sources, but the episode is not so appraised by the self. The image seems strange and vivid and appears to have entered the mind without conscious intent. Such experiences occur. But experiences further away from "ideal" on one or more of the foregoing dimensions are more frequent. The following discussion is not restricted to "ideal" hallucinatory experiences but includes episodes that by strict definition might be called pseudohallucinations, illusions, or hypnagogic events.

One reason the concept of hallucination has implied extreme forms of image phenomenon, and the shadings into other types of experiences have been ignored, is a tendency toward horrification or romanticization. Since these two divergent types of mystification tend to separate hallucinations from other forms of thought experience, they merit brief acknowledgment.

One "push" is from the traditional and conservative horror of deviant behavior and lapses in control. This results in extreme attitudes such as those which imply that hallucinations are signs of insanity, demonic possession, or degeneracy. The second push is from radical wishes for an altogether new "way" to something beyond all known forms of thinking. Here, the hallucinatory experience is a potential source of profound, transcendental, redemptive, and transformative knowledge. In contrast to such motives for exaggeration of reports of hallucinations, an hallucination can be seen as an understandable and even ordinary form of thought by discussing the four rather obvious determinants of the experience: the use or activation of the image system of representation, the intensification of internal input into the image system, the impairment of information processing of the experience, and the alteration in cognitive control over image formation.

DETERMINANTS OF HALLUCINATORY EXPERIENCES

The Activation of an Image System of Representation.   If hallucinations are to be considered a form of thinking, they must be compared with other forms of thinking for similarities and differences. Hallucinations, as defined earlier, are one form of image representation, and image representation can be contrasted with other systems for representation of thought (Horowitz, 1967; 1970). I have modified Bruner's (1964) fundamental concept and categorized three basic modes of representation. The following excerpts on the enactive, image, and lexical systems of representation are from a recent detailed examination of the topic (Horowitz, 1972a).

Enactive Thought

Infants begin with innate motor response systems. These rudiments of thought are then modified by interaction with the environment. A memory of a reflex response such as withdrawal from pain is retained, and this memory is a new patterning because it establishes associations between response and effect of response on stimulus. The recorded motor action plan will tend to be reactivated in similar sensory situations.

Later, trial action may take place through minor movements. Competing response tendencies can be compared, and the most appropriate response selected for major movements. These trial actions, through anticipatory tensing of various muscle groups, may be regarded as thinking by enactive representation. The memory of information capable of transformation into enactive representations would grow from two sources: the memory of motor actions by the self which have a successful effect, and the retention of mimicry responses to the motor activity of someone else (Schilder, 1935).

Image Representation

Images allow continued information processing after perceptual events. In this process, sets of information derived from perception, memory, thinking, and fantasy are combined, compared and recombined. There are separable subsystems of image representation based on the separate sensory systems of organization. Visual images will provide the main illustrations although many of the concepts would also apply to auditory, olfactory, gustatory, and tactile–kinesthetic image systems.

Skill at refiguration through image formation allows one to review information for new meanings, to contemplate objects in their absence, and to seek new similarities and differences. Skill at conceptual manipulation by formation of visual images is useful to architects, painters, and surgeons, and to psychoanalysts during dream interpretation. Skill at auditory image formation is useful in poetry and music, kinesthetic imagery in dance, gustatory imagery in cooking, and so forth.

Visual images are excellent for representation of information about the form and spatial relationships of objects. As Freud (1900) demonstrated for the plastic properties of dream imagery, this makes for ease in the shifts of emphasis used to accomplish symbolization, condensation, and displacement. One can "play around" with the meanings of images. Words (and enactions) can be "played around" with too but, in the case of words, the play is often in the form of auditory or visual images of words (e.g. rhyme, rebus).

It is well known that images are useful for expressing the immediate quality and degree of emotion. This is especially true of complicated affective states which are hard to articulate. For example, a patient's sense of psychic disintegration can be visually symbolized as fragmentation or loss of cohesion of his body, an object, or a landscape.

Lexical Thought

The lexical mode of representation is so familiar and yet so highly complex that only a few statements will be made to orient the place of the lexical system in the model of various modes of representation.

The relationship between words and what they signify is established in the course of human development. The child moves beyond the use of interpretation of sounds, inflections, and tonalities to include words as a means of thinking in the absence of real objects, and in the absence of intense images of objects. The acquisition of lexical representation allows progression to new levels of conceptualization, abstraction, and reasoning.

In the present model, the lexical system is regarded as an epigenetic development from the earlier modes of enactive and image representation, in a manner similar to Erikson's epigenesis of modes in zonal development (Erikson, 1950). The enactive and image modes also continue an epigenetic development fostered by the acquisition of lexical capacity. "Pure" lexical representation is conceptualized as actionless (no subvocal speech) and imageless (no auditory, visual, or kinesthetic accompaniments). But such "purity" is seldom found. Rather, there are conscious experiences that are relatively more or less "purely lexical" in representational quality (pp. 797–805).

Hallucination as Image Thinking. One of the obvious determinants of "hallucination" is the representation of thought in an image rather than an enactive or lexical mode. The experience may also be an "orchestration" of representations in several image modes, such as combined auditory and visual representations.

Let us suppose that an image system can be activated by physiological or psychological changes. *High activations of an image system relative to the level of activation of lexical systems may be one way to predispose a person toward hallucination.* As a first illustration let us consider the effects of electrochemical stimulation anywhere along the tract from eyes to cortex. Such irritants or stimulants usually give rise to simple sensations of some description.

One illustration is the work of Knoll and his co-workers (Knoll et al., 1962, 1963) who continued the nineteenth-century work of Volta, Purkinje, and von Helmholtz by studying the effects of stimulation of the optic system. The experiments involved placing electrodes on the eyes, temples, or occiputs of subjects, and passing a small current between the electrodes. This resulted in a marked increase in the conscious experience of visual images, images that were often "perceptual" in terms of subjective quality. The image experiences were flashes of colored light, or elementary to complex figures of geometrical quality. Similar effects, that is, sensations of geometrical designs, can be produced simply by photostimulation of a flickering sort, especially if the frequency is slowly altered between 10 and 80 flashes per second (Horowitz, 1967).

Similar visual images may be produced by electrical, chemical, or mechanical stimulation anywhere along the optical pathways from the retinae to the calcarine cortex and other cortical areas of the brain. The more "cortical," however, the greater the likelihood of more elaborate images, including images of meaningful objects such as faces, animals, and scenes. Penfield and his co-workers stimulated the exposed brain of persons with intractable temporal-lobe epilepsy undergoing surgical treatment (Penfield and Rasmussen, 1950; Penfield and Jasper, 1954; Penfield, 1966). Since the procedure was done under local anesthetic, the patients were conscious. Depending on localizations of brain stimulation, subjects reported image sensations in various modes. The visual events included vivid and hallucinatory experiences of people and things.

An increase of visual experience may also occur with subcortical electrical stimulation, at least in persons with temporal-lobe epilepsy studied or treated by means of depth electrodes (Horowitz et al., 1968). The latter findings suggest that the visual events were not so much reactivation of particular memories as the result of a sudden increase in image thinking (Mahl et al., 1964; Horowitz and Adams, 1970).

The point is that the system for visual representation can be stimulated in the absence of external objects. When the system substrates are activated, more conscious visual image experiences occur. The same would hold true for other modes of image representations. *Such heightening of one representational system relative to others might give a quasi-perceptual quality to the resultant mental content, hence might contribute to qualities that obtain, in composite, a label like "hallucination."*

Although separable modes of representation have been defined, ordinary cognitive experience consists of such fluid translation across modes that rather than distinct cleavages, there is an "orchestration" of representation in multiple modes. But let us suppose some sudden change activates an image system of representation relative to the lexical system. *The factors leading to activation of the image representational system may at the same time reduce sequential processing capacity, a capacity necessary for coherent organization of information in the lexical system. Were this so, information represented with increased intensity in the image representational system would be inaccurately and poorly translated into the lexical system. Image representations would be experienced consciously as estranged from the usual "orchestration" of thought, since accurate word meanings would not be available. This "standing alone" quality of the images would resemble that of unlabeled percepts.*

Psychological Motives for Shifts to Image Representation. If changes in physiological substrates can change functional capacity and interrelationship of representational systems, so too can changes in psychological motives. Without delving too far into drives or defensive motives for the use of one representational system or another, one can think of the utilities of each representational system. The properties of an emerging set of ideas and feelings may direct the choice of the representational system that will be activated and entered by this information. The image system has particular utility for representation of certain ideas and feelings, especially those involved in self-object aims and fears. Sudden or strong emergence of these ideas and feelings may provoke a shift in state from a relative dominance of lexical representation to relative dominance of visual images. Following is a previously described means of conceptualizing such psychological "utilities" of image representation.

Because images are so evocative of emotion, selective image formation can be used to modify or transform emotional and motivational states. Signal anxiety or a sense of danger can be activated by formation of threatening images, libidinal tension can be increased or decreased by erotic images, anger can be fostered or discharged by images of insult and outrage. In psychoanalytic work we are perhaps most alert to the defensive uses of images to transform emotional states, as when a patient forms anger-provoking images in order to become angry and thereby ward off the experience of fear or guilt (Jones, 1929).

Visual images allow immediate depiction of objects in relationship because of the simultaneous organization of information in a single image. The objects of greatest emotional importance we usually characterize as self and other. Even a single image can instantly show self and object in some kind of transaction. The transactions and images that are associated with important drive derivatives will be repeated and, with repetition, will gain in structural clarity and development so that they come to act as organizers of new information.

Such schematic images can, for discussion, be considered as two-person dyads (Perry, 1970). As an example, consider a sadomasochistic image which depicts an aggressor hurting a victim in some particular way. The sadomasochistic person who habitually uses this image schemata in fantasy or as a mode for interpreting current real experiences may identify himself at different times with different roles of the dyad. When he experiences some version of this repetitive image, he sometimes links himself conceptually with the aggressor, sometimes with the victim. If one role is anxiety-provoking, the other role can be chosen for self-representation in order to reduce anxiety. This role reversal may still lead to some wish fulfillment because in childhood development persons learn both roles and wish sets in Oedipal dyads. If either role is dangerous because of fear or guilt, then an undoing defense can be accomplished by shifting the designation of self from role to role and back.

One important aspect of image representation of object relationships is that the identity of the person need not necessarily be applied to *either* role. In other words, the person may experience the image without awareness as to who is hurt, who hurting. Guilt or fear can be averted, since the responsible person and the injured person are not the self or a particular other. Lexical representation, with its primarily sequential organization, identifies persons more clearly because word names are used. Defensive operations tend to be also serial (if repression fails) and involve shifts in identification such as "I hurt her, no, she hurts me." With such clarity of identity designation, the defensive operations are in danger of creating self-observable contradictions so that the aim, which is hurting, is kept relatively ambiguous. In image representation, the aim can be clear because the name is ambiguous. The fluidity and ambiguity of identification in image representation may be one reason that this system may have a greater escape from censorship than the lexical system (Horowitz, 1972a, pp. 801–802).

Censorship may, of course, be set aside to accomplish a purpose. *The concrete and all-at-once object depiction, the ambiguity of self, and the resemblance to perceptual experience of image representations also contribute to their well-known wish-fulfillment capacity (Freud, 1900). That is, images can substitute, partially, for immediately unavailable external objects in the world of "as if" fantasy.*

Habitual Experience of Images.   So far, we have engaged in speculations about upsurges in the activation of image systems relative to activation or degree of representation in nonimage modes. How such emergence of image representations would be experienced by a person depends on how it compared with his or her ordinary consciousness of thought representations. As it happens, not all persons have the same kind of "ordinary" conscious experience of thought. Some are habitual imagers; others find image formation a strange experience.

In earlier days, as during the turn of the century when research in psychology focused heavily on thought processes, it was believed that all thought was represented in some form of imagery. In fact, an early personality typology was based on how persons differed according to their habitual image mode of thought. There would thus be "audiles," "visiles," "kinesthetics" and so on (Betts, 1909; Galton, 1919). Now it appears that there are only a few persons whose thoughts move primarily in a single mode of image representation, like Luria's mnemonist (1968). The main difference is simply that some persons have more intense or more frequent use of all image modes of representation and others have only dim or scanty use of image modes (Sheehan and Neisser, 1969).

The most intriguing aspect of the visual mode of representation is, after all, the surprise a person may have on contemplating these forms of self-generated thought. Some romanticism about this is all right because a phenomenon such as a parade of pictures in the mind's eye is remarkable to all who experience it. The images flow effortlessly without volitional direction, and conceptual understanding of what it all means is often impossible. I have now seen a few persons who have such experiences *continuously* in ordinary wakefulness. They describe them as a sense of internal "movies," often with several different "screens" going on simultaneously (see Luria, 1968, and McKellar, 1957). Many more persons can "turn it on" at will, perhaps by closing their eyes and avoiding plans for thought.

Freud and Jung capitalized on such "freedom" from planfulness in their use of image formation to subvert censorship. Freud (Breuer and Freud, 1895) would place his hand on a patient's forehead and "command" him or her to have and report visual pictures when he released the pressure. Jung developed an "active imagination" technique in which he told patients to "tune out conscious thought and "tune in" on the flow of mental pictures (Adler, 1967).

Probably all persons can have such flows of uncontrolled images by entering what Kubie (1958) has called the "preconscious stream." But only a few persons are subjectively involved in nonvolitional series of images much of the time. Others can enter and leave this state deliberately. Some persons, however, are unfamiliar with such flows of imagery. Were the latter to have a sudden experience of such states (as in hypnagogic reveries, dream scintillations, or other unexpected shifts to use of image representation), they might become frightened about what such novel (to them) experiences mean—"going insane," "losing control," "thoughts running away with me." . . . The same subjective experience does not scare a habitué. It may be quite frightening and strange to those who ordinarily do not experience such a flow of involuntary images. *Because of their emotional and evaluative response, neophytes may experience or describe the phenomenon in such a way that they or others would label it as hallucinatory.*

Some data are perhaps supportive of such a line of reasoning. Psychotic hallucinations were studied by Cohen (1938), using the Griffitts word-image association test for prevailing mode of concrete images. In the Griffitts (1924) test, a subject is given a phrase and asked to report the content and sensory mode of his intrapsychic response. For example, the stimulus could be "whistle of a train" and the subject would report whether she had an auditory image response, such as hearing the whistle, or a visual image, such as seeing a train. The results were scored in terms of the percentage of responses in each sensory mode of thought images. Cohen contrasted schizophrenic patients who had reported hallucinations in different sense modes with normal subjects who did not report hallucinations. He found that the subgroup with visual hallucinations had fewer visual thought images than the group average. Similarly, those persons with a history of auditory hallucinations had fewer than average auditory thought images in associational response to stimuli.

In 1945 Roman and Landis reported another study correlating style of mental images with the modality of reported hallucinations. A standardized psychiatric interview focused on self-reports of the subjective intensity of various modes of images. They reported data only on auditory and visual hallucinations, since these were most prevalent. Like Cohen, these investigators concluded that the results contradicted the hypothesis that hallucinations are exaggerations or projections of the person's usual thought images.

Based on these previous studies, Seitz and Molholm (1947) examined persons with schizophrenia, persons with alcoholic hallucinations, and normal controls. They used the same test of concrete images developed by Griffitts and used by Cohen. In patients with auditory hallucinations, the mean percentage of auditory image responses to stimuli was less than the percentage in patients with no hallucinations. Similar results occurred in patients with visual hallucinations, who gave fewer visual responses than patients without visual hallucinations. Interestingly, the numbers in the percentage data were quite similar to those reported earlier by Cohen. Seitz and Molholm concluded that "one of the factors responsible for auditory hallucinations is relatively deficient auditory imagery." This conclusion is not warranted because it implies an undemonstrated causality. Nonetheless, such data may indicate that persons with less flexible controls over a given mode tend to experience mental episodes in that mode as un-self-generated; they may describe them in a manner that labels them "hallucinations."

The "less flexible controls" over a given mode are meant to imply both an inability to form images at will and an inability to avoid forming images of warded-off ideas and feelings. Because of the absence of flexible controls, such persons might tend to inhibit an entire representational system because they cannot prevent representation of specific contents predisposed to expression in that system. This would be especially true if the subjects had already experienced frightening images in a particular mode: when tested for associations, they would tend to inhibit that mode. In intensive single case studies of hallucinating patients, even after the phase of hallucinations, I have used the Griffitts image association test. I found this to be the case: in the mode of hallucination (visual in my studies) the person was less flexible in association. He either inhibited response (e.g., "I can't") or had an intrusive response related to warded-off ideas and feelings. Summary of data from groups of such patients would give low percentages in the "dangerous" mode, since intrusive responses are counted as any other image response, and inhibitions are counted as nonmodal responses.

To summarize, one determinant of an experience labeled as "hallucination" is an accentuated use of an image system of representation. Persons not accustomed to such accentuation may be more likely to react to and/or to describe the experience as perceptual in quality. This aspect of evaluation is described further after we consider internal input to image-forming systems as a second determinant of hallucinatory experience.

Relative Intensification of Internal Input into the Image System of Representation.   To understand dedifferentiation of internal and external sources of information, it is necessary to postulate a dual-input model of image formation, as nearly every interested investigator has suggested (West, 1962; Arlow and Brenner, 1964; Arlow, 1969). Before discussing this model, however, we present samples of findings that necessitate a "dual-input" model because they set the stage for complex considerations. These samples of findings include illusion experiments, cross-modal information-processing experiments, and clinical observations of transitions into hallucinatory states.

Illusions.   Illusions fall roughly into two types, general and idiosyncratic. General optical illusions often consist of tricks of perspective. These ways to "fool" the eye-brain are not of direct interest here. Idiosyncratic illusions, like interpreting the shadow of a tree as a menacing figure, are more pertinent. They tend to occur with greater frequency when there is high expectancy and a high level of ambiguity in available stimuli (sometimes called a low signal-to-noise ratio).

Segal (1968a; 1968b; 1969) developed an experimental analog to such illusions. She replicated and extended Perky's (1910) demonstration that normal persons may completely confuse internal and external signals when external signals are vague or dim. The subjects sat inside a semiopaque white plastic hood. Images were periodically projected onto the hood as subjects looked at a fixation point. By use of two coordinated projectors, total illumination was held constant. One projector had slides of particular images, the other projected light only. By varying illumination of each, the projections had differing levels of stimulus clarity.

Subjects were asked to try and form various types of visual images as they looked at the fixation point. Sometimes similar images, sometimes different images, and sometimes no images were projected on the hood. Subjects were then asked to report their experiences and to tell whether what they "saw" was a picture in the "mind's eye" or a "real" image on the hood. Subjects erred. At times they misinterpreted their internal images and called them "perceptions," or they misinterpreted external images and called them "thought images." Sometimes they formed composite images of external and internal information into a single experience. For example, if shown a red circle image and asked to visualize the New York skyline, they might report, "the New York skyline at dusk with the sun setting," or if asked to visualize a plant would report, "a tomato plant." Such composites, as in clinical observation of idiosyncratic illusions, suggest that the image system has a dual input of information—in other words, that perception and image formation share, to some extent, the same processes.

Reciprocal Limitation of Information Processing in the Same Mode.   One of Segal's methods was to systematically vary the mode of internal and external information representation. Some subjects were instructed to form internal visual images but also told to respond when they saw external visual signals. Others formed visual images and responded if auditory signals were detected. Similar variations included the formation of auditory thought images while being alert to auditory or visual external signals.

The results indicated that subjects were more often correct about external signals when they were not forming internal images in that mode. For instance, a person contemplating his own image of "a pair of glasses" would be less likely to notice a visual image of a banana projected on the screen than he would be to notice a voice whispering, "banana." If he were contemplating an auditory image of a train whistle, however, he would have more correct "hits" on visual projections than on auditory signals. Such systematic variations suggested that these results were not due to distraction but to an overlapping usage of channels of information processing within a given system of representation.

A similar conclusion was arrived at independently, using a different experimental paradigm, by Antrobus and Singer (1969). Subjects spent time in a lightproof, soundproof booth. The amount of information in external auditory or visual signals was systematically controlled in terms of intensity, rate, and number of "bits" of information per unit of time. Subjects also reported their "stimulus-independent" thought and the modality of such thought, such as whether they had visual or auditory images. They found that increasing the information rate in the visual signal detection task interfered more with the production of visual imagery than with auditory imagery. Similarly, increasing the rate of auditory external signals decreased the frequency of internal auditory imagery.

The Transition to Hallucination.   Persons shift from nonhallucinatory to hallucinatory states of consciousness in a variety of contexts such as the onset of schizophrenic episodes, entry into delirium tremens, or the gradual change in experience after taking LSD. Although contexts vary, similar transitions have been abstracted. Both show a phase of blending information of immediately internal and external origin.

One progression into hallucinations is direct sequential intensification of internal input. The first experience is the emergence of surprising or warded-off memory or fantasy images. The sense of what is external (i.e., perception) and what is internal (i.e., thought) is unimpaired, although there may be a sense of reduced volitional control over thought. Next the fantasy or memory images seem to be increasingly intrusive and may be appraised as quasi-real in subjective experience. At this point the person may attempt to stabilize a sense of reality through the use of checking maneuvers, including changes in perception (looking "harder," closing the eyes, looking away) and in thought (trying to suppress the image, trying to think of something else, evaluating the probability of such events being real).

In the next stage, the experienced intensity of thought images may resemble that of perceptual images, but the person is still able to label the experience as nonperceptual because he applies a cognitive counterweight such as "I know it can't be so," or "This is only a dream or hallucination." In the most advanced stage of hallucination, the person regards, or reacts to, the intense images of internal origin as if they were real.

The second type of progressive loss of differentiation between external and internal sources of information begins with an alteration of perceptual images. An initial stage such as blurring, graying, bending, halo effects, shimmering, reduplicating of forms, or other types of perceptual distortion, may be followed by a phase of vivid entoptic images such as spots, flashes, and geometric patterns. Finally, pseudohallucinations or hallucinations may be elaborated by adding internal information to these basic forms (Jackson, 1932; Penfield and Rasmussen, 1950; Horowitz et al., 1968; Horowitz, 1969). The latter type of transition is seen more commonly in drug-induced hallucinations, organic changes, and sensory deprivation.

Both of these transitions, like illusions, involve a dedifferentiation of information in the image mode so that the "inner–outer" distinction is lost and the "inner" takes on "outer" qualities in subjective experience. Such composite experiences, and the continuous nature of their development, support a dual-input model.

A Dual-Input Model of Image Formation.   Evidence suggests, as a model criterion, a central image-forming system that receives information from internal and external sources. The model must allow for both correct and incorrect discriminations between the sources of input. West (1962) and Arlow (1969) have formulated such dual-input models.

An oversimplified but perhaps helpful model of these conditions pictures a man in his study, standing at a closed glass window opposite the fireplace, looking out at his garden in the sunset. He is absorbed by the view of the outside world. He does not visualize the interior of the room in which he stands. As it becomes darker outside, however, images of the objects in the room behind him can be seen reflected dimly in the window glass. For a time he may see either the garden (if he gazes into the distance) or the reflection of the room's interior (if he focuses on the glass a few inches from his face). Night falls, but the fire still burns brightly in the fireplace and illuminates the room. The watcher now sees in the glass a vivid reflection of the interior of the room behind him, which appears to be outside the window. This illusion becomes dimmer as the fire dies down, and finally, when it is dark both outside and within, nothing more is seen. If the fire flares up from time to time, the visions in the glass reappear.

In perceptual release, the daylight (sensory input) is reduced while the interior illumination (general level of arousal) remains bright, and images originating within the rooms of our brains may be perceived as though they came from outside the windows of our senses.

The theory thus holds that a sustained level and variety of sensory input normally is required to inhibit the emergence of percepts or memory traces from within the brain itself. When effective (attention-commanding) sensory input decreases below a certain threshold, there may be a release into awareness of previously recorded perceptions through the disinhibition of the brain circuits that represent them. If a general level of cortical arousal persists to a sufficient degree, these released perceptions can enter awareness and be experienced as hallucinations. The greater the level of arousal, the more vivid the hallucinations (West, 1962, p. 275).

According to this model, there is an intensification or "release" of images of internal origin when external image information decreases but the representational system is still "on." I would like to complicate this metaphor because of a concern with variations in controls at the psychological level. Instead of one "pane," consider a metaphor of multiple panes. Each would operate as a matrix for the representation of otherwise coded information. As coded information passes through the panes, there would be a transformation of information into visual (or other modal) representation. Without such transformation, no conscious experience of images in that mode could occur.

Each pane or matrix could be slightly different in terms of intrinsic orientation. Some could be oriented relatively toward information arriving from optical sources; others could be oriented relatively toward information arriving from memory and fantasy sources. But any pane could be stimulated by information from either source. The panes could be considered to be stages of information processing, with multiple representations created by optical stimuli and by internal schemata. Comparisons back and forth and revisions of information to obtain good matchings between matrices would be made. With good matches there would be reduplication of information over a number of panes, or some type of enlargement of the "right image." As Pribram (1971) has suggested, the whole system could be conceptualized holographically with increasing clarity and intensity as the hologram is enlarged.

The dual inputs to these matrices or "panes," the transitions between matrices, and the matrices themselves would be interrelated with feedback processes through which the outcomes we call checking, reality-testing, or revisions of information, could be accomplished. These regulatory processes would provide for matching perception images with schemata, with memory images, with expectancy, and so forth. Information in the image matrices would also be interrelated with information in sensory-motor control systems, especially those involving schemata for eye movements, binocular focus, head position, vestibular sensation, and so forth. The regulatory operations would include means for facilitation, inhibition, perseveration, short-term storage, and extension of short-term storage until conflicts or ambiguities were resolved. These regulatory operations could work harmoniously or disharmoniously with higher or lower levels of capacity, and in discrete or global areas of application.

In such a model, relative intensification of internal sources of information could occur under divergent circumstances. These circumstances would include:

1. Relative reduction of external input with no relative lowering of activity (receptivity) of the representational system.

2. Increase in activity of the representational system without increase in availability of external signals.

3. Augmentation of internal input due to arousal of ideas and feelings secondary to drive states.

4. Reduction of usual or "homeostatic" levels of inhibition over the internal inputs.

5. Alteration of the transition between "matrices," permitting internal inputs to gain more representation on matrices oriented to, and more often associated with, perception.

Ambiguous external signals ("high noise-to-signal ratio") might allow the internal schemata more access to these more "perceptual" matrices. That is, the ambiguous stimuli might activate that matrix but allow patterns of internal origin to serve as organizers. The resultant reduplication or enlargement would lend the image an intensity in conscious experience as well as association with "out-thereness." According to this model, then, an unclear perceptual nidus might provide vividness for internal elaborations. There is evidence suggesting just such contributions in a variety of hallucinatory experience.

Perceptual Nidus Theory. Idiosyncratic illusions can now be considered further. Frequency of occurrence—assuming constancy of external factors, such as ambiguity—is heightened by internal factors that augment or reduce expectancy schemata according to current wishes* and fears. Thus the same ambiguous round shape on initial perceptual representation can be "illusioned" into an orange (if the subject is hungry), a breast (if he is in a state of heightened sexual drive), a cup of water (if he is thirsty), or an anarchist's bomb (if he is hostile or fearful).

Ordinarily, the source of information for the ambiguous shape is outside. It can be checked perceptually or consensually validated in another state (a different

---

*Included with wishes are such nonnecessarily conscious needs as information or "stimulation" seeking to maintain arousal.

state of the same person or a different person). With such validation, the initial image experience may be corrected and labeled as "illusion" rather than "perception" or "hallucination." But, as mentioned earlier, *there may be instances when the perceptual nidus of the experience cannot be validated as external because it is not extracorporeal but is rather within the optic system itself.* What was not considered earlier is the frequency of certain "constancies" in such optical system contributions. These "constancies" are repetitive forms abstracted from reviews of hallucinatory experiences.

Lack of knowledge allowed me to empirically "rediscover" observations made earlier by Klüver (1942). Unaware of his work, I studied varieties of hallucinatory experience and abstracted redundant elements. These corresponded with Klüver's categorizations, although theoretical explanations differ somewhat. Klüver abstracts three levels in the mechanisms of hallucination formation. The first level is that of form constants which are variations on simple motifs of *(a)* gratings or lattice work, *(b)* cobwebs, *(c)* tunnels or funnels, and *(d)* spirals. The second level consists of changes of number, form, and shape of visual material. The third level is alteration of spatial and temporal relations, including translocations, rotations, and fragmentations.

The important idea is that there may be basic perceptual information involved in some hallucinations. This information would be elaborated by contributions from memory and fantasy. *This "mechanism of hallucination," (Klüver's term) would thus be a way of "intensifying" input from memory or fantasy by contiguity of such information with perceptual elements and perceptual processing.*

Like Klüver, I suggested that entoptic contributions may be elaborated into meaningful images and may add a perceptual type of intensity to the resultant constructions. Like Klüver, I abstracted redundant elements of simple form in hallucinatory and pseudohallucinatory images (see Fig. 2).

The similarities between Klüver's constants and my abstraction of formal elements (Horowitz, 1964) are as follows:

1. Klüver's "gratings and lattice-work" are the same as the "grids and filigrees" of Fig. 2. Hexagonal patterns are very prominent in such forms.

2. Klüver's "cobwebs" seem to be a combination of such filigrees, parallel lines, and portions of radiating circular figures.

3. Similarly, "tunnels and funnels" and "spirals" are a combination of "circular figures" and the tendency to "parallel lines." The spatial quality often experienced, that is, the sense of a receding center to the visual field, is a definite recurrent formal element. This effect, which may be due to rapid enlargements and reductions of figures, possibly is related to micropsia and macropsia experiences. The underlying purpose of such size alterations might have to do with efforts to match registered information with schemata of recognition. This again, is quite speculative.

If one presumes a perceptual nidus for some hallucinations, one is, in effect, redefining these experiences as a variety of illusion. These entoptic contributions to the construction of a conscious image could come either from the firing of neurons or from sets of neurons anywhere in the optical-cortical system or from

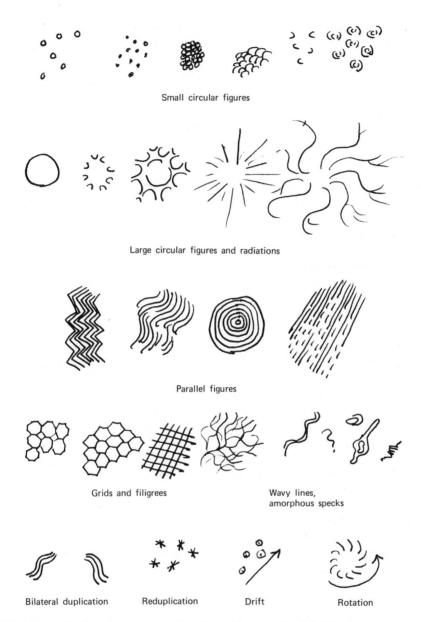

Small circular figures

Large circular figures and radiations

Parallel figures

Grids and filigrees

Wavy lines,
amorphous specks

Bilateral duplication   Reduplication   Drift   Rotation

Figure 2 Redundant form elements from hallucinatory and pseudohallucinatory images.

actual perceptions of orbital anatomy (see also Siegel and Jarvik, Chapter Four, this book). I have reasoned this as follows (based on Horowitz, 1964, pp. 519–520).

The early view of the optic pathway—as a kind of telegraphic system with point-to-point retinal-cortical representations—has been discarded. The retina and optical-cortical pathways appear to do more work in terms of codifying information through special receptivity to patterns in the complex tangle of retinal neurons, feedback circuits, and ganglia (Granit, 1955; Letvin et al., 1959; Neisser, 1967). It is postulated that the basic coding forms include: (1) straightness of line, (2) regularity of arc, (3) circularity, (4) parallelisms of straight lines, arcs, and circles, and (5) congruence of figures, equidistance, and equiangularity (Pitts and McCulloch, 1947; Platt, 1960). These forms resemble, in part, the images abstracted earlier from clinical material, and they also fulfill the gestalt criterion of *pregnanz* and figural goodness—the qualities found in figures most readily perceived (Hochberg and McAlister, 1953; Attneave, 1955; Woodworth, 1958). It is conceivable, then, that the images so repetitive in the clinical material may relate to the nature and function of circuitry and pattern receptivity in the optical-cortical pathway.

Anatomic Structure of the Eye.   The eye usually does not see its own contents, yet most people have visualized one or another of their entoptic elements. These are usually called floaters and are commonly seen while staring at a blank source of illumination such as an overcast sky or a sunlit wall. It seems likely that the figures abstracted in Fig. 2 could arise, in part, from anatomic forms. The patterns of the retinal blood vessels affect the light-sensitive rods and cones peripheral to the macula lutea, the area of precise vision. The shadows of such vessels could give rise to the wavy, radiating, filigreed elements; the blood cells within them might produce dotlike apparitions. The optic disk (i.e., the central scotoma) could give rise to the large circular figures, and the layers of rods, cones, and neural bundles, to the parallel figures. The fibers of the lens are arranged around six diverging axes, and this arrangement causes the rays seen around distant lights, giving them a starlike luster. They can also produce a sense of parallel fibers, swirls, or spots when such defective structures are present in the lens (von Helmholtz, 1962). The muscae volitantes, or floaters in the vitreous humor, like the artifacts in the lens, are produced by the invagination of integument during embryonal development of the eye and can give rise to oval or irregular shapes in entoptic visions. The movement of dots could be the flow of formed blood elements. The constant variations in optic movement caused by tremor, flicker, and drift would also impart a sense of movement to the elements. Optic rotation could cause circling effects, and bilateral orbital stimuli could result in the reciprocal duplications. Other features of imagery might be related to such optical phenomena as the production of figural after-effects (Hanawalt, 1954; MacKay, 1961).

To restate the hypothesis, redundant clinical material of visual images can be abstracted into simple forms, and the origin of some such forms may be entoptic—either from the anatomic characteristics of the eye or arising in the bioelectrical circuits for pattern receptivity in the retinal ganglionic network or at higher cell arrays in the optical-cortical pathway.

Why are entoptic images seldom consciously perceived? Stationary images on the retina fade out in six seconds. The natural involuntary movements of the eye, especially flicker and tremor, regenerate the image and compensate for drift (Ditchburn et al., 1959; Pritchard, 1961). Certain entoptic elements, especially the optic disk and the retinal blood vessels, would not generate many impulses because of their relatively stable retinal position. Their shadows, however, would shift under certain circumstances of moving illumination. In addition to fadeout, then, there must be other ways of limiting the penetration of such stimuli.

There is continuous retinal activity, even with the eye at rest, and continuous forces of inhibition and facilitation alter receptivity to various stimuli and patterns (Bartley, 1959; Granit, 1955). It is known that the visual field varies with the deployment of attention and that receptivity to visual messages depends on the state of visual pathway excitability (Lindsley 1956; Callaway, 1962; Williams and Gassel, 1962; Oswald, 1963). With the evidence for centrifugal control (i.e., for optic nerve impulses moving toward the retina) comes the realization that inhibition and facilitation may operate at a peripheral locus as well as in the brain (Pitts and McCulloch, 1947; Granit, 1955). Cortical responses to stimulation of the retina show: (1) a topographic, organized process, and (2) a slower, more diffuse process, partially intraretinal, which activates major portions of the visual cortex. Vision is a complex transactional process in which the eye tells the brain what it sees and the brain tells the eye what it should look for and what it should not look for. Stimuli originating within the eyeball or in the optical-cortical pathway might register at lower levels but, under normal circumstances, be kept from higher perceptual experience by active inhibition or lack of facilitation. With an increase in the need to see, as in sensory deprivation, entoptic imagery would be facilitated or "tuned up." The somatic purpose would be to prevent optically dependent areas of the brain from being lulled by insufficient afferent stimulation.

What might happen when entoptic images or vague "noisy" perceptions are disinhibited or especially facilitated? This raw material would then impinge on higher centers for image representation and would undergo a variety of secondary elaborations leading to the final conscious image. The nature of the secondary elaborations would depend both on current motivational states and on current regulatory capacity. In persons with relatively stable controls, simple and momentary illusions or hypnagogic images of pleasing lights and patterns might result. With impairment of regulatory function or intensification of motives, the images might become illusions or pseudohallucinations of current wishes, needs, or fears. In states of impaired control, hallucinations might be elaborated out of the entoptic raw material. Entoptic sensations might also contribute sensory quality to dream images. Some subjects, awakened from dreaming sleep, have reported an increase in entoptic sensations as they look with open eyes into the darkness of their room.

An example of a nidus elaboration is provided with the following clinical vignette (based on Horowitz, 1964, pp. 519–522.)

An 18-year-old man was hospitalized when discovered roaming the streets in a confused and disoriented state. In the corner of his visual field he had "hallucinations" of dots (Fig. 3,a), which occurred almost constantly during certain hours of the day, especially if he were not occupied in some distracting activity. During an interview he pointed to the dots with his finger, but when he attempted to focus them, they drifted to the periphery of his visual fields. At times he was convinced they were "cosmic balls of fire sent to punish me." Treatment was started with chlordiazepoxide (Librium), 20 mg four times daily. He reported a marked worsening of the visual disturbances and made drawings of what he saw (Fig. 3,b).

Examination of the subject's visual fields showed a left central scotoma. With the opposite eye closed he could see different figures in each eye (Fig. 3,c). With an exclamation of surprise, he identified the figure in his right eye as "the snakes" he had been "hallucinating." He then reported a psychotic episode that had occurred 18 months previously, which he had kept secret, hoping to remain in the service. He stated he had not had visual hallucinations then until he received medication which, by his description of the capsule colors and recognition of the current

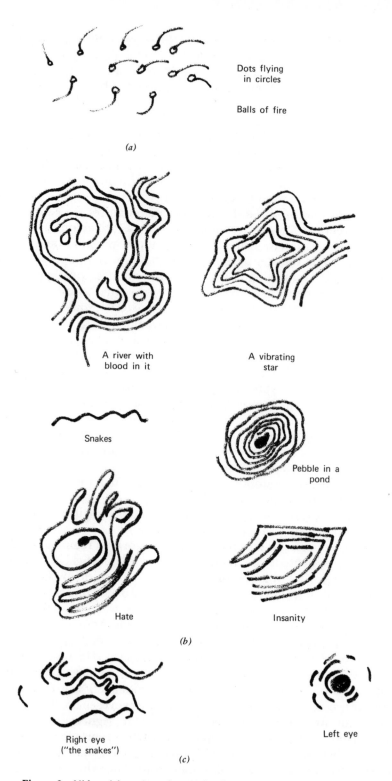

Dots flying
in circles

Balls of fire

(a)

A river with
blood in it

A vibrating
star

Snakes

Pebble in a
pond

Hate

Insanity

(b)

Right eye
("the snakes")

Left eye

(c)

Figure 3 Nidus elaboration of entoptic phenomena drawn by a patient.

medication, had been chlordiazepoxide. After chlordiazepoxide was discontinued, the visual phenomena diminished markedly, although the dots persisted; the scotoma disappeared subjectively and by campimetry. Later, another dose of chlordiazepoxide caused these particular symptoms to recur, and the medication was permanently discontinued. When the patient was treated with thioridazine, there were no similar effects.

In brain-stimulation studies of temporal-lobe epileptics, it has occasionally been possible, in single cases intensively investigated, to observe progressions from elementary sensations to figurally and meaningfully elaborated images (Horowitz et al., 1968).

The preceding discussion on the perceptual system contributions to images experienced as "hallucinatory" focused on the visual mode of representation. Gross et al. (1963, 1970), in a series of studies with alcoholic patients, described parallel findings for auditory perceptual contributions to auditory hallucinations. This information conforms to Klüver's predictions that his "mechanisms" applied to multiple sensory systems. In essence, Gross and co-workers found a progression from clouded sensorium to hallucination and a correlation between the degree of perceptual disturbance and the frequency of hallucinations. In particular, buzzing and clicks seem to provide an "ent-otic" nidus, one that may originate in the physical apparatus of the inner ear or in the auditory-cortical pathways. This raw material may be elaborated into auditory hallucinations (or "illusions") of pistol shots, roaring, or murmuring voices.

Expectancy Schemata Plus a Perceptual Nidus May Intensify Internal Input.   As so ably reviewed by Neisser (1967), perception is a constructive process governed by at least two needs. One need is for accurate knowledge of reality. The other is to find what one hopes or fears *may* be "out there." The latter purpose directs perception and is called expectancy, a priming of certain available schemata for matching with potential patterns.

Suppose there is a highly "tonic" schemata, the result of an intense need-state. Because of dual input, a thought image might be "matched" with it, and this matching could yield a perceptionlike experience. The speculation is that high-drive states may activate not only memories and fantasies but also relevant schemata of recognition. The two may interact in a way ordinarily "reserved" for matching of perceptual stimuli with expectancy. *A fusion of an ambiguous perceptual nidus, a template of expectancy, and an active memory or fantasy image would provide the "information" and perceptual quality of an hallucination.* Of course, if need or fear is great enough, no nidus is necessary.

Freud called this process "topographic regression" and suggested that such disinhibitions of internal input might have adaptive purposes. For example, Freud speculated that a very hungry baby hallucinates a breast, the image associated with prior satisfaction of similar needs (Freud, 1900; Rapaport, 1950). With the baby in danger of physiologic shock (hypoglycemia), further agitation and crying may be maladaptive. The "unreal" gratification of the breast may "really" help by inducing a quieting period in which physiologic homeostasis may be regained. The same may be true of our starving man and his turkey dinner. After a period of time, in cognitive development, physiological restorations might grow into psychological restorations (e.g., hope rather than despair). Thus the intensifications of internal input obtained by modifications in usual levels of control are not only *efforts* at wish fulfillment. The hallucination *does* fulfill some aspects of wishes and needs, and these satisfactions would reinforce whatever control changes (disinhibition or facilitation) made hallucinations possible in the first place.

Impairment of Information Processing May Contribute to the Experience of an Image as a Perception Rather than as a Thought.   Construction of a conscious image from dual-input sources does not necessarily complete an information-processing cycle. If the image episode is important, it must be interpreted to a point of completion before it, or its representative in short-term (active) memory, is erased. Disruption of such information processing *after* image formation (of what is henceforth called the baseline image) but before meaningful completion of appraisal will lead to conceptual isolation of the baseline image, and a quasi-perceptual rather than thoughtlike quality will be associated with the experience.

The Blue Dragon Problem.   Stated so abstractly, these ideas must seem obscure. Consider a concrete, conjectural analogy. Suppose a person, without conscious intent, forms an intense visual image synthesizing determinants such as (1) a currently intense state of expectancy of assault (e.g., as retribution for bad thoughts), (2) memories of childhood terror-dreams of monsters, and (3) entoptic stimuli of blueness, jagged lines, and circles with bilateral duplication. We will call the composite baseline image a "blue dragon" but will not suppose any such lexical labeling in our subject: just an intense, unbidden, visual image of blue color and eyelike, dragonlike shapes.

    Stage 1. The first stages of information processing are completed so rapidly that for discussion of subjective experience they can be called "instant." These "instant" processes establish the spatial characteristics of the object image. They include comparison of the image with current schemata for assessing the sameness or difference of the environment. If the comparison leads to a things-are-the-same-as-always result, nothing further might happen. But in this case, something is different—no blue dragon was "there" before. Also, no clear localization in space relative to the self is established. Vividness indicators may be "like perception" and the dragon could be "out there" on this basis. But since binocular and other cues do not match with such cues, there is "doubt."
    Instant (and automatic) conceptual processes have not solved the blue dragon problem; thus other stages of information processing are set in motion.

    Stage 2. The second stage of information processing includes translation across modes of representation. This "stage" decides if a conscious image experience relates to major current issues by simple comparisons with "templates" of dangers and gratifications. In this case, the dragon signifies potential danger. But for speedy translation to other modes such as verbal representations, some familiarity is required. This image is novel. The absence of a label, such as "dragon," would leave the image isolated in our subject's visual system, render it hard to think about, and give it the strange quality here under discussion.

    Stage 3. A third stage might be called "appraisal" of the image and any cross-modal translations such as "dragon." What does it mean in terms of past experiences, latent fantasies, current conflicts, goal hierarchies, and coping resources? The blue dragon is a "never seen before," "is it real?" "am I crazy?" and "what do I do about it?" problem. The absence of quick solutions to a potential threat means that the image or a memory of the image episode would tend to remain active in terms of consciousness, but unusual, weird, alien to past experience. These qualities are more frequently associated with perceptual input; hence the intensified internal information will tend to be labeled as if perceptual.

Individual Differences.   Suppose, now, two separate episodes of conscious experience, both of visual images, both of identical vividness, clarity, and conceptual "space." Suppose these episodes occur to two identical persons who differ in only one respect. To one the image content is familiar, to the other it is novel. The first person rapidly processes and is done with the image. "Oh, that again," in effect. The second person holds the novel image in active memory; it is isolated conceptually from cross-modal translation and hard to appraise. The latter image in the ongoing conscious experience would be more likely to be labeled "hallucinatory" when described to the self or to another person.

Impairments of Information Processing.   Novelty contributes to doubts, but so too does brevity and ambiguity of an image experience. One aspect of the mystification of hallucinations is the tendency to consider them as dramatically intense images. *But many hallucinations are dim and brief episodes of awareness. When the episode is brief, there is insufficient time for appraisal, in addition to poor memory encoding. These conditions foster misinterpretation, especially during states of cognitive impairment or high conflict.*

The impairment in information processing alluded to previously could occur under a variety of circumstances. Translation into word representations is probably important to many kinds of logical appraisal. For such appraisal, the lexical system requires sequential organizational capacities. These organizations are one of the "highest" cognitive functions (Luria, 1966) and one of the first to be disrupted with impaired cognitive function. An episode of image experience that was easier to process in a state of "higher" functional capacity would be harder to process in a state in which sequential organization, or the lexical system in general, were operative at reduced capacity.

A closely related possibility could be called "overloading" or "disjunctive arousal." As discussed earlier, suppose the visual image system of representation were highly active. In "ordinary" consciousness all systems of representation might have the same potential for activity with ready shifts for utilitarian purposes. But the systems might be activated disjunctively in various "altered" states of consciousness. *A "lit up" image system and a "tuned down" lexical system could result in more images than could be processed for meanings, hence could contribute "strangeness" to the subjective experiences.*

A completion tendency, in terms of a path of information processing directed toward assimilation, was postulated earlier. Defenses and controls may interfere with such processing, even when adequate capacity exists in terms of physiochemical substrates. One cognitive way defense mechanisms may operate is by controlling information transformation at the interfaces between representational systems (Horowitz, 1972b).

For example, inhibition of entry into any system of representation would accomplish *repression* if the information were internal (e.g., memory) or *denial* if the information were external (e.g., perceivable). Thus a given set of ideas and feelings may be functionally conscious in one mode of representation, functionally preconscious in another and functionally unconscious in a third. *Suppression* would refer to a conscious effort to terminate representation in all systems, or in one system in particular. *Isolation* could be accomplished by inhibition of translation between one system and another. For example, a warded-off idea or affect that gained representation as an image would be inhibited from translation to lexical representation. This maneuver would reduce conceptual meanings or implications, hence lower emotional response. *Splitting* could be accomplished by allowing one facet of information to gain representation in the image mode but not in the lexical mode, while permitting a different facet of information representation in the lexical mode but not in the image mode. Mistranslation between systems would be a cognitive maneuver that could accomplish *displacement* and *distortion*. Altering the role labeled as self in a self–object dyad can accomplish *reversal*. Some image representations would tend to activate excessive emotional responses if they were translated into words, and if their meanings and implications were to become fully conscious. Because of the threat of excessive emotional responses (signal anxiety), controls are motivated. These defensive operations may interfere with "ideal" cross-modal translation of information and the sequential matchings and appraisals necessary to establish complete integration with already ordered information. *The result is isolation of some representations in the image system, an isolation that lends a strange, alien, unwelcome, and even "out-there" quality to the episode of image experience.*

One objection has continuously been raised to this line of psychoanalytic reasoning since Freud's (1926) formulations: the explanation seems to be teleological and mechanistic. How does the person *know* what to inhibit if by that inhibition knowledge is itself prevented?

The answer, proposed by Freud, has recently been rearticulated by Sperry (1969) in terms of premonitory information sampling and the intrinsic properties of information itself. Sampling the intrinsic properties of information involves many circuits, at different levels of intensity, in the same cycle and in the presence of feedback. For example, a threatening idea is represented as an image and tends toward transformation into lexical representations. Such transformation would lead perhaps to even clearer, hence more threatening, expression and realization of the dangerous ideas. The danger of the excessive emotion (e.g., fear) that might result motivates controls that impede the translation, leaving the image incompletely translated.

The "strangeness" of the image may be contributed to by controls operative at the other boundary of the image system, not just the translation from images to words (or other modes) but the transformation of internal codings into images in the first place. I refer here to what Freud explained so clearly in *The Interpretation of Dreams* (1900): condensation, displacement, and symbolization, as well as other defensive mechanisms. There are many works on how such processes distort "latent" meanings and render manifest contents "strange" to the very thinker of the thought, and this point is not discussed further (Sharpe, 1937; French and Fromm, 1964).

Derailment of the Reality Principle.   "Strangeness" of an initial image may be maintained in the phases of appraisal *after* the initial image episode, phases that may
relate to a memory of the image episode, a memory itself subject to continuous
revisions. This kind of information processing follows rules or plans governed by
kinds of comparisons between current concepts and schemata or associative
meanings that are acceptable or preferable. One set of rules corresponds to the
Reality Principle (the most important rule, hierarchically, in the differentiation of
reality from fantasy). But, as in the example of hallucinating food to restore
physiological homeostasis or to sustain psychological hope, the most adaptational
path may be to discard ordinary rules and accept fabrications "as if" real. *Such
conditions—states of intense need, for example—would selectively "derail" the Reality
Principle in favor of the Pleasure Principle (Freud, 1911). Such "derailment" would
contribute to the acceptance of image experiences "as if" real.* Restitutional hallucinations
in schizophrenia might be a case in point (Arlow and Brenner, 1964).

Disruption of a Memory as a Factor in "Strangeness".   As the baseline image episode
occurs, and as the appraisal processes continue to take place over time, the
attempts at appraisal may involve matchings with a *memory* of the baseline image
experience rather than the baseline image *itself.* To provide a concrete illustration
of this subtle but important factor, let us reconstruct a hashish-induced image as
experienced by a man at different times. The image is the hand of a woman
companion reaching to touch his face.

Moment 1. The man is relaxed and peaceful. Random thoughts about his
companion enter awareness. He would like to be touched, and he has a visual
thought image of her hand touching his face. This baseline image is more lucid or
clear than his ordinary visual thought images but not "hallucinatory" in quality.

Moments 2 and 3. His thought moves to other topics.

Moment 4. He tries to recall what has been happening over Moments 1 to 3. He
remembers and reproduces an image of the hand touching his face. He cannot
recall whether it just happened, because he has lost memory for the sequence of
mental contents from Moments 1, 2, and 3. If he were touched, what happened
before and after? If not, what fantasy was he having before and after what
thoughts? Because he cannot reconstruct sequences (a drug-induced impairment
of short-term memory), he also cannot recall whether the image he *now* reexperi-
ences was *then* (at baseline) a perceptual or conceptual image.

As he reviews his memory now in Moment 4, it seems to him that the baseline
image was experienced as a perception rather than as a thought. *He has developed,
then, what could be called a retrospective hallucination.* The baseline image during
Moment 1 was *not* hallucinatory, but is now, in Moment 4, appraised erroneously
as a real past happening. If he believed in the real occurrence of the episode and
told his companion in Moment 5, she might label his experience an hallucination.
This revision of belief might of course go on. In Moment 6, he could use her new
information and reappraise the memory on the baseline image as a fantasy.

A nonbizarre image was deliberately used as illustration to make the point that impaired cognitive appraisal—*in this instance loss of sequential short-term memory, hence poor reconstructive capacity—may contribute "hallucinatory" quality to an experience.*

Suppose the image is bizarre. In the rechecking of Moments 4 and 5, a "normal-minded" subject might "reality-test." If the image were a blue dragon, he might conclude that the experience was unreal on the grounds that he has no evidence for the existence of blue dragons and he has heard that persons have weird images on drugs. But suppose he is in a paranoid state and has a delusional system that requires belief in the existence of blue dragons to maintain internal consistency. He will more likely accept the idea of the image episode as real. Thus aspects of hallucinatory quality are determined by the nature of information processing after the episode of awareness has occurred.

When Control over Cognition Is Impaired, Intrusive Images Emerge. The preceding section discussed defensive *overcontrol* which might impede cognitive appraisal of images so greatly that they were left strangely isolated from other concepts. This section describes *undercontrol,* which results in intrusive or unbidden image experiences. The unplanned emergence of such images contributes a quasi-perceptual quality and a sense of estrangement of the images from thoughtlike domain of meaning. Unbidden images occur in a variety of states, but three instances stand out: *(a)* unbidden images as sequels to stressful perceptions, *(b)* unbidden images as eruptive representations of usually warded-off ideas and feelings, and *(c)* unbidden images as the result of unconscious defensive operations aimed at transformation of affective states.

Intrusive Images After Stressful Events. Breuer and Freud (1895) investigated hysterical symptoms, including hallucinations, and found them to be direct or symbolic repetitions of psychic traumas. Nearly 25 years later, Freud was impressed with recurrent nightmares of terrifying combat scenes experienced by veterans of World War I. He revised his theory of dreams and cited a compulsion toward repetition that was more primitive and urgent than wish fulfillment, hence *Beyond the Pleasure Principle* (1920). Unbidden images of powerful intensity, although *usually* not hallucinations in the strict definitional sense, occur in waking life also, after shocking visual perceptions.

I have attempted to develop an experimental analogy of such unbidden images after stress, to determine the generality of the response tendency. In a series of replicated studies, findings indicated a general tendency toward intrusive and stimulus-repetitive images after stressful events, general in that more than 50% of the subjects reported such experiences and the experiences occurred after mild to moderate events as well as after major stresses (Horowitz, 1969, 1970; Horowitz and Becker, 1971; Horowitz and Becker, 1972).

Clinical, field, and experimental findings confirm a tendency toward repetition, as unbidden images, of contents derived from shocking perceptions. One explanation for this aspect of the repetition compulsion is that the shocking perceptions are quickly realized to be of major adaptational importance, but the information is so novel or of such magnitude that it cannot be quickly processed to a point of completion (Freud, 1920). The relevant images are thus retained in what Broadbent (1971) has called "rehearsal" storage or "buffer" storage. This retention might be called "active memory" rather than "short-term memory" because it may last a long time and because an intrinsic tendency toward repeated representation can be postulated.

Whenever a stress-related content goes from coding in active memory to image representation, cognitive appraisal will be resumed. But the current image is incongruent with enduring concepts in a qualitative or a quantitative sense; otherwise it would not be stressful. Emotional responses occur in reaction to the discrepancy between current meanings and schematic memories or attitudes, and these emotional responses are themselves represented. As a concrete illustration, suppose a person has run over a child by accident, has looked with horror at the body under the car, and has realized that a terrible thing has happened. This horrible image remains in active memory until cognitive appraisal—assimilation and accommodation in Piaget's terms—is relatively complete. But assimilation and accommodation are difficult to complete. The "news" does not match with the person's ideal self-image, to mention just one of many "matches" that would have to occur to complete cognitive processing of the stressful event.

Suppose now that every recurrent representation of the child's body reinitiates the ideational processing, which can be abbreviated as, "how does this new information about my acts relate to my ideal self?" Since it relates badly, intolerable levels of guilt, shame, and fear tend to occur. Because of these unbearable emotional responses, there are motives for inhibition of transformation of the information from active memory to active representation. As Klein (1967) has recently reconceptualized, such repression "fresh freezes" the memory: the cognitive process remains incomplete, the memory remains "active." *With any triggers or shifts in capacity, the impulse-defense "kinetic homeostasis" may shift in favor of impulse. The result would be an unexpected episode of the intense, unpleasant, and warded-off images. This intrusion might then become an "hallucinatory experience" depending on other factors, already discussed, such as the kind of cognitive appraisal of the episode that is possible, the intensity of the images in experience, the size of the shift in representational mode, the labeling tendencies, and the degree of general disorganization in the regulation of thought.*

In psychological function there are many other determinants, such as tendencies to reduce threat by denial, projection, and externalization and tendencies toward self-punishment by repetitious reminders of personal guilt. Too complex for discussion here, these factors contribute an "alien" or "not-of-the-self" quality to such images, thus lending a quasi-perceptual or "out-there" quality either to the image experiences or to later interpretation and description of them.

Images of emotionally neutral contents are of marginal interest. They may also have intrusive qualities. That is, repetitive perceptual stimulations may result in expectancy schemata as part of "active memory." A relevant observation can be noted when medical students or laboratory technicians learn to count white blood cells for the first time. After long hours at the microscope, searching for a precise visual form, they go home to sleep and develop intrusive hypnagogic images of "cells." In such instances, afterimages may supply the perceptual nidus for the experience. Skiers report similar kinesthetic images of lifting and turning, drivers report visual images of headlights after night driving, and so on. *Such episodes may be quite startling because they enter awareness without intention or relevant set and resist conscious efforts to prevent recurrence.*

Intrusive Images as Eruptive Representation of Usually Warded-off Ideas and Feelings. The emergence of threatening, conflicted ideas and feelings can be conceptualized as an internal stress event. The analogy to the "active memory hypothesis" outlined previously would be this: ordinarily inactive memories or fantasies are activated by current motivational states resulting in a baseline image experience. This representation and the processing it initiates activate strong unpleasant emotional responses. To avoid continuation or increase of emotional disruptions, emergent representations are inhibited. As inhibitions weaken relative to motives for representation, intense unbidden images recur. The following is an oversimplified case.

A 15-year-old girl entered rapidly into an intense love affair with an older boy. Her lover encouraged her to form a union with him in a mystical and literal sense. A process of nondifferentiation between self and other was "encouraged" by use of marihuana, sensory awareness techniques, and his insistence that she not hold back. The girl experienced altered states of consciousness that were usually pleasant. Her boyfriend left town abruptly after two weeks of this extraordinary relationship. He said he "would return to her in some way," implying unusual "presences" or extrasensory perception. She felt jarred but did not mourn the loss. She did not think about the implications of the affair or his abrupt departure. In a few days she began having hypnagogic hallucinations of his face and illusions of seeing him on the street. She became progressively withdrawn, had fits of weeping and yelling, and reported seeing and hearing him when he was not there.

At no time would she talk with anyone about her affair and the sudden separation. Ideas were warded off to avoid painful feelings. Nonetheless, the need to understand, think through, or undo the loss was intense. She wished to find him again, and did so in her images. The images, however, entered consciousness without deliberate intent, a failure in repressive operations. The resultant intrusiveness of the images contributed to her fear because of a sense of loss of control. The explanation as repressive failure holds, even though there were secondary gains from the syndrome because it operated as a "call for help."

Another "stress event image" of internal origin can be found in extreme instances of flashback phenomena. During an hallucinatory experience, as evoked by LSD, symbolic images of great personal impact may emerge and may have stressful implications that are impossible to process at the moment (Horowitz, 1968). These images may be stored in active memory, having an impulsive tendency toward repeated representation; each episode would have the intrusive quality under discussion. *The drug-induced state may also lead to prolonged reduction of functional inhibition of internal inputs to image formation.*

Intrusive Images as the Result of Unconscious Defensive Operations Aimed at Transformations of Affective States. Like any form of thought, hallucinations may represent current emotional states directly or symbolically. A person who is fearful of others may hallucinate monsters or attackers. A person fearful of himself may give concreteness to vague ideas of disintegration as fragmented or diseased body images. A guilty or ashamed person may hallucinate accusatory voices or faces; an angry person will tend to hallucinate destructive scenes. *But like other kinds of thought, hallucination formation may occur not only to express an emotional state but also to alter one. A despairing and fearful person will try to relieve sadness by hallucinating a replica of a lost object.* This, perhaps, is one determinant of content in the vignette about the teen-aged girl. A person who feels bad, worthless, and alone, may hallucinate voices or figures that praise him, love him, or give helpful advice.

Perhaps the most interesting episodes of hallucination to alter affective states occur in persons who are threatened by loss of control over their own destructive rage. Such persons seem, at times, to hallucinate not only destructive themes but also images that tend to generate guilt or fear in them. It appears that activation of these affects can reciprocally inhibit anger, and vice versa. The fear-generating images such as an accusatory face or monster or a prior traumatic perception will enter awareness intrusively because the processes and purposes of formation are not conscious. Also, *the affect reversal is "helped" if reflective self-awareness of being the thinker of a thought is set aside and the image is regarded as if really perceptual.* Clinical examples of this type of observation and inference have been reported in detail elsewhere (Horowitz, 1970).

During those rare instances when good reports of the sequence of hallucinatory experience can be obtained, one notes a flow and change showing contrasting sets of ideation in which thoughts (i.e., the changing images of the hallucinations) reflect not emergent ideas and feelings *alone* but also active attempts to transform affective states with other ideas and feelings. Here is an example. A teenager described a series of hallucinations experienced during induction of anesthesia. He saw and felt a huge metal cylinder weighing heavily on his chest and saw the faces of surgeons bending over to cut him open. Then the cylinder was opened and a pleasant pink gas came out and everything became "nice" like the cartoon figures in the film *Yellow Submarine.* The first image, as revealed by associations, was connected with a fearful train of thought revolving on the idea of helplessness and a particular fear that he would be cut open while still awake but unable to talk and protest. A physical sense of chest pressure contributed a sensory "nidus," which was elaborated according to the emergent fear. The change in images reflected a self-reassuring thought that all was benign and secure and that anxiety was not indicated. If the experience had lasted longer, there might have been an oscillation between fearful and reassuring images.

SUMMARY

The prototypic hallucination is an image of internal origin that is erroneously regarded as a perception by the subject. The episode is usually nonvolitional and intensive, although voluntary, dim, and fleeting episodes may occur. These properties, which define the label "hallucination," were subjected to detailed discussion. The aim is a theory of information processing to model or explain *how* each property of the hallucinatory experience occurs.

Hallucinations are a type of image-thinking and take their place amid varieties of image experiences. A model with three basic types of representation was used to contrast image representation with enactive and lexical expressions. Activation of the image system, for psychological or physiological reasons, provides one determinant of the hallucinatory experience. Relative deactivation of other systems, especially those which serve word meanings, leaves the image episode "unnamed," hence like a perception that has not yet been translated into other meanings.

The concrete and all-at-once object depiction, the ambiguity of self, and the resemblance to perception that characterize visual image-thinking, indicate that intense images may be formed for psychological reasons. These images may serve as substitutes for unavailable persons or objects in a form of wish fulfillment or mastery of fears. Habitual experience will determine, in part, appraisals of such intense image experiences. Persons unused to spontaneous or vivid images may react more anxiously than habitués and may describe or regard the image experience as if it were a perception.

The image system of representation derives input from internal and external sources that occupy, in part, overlapping channels for the processing of information. This concept of dual input is based on evidence from experimental studies of perception and imagining, as well as clinical observations of illusion and the transition into hallucinatory states. Many conditions might lend internal information an unusually "perceptual" intensity of representation in this dual-input system. These include relative reduction of external input without lowering of receptivity of the image representational system, increased activity of the system without increased availability of external signals, augmentation of internal input due to motivational pressures, reduction of the usual levels of inhibition over internal inputs, and alteration in regulation of the matrices for representation themselves. Altered regulation might occur when ambiguous or unrecognizable external stimuli provide a nidus for elaboration by internal sources of information. In altered states of perceptual physiology, entoptic or entotic sources could provide a latticework on which unusually intense experiences could grow. Certain constantly recurring forms in hallucinations may be derived from such perceptual, although not extracorporeal, sources.

Thoughts, such as images, are differentiated from perceptions not only by intensity and quality but also by a sense of autoformation and knowledge of meanings. Relatively impaired information processing can isolate image thoughts and evoke an alien quality that contributes to the prototypic hallucinatory experience. It is impairment of information processing that probably accounts for the experiencing or labeling of some quite dim and fleeting images as hallucinations. States of general cognitive impairment, high conflict, stress, or great need for fantasy gratifications will increase the likelihood of such episodes. Disruption in short-term memory can lead to a "retrospective hallucination"—that is, a misjudgment about a remembered image. Such dim images and retrospective errors are more frequent in the domain of hallucinations than is commonly believed because the more dramatic and intense hallucinatory episodes tend to take center stage.

Sudden lapses in control occur after stressful perceptions, when warded-off ideas and feelings gain eruptive intensity, and when motivated by unconscious defensive operations. These episodes are experienced as unrelated to the immediate context of ongoing thought. Such impairments in regulatory function lend an intrusive quality to an experience, contributing to labeling an image as hallucinatory.

Hallucinations are a final common pathway entered because of various determinants. By variation of the properties described in this chapter, one could evolve myriad forms of hallucinatory experience. The riddle of hallucinations will never be solved by single models or succinct statements. The mystery and fascination of these strange experiences will, nonetheless, lure us toward the many unexplored contributory processes and into the greatest riddle of all, the operation of the mind.

REFERENCES

Adler, G. Methods and treatment in analytical psychology. In B. B. Wolman (Ed.), *Psychoanalytic techniques*. New York: Basic Books, 1967.

Antrobus, J. S., and Singer, J. L. Mind wandering and cognitive structure. Paper presented to New York Academy of Science, October 20, 1969.

Arlow, J. Unconscious fantasy and disturbances of conscious experience. *Psychoanalytic Quarterly*, 1969, **38**, 1–27.

Arlow, J and Brenner, C. *Psychoanalytic concepts and the structural theory*. New York: International Universities Press, 1964.

Attneave, F. Symmetry, information and memory for patterns. *American Journal of Psychology*, 1955, **68**, 209–222.

Bartley, S. H. Some facts and concepts regarding the neurophysiology of the optic pathway. *AMA Archives of Ophthalmology*, 1959, **60**, 775–791.

Betts, G. H. *The distribution and function of mental imagery*. New York: Columbia University Teachers College Press, 1909.

Breuer, J., and Freud, S. (1895) *Studies on hysteria*, standard ed., Vol. 2, 1954.

Broadbent, D. E. *Decision and stress*. London: Academic Press, 1971.

Bruner, J. S. The course of cognitive growth. *American Psychologist*, 1964, **19**, 1–15.

Callaway, E. Factors influencing the relationship between alpha activity and visual reaction time. *Electroencephalography and Clinical Neurophysiology*, 1962, **14**, 674–682.

Cohen, L. H. Imagery and its relations to schizophrenic symptoms. *Journal of Mental Science*, 1938, **84**, 284–346.

Ditchburn, R. W., Fender, D. H., and Mayne, S. Vision with controlled movements of the retinal image. *Journal of Physiology*, 1959, **145**, 98–107.

Erikson, E. H. *Childhood and society*. New York: Norton, 1950.

Esquirol, J. E. D. *Des maladies mentales*. Paris: Baillière, 1838.

French, T. M., and Fromm, E. *Dream interpretation*. New York: Basic Books, 1964.

Freud, S. (1900) *The interpretation of dreams*, standard ed., Vol. 5, 1953.

Freud, S. (1911) *Formulations on the two principles of mental functioning*, standard ed., Vol. 12, 1958.

Freud, S. (1920) *Beyond the pleasure principle*, standard ed., Vol. 18, 1962.

Freud, S. (1926) *Inhibitions, symptoms, and anxiety*, standard ed., Vol. 20, 1959.

Galton, F. *Inquiries into human faculty*. New York: Dutton (Everyman), 1919.

Granit, R. *Receptors and sensory perception*. New Haven, Conn.: Yale University Press, 1955.

Griffitts, C. H. *Fundamentals of vocational psychology*. New York: Macmillan, 1924.

Gross, M. M., Halpert, E., Sabot, L., and Polisoes, P. Hearing disturbances and auditory hallucinations in the acute alcoholic psychoses: I. Tinnitus: Incidence and significance. *Journal of Nervous and Mental Disease*, 1963, **137**, 455–465.

Gross, M. M., Rosenblatt, S. M., Lewis, E., Malinowski, B., and Broman, M. Hallucinations and clouding of sensorium in acute alcohol withdrawal syndromes. In W. Keup (Ed.), *Origin and mechanisms of hallucinations*. New York: Plenum Press, 1970.

Hanawalt, N. G. Recurrent images: New instances and a summary of the older ones. *American Journal of Psychology*, 1954, **67**, 170–174.

Helmholtz, H. von. *Popular scientific lectures*. New York: Dover, 1962.

Hochberg, J., and McAlister, E. A. A quantitative approach to figural "goodness." *Journal of Experimental Psychology*, 1953, **46**, 361–364.

Horowitz, M. J. The imagery of visual hallucinations. *Journal of Nervous and Mental Disease,* 1964, **138,** 513–523.

Horowitz, M. J. Visual imagery and cognitive organization. *American Journal of Psychiatry,* 1967, **123,** 938–946.

Horowitz, M. J. Spatial behavior and psychopathology. *Journal of Nervous and Mental Disease,* 1968, **164,** 24–35.

Horowitz, M. J., Adams, J., and Rutkin, B. Visual imagery on brain stimulation. *Archives of General Psychiatry,* 1968, **19,** 469–486.

Horowitz, M. J. Psychic trauma: return of images after stress films. *Archives of General Psychiatry,* 1969, **20,** 552–559.

Horowitz, M. J. *Image formation and cognition.* New York: Appleton-Century-Crofts, 1970.

Horowitz, M. J., and Adams, J. Hallucinations on brain stimulation: Evidence for a revision of the Penfield hypothesis. In W. Keup (Ed.), *Origin and mechanisms of hallucinations.* New York: Plenum Press, 1970.

Horowitz, M. J., and Becker, S. Cognitive response to stressful stimuli. *Archives of General Psychiatry,* 1971, **25,** 419–428.

Horowitz, M. J. The modes of representation of thought. *Journal of the American Psychoanalytic Association,* 1972, **20,** 793–819. (a)

Horowitz, M. J. Image formation: Clinical observations and cognitive model. In P. W. Sheehan (Ed.), *The nature and function of imagery.* New York: Academic Press, 1972. (b)

Horowitz, M. J., and Becker, S. Cognitive response to stress: Experimental studies of a "compulsion to repeat trauma." *Psychoanalysis and Contemporary Science,* 1972, **1,** 258–305.

Jackson, J. H. *Selected writings (1932),* J. Taylor (Ed.), Vol. 2. New York: Basic Books, 1958.

Jones, E. Fear, guilt, and hate. *International Journal of Psychoanalysis,* 1929, **10,** 383–397.

Klein, G. S. Peremptory ideation: Structure and force in motivated ideas. *Psychological Issues,* 1967, **5,** 80–128.

Klüver, H. Mechanisms of hallucinations. In Q. McNemar and M. A. Merrill (Eds.), *Studies in personality.* New York: McGraw-Hill, 1942.

Knoll, M., Kugler, J., Echmeier, J., and Höfer, O. Note on the spectroscopy of subjective light patterns. *Journal of Analytical Psychology,* 1962, **7,** 55–70.

Knoll, M., Kugler, J., Höfer, O., and Lawder, S. D. Effects on chemical stimulation of electrically induced phosphenes on their bandwidth, shape, number, and intensity. *Confinia Neurologica,* 1963, **23,** 201–226.

Kubie, L. S. *Neurotic distortion of the creative process.* Lawrence: University of Kansas Press, 1958.

Lettvin, J. Y., Maturana, H. R., McCulloch, W. S., and Pitts, W. H. What the frog's eye tells the frog's brain. *Proceedings of Institute of Radio Engineers,* 1959, **47,** 1940–1945.

Lindsley, D. B. Basic perceptual processes and the electroencephalogram. *Psychology Research Reports,* 1956, **6,** 161–170.

Luria, A. R. Higher cortical functions in man. New York: Basic Books, 1966.

Luria, A. R. *The mind of a mnemonist.* New York: Basic Books, 1968.

MacKay, D. M. Interactive processes in visual perception. In N. Rosenbluth (Ed.), *Sensory communication.* Cambridge, Mass.: MIT Press, 1961.

Mahl, G. F., Rothenberg, A., Delgado, J. M. R., and Hamlin, H. Psychological responses in the human to intercerebral electrical stimulation. *Psychosomatic Medicine,* 1964, **26,** 337–368.

McKellar, P. *Imagination and thinking.* New York: Basic Books, 1957.

Miller, G., Galanter, E., and Pribram, K. *Plans and the structure of behavior.* New York: Holt, Rinehart & Winston, 1960.

Neisser, U. *Cognitive psychology.* New York: Appleton-Century-Crofts, 1967.

Oswald, I. Sleeping and waking: Physiology and psychology. New York: Elsevier, 1963.

Penfield, W., and Rasmussen, T. *The cerebral cortex of man.* New York: Macmillan, 1950.

Penfield, W., and Jasper, H. *Epilepsy and the functional anatomy of the human brain.* Boston: Little, Brown, 1954.

Penfield, W. *The excitable cortex in conscious man.* Springfield, Ill.: Charles C Thomas, 1958.

Penfield, W. Speech, perception, and the cortex. In J. C. Eccles (Ed.), *Brain and conscious experience.* New York: Springer-Verlag, 1966.

Perky, C. W. An experimental study of imagination. *American Journal of Psychology,* 1910, **21,** 422–452.

Perry, J. W. Emotions and object relations. *Journal of Analytic Psychology,* 1970, **15,** 1–12.

Peterfreund, E. Information, systems and psychoanalysis. *Psychological Issues,* 1971, **VII,** (1/2), Monograph 25/26.

Pitts, W., and McCulloch, W. S. How we know universals: The perception of auditory and visual form. *Bulletin Mathematical Biophysics,* 1947, **9,** 127–147.

Platt, J. F. How we see straight lines. *Scientific American,* 1960, **202,** 121–129.

Pribram, K. H. *Languages of the brain: Experimental paradoxes and principles in neurophysiology.* Englewood Cliffs, N.J.: Prentice-Hall, 1971.

Pritchard, R. M. Stablized images on the retina. *Scientific American,* 1961, **204,** 72–78.

Rapaport, D. The psychoanalytic theory of thinking. *International Journal of Psychoanalysis,* 1950, **31,** 161–170.

Roman, R., and Landis, C. Hallucinations and mental imagery. *Journal of Nervous and Mental Disease,* 1945, **102,** 327–331.

Schilder, T. *The image and appearance of the human body.* London: Routledge & Kegan Paul, 1935.

Segal, S. Patterns of response to thirst in an imaging task (Perky technique) as a function of cognitive style. *Journal of Personality,* 1968, **36,** 574–588. (a)

Segal, S. The Perky effect: Changes in reality judgments with changing methods of inquiry. *Psychonomic Science,* 1968, **12,** 393–394. (b)

Segal, S. Imagery and reality: Can they be distinguished? Paper presented at conference of the Eastern Psychiatric Association on Origin and Mechanisms of Hallucinations, New York, November 14–15, 1969.

Seitz, P. F., and Molholm, H. B. Relation of mental imagery to hallucinations. *Archives of Neurologic Psychiatry,* 1947, **57,** 469–480.

Sharpe, E. F. (1937) *Dream analysis.* London: Hogarth Press, 1949.

Sheehan, P. W., and Neisser, U. Some variables affecting the vividness of imagery in recall. *British Journal of Psychology,* 1969, **60,** 76–80.

Sperry, R. W. A modified concept of consciousness. *Psychological Bulletin,* 1969, **76,** 532–536.

West, L. J. A general theory of hallucinations and dreams. In L. J. West (Ed.), *Hallucinations.* New York: Grune & Stratton, 1962.

Williams, D., and Gassel, M. Visual function in patients with homonymous hemianopia. Part I: The visual fields. *Brain,* 1962, **185,** 175–251.

Woodworth, P. S. *Dynamics of behavior.* New York: Holt Rinehart & Winston, 1958.

ACKNOWLEDGMENTS

Research on which this chapter is based was made possible by a Research Career Program award from the National Institute of Mental Health.

CHAPTER SIX

CARTOGRAPHY OF INNER SPACE

ROLAND FISCHER, Ph.D.

They will say that I, having no literary skill, cannot properly express that which I desire to treat of; but they do not know that my subjects are to be dealt with by experience rather than by words.

Leonardo da Vinci (*The Literary Works of* Leonardo da Vinci, Jean Paul Richter, 2nd ed., p. 116. Oxford University Press (1939).

Consciousness has at least two connotations (1) knowing with (i.e. to share knowledge—from the Latin *con-scientia*) and (2) self-awareness (i.e., to know in oneself). Both meanings refer to the domain of self-description (i.e., self-observation). According to Maturana (1970), if an organism can generate a communicable description of its interactions and interact with the communicable description, the process can, in principle, be carried out in a potentially infinite recursive manner, and the organism becomes an observer. It can describe its interactions and communicate its descriptions to others or to itself, and through the very same process it can describe itself describing itself.

"Thus we cannot escape the fact that the world we know is constructed"—or in my words: perceived-conceived—"in order (and thus in such a way as to be able) to see itself" (Brown, 1969). Apparently, consciousness has no structure, no form, and no content; indeed, consciousness *is* structure, *is* form, and *is* the content. Or simply: I am conscious, therefore the world is.

ON THE STATE-BOUND NATURE OF EXPERIENCE, ON PERCEPTIONS, AND HALLUCINATIONS

Conscious experience, we postulate, arises from the coupling of a particular state of subcortical *arousal** with the cortical (cognitive) *interpretation* of that arousal.

---

* There are two types of arousal, according to Hess (1961): ergotropic and trophotropic. Ergotropic arousal denotes behavioral patterns characterized by increased activity of the sympathetic nervous system and an activated psychic state. Trophotropic arousal results from an integration of parasympathetic with somatomotor activities to produce behavioral patterns that decrease the sensitivity to external stimuli.

Experience thus is symbolic and may be *state-bound* and can be evoked by inducing—naturally, hypnotically, or with the aid of drugs—a particular level of arousal, or by presenting some symbol of its interpretation such as an image, melody, or taste. The following passage from Juan Luis Vives is perhaps the oldest description of what we call *stateboundness:* "When I was a boy in Valencia, I was ill of a fever; while my taste was deranged I ate cherries; for many years afterwards, whenever I tasted the fruit I not only recalled the fever, but also seemed to experience it again" (Vives, 1538, p. 192).

Another passage, a contemporary example of stateboundness, is from *Swann's Way:*

And so, mechanically, weary after a dull day with the prospect of a dull morrow, I raised to my lips a spoonful of the tea in which I had soaked a morsel of the cake. No sooner had the warm liquid, and the crumbs in it, touched my palate than a shudder ran through my whole body, and I stopped intent upon the extraordinary changes that were taking place . . . .

Undoubtedly what is thus palpitating in the depths of my being must be the image, the visual memory which, being linked to that taste, has tried to follow it into my conscious mind (Proust, 1928, pp. 62, 64).

But Wordsworth goes even further. For him:

. . . all good poetry is the spontaneous overflow of powerful feelings: it takes its origin from emotion recollected in tranquility: the emotion is contemplated till, by a species of reaction, the tranquility gradually disappears, and an emotion, kindred to that which was before the subject of contemplation, is gradually produced, and does itself actually exist in the mind (p. 501).

In our terminology, Wordsworth's "emotion" can be equated with our "subcortical arousal" and his "contemplation" with our "cortical interpretation."

Another illustration of stateboundness is T. S. Eliot's:

. . . way of expressing emotion in the form of art [is] by finding an "objective correlative"; in other words, a set of objects, a situation, a chain of events which shall be the formula of that particular emotion; such that when the external facts, which must terminate in sensory experience, are given, the emotion is immediately invoked. . . . The artistic "inevitability" lies in this complete adequacy of the external to the emotion (1932, p. 711).

Like Wordsworth, Eliot uses "emotion" for "arousal" and his "objective correlative" seems to be analogous to our "cortical interpretation."

Maybe the criterion of masterful, hence effective, poetry is its ability to induce stateboundness for such eternally stereotyped (or archetypal) human experiences as deep love, intense hate, overwhelming joy, loneliness, ultimate dread, despair, searching hope, and cosmic ecstasy.

But state-bound recall can be evoked not only by imagery, melodies, and other symbols of the content of an experience, but also by simply inducing that particular level of arousal that prevailed during the initial experience, as in the next example. A young man complaining of unpleasant flashbacks from an LSD experience remembered on questioning that the events seemed to occur each time he took some pills prescribed for him (in the emergency room of a university hospital) "to drain my sinuses." The tablets were soon identified as amphetamine, which apparently produced the level of arousal necessary for recall of his previous (state-bound) drug experience. This, then, is the very nature of a flashback: the coupling of an experience to a level of drug-induced arousal that may be reinduced at a later time. In our opinion, LSD flashbacks are only a special case of the general phenomenon of stateboundness, and their unpleasant nature is likely due to the anxiety associated with a seemingly unprovoked experience.

The (common) experience in which alcohol induces the state of arousal necessary for the recall of a state-bound experience is depicted in the film *City Lights*. Here Charlie Chaplin saves a drunken millionaire from attempted suicide and so becomes his good friend. When sober, however, the millionaire does not remember Charlie. But:

> The millionaire does not stay sober long. When he is drunk again, he spots Charlie and treats him like a long-lost friend. He takes Charlie home with him, but in the morning, when he is again sober, he forgets that Charlie is his invited guest and has the butler throw him out (McDonald et al., 1965, p. 191).

Evidently, anamnesis or recollection extends either between states of drunkenness or between sober states, but there is complete amnesia (no recall) between the two discontinuous states of sobriety and drunkenness.

Another illustration of the discontinuity between states of sobriety and drunkenness is given in a recent letter written to me by an older member of Alcoholics Anonymous:

> ". . . there was a time when I was drinking . . . there was a lady in San Antonio. . . . I could find her home when I was drunk. But I could not find it when I was sober" (Personal communication, Jan. 20, 1972.)

Charlie's story has been recently remodeled and scientifically validated by Goodwin et al., (1969), who had 48 subjects memorize nonsense syllables while drunk. When sober, the subjects had difficulty recalling what they had learned, but could recall significantly better when made drunk again. The authors suggest that "the memory-deficit associated with changed state may reflect an impairment of retrieval, rather than of registration and retention." They list a dozen references on "state-dependent learning" in animals and man. Bustamante et al., (1970) also observed excitatory (induced by 20 mg of amphetamine) and inhibitory (induced by 200 mg of amobarbital) state-dependent recall of geometric configurations. Their volunteers memorized and later recalled the configurations under one of the two drugs. We submit, however, that although remembering from one state to another is usually called "state-dependent *learning*," extended practice, learning, or conditioning is *not* necessary for "stateboundness" to occur.*

* It is not easy to explain why stateboundness is somewhat similar to but nevertheless not quite the same as state-dependent learning. State-dependent learning implies that the individual is confronted with a learning task that may involve many trials and much practice. Conversely, a single experience may be sufficient to establish stateboundness. Moreover, state-dependent learning may be induced in any member of a population, whereas stateboundness can only be elicited in hypnotizable subjects who display a large standard deviation on a perceptual and/or behavioral task. (See the section "Interlude on Remembering (Perceiving) an Experience and Reexperiencing (Hallucinating) a Memory," and note, p. 210)

Charlie's story is a good illustration of the amnesia between different states of arousal; apparently, the more different these states are, the more complete is the amnesia. It is a well-known characteristic of so-called dissociated trance states that participants are unable to recall their content afterward. Prince (1968) describes a complete amnesia for the period of dissociation, and Bourguignon (1970) reports a brief period of disorientation as consciousness is regained after the amnesic dissociated state, as if one were "waking from sleep in unfamiliar surroundings." An analogous amnesia may follow violent acts of crime, enabling a criminal to deny sincerely an act he cannot recall. The partial amnesia of excited eyewitnesses for what actually happened may also explain the conflicting accounts reporters invariably obtain from honest, qualified witnesses (Fischer and Landon, 1972).

The implications of amnesia between different levels of arousal for criminology, jurisprudence, and psychotherapy have not yet been realized. Such amnesia explains why Sirhan Sirhan "had no recollection of shooting [Robert F.] Kennedy," and why hypnosis could clear up many details of the assassination. In our interpretation, psychiatrist Bernard L. Diamond (1969) hypnotically induced in Sirhan on several occasions that state of (ergotropic) hyperarousal during which the murder was committed. Only in this state could Sirhan reexperience and reenact the murder. The amnesia between this state and the normal waking state of interrogation was so complete that Sirhan denied having been hypnotized and "would say that the tape recordings made by Diamond during each session were fake or that the psychiatrist had a handwriting expert fake his writing."

(It is interesting that of a group of habitual LSD users, those who reported flashback experiences had a significantly higher mean score on a hypnotic susceptibility test than those who reported never having had a flashback [McGlothlin and Gattozzi, 1971].)

The examples with which we have so far illustrated the subcortical, arousal-state-bound nature of experience were exciting or ergotropic experiences. We contend, however, that stateboundness can also occur during states of tranquility or trophotropic arousal. For example, Barbara Brown (1971) has demonstrated that the association of "biofeedback-controlled" alpha state with a particular color may supplant the habitual feelings associated with that color. People who received a red feedback signal during the relaxed alpha state no longer gave the habitual associations of aggressiveness and anger with the color red. In our interpretation, the red color has been state-bound to the same serene feelings that were associated with the color blue by those people who had received blue feedback during alpha.

If a state-bound experience, or flashback, results from the coupling of arousal with its cortical interpretation, then *déjà vu* may be regarded as a dissociation of interpreting (cortical) and interpreted (subcortical) functions with strong emphasis on the subcortical or, emotional component. On the other hand, the depersonalization phenomenon can be conceived of as mainly cortical experience with emotional or affective dissociation or detachment (arousal deficit).*

---

* What is a "person"? The Romans conceived of "persona" as that which *per sonat* (sounds through the theatrical mask of the role player). According to our classification and terminology of depersonalization, the role player's sound is of a subcortical nature, whereas the role he plays appears to be his personal cortical interpretation.

The subcortical nature of that which *per sonat* seems to be borne out by Schaltenbrand's (1965) data. Through electrical stimulation of subcortical structures, he evoked speech. In contrast, Penfield and

A clinical example should illustrate this point.

A young woman experiences a derealization experience when she answered the door of the house she was living in with her in-laws to be. She stood there, petrified, overwhelmed by the feeling that the man who was standing at the door, her fiancé, was a person she had never seen before, a stranger. This lasted for a few seconds and during this time she wondered in embarrassment: *"How can I throw my arms around a stranger?"* The history revealed that she was dissatisfied, for various reasons, with her fiancé, and for some time before the incident she contemplated separation (Siomopoulos, 1972, p. 86).

If the main feature of depersonalization phenomena is pure detached cognition, *déjà vu* is a counterpart of depersonalization; *déjà vu* is pure affect, emotion, or arousal without specific cognitive or cortical interpretation.

Depersonalization phenomena which have been regarded as disturbances of body image or a loosening of ego boundaries, may occur during psychosis, in temporal-lobe epilepsy, in creative or ecstatic states, and while falling asleep (Fischer, 1969a).

Hallucinogenic drugs can also induce depersonalization experiences, but these occur rather rarely—about 3 to 4% of the time, according to McGlothlin and Gattozzi (1971), who obtained their data from a follow-up of 247 LSD users.

During depersonalization, subjects may feel temporarily like disembodied spirits, because of what MacLean (1964) calls "the 'schizophysiology' of limbic and neocortical systems." The findings in psychomotor epilepsy suggest that without a simultaneous integration of somatovisceral functions by the limbic brain, or cortical interpretation, there is inability to identify with and remember what is transpiring in the external environment. During depersonalization, therefore, the subject feels as if he is viewing himself and what is going on from a distance.

The first LSD-induced depersonalization was recorded by the discoverer of LSD himself, Hofmann (1968), who "observed, in the manner of an independent neutral observer . . ." and "occasionally felt as if I were out of my body."

One of our volunteers, during a psilocybin-induced religious conversion, described her experience with the words "as if I were outside my body" (Fischer, 1970c).

For Celia Green's (1968) subjects, who were under the influence of mescaline, "the visible world . . . [is] seen in the out-of-the-body state." But not only hallucinogenic [i.e., hyperthermia-inducing drugs like mescaline, LSD, and psilocybin (Isbell et al., 1961; Wolbach et al., 1962; Hebbard and Fischer, 1966)] can evoke out-of-the-body experiences. Fever can do the same: "As my temperature was getting higher and higher I became aware that I was no longer in my body but up in the corner of my cubicle watching the nurses flitting about . . . bathing the body lying in my bed. . ." (Green, 1968, p. 24).

---

other investigators could never do this when stimulating cortical structures, and they obtained only unintelligible vocalizations.

Note also the involvement of subcortical structures in dreams: "Coincident with the occurrence of rapid eye movements during sleep ponto-geniculate-occipital spikes (PGO spikes) emanate from the brainstem reticular system" (Jouvet, 1969). PGO spikes, as their name implies, reach the lateral geniculate body and occipital cortex. Thus the brainstem and the visual cortex are linked functionally during the stage of sleep in which there is active visual imaging (Smith et al., 1971, p. 166).

The "realism" of an out-of-the-body experience, however, breaks down when the subject attempts to touch or handle something (willed motor performance). In fact, there is an exclusive relationship between willed motor performance and the ability to maintain apparitions. Ahlenstiel's (1954) self-observations convincingly illustrate this inverse relationship: the image of an illusory poodle disappeared not at the instant he moved his hand to touch the poodle, but at the very moment he decided to reach out. It thus appears that not only the voluntary motor component but also the willed intention remain inhibited during apparitions or visions.

Ergotropic (or hyper-) arousal, the central sympathetic excitation induced by hallucinogenic drugs, is not a prerequisite for body-image changes leading to the experience of disembodiment. Feedback-controlled meditation, a physiological state of trophotropic (or hypo-) arousal, associated with striated muscle relaxation, may also result in profound changes in body image. Subjects with such changes report: "I am not even sitting here. I feel like I'm just detached in some way . . ." (Green et al., 1970, p. 8).

Moreover, exceptional individuals in deep meditation, with the "attention drawn to the crown of the head, contemplating an imaginary lotus in full bloom" (i.e., during *dhyān*, a yogic meditation practice and meditation state), while seated motionless and erect, may have a Kundalini experience (Krishna, 1971), an all-embracing oceanic experience that can be translated into the language of neurophysiology. The Kundalini experience apparently starts with a meditation linked to trophotropic arousal and rebounds into an out-of-the-body type of depersonalization phenomenon that is linked to ergotropic arousal:

> . . . the illumination grew brighter and brighter, the roaring louder, I experienced a rocking sensation and then felt myself slipping out of my body, entirely enveloped in a halo of light . . . .
> . . . I was no longer myself . . . a small point of awareness confined in a body, but instead was a vast circle of consciousness in which the body was but a point, bathed in light and in a state of exaltation and happiness impossible to describe. After some time, the duration of which I could not judge, the circle began to narrow down; I felt myself contracting, becoming smaller and smaller, until I again became dimly conscious of the outline of my body . . . (Krishna, 1971, pp. 61, 66).

Another "trophotropic rebound" (Gellhorn, 1969, 1970) follows then in form of a "fatigued depression."

At this point, we may ask whether state-bound flashbacks, *déjà vu* experiences, and depersonalization phenomena are perceptions or hallucinations. This of course depends on the definitions given for perception and hallucination.

Are the physicist's tracks produced in cloud chambers, bubble chambers, or nuclear emulsions, hallucinations because they are "perceptions without an object," thus conforming to Lhermitte's (1951) definition of hallucinations? And what about other forms of energy (e.g., pulsed microwaves that induce the hearing of hissing and clicking sounds, or magnetic fields provoking phosphenes)? And did the Apollo astronauts, while in translunar flight, hallucinate the flashes of light evoked by the action of cosmic rays, which are definitely not "objects" (Charman and Rowlands, 1971)? Evidently, selective attention is to be paid to the very logic of language and to that logic which is based on sensory observation—or first-order interaction—and willed motor verification—or second-order interaction—with the observed.

We posit that for self-referential, self-organizing man the proof of the sensory pudding is in the motor eating; that is we regard perceptions as exteroceptive sensory experiences that one is able and willing to check out through voluntary motor activity. Perceptions, however, are gradually transformed into hallucinations when the arousal level of daily routine is either raised or lowered. It is at these ergotropic or trophotropic levels of arousal that one is unwilling and unable to verify intense interoceptive sensory experiences. Without motor verification or measurement, the system is not constrained, and things that appeared are re-presented as appearances of things (i.e., dreams or hallucinations). Dreams and hallucinations are therefore aroused experiences characterized by high sensory-to-motor ratios. In perceptions, however, appearances of things are transformed into things that appear (Straus, 1962). In other words, perceptions are experiences characterized by a low sensory-to-motor ratio and by a level of arousal that corresponds to that of normal daily routine. Our definition, therefore, implies that any method, be it chemical, electrical, or hypnotic, that raises the sensory-to-motor ratio can be instrumental in producing hallucinations.

A technological, material culture preoccupied with perception of the real and measurable, a society changing its environment to fit the goals of its restless Faustian explorers and developers—such a society, whose individual members display a strong *I*-in-the-world awareness, has to stigmatize those who are preoc-cupied with the imaginary and unmeasurable. People who have hallucinations may not have strong drives or objectives in the outer world and are not impressed by objects. Thus when they hallucinate, they have "perceptions without an object" (Lhermitte, 1951). And the American Psychiatric Association's official glossary defines hallucination as "a false sensory perception in the absence of an actual external stimulus" that "may be induced by emotional and/or such other factors as drugs, alcohol and stress" (*Psychiatric Glossary*, 1964).

In religious, inner-*self*-oriented civilizations that put more value on meditation, prayer, insight, and revelations than on perceptible objects and objectives, hal-lucinations are not regarded as pathological. Introspective, or inner, sensations apparently are in no need of verification in the outer dimensions of physical reality. Each reality is to be tested in the proper dimension to which it belongs: "If there is a prophet among you, I the Lord make myself known to him in *vision*, I speak with him in a dream . . . in dark speech" (Numbers 12:6, 8).

Historically, we seem to oscillate between one culture that puts high value on outer perception and another that puts high value on inner hallucination. This may well be because both the 10% of the normal population that experience vivid visual imagery and the 48% that experience vivid auditory imagery have unim-paired reality-testing capable of correctly differentiating extrinsic from intrinsic stimuli (Mintz and Alpert, 1972).

Since it is plausible that those who do not experience vivid imagery in any modality have difficulty believing the reports of those who do, visionaries will always be explained, according to the prevailing zeitgeist, as somnambulists, endowed with animal magnetism, or as hallucinating sick people.

We do not imply that the hallucinations of schizophrenics should be regarded as healthy phenomena, and we refer the reader to a more detailed treatment of this topic (Fischer, 1972a). It is, however, important to distinguish between the inability of an hallucinated person to verify the nature of his experience (impaired reality-testing) and the vivid visual or auditory imagery of a person who is able and willing to verify his experience through voluntary motor activity.

A CARTOGRAPHY OF INNER SPACE

In attempting to map inner space, we have placed perceptions and hallucinations on a continuum of increasing ergotropic arousal (Fischer, 1971a). Along this continuum of increasing ergotropic, apparently norandrenergic (Brodie, 1958), arousal, man—the self-referential system—perceptually and behaviorally (cortically) interprets the change (drug-induced or natural) in his subcortical activity as creative, psychotic, or ecstatic experiences. These states are marked by a gradual turning inward toward a mental dimension at the expense of the physical. The normal state of daily routine, our point of departure, is followed by an aroused, creative state, which can be characterized by an increase in both data content (a description of space) and rate of data processing (flood of inner sensation, or more intense time) (Fischer, 1967, 1970a). However, in the next aroused state on the continuum, the acute schizophrenic (or rather, hyperphrenic) state, a further increase in data content may not be matched by an increase in the rate of data

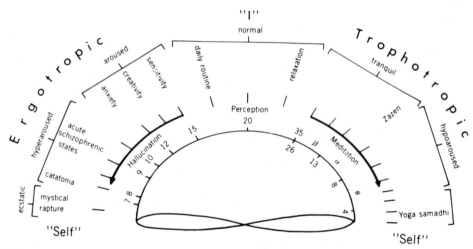

Figure 1. Varieties of conscious states mapped on a perception–hallucination continuum of increasing ergotropic arousal (left) and a perception–meditation continuum of increasing trophotropic arousal (right). These levels of subcortical hyper- and hypoarousal are cortically or cognitively interpreted by man as normal, creative, hyperphrenic, and ecstatic states (left) and *zazen* and *samādhi* (right). With increasing hyperarousal—from relaxation to catatonia—there is a decrease in variability of the EEG amplitude, measured as the coefficient of variation, which decreases from 35 to 7 (Goldstein et al., 1963). The similarity between horizontally corresponding states of hypo- and hyperarousal from the left to the right may be understood by noting that the coefficient of variation is in the same low range of magnitude during deep meditation (Goldstein and Stoltzfus, 1973) as it is in catatonia (i.e., 7 to 8). With increasing hypoarousal (i.e., from relaxation to *samādhi*), there is a gradual emergence of beta, alpha, and then theta EEG waves with their characteristic hertz frequencies of 26 to 13, 12 to 8, and 7 to 4 Hz. The loop connecting ecstasy and *samādhi* represents the trophotropic rebound, which is observed in response to intense ergotropic hyperarousal.

processing. Whereas the creative state is conducive to the evolution of novel relations and new meaning, the psychotic "jammed computer" state interferes with the individual's creative interpretation of the activity of his central nervous system. At the peak of ecstatic rapture, the outside physical world "retreats to the fringe of consciousness" (St. Teresa, 1957), and the individual reflects himself in his own "program" (Fig. 1).

One can conceptualize the normal, creative, hyperphrenic, and ecstatic states along the perception–hallucination continuum as the ledges of a homeostatic step function (Ashby, 1960). Whereas the creative person may travel freely between "normal" and creative states, the chronic schizophrenic patient is stranded in the "jammed computer" state. And the talented mystic, of course, does not need to go through every intermediate step to attain ecstasy.

The mutually exclusive relationship between the ergotropic and trophotropic systems (Gellhorn, 1970) justifies a separate perception–meditation continuum of increasing trophotropic, apparently serotonergic (Brodie, 1958) arousal (hypo-arousal) that is continuous with, and to the right of, the perception–hallucination continuum (Figs. 1 and 3). Along this tranquil perception–meditation continuum, man may cortically interpret his gradually increasing trophotropic arousal as *zazen, dhārnā, dhyān, savichār samādhi,* and, ultimately, *nirvichār samādhi* (for the meaning of these Sanskrit words denoting focused meditative states, see Jain and Jain, 1973).

We can describe verifiable perceptions, therefore, by assigning to them low sensory-to-motor (S/M) ratios (Fischer et al., 1970b; Thatcher et al., 1970), whereas nonverifiable hallucinations and dreams can be characterized by increasing S/M ratios as one moves along the perception–hallucination or perception–meditation continua toward ecstasy or *samādhi,* the two most hallucinatory states (Fischer et al., 1969; Strauss, 1969; Fischer, 1971a) (Figs. 1 and 3, left and right, respectively). Moderate doses of the hallucinogenic drugs LSD, psilocybin, and mescaline can start one moving along the perception–hallucination continuum, whereas minor tranquilizers and some muscle relaxants may initiate travel along the perception–meditation continuum.

We have given a quantitative meaning to the S/M ratio by measuring the components of a psychomotor performance—specifically, handwriting area and handwriting pressure in volunteers during a waking-dream state induced by an hallucinogenic drug.

The techniques for measuring handwriting area (S, in square centimeters), as well as for obtaining handwriting pressure (M, in 10^4 dynes averaged over time), with an indicator that operates on a pressure-voltage-to-frequency basis, have been described elsewhere (Fischer et al., 1970a; Thatcher et al., 1970). Using these two parameters prior to T_1 and at the peak (T_2) of a psilocybin-induced experience (160 to 250 μg of psilocybin per kilogram of body weight), we found in a sample of 47 college-age volunteers a 31% ($T_2 - T_1$) increase in mean S/M ratio.

We should note that the standard deviation (S.D.) on handwriting area or another more complex perceptual-behavioral task at T_1 is significantly related to the S/M at T_1 ($r = 0.4888, P < .01, N = 47$) and that the standard deviation is a simple and useful indicator of the ensuing drug-induced increase in S/M ratio ($r = 0.372, P < .01, N = 47$). The S.D. is a measure of intraindividual variability computed from subjects who would copy a 28-word text four times on separate sheets of paper under standardized conditions. The surface area of each sample is then determined (cm²) and the standard deviation on the handwriting area is computed. The degree of variability is significantly related to and a reliable predictor of the intensity of behavior displayed during the six-to-eight-hour period following the test. The predictive character of the S.D. holds up irrespective of whether the ensuing behavior was drug-induced, hypnotically induced, or modified by sensory attenuation (Panton and Fischer, 1973). The S.D. apparently reflects organismic variability in terms of the "size" of the cortical repertoire (variance being operationally identified with information, i.e., cognitive interpreting ability).

We have interpreted this arousal-induced increase in handwriting area as a foreshortening of nearby visual space. In fact, we have measured such an hallucinogen-induced contraction of nearby visual space with another direct technique by monitoring the apparent frontoparallel plane. The frontoparallel plane corresponds to that fixation distance at which subjects are able to align linearly pins that are positioned one to two meters in front of them (Fischer et al., 1970b; Hill and Fischer, 1970). Such transformation of perceptual constancies under ergotropic arousal can also be observed in acute schizophrenics under natural ergotropic arousal (i.e., without hallucinogens). The transformation of constancies during acute psychotic episodes apparently gives rise to a "vertical displacement of the visual angle," which is implicit in a contraction of visual space and results in an elevation of the horizon. Rennert (1969), who for years has studied the angle of perspective in the drawings of schizophrenic patients, finds the acuteness of a schizophrenic episode to be significantly related to the height of the horizon in the patient's drawings. In fact, Rennert claims to be able to predict

Figure 2. Etching, made during an acute schizophrenic episode, demonstrates the contraction of nearby visual space, which results in a raised horizon (original size, 130 × 100 mm.; reduced 62%). (Through the courtesy of Dr. Leo Navratil, Niederoesterreichisches Landeskrankenhaus für Psychiatrie und Neurologie, Klosterneuburg, bei Wien, Austria.)

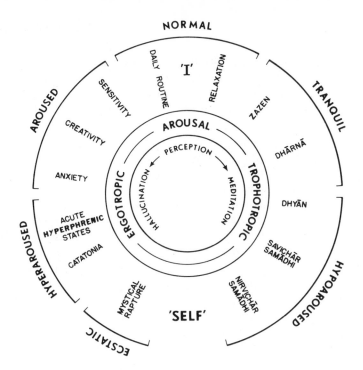

Figure 3. Varieties of conscious states mapped on a perception–hallucination continuum of increasing ergotropic or hyperarousal (left half) and a perception–meditation continuum of increasing trophotropic or hypoarousal (right half). These levels of subcortical arousal are cortically or cognitively interpreted by Western and Eastern man as normal, creative, hyperphrenic, catatonic, and ecstatic states (left) and *zazen, dhārnā, dhyān,* and *samādhi* (right), respectively. During both increasing hyperarousal (characterized by EEG desynchronization) and increasing hypoarousal (characterized by EEG synchronization), there is a decrease in variability of the EEG amplitude. The similarity between horizontally corresponding states of hypo- and hyperarousal from the left to the right is borne out, for instance, by the observation that Goldstein's coefficient of variation is in the same low range of magnitude during deep meditation as it is in catatonia (7 to 8). For the specific meaning of the focused meditative states *dhārnā,* and *dhyān* and the two *samādhi* states, namely *sa-vichār* (with thought) as well as *nir-vichār* (without thought) *samādhi,* see Jain and Jain (1973). *Nir-vichār samādhi* may be consciousness without content, a right-hemispheric cognition of the vivid. The shift from *sa-vichār* to *nir-vichār samādhi* may indeed mark the completion of the shift of information processing from the dominant to the nondominant cerebral hemisphere.

In this circular and more detailed version of the map in Fig. 1, it is perhaps easier to discern that the *Self* of ecstasy and *samādhi* are one and the same. Travel to inner space may proceed from the *I*-state (top) to the *Self* (bottom) on either the perception–hallucination (left) or perception–meditation continuum (right). Return to the *I*-in-the-world state is possible either by using again the path of travel or through horizontal rebound(s) in a zigzag manner. Rebounds may also be labeled as physiologically protective (or if you wish, therapeutic) abreactions.

The physiologically most important rebound proceeds from ecstasy to *nir-vichār samādhi;* it is a rebound from a Faustian trip of creative-psychotic fragmentation or individuation into the cosmic-oceanic peace of unity. Another culturally determined rebound—namely, that which proceeds from *samādhi* to ecstasy—is called the *Kundalini* experience.

The autonomic or subcortical part of experiences on the perception–hallucination continuum can be said to be governed by norepinephrinergic mechanisms, whereas catatonia is conceptualized to follow in response to a switchover to dopaminergic mediation. In certain subjects, however, there is no switchover; hence a full blown mania develops, which—in bipolar patients—may rebound into a depression. Such a depression may be the *dhyān* state if experienced by an Eastern Sanyasi, one of the 17,000,000 holy men who live secluded in forests as religious mendicants. If such a holy man is given a very high dose of LSD, "nothing happens" (Ram Dass, 1973), illustrating the culture-bound nature of consciousness in general and certain rebound states in particular. Note also that consciousness creates culture and culture creates consciousness.

remissic n or relapse from the position of the horizon in a drawing: the more severe the schizophrenic episode, the higher the position of the horizon, as measured by a ruler. Ultimately, the horizon may even disappear. At the same time, a maplike perspective, or bird's-eye view, of the landscape results in houses' and other significant figures appearing in the foreground (Fig. 2). According to Navratil (personal communication), this etching was made during an acute (hyperaroused) schizophrenic episode and demonstrates the contraction of nearby visual space, resulting in a raised horizon. Note that the elevation of the horizon forces the animals to walk at a steep angle. In another etching executed by the same patient after remission, the horizon is low (Navratil, 1969).

The arousal-induced increase in handwriting area or contraction of nearby visual space during hallucinatory or waking-dream states is one example of the transformation of perceptual constancy (Fischer, 1970a). These information or signal/noise ratios (i.e., dimensionless quantities) are part of our learned projections associated with physical space-time and daily routine levels of arousal. Other constancies, or invariants, such as those of size, hue, color, and taste, are also gradually transformed or unlearned when one progresses on the perception –hallucination continuum from the normal through the creative, psychotic, and, ultimately, to the ecstatic state (Fig. 1). The further we progress on the continuum, the more complete is the transformation, or unlearning, of the constancies of the physical dimension. Thus St. Teresa of Avila tells us in her autobiography that at the peak of a mystical experience, "the soul neither hears nor sees nor feels. While it lasts, none of the senses perceives or knows what is taking place" (St. Teresa, 1957, p. 143). Space and time, then, which were gradually established in ever-widening circles during childhood, gradually contract with increasing arousal and ultimately disappear (Fischer et al., 1970b).

With rising levels of ergotropic and trophotropic arousal, interpretive behavior becomes increasingly dependent on (or less free of) the subcortical substratum that generates it. A cat responds to ergotropic hyperarousal with rage, whereas at the peak of trophotropic arousal the animal always yawns, curls up, and falls asleep. But man may be compelled to interpret these two extreme states of hyper- and hypoarousal as ecstasy and *samādhi*. This increasing stereotypy (loss of freedom) with increasing ergotropic arousal can be observed, for example, as a decrease in the variability of the EEG amplitude, which Goldstein and others have measured with the Drohocki integration method (Goldstein et al., 1963; Marjerrison et al., 1967). A decrease in variability is expressed as the coefficient of variation for states ranging from relaxation to catatonia in Fig. 1 (Thatcher et al., 1971). Increasing stereotypy also manifests itself as an increase in the S/M ratio (Fischer et al., 1970a; Thatcher et al., 1970), thus indicating an intensification of inner sensations, accompanied by a loss in the ability to verify them through voluntary motor activity. Such high S/M ratios are implicit in the statements uttered during both drug-induced hallucinations and the hallucinations of schizophrenics: "of being hypnotized," "of being not free," "of being overpowered," "of being paralyzed," and so on, and in the mystic's inability to experience the subject–object dichotomy of daily routine in the physical dimension.

Apparently, then, an increase in ergotropic arousal is paralleled by a restriction in the individual's repertoire of available perceptual-behavioral interpretations.

This restriction implies that certain levels can only be interpreted as creative (artistic, scientific, religious) or psychotic experiences (Fischer, 1972a). Although a religious interpretation is a common feature of catatonia (Weitbrecht, 1948), ecstasy, which is the mystical experience of the Oneness of everything, results from a creative breakthrough out of catatonic hyperarousal. During the ecstatic state, there is neither capacity nor necessity for motor verification of the intense sensations. In the mental dimension, in contrast to the physical, the all-pervasive experience of absolute certainty does not require further verification* and will be structured according to current mythology or the belief system of a St. Francis, Pascal, or Ramakrishna. What is one man's loss of freedom, therefore, may be another's gain in creativity.

An increasing stereotypy can also be observed along the perception–meditation continuum of increasing trophotropic arousal (Fig. 1, right). This enables one to gradually exclude stimulation from without and turn attention inward. Continuous trains of alpha waves accompany these changes, and the dominant frequency of the alpha pattern decreases toward the alpha–theta border region (Fig. 1, right), until some subjects, in a state of reverie, produce long trains of theta waves† (Kasamatsu and Hirai, 1966). According to Green et al. (1970), the "alert innerfocused state is associated with the production of alpha rhythm" (p. 10). In this state, Zen masters show an alpha-blocking response to auditory clicks; in contrast to normal controls, they do not habituate to these stimuli (Kasamatsu and Hirai, 1966). Since the alpha rhythm is not altered or blocked by flashing lights, sounding gongs, or the touch of a hot test tube during the deep meditation of Indian Yoga masters (Anand et al., 1961) the yoga *samādhi* apparently represents a more intense state of trophotropic arousal than *zazen* does and must also express a greater inability to function in physical space-time than *zazen*. In fact, a yoga master denies noticing any outside stimuli during deep meditation, whereas control subjects show alpha-blocking with as little stimulus as a flashing light.

The difference in intensity between *zazen* and *samādhi* can also be illustrated when approaching these experiences *qua* experience. "Not to be attached to something is to be aware of its absolute value" says the Zen Master Shunryu Suzuki (1970, p. 75). This nonattachment is in our terminology a detachment of the cortical "self-centered ideas of value" from the subcortical arousal or emotional activity; *zazen* teaches us how to detach, hence not to be (state-) bound. The aim of *zazen* is to experience everything on the same low level of subcortical arousal but nevertheless to be receptive and appreciating.

But for the yoga master in deep meditation

> . . . here in this emptiness there is no form, no perception, no name, no concepts, no knowledge. No eye, no ear, no nose, no tongue, no body, no mind. No form, no sound, no smell, no taste, no touch, no objects. There is no knowledge, no ignorance, no decay nor death. It is the Self (Cowell et al., 1969, p. 148).

* Pascal, at the peak of his decisive religious illumination, recorded: "Fire. /God of Abraham, God of Isaac, God of Jacob, /not of the philosophers and the scientists. /Certainty." (Arland, 1946).

† It is likely that these parietal, low-frequency EEG waves are related to dendritic field-potential charges.

INTERLUDE ON REMEMBERING (PERCEIVING) AN EXPERIENCE AND REEXPERIENCING (HALLUCINATING) A MEMORY

Given the state-bound nature of experience, and because amnesia exists between the state of normal daily experience and all other states of hyper- and hypo-arousal, it follows that what is called subconscious is but another name for this amnesia. Therefore, instead of postulating *one* subconscious, I recognize as many layers of self-awareness as there are levels of arousal and corresponding symbolic interpretations in the individual's interpretive repertoire. The many layers of self-awareness remind one of the captain with girl friends in many ports, each girl unaware of the existence of the others, and each existing only from visit to visit (i.e., from state to state). This is how multiple existences become possible: by living from one waking state to another waking state; from one dream to the next; from one amobarbital narcoanalysis session to the next; from LSD to LSD; from epileptic aura to epileptic aura; from one creative, artistic, religious, or psychotic inspiration or possession to another; from trance to trance; and from reverie to reverie (Fischer, 1971a).

Only certain people can recall a state-bound experience with an intensity indistinguishable from that of the initial experience. We contrast these recallers (Fischer, 1969b) with those who only remember an experience. Recallers as a group are variable subjects, as illustrated by the following example.

We repeatedly exposed to psilocybin one of our variable college-girl volunteers (Gwynne et al., 1969, p. 225, subject N.B.). The subject exhibited a consistently large standard deviation on perceptual (Gwynne et al., 1969, p. 225) and behavioral (*ibid.*, p. 227) tasks,*–hence the designation "variable." Later, a hypnotically induced drug experience (Gwynne et al., 1969) was substituted for the psilocybin experience. The hypnotic induction placed the subject in a peaceful beach scene with waves lapping at the seashore. Our experiments had to be interrupted after two sessions, since N.B. left for a Florida vacation. On her return, she reported a surprising event while walking down to the beach for the first time: when gazing at the seashore the whole scene suddenly "blacked out," and instead her "old beach" returned—the beach of the hypnotically induced psilocybin experience. Just as Sirhan's state-bound experience may have been evoked by hypnotically inducing the appropriate level of arousal and/or by presenting symbols of its experiential content, our variable college girl's hypnotically induced experience could be recalled (and relived) by exposure to an aspect of ordinary reality that represented the hypnotic experience.

An evaluation of our data (Gwynne et al., 1969; Landon and Fischer, 1970) shows that a variable subject with a large standard deviation, the recaller of an experience in the mental dimension, possesses a larger perceptual-behavioral or

---

* A subject's stability or variability can be measured with a large variety of perceptual and/or behavioral tasks. The simplest and most convenient method is to compute a subject's standard deviation on repeated measurements of his handwriting area, as described earlier (Fischer et al., 1970d; Landon and Fischer, 1970; Thatcher et al., 1970).

The standard deviation on handwriting area apparently reflects organismic or intraindividual variability in terms of information available as cortical repertoire. Note that we operationally identify variability with information (i.e., cognitive interpretive ability).

interpretive repertoire than a stable subject, whose small standard deviations characterize his smaller repertoire. Moreover, variable recallers and stable performers retain their characteristics not only without drugs but also at the peak of a psilocybin experience, during an hypnotically induced hallucinatory experience (Gwynne et al., 1969), and even under both sensory attenuation and hallucinogen induction (Panton and Fischer, 1973). Bourguignon (1970), emphasizing the distinction between trance and possession trance, concludes that the differences are implicit in two types of subjects: "the trancer . . . *experiences* (sees, hears, etc.) while the possession trancer, once he learns his expected role, *performs* for an audience" (p. 90). We would describe Bourguignon's "trancers" and "possession trancers" as variable and stable subjects, respectively.

At this point we reemphasize the two criteria necessary for an individual to experience stateboundness, or flashbacks, on the perception–hallucination or perception–meditation continua: high score on hypnotic suggestibility and large standard deviation on a variety of perceptual and/or behavioral tasks.

SELF: THE KNOWER AND IMAGE MAKER, AND I: THE KNOWN AND IMAGINED

The departure from the physical dimension during a voyage on the perception –meditation continuum is accompanied by a gradual loss of freedom, which is manifested by the increasing inability to verify the experience through voluntary motor activity. At the peak of trophotropic arousal, in *samādhi*, the meditating subject experiences nothing but his own self-referential nature, devoid of compelling contents. It is not difficult to see a similarity between the meditative experience of pure self-reference and St. Teresa's description of her ecstasy: in both timeless and spaceless experiences, the mundane world is virtually excluded. Of course, the converse is true of the mundane state of daily routine, in which the oceanic unity with the universe, in ecstasy and *samādhi*, is virtually absent. Thus the mutual exclusiveness of the normal and the exalted states, both ecstasy and *samādhi*, allows us to postulate that man, the self-referential system, exists on two levels: as *Self* in the mental dimension of exalted states; and as *I* in the objective world, where he is able and willing to change the physical dimension "out there." In fact, the *I* and the *Self* can be postulated on purely logical grounds. Consider, for instance, Brown's reasoning that the universe is apparently

. . . constructed in order (and thus in such a way as to be able) to see itself. But in order to do so, evidently it must first cut itself up into at least one state which sees, and at least one other state which is seen. In this severed and mutilated condition, whatever it sees is only partially itself . . . but, in any attempt to see itself as an object, it must, equally undoubtedly, act so as to make itself distinct from, and therefore, false to, itself. In this condition it will always partially elude itself (Brown, 1969, p. 105).

In our terminology, the *Self* of exalted states is that which sees and knows, and the *I* is the interpretation, that which is seen and known in the physical space-time of the world out there. The mutually exclusive relationship between the "seer" and the "seen," or the elusiveness of the *Self* and the *I*, may have its physiological basis in the mutual exclusiveness* of the ergotropic and trophotropic systems (Gellhorn, 1969).

A discernible communication between the *Self* and the *I* is possible only during the dreaming and hallucinatory states, whether drug-induced or natural. These states are approximately halfway between the *I* and the *Self* on the perception –hallucination and perception–meditation continua. Such *I–Self* communication is the creative source of art, science, literature, and religion (Fischer and Landon, 1972).

Despite the mutually exclusive relationship between the ergotropic and trophotropic systems, there is, nevertheless, a phenomenon called "rebound to superactivity," or "trophotropic rebound," which is a response to intense sym-pathetic excitation (Gellhorn, 1970), that is, at ecstasy, the peak of ergotropic arousal. A rebound into *samādhi* at this point can be conceived of as a physiological protective mechanism. Gellhorn (1968, 1969, 1970) was among the first to notice that the rebound of the trophotropic system is not confined to the autonomic branches but causes significant changes in behavior as well. Thus repetitive stimulation of the reticular formation in the midbrain increases the arousal level in awake cats, but this phase is followed by one in which the animal yawns, lies down, and finally falls asleep. This rebound phase is associated with the appear-ance of theta potentials in the hippocampus (Fischer, 1971a), just as the corres-ponding human trophotropic rebound or *samādhi* (Fig. 1, right) is characterized by EEG theta potentials (Green et al., 1970). These rebound or reversal phenomena between ecstasy and *samādhi* (Gellhorn 1968, 1969, 1970) are implicit in the proximity between the two extreme exalted states in Fig. 1 and in the circular version of the same model in Fig. 3.

The *Self* of ecstasy and *samādhi* are one and the same, as if the reflecting surface of a lake in Fig. 1 or in Fig. 3 embraced both exalted states. If the level of water in such a lake were gradually raised, it would intersect successive and corresponding hyper- and hypoaroused states. The intersected states represent levels of gradu-ally diminishing subjectivity (less *Self*) and increasing objectivity (more *I*), until eventually the objective *I*-state-of-the-world is reached. The inner space walk on a water level of corresponding hyper- and hypoaroused states may be referred to as experiencing a stratum of consciousness, and it should be noted that some of us have more of these strata than others. The inability to "walk" may be the impaired ability for physiological rebound;† that is, the tendency to maintain ergotropic- –trophotropic balance (Gellhorn, 1969).

---

* Apparently the same exclusiveness makes St. Augustine (399, p. 186) and Angelus Silesius (1657, p. 149) exclaim in wonder: "Thus the mind is not large enough to contain itself: but where can that part of it be which it does not contain?" and "I don't know what I am, I am not what I know."

† Not everybody is capable of "rebounding," as we have observed when measuring time and space contraction under the influence of 160 μg/kg psilocybin. The larger the S.D. of a volunteer on a perceptual or behavioral task prior to the drug, the more extreme will be his drug-induced time contraction (i.e., the experiencing of more data content within a chronological time unit resulting in an overestimation of time, and space). Such *variable* volunteers will experience a strong rebound 24 hours after the drug; that is, they will greatly underestimate time and space. The smaller a subject's S.D. under predrug conditions, the closer to normal will be his time and space estimation at drug peak and, accordingly, smaller his rebound 24 hours later. The most *stable* subjects—those rather rare individuals with the smallest standard deviations—will not experience either a contraction of time at drug peak or a rebound during the next day (Fischer, 1970a).

Thus each level of water would connect a hyper- and hypoaroused state with a specific subjectivity/objectivity (or *Self*-to-*I*) ratio, implying a similarity between states connected by each level. For example, this similarity might be used to account for the success of the widely practiced narcoanalytic technique of abreacting or rebounding a traumatic, hyperaroused experience in a hypoaroused state of similar *Self*-to-*I* ratio. The similarity between corresponding hyper- and hypoaroused states could also account for the hypermnesic phenomena of the hypoaroused elderly, who clearly recall the hyperaroused experiences of their youth but do not recall more recent experiences (as suggested by L. Navratil).

During the *I*-state of daily routine, the outside world is experienced as separate from oneself, and this may be a reflection of the greater freedom or separateness of cortical interpretation from subcortical activity. With increasing ergotropic and trophotropic arousal, however, this separateness gradually disappears, apparently because in the *Self*-state of ecstasy and *samādhi*, cortical and subcortical activity are indistinguishably integrated. This unity is reflected in the experience of Oneness with everything, a Oneness with the universe that is oneself.

ON PEACE OF MIND(s), OR THE BIHEMISPHERIC INTEGRATION OF ARISTOTELIAN CATEGORIES AND PLATONIC IDEAS

The discontinuity between perceptions and hallucinations posited by the scholastics and eloquently represented by St. Thomas Aquinas (Sarbin and Juhasz, 1967), may have its roots in the dual—objective and subjective—facets of our nature. Although we experience the universe inside ourselves as *Self*-referential *sensation*, we can still change that universe outside through willed *motor* activity or goal-seeking verification. The discontinuity, however, may also be a reflection of our brain and its two minds.

It is well to remember that in the split brain, each cerebral hemisphere can process information independently with respect to nearly all higher functions (Bogen, 1970). Decision and verification-demanding tasks of daily routine which subserve survival and are processed at moderate (lower) levels of arousal are solved with our left, rational, analytical mind, whereas the activity of the other hemisphere is inhibited or, if you wish, disengaged. Such disengagement can be measured: more alpha activity is recorded from the back of the head (occipital area) in the right or nondominant side of the brain (Morgan et al., 1971).

The right hemisphere is concerned with nonverbal information processing, visuospatial gestalts and fields, multivalued metaphors, music, and imagery: it is our analogical, intuitive mind.

The left hemisphere, the dominant one in most right-handed and in two-thirds of left-handed people (Zangwill, 1960), functions within the framework of a two-valued or Aristotelian (yes–no; true–false) digital logic underlying speech, language, and arithmetic.

The two cerebral hemispheres communicate with each other (transfer of information) through the *corpus callosum* (Bogen, 1969 a, 1969b; Bogen and Bogen, 1969; Bogen et al., 1972). Although each hemisphere can process information independently, the right hemisphere, being nonverbal, cannot "talk." Moreover, certain kinds of left-hemispheric activity may directly suppress or inhibit certain kinds of right-hemispheric action, and vice versa. Or in the words of Bogen and Bogen:

> If transcallosal inhibition is indeed a prominent aspect of cerebral function, we can see a physiological basis for the fact that failure to develop fresh insights (in the sense of new understanding of the outside world) is closely related to a failure to gain further sight into one's other self (1969, p. 201).

At this point, we may specify that the rational I-state of daily routine—illustrated on the top or the starting point (i.e., between the two continua of our model, Figs. 1 and 3)—may be relegated to left-hemispheric or propositional activity, whereas the *Self* (Figs. 1 and 3, bottom) may be experienced as right-hemispheric appositional or intuitive activity.*

Interhemispheric communication [i.e., integration of verbal (left) and visuo-spatial (right) ideas] may then be the basis of innovative ideation or creativity. So-called ordinary people may have creative experiences, but they are unable to communicate them intraindividually (i.e., even within themselves), whereas the ecstasies of St. Teresa, St. Francis, and the *samādhis* of Ramakrishna, although ineffable, become hemispherically integrated and interindividually communicable creative performances—peace of mind(s).

It is now becoming experimentally established that data processing is preferentially shifted to the visuospatial, the *right* cerebral hemisphere, whenever one departs on the perception–hallucination continuum naturally, as, for example, during the REM-dream state (Goldstein et al., 1972), through the assistance of waking-dream-state-inducing hallucinogenic drugs (Goldstein and Stoltzfus, 1972), or on the perception–meditation continuum (Goldstein and Stoltzfus, 1973).

Let us consider the experimental support for this notion. Etevenon (1967) was the first to notice that the functional hemispheric asymmetry of rabbits present during the predrug state can be abolished by LSD. Both the mean amplitude of the EEG and the variability of electrical activity of the geniculate body on the *left* side are greater *prior* to drug administration. But under the influence of the drug, the two geniculate bodies respond to visual stimulation in an identical way; apparently, a shift from the left to the right has occurred.

Similarly, the sleep studies of Goldstein et al. (1972) in men, cats, and rabbits demonstrate a relative decrease in EEG amplitude in the right cerebral hemisphere—as measured by a Drohocki-type integrator—when NREM sleep was followed by REM (dream) activity. The interpretation of the relatively higher initial amplitude in the right hemisphere is that the left hemisphere is more active; but with the onset of REM sleep, which is marked by ergotropic arousal, the amplitude relationship is reversed (i.e., a shift occurs from the left to the right hemisphere).

Furthermore, stimulants decrease the amplitude and its variability and render the *R*ight/*L*eft amplitude ratio nearly equal to one. Hallucinogens, however, completely reverse amplitude laterality, according to Goldstein and Stoltzfus

---

* "Propositional" and "appositional" are Bogen's terms.

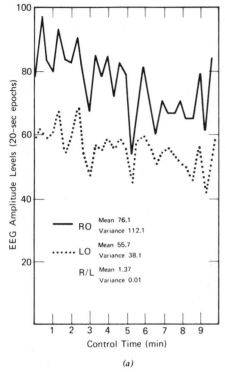
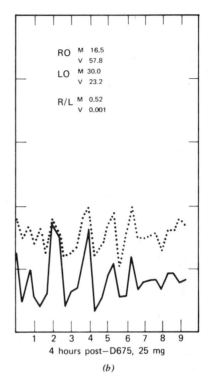

Control Time (min)

(a)

4 hours post—D675, 25 mg

(b)

Figure 4. Chronograms of the electrical activity from left and right occipital EEGs of a 25-year-old, right-handed male volunteer: *(a)* prior to and *(b)* four hours after the oral administration of 25 mg of the hallucination-inducing analgesic drug Exp-675 (duPont de Nemours). Solid lines: right occipital (RO); dotted lines: left occipital (LO) recordings. Note the reversal of amplitude–laterality relationship (i.e., the drug-induced shift to the right hemisphere): *(a)* R/L, mean 1.37, variance 0.01; *(b)* RO, mean 16.5, variance 57.8; LO, mean 30.0, variance 23.2; R/L, mean 0.52, variance 0.001. (Through the courtesy of Drs. L. Goldstein and N. W. Stoltzfus, Princeton, N.J.; and with the permission of the Swiss journal of pharmacology *Agents and Actions,* 1973, **3,** 124–132.)

(1973). Such a reversal could not be observed when sedatives and/or minor tranquilizers and placebo were administered. Figure 4 illustrates this reversal of amplitude laterality under the influence of the experimental drug "Exp-675," an hallucinogenic analgesic (N-isotropyl-N-methyl-3-formamido-l-pyrazole-carboxamide). Note that during hallucinatory states the L/R amplitude ratio is significantly higher than normal.

A similar decrease in variability of the amplitude (C.V.) was observed by Goldstein and Stoltzfus (1973) during deep meditation in trained subjects, affiliated with the International Meditation Society. The magnitude of decrease is comparable to that which becomes manifest in a normal subject on becoming catatonic. Thus hyper- as well as hypoaroused states induce a similar decrease in the C.V. Moreover, a reversal of amplitude laterality, similar to that obtained after the transition from NREM to REM-sleep, can be observed when one departs on the perception–meditation continuum. There is less hemispheric switching or, in other words, data are preferentially processed in the visuospatial or right cerebral hemisphere. This left-to-right hemispheric switch can also be induced by the intravenous administration of 5 mg of the major tranquilizer chlorpromazine or when verbalization, which is left-hemisphere specific, is followed by right-hemisphere-specific music (Goldstein and Stoltzfus, 1973). According to most recent and yet unpublished results by Goldstein and associates: the left-to-right hemispheric switch also obtains at the peak of sexual ecstasy (i.e., orgasm) and has been measured in both males and females ($N = 6$); the right-hemispheric switch can be characterized by a 4/sec frequency, which is below theta and above delta activity and accompanied by a 200-μV 3/sec, a very large, amplitude. During this *right*-hemispheric switch there is little change in the left hemisphere, which displays a persistent preorgasmic alpha activity (personal communication of Dr. L. Goldstein, 1974). It is intriguing to speculate about the nondominant or spatial nature of ecstatic experiences, especially today, when the "container" concept of space, a nineteenth-century remnant, is undergoing a "Leibniz-ian—Chinese" transformation into a *force field*. With due apologies to the reader for calling an orgasm "a poor man's ecstasy," we should like to recall that all ecstatic experiences may be characterized by an hallucinatory high S/M ratio and a very low coefficient of variation.

In summing up the novel findings of Goldstein and his associates, we refer to their conclusions that:

"Relaxing" or "restful" states correspond to a separation of the amplitudes on both sides of the brain, while, on the contrary, states of stimulation, excitation, anxiety and hallucination correspond respectively to a progressive narrowing of interhemispheric amplitude differences with eventually a complete reversal of their relationships (Goldstein and Stoltzfus, 1973, p. 130).

ONE MAN'S BRAIN DAMAGE IS ANOTHER'S CREATIVITY

In some sense one spends more and more time in the right cerebral hemisphere when traveling on *either* the hyperaroused hallucination or hypoaroused meditation continuum (to the left or to the right in Figs. 1 and 3). If such reversal of laterality relations is reproducible by others, it is an extremely significant phenomenon.

The first amendment we have to make when updating our cartography of inner space in the light of this information is that creativity (Figs. 1 and 3, left upper-third) is not confined to the creative dream and waking-dream states (Fischer, 1969c; Fischer et al., 1972) but should also be tentatively inserted in the right upper third of the meditation continuum. Apparently, the practice of spending more time in the right (the visuospatial, intuitive, gestalt-making) hemisphere while at the same time not being too strongly aroused, may allow creativity to unfold and missing clues to appear in symbolic new gestalts or nonverbal meaning schemata. Recurring dreams, transcendental visions, fantasies rooted in mythology—in short, nonrational, right-hemispheric, visuospatial ideation (called primary process by Freud)—is the basis of creative intuition in artists, scientists, and discoverers. Whether these experiences are called dreams or hallucinations, visions, waking dreams or daydreams, may depend on how far the subject was traveling on either of the two continua (Figs. 1 and 3). Most people have heard of Kekulé's dream of a snake biting its tail, inspiring that scientist's conception of the benzene ring; Niels Bohr's concept of the atom as a miniature planetary system also originated in dreams. Right-hemispheric (visuospatial and musical) dreamy intuition may have led to the creation of books, pictures, and compositions originated by Robert Louis Stevenson, Tolstoy, Goethe, Blake, Wagner, Tartini, Schumann, Mozart, and many others (for these and other examples of creative experiences, see Fischer and Scheib, 1971).

It also becomes clear now why painter naïfs, aboriginal artists, children, hyperphrenic patients, and some of the mentally retarded can paint esthetically pleasing pictures without much, or sometimes any, training. These people may be creative because they preferentially shift data processing to the visuospatial, the right hemisphere. But creativity gradually declines and ultimately comes to a halt when hyperphrenics recover (i.e., are beginning to function in the normal, conforming, and rational *I*-state-of-the-world), or when children reach the age of about 10 and perhaps become overdeveloped in the left hemisphere (at the cost of the right one), as a result of compulsory attendance at our schools geared for verbal-writing-mathematic skills.

The creative pictorial artist among the mentally retarded is perhaps more retarded with respect to his left-hemispheric activity. The low I.Q. assigned to mental retardates is based on tests relying to a large part on analytical left-hemispheric ideation, disregarding capabilities associated with the right hemisphere. Apparently, in the same category belong the idiot savants, with an I.Q. range of 58–67 (WAIS), who usually cannot count higher than 30 and are generally unable to learn the simplest mathematical operations. Yet such left-hemispheric idiots show an uncanny ability at calendar calculations, and it is documented that many of them can identify the day on which a given date will fall for a range of centuries beyond our present perpetual calendars. Moreover, some of these patients not only display an admirable acoustic imagination and memory but an astonishing ability to perform on the piano as well, despite their difficulties with motor coordination in relation to simple tasks of daily routine (Leonhard and Berendt, 1968). We are tempted to assume that most of these idiot savants perform their calendar calculations and display musical knowledge largely with their Platonic hemisphere and that the art of the mentally retarded may involve nonrational ways of problem solving. Indeed, it appears that we are "rational idiots" in understanding and explaining their nonrational sophistication. (For more details about the art of the mentally retarded and the abilities of idiot savants see Fischer, 1970c; Fischer and Scheib, 1971; and Fischer et al., 1972).

Years ago (Fischer and Rockey, 1967), we asked volunteers to read texts in which up to 74% of the upper part of each line was deleted. Four of our 17 subjects were able to read more than a third of these topless texts, but only when under the influence of the hallucinogenic drug psilocybin. During the subsequent years we have found, and could repeatedly verify, that 2 out of about 800 second-year medical students can read 100% of the topless texts without any drug. Eidetic ability could not be implicated because testing the subjects with a method adapted from Stromeyer and Psotka (1970) revealed that they were definitely not eidetics. In the light of data from Goldstein's laboratory (Goldstein and Stoltzfus, 1973), we may now reinterpret both the increased ability to make visuospatial gestalts during an hallucinogenic-induced state as well as the ability of 2 out of 800 medical students—with what we take to be unusual visuospatial talent and training—to dream up or hallucinate the gestalts from topless parts of deleted lines. Some of our ordinary volunteers evidently need the psilocybin to spend more time in (i.e., to shift information processing to) the right hemisphere, to make the gestalts. On the other hand, the very few and unusually gifted visuospatial savants need no drug at all for a performance superior to that of any other volunteer under psilocybin.

We knew for some time that the majority of our volunteer subjects were generally quiet, intuitive, and not very verbal. During the last five years or so, however, we became aware that the majority of our subjects were taste-sensitive, thus also drug-sensitive; that is, in general, *sensitive* individuals came to us to enjoy the travel into inner space (Fischer, 1971b). Interestingly, about 90% of these college students score as introverts (I), intuitors (N), feelers (F), and perceivers (P) on the Myers-Briggs-type indicator (MBTI), a brief, self-reporting Jungian personality inventory, although in the general United States population, according to MacKinnon's estimate, intuitors constitute 25% of the total (Corlis et al., 1967). Given our present state of knowledge, the INFP score seems to denote volunteers with preferentially right-hemispheric involvements and interests, whereas high scores on the extroversion (A), down-to-earth sensation (S), thinking (T), and judging (J) scales on the MBTI point to left-hemispheric predominance (called secondary process by Freud).

When we test not the left-hemispheric I.Q. of our volunteers but a right-hemispheric intelligence, by administering to 21 of our (mostly INFP) subjects the visuospatial Minnesota Perceptual Diagnostic Test (MPDT), a test for brain damage, we obtain most interesting results. Half of our volunteers become *less* "brain damaged" under the influence of psilocybin (i.e., they show less rotation on the MPDT at hallucinogenic drug peak than at predrug), whereas the others display *increased* rotation on the MPDT from predrug to drug peak, showing more drug-induced "brain damage." Perhaps a drug-induced reversal of laterality raises the appositional to propositional or A/P ratio (Bogen et al., 1972), hence improves visuospatial performance in volunteers who were less creative to begin with in terms of MacKinnon's creativity score [i.e., $\sum (N + P)$ of the MBTI; see Fischer, 1970b] and whose predrug performance, as measured by the "visuospatial I.Q." implicit in the MPDT, was quite poor. The beneficial effect of the drug (i.e., the temporary cure of the "brain damage" in our field-independent subjects) is also reflected in the original and sophisticated figure drawings created at drug peak (Fischer and Scheib, 1971).

In the other field-dependent group of volunteers who were more creative under predrug conditions [i.e., produced higher scores on the $\sum (N + P)$ of the MBTI], the hallucinogenic drug provoked signs of a temporary and reversible "brain damage," as indicated by the MPDT.

In summary: a self-selected college population, homogeneous with respect to age, race, socioeconomic status, education, interests, and goals could be divided into superior and inferior peformers based on a visuospatial (right-hemispheric) test. The results could be completely reversed under the influence of an hallucinogenic drug, that induced a high A/P ratio.

Evidently, it is misleading to rely solely on right-hemisphere-specific testing when judging aptitudes in individuals who were preferentially trained for (most) problem solving in the left hemisphere. It may also be restrictive to administer only left-hemispheric (I.Q.) tests to (minority) groups who are used to solving most of their problems with the right hemisphere. Apparently, one man's brain damage is another's creativity (Fischer and Scheib, 1971).

We have used the expression "shifting data processing to the right hemisphere"; included, however, should be the ability to alternate between hemispheres*—between the primary and the secondary processes—to integrate right-hemispheric patterns into bihemispheric, communicable ideation. Or in other words, left-hemispheric, digital or Aristotelian signification and right-hemispheric analogical or symbolic meaning have to be integrated into a bihemispheric cortical interpretation of subcortical activity.

Let us now look at the schizophrenic or hyperphrenic and catatonic states (Figs. 1 and 3, left), the "jammed computer" states, characterized by hyperarousal. A sustained high level of arousal is bound to culminate in overinclusion in the unsystematic group of schizophrenias (Payne, 1962). Overinclusion is likely to result from an inability to separate symbolization from rational thinking (Fischer, 1972a), or to perceive-behave the digital as though it were analog. Inability to separate is a disturbance of lateral balance (Venables, 1969) that may interfere with bihemispherically integrated ideation. Indeed, Oddy and Lobstein (1972) recently found an unusual prevalence of cross dominance (e.g., right-hand but left-eye dominance) in a group of 140 schizophrenics. It is yet to be shown whether these findings are but another manifestation of the schizophrenic's confusion when confronted with words and phrases having both a literal and figurative (or metaphoric) usage (Chapman et. al., 1964). The confusion of metaphoric and literal usages is an important feature of schizophrenic ideation and points toward a disturbance of the cortically integrated or bihemispheric interpretation of subcortical activity.

Recent data support Luria's (1966) contention that cerebral dominance varies intraindividually from function to function (Berman, 1971). The incompletely lateralized individual may exhibit laterality differences that upset the uniformity of dominance among preferences, controls, and functions. Apparently dominance is one of the significant factors related to, maybe even determining intelligence; therefore, dominance has to be assessed by tasks measuring preference, control, and function (Berman, 1971).

Another intriguing aspect of cerebral dominance is that lesions of the dominant hemisphere are usually associated with depression, whereas lesions of the non-dominant hemisphere contribute to euphoria (Hommes, 1965). Moreover, the intracarotic injection of sodium amytal on the speech-dominant side results in a catastrophic depressive reaction, whereas the same injection on the contralateral side results in an euphoric, manic type of response (Terzian and Cecotto, 1960). But according to Hommes and Panhuysen (1971), sodium amytal induced euphoria irrespective of the side of the injection, in 11 untreated patients hospitalized for depression, since both hemispheres displayed nondominant behavior. Hommes and Panhuysen (1971) favored the conclusion that depression changes cerebral dominance. Interestingly, manic-depressive patients have been found to be manic and depressed at the same time (Kotin and Goodwin, 1972).

---

*   There are methodological errors related to this very problem when autoregulation is to be attained by means of biofeedback. For instance, alpha control training should be based on two different tones independently indicating the presence of alpha in each hemisphere (Peper, 1971).

Flor-Henry's (1971) review of the literature concluded that dominant temporal pathology seems to be positively correlated with psychotic (schizophrenic) manifestations, whereas affective (manic-depressive) disorders correlate significantly with nondominant (temporal and frontal) hemispheric pathology. Or, with a different twist: the critical function of assigning values or response probability involves subcortical neural systems that can maintain a mutual independence after cortical–cortical disconnection (Gazzaniga, 1972). Now there is evidence that after commissurotomy, a single hemisphere can operate alone to initiate an emotional response (in using "arousal" instead of "emotional response," we are reminded that stateboundness most likely can be initiated in a particular hemisphere.) For example, a broad smile, which the subject is unable to explain, has often been seen after the completion of a task by the right hemisphere (Sperry, 1965). The intriguing possibility remains that even in the intact state, the corpus callosum may not necessarily keep each hemisphere fully acquainted with what is proceeding in the other; specifically, those functions which are the prerogative of the nondominant hemisphere will possibly be less accessible to the conscious awareness of the subject (Lishman, 1971).

SIGN–SYMBOL–MEANING TRANSFORMATIONS

The separateness of subject and object during the daily routine levels of arousal (in the I-state) has been elaborated in our customary, rational Aristotelian logic and language—a two-valued (either-or, true-false) logic that discounts the creative interaction between observer (subject) and observed (object).* This separateness of object and subject, as we have seen, is a reflection of the relative independence of cortical interpretation from subcortical activity and reflects a predominantly rational left-hemispheric, analytical, time-bound, and objective ideation. Such left-hemispheric preponderance is of survival value in the I-state, when the subject must make decisions of life and death by manipulating objects (through voluntary motor activity).

But when we depart along the perception–hallucination continuum of hyperarousal from the I toward the *Self*, the separateness of object and subject gradually disappears and their interaction becomes the principal content of the experience. This interaction, again, is a reflection of the gradually increasing integration of cortical and subcortical activity on the one hand and preferential information processing in the visuospatial, nonverbal hemisphere on the other. In this state of unity, the separateness of subject and object implicit in dualistic, Aristotelian logic and language becomes increasingly meaningless; only an analogical or postlogical, a visuospatial mode of computation can convey the experience of intense meaning. Apparently, then, meaning is meaningful only at that level of arousal and that particular A/P ratio at which it is experienced. Thus experience has a state-bound meaning. The more the arousal level and its A/P

---

* For example, neither quinine molecules nor a subject's taste receptors are bitter per se—bitterness results only during interaction of the two. Therefore, no taster, no bitterness, just as there can be no image or sound of a falling tree without a viewer or listener (Fischer, 1969b). That the brain is the only organ to develop through experiencing itself already implies the interactional nature of reality (Ey, 1963).

ratio are altered, the further the meaning is removed from its most relevant context. For example, at the peak of an analogical psilocybin experience, our volunteers found the digital or true-false questions of the Minnesota Multiphasic Personality Inventory "childish baby talk and completely irrelevant gibberish at best." In the rational, digital *I*-state of daily routine, however, they did not object to the Aristotelian nature of the test.

During the *Self* or analog state of highest levels of hyper- or hypoarousal, meaning can no longer be expressed in dualistic terms, since the experience of unity is born from the integration of interpretive (cortical) and interpreted (subcortical) structures. Because this intense meaning is devoid of specificities, the only way to communicate its intensity is the metaphor; hence only through the transformation of objective sign into subjective symbol in art, literature, and religion can the increasing integration of cortical and subcortical activity be communicated.

The transformation of sign and symbol is of course most apparent in the visuospatial realm. The objective constancies of the *I*-state gradually vanish and are replaced by geometric-ornamental rhythmic structures, the "hallucinatory form-constants" of Klüver (1966, p. 66), which we consider to be visuospatial metaphors of the waking-dream states. Klüver classified the form-constants of his own *mescaline* experiences into four categories: "*(a)* grating, lattice, fretwork, filigree, honeycomb, or chessboard; *(b)* cobweb; *(c)* tunnel, funnel, alley, cone, or vessel; *(d)* spiral" (p. 66) and assumed that any other varieties are but modifications of these basic designs. Our own experience suggests an extension of Klüver's observations to include hyper- and hypoaroused hallucinatory experiences in general, whether induced electrically (Knoll et al., 1963), naturally, or by hallucinogenic drugs other than mescaline (Fischer, 1970c).

The hallucinatory constancies are magic symbols, visible or audible metaphors within a structure of symbolic logic and language, the language of hyper- and hypoaroused hallucinatory states; they are at the base of the general tendency toward geometric-rhythmic ornamentalization. For example, the rose windows of Gothic cathedrals and the mandalas of Tantric religious art (Mookerjee, 1967) are ritualized hallucinatory form-constants. The tendency toward ornamentalization, however, is not only restricted to visual imagery but also governs the order of poetic and musical rhythm, imposing an all-pervasive meter and harmony on the hallucinatory creative-religious states (Fischer, 1970c). Since the rhythm of music and poetry corresponds to the geometric-ornamental rhythm of the visuospatial realm, the manneristic (Navratil, 1965, 1966) hallucinatory-creative style of art and literature is regarded as a projection and elaboration of the geometric-rhythmic-ornamental fabric of hyper- and hypoaroused states.

ON GEOMETRIC HALLUCINATORY CONSTANCIES, VISUAL NOISE, PYTHAGOREAN HARMONIA, AND A BOUNDARY CONDITION: THE "SOUL"

What factors may be operational during the transformation of sign to symbol in visual space?

It has been shown that ergotropic arousal or central sympathetic excitation interferes with the visuocortical optimization, that is the process of counteradaptation to optically provoked distortions (Fischer and Hill, 1971). This interference, or the impaired ability to see this best of all possible worlds as it should be, may facilitate the emergence of nonordinary varieties of visuospatial experiences. It does not, however, account for the ornamentalization phenomenon, the continuous transformation into a Pythagorean *harmonia,* "an orderly adjustment of parts in a complex fabric" (Santillana, 1961).

If we assume that both ergotropic hyper- and trophotropic hypoarousal increase random noise in the visual system, such noise has to be viewed through a spatially repetitive pattern—and such patterns are ubiquitous in our symmetrically ordered environment. Thus the otherwise chaotic disposition of particles is at once organized into one or several superimposed geometric figures (MacKay, 1965).* Moreover, the principal directions of such a complementary image run at right angles to the lines of the repetitive pattern. If the stimulus figure is a grid formed by superimposing sets of parallel lines at right angles, the complementary image lines run diagonally. The complementary figures so generated are usually seen in motion, and the speed of rotation of a rosette of this type depends on the spacing of the lines of the pattern (on wallpaper or an oriental rug, for instance), which the subject may fixate during an hallucinatory experience. The geometric patterns may be seen as counterrotating or rotating clockwise or anticlockwise, more or less at will. These geometrizations seem to be stimulus-locked and may be elicited from the outside or through in-sight (i.e., by viewing with closed eyes the repetitive pattern of intraocular structures).

Such symmetrical geometrizations may, however, involve other than the visual domain and may develop into synesthesia. Hence one of Beringer's (1927) volunteers saw and felt the sounds of a concertina. The pain produced by the experience coagulated as luminous curves in the spiral turns of his body, the lower part of his body being a green varnished cone with spiral windings.

The translation of visual geometrizations into synesthesia involving drastic changes in body image may be another way of expressing the observation that certain subjects after from eight to twelve psychotherapeutic LSD sessions cease to experience visual geometrizations. Thus the experience of meaning becomes the main feature and perhaps the sole meaning of the experience.

In creative writers such (physical) timeless and spaceless moments of insight come as an undefined mass of significance, fused in a glow of intense feeling. It may take years or generations for all the meaning and implications to be expressed in words. When this feeling has passed, the thought is felt and an intellectual content is distilled into the language of prose (Cornford, 1937).

The visuospatial and audiospatial domain of the nondominant Platonic hemisphere may be the creative source of geometric-rhythmic hallucinatory form-constants. Geometrization may be the representation of a mediating factor "in charge" of the union between the object and subject, the *I* and the *Self,* the

---

* Visual noise is regarded by MacKay (1965) as the neutral member of a family of stimuli, analogous to those used by communication engineers in the time domain, at the extremes of which are stroboscopic illumination (spatially uniform, temporally periodic) and our parallel-line patterns (temporarily uniform, spatially periodic).

observed and the observer. Using some of Santillana's (1968) words, we may juxtapose our Platonic visual space with the closed arrangement of a multiplicity of things on the dominant Aristotelian side. The Platonic visual space closely resembles that of the Renaissance: a pure space of diaphanous light, articulated throughout by a central design bringing into action the law of forms from every point of view. It is described by Cusanus—who borrowed his famous phrase from the description that Hermes Trismegistus gives of the soul—"that whose circumference is nowhere and the center everywhere" (Santillana, 1968, p. 165). Such a transfer of the properties of the soul to cosmic space, with the accent on a central perspective of the intellect is, then, a vision of the Pythagorean system becoming truly universal and permeating all reality.

I believe that during depersonalization or out-of-the-body experiences the subject takes leave of the body (Plato, 398 B.C.) and travels in a visual space with its center everywhere. This space with its "circumference. . . nowhere" is the domain of Platonic ideas, the realm of the pure, eternal and immortal, the domain of intelligible archetypes, which are painless, divine, immanent, simple, and indestructible (Plato, 398 B.C.).

It seems clear, in retrospect, that the image of a timeless visuospatial realm of perfect archetypal images or ideas (connected with ecstatic-shamanistic, hyperaroused out-of-the-body experiences) has given rise to the esoteric concept of the "soul." But for Aristotle, consciousness can only exist within the body and is distributed, so to speak, over the whole body. We tend to regard this technomorphic and psychophysiological view of the soul (Topitsch, 1965) as a typical Aristotelian analytical ideation. For us, the soul is a *boundary condition* between the *I* and the *Self*; and only those whose *I* and *Self* can communicate with each other become conscious of it. The soul, we may say, becomes manifest through transcallosal and corticosubcortical (hyper- or hypoaroused) communication. A characteristic feature of this communication is a high R/L or A/P ratio. The unknowable transcallosal code (Gazzaniga, 1971) and the neuronal firing pattern of the cortical--subcortical systems during hyper- and hypoarousal are the sphere of the *I–Self* dialogue. The creative act is a luxurious byproduct of this dialogue. Most great artists and scientists, at some point in their lives, have a decisive conversion experience of an hallucinatory-religious nature which results in the creation of a more consistent personality—one that has "found its style." (For examples that substantiate the point that great discoveries, and creative performance in general, are preceded by hallucinatory experiences, see Fischer, 1970c.)

But the *I–Self* dialogue on the perception–hallucination continuum is not the only creative experience. A comparable dialogue is initiated during that classic *folie à deux* we call being in love, but it is between the *Selves* of Lover and Beloved, and Lacan's (1968) question, "Who is speaking, and to whom?" is transmuted to Ibn Arabi's questions: "Who is the Beloved, and who is the Lover?" (Corbin, 1969). For the Sufi, however, they are "not two heterogeneous, but one being encountering himself."

But the *I–Self* dialogue is not concerned solely with the creative emergence of art, science, literature, and religion: conversion experiences of the Saul-to-St. Paul type are also hallucinatory and also involve communication between the *I* and the *Self*.

THE PROOF OF THE SENSORY (BIHEMISPHERICALLY INTEGRATED) PUDDING IS IN THE MOTOR EATING

We define reality, that evolving and fluctuating process, forward-driven on all levels of systemic organization, from the biochemical to the intentional, as an actualizing appearance of observational relations—specifically, the cortical interpretation of subcortical activity. By subcortical activity we refer to the raw sensory experience of observational relations, or first-order interaction (e.g., the image of an external stimulus configuration on the retina, a subcortical structure). The subsequent cortical interpretation of this low-to-moderate level of subcortical activity can be characterized by an *appositional* (A) to *propositional* (P) or R/L hemispheric alternation ratio A/P = 1. Throughout such *perceptual* (i.e., exteroceptive) behavior, the subject may utilize two methods of verification: (1) he may use his two hemispheres at will to check out—in the light of past experience and expectation—one hemisphere against the other concerning the appropriateness of the most probable cortical interpretation, and (2) he may verify the content of his sensory (S) experience through willed motor (M) activity: second-order interaction with S/M = 1.

With increasing hyper- or hypoarousal, however, the subject's capacity to verify gradually wanes and the intense sensory experience becomes an internal, interoceptive event that cannot be verified externally. To begin with, the ability to check out the ideation of the right hemisphere with the left hemisphere is diminished—which is another way of stating that the subject spends significantly more time in the right hemisphere than in the left one (high A/P ratio). Another corollary of hyperaroused hallucinatory (REM sleep and waking dream) states as well as hypoaroused meditative (*zazen* to *samādhi*) states is an increasing inhibition and, finally, blocking of the intention and ability for verification through peripheral voluntary motor activity* (high S/M ratio). Hallucinatory behavior thus gradually evolves from perceptual behavior under conditions conducive to and characterized by a high A/P and high S/M ratio.†

How high these ratios have to be to indicate hallucinatory behavior will depend

---

* Interestingly, drugs that can elicit hallucinations—certain corticosteroids, cannabinols, LSD, psilocybin, mescaline, and alcohol—also dampen willed motor performance *and* are in fact anesthetics and/or analgesics (Kuromaru et al., 1962; Kast and Collins, 1964; Buxbaum, 1972). In higher doses these drugs can produce catalepsy in animals (Fischer, 1969b) and, in man, cataleptic anesthesia—as ketamine, a derivative of phencyclidine does (Winters et al., 1972).

What is striking about LSD—and other hallucinogens—is that they disrupt the normal integration of motor programs by the nervous system in animals and produce ineffective motor behavior patterns; in other words, hallucinogens impair reality-testing. In humans, however, full expression of the disintegrating action of LSD on central coordination of motor activity is less obvious because of the small doses employed (Pscheidt, 1968).

The phenylethylamine pattern present in LSD as a rigid 2-amino-tetralin structural element, I find, is not restricted to hallucinogenic drugs of the LSD-type, indolealkylamine-type, and methoxylated amphetamine type but it is also a common feature shared by certain corticosteroids, tetrahydrocannabinols, anaesthetics like ketamine, and analgesics, including morphine and some of its antagonists, such as cyclazocine. A careful reevaluation of the concept of hallucinations is prompted by the ability of all these drugs to impair reality-testing, or more specifically, to raise the S/M ratio (Fischer, 1975).

† "Hallucinations can be characterized not only by a high sensory to motor but also by a high symbolic to cognitive ratio" (Fischer, 1969b, p. 166). The symbolic to cognitive or R/L (or A/P) ratio can be expressed as successive levels of EEG amplitude recorded separately from the right and left occipital area and can be represented as reversal of the amplitude–laterality relationship (see data of Goldstein and Stoltzfus, 1972, in Fig. 4).

on a subject's systemic sensitivity, which can be determined by measuring his (1) gustatory threshold, (2) drug-reactivity, and (3) personality-reactivity, all of which covary (Fischer, 1971b). We have found that intuitive and introverted subjects on the MBTI (the majority of our sensitive tasters and sensitive drug reactors) are also frequent dreamers, dream more in color than in black and white, prefer color to form, and display high mean energy content, as well as greater C.V.s in the EEG.* In contrast, our down-to-earth sensor and extroverted subjects (the insensitive tasters and insensitive drug reactors) dream infrequently, dream in black and white rather than in color, prefer form to color (Fischer et al., 1969), and display low mean energy content, as well as lower C.V.s on the EEG (Thatcher et al., 1971).

How fast the subject will move on the perception–hallucination and perception–meditation continua will also depend on the size of his cortical repertoire, which is implicit in a small or large S.D. of a stable or variable subject when tested just prior to a drug-induced hallucinatory experience (Gwynne et al., 1969; Fischer, 1970b, 1971a; Panton and Fischer, 1973).

It should be obvious by now, as Maturana wrote, that

> From the point of view of the observer the nervous system, as a mode of organization, seems to begin at any arbitrary point that the observer may choose to consider and hence the answer to the question what is input to the nervous system depends entirely on the chosen point of observation. Any given state of activity of the nervous system consists of states of relative activity holding between neurons and thus there is no possible distinction between internally and externally generated states of nervous activity (1970, p. 17).

In further refining the concept of hallucinations, we may distinguish two types of hallucinatory behavior: that which increases in intensity when one moves along the perception–hallucination continuum of ergotropic or hyperarousal and that which spiritualizes when a subject departs on the trophotropic or hypoarousal continuum. We contend that although both continua are hallucinatory, there are important differences between them. The physiological substrate of hyperaroused hallucinations may be characterized by heightened sympathetic responsiveness and increased tone of the striated muscles—the "excitation syndrome" (Hofmann, 1968). Conversely, the substrate of hypoaroused hallucinations (transcendental meditation) involves increased parasympathetic responsiveness and muscular relaxation (Gellhorn, 1969; Wallace, 1970). Accordingly, during hyperaroused hallucinatory states the separateness of object and subject, or *I* and *Self,* or observed and observer, gradually disappears, and their fusion becomes the principal content of the experience. During hypoaroused hallucinatory or meditative states, however, the detachment of the subject from object and events becomes the meaning of the experience. This detachment may be referred to as "arriving at the source of thought" (Mahesh Yogi, 1969) or as pure self-reference without content (Fischer, 1971a).† The fusion, or interaction, is, of

---

* The 10% of the normal population, cited previously, who experience vivid visual imagery—an ability with high intermodality correlations (Zuckerman et al., 1962)—may belong to this taste- and drug-sensitive group.

† One could argue, however, that both linguistic renderings: (1) "fusion or interaction of object and subject" and (2) "arriving at the source of thought" are hyper- and hypoaroused attempts to express the *unity* or identity of self-reference and cognitive content (i.e., the meaning of an experience in which "to know is to be"). Stated differently: sentences 1 and 2 may illustrate the relation between self-reference in language and experienced self-reference and may point to the arousal-dependent *and* culture-dependent transformations in denotation.

course, the cultural feature of our "progressive" Faustian-Western civilization, whereas detachment may be regarded as a typical feature of the nontechnological Eastern civilization.

Despite their physiological and cultural differences, both hyper- and hypoaroused hallucinatory experiences display a high hemispheric A/P ratio. There is another common feature, particularly during the culmination points (i.e., during ecstasy and *samādhi*) of both continua (Figs. 1 and 3), and that is the apparently unimpaired ability for recall during the normal state of daily routine. Gopi Krishna's (1971) account, which is representative for such an intact recall of ecstatic experiences,* points to the possibility that the A/P ratio may be lower during these peaks than prior to the breakthrough. The highest states, therefore, may indeed be peace of mind with a characteristically high S/M ratio; but they also may involve bihemispheric integration, that is, peace of mind(s) necessary for an unimpaired recall:

. . . because during the vision I still possessed the capacity to make a comparison between the extended state of consciousness and the normal one, and when it began to fade, I could perceive the contraction that was taking place. It was undoubtedly a real experience, and has been described with all the power of expression at their command by mystics and saints all over the world (Krishna, 1971, p. 60).

Such recall transgresses the rules of stateboundness. Does this happen because the return to the normal *I*-state is gradual and rather slow? And is this recall comparable to that which is displayed by creative people who dream and/or hallucinate first and execute, formulate, write, paint, or compose later?

Apparently the overriding common feature of creative hyper- or hypoaroused hallucinatory experiences is the unification of diversity or the meaning of Oneness. Sewell (1952) observes with clarity that:

If everything becomes one and the same, the notion of similarity vanishes in identification. The last poem quoted from Rimbaud's *Illuminations,* "Marine," shows this well; in it the land is not compared to the sea, it has become the sea, and the sea the land. It is a world where a house does not resemble its owner, it *is* its owner, so that if the house is the March Hare's, the chimneys are ears and the roof is thatched with fur (p. 130).

Sewell goes on to say that "the world of the *Illuminations* may be constructed according to the principles of Dream and Nightmare (the right cerebral hemisphere) rather than those of Number and Logic" (i.e., in the domain of the speech-dominant left hemisphere).

Let us digress for a moment. Wittgenstein (1922) writes "Roughly speaking, to say of *two* things that they are identical is nonsense, and to say of *one* thing that it is identical with itself is to say nothing" (p. 147). But where is mind? Is it in the mind as a map of a map of a map? We never know what a territory is (Iberall, 1972).

* Disciples of krya yoga do not pursue a detached *zazen* meditation "to empty the soul" but concentrate with unwavering attention on a vision (as Gopi Krishna does at the image of a lotus in full bloom, radiating light in the crown of his head). The Kundalini experience then comes quite close to that which we in the West call "ecstasy," a hyperaroused excited state characterized by fast beta (EEG) activity—frequency up to 40 Hz and an amplitude of 30 to 50 μV—and just as in St. Teresa's description of her ecstasy "the outside world retreats to the fringe of consciousness," stimuli applied during this *"extase yogique"* do not alter the EEG (Das and Gastaut, 1957).

What we obtain are representations on the retina which we have to interpret cortically in terms of differences: a visuospatial difference in pattern, differences between gestalts, abstract differences between propositions, differences in information content.*

Now, back again, we may formulate the question: what is the method in the "madness" of identification and Oneness? Coleridge (1907) as quoted by Sewell (1952) remarks in the second passage of *Biographia Literaria* that *"images* (italics added) may have the function of reducing multitude to unity, or succession to an instant." Images, those visuospatial patterns of meaning, may be *the* vehicle that enables a subject to abreact an exciting but traumatic state-bound experience,† located at a particular point on the left of our continuum (Figs. 1 and 3), during a hypoaroused state (represented by a point on the right side while both are connected with an imaginary water level). Both the traumatic and the abreactive experiences imply similarly high A/P ratios, which makes a therapeutic "walk on the water," from the left to the right, possible. Each step of this walk is performed in imagination, images being the nonverbal communication between corresponding hyper- and hypoaroused states.

It is indeed a bit of a work of art for both guru and disciple, or doctor and patient, to teach and to learn or to enact and to interpret this walking on water in the most meaningful dimension that exists—imagination.

VARIATIONS ON THE THEME: PRO DOMO AND CODA

It is "regrettable" indeed that the scientific, rational study of hallucinations or visions is hampered by the scientific discovery "that strictly causal brain mechanisms underlie all rational thought-processes—*including* the scientific discovery that strictly causal brain mechanisms underlie all rational thought-processes" (Toulmin and Peters, 1971).

The general relationship of genius to insanity was first formulated by Moreau de Tours (1859) in whose paradigm the same constitutional mental disposition leads to both genius and insanity, the former being a disease caused by overexcita-

---

* Semmes (1968), from direct experimental evidence, suggests that the functional capacities of the two hemispheres may be differently organized in a fundamental way, with more focal representation of functions in the dominant hemisphere—the integration of similar units, fine sensory motor control, such as manual skills and speech—and more diffused representation in the nondominant, that is, the integration of dissimilar units and multimodal coordination.

† More recent evidence (Roffman and Lal, 1972) confirms our earlier statement, which was based on experimentation with psilocybin and an evaluation of the pharmacological research literature- —namely, that stateboundness refers to an experience bound to a *central* sympathetic (or ergotropic arousal) state. Roffman and Lal have shown that amphetamine but not hydroxyamphetamine—which is devoid of central action although peripherally equipotent with amphetamine—can induce state-dependent learning in rats. Dihydroxyphenylalanine (DOPA) but not hydroxytryptophan (5-HTP) can substitute for amphetamine, whereas reserpine but not syrosingopin eliminates the amphetamine state. DOPA and 5-HTP, only when given together, restore the amphetamine state in reserpinized animals. DOPA alleviates the deficit in retention which was caused by methyl-*p*-tyrosine. 5-HTP alleviates the similar deficit caused by *p*-chlorophenylalanine. And last, chlorpromazine or cyproheptadine can antagonize the amphetamine state. Evidently the amphetamine state can be induced by (i.e., it depends on) newly synthesized catecholamines that stimulate central catecholamine receptors through serotonin modulation.

tion of the brain. The arousal theory of creativity and hyperphrenia—both cartographed on a perception–hallucination continuum—is, therefore, a contemporary reformulation of the Moreau de Tours tour de force. Clinical psychiatrists will of course object to our normalization of the concept of hallucinations. We contend, however, that much communication on a sophisticated and creative level originates in hallucinatory experiences. These include the often politically operational predictions of religious prophets, myth and fable, preliterate as well as scientific, and creative and original structures and styles in fine art and literature, as well as abstract ideas in mathematics or architecture.

And if hallucinations should be an exclusive property of clinical psychopathology, why not perceptions too? Both ends of the perception–hallucination continuum can be labeled either "normal" or "pathological." Paranoid patients may give a pathological interpretation to their percepts, whereas creative people may have unusual, innovative, but still "normal" hallucinations. The common misconception that labels all hallucinatory experiences as pathological is rooted in the fact that psychiatrists usually see hallucinating mental patients—and not a Poincaré, a Max Ernst, or an Einstein.

On the other hand, we are aware of our personal bias for the opposite reason. We are confronted with relatively few patients per se but rather with young men and women in a university setting, volunteers who come to us to participate in drug research; most of them are bright, intuitive, and sensitive, and some are outright creative.

The fluctuating borderline between creativity and hyperphrenia may be hypothetically drawn as a boundary condition between the two hemispheres and may have something to do with the ideational porosity of the corpus callosum and the high A/P ratio during increasing ergotropic and trophotropic arousal. It may also have to do with the ability of certain subjects—well trained in their art or science to begin with—to accept the increasing loss of freedom in the cortical repertoire as a loss from the confines of the rational, dominant, Aristotelian hemisphere. Such loss may then be experienced as a gain in creative Platonic inner inspiration.

The hyperphrenic's complaint of powerlessness, of being in mortal danger, of being overwhelmed by external forces beyond his control, is strongly reminiscent of the symptomatology of all the hallucinogen-induced bad trips* I have witnessed. Both types of subjects—the patients as well as the drugged individual(ist)s—report themselves as losers in their struggle against externalized forces that have taken over their rational (dominant) thinking routine. Possession is felt here instead of inspiration.

---

* Among the many good Kundalini "trips" of Gopi Krishna, there was a memorable bad one, which deserves our attention. The bad trip was characterized by a full-fledged depression, burned-out emotions, loss of appetite, and hyperpyrexia lasting for weeks. Thermoregulation was out of control and restlessness as well as extreme fatigue prevailed to an alarming extent. In this critical situation, Krishna learned that if Kundalini were aroused through any other nerve except *Sushuma*, there was every danger of serious psychic and physical disturbances . . . ultimately ending in death. This was particularly the case, if the awakening occurred through *pingala* on the right side of the spine when the unfortunate man is literally burnt to death . . . [Gopi Krishna asked himself:] Could it be that I had aroused Kundalini through *pingala* or the solar nerve which regulates the flow of heat in the body and is located on the right side of *Sushuma?*

In a last-minute attempt, Gopi Krishna roused *Ida*, or the lunar nerve on the left side, to activity by

But it is sometimes quite difficult to distinguish between possession and inspiration. At one time or another, most of us have had a very (un)certain kind of dream, a dream that was somewhat frightening as well as captivating and enthralling, thus making it difficult to decide whether one felt possessed or inspired.

It appears that visuospatial gestalts are externalized as real happenings during possession, whereas rational thinking intrudes into the non-dominant hemisphere during inspiration. Different baselines may be additionally involved in terms of arousal thresholds conducive to or hindering at least partial bihemispheric integration. Here again, there is a delicate balance and one man's inspiration may be another's possession.

Harnad (1972) proposes an asymmetry model* in which the nondominant hemisphere is characterized as less bound by sensory and logical reality than the dominant hemisphere. It has its output monitored and evaluated by aesthetic emotions, whereas the output of the dominant hemisphere is monitored and evaluated by "emotions arising from inconsistency." Such an asymmetrical subcortical–cortical equilibrium may account for, or in any case may be consistent with, the already mentioned coexistence of mania and depression in manic-depressive patients on the one hand (Kotin and Goodwin, 1972) and the simultaneous presence of inspiration and possession, or terror and enchantment, in the creative writings of mad poets—such as Gerard de Nerval (1854, p. 269)—on the other.

I attributed a mystic sense to the conversations of the warders and of my companions. It seemed to me that they represented all the nations of the world, and that between us we had to regulate in a new way the paths of the stars and to widen the bounds of the solar system. . . . My role seemed to me to be the reestablishing of universal harmony. . . . This thought led to another: that there existed a vast cabal of all living creatures, with the aim of reestablishing the world in its primal harmony, and that communication took place by means of the magnetism of the stars; that an unbroken chain linked those minds the world

---

* The direction of lateral eye movement elicited by reflective questions is strongly modified by the cognitive demands of the question; verbal and arithmetical questions elicit more movements to the right than do spatial and musical questions. This is consistent with the asymmetric specialization of the human brain for these cognitive processes. Apparently, the direction of the lateral eye movement indicates the activation of the contralateral cerebral hemisphere (Kocel et al., 1972). In left-handers, however, both verbal and spatial processes appear to be programmed from one hemisphere at a given time (Kinsbourne, 1973).

---

focusing his attention—with all the willpower at his command—to bear on the left side of the seat of Kundalini, and he tried to force an imaginary cold current upward through the middle of the spinal cord. And the miracle happened . . . (Krishna, 1971, pp. 59–67).

Note that many neurons of the heat-dissipating system are located in the anterior part of the hypothalamus, with their descending pathways passing down the brain stem in or near the central gray and setting up connections with respiratory and cardiovascular mechanisms of the brain stem and spinal cord. Localization of thermoregulation within a hemispheric site is not possible, however, because the relevant fibers are all crossed. But around the spinal cord the fibers are not yet crossed; moreover, both ascending as well as descending dopaminergic, serotonergic, as well as noradrenergic fibers are uncrossed (Ungerstedt, 1971). Krishna's description allows us, therefore, to speculate that he indeed may have been able to reinstate thermoregulation after a bad Kundalini trip that was induced on the right side (spreading contralaterally into the left or dominant hemisphere). Since during ergotropic hyperarousal it is physiologically appropriate to spend significantly more "space" in the nondominant hemisphere (Goldstein and Stoltzfus, 1972), a Kundalini ecstasy with left-hemispheric predominance may have been the physiological factor involved in this bad trip.

over that were dedicated to this universal communication; and songs, dances, glances of the eye, magnetized from one to the next, interpreted the same aspiration. . . . The whole of nature took on a new appearance. The speech of my companions was turned in mysterious ways of which I understood the meaning. Even formless and lifeless objects lent themselves to my mental calculations. And from collections of pebbles, shapes of angles or cracks or openings, from patterns of leaves, from colors, scents, and sounds I sensed harmonies emerging, unknown till then (translation of Sewell, 1952, pp. 106–107).

Perhaps it is not necessary to postulate a "code" as the basis of effective communication between the hemispheres. Could we not look at cerebral functioning, and specifically interhemispheric integration, in terms of a two-oscillator model involving synchronization or frequency entrainment analogous to the two clocks of Huygens (1673), which "—although slightly out of step initially—became synchronized when fixed on a thin wooden board."? Such synchronization was later rediscovered with electric circuits.

Or, based on Etevenon and Boissier's (1972) finding of an increase of the lateralization index and signal-to-noise ratio in rabbits, especially during contralateral intermittent photic stimulation under LSD, we may model certain aspects of interhemispheric functioning as a most efficient signal detection scheme, the parallel coherent detector that maps coherent signals as correlation functions.

Or, we may go one step farther by contemplating the two logical systems implicit in the functioning of the two hemispheres. In our two-valued or Aristotelian logic, the subject is hidden in the reflection process that prevails between subject and object. For example, when you reflect yourself in the mirror-surface of a lake, you—the subject—appear to yourself as an object. Analogously, two-valued or digital logic disregards the difference between an object and its image. But by introducing further values through three, four, and multivalued logic we may multiply the reflections between object and subject, thus lifting the classic symmetry that exists between them. For example, by introducing another, a third value (the second mirror) into the Aristotelian or two-valued situation, we may suddenly see ourselves in the second mirror as a subject reflecting itself in the first mirror as an object. My contention is that the multivalued logic of the nondominant hemisphere is a speculation (from: *speculum* [lat.] mirror) through visuospatial reflections.

Rational or Aristotelian thinking is literally objective, but it is fragmented and thus out of context. Only through visuospatial or audiospatial gestalts can we reflect ourselves as part of the universe of which we may be the consciousness. Are you in the audiovisual picture? Do you feel part of the gestalt? Günther (1971) defines such a non-Aristotelian situation as a dilemma arising from further values being added to classic two-valuedness. He believes that such an "intra-contextural system" cannot dispense with that "multivalued" nonrationality inaccessible to a rational approach. But multivalued systems may also represent rational structures, the more since they can be dissolved into two-valued subparts. A three-valued analogical proposition, for instance, can be dissolved into three digital propositions. If this were the code for interhemispheric communication, the transfer of meaning from the Platonic (right) to the signifying Aristotelian (left) hemisphere would correspond to the checking operation we postulated earlier as part of reality-testing.

In the process of evolution, man seems to have gradually begun to grasp that the realm of Platonic archetypal images or ideas is not within the realm of projected objects "out there" but is generated inside during hallucinatory (waking and REM) dream states. In such states, laterality relations change and we are capable of holding up a series of visuospatial mirrors of multivalued reflection and self-reflection in context. If there is irrationality in subjectivity and rationality in objectivity, we can be sure that *we* generate them both. We are the source of science, mythology, religion, literature, and art by generating images "in this prison" that are "sufficiently powerful to deny our insignificance" (Malraux, 1948).

But what are dimensions of that prison, or more specifically, the verifiable limits of the human cortical repertoire? And is verification possible if the same sensory-motor structures and processes that generate the inner experience of an observer are also involved in the verification of his experience? Note that the two phases of elementary verification behavior, approach and withdrawal, establish the operational origin of the two fundamental axioms of two-valued logic, "the law of the excluded contradiction" and the "law of the excluded middle." Thus not only the logical structure of descriptions but also their truth values are coupled to movement (Foerster, v., 1970). What is already there is the structure or organization of our own nature, an order that is reflected in the eye of the beholder (Fischer, 1972b).

If we consider this speculative structure through which we mirror everything, including the reflection of our own structure, we arrive at a basic dichotomy: that of the analog and the digital. Analog or continuous-function computers operate between continuous physical quantities and some other set of variables, whereas digital computers involve discrete elements and discontinuous—so called on/off—scales. Neurons, for example, may be said to operate digitally, but the synapse and axon that connect them appear to be complex analog devices (Dreyfus, 1965).

Von Neumann (1958) refers to the constant switching between the analog and the digital in the behavior of the message system of the body: a digital command releases a neurohumoral chemical that performs some analog function or other. This release or its result is in turn detected by an internal receptor neuron, which sends a digital signal to command the process to stop or to start some other process. The neuron could be said to fire or not to fire if and only if the requisite analog and digital logical arrangements have been completed. The complexity of such a system would hardly seem to be that of a two-valued, analytic logic, but rather that of a many-valued, dialectical one, a logic of degrees (Wilden, 1972).

The analog computer is an icon or an image of something real, whereas the digital computer speaks about reality in an artificial language. The informational relationship of an organism to its environment is an analog one. From this point of view all nonconventionalized, nonverbal communications (gestures, rhythms, cadences, inflections, etc.) and their contexts are analogical or iconic.

Since verbalization and symbolization involve the digitalization of the analog, the ineffable ecstasies of a St. Teresa or a St. Catherine of Siena may become communicable literary experiences. Obviously without the digital we could not speak of the analog: there is a relationship between the two, and they should not be treated as entities. A digital system is of a higher level of organization but of a lower logical type than an analog system. The digital system has greater semiotic freedom (with reference to an open system's flexibility), but it is ultimately governed by the rules of the analog relationship between systems, subsystems, and supersystems in nature. The analog (continuum) is a set that includes the digital (discontinuum) as a subset (Wilden, 1972).

Perhaps we should do away with expressions like "analog" or "multivalued logic" and conceive of the iconic in hydrodynamic terms (Iberall, 1972) or even better as a hyperspace governed by the ordering principles of broadcast mechanisms, such as wave propagation, diffusion, radiation, convection, and electric field changes.

The all-pervading process of mechanization could be called a digitalization of the analog. The gradual dissolution of the hierarchical structure of the medieval Church was paralleled by a mechanization of the world picture which has been taking place at an ever-increasing rate since the Renaissance. A description of the universe as mechanical system requires a mechanical algorithm with an additional set of statements about the character of the system and the initial conditions. These statements involve the observer, his zeitgeist-dependent cortical interpretations, paradigms—hence his decisions, which transcend the mechanical algorithm and blur the distinction between observer and observed.

The result of this mechanization is a Faustian liberation of the *I*-in-the-world and a relegation of the *Self*—the seer and image maker—to a secondary role. It was this development which brought about the gradual disappearance of the visionary and a proliferation of rationally inclined masses trained from an early age and constantly reinforced thereafter to solve most if not all problems within the Aristotelian hemisphere. No wonder then that in most of these people hallucinatory and meditative experiences often elicit a reversal of EEG amplitude--laterality relationship (Goldstein and Stoltzfus, 1973), that is, a shift to the Platonic hemisphere.

Remember that the first use in English of the word "hallucination" occurs in the translation of a tract by Lavater in 1572, a few years after Michelangelo's death, at the peak of the Renaissance. If Goldstein and Stoltzfus could travel back to preRenaissance times, for instance into the twelfth century when the Gothic cathedrals were built, and were they to perform their EEG measurements, using a representative sample of faithful sons of the Church, we hypothesize that they might not confirm their present results (i.e., an hallucinatory meditative shift to the Platonic hemisphere). The medieval subjects, embedded as they were in the analog world of the Church, may have spent more "space" in their Platonic hemisphere to begin with and were already shifted prior to any experimentation.

In the past 2000 years the pendulum has swung twice from analog to digital and back, and is now swinging toward the analog for the third time. Perhaps we have just about passed the halfway point. The great outburst of creative activity that marked the first few decades of the century may be viewed as a result of an interhemispheric integration of the digital and the analog zeitgeists. Apparently artistic and scientific creativity reaches a maximum at a point midway between a digital and a subsequent analog epoch, as it did in the Elizabethan age. Rattray Taylor (1954) believes that under extreme "patrism"—our digital times--spontaneity is too strongly repressed, whereas under extreme "matrism"—our analog times—there may be insufficient discipline to school and direct the creative urge.

A complementarity* seems to exist between hallucination and vision, the two aspects of vivid visual imagery. Apparently it is this complementarity which compels historical epochs to devise rituals for beatification and exorcism, to sanctify or to burn at the stake, to heal or to institutionalize the individual whose imagery has strengthened or weakened the fabric of society.

From the point of view of the individual, hallucinations may be considered to be Platonic reformulations of Aristotelian propositions, hence hallucinatory and dream experiences may have strong symbolic significance for the individual in relation to his unresolved (and sometimes unresolvable) problems. Such problems closely resemble certain mythical patterns; that is, they center around unresolved (and sometimes unresolvable) archetypal or stereotypic problems of the human condition.

Hallucinations are too important to be left entirely to clinical psychiatrists. The common misconception that labels all hallucinatory experiences as pathological is reinforced by a previously noted limitation—namely, that the average psychiatrist is confronted all too often by uncreative hallucinating patients who are stuck with conflict and unable to follow that "vast and painful initiation rite" (Bateson, 1972), the path from agony to ecstasy: the process of disintegration and rebirth through symbolic experiences.

CODA

Self-referential man's consciousness contains both the *I*-awareness of the observed and the *Self*-awareness of the observer. Hence it well could be, although it may be impossible to prove, that the world is becoming aware of itself through little islands of "rational" *I*'s and "hallucinated" *Selves* that are experienced in, and recognized as, "normal" and "exalted" states.

Or simply: the world is becoming conscious, therefore I am.

ACKNOWLEDGMENTS

I am indebted and express my thanks to friends and colleagues whose stimulating and critical remarks contributed significantly to the formation of some of my pet concepts. I am particularly grateful to Blair Burns, Washington, D.C.; Harold Goldman, Columbus, Ohio; Leonide Goldstein, New Brunswick, New Jersey; Arthur Iberall, Upper Darby, Pennsylvania; Patrick Milburn, New Rochelle, New York; and last but not least to Stevan Harnad, Princeton, New Jersey. Steve has read the manuscript and in the light of his incisive remarks and clarifying editorial suggestions I could reduce uncertainties and raise the signal-to-noise ratio to some extent.

The assistance and cooperation of my creative artist wife Trudy cannot be verbalized, and I shall have to dream up a visuospatial pattern that contains both

---

* By "complementarity" it is meant—in analogy to an electron, which has no properties such as position or momentum—that vivid visual imagery has no religious or psychopathological connotations. Position and momentum or visions and hallucinations represent informational properties that arise only from the act of observation or measurement.

her intuition-devotion and my gratitude. That the essay is still somewhat hard on the reader may be due to the interdisciplinary language of my hallucinatory style, which abounds in rhythmic-ornamental geometrizations.

REFERENCES

Ahlenstiel, H. Selbstbeobachtung einer von der Basis gelösten Illusion; Betrachtung zur Frage einer rationalen Unterbringung bei Trugbildern. *Nervenarzt*, 1954, **25**, 295–297.

Anand, B., Chhina, G., and Singh, B. Some aspects of electroencephalographic studies in yogis. *Electroencephalography and Clinical Neurophysiology*, 1961, **13**, 452–456.

Angelus, S. (1657) In *Gesammelte Werke*. Munich: Carl Hanser Verlag, 1949.

Arland, M. *Pascal*. Paris: L'enfant poète, 1946.

Ashby, W. *Design for a brain*. New York: Wiley, 1960.

St. Augustine. (396) *Confessions*. Book 10, paragraph 8. Sheed (Transl.). London: Sheed and Ward, 1943.

Bateson, G. *Steps to an ecology of mind*. New York: Ballantine, 1972.

Benz, E. *Die Vision*. Stuttgart: Ernst Klett, 1969.

Beringer, K. *Der Meskalinrausch*. Berlin: Julius Springer, 1927.

Berman, A. The problem of assessing cerebral dominance and its relationship to intelligence. *Cortex*, 1971, **7**, 372–386.

Bogen, J. E. The other side of the brain. I. Dysgraphia and dyscopia following cerebral commissurotomy. *Bulletin of the Los Angeles Neurological Society*, 1969, **34**, 73–105. (a)

Bogen, J. E. The other side of the brain. II. An appositional mind. *Bulletin of the Los Angeles Neurological Society*, 1969, **34**, 135–162. (b)

Bogen, J. E., and Bogen, G. M. The other side of the brain. III. The corpus callosum and creativity. *Bulletin of the Los Angeles Neurological Society*, 1969, **34**, 191–220.

Bogen, J. E. The corpus callosum, the other side of the brain and pharmacologic opportunity. In W. L. Smith (Ed.), *Drugs and cerebral function*. Springfield, Ill.: Charles C Thomas, 1970.

Bogen, J. E., DeZure, R., Tenhouten, W. D., and Marsh, J. F. The other side of the brain. IV. The A/P ratio. *Bulletin of the Los Angeles Neurological Society*, 1972, **37**, 49–61.

Bourguignon, E. Ritual dissociation and possession belief in Caribbean Negro religion. In N. Whitten and J. Szwed (Eds.), *Afro-American anthropology*. New York: Free Press, 1970.

Brodie, B. B. Interaction of psychotropic drugs with physiologic and biochemical mechanisms in the brain. *Modern Medicine*, 1958, **26**, 69–80.

Brown, B. B. Studying aspects of consciousness with the physiological feedback technique. In J. Segal (Ed.), *Mental Health Program Report 5*. Rockville, Md.: National Institute of Mental Health, 1971.

Brown, S. *Laws of form*. London: Allen and Unwin, 1969.

Bustamante, J., Jordan, A., Vila, M., Gonzales, A., and Iusua, A. State-dependent learning in humans. *Physiology and Behavior*, 1970, **5**, 793–796.

Buxbaum, D. M. Analgesic activity of Δ^9-tetrahydrocannabinol in the rat and mouse. *Psychopharmacologia (Berl.)*, 1972, **25**, 275–280.

Chapman, L. J., Chapman, J. P., and Miller, G. A. A theory of verbal behavior in schizophrenia. In B. A. Maher (Ed.), *Progress in experimental personality research*. New York: Academic Press, 1964.

Charman, W. N., and Rowlands, C. M. Visual sensations produced by cosmic ray muons. *Nature*, 1971, **232**, 574–575.

Coleridge, S. T. *Biographia literaria*, Vols. I and II, J. Shawcross (Ed.). Oxford: Clarendon Press, 1907.

Corbin, H. *Creative imagination in the Sūfism of Ibn 'Arabī*. London: Routledge and Kegan Paul, 1969.

Corlis, R., Splaver, G., Wisecup, P., and Fischer, R. Myers-Briggs type personality scales and their relation to taste acuity. *Nature*, 1967, **216**, 91–92.

Cornford, F. (1937) *Plato's cosmology. The Timaeus of Plato*. Translated, with a running commentary. New York: Liberal Arts Press, 1957.

Cowell, E. B., Müller, F. H., and Takakusu, J. (Eds.) *Buddhist Mahâyâna texts.* New York: Dover, 1969.

Das, N. N., and Gastaut, H. Variations de l'activité électrique du cerveau, du coeur, et des muscles squelettiques au cours de la méditation et de l'extase yogique. *Electroencephalography and Clinical Neurophysiology,* 1957, Supplement **6,** 211–219.

Diamond, B. Sirhan B. Sirhan: A conversation with T. George Harris. *Psychology Today,* 1969, **3,** 48–55.

Dreyfus, H. L. *Alchemy and artificial intelligence.* Santa Monica, Calif.: Rand Corporation, Publication No. P–3244, 1965.

Eliot, T. S. *Selected essays.* New York: Harcourt, Brace, 1932.

Etevenon, P. R. Effects de la S. L. I. différentielle sur les structures visuelles du lapin. Variations de l'électrogenèse et de la dominance cérébrale sous l'action du LSD-25. *Revue de Médecine Aéronautique,* 1967, **21,** 35–47.

Etevenon, P., and Boissier, J. R. LSD-effects on signal-to-noise ratio and lateralization of visual cortex and lateral geniculate body during photic stimulation. *Experientia,* 1972, **28,** 1338–1340.

Ey, H. *La conscience.* Paris: Presses Univérsitaires de France, 1963.

Fischer, R. The biological fabric of time. In R. Fischer (Ed.), Interdisciplinary perspectives of time. *Annals of the New York Academy of Sciences,* 1967, **138,** 440–488.

Fischer, R., and Rockey, M. A. A heuristic model of creativity. *Experientia,* 1967, **23,** 150–151.

Fischer, R. Out on a (phantom) limb; variations on the theme: Stability of body image and the golden section. *Perspectives in Biology and Medicine,* 1969, **12,** 259–273. (a)

Fischer, R. The perception–hallucination continuum, a re-examination. *Diseases of the Nervous System,* 1969, **30,** 161–171. (b)

Fischer, R. On creative, psychotic and ecstatic states. In I. Jakab (Ed.), *Art interpretation and art therapy. Psychiatry and art,* Vol. 2. Basel/New York: S. Karger, 1969. (c)

Fischer, R., Thatcher, K., Kappeler, T., and Wisecup, P. Unity and covariance of perception and behavior. *Arzneimittelforschung* (Drug Research), 1969, **19,** 1941–1945.

Fischer, R. Psychotomimetic drug-induced changes in space and time. *Proceedings of the Fourth International Congress of Pharmacology,* 1969, **3,** 28–77. Basel: Benno Schwabe, 1970. (a)

Fischer, R. Prediction and measurement of perceptual–behavioral change in drug-induced hallucinations. In W. Keup (Ed.), *Origin and mechanisms of hallucinations.* New York: Plenum Press, 1970. (b)

Fischer, R. Über das Rhytmisch-Ornamentale im Halluzinatorisch–Schöpferischen. *Confinia Psychiatrica,* 1970, **13,** 1–25. (c)

Fischer, R., Kappeler, T., Wisecup, P., and Thatcher, K. Personality trait-dependent psychomotor performance under psilocybin. *Diseases of the Nervous System,* 1970, **31,** 91–101. (a)

Fischer, R., Hill, R., Thatcher, K., and Scheib, J. Psilocybin-induced contraction of nearby visual space. *Agents and Actions,* 1970, **1,** 190–197. (b)

Fischer, R. A Cartography of the ecstatic and meditative states. *Science,* 1971, **174,** 897–904. (a)

Fischer, R. Gustatory, behavioral and pharmacological manifestations of chemoreception in man. In G. Ohloff and A. E. Thomas (Eds.), *Gustation and olfaction.* New York: Academic Press, 1971, (b)

Fischer, R., and Hill, R. M. Psychotropic drug-induced transformations of visual space. *International Pharmacopsychiatry,* 1971, **6,** 28–37.

Fischer, R., and Scheib, J. Creative performance and the hallucinogenic drug-induced creative experience; or one man's brain damage is another's creativity. *Confinia Psychiatrica,* 1971, **14,** 174–202.

Fischer, R. Schizophrenia research in biological perspective. In A. Kaplan (Ed.), *Genetic factors in "schizophrenia."* Springfield, Ill.: Charles C Thomas, 1972. (a)

Fischer, R. On separateness and oneness, an I–Self dialogue. *Confinia Psychiatrica,* 1972, **115,** 165–194. (b)

Fischer, R., and Landon, G. On the arousal state-dependent recall of 'subconscious' experience: Stateboundness. *British Journal of Psychiatry,* 1972, **120,** 159–172.

Fischer, R., Navratil, L., and Rainer, R. Der Wahn als das Schöpferische. Kreativität, psychopathologische Kunst, Kunst. Ein Dreier-Gespräch, In O. V. Breicha (Ed.), *Wiener Halbjahresschrift für Literatur, bildende Kunst und Musik.* Protokolle 1972, Nr. 1.

Fischer, R., A pharmacological and conceptual reevaluation of hallucinations. *The Pharmacologist,* 1974, **16,** 237; and *Confinia Psychiatrica,* 1975 (in press).

Flor-Henry, P. Laterality effects in organic, epileptic and functional psychoses. Paper presented at the Fifth World Congress of Psychiatry, Mexico City, 1971.

Foerster, H. v. Thoughts and notes on cognition. In P. Garvin (Ed.), *Cognition: A multiple view.* New York: Spartan Books, 1970.

Gazzaniga, M. S. One brain—two minds? *American Scientist,* 1972, **60,** 311–317.

Gellhorn, E. Central nervous system tuning and its implications for neuropsychiatry. *Journal of Nervous and Mental Disease,* 1968, **147,** 148–162.

Gellhorn, E. Further studies on the physiology and pathophysiology of the tuning of the central nervous system. *Psychosomatics,* 1969, **10,** 94–104,

Gellhorn, E. The emotions and the ergotropic and trophotropic systems. *Psychologische Forschung,* 1970, **34,** 68–94.

Goldstein, L., Murphree, H., Sugerman, A., Pfeiffer, C., and Jenney, E. Quantitative electroencephalographic analysis of naturally occurring (schizophrenic) and drug-induced psychotic states in human males. *Clinical Pharmacology and Therapeutics,* 1963, **4,** 10–21.

Goldstein, L., and Stoltzfus, N. W. Drug-induced changes of interhemispheric EEG amplitude relationships in man. Fifth International Congress on Phamacology, July 23–28, 1972, San Francisco. (Abstracts, 505, p. 85)

Goldstein, L., Stoltzfus, N. W., and Gardocki, J. F. Changes in interhemispheric amplitude relationships in the EEG during sleep. *Physiology and Behavior,* 1972,**8,** 811–816.

Goldstein, L., and Stoltzfus, N. W. Psychoactive drug-induced changes of interhemispheric EEG amplitude relationships. *Agents and Actions,* 1973, **3,** 124–132.

Goodwin, D., Powell, B., Bremer, D., Hoine, H., and Stern, J. Alcohol and recall: State-dependent effects in man. *Science,* 1969, **163,** 1358–1360.

Green, C. *Out-of-the-body-experiences.* Oxford: Institute of Psychophysical Research, 1968.

Green, E. E., Green, A. M., and Walters, E. D. Voluntary control of internal states: Psychological and physiological. *Journal of Transpersonal Psychology,* 1970, **1,** 1–26.

Günther, G. Die Theorie der mehrwertigen Logik. In R. Berlinger and E. Fink (Eds.), *Philosophische Perspektiven. Ein Jahrbuch,* Vol. 3. Frankfurt: Vittorio Klostermann, 1971.

Gwynne, P., Fischer, R., and Hill, R. Hypnotic induction of the interference of psilocybin with optically induced spatial distortion. *Pharmakopsychiatrie Neuro-Psychopharmakologie,* 1969, **9,** 146–156.

Harnad, S. Creativity, lateral saccades and the nondominant hemisphere. *Perceptual and Motor Skills,* 1972, **34,** 653–654.

Hebbard, F., and Fischer, R. Effect of psilocybin, LSD and mescaline on small involuntary eye movements. *Psychopharmacologia (Berl.),* 1966, **9,** 146–156.

Hess, W. Quoted in H. Beckman, *Pharmacology,* 2nd ed. Philadelphia: Saunders, 1961, p. 292.

Hill, R., and Fischer, R. Psilocybin-induced transformations of visual space. *Pharmakopsychiatrie Neuro-Psychopharmakologie,* 1970, **3,** 256–267.

Hofmann, A. Psychotomimetic agents. In A. Burger (Ed.), *Chemical constitution and pharmacodynamic action,* Vol. II, New York: Dekker, 1968.

Hommes, O. R. Stemmingsanomaliën als neurologisch symptoom. *Nederland Tijdschrift for Geneeskunde,* 1965, **109,** 588–593.

Hommes, O. R., and Panhuysen, L. H. H. M. Depression and cerebral dominance. *Psychiatria, Neurologia and Neurochirurgia,* 1971, **74,** 259–270.

Huygens, C. *Horologium oscillatorium; Sive de motu pendulorum ad horlogia aptato demonstrationes geometricae.* Paris: 1673.

Iberall, A. S. *Toward a general science of viable systems.* New York: McGraw-Hill, 1972.

Isbell, H., Wolbach, A., Wikler, A., and Miner, E. Cross-tolerance between LSD and psilocybin. *Psychopharmacologia (Berl.),* 1961, **2,** 147–159.

Jain, M., and Jain, K. M. The science of Yoga, a study in perspective. *Perspectives in Biology and Medicine,* 1973, **17,** 93–102.

Jouvet, M. Biogenic amines and the state of sleep. *Science,* 1969, **163,** 32–41.

Kasamatsu, A., and Hirai, T. An electroencephalographic study on the Zen meditation (Zazen). *Folia Psychiatrica Neurologica Japonica,* 1966, **20,** 315–336.

Kast, E. C., and Collins, V. J. Lysergic acid diethylamide as an analgesic agent. *Anesthesie et Analgesie,* 1964, **43**, 285–291.

Kinsbourne, M. The control of attention by interaction between the cerebral hemispheres. In S. Kornblum (Ed.), *Attention and performance.* New York: Academic Press, 1973.

Klüver, H. *Mescal and the mechanism of hallucinations.* Chicago: University of Chicago Press, 1966.

Knoll, M., Kugler, J., Hofer, O., and Lawder, S. D. Effects of chemical stimulation on electrically induced phosphenes on their bandwidth, shape, number and intensity. *Confinia Neurologica,* 1963, **23**, 201–226.

Kocel, K., Galin, D., Ornstein, R., and Merrin, E. L. Lateral eye movement and cognitive mode. *Psychonomic Science,* 1972, **27**, 223–224.

Kotin, J., and Goodwin, F. K. Depression during mania: Clinical observations and theoretical implications. *American Journal of Psychiatry,* 1972, **129,** 679–686.

Krishna, G. *Kundalini, the evolutionary energy in man.* Berkeley, Calif.: Shambala, 1971.

Kuromaru, S., Okada, S., Hanada, M., Kashara, Y., and Sakamoto, K. Effect of LSD-25 on the phenomenon of phantom limbs. *Psychiatria et Neurologia Japonica,* 1962, **64**, 604–613.

Lacan, J. *The function of language in psychoanalysis.* A. Wilden (Transl.) Baltimore: Johns Hopkins Press, 1968.

Landon, G., and Fischer, R. On common features of the language of hallucinogenic drug-induced and creative states. *Confinia Psychiatrica,* 1970, **13,** 115–138.

Lavater, L. *Of ghostes and spirites walking by nyght.* London: Watkins, 1572. (Quoted by T. R. Sarbin, and J. B. Juhasz, The historical concept of hallucination. *Journal of the History of the Behavioral Sciences,* 1967, **3,** 339–358.)

Leonhard, K., and Berendt, H. Musikalische Leistung einer Idiotin. *Confinia Psychiatrica,* 1968, **11,** 106–118.

Lhermitte, J. *Les hallucinations.* Paris: G. Doin, 1951.

Lilly, J. Mental effects of reduction of ordinary levels of physical stimuli on intact, healthy persons. *Psychiatric Report No. 5.* Washington, D.C.: American Psychiatric Association, 1956.

Lishman, W. A. Emotion, consciousness and will after brain bisection in man. *Cortex,* 1971, **7,** 181–192.

Luria, A. A. *Higher cortical functions in man.* New York: Basic Books, 1966.

MacKay, D. M. Visual noise as tool of research. *Journal of General Psychology,* 1965, **72,** 181–197.

MacLean, P. Man and his animal brains. *Modern Medicine,* 1964 (February 3), 95–106.

Mahesh Yogi, M. *Maharishi Mahesh Yogi on the Bhagavad-Gita.* Baltimore: Penguin, 1969.

Malraux, A. *Les noyers de l'Altenburg.* Paris: Gallimard, 1948.

Marjerrison, G., Krause, A., and Keogh, R. Variability of the EEG in schizophrenia: Quantitative analysis with a modulus voltage integrator. *Electroencephalography and Clinical Neurophysiology,* 1967, **24,** 35–41.

Maturana, H. Neurophysiology of cognition. In P. L. Garvin (Ed.), *Cognition: A multiple view.* New York: Spartan Books, 1970.

McDonald, G., Conway, M., and Ricci, M. (Eds.), *The films of Charlie Chaplin.* New York: Bonanza, 1965.

McGlothlin, W. H., and Gattozzi, A. A. Long-term effects of LSD—A follow-up survey. In J. Segal (Ed.), *Mental Health Program Reports, 5.* Rockville, Md.: National Institute of Mental Health, 1971.

Mintz, S., and Alpert, M. Imagery vividness, reality testing and schizophrenic hallucinations. *Journal of Abnormal Psychology,* 1972, **79,** 310–316.

Mookerjee, A. In R. Kumar (Ed.), *Tantra Kunst.* Basel: Basilius, 1967.

Moreau de Tours. J. *La psychologie morbide dans ses rapports avec le philosophie de l'histoire, ou l'influence des neuropathies sur le dynamisme intellectuel.* Paris: 1859.

Morgan, A. H., McDonald, P. J., and MacDonald, H. Differences in bilateral alpha activity as a function of experimental task; with a note on lateral eye movements and hypnotizability. *Neuropsychologia,* 1971, **9,** 459–469.

Navratil, L. *Schizophrenie und Kunst.* Munich: Deutsches Taschenbuch Verlag, 1965.

Navratil, L. *Schizophrenie und Sprache.* Munich: Deutsches Taschenbuch Verlag, 1966.

Navratil, L. Krankheitsverlauf und Zeichnung (im Hinblick auf Kreativität). *Confinia Psychiatrica,* 1969, **12,** 28–39.

Nerval, de G. (1854) *Les filles du feu, suivi de l'Aurélia.* Présenté par Kléber Haedens. Paris: Gallimard, 1961.

Neumann, J. v. *The computer and the brain.* New Haven, Conn.: Yale University Press, 1958.

Oddy, H. C., and Lobstein, T. J. Hand and eye dominance in schizophrenia. *British Journal of Psychiatry,* 1972, **120,** 331–332.

Panton, Y. A., and Fischer, R. Hallucinogenic drug-induced behavior under sensory attenuation. *Archives of General Psychiatry,* 1973, **28,** 434–438.

Payne, R. W. An object classification text as a measure of overinclusive thinking in schizophrenic patients. *British Journal of Social and Clinical Psychology,* 1962, **1,** 213–221.

Peper, E. Comment on feedback training of parietal–occipital alpha asymmetry in normal human subjects. *Kybernetik,* 1971, **9,** 156–158.

Plato. (398 B.C.) Phaedo. In S. Buchanan (Ed.), *The portable Plato.* New York: Viking, 1948.

Prince, R. Can the EEG be used in the study of possession? In R. Prince (Ed.), *Trance and possession states.* Montreal: R. M. Bucke Memorial Society, 1968.

Proust, M. *Swann's way.* C. S. Moncrieff (Transl.). New York: Modern Library, 1928.

Pscheidt, G. R. Comparative aspects of selected psychoactive compounds: Biogenic amines, MAO-inhibitors and LSD. *Comparative Biochemistry and Physiology,* 1968, **24,** 249–265.

Psychiatric Glossary. Washington, D.C.: American Psychiatric Association, 1964.

Ram Dass, B. Lecture at the Maryland Psychiatric Research Center, Part I. *Journal of Transpersonal Psychology,* 1973, **5,** 75–103.

Rennert, H. Die prognostische Bedeutung der "Horizontverschiebung" in der schizophrenen Bildnerei. *Confinia Psychiatrica,* 1969, **12,** 23–27.

Roffman, M., and Lal, H. Role of brain amines in learning associated with "amphetamine-state." *Psychopharmacologia (Berl.),* 1972, **25,** 195–204.

Santillana, G. di. *The origins of scientific thought.* New York: New American Library, 1961.

Santillana, G. di. *Reflections on men and ideas.* Cambridge, Mass.: MIT Press, 1968.

Sarbin, T. R., and Juhasz, J. B. The historical background of the concept of hallucinations. *Journal of the History of the Behavioral Sciences,* 1967, **3,** 339–358.

Schaltenbrand, G. The effects of stereotactic electrical stimulation in the depth of the brain. *Brain,* 1965, **88,** 835–840.

Semmes, J. Hemispheric specialization: A possible clue to mechanism. *Neuropsychologia,* 1968, **6,** 11–26.

Sewell, E. *The structure of poetry.* New York: Scribner, 1952.

Shaffer, J., Hill, R. M. and Fischer, R. Δ^9-THC and psilocybin-induced changes in sensory magnitude estimations, *Agents and Actions,* 1973, **3,** 48–51.

Siomopoulos, V. Derealization and déjà vu: Formal mechanisms. *American Journal of Psychotherapy,* 1972, **26,** 84–89.

Smith, R. A., Gelles, D. B., and Vanderhaeghen, J. J. Subcortical visual hallucinations. *Cortex,* 1971, **7,** 162–168.

Sperry, R. W. Brain bisection and mechanisms of consciousness. In J. Eccles (Ed.), *Semaine d'étude sur cerveau et expérience consciente.* Rome: Pontificalis Academia Scientiae Scripta Varia, 1965.

Straus, E. W. Phenomenology of hallucinations. In L. J. West (Ed.), *Hallucinations.* New York: Grune & Stratton, 1962.

Strauss, J. S. Hallucinations and delusions as points on continua functions. *Archives of General Psychiatry,* 1969, **21,** 581–586.

Stromeyer, C. F., III, and Psotka, J. The detailed texture of eidetic images. *Nature,* 1970, **225,** 346–349.

Suzuki, S. *Zen mind, beginner's mind.* New York and Tokyo: Weatherhill, 1970.

Taylor, R. G. *Sex in history.* London: Thames and Hudson, 1954.

St. Teresa. (1565) *The life of St. Teresa,* J. M. Cohen (Transl.). Baltimore: Penguin, 1957.

Terzian, H., and Cecotto, C. Amytal intracarotideo per lo studio della dominanza emisferica. *Rivista Neurologica,* 1960, **30,** 460–471.

Thatcher, K., Kappeler, T. Wisecup, P., and Fischer, R. Personality trait-dependent psychomotor performance under psilocybin. *Diseases of the Nervous System,* 1970, **31,** 181–192.

Thatcher, K., Wiederholt, W., and Fischer, R. An electroencephalographic analysis of personality-dependent performance under psilocybin. *Agents and Actions,* 1971, **2,** 21–26.

Topitsch, E. Mythische Modelle in der Erkenntnislehre. *Studium Generale,* 1965, **18,** 400–418.

Toulmin, S., and Peters, R. S. A debate. In R. Borger and F. Cioffi (Eds.), *Explanation in the behavioral sciences.* Cambridge: Cambridge University Press, 1971.

Ungerstedt, U. Stereotaxic mapping of the monoamine pathways in the rat brain. *Acta Physiologica Scandinavica,* Supplementum **367,** 1971.

Venables, P. H. Sensory aspects of psychopathology. In J. Zubin and C. Shagass (Eds.), *Neurobiological aspects of psychopathology.* New York: Grune & Stratton, 1969.

Vives, J. L. (1538) Quoted by G. Zilboorg and G. W. Henry (Eds.), *A history of medical psychology.* New York: Norton, 1941.

Wallace, R. K. Physiological effects of transcendental meditation. *Science,* 1970, **167,** 1751–1754.

Weitbrecht, H. *Beiträge zur Religionspathologie, insbesondere zur Psychopathologie der Bekehrung.* Heidelberg: Scherrer, 1948.

Wilden, A. *System and structure; essays in communication and exchange.* London: Tavistock, 1972.

Winters, W. D., Ferrar-Allado, T. Guzman-Flores, C., and Alcaraz, M. The cataleptic state induced by ketamine; a review of the neuropharmacology of anesthesia. *Neuropharmacologia,* 1972, **11,** 303–315.

Wittgenstein, L. *Tractatus logico-philosophicus.* London: Routledge & Kegan Paul, 1922.

Wolbach, A., Isbell, H., and Miner, E. Cross tolerance between mescaline and LSD. *Psychopharmacologia (Berl.),* 1962, **3,** 1–14.

Wordsworth, W. Observations prefixed to the second edition, *Lyrical Ballads.* Quoted in J. H. Smith and E. W. Parks (Eds.), *The great critics.* New York: Norton, 1960.

Zangwill, O. L. *Cerebral dominance and its relation to psychological function.* Edinburgh: Oliver & Boyd, 1960.

Zuckerman, M., Albright, R. J.; Marks, C. S., and Miller, G. L. Stress and hallucinatory effects of perceptual isolation and confinement. *Psychological Monographs,* 1962, **76** (30, Whole no. 549).

CHAPTER SEVEN

THE SOCIAL CONTEXT OF HALLUCINATIONS

THEODORE R. SARBIN, Ph.D.

JOSEPH B. JUHASZ, Ph.D.

The behavior and experience of an individual cannot be understood without taking into account the texture of his social environment. We see the significance of behavior and experience arising out of the context of social roles enacted by a person and the reciprocal roles enacted by others. Thus within the field of social psychology itself, our approach to the understanding of the behavior traditionally labeled hallucinatory is a role-theoretical one (Sarbin, 1956; Sarbin and Allen, 1968).

Role theory employs a dramaturgical model to describe human behavior. The concept of role implies that persons can be described as actors: they are active and they influence the context in which their actions occur. "Role," a term borrowed directly from the theatre, is a metaphor intended to communicate that conduct adheres to certain "parts" rather than to the particular players whose interpretation we observe. Any piece of conduct is then understood as having two components: the actor's interpretation and the underlying role structure of which it is an exemplar.

The underlying role structure, the central metaphor of role theory, includes the following components: role expectations and their validity, role locations and their accuracy, congruence of role and self, general and specific skills in interpretation, sensitivity to ecological demands for nonstructural role performances, and the properties of audiences for guiding overt performances of actors.

The study of isolated individuals per se has no place in role theory. Roles can only be enacted in the context of others. It is absurd to consider such a role as *teacher* without at the same time considering the reciprocal role of *student*. Similarly, to analyze a person's performance as *physician* is empty without reference to the reciprocal role of *patient*.

It is the burden of this chapter that any performance diagnosed as "hallucinating" is not adequately described unless there is reference to complementary roles, the audience, the expectations of others, the role skills of the performer, and so on.

DEFINITIONS OF HALLUCINATION: PAST AND PRESENT

The word "hallucination" is an anglicized form of the Latin word *alucinatio*, which means a wandering of the mind, idle talk, prating. Its first use in English is in a translation of a tract by Lavater (1572), who used the word to refer to "ghostes and spirites walking by nyght," that is, to apparitions.

The original use of the word assumes that talk of ghosts and spirits is idle talk or prating. Some observer or observers make a judgment, one which is at odds with that of the speaker (the prater or hallucinator). Lavater implies that talk of ghosts and spirits is idle talk. To label certain talk "hallucination" is to pass judgment that certain talk is idle. The observer (the person who is making the judgment of the appropriateness of the behavior) discounts the possible seriousness of the behavior of the observed. Lavater's use of the word was pejorative. In it was embedded a metaphysical assertion that ghosts and spirits have no ontological status; therefore, talk about them is foolish by definition.

From the beginning of its usage in the English language, the word "hallucination" has in fact referred to two conjoined but analyzable elements: (1) the serious talk by some person about ghosts and spirits or other apparitions, and (2) the labeling by another of such talk as heedless, foolish, lacking in credibility (i.e., representing no ontological validity). "Hallucination," then, has traditionally been used to describe behavior that is intended as serious by the speaker but is perceived as heedless and foolish by an observer.

"Hallucination" became a technical term in psychology and medicine in the hands of Esquirol in the nineteenth century. He defined the term as "ascribing a body and actuality to images" (1838, p. 7) and took the content element out of Lavater's implicit definition. The phenomena were no longer restricted to apparitions; under the heading of hallucination were included *any* ascribing of a body or actuality to images. To hallucinate was to be "out of touch with reality"; and to be out of touch with reality was to be insane. According to Esquirol, hallucination is a *species* of the *genus* "image," whose defining characteristic is the imaginer's declaration that the referent for the observer's *"image"* is the subject's *"perception."* Thus Esquirol continued to employ "hallucination" so that the observer's declaration was a necessary condition; that is, (1) a person has certain imaginings, and (2) some other person makes the judgment that the imaginer has ascribed a body and actuality to a noncorporeal image.

The person who ascribes the body and the actuality to the image is in no position to make a self-diagnosis, for then he would be behaving in a clearly self-contradictory way. To say, "I actually see the body of the Virgin Mary before me, and I know that it is neither actual nor a body" is a self-contradiction. Although a person can take the position of self-accusation, the *judgment* has to be made by an outsider (Malcolm, 1959).

From the point of view of the person making the judgment, the hallucinator is imagining but claiming to be perceiving; he is responding to stimuli that are not there. Juhasz (1973) has attempted to show that inability to tolerate such paradoxical behavior is the usual precondition to declaring another person insane, mentally ill, or otherwise psychologically incompetent. From our point of view, hallucination still remains one of the cornerstones of the mental illness edifice. In *New Introductory Lectures on Psychoanalysis* (1933), Freud says "the logical laws of thought do not apply in the id, and this is true above all of the law of contradiction" (p. 73).

Hallucination, for Freud, was the most fundamental contradiction of all, and it remains one of the principal conceptual bases of the unconscious for psychoanalytically oriented writers (Rapaport, 1951).

In Esquirol's definition, the insanity—the inability to distinguish image from perception—is placed *inside* the hallucinator. The hallucinator possesses the intrapsychic flaw of being unable to distinguish between his perceptions and his fantasies.

This definition was congruent with contemporary ideas of medical science in two very significant ways:

1. Esquirol's definition did not specify *content*. Because the definition is content-free, it appears to be judgment-free, or *objective*. Lavater's restriction to apparitions was lifted; thus seemingly *any* phenomenon that fit this structural definition would be accepted as an hallucination.

2. Esquirol's definition pretended to be *intrapersonal*, locating the pathology inside the sufferer. Suppressing reference to the interpersonal feature of hallucination allowed Esquirol to apply the medical model of illness to hallucination. The intrapersonal definition provides the practitioner with a *tangible patient to treat*, ignoring the participation of the practitioner in the identification of the patient's imagining as hallucinatory.

As Sarbin (1967), Sarbin and Juhasz (1967), Fischer (1969), and others have pointed out, "hallucination" is perhaps unique among psychiatric terms in having remained essentially unaltered from the late nineteenth century to the present. "A false sensory perception in the absence of an actual external stimulus" is the American Psychiatric Association's official *glossary* definition (1969).

Like the nineteenth-century definition, the 1969 definition operates as a result of yoking together two processes: (1) a person claims that he is perceiving, and (2) an observer claims that the person is not perceiving but is imagining. That is, as with the previous definitions, the hallucinating person is in no position to evaluate the truth of the diagnostic statement that he is hallucinating. Given the usual meanings of the words *perception, false,* and *external stimulus,* he is in no position to take the role of psychiatric diagnostician and *assert* "I am hallucinating." Only another person is capable of making the diagnosis. This definition, like previous ones, *ignores the role of the behavior analyst and pretends that the phenomenon is exclusively intrapersonal.*

The *Glossary's* definition sees the hallucinator as one acting in a senseless manner and implies that he is unable or unwilling to distinguish between true and false sensory impressions and between honest-to-goodness stimuli and fantasies or dreams. Thus from the point of view of the diagnostician, the hallucinator manifests contradictory behavior. Therefore, he is illogical, irrational, mad, crazy—hallucination is a sign of mental illness. Used in this way, "hallucination" refers to a situation in which one person places a negative valuation on the reported imaginings of another, which serves to exclude and degrade the hallucinator. The person passing the judgment usually occupies a more powerful status than the person on whom the judgment is being passed.

More recently, however, in the popular culture the word "hallucination" is sometimes applied with a *positive* valuation, showing a general change in sentiment toward reported imaginings (Juhasz, 1969, 1971). The writings of Laing (1967), Castaneda (1968, 1972), Jung (1968, 1970), Mutwa (1969), and Fischer (1971) point to the evolution of a new lexicographic definition: enacting the social role of hallucinator means that the second person empowered to label the reported imaginings is often a person such as a priest, psychiatrist, or shaman who brings to bear a significant influence on the fantasy life of the hallucinator. Used in this way, "hallucination" may be employed to represent involved imaginings of estimable, honored, and respected persons.

TOWARD A CONTEXTUAL THEORY

Our central thesis can be stated as follows: in Western medicine and psychology, a reported imagining is labeled as hallucination if the individual reporting the experience is identified as occupying a degraded or nonvalued status. In the most typical case, the degraded status is that of a mental patient, an individual whose choice of metaphysical heterodoxy has been rejected by those who have the power—legitimate, coercive, or expert—to declare a negative valuation on the reported imagining and, by extension, on the imaginer. To develop this thesis, it is necessary to locate our observations within a social psychological framework, first addressing ourselves to the question of social degradation.

The Social Psychology of Degradation.   As Goffman (1961), Becker (1963, 1964), Scheff (1966), Szasz (1970), and others have repeatedly pointed out, the use of diagnostic labels occurs *after* the putative patient has violated propriety norms. Such violations lead to declarations of negative valuation—a moral enterprise. The diagnostician, as a representative of legitimate power, can formalize the negative valuation in his employment of terms such as psychosis, hallucination, and schizophrenia. The effect of such moral judgment is to degrade the actor from a position of at least neutral respect to one of lack of respect. A felicitous way of denoting the position occupied after the moral judgment is that of nonperson. Because the diagnosis is a moral judgment, the labels used by the diagnostician stigmatize the patient (Osborne, 1974).

In general, one person degrades another when the reciprocal role relation that exists between them comes under strain. Successful degradation involves the use of legitimate, expert, and/or coercive power. It involves capitalizing on the asymmetrical aspects of role expectations embedded in role systems. The attempt of A to degrade B is an attempt at redefinition of the mutually held role expectations. Since the role expectations of A are not being fulfilled by B, A tries to redefine the role relation by degrading B. For example, parent–child role relations often come under strain. If the child does not do well in school, the parent may attempt to redefine the situation by labeling the child "dumb-ox," "stupid ass," or "idiot."

The precipitating cause of some degradation procedures often has to be enlarged to at least a triad before the degradation can successfully be carried out. Consider, for example, a police officer "busting" a juvenile pot smoker on the complaint of the school principal. The juvenile's identity is subject to degradation because of the police officer's legitimate and coercive power. Again, a forensic psychiatrist who testifies that a defendant is a paranoid schizophrenic has used his expert power to degrade the defendant in the eyes of the jurors.

The actor's interpretation of a role, in particular in the case of achieved roles (roles chosen *by* rather than chosen *for* actors), allows for a good deal of latitude in jockeying for the more powerful position. In the case of ascribed roles (roles chosen *for* rather than chosen *by* actors), the situation tends to be far less fluid. For example, in a father–son role relation, the son will have the less powerful short-range position and the father the less powerful long-range position. This tends to be a general "truth," for it relies on the mortality of the father, the helplessness of the babe, and some series of role and power changes in the interim.

In any case, the greater the perceived power difference between the two actors, the easier the prediction of who will come out with a degraded identity in a strained role relation.

The relation existing between two actors performing reciprocal roles may come under strain from either of the two performers or from some source outside the dyad. In the former case new obligations or rules of procedure in other roles may be in conflict with the implicit rules defining the role structure coming under strain. The latter case involves the actual penetration of outsiders into the role structure or set of implicit rules defining the relation. To be sure, there are means of dealing with either type of role strain other than the attempt by one party to degrade the other (e.g., Toby, 1952; Sarbin, 1954; Goode, 1960).

One of us (J.B.J.) has examined reports from a number of cultures and histori-cal epochs to generalize about the conditions under which one person degrades another through the accusation of witchcraft. The antecedent condition most typically preceding the accusations is a strained relation between two persons, usually of unequal power: the assertion of witchcraft by the person in the superior role position tended not only to annul the strained role relation but generally to enhance the position of the accuser in the community as well. The cause of the role strain often involved the sickness (incapacity to perform expected role obliga-tions) of some third party, or political upheaval in the life of the accuser, making his or her relation with the accused no longer tenable. Such "political upheaval" might involve avoidable or unavoidable role changes, such as *rites de passage* or natural calamities, with which unavoidable changes in the exercise of power coincide. In many cultures, for example, becoming a widow is occasion for a general redefinition of social power, one that changes uncountable role relations with everyone in the community. Such persons are frequently both the targets and the makers of witchcraft accusations. Whether they become makers or receivers of accusation depends on the perceived power relation between the new widow and the role partner.

Szasz (1970) has convincingly argued that the accusation of "mental illness" in our society is functionally equivalent to accusations of witchcraft in other com-munities. The "mentally ill" as well as witches are persons who are declared intolerable by the community and with whom reciprocal role relations can safely be abrogated. In effect, the declaration of "mental illness," like witchcraft, places the accused in a nonperson status.

Goffman (1961), Becker (1964), Foucault (1965), Sarbin (1968), and Rosenhan (1973) have demonstrated that it is not any particular set of behaviors of the individuals under question that lead to their expulsion; rather, *after* the expulsion their behavior becomes intolerable. At times the situation is more complex. The process of expulsion involves a slow process of redefining behaviors and altering perceptions. The moment of expulsion may coincide with the moment when the person in the more powerful role redefines the reciprocal other as hopeless, dangerous, or inhuman (i.e., as a nonperson). The more powerful individual alters the categories under which the conduct of the individual to be degraded is to be subsumed. That is, not all changes in the classifying of conduct to support the degrading label need be *ex post facto,* although perhaps most are.

In the case of hallucinations, a reported imagining becomes an hallucination after the identity of the person in question has already been degraded to that of mental patient, with the implication that the patient's claim to personhood is no longer honored (Sarbin, 1967; Sarbin and Juhasz, 1967; Sarbin et al., 1971; Juhasz, 1972). Undoubtedly, this is what happens in most instances, but there are times when the degradation process occurs before the official transvaluation of identity is carried out. A reported imagining may be declared a "symptom" of an individual's inability to maintain satisfactory role relations. Such a declaration may convince the person making the declaration (and perhaps others) that a nonperson label needs to be attached to the deviating or disturbing person. Whether before the official degradation ritual, or after, when an individual is perceived as having violated ascribed role expectations, behavior that is routinely tolerated becomes intolerable.

Another category of degraded identity similar to that of mad or crazy is that of the criminal. The principal traditional distinction between the insane on the one hand and the criminal on the other is that the criminal is seen as the causative locus of his or her own actions. By and large (although distinctions in practice are never as neat as they are in writing), becoming crazy is something that *happens* to a person, whereas becoming a criminal is something that a person *does.* From this distinction flow a number of implications about the treatment and perception of the insane and criminals. The insane, like witches in other cultures or in the Middle Ages in Europe, are incapacitaed because of some outside force or power.

Becoming a witch or becoming a mental patient involves such fundamental departures from normal conduct and the carrying out of normal responsibilities that a force from outside the person is assumed. The expectations associated with the performance of one's set of ascribed or granted roles amount to an operational definition of one's "human nature" as seen by his or her society. Not carrying out the expectations associated with such granted roles amounts to "unnatural" behavior. Such unnaturalness cannot be conceived as a matter of choice, for it is not evil as such, but rather beyond evil, beyond human. It means a forfeiture of the claim to *being* human. The actor who is in a strained granted role, then, is most often a candidate for degradation to the status of temporary or permanent nonhuman, hence nonperson. He or she is given over to the care of experts at warehousing or repairing those whose humanity has lapsed or come under question.

The bulk of one's ascribed roles in this society, as in most others, involve familial relationships and responsibilities. In terms of our discussion, it is amply documented (e.g., Hollingshead and Redlich, 1958) that in the case of the "mentally ill" the accuser is most apt to be a person in a complementary familial role. In a strained role relation with a teen-aged son, a father is unable or unwilling to take the son's perspective. The father is more likely than the son to entertain the notion that the other is mad. Once this classification is made, the son's talk about his imaginings will take on new meaning and may even be identified as hallucination.

In choice (achieved) role relations, the situation is different. In a strained relation with an employee, an empoyer is more likely to see the employee as lazy or inefficient or larcenous, depending on the kind and degree of strain. The employee's reported imaginings would not likely come under close scrutiny, and hallucination would not be involved as a "symptom." The employee *can* strain interpersonal role relations by reporting unusual imaginings. The employer--employee role relation is then set aside.

The recent interest in the relationship between being female and being mad (e.g., Chesler, 1972) points up the generally weaker political position of females in our society as well as the fact that they are perceived to be occupying *granted* rather than achieved status. Since the relative involvement of males in achieved roles continues to be much greater than that of females, we predict (as is the case) that the deviant female is more likely to be perceived as mad or hallucinating, whereas the deviant male is more likely to be perceived as antisocial or criminal. According to Chesler, the strained husband–wife and parent–daughter relations are particularly likely to lead to accusations of madness in our society. Although madness is no longer purely sex-linked as witchcraft or hysteria was, under present arrangements it has remained a condition to which a significant number of females are degraded (or depersoned) by male judges and accusers. When a housewife refuses to dress her children, clean the house, and do the dishes, the explanation sought is usually one that assumes such behavior to be "unnatural." As a result she is likely to be stigmatized as an "unnatural" mother, therefore a nonperson and a candidate for a mental hospital. When males go deviant, they are more likely to be caught stealing, acting in a violent manner, or otherwise misbehaving outside the family. Their unwanted behavior is regarded as self-caused, therefore criminal.

Especially interesting are the cases of persons whose social roles usually render them immune to accusations of irresponsible conduct, such as the poet Ezra Pound, or Mad Ludwig of Bavaria. Ordinarily, poets and princes enjoy a certain degree of "idiosyncrasy credit" (Hollander, 1958) and, as a result, are relatively shielded from usual valuational practices. When they have exhausted their idiosyncrasy credit, the valuational problem becomes one of establishing whether the deviant conduct was intentional or not intentional (i.e., crime or madness). Ezra Pound, for example, violated the role expectations associated with the granted status of a citizen of a democratic state. Mad Ludwig violated the expectations associated with the granted status of prince.

The public declarations and denunciations of such persons as criminals would strain and perhaps tear the fabric of assumptions that provide the moral base for a society. Therefore, the practice is to assign the unwanted conduct to the class "madness," implying that the actor was not the responsible agent and that "forces beyond the control" of the actor were responsible. (We are reminded of the publicized psychiatric labeling of Soviet scholars who openly criticize the political system.)

To bring arguments into sharper focus, we recapitulate: we have described how accusations of hallucination are a part of the process of the transvaluation of social identity (Sarbin and Scheibe, *in press*), wherein the valuations degrade, demote, and disparage the actor. The result of the transvaluation is the assignment of the actor to a nonperson status, variably labeled mental illness, insanity, or madness, or a suspicion of mental illness, insanity, or madness. If such classification or suspicion does not preexist, the reported imagining will be classified as fantasy, preoccupation, meditation, play, religious exercise, idiosyncratic conduct, creative achievement, or any one of a number of other excuses for lapses of attention to the requirements of social role enactment. It should be clear that our arguments are directed toward the employment of the definition that identifies current psychiatric practice.

Fictive Behavior Perspectives.   The use of the concept "hallucination" by responsible, honest, and well-intentioned scientists and religious healers is justified by invoking the explanation that the actor's reported imaginings indicate that he or she is "out of touch with reality."

Discussions of imaginings, visions, hallucinations, almost invariably invoke the concept of "reality." In recent times Castaneda (1968, 1972), Roszak (1969), and others have argued for the existence of multiple realities. Although these writers are concerned with issues that need clarification, calling on the concept of "reality" obscures rather than clarifies.

For those who hold the belief that "reality" is a term with venerable history, we are quick to point to its etymology. The Latin root *res* (thing, material object) tells the story. In the first place, whatever had thing-character—that is, ponderability, mass, tangibility—was an instance of *res* (adjective, *real*). Where biological survival depended on the ability to differentiate *things* from shadows, mirages, optical illusions, words, rememberings, dreams, and imaginings, to be "in touch with reality" meant no more than its literal denotation. "To be in touch with reality" meant only that the individual did not embrace wood nymphs, or bump into trees, horses, or people. Thus the original use of the word "reality" was in the service of denoting the world of ponderable things.

It was not until the seventeenth century, at the earliest, that the word "reality" was made to do double duty. The word was employed not only to denote things or thinglike characteristics, but also highly valued abstractions. We take an example from the *Oxford English Dictionary* (1928): Melton, writing about astrology in 1620, said "your discourse . . . hath no Realitie or Essence in it." This equating of thinglike character with essence is an innovation of the Renaissance and was certainly not understood to be commonsensical until very recently.

To denote events that are not based on things, we need special linguistic devices. Usually we borrow a term through figurative language. For example, a child in describing a night terror may search for a word to express his high involvement. The child might say "it was like real." He might compress the simile and say "it was real," thereby constructing a metaphor. The child's audience may interpret the child's expression literally rather than metaphorically; thus the audience would assume that the child did not distinguish between the world of things and the world of dreams. Let us put it another way. That abstractions such as "spirit," "angels," "devils," and "elves" may be highly valued in one's transcendental world is well known. To imagine, for example, an encounter with Mephistopheles would be highly involving, to say the least. In an effort to communicate to others, the imaginer might say "Mephistopheles was vivid" and decide that the expression was too weak to convey the intensity of the experience. To say "it was as if Mephistopheles had thing-character" is a bit stronger. To make the utterance more emphatic, the imaginer could drop the "as if" and say "Mephistopheles had thing-character" or, translated into the vernacular, "Mephistopheles was real."

In *Paradise Lost,* Milton has Adam say to the angel Raphael: "whereat I wak'd, and found before mine eyes all real, as the dream had lively shadowed" (Book VIII, pp. 309–311).

Eventually the meaning becomes turned completely upside down, as when the nineteenth-century philosopher-psychologist Bradley (1897) wrote: "the more that anything is spiritual so much the more is it veritably real" (p. 552).

The foregoing account is instructive in that any effort to understand conduct that is not predicated on the world of things requires a special vocabulary. "Reality" is a confusing rather than a helpful concept.

We subscribe to the point of view that the human being is no passive receptor of stimulation but rather an active constructor. We construct and reconstruct our world, taking into account stimuli of various kinds, together with the residue of past experience. As a shorthand to deal with the constructive aspects of knowing, we borrow from Vaihinger (1924) and Ogden (1932) the notion of fictions. We use *fictions* in the dual sense of *makings* (from the Latin *fingere*) and of hypotheses, things that are "made up." In our analysis, we describe people as actors, engaged in viewing the world and themselves from a variety of interpenetrating perspectives. They deal with the world at various levels of fictiveness.

One cannot adequately account for human conduct without recognizing that persons behave from a variety of fictive perspectives; the actions of human beings may follow from the actor's location of self in more than one perspective. Singer (1966), among others, has experimentally demonstrated that most people are continually shifting back and forth between different perspectives. A person who is driving a car may engage in a rich fantasy life. Thurber's (1940) portrayal of Walter Mitty nicely illustrates simultaneous performance in both the workaday world and in the world of fantasy.

A more complex situation arises when one views the "same scene" in several ways at once. In describing a sunrise, William Blake, the eighteenth-century poet and mystic, considers two perspectives and in no uncertain terms expresses which perspective has top priority.

"What," it will be "questioned," when the sun rises, do you not see a round disk of fire somewhat "like a guinea?" O, no, no, I see an innumerable company of the Heavenly host crying 'Holy, Holy, Holy, is the Lord God Almighty.' I question not my corporeal or vegetative eye any more than I would question a window concerning a sight. I look through it and not with it (p. 617).

Similarly, an astronomer will view the same sunrise from the perspective of modern astronomy. At the same time, he can "see" Rosy Fingered Dawn preceding the Chariot of the Sun God. None of these perspectives is mutually exclusive, nor is any one more credible than any other; they refer to different kinds of fictions. Certain of the astronomer's observations, or that of a navigator taking a morning sun line, may suffer from too much involvement in the poetic or mythic perspective. A poet, on the other hand, might be unnecessarily encumbered by too great an involvement in the perspective of astronomical science.* It is *not* that the mythic perspective is less useful than the astronomical; both are useful.

---

*We also note that imaginings need not be expressed in poetic, fanciful, or esoteric language. An unconventional perspective need not lead to language in an unconventional form. Some reports may emphasize angels and unicorns; others, snakes and telephones.

However, preoccupation with one ecology may impede certain but by no means all role performances. Furthermore, certain perspectives may be proscribed by certain societies at certain times. Unrestrained talk about the results of participating in a fantasy world, for example may be *ipso facto* grounds for suspicion.*

Epistemological Considerations.   Thinking, remembering, and imagining are all actions that tend to move the person from one perspective to another, for example, from the perspective of the world of things to the world of abstractions. Remembering refers to movement along a time dimension, and of course that dimension is backward. Imagining and thinking are not limited either to the time dimension or to backward movement—thus they are particularly useful when preparing future interpretations or moves or actions.

Imagining and thinking are muted actions that can involve absent events. To separate the two actions is arbitrary. It is helpful to regard thinking as muted discourse more akin to talk, and imagining appears to be closer to sensory processes. Piaget and Inhelder (1971) define imagining as a signifier that is similar to the signified (i.e., iconic). They distinguish images from signs, where the link between signifier and signified is arbitrary. Thinking, as employed here, involves the use of signs and is contrasted to imagining, which employs muted iconic behaviors (i.e., images). In both activities of thinking and imagining, of course, overt behaviors usually associated with the activities in question are attenuated. In their use of the concept "deferred imitations," they assert that imagining is clearly of a much more sensory character than is thinking.

We have elsewhere developed a theory of imagination based on these premises (Sarbin, 1952; Sarbin and Juhasz, 1970) and have tested its implications in a set of empirical studies (Juhasz, 1969, 1972). Here we merely wish to stress that the imaginer as defined previously is far less under social control than is the thinker. The series of papers by Paivio and associates (1971) uses the same distinctions employed here. The series of experiments conducted by Juhasz and associates (Juhasz, 1969, 1972; Juhasz et al., 1974), has as its goal the correct performance of tasks not amenable to verbal coding. For example, a subject is required to smell seven substances and to state which one of the last five is a 1–1 combination of the first two substances. Exhaustive pretesting established that the seven substances are olfactorily discriminable but not readily and efficiently discernable on verbal dimensions. It appears clear from this set of experiments that human beings are able to solve such problems with varying degrees of effectiveness. Furthermore, such effectiveness does not appear to be coincident with usual measures of "intelligence" but rather those of "creativity."

Incoming stimulation can be coded in various ways (Sarbin and Bailey, 1966). The fact that there are *parallel* means of coding is a recent conception. One means of coding is sensory—the world cannot be perceived as an undifferentiated field of gradations of light, shade, and contour—we *instantiate* (classify, perceive, categorize) inputs according to our needs, interests, and the structural features of

---

*The attitude that differing perspectives are in fact identical can overcome some of the difficulties. The orthodox doctrine of the Eucharist in Christianity as well as traditional alchemy and Sufism represents such attempts to view events as simultaneously occurring in two (or more) ecologies.

our perceptual systems. Instantiation or perception precedes language use by a good two years in the case of most humans. The use and reuse of such sensorily coded information for whatever purpose is what we mean by imagining.

As the child masters the use of vocabulary and the rules of language, a more clearly socially imposed set of categories is provided. Although this set of socially imposed categories of syntax and vocabulary is certainly constrictive of a person's freedom of "vision," it enables people to communicate with one another in a way far more efficient and precise than that available to any other organism. When a person wishes to escape from social control, however, he or she will most likely turn to imagining (i.e., to an alternate perspective).

In desiring to communicate about personal imaginings, the problem of translation enters. The imaginer must go from a cognitive mode that is in part alinguistic and asocial to a linguistic and social mode. The sticky problem of translating from imagining to speech or some other overtly communicative behavior has been the concern of artists, writers, mystics, philosophers, and most other reflective persons.

The translation is facilitated by the use of figures of speech and action, such as similes and metaphors. To make sense of the inputs from sensory activities, the perceiver will use whatever linguistic tools are available. Consider a California sunrise in November. The sensory inputs are uncountable—hues, saturations, luminosities, forms, textures, and so on. To translate such an infinitude of sensory experience into communicative acts, the actor may employ a variety of techniques, such as oil paints on canvas, Italian melodies, choreography, and/or speech. When employing these communicative acts, the actor has considerable freedom in labeling them. If, for example, speech is employed, the actor may say "the sunrise is *like* a fireball," and we know that only similarity is intended. If he says "it is *as if* the sunrise is a flaming sphere," we can safely assume that he is taking another perspective and wants us to know that he is still "in touch" with the listener's perspective. The use of *as if* is intended to guarantee that the speaker and listener share the same perspective. If he says "it is a spouting blast furnace," the listener must construct from the context whether the speaker intends similarity or identity. If the listener concludes that the speaker intends identity, at that moment he concludes also that the speaker is operating from a nonordinary, nonphysicalistic perspective.

Translation from imagining to speech involves shifting from one fictional perspective to another. The perspective of hues and luminosities is no more fictive than Blake's mystical perspective. At this point, it is instructive to remind ourselves of the "stimulus error" concept advocated by Titchener (1901). The stimulus error was defined as the "mistake" of seeing an ecological object *qua* object rather than as a set of discrete sensations. One who had been trained in the introspective methods of Wundt and Titchener would not "see" and report a table (if he did, he would be guilty of the "stimulus error"); rather he would utter a report something like "a brownish plane tilted about 15 degrees from the horizon, alternating striata of darker and lighter brown, increasingly luminous from top to bottom, surrounded by a homogeneous field of grey, . . ."

The problem of translating is nowhere better illustrated than in the perceptual constancies. Take the stock illustration of comparing a piece of white chalk and a chunk of anthracite coal. Illumination can be arranged in such a way that the coal reflects more light than the chalk. From the perspective of a physicist measuring reflected light energy, the coal is brighter. This leads to the inference that the coal is whiter, white being defined as greater brightness.

From the perspective of the ordinary human observer, the chalk continues to be perceived as white and the coal as black. No one concludes from the perceptual constancy experiments that the perspective of the physicist is more or less fictive than the perspective of the ordinary perceiver. Neither is declared to be "out of touch with reality," although they approach the cognitive task from mutually contradictory perspectives. In the case of the perceptual constancies, departure from the physicalistic perspective is the ordinary approach and is taken as the measure of normalcy. Alternatively, *not* to commit the stimulus error would be seen by many psychiatric observers as a sign of deviance. For example, in examining a person suspected of psychiatric abnormality, the psychiatrist points to an orange on the table and says, "What is this?" The putative patient replies: "alternating bands of brown and grey, bluish hues interposed in a luminescent sheen on which is superimposed an elliptical form, predominant hue varying from 580 to 660 millimicrons, with punctiform grey masses in a regular grid tightly packed around the edges of the irregular ellipse, et cetera, et cetera."

As we can shift perspective by not committing the "stimulus error," thus verbalizing about "sense data," so can we shift perspective by changing our cognitive mode from thinking to imagining. In attempting to translate an imagining into speech a person might say "it is as if I saw the Virgin Mary." The moment he says it, he knows that the rendering of the experience (making public what was private) was grossly inadequate, that something was lost in the translation.

The situation of the person adopting several perspectives simultaneously is even more difficult. In translating the experience "Rosy Fingered Dawn," an actor is constrained to use nonphysicalistic language, for he or she is "seeing" in a mode not covered by the conventions defining the ordinary perspective. To be sure, the reporter "sees" "Rosy Fingered Dawn," but another observer might easily misinterpret and/or misrepresent such a statement as an absurdity because dawn has no fingers. But "Dawn" has. It requires attention to the possibilities of multiple interpretation not to make a fool of a person who talks about personally meaningful imaginings.

He that would speak exactly must not name it [a platonic form, e.g., justice] by this name or that; we can but circle, as it were, about its circumference, seeking to interpret in speech our experience of it, now shooting near the mark, and again disappointed in our aim by reason of the antinomies [dialectical opposites] we find in it. The greatest antinomy arises in this: that our understanding of it is . . . by a Presence higher than all knowing. . . . Hence the word of the Master [Plato] that it overpasses speech or writing. And yet we speak and write seeking to forward the pilgrim on his journey thither (Plotinus, *Enneads VI,* ix, 3–4; Transl. Dodds, 1962, p. 57).

Reporting Imaginings.   We have seen that before a report or other action can be called "hallucinatory" a person must engage in and report his imaginings. In this section we discuss some of the variables affecting a person's disposition toward translating his imaginings into social communications.

The imagining mode is particularly suited to avoid or escape from role expectations that require attention to socially construed features of the here-and-now standard world of occurrences. To put it in another and less mystifying way, imagining is a felicitous vehicle for creating a fantasy world, for entering another ecology not burdened with demanding conventional role expectations. We assume that the role relation that has come under strain would be a particularly likely situation for an actor to shift his perspective from the here-and-now to another perspective, from socially constrained to idiosyncratic categorizations. It is the person in the less powerful social role—the person with fewer choices—for whom the socially constrained perspective or level of discourse is likely to be the less bearable. Such a person is likely to dismiss all the implicit rules that define *the* commonly held perspective of the moment, shifting the rules to some interpenetrating ecology that by the implicit rules of the moment is understood to be "unreal." He is actively construing a world separate from the physical here-and-now. This is what we mean by imagining and fantasy. To fantasize is to remove one's self from the currently existing set of implicit, agreed-on rules that define the literal world of occurrences, and actively to construe one's self in another perspective.

We have argued that the occupant of the less powerful role in a strained role relation may be declared ill or criminal or crazy. The diagnoser has the option of declaring the fantasizer to be an artist or daydreamer or harmless eccentric. At this point the relation between social degradation, and hallucination should become clear. It is not the overt, autochthonous features of the behavior that determine whether the reported imagining is diagnosed as hallucinatory or creative imagining. It is rather the social variables that single out the individual as a proper candidate for degradation to the status of the mentally ill. Any reported imagining now labeled hallucinatory could as easily be labeled artistic, eccentric, or distracted. Whether the reported imagining is declared an instance of hallucination or of creativity depends on the kind of social role relation that is under strain, and the relative power of the reciprocal others in the role relation.

Search for Alternate Perspectives. Hypnotism in our society, the vision quest among the Plains Indians, and the spirit quest and other forms of seeking for alternate perspectives in other societies, confer on the actor a form of social permission to escape the ecologies circumscribed by here-and-now conventional role demands. The hypnotist, like the medicine man or spirit guide, involves the actor in a social role in which reported imaginings are *not* evidence of strained role relations but are indeed *role-relevant* behaviors. Thus it is clearly possible for societies to be more or less tolerant of people who withdraw from one set of rules for perceiving the world in favor of another.

The implication of this notion is patent. Professional behavior analysis ought to be sensitive to the following propositions: (1) the traditional labeling of a person as hallucinator means that the labeler refuses to share the person's current perspective; (2) such labeling is a moralistic rather than a scientific undertaking; and (3) sharing another person's unconventional perspective need not be considered a traumatic event fraught with dire possibilities, such as the inability of the client or professional to maintain his other social relations.

The diagnoser who labels another as hallucinator fails to recognize that the actor is attempting to *translate* his imaginings from a special perspective. Such a diagnoser usually insists that his (and not the actor's) perspective is the only legitimate one. Unfortunately, under high strain, particularly when under suspicion of madness, the accused may not be aware that he or she *is* translating imaginings into communications, and this condition is an especially difficult complication. This, indeed, is what people mean when they say that they are being "driven crazy." Consider the case of the woman being divorced by her husband. She asserts that she is "persecuted by the devil," but if she had said, "it is as if I am persecuted by the devil," the audience would know that she was using a figure of speech. However, if she did not include *as if* in her assertion, the audience would have to assess whether "the devil" was used metaphorically or was used to communicate an experience from an altered perspective. She can convince her audience that from her perspective, she *is* being persecuted by the devil. To say "she is deluded" or "she is hallucinating" contributes no understanding to the problem (a strained role relation) or to helping the persons involved (husband or wife or both). Such diagnostic statements mislabel the problem as one of intrapsychic pathology in the woman. A more useful approach to the problem would involve an understanding of the legitimacy of the woman's fantasy and a stance that avoids taking sides in the strained role relation by a willingness to share her perspective. The "cure" would consist not in convincing the woman to overcome her "delusion" but rather to help *in aiding* her and the husband to establish new role relations, compatible with their present status. After such treatment the woman should no longer need to fantasize that her husband is a devil—he would cease being a devil in precisely the same way he had become one.

Consider the case of a sexually exploited adolescent girl who "hears voices." To say that she is hallucinating helps neither to understand the problem (strained relation with lovers and mother) nor to help those involved (since it focuses the behavior analyst on the girl exclusively, and she is only part of the problem). To translate the multiple cognitive and somatic effects of ongoing strain leads inexorably to an alternate perspective for perceiving the complex world of occurrences. Under these conditions, "hearing voices" would be predictable. Sensible treatment will not focus on the ablation of the girl's "pathology" but rather on readjusting the role relations that have become strained beyond tolerability. The implications that follow from an understanding of her situation as incapacity due to psychological infirmity is not only incorrect but impractical in its consequences as well. The voices she *"hears"* are for the healer as valid, important, and worth attending to as the voices she merely *hears*.

Furthermore, being sensitive to the human condition involves an understanding that certain role changes normally attended by *rites de passage,* such as birth, marriage, death, bereavement, and aging, are *properly* occasions for exploring the utility of taking new perspectives, and it is the proper role of the psychiatrist, psychologist, spirit guide, or medicine man, to see to it that such explorations do not totally destroy the client's ability to shift to the use of more traditional perspectives. Much of the present criticism of the psychiatric profession comes because the behaviors of therapists often function to freeze patients in the nonhuman role of mental patient. This follows from the unwillingness of conservative professionals to grant legitimacy to the fantasies of their patients.

The predilection for identifying practitioners as scientists has interfered with effective understanding of the phenomena under study. To study the social psychology of hallucination, the scientist must here and elsewhere encounter the phenomena as they occur. The scientist must be willing and ready to hold in abeyance the conventional categories of "reality" and "scientific method."

We do not see through our eyes alone, and the person who fails to see with the eyes is neither blind nor "primitive" (subintellectual). *"Ideo amor ab Orpheo sine Oculis dicitur, quia est supra intellectum"* Pico della Mirandola, 1504, p. 96).*

*J.B.J. translates as follows: Love is said to be blind because it is *above* the intellect.

REFERENCES

A psychiatric glossary. Washington, D.C.: American Psychiatric Association, 1969.

Becker, H. S. *Outsiders: Studies in the sociology of deviance.* New York: Free Press, 1963.

Becker, H. S. (Ed.) *The other side; perspectives on deviance.* New York: Free Press, 1964.

Blake, W. *Complete writings.* London: Oxford University Press, 1971.

Bradley, F. H. *Appearance and reality.* London: Swan Sonnenschein, 1897.

Castaneda, C. *The teachings of Don Juan: A Yaqui way of knowledge.* Berkeley: University of California Press, 1968.

Castaneda, C. *Journey to Ixtlan.* New York: Simon & Schuster, 1972.

Chesler, P. *Women and madness.* Garden City, N. Y.: Doubleday, 1972.

Esquirol, J. E. D. *Des maladies mentales.* Paris: Baillière, 1838.

Fischer, R. The perception–hallucination continuum. *Diseases of the Nervous System,* 1969, **30,** 161–171.

Fischer, R. A cartography of the ecstatic and meditative states. *Science,* 1971, **174,** 897–904.

Foucault, M. *Madness and civilization.* Translated by R. Howard. New York: Pantheon, 1965.

Freud, S. *New introductory lectures on psychoanalysis.* Translated by W. J. H. Sprott. New York: Norton, 1933.

Goffman, E. *Asylums.* Chicago: Aldine Press, 1961.

Goode, W. J. A theory of role strain. *American Sociological Review,* 1960, **25,** 483–496.

Hollander, E. P. Conformity, status, and idiosyncracy credit. *Psychological Review,* 1958, **65,** 117–127.

Hollingshead, A. B., and Redlich, F. C. *Social class and mental illness.* New York: Wiley, 1958.

Juhasz, J. B. Imagination, imitation and role taking. Unpublished doctoral dissertation, University of California, Berkeley, 1969.

Juhasz, J. B. Greek theories of imagination. *Journal of the History of the Behavioral Sciences,* 1971, **7** (1), 39–58.

Juhasz, J. B. An experimental study of imagining. *Journal of Personality,* 1972, **40** (4), 588–600.

Juhasz, J. B. The psychology of paradox and vice-versa. Paper presented at the meeting of the American Psychological Association, Montreal, 1973.

Juhasz, J. B., White, K. G., and Gosling, A. Recognition memory for compound tones and for single tones as a combination. *Perceptual and Motor Skills,* 1974, **39,** 387–394.

Jung, C. G. *The collected works of C. G. Jung. Vol 12. Psychology and alchemy.* Translated by R. F. C. Hull. Princeton, N.J.: Princeton University Press, 1968.

Jung, C. G. *The collected works of C. G. Jung. Vol 14. Mysterium conjunctionis.* Translated by R. F. C. Hull. Princeton, N. J.: Princeton University Press, 1970.

Laing, R. D. *The politics of experience and the bird of paradise.* New York: Pantheon, 1967.

Lavater, L. *Of ghostes and spirities walking by nyght.* Translated by R. Harrison. London: Watkyns, 1572.

Malcolm, N. *Dreaming.* London: Routledge and Kegan Paul, 1959.

Melton, J. *Astrologaster or the figure caster.* London, 1620.

Milton, J. *Paradise lost.* M. Y. Hughes (Ed.) Indianapolis: Odyssey Press, 1962.

Mirandola, Pico della. *Opera.* Strassberg: 1504.

Mutwa, C. V. *My people, my Africa.* New York: John Day, 1969.

Ogden, C. K. *Bentham's theory of fictions*. London: Kegan Paul, Trench, Trübner, 1932.

Osborne, L. *The ethics and aesthetics of crime: A study of Jean Genet*. Unpublished dissertation, University of California at Berkeley, 1974.

Oxford English dictionary, J. A. H. Murray (Ed.) Oxford: Clarendon Press, 1888–1928.

Paivio, A. *Imagery and verbal processes*. New York: Holt, Rinehart & Winston, 1971.

Piaget, J., and Inhelder, B. *Mental imagery in the child*. Translated by P. A. Chilton. New York: Basic Books, 1971.

Plotinus. *The enneads. Vol VI. Selected passages*. Translated by Dodds. London: Faber & Faber, 1962.

Rapaport, D. Toward a theory of thinking. In D. Rapaport (Ed.), *Organization and pathology of thought*. New York: Columbia University Press, 1951.

Rosenhan, D. L. On being sane in insane places. *Science*, 1973, **179,** 250–258.

Roszak, T. *The making of a counter culture*. Garden City, N. Y.: Doubleday, 1969.

Sarbin, T. R. Contributions to role-taking theory. I: Preface to psychological analysis of self. *Psychological Review*, 1952, **59,** 11–12.

Sarbin, T. R. Role theory. In G. Lindzey (Ed.), *Handbook of social psychology*. Reading, Mass.: Addison-Wesley, 1954.

Sarbin, T. R. Physiological effects of hypnotic stimulation. In R. M. Dorous (Ed.), *Hypnosis and its therapeutic applications*. New York: McGraw-Hill, 1956.

Sarbin, T. R. The concept of hallucination. *Journal of Personality*, 1967, **35,** 359–380.

Sarbin, T. R. Ontology recapitulates philology: The mythic nature of anxiety. *American Psychologist*, 1968, **23,** 411–418.

Sarbin, T. R., and Allen, V. L. Role theory. In G. Lindzey and E. Aronson (Eds.), *Handbook of social psychology*. Reading, Mass.: Addison-Wesley, 1968.

Sarbin, T. R., and Bailey, D. E. The immediacy postulate in the light of modern cognitive theory. In K. R. Hammond (Ed.), *The psychology of Egon Brunswick*. New York: Holt, Rinehart & Winston, 1966.

Sarbin, T. R., and Juhasz, J. B. The historical background of the concept of hallucination. *Journal of the History of the Behavioral Sciences*, 1967, **3** (4), 339–358.

Sarbin, T. R., and Juhasz, J. B. Toward a theory of imagination. *Journal of Personality*, 1970, **38,** 52–76.

Sarbin, T. R., Juhasz, J. B., and Todd, P. The social psychology of "hallucinations." *The Psychological Record*, 1971, **21,** 87–93.

Sarbin, T. R., and Scheibe, K. E. Transvaluation of social identity. In C. Bellone (Ed.), *The normative dimension in public administration*. New York: Academic Press, in press.

Scheff, T. J. Typification in the diagnostic practices of rehabilitation agencies. In M. B. Sussman (Ed.), *Sociology and rehabilitation*. Washington, D.C.: American Sociological Association, 1966.

Singer, J. L. *Daydreaming*. New York: Random House, 1966.

Szasz, T. S. *The manufacture of madness*. New York: Harper & Row, 1970.

Thurber, J. G. The secret life of Walter Mitty. In J. G. Thurber, *Fables of our time*. New York: Harper & Row, 1940.

Titchener, E. B. *Experimental psychology. Vol 1*. New York: Macmillan, 1901.

Toby, J. Some variables in role conflict analysis. *Social Forces*, 1952, **30,** 323–337.

Vaihinger, H. *The philosophy of "as if."* Translated by C. K. Ogden. London: Routledge and Kegan Paul, 1924.

CHAPTER EIGHT

THE CONTINUITY OF PERCEPTUAL AND COGNITIVE EXPERIENCES

C. WADE SAVAGE, Ph.D.

On the 30th of December, about four o'clock in the afternoon, Mrs. A came downstairs into the drawing-room, which she had quitted only a few minutes before, and on entering the room she saw her husband, as she supposed, standing with his back to the fire. As he had gone out to take a walk about half an hour before, she was surprised to see him there, and asked him why he had returned so soon. The figure looked fixedly at her with a serious and thoughtful expression of countenance but did not speak. Supposing that his mind was absorbed in thought, she sat down in an arm chair near the fire, and within two feet at most of the figure, which she still saw standing before her. As its eyes, however, still continued to be fixed upon her, she said after the lapse of a few minutes, "Why don't you speak——?" The figure immediately moved off towards the window at the farther end of the room, with its eyes still gazing on her, and it passed so very close to her in doing so, that she was struck by the circumstance of hearing no step nor sound, nor feeling her clothes brushed against, nor even any agitation in the air. Although she was now convinced that the figure was not her husband, yet she never for a moment supposed that it was any thing supernatural, and was soon convinced that it was a spectral illusion. As soon as this conviction had established itself in her mind, she recollected the experiment which I had suggested, of trying to double the object; but before she was able distinctly to do this, the figure had retreated to the window, where it disappeared. Mrs. A immediately following it, shook the curtains and examined the window, the impression having been so distinct and forcible that she was unwilling to believe that it was not a reality. Finding, however, that the figure had no natural means of escape, she was convinced that she had seen a spectral apparition like those recorded in Dr. Hibbert's work, and she consequently felt no alarm or agitation. The appearance was seen in bright day light, and lasted four or five minutes. When the figure stood close to her it concealed the real objects behind it, and the apparition was fully as vivid as the reality (Brewster, 1832, pp. 40–41).

It is important to realize that many hallucinations are quite unlike Mrs. A.'s. Some hallucinations are neither perceptionlike nor particularly deceptive; some bear little or no resemblance to the subject's previous experience. These are often described in the literature, but rarely in great detail. Fortunately for the science of hallucinations, recent intense interest in hallucinogens has produced numerous subjects willing to spend hours introspecting and reporting their visual experience. Current research in this area may supply the needed detail. (There are also numerous experiments with hallucinations in several modalities produced by sensory deprivation, sleep deprivation, and food deprivation.)

A useful series of experiments with drug-induced hallucinations has been performed by Siegel (1973). The subject was given either a behaviorally effective dose of one of five hallucinogens (marihuana, tetrahydrocannabinol, psilocybin, mescaline, or LSD) or a dose of a control substance (amphetamine, barbiturate, or inactive placebo). Dosage was by mouth in standardized capsules that could not be distinguished by the subject. The subject was then placed in a lightproof, sound-proof room, supine on a bed, and asked to provide, with eyes open, a continuous report of what he or she saw. The report was recorded on tape. Some subjects were given prior training in describing their visual experience; the others were untrained. What follows are condensed segments of the transcript of one such report from an untrained, 21-year-old, subject, Ms. C. She had ingested 20 mg of psilocybin.

An initial segment of the report, which was begun 25 minutes after ingestion, is presented first.

It looks like several different whirlpools, with lots of spirals divided up into checks. It's pretty black. There's purple and green glowing areas in the middle of the spirals, kind of clouds around. There are lines going from top to bottom, kind of a grid, but the lines squiggle around. There's odd shapes, but still lots of right angles in them. Seems really bright. There's little prismatic things happening next to the lines. I mean, where there's a cloud or a line on the screen, its edge goes through this little narrowed-down rainbow. There's like an explosion, yellow in the middle, like a volcano gushing out lava, yellow, glowing. There's a black square with yellow light coming behind it. There's a regular pattern superimposed on everything, lots of curlicues, with dots in the middle. Lot of little paisley things that fill up the spaces between patterns of triangles, squares, or crown-shaped things. And there's a little white star that floats around the picture and sometimes goes behind what's on the screen and illuminates from behind.

In this segment Ms. C. had only abstract visual experiences of forms, patterns, colors, lights, and movements of and other changes in these. Such experience is often called "simple imagery." But the term is misleading, since the imagery is in one sense quite complex. The term "abstract" is used here instead, in the sense in which a nonrepresentative painting is abstract. Notice that there is no tendency for the subject to confuse her experience with veridical perceptions. Quite the contrary, for she describes what she sees as occurring on a screen. However, the experiences seem to be as little under her conscious control as are veridical perceptions. Most of the experiences—the checkered spirals, the explosion from a center, the paisley patterns superimposed on everything—are frequently found in the early stages of drug experience, so frequently that some researchers believe them to be hallucinatory constants. In one tentative hypothesis, these constants are, like entoptic phenomena, perceptions of the anatomy of the visual system. In another, they are viewed as a kind of visual noise enhanced by drug stimulation. Neither hypothesis seems to account for the complexity and "imaginativeness" of the experience.

Several minutes later, representative experience (usually called "complex im-agery") enters, mixed with abstract.

Now there's a kind of landscape. Very flat, flat country. The picture is very narrow. In the middle part a tree at the left and then flat with green grass and blue sky above. There are orange dots, oranges hanging all over, in the sky, on the tree, on the ground. A bicycle! Oh, my! It's headed down, not horizontal, like someone's holding it up on end. It's on the left hand of the screen. The wheel's turning very fast. No one's on it. There's a checkerboard superimposed on everything, like the flags they wave at the races. Oh right! Yeah! O.K., right! The bicycle's obviously racing somewhere, and there's flags.

In the first half of this segment the experience again does not seem to be under the conscious control of the subject. Although she speaks of seeing things in a "picture" and on a "screen," she otherwise describes her experience as she would veridical perceptions. There is even what seems to be an act of perceptual recognition, described in the phrase, "A bicycle! Oh my!" But in the last half of the segment it seems that the subject is interpreting her experience and the interpretation is guiding the course of the experience. The turning of the bicycle wheel suggests to her a race, the checkerboard pattern suggests racing flags, and the flags and the race "materialize." It seems that thought is translated into experience.

In a still later segment, abstract experience gives way entirely to representative, and the experience becomes dreamlike, and almost totally coherent.

It's on a city street, I think it's Portland actually, but it's that kind of place, not a huge, booming metropolis, you know, but a city nonetheless. I can see a brick wall—there's a gray edge—and at the corner they put this gray cement edge to it, a kind of edging, right, trim of some sort. I can see the street out there.... Well, it's old—golly—interesting! It's like in the forties, I guess, or maybe the fifties ... I don't know. And there are people riding their bicycles, and there are, like, boys in plaid vests and those funny kind of hats. And you get the impression they are newspaper boys and they're real smart aleck and they'll have red hair and lots of black and white loafers and—I mean, not loafers, oxfords. And, umm, I can't see that one too much. The street kind of widened, was what happened. I was at the side walking on the sidewalk, so it wasn't like I was in the middle of the street and [laughter] you can't laugh very long in the middle of the street in the city, so that image kind of went away [laughter].

The role of the subject's thinking is even more apparent here than in the previous segment. She seems not merely to be seeing scenes, but also contributing to their fabrication, as when she says, "and they'll have red hair and lots of black and white loafers," seeming to endow the hallucinatory objects with features she thinks appropriate. The most notable feature of the segment is its similarity to dream reports, the difference being that the experience is not being recalled but observed and reported as it takes place. Toward the end the subject herself is part of the experience, in much the same way that dreamers are sometimes in their own dreams. And the experience becomes inexplicably incoherent, in the manner of dreams, when the subject suddenly finds herself in the middle of the street rather than on the sidewalk. This similarity to dreams prompts one to ask whether the subject is seeing the things described or merely imagining (or thinking) them. This question assumes that the distinction between seeing and imagining is a sharp one. It is argued later that this assumption is false.

THE CONTINUITY HYPOTHESIS

There is a view—which may be called the continuity hypothesis—that seems to be part of traditional scientific and philosophical wisdom concerning such experiences as sensations, perceptions, hallucinations, dreams, fantasies (experiences of imagination), and thoughts. It is, unfortunately, difficult to formulate with precision. Any of the following formulations are candidates:

1. The experiences listed are composed of the same stuff, so to speak; they differ not in kind, but in degree—degree of vivacity, coherence, voluntariness, creativeness, concreteness, and veridicality. For example, perceptions are often more vivid than dreams; fantasies are usually more voluntary than perceptions.

2. The experiences listed are not sharply distinguishable from one another, as the existence of intermediate cases shows. For example, between a vivid hallucination and a not-so-vivid dream, we can find an experience intermediate in vivacity, and we may be unsure whether to call it a dream or an hallucination.

3. The experiences listed can evolve into, become transformed into, one another. For example, a dream, on waking, may evolve into a fantasy; a perception, on falling asleep, may evolve into a dream.

4. The internal mechanisms of the experiences listed, the processes by means of which they are produced, are similar.

Formulations 2 and 3 are phenomenal, introspective, descriptive formulations of the hypothesis; 4 is a theoretical, explanatory formulation; 1 is ambiguous and can be interpreted either as a descriptive or as an explanatory formulation. The descriptive formulations, associated mainly with the British empiricist philosophers, are suggested also by certain rationalists and by other philosophers and scientists of no definite school. The hypothesis has been out of fashion for most of the present century, but it is beginning to reappear, at least in the theoretical formulation. Haber says: "Sensation, perception, memory, and thought must be considered on a continuum of cognitive activity. They are mutually interdependent and cannot be separated except by arbitrary rules of momentary expediency" (1969, p. 1). Arnheim writes: ". . . the remarkable mechanisms by which the senses understand the environment are all but identical with the operations described by the psychology of thinking. Inversely, there [is] much evidence that truly productive thinking in whatever area of cognition takes place in the realm of imagery" (1969, p. v). It seems clear that converging lines of speculation and theory are being developed in cognitive psychology, psycholinguistics, information theory, and the study of creativity. In my opinion, one of the major points of convergence is the continuity hypothesis.

Both empiricists (Locke, 1690; Berkeley, 1710; Hume, 1739, to mention the classic three) and rationalists (e.g., Descartes, 1641) have subscribed to the continuity hypothesis. Empiricists take the perception end of the continuum to be primary: they view all experiences as more or less vivid, voluntary, concrete perceptions. The opposite position takes the thought end of the continuum to be primary: it views all experiences as more or less vivid, voluntary, concrete thoughts. Rationalists have tended to hold this opposite position—tended, one must say, because it has been difficult for anyone, even a rationalist, to be persuaded that perceptions and vivid hallucinations are thoughts. Empiricists hold that perceptions (or sensations) are primary also in the sense that they are the "materials" for the other experiences. Thus hallucinations, dreams, fantasies, and thoughts are retrieved perceptions. Hobbes, the most extreme of the empiricists, says: ". . . there is no conception in a man's mind which has not at first, totally or by parts been begotten upon the organs of sense. . . . Imagination is nothing but decaying sense. . . . We have no transition from one imagination to another whereof we never had the like before in our senses" (1651, Chs. 1–3). Rationalists oppose Hobbes's theory on the ground that it does not account for the creativity and freedom often exhibited by thought. Hobbes's successors (Locke, Berkeley, and Hume) softened his theory. They maintained that novel complex thoughts are possible, since only the *elements* of thought need be retrieved perceptions; and they held that the elements of thought are often combined, according to the laws of association, in novel arrangements. Whether this more sophisticated and flexible empiricism is compatible with the creativity and freedom of thought, language, and perception, is one of the most important questions of current cognitive psychology and psycholinguistics.

The study of hallucinations is an important enterprise in its own right. But it also has a central role in the far-reaching theories and issues described earlier. Hallucinations obviously have many of the features of perceptions, otherwise they could not deceive the hallucinator into believing that he perceives. But they also often have some of the features of thoughts, most notably, novelty and freedom from sensory stimuli. Visual hallucinations (and dreams and fantasies, to which they are similar) are thus a bridge between perception and thought. The study of visual hallucinations seems to lead inexorably to the continuity hypothesis: the hypothesis that at both the descriptive and explanatory levels, sensations, perceptions, hallucinations, dreams, fantasies, and thoughts are similar. Whether it leads to the empiricist or to the rationalist version of the hypothesis is not at all clear.

Despite the favorable indications already described, the continuity hypothesis may turn out to be wrong. Indeed, difficulties in the hypothesis readily come to mind. The hypothesis that sensations, perceptions, hallucinations, dreams, fantasies, and thoughts are the same in kind may seem plausible as long as attention is restricted to vision. But olfactory perceptions and gustatory perceptions do not seem to be anything like thoughts. (Note that although there are olfactory and gustatory hallucinations, there do not seem to be olfactory or gustatory dreams and fantasies. For these senses, part of the "bridge" between perception and thought seems not to exist.) The hypothesis may not be as plausible as it seems, even for vision. If sensations, perceptions, hallucinations, dreams, fantasies, and thoughts are the same kind of things, it must be possible to say what kind of thing they are. And every attempt to do this seems to be unsatisfactory. The most familiar suggestion is that all the experiences listed are images. Against this suggestion, there seem to be imageless thoughts, and it is difficult to see how sensations of unpatterned light and color can be construed as images.

Even if the continuity hypothesis is finally proved false, it has a useful life ahead of it. Proving a stimulating hypothesis false can be as fruitful as proving a dull hypothesis true. The continuity hypothesis continues to stimulate theoretical speculation and promises to stimulate experimental research in the future. It is a sweeping hypothesis that attempts to integrate all perceptual and cognitive experience into a single theoretical scheme. It thus attempts to unify a large part of psychology, a science noted for its disunity. It encourages psychologists and other investigators to consider many types of psychological phenomena at once, rather than separately, as is the custom of much recent research. The purpose of such comprehensive consideration is, of course, to arrive at general theories, theories concerning all or most experience. The most successful science—physics—has sought and produced general theories. Why should psychology settle for less? Even if the continuity hypothesis is false, it would surely be beneficial to psychological research to assume that sensing, perceiving, hallucinating, dreaming, fantasizing, and thinking cannot be understood in isolation from one another, that no one of these experiential processes will be completely understood until all are understood.

THE CONTINUUM OF EXPERIENCES

The literature on hallucinations contains much evidence in favor of the continuity hypothesis in its clear descriptive form. In this form, the hypothesis is that sensations, perceptions, hallucinations, dreams, fantasies, and thoughts are not sharply distinguishable from one another and that the experiences are capable of evolving, one into the other. Almost exclusively, the evidence is introspective reports of experience. Owing to behaviorist reluctance to use introspective data, the bulk of this evidence is found in the older literature, particularly that of the second half of the nineteenth century and the first quarter of the twentieth. Fortunately for the science of cognition and perception, psychologists are losing their behavioristic inhibitions and are beginning to introduce introspective evidence into the current literature. Much of it is being obtained from research on drug-induced hallucinations, and some specimens are examined later in this section.

Intermediate cases between perceptions and hallucinations are usually called illusions. Examples are the tactual experience of something hot caused by touching ice, the auditory experience of one's name being called caused by the sound of wind blowing, the visual experience of a person standing in a dimly lighted room caused by looking at a hanging garment. In these cases, since the experience does not completely correspond to its cause, it is not properly called a perception; and since it partially corresponds to its external cause, it is not properly called an hallucination. There is a full spectrum of cases, from experiences that completely correspond to their external causes to experiences that do not correspond at all. An example of the latter: by hypnotic suggestion a subject was given an hallucination of a top spinning on a (real) sheet of white paper before him. When asked to point to the top, he pointed to a tiny black speck on the paper (Sidgwick, 1894, p. 109).

Excellent examples of perception evolving into hallucination can be found in drug-intoxicated subjects. One subject told the writer that while under the influence of LSD he saw a painting on the wall slowly separate into loosely connected parts. At what point did his perception become an illusion? At what point did the illusion become an hallucination? It seems impossible to say. Cases of the reverse evolution have also been reported. Intoxicated subjects have sometimes reported seeing the face of a companion turn into a grotesque animal head (or other form) and then turn back into the face of the person. Hallucinations are commonly said to be nonveridical perceptions. In view of cases such as those cited, it seems just as appropriate to say that perceptions are veridical hallucinations.

Intermediate cases between dreams and hallucinations can be found among the so-called hypnagogic (sleep-inducing) hallucinations and hypnopompic (sleep-terminating) hallucinations. One researcher describes several of the former occurring on a single occasion:

My general mental state throughout the series was of alternate drowse and awakening, never real sleep, yet a curious mingling of sleep and waking strata. . . . Landscape: stormy clouds, clear detail. . . . Six-leaved plant, seen from above; reddish stalk at center; counted the leaves twice, only five of them visible, but the structure demanding six. . . . Nearly asleep: was saying to myself, "no one of these images very clear," when suddenly aroused by figure of gorilla-like face (Alexander, 1909, pp. 628–629).

These images are the stuff of which dreams are made. None of them is as extended as an average dream; but extended hypnagogic hallucinations have been reported. For example:

The pictures I see generally appear at night before going to sleep, always in complete darkness, and I believe usually when I am rather tired. I can see them with my eyes open, but the colours are much less brilliant than when my eyes are shut. I am quite conscious at the time of the unreality of the scenes. . . . Once or twice I have seen a little scene enacted. I remember one distinctly. I saw a man in the dress of the last century riding down a lane. As he came forward, two men, also on horseback, rushed out on him from behind some trees and knocked him down. I longed to know the end of this little story, but it disappeared (Gurney et al., 1886, p. 474, footnote).

There is evidence that hypnagogic hallucinations sometimes become, or become incorporated into, dreams. Maury (1865, p. 108) reports a case of his own in which he first had two hypnagogic hallucinations: one of a green-winged, red-headed bat; the second of a Pyrénées-type landscape. He then fell asleep, and in his dreams the same two images appeared in the same order. Archer claims that hypnagogic hallucinations differ only in brevity from dreams (note, however, that many hypnagogic hallucinations exhibit lilliputianism—reduced size of the experienced object, and sensory unreality—whereas dreams rarely do), and that all dreams begin with experiences of the hypnagogic type:

In my view they [hypnagogic hallucinations] *are* dreams and nothing else—at all events they are such stuff as dreams are made of, and differ only from full-grown dreams in the fact of being nipped in the bud. They should, in fact, be called "oneirogogic" [dream-inducing] rather than "hypnagogic" [sleep-inducing]. I have little doubt that all dreams begin in some such fashion, and that, when we have time to dream the dream out, we forget the induction, the opening vision or phases. Our memory of dreams almost always plunges *in medias res*. We suddenly find ourselves included in some experience or action, with no idea how we got there. But this only means we have forgotten what may have been quite a long train of preceding incidents . . . (Archer, 1947, p. 754).

Hypnopompic hallucinations provide striking examples of dreams turning into hallucinations. Consider the following report:

About fifteen years ago . . . I had gone to sleep without knowing it, a fire burning opposite the foot of my bed. Thinking I was awake, I thought I saw standing before my fire, at the right hand side, looking into it, with her back turned to me, so that I could not see her face, an elderly woman, rather stout, and dressed like an old-fashioned nurse or housekeeper, in a black cap tied close round the ears, and a large-checked shawl. The check was about four inches square, and black, pink, white and grey, the pink squares being specially distinct. Wondering what she was doing there, I sat up in bed to look at her, and the action of doing so woke me. I was fully conscious of suddenly waking, fully conscious that I had been asleep, and had awoken with a shock, yet I still saw the woman distinctly, with my eyes open and wide awake. She faded gradually. My heart beat for a moment; but I thought it was only the impression of a dream still remaining in my brain that appeared to be seen with my eyes. So I lay down and went to sleep again, and saw no more (Sidgwick, 1894, pp. 71–72).

Dement et al. claimed that "dreaming is the prototypical hallucinatory experience" and advanced the hypothesis that "the occurrence of hallucinatons may be generally defined as 'dreaming while awake' " (1970, p. 335). Cases such as the one just given are excellent support for this hypothesis. But it seems to matter little whether we say that hallucinations are waking dreams or that dreams are hallucinations during sleep. (Attempts have been and are being made to develop theories that will explain both hallucinations and dreams. A notable example is the "perceptual release" theory developed by West [1962]).

Examples of fantasies—as the term is used here—are the daydreams and reveries that sometimes occur during moments of abstraction and relaxation, and the experiences of imagination that often occur while the subject is reviewing the past (and, perhaps, changing it in imagination) or planning the future. (There is no commonly accepted term for this group of experiences. "Imaginations" might be employed for the purpose; but it is awkward and is frequently employed broadly to refer also to experiences of dreams and hallucinations.) In some cases (e.g., those cited previously), hypnagogic and hypnopompic hallucinations are more vivid and compelling than the average fantasy. But in other cases they are virtually indistinguishable from fantasies, providing examples of experiences intermediate between hallucinations and fantasies, or between fantasies and dreams. They also supply examples of fantasies evolving into hallucinations, and conversely, and of fantasies evolving into dreams, and conversely. Many hypnagogic and hypnopompic experiences are just as appropriately called fantasies, or dreams, as hallucinations. Indeed, in this area of experience, the terms "hallucination," "dream," and "fantasy" are often interchangeable.

The word "thought" is more often applied to nonsensory, voluntary experiences than to sensory, involuntary experiences; and the word "hallucination" is more often applied to experiences of the latter type than to the former. Experiments such as those involving Ms. C. show that this usage is more convenient than essential. But if we adhere to the usage, we can say that these experiments provide numerous examples of experiences intermediate between hallucinations and thoughts. Ms. C. occasionally reports experiences that could as easily be thoughts as hallucinations, as in her description of the newsboys with red hair and black and white oxfords, in the third segment. At one point she says: "I don't feel like I'm seriously stoned. There are just a lot of interesting things happening, and I'm just kind of allowed to fool around with it." At another: "It's like I had to hallucinate conscientiously." These statements indicate that her hallucinatory experience is often as voluntary as her thoughts.

Other subjects (identified by code names) in the same series of experiments (Siegel, 1971) provide explicit examples of experiences intermediate between thoughts and hallucinations:

I see water, sort of like bluish. I don't think I'm seeing it, I'm thinking it, but I'm not seeing colors really. At the beginning, I was seeing the colors, then I started getting into thinking the colors, but when things were going back—passing back—I think I was seeing them. (Saffron)

My thoughts are sort of visualized, so, so it's somewhat like moving pictures of what I'm thinking and [they] change with the thoughts. All my thoughts have an element of sight, that's all, so they just changed arbitrarily as my thoughts would. (Curry)

The first of these examples also seems to illustrate the phenomenon of hallucinations (sensory experiences) evolving into thoughts. The second definitely provides an example of thoughts guiding sensory hallucinations, and possibly an example of thoughts evolving into hallucinations.

The foregoing use of "hallucination" and "thought" is rather artificial. Suppose we abandon these terms, distinguishing instead between sensory experiences and mental experiences. Again we find evidence that the distinction is not a sharp one.

I see the outside of the hospital . . . although it's more a mental image than a visual image. (Sesame)

. . . and a nice green basket. That's a mental image not a real one. I guess it's hard to tell the difference. (Alfalfa)

Finally we come to sensations, and the terminological problems are even more acute. The distinction between sensations and perceptions is one of the most popular and yet one of the most obscure distinctions in psychology. It is connected with a deep theoretical problem in the science: the problem of how physical stimulation is converted into experience. Moreover, the terms of the distinction are employed in different ways by different writers. In this chapter, both "sensations" and "perceptions" refer to experiences. This much settled, the distinction can be construed as (a) that between abstract sensory experiences and representative sensory experiences, or (b) that between indescribable or "meaningless" sensory experiences and describable or "meaningful" sensory experiences. On either construction, evidence for the continuity between sensations and perceptions is available.

a. The distinction between abstract and representative sensory experiences is excellently illustrated by the three segments of Ms. C.'s report. The first of these contains only abstract experiences: of shapes, colors, and movements. The third contains only representative experiences: of streets, boys, a wall. The second contains abstract mixed with representative and is therefore an intermediate case. It is also an illustration of abstract imagery evolving into representative: orange dots become oranges, a checkerboard pattern turns into checkered flags. The experiences in each of these segments are described by the subject with comparative ease. None of them is "meaningless," although some do not represent items of familiar experience. (In one sense they are all representative. If the experience of a bicycle is representative—representative of a bicycle—the experience of a right angle is representative—representative of a right angle.)

b. Good examples of "meaningless," or virtually indescribable, experiences are found in subjects in the baseline state (state of a normal, nonintoxicated subject) and in subjects who had ingested a placebo.

It's fuzzy, fuzzy blots . . . no colors, no vividness, no patterns, just fuzzy white on black, no dynamic qualities, no movement . . . I promise I'm not seeing things, no pink elephants, no lines, no nothing, just white on black, well, gray on black. . . . (Saffron)

The imagery is nonexistent . . . a large . . . there are shapes . . . just the entire field of vision collecting uniformly with different parts to it . . . very unusual . . . very hard to comprehend exactly what is going on. Quite a different effect. (Coriander)

Most of this is . . . impossible to describe . . . and it's sort of like describing a red color with blue words, I mean it just doesn't fit. (Oregano)

There is a logical difficulty in trying to provide examples of meaningless, or indescribable, experiences. For if the experience is totally meaningless, the subject will not be able to say what its meaning is and will say, like Coriander, "very hard to comprehend exactly what is going on." And if the experience is indescribable, the subject will be able, like Oregano, to say only that it is indescribable. Nonetheless, it is clear from the examples that there is no sharp distinction—that there *are* intermediate cases—between meaningless, indescribable experiences and meaningful, describable experiences. Longer segments could be presented to show also that the one kind of experience often evolves into the other kind, and conversely.

These experiments with hallucinogens reveal the full qualitative and developmental continuum of perceptual-cognitive experience: from meaningless to abstract to representative sensory experience, to dreamlike and fantasylike experience, to nonsensory experiences the subjects call mental images or thoughts. It is for this reason, as noted earlier, that the study of drug-induced hallucinations seems to lead inexorably to the continuity hypothesis, at least in its introspective, descriptive form—formulations 2 and 3 of a previous section.

THE SIMILARITY BETWEEN EXPERIENCES

The most striking feature of hallucinations such as that of Mrs. A. is their similarity to perceptions. Her hallucination of her husband is—to mention the traditional criteria for distinguishing perceptions from hallucinations—as vivid, coherent, and involuntary as a visual perception of him. The similarity between the two sorts of experience has been used by many philosophers as the basis of the first premise in an argument for solipsism, or skepticism, concerning the external world. It is usually called "the argument from illusion"; but this is misleading because the argument is most successfully and dramatically constructed in terms of hallucinations. It can also be constructed in terms of dreams, fantasies, thoughts, and sensations. It may be called the similarity argument. For the moment, thoughts and sensations are excluded from consideration. Although the argument fails to establish its skeptical conclusion, it provides powerful support for the continuity hypothesis in its most extreme, and most obscure form —formulation 1 of a previous section.

The Similarity Argument.   Stated in terms of hallucinations, and from the point of view of the subject, the similarity argument is as follows:

1. Some of my hallucinations are indistinguishable to me from perceptions; so,

2. There are no reliable criteria to determine which of my experiences are hallucinations and which perceptions; consequently,

3. I cannot know for certain whether a given experience is an hallucination or a perception; therefore,

4. I cannot know for certain whether the things I experience exist in an external world (since the thing experienced exists in my mind if the experience is an hallucination).

The argument can also be constructed in terms of dreams. This version is suggested by Descartes:

How often has it happened to me that in the night I dreamt that I found myself in this particular place, that I was dressed and seated near the fire, whilst in reality I was lying undressed in bed! At this moment it does indeed seem to me that it is with eyes awake that I am looking at this paper; that this head which I move is not asleep, that it is deliberately and of set purpose that I extend my hand and perceive it; what happens in sleep does not appear so clear nor so distinct as does all this. But in thinking over this I remind myself that on many occasions I have in sleep been deceived by similar illusions, and in dwelling carefully on this reflection I see so manifestly that there are no certain indications by which we may clearly distinguish wakefulness from sleep that I am lost in astonishment. And my astonishment is such that it is almost capable of persuading me that I now dream (1641, pp. 145–146).

Descartes attempts to overcome his skepticism at a later stage; but at this point he can be taken to argue as follows. Some of my dreams are indistinguishable to me from perceptions. So, there are no reliable criteria to determine which of my experiences are dreams and which are perceptions. Consequently, I cannot know for certain whether a given experience is a dream or a perception. Therefore, I cannot know for certain whether any of the things I experience exists in an external world.

Surprisingly enough, it is also possible to construct the argument in terms of fantasies (experiences of imagination). In her classic study of imagination, Perky (1910) showed that it is possible to induce perceptions in a subject that he cannot distinguish from the images of his imagination. In one experiment the picture of a banana was projected onto a one-way window; the subject sat on the other side and was able to see the picture but not the projecting device. S was asked to imagine a banana on the window, and a few seconds later the picture of the banana was flashed at low illumination on the window. S was convinced that the banana was the product of his imagination. (These results have been replicated in other laboratories [Segal, 1970, pp. 104–105].)

From what we have just said, it is possible to argue as follows. Some of S's perceptions are indistinguishable to him from his fantasies (those he projects externally). Thus there are no reliable criteria by which S can determine which of his experiences are perceptions and which are fantasies. Consequently, S cannot know for certain whether a given experience of his is an hallucination or a perception. Therefore, S cannot know for certain whether any of the things he experiences exists in an external world.

These arguments are open to several objections, and two are important for present purposes. For brevity, these objections are directed only against the argument stated in terms of hallucinations. First, the argument's first premise is true only of subjects who, like Mrs. A., have had an hallucination that was indistinguishable from a perception. To any subject who has never had such hallucinations—and there are many—the argument does not apply. Second, the first premise of the argument is inconsistent. If a particular hallucination is indistinguishable to me from a perception, then I cannot know that it is an hallucination rather than a perception. Therefore, I can never know that the first premise of the argument is true. To know that it is true, I would have to be able to distinguish from a perception an hallucination that is indistinguishable to me from a perception, which is contradictory.

To avoid these objections, the first premise of the argument has sometimes been stated as follows: hallucinations (dreams, fantasies) are *intrinsically* indistinguishable from perceptions. This restatement is believed to avoid the two objections in the following way. To show that hallucinations are intrinsically indistinguishable from perceptions, it is not necessary to present actual, known examples of hallucinations that are indistinguishable from perceptions. It is sufficient to show that hallucinations indistinguishable from perceptions are possible. And this can be done simply by reflecting on the nature of experience. I now believe myself to perceive a white paper with black writing on it. But it is possible that I am hallucinating (or dreaming, or fantasizing) and that there does not exist any white paper with black writing on it in my external environment. This reflection does not require that the present experience be an hallucination, or that I know it to be an hallucination.

With its revised first premise, the similarity argument becomes a philosophical, or at least a very high-level theoretical, argument. For it no longer depends in any straightforward way on empirical evidence. It also becomes obscure. What is meant by the phrase "intrinsically indistinguishable"? What is the difference between an "intrinsic" and an "extrinsic" distinction? It is left for the reader to discover that there is no easy answer to these questions. Nevertheless, the first premise attempts to state what, in the opinion of the writer, is an old and profound insight concerning the nature of experience. It appears that merely philosophical investigation cannot clarify the insight, that only future theoretical developments in psychology and related fields can reveal in what sense (if any) it is true.

The revised formulation of the first premise avoids the objections to its predecessor but at the same time creates new ones. Although the premise is no longer false or inconsistent, it no longer entails the next step in the argument. That hallucinations are intrinsically indistinguishable from perceptions does not entail that there are no reliable criteria for distinguishing them. Hallucinations may be extrinsically distinguishable, in which case there will be reliable extrinsic criteria for distinguishing them. That my present experience of a white paper with black writing on it *may* be an hallucination does not entail that the experience *is* an hallucination, or that I cannot know whether it is an hallucination or a perception.

In either of the two versions criticized, the similarity argument fails to establish its skeptical conclusion. All the same, it is a crucially important argument for the science of perceptual-cognitive experiences. It forces us to make a critical examination of the traditional criteria for distinguishing sensations, perceptions, hallucinations, dreams, fantasies, and thoughts from one another. For simplicity, discussion of sensations and thoughts is postponed until the end of this section.

The three most familiar criteria are vivacity, coherence, and voluntariness. Examination shows, as the similarity argument suggests, that all three are unreliable.

Vivacity.   Vivacity is the most popular of the three criteria. It is used (under other names) by Locke (1690, Book IV, Ch. II) and Berkeley (1710, Pt. I, para. 30). But it is with Hume that the criterion achieves primary status. Hume (1739, pp. 1–2) divides experiences ("perceptions," he calls them) into "impressions" (sense perceptions) and "ideas": the former distinguished from the latter by their greater vivacity; the latter "faint copies" of the former. Unlike proponents of the view to be criticized, Hume realized that ideas can and sometimes do achieve the vivacity of impressions.

It may be supposed that however similar an hallucination and a perception may be, no hallucination is as vivid as a perception, and if the subject will only pay close attention to his experience, its vivacity will show whether the experience is a perception or an hallucination. This supposition is refuted by examples of hallucinations like that of Mrs. A. Her visual hallucination of her husband was as vivid (lifelike) as any visual perception of him—so vivid that at first she was deceived. It was not any quality of her visual experience that convinced her she was hallucinating, but rather her inference (reasoning) that her husband was not in the room at the time and could not have disappeared as did the apparition. The supposition is also refuted by the converse case: that of a perception which is less vivid than many hallucinations. The perceptions in a house of horrors, or the Alice in Wonderland exhibit at Disneyland, are not at all lifelike. And some of them are literally quite dim, because the lights are low.

Parallel criticisms apply to the view that dreams are invariably less vivid than the perceptions of waking life. Some dreams—"nightmares" or night terrors—are so vivid that they rouse the dreamer. Some dreams are so like waking experience that they are remembered as perceptions, as experiences of events that really happened. Children, when they begin to dream, often (if not usually) report their dreams as perceptions of waking life and respond to them with the same fear or pleasure they exhibit in waking life. It is quite difficult to convince a young child who has awakened from an unpleasant dream that it was "just a dream" and that the dream monster cannot harm him. It is difficult to explain to the child even the distinction between dreams and perceptions: the "explanation" usually takes the form of saying "You were asleep; you were having a dream." The child thus learns that those experiences he remembers on waking are the things we call "dreams" and learns to treat them (discount them) as we do. The converse case also exists: some perceptions are remembered as dreams:

A young nobleman, mentioned by Horatius, living in the citadel of Breslau, was observed by his brother, who occupied the same room, to rise in his sleep, wrap himself in a cloak, and escape by a window to the roof of the building. He there tore in pieces a magpie's nest, wrapped the young birds in his cloak, returned to his apartment, and went to bed. In the morning he mentioned the circumstances as having occurred in a dream, and could not be persuaded that there had been anything more than a dream, till he was shown the magpies in his cloak (Abercrombie, 1833, pp. 218–219).

Fantasies that are as vivid as perceptions are sometimes found in the psychotic, who may imagine that he has been threatened or attacked, or that he has killed someone. Or, to consider examples from everyday life, a mother may imagine hearing a door opening because she expects her child to come home from school at that time; or one member of the household may imagine that her name has been called by another. There are also cases of the converse type: those in which a perception is no more vivid than a fantasy. The Perky experiment, cited in a previous section, provides an example. The subject thinks he is imagining a banana on the wall, when in fact it is a faint picture projected on a screen by an experimental device. It is commonly supposed that fantasies are always less vivid than perceptions. This supposition may rest in part on the dubious belief that fantasies are manufactured in the subject's mind and that he could not thus manufacture a vivid, sensory experience like a perception. In any event, the examples presented here show that the supposition is false.

So far the term "vivid" has been employed as if it referred to a single characteristic of experience. In truth, the term is ambiguous. At least four meanings can be distinguished (they are illustrated with hallucinations only, for simplicity):

1. "Vivid" may mean "bright." Some hallucinations are rich in content, highly colored, so to speak; others are anemic, sketchy, faint.

2. "Vivid" may mean "lifelike." The objects of some hallucinations are described as "looking like the real thing." In other cases the subject may say his hallucination "does not look real."

3. "Vivid" may mean "projected." The objects of some hallucinations—Mrs. A's husband, for example—appear in the space of the normal external environment. Others—Ms. C.'s abstract imagery, for example—appear to be on a screen, in some unusual space, or even at no distance from the subject.

4. "Vivid" may mean "compelling." Some hallucinations (perhaps because of their vivacity, in one or more of the previous senses) compel the subject to believe that their objects exist in external reality. Others are "not believable."

These senses must be kept distinct by the phenomenologist of experience. But they do not affect the point here, which is that hallucinations, dreams, and fantasies can be—and sometimes are—as vivid, in any of these senses, as perceptions.

Coherence.   In Meditation VI, having overcome his earlier philosophical doubt concerning the possibility of distinguishing the experience of sleeping from the experience of waking, Descartes says:

... I find a very notable difference between the two, inasmuch as our memory can never connect our dreams one with the other, or with the whole course of our lives, as it unites events which happen to us while we are awake. And, as a matter of fact, if someone, while I am awake, quite suddenly appeared to me and disappeared as fast as do the images which I see in sleep, so that I could not know from whence the form came nor whither it went, it would not be without reason that I should deem it a spectre or a phantom formed by my brain and similar to those which I form in sleep, rather than a real man (1641, p. 199).

In the first sentence of this passage Descartes suggests a distinction between what may be called the internal coherence of a dream—the way parts of the dream cohere with its other parts, and its external coherence—the way a dream coheres with waking experience or with other dreams.

External Coherence.   Descartes claims that dream experiences can be distinguished from waking experiences by the greater external coherence of the latter. But in fact external incoherence is not a distinguishing feature of dreams, at least not an infallible one. Some dreamers report continuation dreams, a dream that begins where another dream had left off. Indeed, occasionally a dreamer goes back to sleep intending to finish a dream already begun and succeeds in doing so. Such continuation dreams cohere with one another as well as waking experiences cohere with one another—better, in fact, since the waking experiences prior to and following a night's sleep are discontinuous in that the former terminates at night and the latter begins during the day. Other discontinuities are present in the waking experiences of a person before and after anesthesia (he is in the operating room before, in a hospital room after), or of a person who falls asleep on a plane as it takes off in Los Angeles and wakens on arrival in San Francisco. In sum, dreams sometimes cohere with other dreams, and waking experiences sometimes fail to cohere with other waking experiences.

Descartes also claims that dreams do not cohere with waking experiences and can, by this feature, be distinguished from the latter. To defeat this claim it is sufficient to find a dream that continues some waking experience or is continued in some waking experience. Dreams in which the dreamer hears someone calling him and wakens to find that he is indeed being called are perhaps examples. But assume, for argument's sake, that no such examples can be found. If Descartes's claim that dreams do not cohere with waking experiences is true, then of necessity so is the converse claim (i.e., that waking experiences do not cohere with dreams). Consequently, waking experiences are no more coherent than dreams.

Internal Coherence.   The coherence of parts of an experience (dream, perception, etc.) with other parts of the same experience is called "internal coherence." A more common term is "continuity." Thus it has been said—and Descartes would agree—that dreams can be distinguished from perceptions by their greater discontinuity. This claim is not true, at least not universally. In the first place, some dreams exhibit as much continuity as any perceptual experiences of waking life. Some dreams are crafted in much the same manner as a play, with a beginning, climax, and dénouement. Some dreams are extended representations of traveling, skiing, fighting, escaping, and so on; and to be such they must possess a high degree of continuity. In the second place, some waking experiences are as discontinuous as any dream. The experiences of a person who goes to a movie about Henry VIII of England are discontinuous: outside the theater he sees and otherwise perceives twentieth-century streets, people, vehicles,; inside he perceives sixteenth-century streets, persons, vehicles. The experiences of a person who takes an airplane trip from one country to another are in a similar way discontinuous. The experiences of a person involved in a natural catastrophe—tornado, earthquake, flood—may be discontinuous. At one point he may be driving his automobile along a highway, at the next moment picking himself up from a field a hundred yards away, having been carried there by the winds of a tornado.

Thus far we have examined the inadequacies of coherence as a test for distinguishing dreams from (waking) perceptions. As a test for distinguishing waking experiences—hallucinations, fantasies, and perceptions—from one another it is hardly more successful. The test of *external* coherence, as we have seen, is of necessity a double-edged sword. If hallucinations (or fantasies) are externally incoherent with perceptions, then perceptions must be externally incoherent with hallucinations (or fantasies). Hence perceptions cannot be more externally coherent than hallucinations (or fantasies), and external coherence therefore must fail to distingush them. The test of *internal* coherence suffers from the defects mentioned earlier in connection with dreams. Some fantasies are extended sequences of experiences that embody a "story" composed by the subject, perhaps one that satisfies certain wishes. These are as internally coherent, or continuous, as any sequence of perceptual experiences. And, as noted already, some perception sequences exhibit a high degree of discontinuity, as much as any fantasy sequence. Hallucinations, it may be supposed, are surely less continuous than perception sequences. But, again, some perception sequences are quite discontinuous. Furthermore, the belief that hallucinations are usually discontinuous arises from reflecting on too limited a class of cases. Mrs. A.'s hallucination of her husband in the living room is as continuous as any perception sequence; indeed, it is just this continuity that makes it such a compelling hallucination. Some of the extended hallucinations of the intoxicated Ms. C. are also as continuous as any perception sequence.

Voluntariness.   As traditionally employed, the test of voluntariness assumes that nonperceptual experiences such as fantasies, dreams, and hallucinations are under the immediate control of the subject and can be produced by him at will, whereas his perceptions are involuntary (see, e.g., Berkeley, 1710, Pt. I, paras. 28–29). If the assumption were correct, I could determine whether I am fantasizing or perceiving by trying to direct the course of the experience or to terminate it: if I am successful, then I was fantasizing. This test seems especially appropriate for use by the subject of Perky's experiment. The experimenter was able to deceive the subject into thinking that he was imagining a banana by not allowing him to try to manipulate the experience. If S had been allowed to do so, he could have discovered that his experience of a banana could not be altered or terminated, and might have concluded that he was perceiving rather than imagining a banana.

Now it is true of some of our fantasies that they are under our control, but it is not true of all. Some fantasies are obsessive and continue even when the subject tries to terminate them. The fantasies that one has during a hangover are often of this character: they get out of control, so to speak. Even normal daydreams are largely involuntary. The dozing person does not control the reveries he is having, any more than he controls the flow of visual experiences produced by his open eyes. The images seem to flow on by their own laws. It is true that the subject can terminate or modify the reverie in the sense that he can rouse himself; but this is control of an indirect type and does not differ from the control he has over his perceptions. He can terminate his visual perceptions by closing his eyes or anesthetizing himself. His perceptions are, perhaps, involuntary in the sense that he has no *immediate* control of them. But in this sense many fantasies are also involuntary; indeed, most seem to be.

Excellent examples of fantasies under the immediate control of the subject are those produced as an aid to erotic self-stimulation. These are typically of other persons and of genitalia. They are produced on demand, image by image. Few of our fantasies and daydreams are produced in this manner. Undoubtedly some persons are better at controlling their fantasies than others (perhaps adults are better at it than children); and it is perhaps possible for humans to learn how to control all their fantasies in the way that some can control sexual fantasies. But at the present stage of development of the human species, such control is rare. So the test of volition—according to which fantasies but not perceptions can be produced at will—would reveal if strictly and solely applied, that most of what we now call fantasies are in reality perceptions! It will not help to argue that although fantasies, like perceptions, are under indirect control only, the means by which they are indirectly controlled are different. For the means are not essentially different. I can terminate my visual perceptions by closing my eyes, and I can terminate visual fantasies experienced with eyes closed by opening my eyes.

In reply it may be said that those fantasies not under immediate conscious control are under immediate *unconscious* control, whereas perceptions are not under our control in either sense. This reply raises the question of whether "unconscious control" is really control: perhaps what is called unconscious control of experiences is really the involuntary production of those experiences by mechanisms internal to the organism. However this question is answered, the reply that raises it is of no service to the proposition that a subject can distinguish his fantasies from his perceptions by determining which of his experiences are voluntary and which involuntary. For unconsciously controlled fantasies are, from the subject's point of view, involuntary: he finds when he tries to control them that he cannot do so, since his attempts are made at the conscious level. Consequently, he will conclude that they are not fantasies if he uses the proposed test.

This point becomes relevant when we ask whether the volition test can be employed to distinguish perceptions from dreams. Freudian psychoanalysts can be taken to hold that dreams are voluntary, for in their theory, dreams are the deliberately disguised expressions of repressed desires and anxieties. (This interpretation is open to question, because the psychoanalysts might reply that "deliberation" consists merely in control exercised by an involuntary mechanism internal to the organism.) One might suppose that if this theory is true, dreams can be distinguished from perceptions by means of the volition test: for perceptions, unlike dreams, are involuntary. But the suggestion is in error. From the subject's point of view—which is, by definition, a conscious point of view—dreams are as involuntary as perceptions. If his dreams are controlled unconsciously, he is not aware of it in the typical case.

Furthermore, the Freudian theory is controversial. Some theorists believe that dreaming is the unconscious processing of perceptual material acquired while awake. Still others hold that dreaming (and fantasizing) is baseline mental activity that occurs spontaneously in the absence of other mental activity. Whatever the true theory—and none is generally agreed on—it seems to be undeniable that the dreamer has no conscious control over much of his dreaming. Subjects do sometimes have the sense that they construct their dreams, in something like the way in which a play or a film is constructed. But more often than not, the dreams seem to be produced by mechanisms over which the subject has no control; thus they seem to him to be as involuntary as his perceptions. Indeed, some dreams are, apparently, perceptions had during sleep. For example, the sleeping subject dreams that the telephone in his room is ringing when the telephone *is* ringing.

We have finally to ask whether the volition test can be used to distinguish between hallucinations and perceptions. The answer is, obviously, that it cannot. For one of the characteristic (though not essential) features of hallucinations is our inability to control them. Mrs. A.'s hallucination of her husband was as involuntary as her perception of the room the apparition was standing in. To this must be added a somewhat less obvious point. A subject may conclude that he is having an hallucination rather than a perception on the ground that he cannot terminate his experience by any means (short of anesthesia or death), whereas if it were a perception he could terminate it by changing his situation or blocking his sense organs. The same test could perhaps be employed to detect an obsessive fantasy. Thus we have ample evidence of the falsity of the assumption on which the volition test depends—the assumption that experiences of things that exist externally (perceptions) are involuntary, whereas experiences of things that do not exist externally are voluntary.

Stating the false assumption in this way helps us to see how the volition test may have suggested itself. To defeat the skeptical argument from illusion, we require a test that will distinguish our veridical experiences (perceptions) from the nonveridical (hallucinations, dreams, and fantasies). Veridical experiences, it may be supposed, are externally caused, whereas nonveridical experiences are internally caused. Now I cannot directly know, merely from the character of my experiences, what their causes are and whether they are external or internal. But I can directly know whether the experience is voluntary or involuntary. And from that information I can make inferences about the cause of the experience: if an experience is voluntary, it is internally caused; if it is involuntary, it is externally caused. Thus I can know, indirectly and by inference, whether my experiences are veridical.

This argument is riddled with mistakes and questionable assumptions. First, it is doubtful that I can directly know whether my experiences are voluntary, because some voluntary experiences—dreams, for example—are unconscious, therefore inaccessible to direct knowledge. Second, it is doubtful (or false) that all involuntary experiences are externally caused. Dreams are internally caused, and yet some are involuntary. Obsessive fantasies are internally caused and yet are involuntary. Third, it is false that all externally caused experiences are veridical. An hallucination produced by a stroboscope is produced by an external cause and is nonveridical. In conclusion, if the motivation underlying the volition test is the assumption of a connection between the involuntariness and the external causation of experiences, the motivation is flawed because the assumption is false.

SENSATIONS AND THOUGHTS

"Sensations" is used in this chapter to refer either to the abstract experiences exemplified by the first segment from Ms. C.'s report, or to the "meaningless," virtually indescribable experiences exemplified by segments from other drug-intoxicated subjects. None of the subjects give any indication that these experiences are even partly under their conscious control. It is possible that they have no interest in controlling the experiences and make no attempt to do so. But if experiments should show that subjects cannot control such experiences even when they try, it is still possible that some among them could learn to do so, much as some yogis have learned to control their heartbeat and other activities usually supposed to be inescapably involuntary. The point to be made here is a general one. It is customary to suppose that sensory experiences are passions (to use an old term) of the subject, events that happen to him over which he has no control. Perhaps experiences should be regarded instead as actions, or activities, of the subject (or products of activities of the subject), actions that are usually performed unconsciously but through learning can come under the subject's conscious control.

Are sensations generally more coherent than other experiences? Less coherent? It is not clear that the question makes any sense. Ms. C.'s dreamlike experience of a street with newsboys in it becomes incoherent at the end, when the street suddenly widens and she finds herself in the middle of it. In this sense, abstract experiences are not properly said to be coherent or incoherent; the terms properly apply only to representative experience. For example, the experience of a flower opening its petals is coherent; the experience of a flower turning into a dog is incoherent. The reason, presumably, is that flowers often undergo the first transformation, but rarely, if ever, undergo the second. In short, an experience is coherent in this sense if it is an experience of something that might happen in reality, incoherent if it is an experience of something that could not happen in reality. Since abstract experiences do not seem to represent reality at all, it seems improper to call them coherent or incoherent in this sense. And there does not appear to be any other sense in which the terms are profitably applied to such experiences.

Earlier it was pointed out that in its application to experiences, "vivid" may mean (a) bright (not faint), (b) lifelike ("real"), (c) projected (located in external space), or (d) compelling (believable). There are undoubtedly other senses for this difficult term, and even those mentioned here need more analysis. The present lexical machinery is, however, adequate to show that sensations (abstract or obscure experiences) are sometimes vivid and sometimes not. Ms. C. at one point says "seems really bright," and then describes an explosion like a volcano gushing yellow, glowing lava. Saffron, by contrast, says "It's fuzzy, fuzzy blots . . . no colors, no vividness. . . ." It is not clear that the terms "lifelike" and "not lifelike" should be applied to these abstract and obscure experiences. But if we do so apply them, Ms. C.'s experience of a volcano gushing yellow, glowing lava is lifelike. Saffron's experience is not: "I'm not seeing things, no pink elephants, no lines, no nothing, just white on black, well, gray on black." Saffron's experience is also not projected in space: internal or external space. Ms. C.'s experience is projected in at least internal space. For example, the illuminating star she sees "sometimes goes behind what's on the screen." Furthermore, when intoxicated subjects are taken out of the lightproof experimental room, the abstract forms, patterns, and colors they were seeing are often projected on the surfaces of the external environment. None of the subjects quoted in this chapter were inclined to believe that the forms, patterns, and colors they saw existed in external reality. But with larger doses of the hallucinogen, the subject's ability to distinguish between the real and the unreal is lost, and even abstract experiences sometimes become compelling.

The term "thought" has been used in this chapter as roughly synonymous with "mental image in no sensory modality," that is, as referring to a cognitive experience that is neither visual, tactual, auditory, and so on. It is often supposed that thoughts are distinguished from other experiences in being always voluntary. But it is clear that some thoughts are not under the conscious control of the subject: compulsive thoughts—thoughts that a subject "cannot get out of his head"—are examples. It may be said that all thoughts, even compulsive ones, are under at least the unconscious control of the subject. This claim cannot be confirmed or disconfirmed by direct experiment. The experimenter cannot instruct the subject to try to control his thoughts, since subject success or failure would establish *conscious* control or lack of it. Unconscious control of thoughts can be established only indirectly, possibly by psychiatric methods. For example, we might infer that since the subject wanted or needed to have certain thoughts, and did have them, these thoughts were under his unconscious control. If the inference is acceptable in the case of thoughts, it can also be used to establish that sensations, perceptions, and hallucinations are sometimes under the conscious control of the subject. Consequently, there is just as much (or as little) reason to suppose that other experiences are voluntary in the unconscious sense as there is to suppose that thoughts are.

Are thoughts generally more coherent than other experiences? Less coherent? In the sense of "coherent" thus far employed in the chapter, thoughts are coherent if *(a)* they occur in the manner in which the objects of thought can occur in reality. In this sense, some thoughts are coherent, some are incoherent. If I think of myself jumping from a diving board and plunging into a swimming pool below, my thoughts are coherent. But if I think of myself jumping from the board and floating off into space (such experiences sometimes occur in dreams), my thoughts are incoherent. Obviously thoughts of both types occur. To say that thoughts are coherent might also be taken to mean that *(b)* they are well-organized, *(c)* they are clear and unconfused, or *(d)* they conform to the canons of logic. To explicate these various senses would be a formidable task, and fortunately such explication is not required to see that thoughts sometimes do and sometimes do not have the characteristics named in *b, c,* and *d.* (The interesting question of whether sensations and perceptions can be said to be coherent or incoherent in these additional senses is left aside.)

The prejudice of centuries makes it very difficult to believe that a mere thought—a mental image in no sensory modality—could be as vivid as a perception. It is easier to believe the converse claim: that some perceptions are as unvivid as thoughts. The best examples are perceptions under reduced stimulation. Consider one's perceptions of an unlighted landscape on a moonless night: they are anemic and faint. They can also come to seem "unreal." Occasionally the things seen will appear to be at no distance from the subject. And under these conditions, it is not difficult for the subject to believe, or at least come close to believing, that what he sees is a landscape of his dreams. Or consider the perceptions of a person immersed in a fog so thick that he can see only a few inches from his face. The white stuff he sees is anemic, "unreal," and unprojected. Laboratory experiments on reduced stimulation provide further examples. Subjects fitted with translucent goggles, or placed in an all-white room with no contours or shading, tend to lose their sense of reality and virtually cease to see. It would be difficult to contend that their perceptions are more vivid than their thoughts.

More radically, it can be argued that thoughts occasionally achieve the vivacity of perceptions. The argument requires careful attention to the various senses of the difficult term "vivid." Consider a hypothetical example. I am cross-country skiing in a Northern forest in midwinter. I sit down to rest for a few minutes and begin to think of myself—without visual, tactual, auditory, or other sensory imagery—sitting in a cozy cabin before a fire. My thought of the fire is *(a)* bright, since the fire is blazing and bright; *(b)* lifelike, since I am thinking of a real fire that warms; and *(c)* projected, since the fire is thought to be in the space of a fireplace. As I sit in the forest fondly thinking these thoughts, I forget that I am sitting in a forest and not before a fire—the thought has become *(d)* compelling. My thought of the fire is therefore vivid in every sense of the term mentioned. It will be objected that this case cannot be described without supposing that the thought becomes sensory, becomes an image in one or more sense modalities. But surely it is possible for me to have an "imageless thought" of a fire. Surely it is possible for me to think of a warm fire brightly burning in a fireplace without having visual, tactual, auditory, or other sensory imagery. It will be said that it is simply obvious that the thought described is not as vivid as a perception, or even an hallucination or fantasy, of a fire. But in what sense of "vivid"? The various senses of the term have been examined one by one, and it has been seen that in every sense the thought is as vivid as a perception.

It may be said that although my thought is of a brightly burning fire, the thought itself is not bright, and the perception of a brightly burning fire (or even of a faintly burning fire) would itself be brighter than a thought. But it apparently makes no sense to say that a perception or a thought, as opposed to the object perceived or thought of, is bright. Experiences, whether perceptual or cognitive, are experiences *of* objects (this is sometimes expressed by saying that experiences are representations). Experiences are described introspectively by describing the qualities of their objects. All that can be meant by saying that an experience is bright, or red, or rectangular is that the thing experienced is bright, or red, or rectangular. The experience itself is "transparent" to introspection. This feature of experiences makes it possible to prove that thoughts are potentially as vivid as perceptions, where vivacity is defined in terms of brightness or some other quality of the experienced object. Perhaps some objects that can be thought of cannot be perceived, but it seems clear that every object that can be perceived can also be thought of. Now suppose "vivid" means "bright." Then a vivid perception is by definition a bright perception. But a bright perception, owing to the transparency of experiences, is a perception of a bright object. Now it is possible to think of (have a thought of) an object that is just as bright as any that can be perceived, since every object that can be perceived can also be thought of. Consequently, it is possible to have as bright (i.e., as vivid) a thought as any perception.

All the same, one wants to say, there is obviously some difference—perhaps "vivid" is the wrong term for it—between a thought of a fire and a perception of a fire. And indeed there is, given the use of "thought" to mean "a mental image in no sensory modality." According to this definition, a perception is sensory and a thought is nonsensory. This difference between perceptions and thoughts may be an important one. But what it consists in is, at the current theoretical stage, obscure. There is no reason to think that it is an essential, intrinsic difference.

Other Criteria.   It has been argued here that the traditional criteria for distinguishing sensations, perceptions, hallucinations, dreams, fantasies, and thoughts are inadequate. No one of the experiences is essentially more vivid, coherent, or involuntary than any of the others. It has not been argued that there are no differences between our perceptual-cognitive experiences; nor has it been suggested that these are not differences in vivacity, coherence, and involuntariness. What has been maintained here is that the differences that do exist do not divide up the continuum of experiences into sensations, perceptions, hallucinations, dreams, fantasies, and thoughts. To summarize, some perceptions are more vivid than some dreams; some dreams are more vivid than some perceptions. Perceptions are not necessarily, or essentially, more vivid (or coherent, or involuntary) than dreams. If we are to distinguish between sensations, perceptions, hallucinations, dreams, fantasies, and thoughts, it must be by means of criteria other than vivacity, coherence, and involuntariness.

What other criteria? Those that come to mind are just as unsuccessful as the traditional three. Consider *concreteness*. (The usual antonym of "concrete" is "abstract." The latter term is avoided in this context because it has already been used, in a possibly different sense, to label so-called nonrepresentative experiences such as those of Ms. C.'s first segment. It will be evident that "concrete" is an additional possible meaning for "vivid.") A full-color oil painting of a woman is more concrete than a charcoal sketch of the same person. A charcoal sketch is more concrete than a line drawing. And a line drawing is more concrete than a Matisse-like sketch consisting merely of a line here and a line there to suggest essential features of the person. There is an inclination to suppose essential features of the person. There is an inclination to suppose that perceptions are more concrete than dreams and fantasies, and these in turn more concrete than thoughts. But the inclination seems to be wrong. An artist's fantasy may be as rich in detail as an oil painting; indeed, it may have been the complete prior plan of the painting. Moreover, the argument from the transparency of experiences can again be employed to show that thoughts as concrete as any perceptions are possible. Concreteness is, roughly, richness in detail. If I have a thought of a woman that represents all the details of her face and figure—and such thoughts seem as possible as a complete verbal description of her face and figure—the thought is as concrete as any perception of the woman would be. It may be objected that thoughts are coded perceptions in abbreviated form. The reply is that some thoughts are indeed abbreviated, but some are not. Finally, some perceptions are not very concrete. A squash player's perceptions of his opponent and the ball in play are undoubtedly highly schematic, since the player has no time for anything more complete. Perceptions rich in detail require sufficient time to look and to allow the visual images to form.

Or consider *veridicality*. It may be supposed that perceptions can be distinguished from the other experiences by their veridicality (correspondence to reality). But thoughts are just as often veridical, and so sometimes are dreams and fantasies. The skier thinks expectantly of snow in the Sierras, and then discovers that there is snow in the Sierras. The lover fantasizes his loved one appearing at his door, and the loved one does appear at the door. Fortuitous veridicality, but veridicality nonetheless. In the same way, veridical hallucinations are possible. For example, a subject in a sensory isolation booth could hallucinate something happening outside the booth that was in fact happening outside the booth. Finally, some perceptions are at least partly nonveridical: we call them illusions.

Or consider *causality*. It is tempting to suppose that hallucinations are peripherally caused and thoughts centrally caused. But perceptions can be caused by stimulating the central nervous system. Classic examples are found in the reports of Penfield (1958, pp. 21–30) and his associates, who by stimulating the exposed temporal cortex caused the patient to have extended visual and auditory hallucinations and/or memories. And thoughts can be caused by stimulating receptors. Examples can be found in work on subliminal perception. For instance, a picture of an appetizing drink is flashed on a screen before the subject so briefly that the subject does not (consciously) see the picture; a short time later the subject thinks of the drink. In the writer's opinion, the distinction between peripheral and central causation of experiences has been very harmful to the science of perception and cognition. Because the anatomical distinction was clear, researchers supposed that a comparably clear distinction could be found among the experiences caused. For instance, peripherally caused experiences are supposed to be vivid and involuntary, centrally caused experiences faint and relatively involuntary. The hypothesis of such physiological-experiential connections should not be uncritically accepted. Perhaps experiences of all kinds are sometimes the result of activities in the entire peripheral-central nervous system, sometimes the result of activities in a limited part of the system. The distinction between peripheral and central causation of experiences has also obscured the possibility that experiences are not passions—effects passively produced by stimulation of the organism, but actions—active responses of the organism to stimulation.

The failure of the criteria discussed in this section provides excellent support for the first premises of the similarity argument, which states that sensations, perceptions, hallucinations, dreams, fantasies, and thoughts are *intrinsically* indistinguishable from one another. Does it support the stronger conclusion that the experiences listed are totally indistinguishable, that the terms in the list of experiences do not mark out any distinctions whatsoever? This conclusion is, of course, counterintuitive in the highest degree. But one point seems clear. We do not at the moment know how to distinguish between the various experiences named in our list. Psychological theory must be developed to show what the distinction consists in. Perhaps we shall find, to mention just one possibility, that it consists in the use to which the experience is put in the activities of the organism. Thus perceptions may be experiences that require immediate attention for the survival or health of the organism; thoughts may be experiences that enable the organism to act on other experiences; fantasies may be the cognitive play or experimentation of the organism; and so on. This type of distinction can be called an *extrinsic* distinction, since it focuses on the use rather than the construction of the experience (what it is made of). It permits us to say either *(a)* that thoughts are nonsensory perceptions, or *(b)* that perceptions are sensory thoughts. Statement *(a)* is the general form of an empiricist theory of cognition. The next and final section offers tentative arguments against *(a)* and, indirectly, in favor of *(b)*.

CRITICISM OF EMPIRICIST THEORIES

It was noted in the first section of the chapter that cases such as Mrs. A.'s are often taken as paradigmatic of hallucinations. This is dangerous because it can induce us to be satisfied with external, stimulus-type explanations of hallucinations and other perceptual-cognitive experiences. That such explanations are acceptable is the view of what may be called *extreme empiricism*. The three types of explanation countenanced by this view can be labeled—for want of better terms——supernatural, physical, and physiological. The hypothesis that Mrs. A. saw an apparition or ghost of her husband is an example of a supernatural explanation. The hypothesis that Mrs. A. saw a shadow or play of light and mistook it for (inferred it to be) her husband is an example of a physical explanation. The hypothesis that Mrs. A. saw a floater in her eye and mistook it for her husband is an example of a physiological explanation.

In many cases such explanations simply are false to the facts and will be quickly disconfirmed by a researcher with the proper theoretical set. There was no ghost, or play of light, in Mrs. A.'s drawingroom; there was no floater in her eye. But a different theoretical set is possible, one in which the researcher reasons as follows: perception is to be explained in terms of the stimuli acting on the organism; hallucination is like perception; thus there *must* be some stimulus producing Mrs. A.'s hallucination—a play of light, something in her eye, and so on. The proper theoretical set is one in which it is realized that neither perception nor hallucination is that simple, or external, or stimulus-bound. (This point is, of course, tacitly acknowledged by those externalists who say that hallucinations are the effect of plays of light, floaters in the eye, etc. For they admit that these stimuli must be mis-taken, or mis-interpreted, by the subject. The interpretive process is, however, underemphasized or dismissed as a cognitive addition to perception. And perception—as opposed to thought—is held to be completely explicable in terms of its external causes, or stimuli.)

Much of the earlier work on hallucinations (especially that in the later nineteenth century) consists of dogged attempts to provide external, stimulus-type explanations. Some current neurophysiological work in the area exhibits a similar theoretical set. Consider the researcher who believes that by probing the brain with finer and finer electrodes and analyzing the data obtained with more and more sophisticated processing techhiques, he will one day come to understand how hallucinations and perceptions are produced. Like his externalist predecessor, he assumes that perception, veridical and nonveridical, can be understood in terms of what stimuli do to the organism. What in fact, is required, is an understanding of what the organism does to the stimuli. Perception and hallucination should not be thought of as passive, receptive processes, but as active, constructive processes. To explain hallucinations as effects of brain stimulation is as unsatisfactory as explaining them as effects of physical stimulation (plays of light, shadows, etc.). The neurological explanation is indeed more internal than the physical, but not in the required sense of "internal." The required internal explanation must describe for us the internal activity of hallucination (and perception) production. This is a monumental task, requiring the collaboration of psychologists, information theorists, neurophysiologists, psychiatrists, psycholinguists, and others.

The hypothesis that hallucinations are retrieved perceptions—memories, in one sense of the term—is the simplest and most popular explanation of the required kind. It is the hypothesis of what may be called *moderate empiricism,* and it may be illustrated as follows. Mrs. A. had seen her husband stand in front of the fireplace and then walk to the window on several (or at least one) previous occasion. On the occasion described, she expected to see what she had so often seen before and consequently had a visual memory of her husband standing before the fire and then walking to the window, a memory so vivid that for a time she was unable to distinguish it from a veridical perception. Surprising as it may seem, this theory has important resemblances to the externalist theories criticized above. It treats hallucinations as perceptions: delayed perceptions. One might even say that it treats hallucinations as nonveridical perceptions, nonveridical because they are retrieved at a time when they no longer correspond to reality. Furthermore, it treats hallucinations as the effects, delayed or postponed, of stimulation. Perception is taken to be an immediate effect of stimulation, hallucination is taken to be a delayed effect. We can therefore expect deficiencies in the theory.

Even if the retrieval theory is satisfactory in outline, it is surely deficient in detail (i.e., incomplete). This deficiency manifests itself in several different ways when we try to apply the theory to Mrs. A.'s hallucination.

1. It is likely that Mrs. A.'s experience of her husband differs from every one of her past perceptions of him in at least some small detail (the look on his face, the color of his pants, his path through the room, etc.). The theory must explain how this novel detail was added to the memory to form the hallucination, and it cannot do this by a further appeal to past perception.

2. Mrs. A.'s hallucinatory experience of her husband is integrated with her (veridical) perceptual experiences of the room, furniture, fire, and so on. The theory must explain this remarkable accomplishment. Why does the figure of the husband occlude the fire rather than the other way round? Why does the husband walk on the floor rather than in the air? To answer such questions as these, some constructive, creative process must be posited: perception-retrieval alone will not suffice. If the hallucinator is combining materials from perception and memory, he is combining them not at random, but in novel and appropriate ways. To explain the novelty and the appropriateness, processes in addition to perception-retrieval must be posited.

Most fundamentally, the retrieval theory is not generally satisfactory even in outline. For many hallucinatory experiences are novel, that is to say, they bear little or no resemblance to past perceptions of the subject. Recall the three segments from Ms. C.'s transcript. Only in the third of these do we have a strong suspicion that she may be recalling scenes from her past. Even here a complete life history would be required to determine whether she has ever seen city streets, walls, and persons like those described. It will be asked: how then is she able to describe and identify (recognize) what she hallucinates? The answer is: in the same way that she describes and identifies what in normal states she veridically sees. There is no need to speculate here about the nature of the process of perceptual identification (recognition). Perhaps it involves matching current experiences with a previously obtained template; perhaps not. Perhaps the template (if any) is acquired through experience; perhaps it is genetically transmitted. The point is that whatever the process, it is as available for hallucinatory experience as it is for veridical perceptual experience. The former activity is no more mysterious than the latter. If a subject can see and identify as a lion something that she has never seen before, then she can hallucinate and identify as a lion something that she has never seen before.

The retrieval theorist may concede the point yet insist that if the subject has not previously seen the things hallucinated, she must have seen their *elements,* which are perceptions retrieved from memory and combined into the hallucinatory experience. It is important to realize that this may be a major concession, depending on how the theorist intends "perception retrieval." "Perception retrieval" may refer, *first,* to *(a)* the process of bringing a perception stored in memory into consciousness; or, *second,* to *(a)* together with *(b)* the process of selecting a stored perception for entry into consciousness; or, *third,* to *(a)* and *(b)* together with *(c)* the process of combining the perceptions selected into a whole conscious experience. It is obvious that the retrieval theory can explain novel hallucinations (if it can explain them at all) only on the third interpretation. Novel hallucinations are not the result of bringing stored perceptions into consciousness *whole;* otherwise they would not be novel. Nor are they the result of fortuitous combination of elemental stored perceptions into novel wholes: the elemental perceptions must have been selected and combined in such a way as to produce coherent wholes—for example, Ms. C's hallucination of boys in plaid vests, funny hats, and oxford shoes riding bicycles on a city street.

Retrieval theorists usually fail to discuss alternative interpretations of "perception retrieval" and fail to say which of the various interpretations they intend [West (1962) provides an example]. This striking omission is probably not accidental. For it becomes immediately obvious that only on the third interpretation above can the retrieval theory hope to explain novel hallucinations. But the processes of selecting and combining elements seem to be the sort of cognitive activity that retrieval theorists—who lean toward behaviorism—wish to exclude from their explanations. Furthermore, the third interpretation is subversive to the motivation that initially leads to the retrieval theory. For if there can be a process that selects elemental perceptions from memory and combines them into coherent hallucinations, couldn't there be a process that *manufactures* the elemental perceptions as needed, rather than retrieving them from memory? Retrieval theorists of every sort will reply that the elements of experiences must, if manufactured, be manufactured from other elements—otherwise they would be composed of nothing—and that in the final analysis all experiences are composed of simple elements of experience previously acquired in perception and stored in memory.

This brings us to the fundamental objection to the retrieval theory in any of its forms: its hypothesis that experiences are ultimately composed of simple experiential *elements* is—whatever the process of composition—unacceptable. Consider the segment in which Ms. C. hallucinates boys with red hair. Although unlikely, it is possible that she has never before seen red hair. In that event, says the retrieval theorist, she must have seen the elements before, and she must be retrieving these from memory and combining them into an experience of red hair. What are the elements? The most natural suggestion is that they are an experience of red and an experience of hair. But there are insuperable difficulties in this analysis. The experience of hair is either a color experience or it is not. If it is not a color experience, it cannot be an experience at all. In the same way that one cannot see uncolored hair (which would be invisible), one cannot have an experience of hair that is not a color experience. Suppose, on the other hand, the experience of hair is a color experience. Then it is a composite experience and not an element. It is an experience of red hair, or green hair, or black hair, and so on. But if it is an experience of red hair, it is the very experience whose elements we wish to discover. And if it is an experience of green hair, or black hair, the experience of red cannot combine with it to produce an experience of red hair.

Another kind of difficulty arises from the assumption that a property-experience, such as an experience of red, can be an element. Perhaps we can have an experience of red that is not an experience of any red thing; but at least the experience must be of a red spatial expanse. How does it happen that Ms. C.'s experience of red is an exact spatial fit of her experience of hair? It seems unlikely that she has a store of red experiences of every or even most sizes. So we seem forced to the conclusion that the red experience is shaped to fit her experience of hair. Perhaps there is no logical absurdity in this conclusion, but it seems at least farfetched. We do not have any clear notion of what can be meant by "combining an experience of red with an experience of hair." Therefore we are forced to use analogies. The one that naturally comes to mind is a book of paper cutouts, with outline drawings of boys and girls and colored shapes that can be pasted on to make a red dress or a black shoe, blue hair or red hair. It seems farfetched to suppose that such a process literally takes place in hallucinating organisms.

As a final criticism, it is important to realize that with regard to either their dependence on or independence of past perception, hallucinations and veridical perceptions are on a par. If it is possible for the subject to see a red-haired person without having seen one before, it is possible for her to hallucinate a red-haired person without having seen one before. And surely the former is possible; for if it were impossible it would be impossible for anyone to see something for the first time, and consequently impossible for anyone to see anything. If it is impossible for the subject to hallucinate a novel object without having seen its elements before, it is impossible for the subject to see a red-haired person without having seen his elements before. And surely the latter is not impossible. For if it were impossible to see things without having seen their elements before, it would be impossible to see simple elements for the first time (one cannot see the elements of a simple element, since simple elements have no elements), therefore impossible to see anything composed of elements, that is, impossible to see anything.

The conclusion of the foregoing arguments is that hallucinations (and dreams, fantasies, and thoughts) are not composed of elemental experiences, neither retrieved perceptions nor other experiences. This conclusion dissolves one of the problems in explaining the novelty that many hallucinations exhibit. If hallucinations are not composed of retrieved perceptions, there is no reason for them to resemble past perceptions, either in whole or in part. It may seem that this advantage is purchased at a prohibitive price. If hallucinations are not composed of experiences, what are they composed of? Are they perhaps simple, composed of nothing? If hallucinations are simple, they would seem to be inexplicable. For if they are simple, they have no elements. And if they have no elements, they come into being from nothing, which is absurd, or at least supernatural. Hallucinations come into being in a natural, explicable manner only if they are formed from elements. What, then, are their elements?

There is, of course, only one scientific answer to this question: the elements of experiences are neural entities. This answer is, however, almost empty. For we do not know how to identify these neural entities, nor do we know how to conceive the relation between an experience and its neural elements. There is no reason to suppose that the neural elements of experiences are neurons, or synapses, or ion flows. It may be that only some entity as yet unconceived by theory can serve as an element of experience. Furthermore, there is no reason to suppose that science has yet adequately conceptualized the relation between an experience and its elements. Neurons are elements of the nervous system, but it does not follow that they are elements of experiences. The relation between an element of an experience and the experience may not be at all like the relation of a synapse to a neuron or that of a neuron to a neuron-column. The relation in question may be like that between a bit of neural information and the information of which it is a bit. Now the concept of a bit of information is a different kind of concept from the concept of a synapse. Neurons are not composed of bits of information (although bits of information may be stored in neurons). Similarly, experiences need not be composed of synapses. The concept of a bit belongs to one theory—the theory of information, the concept of a synapse to another—the theory of nervous activity, although of course the theories are interrelated (in ways that are exceedingly difficult to describe).

The elements of a thing are entities that theorists posit to explain the behavior of that thing. Elements need not be parts. The physical elements of a desk are not parts of desks: legs, drawers, knobs, surfaces, angles. They are electrons, protons, bonds between these, and so on. Indeed, it is not clear whether the elements of a (material) desk should be regarded as material particles or as energy fluxes. In the same way, the elements of experiences need not be regarded as parts of experiences—little pieces of experiences. They can be construed as theoretical entities posited to explain the behavior of experiences. We may not know what these elements are for some time to come. They will be neural entities, since (so far as we know) experiences are dependent on a nervous system. But, as noted earlier, to say this is to say almost nothing.

The point of these remarks is not to speculate about the nature of the elements of experiences, or to offer even the outline of a scientific theory of experiences. It is merely to show that there is no difficulty whatsoever in the supposition that experiences have elements that are not themselves retrieved perceptions or other experiences. In the opinion of the writer, the science of perception and cognition would greatly benefit from entertaining the supposition.

Consider an analogy (a myth, perhaps, in the sense in which myths can be the precursors of scientific theories). Children make pictures, with crayons, water-colors, and paints. The least creative among them picture things they have seen before: the stereotyped house, tree, and dog. (Even here there is probably some novelty; for it is unlikely that even the stereotyped figures are exactly like their prototypes in memory.) The more creative children picture things whose parts they have seen before even though they have not seen the thing as a whole: a stereotyped window in a novel house, for instance. Children who are even more creative picture things they have never seen before in whole or in part: perhaps a weird creature that reminds one of a bird and a reptile and a cat but looks like none of these. The most creative pictures of all are those that any child can make: abstract finger-paintings that are the result of an attempt to do nothing more than spread some colors on paper in a pleasing way. The child may never have seen the shapes into which he spreads the colors. He could paint a complicated closed curve whose curvature is at every point different from that of any curve he has seen. "But," you will say, "the child must have seen at least the colors before." Not even this is true. Suppose the liquids in the watercolor kit are colorless until they are spread on special reactive paper, at which point they take on colors the child has never seen before. (The child could even plan his painting by the numbers of the colorless liquids, although he would not know before painting it exactly how it would look.)

Some hallucinations are as novel as the most novel pictures. It is not necessary to suppose that even the parts of these are retrieved perceptions. The parts may be themselves manufactured in the hallucinative process. An hallucination can be of a closed curve whose curvature is at every point novel and whose color has never before been seen by the hallucinator. Of course, the subject would not know exactly what to call the curve or the color, but neither does the child with the special watercolor kit. It is possible that those drug-intoxicated subjects who have difficulty describing what they see are seeing things that are, in whole and in part, so unlike anything they have seen before that they do not know what to call them. A satisfactory theory of hallucinations must explain how they can exhibit this radical kind of novelty (if, indeed, they do exhibit it). To do this, it will probably have to be a general theory of the formation of sensations, perceptions, hallucinations, dreams, fantasies, and thoughts.

ACKNOWLEDGMENTS

The author is heavily indebted to Professor R. K. Siegel, co-editor of this volume, for much information concerning contemporary literature and experimental results concerning hallucinations, and for many stimulating discussions while this chapter was being prepared.

The author is indebted to Professor R. M. Yost, of the UCLA Department of Philosophy, for making available his extensive file of references to and excerpts from the older literature concerning hallucinations.

This chapter was brought to completion with a grant-in-aid from the Graduate School of the University of Minnesota, Minneapolis.

REFERENCES

Abercrombie, J. *Inquiries concerning the intellectual powers and the investigation of truth.* New York: Harper and Brothers, 1833.

Alexander, H. B. The subconscious in the light of dream imagery. *Proceedings of the American Society for Psychical Research,* 1909, **3.**

Archer, W. On dreams. In R. L. Woods (Ed.), *The world of dreams.* New York: Random House, 1947.

Arnheim, R. *Visual thinking.* Berkeley: University of California Press, 1969.

Berkeley, G. (1710) A treatise concerning the principles of human knowledge. In A. A. Luce and T. E. Jessop (Eds.), *The works of George Berkeley,* Vol. II. London: Thomas Nelson, 1949.

Brewster, D. *Letters on natural magic addressed to Sir Walter Scott.* New York: J. and J. Harper, 1832.

Dement, W., Halper, C., Pivik, T., Ferguson, J., Cohen, H., Henriksen, S., McGarr, K., Gonda, W., Hoyt, G., Ryan, L., Mitchell, G., Barchas, J., and Zarcone, V. Hallucinations and dreaming. In D. Hamburg (Ed.), *Perception and its disorders*. Baltimore: Williams & Wilkins, 1970.

Descartes, R. (1641) Meditations. In E. S. Haldane and G. R. T. Ross (Eds.), *The philosophical works of Descartes,* Vol. I. New York: Dover, 1955.

Gurney, E., Myers, F., Podmore, W. *Phantasms of the living.* Vol. I. London: Trübner, 1886.

Haber, R. N. (Ed.) *Information processing approaches to visual perception.* New York: Holt, Rinehart & Winston, 1969.

Hobbes, T. (1651) *Leviathan: Parts I and II,* H. W. Schneider (Ed.). Indianpolis: Bobbs-Merrill, 1958.

Hume. D. (1739) Hume's treatise of human nature. L. A. Selby-Bigge (Ed.) Oxford: Clarendon Press, 1888.

Locke, J. (1690) *An essay concerning human understanding.* A. C. Fraser (Ed.) New York: Dover, 1959.

Maury, L. F. A. *Le sommeil et les rêves,* (3rd ed.) Paris: 1865.

Penfield, W. *The excitable cortex in conscious man.* Springfield, Ill.: Charles C Thomas, 1958.

Perky, C. W. An experimental study of imagination. *American Journal of Psychology,* 1910, **21,** 422–452.

Segal, S. J. Imagery and reality: Can they be distinguished? In W. Keup (Ed.), *Origin and mechanisms of hallucinations.* New York: Plenum Press, 1970.

Sidgwick, H. (Ed.) Report on the census of hallucinations. *Proceedings of the Society for Psychical Research,* 1894, **26.**

Siegel, R. K. Cannabis-induced visual imagery. A report prepared for the Commission of Inquiry into the Non-medical Use of Drugs, Ottawa, Canada, December 1971.

Siegel, R. K. Visual imagery constants: Drug-induced changes in trained and untrained observers. *Proceedings, 81st Annual Convention, APA,* 1973, 1033–1034. (Transcript prepared by the writer and quoted by permission of the experimenter and subject.)

West, L. J. A general theory of hallucinations and dreams. In L. J. West (Ed.), *Hallucinations.* New York: Grune & Stratton, 1962.

CHAPTER NINE

A CLINICAL AND THEORETICAL OVERVIEW OF HALLUCINATORY PHENOMENA

LOUIS JOLYON WEST, M.D.

The hallucinatory experience has always held a special fascination for mankind. The visions of prophets and seers were divine gifts. The uses of hallucinogenic substances in the remote past were nearly always connected with religious or mystical rituals.

However, the nineteenth century saw a sharp rise, not only in attempts at rational understanding of all human experience, but also in the secularization of the mystical. It is no wonder, then, that the recreational use of hallucinogenic doses of hashish and other drugs had become widespread in the Paris of Louis Philippe, and that French medical science—perhaps the most advanced of that time—brought the phenomena of hallucinations under sharp scrutiny.

Jean Esquirol pointed out the significant relationship between the content of dreams and of hallucinations in 1838; in fact he did much to distinguish hallucinations from other phenomena in psychopathology before his death in 1840. During the following decade, Esquirol's student, Moreau de Tours, described the occurrence of hallucinations under a wide variety of conditions (including psychological and physical stress), as well as the genesis of hallucinations by such drugs as stramonium and hashish (1845). Moreau pointed out that there are basic similarities in the functions of dream and of delirium, a surprisingly modern concept. Brierre de Boismont in 1853 registered many instances of hallucinations associated with intense concentration, or musing, and extensively documented the symptomatic occurrence of hallucinosis in mental disease.

In the last half of the nineteenth century studies of hallucinations continued. Those in France were particularly oriented to the rising discipline of psychopathology, and from this came Pierre Janet's marvelously lucid description of hallucinosis during somnambulism and other dissociative reactions. Interest in hallucinations spread from France to Germany, Austria, and England as the nineteenth century drew toward its close. Brilliant work on perception, including illusions and hallucinations, was carried out by Galton (1883).

During the first three decades of the twentieth century, neurologists and psychiatrists continued their interest in hallucinations. Freud's concepts of conscious and unconscious ideation gave the content of dreams and hallucinations new significance. During the same period, Mourgue in France and Prince in the United States also worked out theories of hallucinations along psychobiological lines.

The medical and scientific literature has continued to contain many references to hallucinatory phenomena, and by 1932 Mourgue found more than a thousand publications to review. During the next 20 years there was an apparent decrease of interest in the subject. Attention revived, however, stimulated considerably by the upsurge of work on hallucinogenic drugs, other approaches to experimental psychopathology (e.g., sensory isolation, sensory overload, sleep deprivation), and the new psychobiology of dreaming in sleep research. In the United States two major symposia on hallucinations were published in 1962 and 1970 (see Preface). Meanwhile the traditional French contribution to this field has continued and is well represented in the recent magnificent two-volume work by Professor Henri Ey (1973); unfortunately, Ey's magnum opus has not yet been translated into English.

Hallucinations were defined by Bleuler as "perceptions without corresponding stimuli from without." Hinsie and Campbell's *Psychiatric Dictionary* (1960) essentially concurs, calling the hallucination "an apparent perception of an external object when no such object is present." Such definitions avoid the question of the hallucinator's belief in the validity of his apparent perception, or his subsequent interpretation of it. Dreams fall within the definition. So do perceptions that are known to be false at the time they are experienced (often called "pseudohallucinations"). With some exceptions it is in this general sense that the term "hallucination" is employed in the essays collected here.

The use of hallucinogenic drugs stimulated both the early studies of hallucinations and the contemporary upsurge of interest in these phenomena. Therefore, special attention should be paid to the hallucinogenic substances and their current status.

HALLUCINOGENIC DRUGS

Hallucinogenic drugs are discussed extensively throughout this book. They may be defined as substances that create gross distortions in perception without causing loss of consciousness when administered in low doses (not toxic overdoses). These distortions frequently include hallucinations. Such compounds also are likely to exert profound effects on mood, thought, and behavior, which may resemble the disturbances seen in naturally occurring psychoses. Certain hallucinogens have been termed "psychotomimetic" or "psychotogenic" on this account.

Scientists and clinicians have sometimes deliberately taken these compounds as a means of enabling themselves to empathize better with severely ill psychiatric patients. Also, in modern experimental psychopathology, it has been hoped that the study of chemically induced model psychoses would lead to a better understanding of phenomena found in clinical practice. Meanwhile, Osmond's term "psychedelic" (mind-realizing) (1956), to describe the seeming effect of hallucinogenic substances to expand perceptual and experiential horizons, heralded a period of interest in their potential therapeutic value. This orientation led to the use of certain hallucinogens (especially LSD) for the treatment of a variety of patients with alcoholism, rigid personality patterns, frigidity, and other problems.

The psychological changes produced by these chemicals have sometimes been described as a "loosening of ego structure," "dissolving of ego boundaries," or "disrupting of ego defenses." Such changes may include the experiencing of thoughts, feelings, and perceptions that are usually unconscious or repressed: that is, ordinarily outside the individual's awareness. Persons who are unusually suggestible, emotionally labile, or unaware of their own reactions and the reactions of others, may become quite disturbed under the influence of such drugs. Feelings of transcendence of ordinary experience, of leaving one's body, and distortions in time and space perception, are also often reported.

Over the past 20 years an increasing number of people have been taking various hallucinogenic substances (marihuana, hashish, lysergic acid diethylamide, psilocybin, mescaline, dimethyltryptamine, etc.) frequently acquired through illegal channels and employed without medical supervision, to participate in special group experiences with cultlike characteristics, or to satisfy other, more private desires. Although these experiences are often recalled by the participants with great enthusiasm, the unintoxicated observer may find little in the way of verbal or nonverbal communication to account for the joyous sense of communion so often described.

Not infrequently (especially with LSD) a severe emotional disturbance accompanies the intoxication. This was originally described by users as a bad trip; the bad trip (or bummer) has subsequently become standard description of any unpleasant experience. On rare occasions bad trips lead into persistent psychotic syndromes (e.g., prolonged delirious reactions, catatonic excitements, chronic hallucinosis, stupors) following the administration of the hallucinogenic substances. Furthermore, some workers have suggested that chronic use of drugs like hashish and LSD may gradually produce major personality changes, often marked by passivity, habit deterioration, and diminution of the highest integrative mental functions. Such a chronic user is often called a "head." A few develop brief episodes of spontaneous hallucinosis in the absence of drugs—the so-called flashbacks—after chronic or even occasional use.

As Winters has shown in his chapter, most of the hallucinogens affect electrical activity of the central nervous system by shifting it toward an alert or arousal pattern. Cortical alerting patterns are consistently found with active congeners, but these are apparently dependent on intact lower-brain-stem cortical connections, whereas nonpsychotogenic congeners can produce an alerting effect even with these connections severed, thus suggesting action at the level of midbrain or higher subcortical sites. Persistent hippocampal electrical changes, resembling those seen in the orienting response, have been found with low dosages of LSD. Winters has described a continuum of reticular cortical excitability from arousal to excitatory-occlusive blocking and disorganization under the influence of certain excitatory drugs, with staring and hallucinatory-like posturing of experimental animals during the maximum drug effect.

These observations conform with the general proposition (see below) that the combination of cortical arousal and impaired or distorted information input produced by LSD leads to emergent awareness of ongoing information processing by the brain (the so-called preconscious stream), which is then appreciated by the individual in experiences ranging from fragmentary images to well-developed scenarios. The combination of LSD's effect as a sensory poison (it alters retinal cell excitability and electrochemical activity at the sensory synapses) and as a cortical arouser may well account for its hallucinogenic characteristics.

Biochemical research in the area of mechanisms of action of the hallucinogens has been growing, but consistent correlates have not yet been established. This may be partly because one is dealing with a large number of biochemical phenomena, perhaps different for each drug in spite of similarities in the induced behavioral changes. In addition, the theoretical biochemical models explored are not easily integrated with behavioral models; the clinician is more likely to feel comfortable when considering formulations from neurophysiology. Such words as "alerting" and "arousal," which appear to have meaning in both the physiological and behavioral realms (even though they may refer to both related and nonrelated phenomena), are not as available in current neurochemical theory.

A number of the hallucinogens apparently undergo metabolic conversions to more active compounds in the body. Studies of enzymes and urinary metabolites suggest that 6-hydroxylation may convert the indole alkylamines to psychoactive metabolites. Mescaline apparently is less active than the products of its oxidative deamination, the trimethoxyphenylethanol and -aldehyde. Psilocybin is hydrolyzed to psilocin quite rapidly. The significance of the oxy- and hydroxy-metabolities of LSD has not yet been fully evaluated.

The major theme in research on the biochemical mechanisms of the action of hallucinogens centers around their effects on various postulated neurohormones or neurotransmitters, including 5-hydroxytryptamine (5-HT or serotonin), norepinephrine, dopamine, histamine, acetylcholine, and certain brain polypeptides.

There are four major chemical classes of hallucinogens: the indole alkaloid derivatives, the piperidine derivatives, the phenylethylamines, and the cannabinols.

INDOLE ALKALOIDS

Tryptamine Derivatives.   The simplest of the indole alkaloids is tryptamine, which has no hallucinogenic effect. However, *N,N*-dimethyltryptamine is found in the Caribbean cahobe bean, chewed by certain natives to produce religious visions, and in the seeds of the domestic morning glory plant, which are sometimes chewed in the United States to produce hallucinatory experiences.

The hydroxylated *N,N*-dimethyltryptamines are also active. Among these are the 4-hydroxy (psilocin) and its phosphorylated derivative psilocybin (found in the ritually employed hallucinogenic mushroom *Psilocybe* spp. of southern Mexico), the 5-hydroxy bufotenine (originally isolated from the skin of toads), its more active 5-methoxy derivative, and the 5-hydroxy-*N,N*-dimethyltryptamine.

Dimethyltryptamine is a psychotogenic at 1 mg per kilogram levels (administered intramuscularly); effective dosages of the other substances vary. Psilocybin and psilocin produce effects in doses of 4 to 8 mg in man. A recent addition to the tryptamine family is α-methyltryptamine, which has been shown to be effective at a dosage level of 20 mg in man.

Harmine, Harmaline, and Ibogaine.   A drug with a three-ring aromatic system (harmine) and its related dihydro derivative (harmaline) are isolated from shrubs and used by South American Indians to produce hallucinatory states. The indole alkaloids with a larger ring structure include ibogaine, used by African natives to remain motionless for as long as two days while stalking. But confusion, drunkenness, and hallucinations are produced if the drug is taken in large doses.

Lysergic Acid Diethylamide (LSD).   The ergot alkaloids were originally isolated from a grass and rye fungus and were thought to be responsible for the convulsions, mental confusion, and gangrenous changes in the lower limbs associated with the periodic outbreaks of St. Anthony's Fire caused by infected rye in the Middle Ages. All ergot alkaloids can be hydrolyzed to lysergic acid, and various derivatives of this compound have been developed. The diethylamide was synthesized by Stoll and Hofmann in 1938; in 1943 it was discovered by Hofmann to be a potent hallucinogen (see Hofmann, 1963).

LSD is more than 8000 times more potent on a dosage basis than mescaline. Less than 0.3 g has caused death in stafus epilepticus of a 7000-pound elephant (West et al., 1962). This remarkable substance is by far the most potent hallucinogenic agent known, effective at levels as low as 1 microgram (0.000001 g) per kilogram of body weight in man. Originally used experimentally to produce an artificial psychosis lasting several hours, it became widely employed during the late 1950s and early 1960s as a psychedelic agent by a variety of practitioners. Soon it became the basis for a cult, was hailed by Dr. Timothy Leary and others as the key to a new life style, and was extensively distributed by a lively underground illegal market to a wide variety of customers in all walks of life.

Prolonged psychopathological reactions to LSD (i.e., effects lasting more than 24 to 48 hours) are usually viewed as latent psychiatric disorders precipitated or exacerbated by the drug experience. The clinician who sees a number of these casualties may well develop a profound mistrust of the drug. Its unpredictability is second only to its extraordinary potency.

PIPERIDINE DERIVATIVES

Belladonna and stramonium, containing anticholinergic compounds such as atropine, scopolamine, and hyoscyamine, have been known for centuries to produce delirious reactions with hallucinations. Cocaine, belonging to the same family, may produce hallucinations and thought disorders if taken in toxic doses.

Recently there has been a considerable increase in frequency of cocaine use in the United States. Cocaine is considered by users to produce an ideal "high" (elation) with prolongation and enhancement of sexual pleasure an important (if uncertain) component. There are few drug users more preoccupied and emotionally involved with their habits than those who use cocaine. They are enthusiastic proselytizers for the drug.

Long defined as a powerfully addicting substance, cocaine is nevertheless quite different from the opiates in this respect. Habituation to, and craving for, cocaine are powerful. However, there is much less development of tolerance to cocaine than to most addicting drugs, even including amphetamines. Furthermore, the withdrawal syndrome, even after prolonged cocaine use, is considerably less dramatic than that seen on withdrawal from opiates.

The cocaine addict's major psychiatric symptoms result from prolonged periods of intoxication by the drug, which is taken repeatedly to sustain the desired sense of exhilaration and euphoria that it produces and, perhaps, to avoid the depression of withdrawal. A toxic picture develops, often with vivid hallucinations (visual, auditory, and tactile) and delusional thought patterns frequently paranoid in content. The mood is usually elevated, although there may be considerable lability, with outbursts of rage and periods of irritability. The user experiences a sense of great physical and mental vigor, together with hyperalertness and loss of need for sleep, which often leads to a clinical picture of exhaustion overridden by the artificial stimulation of the drug. Crawling sensations (formications) on the skin are very common; scratch marks and excoriations are often seen and the user may be convinced that he is being attacked by insects, with both visual and tactile hallucinatory confirmation. Otherwise, the clinical picture is similar in many ways to that seen in amphetamine addicts.

Piperidine derivatives are perhaps not properly termed hallucinogens (as previously defined) because the effects depend on overdosage. However, a number of compounds have been synthesized and tested recently in which the substituted glycolic acid side chains are *meta* instead of *para* to the nitrogen of the piperidine ring. These changes have resulted in a large series of psychotogens including 1-methyl-3-piperidycyclopentylphenylglycolate (the most powerful) and Ditran (the best known). These compounds can cause delusional thinking, disorientation, and hallucinations.

Another recently synthesized piperidine derivative that has generated much interest is phencyclidine. Originally it was thought to be potentially useful as an analgesic, or an agent that prevented sensory impulses from reaching nerve centers. Then its effects in lower doses were found to mimic the primary signs of schizophrenia (including flattened affect, thought disorder, and emotional withdrawal) without the secondary signs, such as delusions and hallucinations. This was considered to be due to a peculiar effect on the sensory synapses. Subsequent work led to other reports of behavioral aberrations induced by phencyclidine, including phenomena resembling those resulting from sensory deprivation.

Related to phencyclidine is a new synthetic anesthetic called ketamine. Chemically it is *dl*, 2-(o-chlorophenyl)-2-(methylamino) cyclohexanone hydrochloride. It has been widely used as a rapidly acting general anesthetic that produces profound analgesia but maintains respiratory and circulatory reflexes and tone. In fact, it appears to stimulate rather than depress the central nervous system, while selectively interrupting association pathways. The net result has been termed "dissociative anesthesia." On emerging from ketamine anesthesia, between 10 and 15% of patients show hallucinatory reactions. These range from pleasant dreamlike states to highly developed visual or polysensual hallucinosis and even, on occasion, delirium. In some instances, there may be an accompanying confusion, excitement, or panic. Once in a while, there is a "flashback" of the emergence experience hours or even days after the induction. Hallucinations caused by ketamine are apparently enhanced by stimulation from the environment during the period of recovery from general anesthesia. A few psychiatrists have begun to use ketamine deliberately for its dissociative effect, to induce abreactions or to overcome psychological blocks or rigidities in the course of psychotherapy. Sometimes there are transient hallucinatory experiences even with lower doses used for this purpose.

There is also evidence of a small but growing diversion of ketamine from legitimate clinical use in anesthesia, and experimental use in psychotherapy, to the recreational drug subculture. Samples have been found in collections of street drugs by police and other authorities. It is possible that a considerable psychological dependence on ketamine may develop if it is used regularly over a long period of time. A case of apparent ketamine addiction with self-administration through frequent intramuscular injections in doses up to 1500 mg per day for many months has been seen by the author. Hallucinosis was not a significant feature in this case, although vivid mental imagery accompanied the intoxication and was considered a desirable effect by the user.

PHENYLETHYLAMINES

Mescaline.   The most significant member of the phenylethylamines is mescaline. Chemically it is trimethoxyphenylethylamine. Named after the Mescalero Apaches, who developed the cult of peyotism, mescaline is the major active component of the buttons from the peyote cactus *Lophophora williamsii*. Peyote buttons are chewed by Indians of a number of tribes in the southwestern United States and Mexico to induce hallucinatory states in their religious rituals.

Mescaline must be administered in high dosages to achieve a full effect. The experience is usually ushered in by 1 to 3 hours of flushing, vomiting, cramps, sweating, and other autonomic phenomena, followed by several hours (to days in some cases) of visual hallucinations (often colorful), depersonalization, and distortions of time.

The remarkable sensory and introspective effects of mescaline have long fascinated psychopathologists; both S. Weir Mitchell and Havelock Ellis reported on personal experiences with it more than 70 years ago. Aldous Huxley, in *The Doors of Perception,* described mescaline intoxication as providing a "voyage to the Antipodes of the mind."

Amphetamines.   Another phenylethylamine group, the amphetamines, should be mentioned in passing, although certain pharmacological properties of these sympathomimetic amines differentiate them from the true hallucinogens. Chronic administration of large amounts of amphetamine may result in a psychosis with delusions, hallucinations, and dangerous behavior, accompanied by distortions in reality-testing. Sleep deprivation, due to the drug's analeptic effects, may contribute to the syndrome. Such reactions usually remit promptly on withdrawal of the amphetamine, although treatment (including phenothiazine medication) may be required.

Adrenochrome.   A trihydroxyindole called adrenochrome (an oxidation product of adrenaline) has been reported by some workers to be hallucinogenic in intravenous dosages of 0.5 mg. Based on these reports (including the supposed discovery of the presence of increased amounts of this and related metabolites in body fluids of psychiatric patients), an adrenochrome theory of schizophrenia was advanced by Hoffer and Osmond (1967). More recent studies have failed to confirm the proposition that adrenochrome is an autogenous psychotogenic substance. However, other more elaborate work on the role of biogenic amines in the human brain may yet prove to be of significance in the search for hallucinogenic or psychotogenic substances related to errors of metabolism in man. Some of these metabolites, such as porphobilingen, which causes neurologic and psychiatric symptoms including hallucinosis in cases of acute intermittent porphyria, are of course already well known.

CANNABINOLS

The cannabinols have been well known since ancient times as intoxicants and perceptual distorters. Called hashish, bhang, kif, marihuana, and various other names, hemp-derived alkaloids produce excitation, vivid imagery, euphoria, and occasionally depression and social withdrawal. More major effects, such as disorientation and true hallucinations, usually occur only with high dosage. The smoking of marihuana (the most active agent of which is tetrahydrocannabinol, or THC) in cigarette form is quite common in the United States. Recent surveys at major American universities indicate that substantial majorities of the student population had used marihuana at least once during the previous year. Several recent books, and the report of the President's Commission (1972), have made all the known pertinent facts about marihuana readily available.

THC has been shown to produce an LSD-like reaction in higher doses, clearly marking it as hallucinogenic. Some tolerance to THC may develop if the drug is used in large amounts over a long period of time. Nevertheless, although the issue of marihuana is often discussed under drug addictions, the substance is not truly addicting.

HALLUCINOGENS AS TREATMENT: THE LSD EXAMPLE

The use of LSD is not decreasing as much as is commonly thought, in spite of stringent restrictions on its distribution. It is easily synthesized from commercially available starting materials, and a definite demand still exists.

It would be an oversimplification to say that all those who are involved in LSD use of one kind or another are necessarily motivated by a pathological desire to withdraw from reality. The experience is too variable and too complex for such an explanation to hold true; contacts with many LSD users convince the observer that their motives range widely. These motives may include an adventuresome desire to seek new experiences, a craving for shared forbidden activity in a group setting to provide a sense of belonging, a manifestation of adolescent and postadolescent rebelliousness, a simple search for sexual opportunities, a genuine attempt to achieve greater self-understanding and self-fulfillment, the exercise of a truly mystical bent in persons with a philosophical orientation toward the transcendental, and, as Blum had described it (1969), the search for fulfillment of a private utopian myth.

In addition, of course, there is the inevitable variety of clinical psychiatric patients who are searching for treatment or relief through the use of chemicals. Their desire may be related not only to a magical hope for cure (enhanced by the reputation of a substance as mysterious and extraordinary as LSD) but also to a very understandable human wish for a short cut to therapeutic insight, with considerable saving of time, money, and suffering.

The physician may be tempted in some cases to go along with the subject's request for one or more treatments with LSD (if, when, and where it is still in use). Before yielding to this temptation, however, he would do well to remember that there are other therapeutic maneuvers, such as hypnosis and the amytal interview, which have been employed to bypass conscious resistance or temporarily modify ego structure, and for which there were once high hopes indeed. Although valuable, these methods have in the long run been found to be of limited general application. There is also a growing impression that for certain individuals, repeated large doses of LSD may lead to apparently irreversible personality changes. Whether it is related to some poorly understood "biochemical scarring" or to the dangers of overexposure to one's own primary process (normally unconscious) ideation, remains to be seen.

LSD therapy has been tried for alcoholism, narcotic addition, homosexuality, criminal behavior, various neurotic symptoms, psychoses, and resistance in psychotherapy. However, its efficacy remains uncertain. This uncertainty, in addition to the rare but disturbing precipitation by LSD of prolonged psychotic reactions, has led to serious questions about its usefulness in treatment and makes its place in the psychopharmaceutical armamentarium dubious to say the least. Much the same could be said about the recent employment of ketamine for the same general purposes. Yet the possibility remains that certain individuals may benefit from controlled psychoticlike experiences in which primary process information floods the awareness to produce a self-realizing effect. Nevertheless, although careful clinical research on the therapeutic potentialities of hallucinogens should probably continue, great caution must be exercised. The unpredictability of response to most of the known hallucinogens probably limits the likelihood of their regular employment in psychiatry. However, not all the classical hallucinogens have been evaluated for therapeutic efficacy and new hallucinogens may soon be synthesized.

SOCIAL USES OF HALLUCINOGENS

There are many ways that drugs can influence mentation, emotion, perception, and action. The extent to which these effects, actual or potential, are deliberately sought out by people relates to their hopes and expectations about the drug, the social context of its use, and the variability of both subjective and behavioral reaction to it. No discussion of hallucinations can be complete without an analysis of the fact that at least some people develop a veritable appetite for hallucinatory experiences and deliberately take drugs to induce hallucinations in themselves.

Motives for self-intoxication with hallucinatory drugs are not uniform; various purposes are admitted by the users. For example, a drug may be used in an attempt to restore something resembling normal function, under conditions of dissatisfaction, disorder, or discomfort. Hallucinogens are not usually prescribed or administered by a health professional although LSD enjoyed a brief vogue as an adjunct to psychotherapy as noted previously. However, nonprofessional use of drugs, including hallucinogens, remains considerable. The chemicals may be self-administered or provided by an amateur would-be helper. Nevertheless they are often intended as a medicament. This may be to meet purely subjective individual needs, or even to relieve or change troublesome interpersonal situations.

Drugs can also be used to improve performance under various conditions. Amphetamine, for example, helps to overcome the effects of fatigue or to diminish hunger. Local anesthetics have been employed for diverse purposes, from permitting injured athletes to play, to diminishing genital sensitivity in males prone to premature ejaculation. Certain South American Indian laborers in the high Andes, who habitually chew the coca leaf for the cocaine effects while working, will not work without it.

Creative artists have sometimes employed hallucinogens or otherwise sought to produce hallucinatory experiences, to enhance their production of artistic work. These efforts do not always succeed, but sometimes, or in some cases, the results are remarkable. Examples can be found in primitive societies and in café society. Other tasks utilizing hallucinogens relate to religious or even medical employment. For example, the Tarahumara Indian shaman uses peyote (mescaline) to induce in himself a vision of what to do for his patients.

Certain drugs (e.g., glutamic acid) in the past were thought to enhance learning ability. Other substances (e.g., puromycin), may block certain types of protein synthesis in neurons, thus preventing learning from taking place. Learning acquired under the influence of a certain drug may be only (or, at least, most effectively) retrieved when the subject resumes that state. This phenomenon of state-dependent learning has been identified with several substances in man, including tetrahydrocannabinol. There is evidence from clinical psychiatry that certain behaviors linked with certain drug-related states (e.g., alcohol with sexual performance) may in some individuals become almost inevitable partners. The current fashions include high correlation of various behaviors (e.g., those related to the performance or appreciation of music) with the regular use of marihuana or hashish.

Drugs that produce pleasurable subjective states have been proved effective as reinforcers of desired behavior under a variety of conditions. They may also reinforce related or conditional behaviors. In man, a clinical example would be the positive desire for intravenous injections, even of saline, by old main-lining addicts. But the opposite also obtains. A well-known use of this effect is the aversion therapy of alcoholism. Severe nausea and vomiting are produced along with the alcoholic drink (through the use of a substance like apomorphine). With this in mind, it is interesting to reflect that regular users of mescaline are not inhibited from repeatedly seeking its hallucinogenic effects, despite powerfully nauseant and emetic reactions.

The purely recreational use of drugs is well known and need not be extensively reviewed here. Alcohol is probably the most universally employed recreational drug, but cannabis has been utilized this way for centuries. Hallucinogens serve more and more for recreational purposes in Western societies at the present time.

The use of sodium amytal or sodium pentothal in narcosynthesis is now well known. Given intravenously, the "truth serum" may cause the subject to reveal things previously concealed even from himself. However, other substances that cause disinhibition—ranging from alcohol to LSD—have been deliberately administered to cause individuals to reveal things about themselves. For example, stimulants were used by Chinese captors during prolonged forceful interrogation (sometimes improperly called "brainwashing") of American flyers during the Korean war, to elicit confessions of germ warfare. In this case it was sleep deprivation that caused impairment of personality function (including hallucinations) and increased suggestibility; the drugs merely enhanced the captors' ability to keep the prisoners awake. Hallucinogens—especially LSD—have thus been used as political weapons. They have also been used dangerously in pranks to alter behavior without the user's knowledge or permission.

Employment of drugs for self-understanding has a great appeal. Dumas did it; Coleridge did it; so did Aldous Huxley. Along with the sense of self-revealtion that hallucinogenic drugs can produce, there is often a feeling of enhanced creativity, of release of the imagination. Through exploration of the inner world, there may come a sense of great comprehension of the entire universe. This is comparable to the spontaenous variety of the same experience, called "cosmic consciousness" by Bucke (1964).

The hallucinogens appear to be unusually powerful in this effect, probably because of the period of enhanced sensation that marks the early part of intoxication, and also because of the relatively good recall of the experience. However, similar experiences can be elicited in a number of other ways, from meditation to hypnosis. Persons going under anesthesia often have a brief moment of immense self-revealtion. High fevers may have the same effect. As a rule the great revelation induced by hallucinogens proves subsequently to be trivial, and the sense of greatly increased creativity fails in reality to produce results.

The user may employ hallucinogens to show his willingness to take risks. Often seen in indiscriminate drug taking by youngsters, the practice works equally well with known substances, as long as they are thought to be dangerous, exciting, or unpredictable in their effects. The use of certain drugs can also represent a youngster's readiness to function as an adult, if adults are believed or known to use the drug in question, or similar drugs. Getting drunk is a traditional rite of passage, especially to prove one's independence or defiance of prohibitions. However, nowadays youthful takers of barbiturates and amphetamines have parents who use them too. LSD, marihuana, and hashish are beginning to join this category. The use of forbidden drugs to defy restraints and controls is characteristic of—but not limited to—adolescents and young adults. Peer pressures are enormously powerful and can easily induce drug taking (as well as almost any other behavior). Much experimentation with hallucinogens, together with many untoward reactions, begins on this basis.

Cultural transition may involve more than mere rebellion. Drug use can symbolize entering a new way of life and casting off the old. LSD exemplified this function during the early days of the Green Rebellion (West and Allen, 1967) and was extolled by Leary and others as the key to the process of "turn on" (take the hallucinogenic drug), "tune in" (develop new awareness), and "drop out" (assume a totally different mode of existence). LSD was credited with facilitating this process, not only through hallucinosis and self-revelation but also through its power to dissolve old inhibitions, fears, or "hang-ups."

Drugs have played a role in such ceremonies since the earliest records of human affairs, going back to ancient Egypt. Alcohol is commonly employed in religious rites (e.g., Christian communion, Jewish seder). The peyote cult (resulting in mescaline hallucinosis) of the Native American Church is well known. Leary's League of Spiritual Discovery still has a few followers, but LSD and other hallucinogens are also employed in mystical contexts by a great many individuals and small groups in various cultures (see chapter by La Barre).

There are even ways in which drugs may be employed as adjuncts to interpersonal manipulation or assault. These depredations have been known to include blackmail (depending on legal situation, reputation of victim, etc.); addiction or habituation (supplier manipulates the user); kidnaping (the drug renders the victim helpless or more vulnerable); "Manson-ism" (in which a strong-willed psychopath manipulates others made suggestible by drugs or, as "acid heads," suffering from poor judgment and passivity); law enforcement (when police or narcotics agents force drug users to become informers); and, as previously mentioned, political or military intelligence and counterintelligence (agent puts LSD in victim's beer, then gets him to defect or reveal secrets).

There have been many battles won because soldiers were taken by surprise when drunk. George Washington won such a victory. However, the corruption of whole armies, or even countries, by drugs is presently being discussed. China, with its history of victimization by British commercial interests through the use of opium, was recently itself accused of employing cheap hashish and heroin to weaken the American military force in Vietnam. Regardless of whether the charge is true, the potential danger exists for drugs, including hallucinogens, to be misused in this way.

The role of drugs in the exercise of internal political control is also coming under increasing discussion. Control can be imposed either through prohibition or supply. The total or partial prohibition of drugs gives government considerable power, because the mechanisms necessary for controlling drugs can provide leverage for other types of control. An example would be the selective application of drug laws permitting immediate search, or "no knock" entry, against selected components of the population, such as members of certain minority groups or political organizations.

But a government could also supply drugs to help control a population. This method, foreseen by Aldous Huxley in Brave New World (1932), has the governing element employing drugs selectively to manipulate the governed in various ways. A country that requires maximum effort from its total work force (e.g., China today) must take stern measures to eliminate all drug abuse, but a more affluent nation can afford to tolerate large numbers of drug users in various circumstances.

To a large extent the numerous rural and urban communes, which provide great freedom for private drug use and where hallucinogens are widely used today, are actually subsidized by our society. Their perpetuation is aided by parental or other family remittances, welfare and unemployment payments, and benign neglect by the police. In fact, it may be more convenient and perhaps even more economical to keep the growing numbers of chronic drug users (especially of the hallucinogens) fairly isolated and also out of the labor market, with its millions of unemployed. To society, the communards with their hallucinogenic drugs are probably less bothersome—and less expensive—if they are living apart, than if they are engaging in alternative modes of expressing their alienation, such as active, organized, vigorous political protest and dissent. Meanwhile the communards themselves use drugs like cannabis to foster social stability in a setting of relative nongovernance. When tensions or hostilities arise, marihuana or hashish is quickly produced and passed around; the anger literally goes up in smoke (McGlothlin and West, 1968).

The hallucinogens presently comprise a moderate but significant portion of the total drug problem in Western society. The foregoing may provide a certain frame of reference against which not only the social but also the clinical problems created by these drugs can be considered. Before proceeding with further psychiatric considerations, however, a theoretical perspective is in order.

THE HALLUCINATORY EXPERIENCE: THEORETICAL REFLECTIONS

The first major neurophysiological disinhibition theory of dreams and hallucinations was proposed long ago by the great neurologist Hughlings Jackson (see Taylor et al., 1958). Jackson was interested in the relationship of sensory input to the *form* of the hallucinatory experience. In recent years Evarts was one of the first to note a possible relationship between the disruption of information input and the very *occurrence* of disinhibition phenomena of the special senses (particularly in the visual system) in his early experiments with LSD (Evarts, 1954, 1957). There was an obvious connection to be drawn from Evarts's experiments and those of Hebb and his co-workers (see Heron et al., 1953) on the depatterning of sensory input with resultant hallucinosis in many subjects.

In 1958 I proposed a "perceptual release" theory of hallucinations, drawing heavily on Jackson and Evarts, and resting on two fundamental assumptions. The first, generally accepted and well stated by Gerard (1955), is that life experiences affect the brain in such a way as to leave permanent neural traces (templates or engrams). Ideas and images derive from these traces. They provide the neurophysiological substrate of memory, thought, imagination, and fantasy. Papez (1937) suggested, and MacLean (1955a) and others elucidated, how the emotions or affects associated with these intellectual and perceptual functions are mediated by the limbic system or "visceral brain," thus permitting a dynamic interplay between perception and emotion through transactions that take place largely at unconscious levels.

Magoun (1952) and others (Jasper and Ajmone-Marsan, 1952; MacLean, 1955b) have shown that insofar as conscious awarnesss can now be explained neurophysiologically, it is regulated through a general arousal process mediated by the ascending midbrain reticular activating system. Analyses of the relationships of hallucinations to neurological syndromes, and to brain stimulation experiments in neurosurgical patients, have shown the importance of the temporal lobes and such functionally relevant areas as the cingulate gyrus (Baldwin, 1962).

The second basic assumption is that the total personality, as represented by structural, instinctive, and acquired functions, is best understood in terms of the constant interplay of psychobiological forces that continually emanate from inside and outside the individual. This dynamic, constantly changing field of forces is in fact one way to define the individual (Lewin, 1951). It may also be usefully conceptualized in terms of transactions among systems, and information theory. In any case, an integrating and organizing influence on memory traces is undoubtedly exercised by the constant flow of information, both new and stored, that continually affects the patterns whereby sensory engrams are woven into images, fantasies, dreams, or hallucinations, and also the emotions associated with these patterns. Thus we would expect that cultural factors and psychodynamic factors would be of major importance in determining the actual content and emotional meaning of hallucinations, which predictably interact with psychobiologically determined form-constants as explicated by Siegel and Jarvik in their chapter. Such a concept moves us to employ a phenomenological rather than a mechanistic approach to the hallucinatory experience.

The human brain is bombarded constantly by sensory impulses. Most of these sensations are excluded from consciousness in a dynamically selective fashion. The exclusion is accomplished through the exercise of integrative psychobiological mechanisms that permit the small field of awareness to hold selected areas of mental content in clear focus. In this way, the work of concentration may be defined in part as a scanning and screening process, serving to keep a tremendous amount of potentially available information *out* of the sphere of awareness. When material ordinarily or normally expected to be associated with conscious information is blocked off, or conversely appears out of context, we may speak of it as *dissociated* (see below).

During normal wakefulness the input of information through the sensory pathways serves a basic function in maintaining the organization of this scanning and screening activity. As long as it is working well, scanning and screening exclude from awareness not only information from the internal and external environments that is undesired, of low priority, or relatively static, but also the vast bulk of information already stored within the brain in the form of perceptual traces, their derivations and interrelations. Some of this information can be brought into awareness in the service of memory. Many children and a few adults can mobilize and scan perceptual memory traces with great clarity, thereby permitting eidetic imagery. Such images might be considered deliberate, self-generated, healthy (although not statistically "normal") hallucinations.

What happens when sensory input is diminished or impaired? Its *organizing* effect on the screening and scanning mechanism decreases. Simultaneously, as a rule, there is a decrease in the *stimulating* effect of sensory input on the ascending midbrain reticular activating system (through neural connections to the reticular formation from the major sensory pathways as they course upward through the brain stem), and as a result arousal and awareness tend to diminish. But under a variety of circumstances it is possible for great reduction or impairment of sensory input to be accompanied by considerable cortical arousal, thus allowing a residual awareness of significant degree. In such instances, when the usual information input level no longer suffices completely to inhibit their emergence, perceptual traces may be "released" and reexperienced, either in familiar or new—even bizarre—combinations. Some people are able to control this perceptual release to an astonishing degree. Coleridge (1912) described this ability in himself (presumably even without benefit of opium), saying "My eyes make pictures when they are shut."

Released perceptions ordinarily do not become conscious with hallucinatory vividness. There appear to be two prerequisites for their discrete emergence into clear awareness. First, there must be a sufficient general level of arousal for awareness to occur. Second, the particular perception-bearing circuits must reverberate sufficiently to command awareness.

Under certain circumstances the latter conditions can be brought about through direct stimulation of the circuits. Penfield and Jasper (1954) described this in cases of focal temporal-lobe seizures (occurring either spontaneously or under the neurosurgeon's electrode), producing clear, vivid scenariolike imagery that the patient could readily describe. But under other circumstances, perceptual release usually accompanies a change in the flow of forces that ordinarily dominate consciousness and normally help to inhibit the emergence of previously recorded percepts. These inhibiting forces usually include a significant flow of information to the brain from the environment (both external and intracorporeal), possessing certain quantitative, qualitative, and time-related characteristics. If this inflow is significantly altered (as a result of changes anywhere along the line, from external sensory environment to internal sensory neuronal transmission), and at the same time cortical arousal is sufficient to provide awareness, then that sphere of awareness will be occupied by information already in the system. This information can be said to be "released" or "disinhibited" through the impaired integrative or inhibiting power of normal sensory input.

The theory thus holds that a sustained level and variety of sensory input normally is required to inhibit the emergence of percepts or memory traces from within the brain itself. When effective (attention-commanding) sensory input decreases below a certain threshold, there may be a release into awareness of previously recorded perceptions through the disinhibition of the brain circuits that represent them. If a general level of cortical arousal persists to a sufficient degree, these released perceptions can enter awareness and be experienced as fantasies, illusions, visions, dreams, or hallucinations. The greater the level of arousal, the more vivid the hallucinations will be.

In 1958 I presented an oversimplified but perhaps helpful model of these conditions which Horowitz, earlier in this book, was kind enough to cite. A man is standing at a closed, clear glass window opposite a fireplace, looking out at his garden in the sunset. He sees only the outside world. As it becomes darker outside, however, images of the objects in the room behind him can be seen reflected dimly in the window glass. For a time he may see either the garden (if he gazes into the distance) or the reflection of the room's interior (if he focuses on the glass a few inches from his face). Night falls, but the fire still burns brightly in the fireplace and illuminates the room. The watcher now sees in the glass a reflection of the interior of the room behind him, which *appears* to be outside the window. This vision becomes dimmer as the fire dies down, and, finally, when it is dark both outside and within, nothing more is seen. However, if the fire flares up from time to time, the visions in the glass reappear.

In perceptual release, the daylight (sensory input) is reduced while the interior illumination (general level of arousal) remains bright, and images originating within the rooms of our brains may be perceived as though they came from outside the windows of our senses.

The ways in which the reticular formation of the brain act as a regulatory and integrating system for these relationships are still under study. However, as the periodic changes in cortical arousal during sleep and dreams are apparently mediated at least in part by reticular activity, the visions of dreaming may help to define the proposed model. As a person falls asleep, he passes (usually quite swiftly) through a zone in which awareness of the environment is decreased but the level of cortical arousal (which may fall less rapidly) remains sufficiently high to permit some appreciation of reality. Under these circumstances occur the hypnagogic phenomena.

Common hypnagogic hallucinations may be visual (scenes from the previous few hours often appear) or auditory (one's name is called, or a knock is heard at the door). A frequently occurring kinesthetic hypnagogic hallucination is the sensation of loss of support or balance, usually accompanied by a fragmentary dream of missing a step or stumbling, and followed immediately by a jerking reflex recovery movement that may even jolt the sleeper back into wakefulness.

With progressive loss of contact with the environment, sleep begins and is at first dream-free, with large slow waves on the EEG (Stage IV).

Stimuli either from without (e.g., noise or cold) or from within (e.g., dyspepsia, anxiety), interact with the basic 90-minute periodic fluctuation in the sleep state, to bring the sleeper into the zone for spontaneous perceptual release (emergent Stage I EEG with rapid eye movement or REM), in which case dreaming will take place. This occurs several times every night in most normal people, so that perhaps 15 or 20% of an average person's eight hours of sleep is taken up with five or six dreams, shorter early in the night, longer toward the end (see chapter by Hartmann). At the time of awakening, the sleeper again returns through the zone of perceptual release, often experiencing dreams that increase in intensity, and perhaps having hypnopompic hallucinations as he emerges from sleep.

An analogy might be that our dreams, like the stars, are there all the time. We do not often see the stars because by day the sun shines too brightly, and by night we sleep. Suppose, however, that during the day there is an eclipse of the sun, or that we choose to be watchful a while after sunset or a while before sunrise, or that we awaken from time to time on a clear night to look at the sky; then the stars, like our dreams, though often forgotten, may always be seen.

The late Lawrence S. Kubie frequently referred to the concept of a continuous information-processing activity, the "proconscious stream," which flows 24 hours a day under the influence of both conscious and unconscious forces, and constitutes the matrix of dream content. The dream is an experience during which, for a few minutes, the individual has some awareness of the stream of data being processed. Hallucinations in the waking state are undoubtedly to some extent the same.

What of the relationship between level of arousal in the brain and information processing during the waking state? The functions of consciousness apparently reach an optimal point in relation to level of arousal, above which they disorganize progressively as arousal increases excessively. The presence of marked arousal (caused, e.g., by extreme panic or by chemical stimulation of the brain) is accompanied by a picture of marked disturbance of concentration. Again, contact with external reality is impaired, this time by excessive input (input overload), which "jams the circuits." Under these conditions spontaneously dissociative phenomena may occur. Finally, as arousal reaches overwhelming proportions, the hallucinations of full-blown delirium or psychotic excitement may appear with frightening vividness, intensity, and emotional accompaniment. This relationship between arousal and a variety of functions has also been formulated by Burch and Greiner (1960).

In sensory isolation experiments, information input by way of the special senses is artificially depatterned or reduced. If the subject remains alert, he is likely to experience vivid fantasies and perhaps hallucinations. The findings of Vernon and Hoffman (1956) and of other investigators suggest that a slight amount of stimulation of the hallucinated modality enhances the likelihood of the hallucination's appearance. If incoming stimuli are markedly reduced and the level of arousal is high, the hallucinations should be expecially vivid and emotionally charged. Of course numerous factors encountered in experimental sensory isolation situations can influence the experience.

In 1883 Galton declared, "The cases of visions following protracted wakefulness are well-known, and I have collected a few of them myself." Progressive sleep loss appears to cause a decreased capacity for integrating perceptions of the external environment, as described by West et al., (1962). Hallucinations probably occur inevitably if wakefulness is sufficiently prolonged, and the presence of excessive arousal due to anxiety is likely to hasten or enhance hallucinatory production. The disorganizing effect of excessive wakefulness has been exploited in extorting false confessions from prisoners, many of whom experience hallucinations during prolonged sleep deprivation. Other experiences with sleep-deprived subjects suggest that fleeting hallucinations begin after two or three days without sleep, and that after 100 to 200 sleepless hours a progressive personality disorganization will develop gradually and be marked by periods of hallucinosis and, in some cases, by a reappearance of previously existing psychopathology (Brauchi and West, 1959).

Many other examples of hallucinations related to diminution or impairment of sensory input will come to mind from clinical experience. Bartlett (1951) compares visual hallucinations in cases of progressive blindness from cataracts with phantom limb syndromes, citing "absence of normal stimuli from the periphery [as] being an important factor in both syndromes." It is well known that auditory hallucinations may occur in individuals having a progressive loss of hearing, musical perceptions being not uncommon (Rosanski and Rosen, 1952). A most interesting case of combined visual and auditory hallucinations in a patient with progressive cataracts and otosclerosis has been observed by the author. Hallucinations of the phantom limb are probably normal phenomena, arising as the projection of an experientially established template in the absence of long-accustomed input from the missing part. The relative differences in significance of usual sensations from such a part may cause the phantom to be distorted in proportion or in size.

Multiple causes undoubtedly play an *additive* role in bringing about the symptoms of the major psychoses, which are in some ways like waking dreams, and in which hallucinations (usually auditory) may figure prominently. Furthermore, subhallucinogenic doses of LSD will quickly produce hallucinations when administered to moderately sleep-deprived subjects or to subjects in a state of sensory isolation. Continuing attempts, such as that by Deckert (1964), are being made to discover how bioelectric patterns in dreams (e.g., electroencephalographic changes, rapid lateral eye movement, subvocal speech activity, galvanic skin changes) compare with those occurring in sensory isolation, sleep deprivation, LSD intoxication, hypnotically induced hallucinations, and clinical psychiatric syndromes featuring hallucinosis. Certainly in cases of acute psychotic reactions with hallucinosis, we can see combinations of factors at work: genetic and cultural predispositions; excessive arousal with anxiety or panic; autointoxication through stress, exhaustion, sleep loss, hemoconcentration, and the like; and dissociative mechanisms that impair or distort the processing of information from a frightening or threatening interpersonal environment or intrapsychic conflict.

Finally, we return to hallucinations produced by chemicals. These may derive from metabolic disturbances inside of the body or be introduced from the external environment. The chemicals need not always be hallucinogens per se. Dramatic abreactions of intense experiences from the recent past, complete with hallucinatory recall, can be brought about (in narcosynthesis) by intravenous administration of barbiturates in low doses, which reproduce the conditions of perceptual release. Hallucinations during induction of (and emergence from) general anesthesia are well known and can be explained on the same basis. Ketamine, or course, is in a class by itself in this respect.

It is not necessary that an hallucinogenic chemical impair sensory input specifically by *decreasing* synaptic transmission through raising the resistance to the passage of electrochemical impulses. It might just as easily produce its effects by markedly *increasing* synaptic transmission, thus disrupting the orderly input of information and resulting in a "jamming of the circuits." This effect can also be achieved by information input overload of the type described by Miller (1960).

PSYCHOGENESIS AND PSYCHOPATHOLOGY OF HALLUCINATIONS

Although hallucinations may be explained in neurophysiological terms by a perceptual release type of theory, this alone is insufficient to account for the total phenomenology of hallucinations: it tends to picture the human subject in too passive a mode. From the psychodynamic viewpoint, a much more active process is also involved, whereby to a lesser or greater extent the individual participates in creating his own hallucinations. Thus the psychiatric formulation of hallucinatory phenomenology is often put forward in terms of "dissociation."

The four classical dissociative reactions, generally listed under the neuroses, are fugue, amnesia, somnambulism, and multiple personality. However, many other dissociated experiences and behaviors are appropriately classified as dissociative phenomena within the framework of modern dynamic psychopathology. We also speak of dissociation from awareness of expected sensations from appropriate stimuli (as in conversion reactions involving apparent sensory loss, or in hypnotic anesthesia), and the opposite experience, which is the dissociated sense of perception *without* appropriate external or internal stimuli (as in *déjà vu,* feelings of unreality, and, of course, hallucinations of the special senses).

Pierre Janet introduced the concept of dissociation and used hypnosis to explore it. Ever since that time, there have been historical connections between dissociation, hallucination, and hypnotism, which have played key roles in the evolution of contemporary psychodynamic concepts. While considering dissociation, we must hold clearly in mind the phenomenology of hypnosis—including both hallucinations and "negative hallucinations" (which are failures to perceive things that *are* present)—and the classical psychopathology of hysteria that hypnosis can often reproduce. All are undoubtedly manifestations of the same fundamental psychophysiological mechanisms. Additional connections will be found in the study of epilepsy, which involves some similar problems of consciousness; of anxiety, which may provoke the increased exercise of dissociation as a psychodynamic defense mechanism in any given case regardless of diagnosis; and of schizophrenia, in which disturbances of association constitute an important and usually early component of symptomatology. In all these conditions hallucinations may occur.

The basic theory of dissociation originated with Charcot's teaching in 1882 that the stream of consciousness breaks up into diverse elements in cases of hysteria. Janet's famous inquiries in 1889 into clinical instances of somnambulism, with elaborate dreamlike hallucinosis followed by amnesia, firmly connected the conception of dissociation with that of hallucination. This connection has persisted to the present day.

Psychophysiological Basis of Dissociation.   Although there are traditional definitions of dissociation as a mental mechanism, it has not been a lucid concept; it has tended to merge with repression or conversion or both. I have found it more useful to consider dissociation in terms of information processing. If this is accepted, a number of terms (dissociation, suppression, repression, co-conscious, etc.) can be characterized as special instances of a general psychophysiological mechanism for dealing with information.

This master mechanism (or group of mechanisms) of the central nervous system is responsible simultaneously and continuously for (1) scanning and screening incoming information, (2) processing both new and old information in a way that serves to modulate the state and content of conscious awareness, (3) integrating or associating new information with previously stored information, and (4) controlling information output in the form of behavioral responses.

In the past 30 years an increasing fund of data concerning the physiology of awareness has made it possible to conceptualize the clinical dissociative reactions as pathological exercises of these normal functions. Whatever one may choose to call the mechanisms involved (perhaps "integrative" would be an appropriate term as used earlier in this chapter), they subserve the requirements for scanning and screening information, modulating the sphere of awareness moment by moment, controlling the processes of associative thought, relating perception to mentation, and relating both to action.

As noted previously, only a minute portion of total available information (from the external environment, from within the body, and from the brain's own stores) can be held in awareness at any given time. Concentration, reality-testing, and simple survival require the exercise of scanning and screening mechanisms to keep the searchlight of awareness focused on selected areas of psychic content and to keep everything else out of awareness. Because hypnosis has long been used as a laboratory technique to study this process, its relationship to dissociation and the production of hallucinations is worthy of note.

A complete explication of dissociation and the clinical dissociative reactions, many of which may be accompanied by hallucinations, is available elsewhere (West, 1967). However, let us be reminded that the mystic achieves hallucinations by gaining control of his own dissociative mechanisms, perhaps through autohypnosis. Such individuals can accomplish an astonishing withdrawal of contact from the environment by prolonged intense concentration (e.g., gazing into the ink pool). The hallucinations occurring under such circumstances may be of the scenario type, in which the subject's soul seems to leave his body either to view himself (autoscopic hallucination) or to be transported to new surroundings. Or the hallucinations may take the form of visual imagery endowed with unique meaning. For example, the *yantra* is a special visual hallucination of a colored, geometrical image related to the more general mandala form described by Jung. It appears at a level of trance corresponding to that of *samādhi* in yoga. It has been explained by Ahlenstiel and Kauffman (1952) as "an adequate expression of the ecstacy which cannot be translated into concepts." The universality of designs and patterns in human hallucinatory experience is very likely related to structural aspects of the human information receiving and processing systems.

Ordinary experimental hypnotic and posthypnotic suggestions of hallucinations are well known. The hypnotically entranced subject (who might be described as a person in a controlled dissociative state) may on occasion also experience spontaneous hallucinations in the absence of specific suggestions (Schneck, 1953).

Prolonged monotony or fixation of attention may lead to diminished responsiveness to the environment, with a general effect similar to that of absolute reduction of stimulation or of hypnotic trance. Under these conditions occur spontaneous dissociative phenomena such as "highway hypnosis." Similar phenomena that occur among flyers have been called "fascination" or "fixation." During prolonged, monotonous flight, normal flyers may experience visual, auditory, and kinesthetic hallucinations. For example, the pilot may suddenly feel that the plane is in a spin or a dive or that it is upside down. Such a kinesthetic hallucination can be so vivid that the pilot will attempt "corrective" maneuvering of the aircraft, with potentially tragic results. The designation of such episodes as "vertigo" in the literature on aviation medicine is incorrect and misleading.

Although the role of expectation or mental set is still being studied in relation to perception, there can be no doubt of the significance of these factors in determining the nature of hallucinated objects. It may be that the psychophysiologic basis for *recognition* requires the subconscious preparation of a perceptual template (e.g., a previously seen object) against which to match the incoming information for identification, significance, and meaning in terms of past experience. If some real but unrecognized object is present, the perceptual template or engram emerges as an illusion. In the absence of a reality object, it is perceived as an hallucination. This accounts for the specificity of collective visions when they occur. For example, among shipwreck survivors floating at sea, a shouted suggestion may cause everyone to see the same nonexistent ship projected against the blank screen of empty sea and sky (Anderson, 1942).

CLINICAL APPLICATIONS

In dealing with a possibly hallucinating patient, the clinician must be alert to various dimensions. Is the patient denying that he hallucinates when in fact he does? Or pretending to hallucinate when he does not? Is a single sense modality involved or are several? Exactly what is the content of the hallucinated experience? How real does it seem? How vivid? From what source? With what associated ideas, emotions, or feelings? When do the experiences occur—by day or by night? Alone or with others? Constantly or intermittently? In relation to sleep or not? How much insight does the patient have into the unreality of his hallucinations? How much do they affect his judgment? To what extent is he likely to act, and in what way, as a consequence of the hallucinatory experience?

In clinical practice, hallucinations may occur in one or several of the sensory modalities. Auditory hallucinations are the most common, but any of the major senses may be involved. Regardless of the sensory mode, the most frequent types of hallucination are the most undifferentiated: murmuring or nonspecific buzzing sounds in the ears; flashes of light or impressions of darting movements in the periphery of vision; faint, unfamiliar odors; slight bad taste in the mouth; mild parasthesias, and the like. The high frequency of auditory hallucinations in connection with the major psychoses emphasizes the role of hearing in maintaining a constant orientation to the environment. Voices are the most frequently reported *specific* manifestations, with the words being heard either in one or both ears and seeming to emanate either from outside or inside the head. The voices may be familiar or unfamiliar, friendly or hostile, and the message they transmit vague or highly specific. The content of auditory hallucinations is usually associated with concomitant delusional patterns of thought. In other words, a person with delusions of grandeur may hear voices praising him or providing instructions from God; delusions of persecution or of worthlessness are more likely to be accompanied by voices expressing threats, accusations, or contempt.

Visual hallucinations, like those of hearing, often accompany diseases of the sense organs. Progressive loss of either hearing or vision is likely to lead to an increased preoccupation with the affected mode and to hallucinatory experiences. These may be related to the pathological process, to the diminished sensory input, or to both. Visual illusions and hallucinations appear in states of confusion, impaired orientation, or even religious ecstasy. Here again the general mood, and any concurrent pattern of delusional thought, are very likely to influence the hallucinatory content. The roles of culture and of expectation or mental set are also of great significance. For example, Indians taking mescaline in ceremonial rites of the Native American Church used to have visions of the gods appropriate to their animistic religion; in modern times they are likely to see figures having significance to Christianity.

Hallucinations of smell are usually (although not always) unpleasant. Some seem to emanate from the patient's own body and are likely to be tied in with semantic delusions. Others appear to emanate from without and are often suspected by the patient to be manifestations of a plot to annoy or attack him. Epileptic auras may involve any sensory experience; hallucinations of smell should lead the clinician to suspect and rule out an irritative lesion of the uncus.

Sometimes hallucinations of taste accompany those of smell, regardless of whether related to organic disease. Just as the patient is likely to suspect that an hallucination of smell may come from "gas being piped into the room," the hallucinated strange taste is frequently suspected of being caused by "someone trying to poison my food."

There are significant differences between experimentally produced hallucinations and those occurring spontaneously in psychiatric patients. For example, visual hallucinations in the psychoses often appear suddenly and without prodromata; those of mescaline and LSD are heralded by unformed visual sensations, simple geometric figures, and alterations of color, size, shape, movement, and number. The stereotyped visual forms, or form-constants, almost invariably present during the development of certain drug syndromes, are rarely seen in symptomatic hallucinations of the major psychoses and virtually never in hysterical or dissociative reactions.

In schizophrenia, hallucinations often occur in a psychological setting of intense affective need or delusional preoccupation. These features either are spontaneously reported or can be obtained through brief questioning. But mescaline and LSD hallucinations appear to develop independently of such emotional conditions, or else they produce their own affective alterations.

In schizophrenia, hallucinations may be superimposed on a visual environment that appears otherwise normal; more rarely, they may appear with the remainder of the environment excluded. The hallucinogenic drugs produce diffuse distortions of the existing visual world along with the hallucinatory experience. Schizophrenic visual hallucinations are generally seen with the eyes open; those of mescaline and LSD are more readily seen with the eyes closed or in darkened surroundings.

In searching for schizophrenic patients who experience true visual hallucinations, one is struck by their rarity, compared with those who have auditory hallucinations. According to a rough estimate of the frequency of visual hallucinations on the receiving wards of large state hospitals, such phenomena are experienced by fewer than 5% of schizophrenic patients. Other studies suggest a higher incidence, but there is no doubt that visual hallucinations in schizophrenia occur far less often than do auditory hallucinations.

Feinberg (1962) offers the following possible explanations:

1. That the neurophysiologic system underlying visual memory and images is less susceptible to derangement by, or involvement in, the schizophrenic process than is the system underlying verbal memory and images.

2. That stimulation in the auditory environment is more fleeting and transitory than is that of the visual world. Relatively prolonged periods of exposure to the same stimuli are common in vision, but infrequent in audition. The visual background is one of patterned stimuli. The auditory background is, in general, less structured. Thus the latter may be considered more ambiguous, hence more open to misinterpretation, or reconstruction, in the direction of affective need.

3. That the information that must be communicated, for delusional reasons, is more readily expressed in words than in pictures. It is easier to hear "You are a wicked person," or "You are a specially chosen person," than it is to conjure up a visual image which would convey the same message.

Morgenbesser (1962) has suggested that hallucinations in schizophrenia may represent, in part, an attempt to find support for delusional beliefs through sense data. He hypothesizes that the schizophrenic is confronted with a situation in which a delusional idea is primary. Unable to give up this idea, but recognizing the absence of supporting evidence, the patient manufactures the required evidence through hallucinations. In this sense, hallucinations might be considered restitutional in that they restore the normal relationship between sense data and belief. However, this explanation would not encompass hallucinatory phenomena that appear to be unrelated to delusional material, or those that seem to occur prior to the establishment of delusions.

Another possibility is that auditory data may be simpler and more effective than pictorial data for supporting delusional beliefs. It is noteworthy that the majority of visual hallucinations in schizophrenics are of stereotyped content, often religious, usually obvious in their implications, and generally requiring little interpretation.

In a more psychoanalytic vein, Isakower (1939) has suggested that auditory hallucinations are preeminent because they represent criticism by the superego. The superego develops through the incorporation into the psychic structure of normative values previously expressed through the verbal prohibitions or commands of the parents. In hallucinations, the superego speaks with these voices to an individual beset by the eruption into consciousness of intolerable impulses.

It is by no means certain, however, that verbally expressed censure is more potent than censure that is visually perceived, as in facial expressions and gestures. Furthermore, Modell (1958) has objected to Isakower's formulation on the grounds that hallucinated voices frequently give helpful advice or assist in decisions, and in this manner represent executive, or ego, rather than superego functions.

An alternative explanation, offered by Feinberg (1962) is that the early traumata or events responsible for the development of schizophrenic reactions in later life occur at a critical period of development, and this period coincides with the organization of that aspect of the ego concerned with verbal functioning or language mastery. In such discussions "ego" is used according to its specialized psychoanalytic sense, including the mental processes that mediate between inner needs and external reality. The perceptual apparatus is particularly important in this regard. The critical periods hypothesized by Feinberg occur between the first and third years of life. Such a hypothesis requires an assumption that the organization of visual functions of the ego is largely completed by the end of the first year. Recent work on dreams in infants appears to support this possibility.

Hallucinations may occur in relation to a great variety of physical and mental illness. In the practice of neuropsychiatry all major catagories—character and behavior disorders, neuroses, "functional" psychoses, and organic brain syndromes—provide illustrations. Without being comprehensive (which would require a monograph in itself), a sound general textbook of psychiatry will contain literally scores of examples. This is particularly true if the orientation of the textbook is based on a tradition of great attention to psychopathological detail.

For the purposes of this chapter it is not necessary to recapitulate all these examples. Instead, let me simply say in closing that the general theoretical formulations of perceptual release and of dissociation cited herein have been useful to me in comprehending the hallucinatory experiences of subjects or patients, experimental or clinical, in health or disease, regardless of the specific conditions or factors that have produced the hallucinations. One can ask no more of theory than this: that it prove useful, to be employed until new data and new insights lead either to its modification or to its replacement by newer theory, even more useful than that which has gone before.

REFERENCES

Ahlenstiel, H., and Kauffman, R. Über die mandalaform des "linearen Yantra." *Schweizerische Zeitschrift für Psychologie und ihre Anwendungen,* 1952, **11,** 188–197.

Anderson, E. W. Abnormal mental states in survivors, with special reference to collective hallucinations. *Journal of the Royal Naval Medical Society,* 1942, **28,** 361–377.

Baldwin, M. Hallucinations in neurologic syndromes. In L. J. West (Ed.), *Hallucinations.* New York: Grune & Stratton, 1962.

Bartlett, J. E. A. A case of organized visual hallucinations in an old man with cataract, and their relation to the phenomena of phantom limb. *Brain,* 1951, **74,** 363–373.

Blum, R. H. *Society and drugs.* San Francisco: Jossey-Bass, 1969.

Boismont, A. B. de. *Hallucinations: Or, the rational history of apparitions, visions, dreams, ecstasy, magnetism, and somnambulism.* Philadelphia: Lindsay and Blakiston, 1853.

Brauchi, J. T., and West, L. J. Sleep deprivation. *Journal of the American Medical Association,* 1959, **171,** 1–14.

Bucke, R. M. *Cosmic consciousness (or illumination),* (22nd ed.). New York: Dutton, 1964.

Burch, N. R., and Greiner, T. H. A bioelectric scale of human alertness: Concurrent recordings of the EEG and GSR. In L. J. West and M. Greenblatt (Eds.), *Explorations in the physiology of emotions* (April 1957). Psychiatric Research Report No. 12, 1960.

Charcot, J. M. Sur les divers états nerveux déterminés par l'hypnotisation chez les hystériques. *Comptes-Rendus Hebdomadiares des Séances de l'Académie des Sciences,* 1882, **94,** 403–405.

Coleridge, S. T. A day dream. In E. H. Coleridge (Ed.), *Complete poetical works.* New York: Oxford University Press, 1912.

Deckert, G. H. Pursuit eye movements in the absence of a moving visual stimulus. *Science,* 1964, **143,** 1192–1193.

Esquirol, J.E.D. *Des maladies mentales.* Paris: Baillière, 1838.

Evarts, E. V. Personal communication, 1954.

Evarts, E. V. A review of the neuro-physiological effects of lysergic acid diethylamide (LSD) and other psychotomimetic agents. *Annals of the New York Academy of Sciences,* 1957, **66,** 479–495.

Ey, H. *Traité des hallucinations.* Paris: Massou, 1973.

Feinberg, I. A comparison of the visual hallucinations in schizophrenia with those induced by mescaline and LSD-25. In L. J. West (Ed.), *Hallucinations.* New York: Grune & Stratton, 1962.

Galton, F. *Inquiries into the human faculty and its development.* London: Macmillan, 1883.

Gerard, R. W. The biological roots of psychiatry. *American Journal of Psychiatry,* 1955, **112,** 81–90.

Heron, W., Bexton, W. H., and Hebb, D. O. Cognitive effects of a decreased variation in the sensory environment. *American Psychologist,* 1953, **8,** 366.

Hinsie, L. E., and Campbell, R. J. *Psychiatric dictionary.* New York: Oxford University Press, 1960.

Hoffer, A., and Osmond, H. *The hallucinogens.* New York: Academic Press, 1967.

Hofmann, A. Psychotomimetic substances. *Indian Journal of Pharmacology,* 1963, **25,** 245–256.

Isakower, O. On the exceptional position of the auditory sphere. *International Journal of Psychoanalysis,* 1939, **20,** 340–348.

Janet, P. *L'état mental des hystériques. Les stigmates manetaux.* Paris: Rueff, 1892.

Jasper, H., and Ajmone-Marsan, C. Thalamocortical integrating mechanism. *Patterns of organization in the central nervous system. Association for Research in Nervous and Mental Disease Proceedings,* 1952, **30,** 493–512.

Lewin, K. *Field theory in social science: Selected theoretical papers.* New York: Harper, & Row, 1951,

McGlothlin, W. H., and West, L. J. The marijuana problem: An overview, *American Journal of Psychiatry,* 1968, **125,** 370–378.

MacLean, P. D. The limbic system ("visceral brain") and emotional behavior. *Archives of Neurology and Psychiatry,* 1955, **73,** 130–134. (a)

MacLean, P. D. The limbic system ("visceral brain") in relation to the central gray and reticulum of the brain stem. *Psychosomatic Medicine,* 1955, **17,** 355–366. (b)

Magoun, H. W. An ascending reticular activating system in the brain stem. *Archives of Neurology and Psychiatry,* 1952, **67,** 145–154.

Marijuana: A signal of misunderstanding. First Report of the National Commission on Marijuana and Drug Abuse. Washington, D. C.: Government Printing Office, 1972.

Miller, J. G. Information input overload and psychopathology. *American Journal of Psychiatry,* 1960, **116,** 695–704.

Modell, A. Hallucinatory experiences in schizophrenia. *Journal of the American Psychoanalytic Association,* 1958, **6,** 442–480.

Moreau (de Tours), J. *Du hachisch et de l'alienation mentale, études psychologiques.* Paris: Librarie de Fortin, Masson, 1845.

Morgenbesser, S. Personal communication to I. Feinberg. A comparison of the visual hallucinations in schizophrenia with those induced by mescaline and LSD-25. In L. J. West (Ed.), *Hallucinations.* New York: Grune & Stratton, 1962.

Mourgue, R. *Neurobiologie de l'hallucination.* Brussels: Lamertin, 1932.

Osmond, H. Research on schizophrenia. In H. A. Abramson (Ed.), *Neuropharmacology: Transactions of the Second Conference, May 25–27,* 1955. Princeton, N.J., and New York: Josiah Macy, Jr., Foundation, 1956.

Papez, J. W. A proposed mechanism of emotion. *Archives of Neurology and Psychiatry,* 1937, **38,** 725–743.

Penfield, W., and Jasper, H. *Epilepsy and the functional anatomy of the human brain.* Boston: Little, Brown, 1954.

Rosanski, J., and Rosen, H. Musical hallucinations in otosclerosis. *Confinia Neurologia,* 1952, **12,** 49–54.

Schneck, J. M. Hypnotic hallucinatory behavior. *Journal of Clinical and Experimental Hypnosis,* 1953, **1,** 4–11.

Taylor, J., Holmes, G., and Walshe, F. M. R. (Eds.) *Selected writings of Hughlings Jackson,* (Vol. 2). New York: Basic Books, 1958.

Vernon, J., and Hoffman, J. Effect of sensory deprivation on learning rate in human beings. *Science,* 1956, **123,** 1074–1075.

West, L. J. The dissociative reaction. In A. M. Freedman and H. I. Kaplan (Eds.), *Comprehensive textbook of psychiatry.* Baltimore: William & Wilkins, 1967.

West, L. J., and Allen, J. R. The green rebellion. *Sooner Magazine,* November 1967, 2–7.

West, L. J., Janszen, H. H., Lester, B. K., and Cornelison, F. S. The psychosis of sleep deprivation. *Annals of the New York Academy of Sciences,* 1962, **96,** 66–70.

West, L. J., Pierce, C. M., and Thomas, W. D. Lysergic acid diethylamide: Its effects on a male Asiatic elephant. *Science,* 1962, **138,** 1100–1103.

INDEX

Abercrombie, J., 269
Abreaction, 21, 213, 227, 293
Abstract experience, 258
Achieved roles, 245, 247
A. colubrina, 37
Active imagination technique, 171
Adolphus, King Gustavus, 26
Adrenochrome, 68, 293–294
Africa, 23, 28, 29, 33
Afterimages, 166, 189
Agave mexicana, 39
Ajuca, 38
Alcohol, 12, 26, 33, 41, 71, 85, 147, 199, 224, 296, 298
Alexander, H. B., 263
Amanita muscaria, 12, 25, 85, 108
Amantadine, 108
Ambrosia, 33
American Indians, 27, 34, 39
Amnesia, 200, 210
Amok, 22
Amphetamines, 12, 41, 54, 57, 63, 89, 91, 94, 100, 102, 108, 124, 199, 227, 293, 296
Anadenanthera peregrina, 13, 36, 88
Analgesics, 224
Anesthesia, 54, 191, 292–293
Anesthetics, 54, 59, 71, 108, 224, 292–293
    drug effects on, 82–83, 100, 103–104
        see also individual drugs
    stereotypy in, 101–102
Animal behavior, 82, 83, 101, 103, *see also* individual animals
Animism, 10, 41
Anticholinergics, 71, 108
Antihistamines, 108
Anxiety, 302, 303
Apollo, 15
Apparitions, 146, 257, 280
Archer, W., 263
Archetypal experiences, 198
Archetypal images, 136, 137, 223, 231
Arctic hysteria, 15, 22, 41
Argument from illusion, 266
Aristotle, 11, 223
Arnheim, R., 148, 260
Arousal, 61, 73, 197, 200–201, 208, 209, 210, 290, 301, 302

cortical interpretation of, 197, 200–201
experience of, 209, 210
    see also Central Nervous System, excitation;
        Hyperarousal; Hypoarousal
Art, 2, 106, 222, 223, 284–285
Ascribed roles, 245, 246
Assimilation, 185
Asymmetry model, 229
Atropa belladonna, 25
Auditory Evoked Response, 61
Auditory hallucinations, 10, 19, 54, 65, 72, 105, 107, 173, 183, 254, 307, 308
Auditory system, 61, 62, 64
Aura, 60
    see also Epilepsy
Authoritarian personality, 40
Autoscopic phenomenon, 167
Avicenna, 30
Avoidance behavior, 86, 87, 95, 100, 102, 103
Ayahuasca, 137
    see also Harmala alkadoids
Aymara, 15
Aztec, 38

Baldwin, M., 93, 103
Balzac, H. de, 107
Bamboo grub, 24
Banisteriopsis spp., 37, 38, 108, 137
Barbiturates, 71
Baudelaire, C., 27, 107, 149
Becker, H. S., 244
Beer, 34, 36, 39
Bees, 84
Belladonna, 25, 104, 291
Benedict, R., 20
Berkeley, G., 260, 269
Black Drink, 34
Blake, 2, 249
Boars, 84
Boismont, B. de, 141, 147, 287
Bourguignon, E., 21–22, 211
Bridger, W. H., 95
Brazil, 29
Bromo-Lysergic Acid Diethylamide (BOL), 94, 98, 124
Brunfelsia, 38
Bufo marinus toads, 84

Bufotenine, 13, 67, 88, 109, 290
Bushmen, 18, 24
  African, 24
  Australian, 18, 24
Byrd, Admiral R. E., 14

Calomel (*Acorus calamus*), 38
Cannabinols, 224, 294
  see also Cannabis; Hashish; Marihuana
Cannabis, 27, 28, 39, 84, 85, 97, 98, 108, 115,
    147
  see also Cannabinols, Hashish; and Marihuana
Cannibalism, ritual, 15
Carbon dioxide, 108
Carroll, L., 144
Cataléptic behavior, 10, 55
Catatonia, 208, 219
Catecholamines, 76, 227
Catha edulis (qat), 33
Catharsis, 21
Catnip, 37, 85
Cats, 54, 63, 90–92, 101, 102, 143, 208
Central Nervous System (CNS), 3, 5, 54, 55,
    57, 66–68, 73, 75–76, 107, 145, 197,
    289, 302
  depression, 54
  excitation, 3, 5, 54, 58, 63, 66, 68, 75–76,
      107, 145, 197, 289, 302
    see also Arousal
Cerebral hemispheres, 213, 220
Charcot, J. M., 305
Charisma, 41
China, 20, 28, 30, 33
Chlordiazepoxide, 181, 183
Chloroform, 147
Chlorpromazine (CPZ), 94, 215
Clairvoyance, 10
Club des Haschichins, 107
Coca, 37
Cocaine, 93, 291, 296
Cocteau, J., 106
Coffee, 26, 84
Cognition, 148, 188, 189, 197, 251, 261, 279,
    282
  overcontrol, 188
  undercontrol, 188
Cohoba snuff, 37
Coleridge, S. T., 4, 27, 227, 301
Communes, 298
Concept formation, 121
Consciousness, 81, 149, 197, 205, 212, 223
Congo, 29
Contraction of visual space, 206
Consensual validation, 2
Continuity, 271
Continuity hypothesis, 259–262
Continuum, 4, 5, 6, 53, 61, 64, 67, 68, 72–73,
    74, 148, 204, 209, 257, 260, 266,271,278

  of CNS states, 4, 53, 54, 64, 67, 68, 73
  of cognition, 6, 74, 257, 260
  of dreams and hallucinations, 4, 5, 73, 74,
      271–272
  of ergotropic arousal, 204
  of experiences, 5–6, 260, 266, 277
  of hallucinosis, 53, 60
  of information processing, 5
  of mental imagery, 148
  of perception and cognition, 257
  of perception-hallucination, 205
  of perception-meditation, 209
Corticosteroids, 224
Cortisol, 108
Crabbe, G., 4
Creativity, 205, 214, 216, 217, 218, 222, 223,
    228, 229, 232, 250, 260
Crisis cult, 23
Culture, 41–42
  sacred, 42
  secular, 42
Culture shock, 14
Cyclosersine, 108
Cytisus (Genistus) canariensis, 37

Dagga, 20
Dancing, 19, 23, 24, 33
Daturas, 35, 39, 42
Datura stramonium, 108, 141
Daydreams, 147, 216, 264, 272
D. candida, 36
Defense mechanisms, 186
  condensation, 186
  denial, 186
  displacement, 186
  distortion, 186
  isolation, 186
  repression, 186
  reversal, 186
  splitting, 186
  suppression, 186
  symbolization, 186
Degradation, 244, 253
Deja vu, 42, 166, 200, 201
Depersonalization, 200–201
  see also Dissociation
Delirium, 303
Delirium Tremens, 12, 108, 175
Delusions, 9, 13, 23, 41, 54, 103, 105, 188,
    307
  in animals, 103
Dement, W., 11, 87, 91–92
Dementia, 71
De Quincey, T., 4–5, 27
Descartes, R., 260, 267, 270
Dhārnā, 205
Dhyān, 202, 205
Diethyl ether, 58

Diethyltryptamine (DET), 91
Digitalis, 106, 108
3, 4-Dimethoxyphenylethylamine, 67
N, N.-Dimethyltryptamines (DMT), 67, 94, 100,
    121, 143, 290
Dionysian Mysteries, 33
Disinhibition Theory, 73, 146, 299
Disjunctive Arousal, 185
Dissociation, 3, 16, 20, 138, 200, 292, 303, 304
    see also Stateboundness
Dissociative reactions, 304
Divination, 10, 36
Dogs, 84, 90–92
Dopamine, 77
Dopamine Beta Hydroxylase, 77
Dramaturgical model, 241
Dreams, 3, 5, 10, 13, 18, 35, 36, 40, 41, 53, 71,
    72, 74, 77, 172, 181, 203, 216–217, 225,
    248, 263, 267, 269, 270–274, 287, 288,
    299, 302
    external coherence of, 271
    internal coherence of, 271
    unconscious control of, 273
    voluntariness of, 273
Dreaming, 13, 20, 148
Drumming, 10, 19
D. sanguinarea, 36
D-Sleep, 74, 75, 77
    see also REM
Dual-input model of image formation, 175–177
Duboisea hopwoodii, 24
Dumas, A., 107
Dyads, 171

Eccles, Sir J., 2
Ecstacy, 6, 13, 205, 208, 211, 214, 216, 226,
    307
EEG, 54, 55, 59, 62, 143, 145, 214, 232
    desynchronizations, 55, 59, 61
    electrical silence, 55
    hypersynchrony, 55, 57–59, 61
    seizure, 57
    slow waves, 54
    spike bursts, 55, 62
Ego, 19, 20, 22, 41
    differentiation, 22
    function, 19, 20, 21, 41
Electroencephalogram, *see* EEG
Elephants, 85, 291
Eleusinian Mysteries, 33
Eliot, T. S., 198
Ellinwood, E. H., 91, 102, 103
Empiricism, 260, 279
Empiricist Theory of Cognition, 279
Enactive thought, 168
Endogenous Psychotomimetic substances, 67
Entoptic phenomena, 110, 141, 143, 175, 178–
    183

Epilepsy, 20, 110, 169, 183, 210
Ergotropic arousal, 197, 202, 204, 206
Erythroxylon coca, 37
Esquirol, J. E. D., 166, 242, 287
Ethanol, 12
    see also Alcohol
Ether, 58, 62
Ethnopsychiatry, 23
Ethrane, 59
Etoxidrol, 59
Evoked responses, 54
Expectancy schemata, 183, 189
Experiences, 148, 257, 259–260, 262, 263, 265–285
    abstract, 258, 265, 274–275
    causes of, 274, 279
    coherence of, 260, 266, 269, 270–271
    compelling, 270
    concreteness of, 260, 278
    creativeness of, 260
    criteria of, 172, 266–269
    distinctions between, 184, 197, 250, 268, 279
    elements of, 283–284
    evolution of, 118, 130, 175, 260, 262, 265
    indescribable, 265–266, 274
    intermediate, 260, 265
    meaningless, 265, 274
    mechanism of, 273
    mental, 265
    projection of, 109, 147, 270
    reality of, 263, 276
    reports of, 119, 251, 252–253, 262
    representative, 258–259, 265
    similarity between, 266–274
    simple, 283
    transparency of, 277, 278
    veridical, 274, 283
    veridicality of, 260, 278
    vivacity of, 260, 266, 269–270
    voluntariness of, 260, 266, 269, 272–274
    see also Hallucination, experience of
Experiential Projector Model, 148
Experiential Typewriter, 120
Experimental neuroses, 93
Extreme empiricism, 280

Fantasies, 6, 72, 105, 216, 260, 264, 269–270,
    271, 272, 273, 274, 303
    coherence of, 271–272
    erotic, 119, 272, 273
    obsessive, 272, 274
    unconscious control of, 273
    vivacity of, 269–270
    voluntariness of, 272
Fatigue, 77
Fever, 201
Fever deliriums, 109
Fischer, R., 5–6, 22, 101, 132, 197, 243, 244
Fish, 24

Flashbacks, 132–135, 146, 167, 190, 199, 200, 289, 292
Form-Constants, 108, 109–112, 139, 178, 221
Form-Constants induced by:
  crystal gazing, 110
  drugs, 108, 111, 115, 119, 125, 137–138
  electrical current, 110
  migraine, 110
  sensory deprivation, 110
  swinging, 110
Formications, 292
Fortification "illusions," 144
Freud, S., 11, 16, 22, 171, 172, 183, 186, 188, 242, 243, 288
Fusaric acid, 77

Galbulimima belgraveana, 24
Galen, 28
Galton, F., 287, 303
Gamma-hydroxybutyrate (GHB), 59, 62
Ganja, 28
Gautier, T., 27, 107
Geometric imagery, 108, 110, 112–113, 138, 169, 221–223
  see also Form-Constants
Ghost Dance, 23, 40
Glossolalia, 23
Goats, 83
Goethe, J. W. von, 106
Goffman, E., 244
Goode, W. J., 245
Grasshoppers, 84
Greeks, 16, 20, 25, 31, 33
Gustatory hallucinations, 10, 13

Haber, R. N., 260
Hallucinations, 1–7, 9, 10, 13, 15, 16, 17, 19, 21, 41, 54, 60–61, 63, 71–78, 81–82, 84–85, 104, 106, 128, 130, 137, 139, 141, 145, 146, 149, 172, 173, 176, 202, 203, 208, 213, 216, 228, 232, 248, 257, 260, 264, 269, 271, 278, 280, 282, 283, 285, 287, 288, 289, 292, 299, 303, 304, 307–310
  in alcoholics, 12, 85, 108–109, 172, 183
  in amphetamine addicts, 102
  in amputees, 2
  in animals, 4, 5, 81, 87–104
    laboratory animals, 87–100
  of apparition, 257
  as image thinking, 169
  as thoughts, 264, 266
  in astronauts, 202
  in blind subjects, 143
  of "blue dragon," 184
  of cars, 2
  of cartoons, 110, 115, 116–117, 141
  in cats, 4, 55, 58, 90–92, 101
  in children, 3, 72, 101

  clinical assessment of, 6, 13, 20, 228, 243, 253, 307–310
  coherence of, 271
  of colors, 127
    see also Imagery, color
  definitions of, 2–3, 4–5, 9, 10, 40, 53, 71, 73, 82, 92, 94, 103, 104, 107, 163, 165, 167, 202, 203, 224, 225, 242–244, 253, 257, 260, 288
  of demons, 9, 15, 16, 17, 141
  determinants of, 5, 53, 72, 136, 138, 164, 168–191, 224–225, 246, 252, 259, 303, 304
  of devils, 39, 248, 254
  in driving, 2, 189, 306
  elements of, 282
  of entoptic phenomena, 181
    see also Entoptic phenomena
  in epileptics, 3, 110
  experience of, 14–15, 17, 24, 111–112, 119, 128, 146, 149, 167, 188, 189, 190–191, 207, 208, 226, 258–259, 289
  in flashbacks, 132–134
    fever delirium, 109
    see also Flashbacks
  of food, 72, 164
  of ghosts, 166, 242
  of gods, 3, 10, 38, 81, 118, 138
  of heaven, 3
  of hell, 3
  history of, 3, 287–288
  of Holy Ghost, 3
  of imagery constants, 108
    see also Form-Constants, 108
  induced by:
    alcohol, 107
    alcohol withdrawal, 5
    amanita, 12
    belladonna, 107
    cocaine, 93–94, 291
    convulsions, 107
    disease, 109
    dizziness, 107
    drugs, 2, 4, 5, 53, 75–76, 258
      see also individual drugs
    drumming, 10, 13
    electrochemical stimulation, 169
    epileptic convulsions, 3
    experimental neuroses, 93
    fevers, 3, 107
    henbane, 107
    hunger, 3, 107
    hypnosis, 210, 211
    intense cold, 3, 107
    ketamine, 116
    migraine, 144–145
    nervous excitement, 3
      see also Central Nervous System
    nitrous oxide, 107

opium, 4, 106, 107
photostimulation, 169, 274
thirst, 3
sensory deprivation, *see* Sensory deprivation
sensory uncertainty, 72
severe hunger, 72
severe pain, 3
sleep, *see also* Dreams, 107
sleep deprivation, 72
thirst, 107
thorny apple, 107
of jackrabbits, 2
of jaguars, 137
of movement, 111
see also Imagery, movement of
novelty of, 111, 185, 281, 282, 283, 285
of pain, 16, 17
in pilots, 143, 149, 306
of pink elephants, 167
of "presences," 190
projection of, 109, 128, 137
of reality, 19
in schizophrenics, 13, 65, 66–67, 107–108,
110, 172, 187, 203, 308
sensory distortions, 4
in shipwreck survivors, 306
in skiers, 189
of skulls, 132
of spirits, 16, 34, 35, 36, 38, 40, 242, 248
in terminal patients, 2
theories of, 6, 64–66, 68–69, 75, 76–77, 78,
102, 136, 139, 145–149, 176–180, 241,
244, 261, 280, 281, 285, 299, 309–310
transition to, 175
of tunnels, 115, 116–117, 134, 135, 137,
139–140, 141, 178
veridical, 278
vivacity of, 167, 269
of voices, 254
see also Auditory hallucinations
Hallucinatory constants, *see* Imagery, constants;
Form-Constants; and Geometric imagery
Hallucinogens, 3, 12, 24–40, 41, 57, 63, 64, 67,
81, 82–83, 84–85, 86, 87, 88, 92–93, 94,
96, 97, 100, 102, 103, 104, 108, 145, 201,
205, 206, 211, 217, 224, 228, 257, 266,
288–290, 294–299, 304
in the cat, 4, 57–58, 63, 85, 90
see also Cat
in animals, 81–104
see also individual animals
in laboratory animals, 87, 95–100
social uses of, 295–299
self-administration of (in animals), 83–87
self-administration of (in man), 295–296
see also individual drugs
Hallucinosis, 5, 22, 53, 69, 289
see also Hallucinations

Harmala alkaloids, 108
Harmaline, 291
Harmine, 91, 291
Hartmann, E., 5, 71
Harvey, N. A., 3
Hashish, 26, 28, 29, 42, 86, 104, 107, 146, 147,
149
see also Cannabis; Marihuana
Hashish hallucinations, laws of, 108
Head twitch response, 88–90, 102
Hebb, D. O., 105, 145
Hebrews, 25
Heimia salicifolia, 39
Hemp, 27, 28, 29
Hempseeds, 28, 85–86
Herodotus, 28
Heroin, 30, 298
Hervey, Marquis D', 109
Hindu, 28, 31, 32, 42
Hippocrates, 15
Hobbes, T., 260, 261
Hofmann, A., 201
Homalomena ereriba, 24
Homosexuality, 20
Hops, 27
Horowitz, M. J., 5, 163, 301
Hugo, V., 27, 107
Huichol Indians, 138–139
Human development, 169
Hume, D., 260, 261, 269
Huxley, A., 106, 293
6-Hydroxydopamine, 67
5-Hydroxytryptophan (5-HTP), 90
Hyoscyamus niger (Henbane), 25, 87
Hyperarousal, 208, 212, 215, 219, 224
Hyperaroused hallucinations, 225
Hypermnesic phenomena, 213
Hyperphrenic, 6, 204, 219, 228
Hypnagogic hallucinations, 4, 5, 72, 109, 115,
147, 167, 172, 181, 189, 263, 302
Hypnopompic hallucinations, 72, 147, 167, 263
Hypnotism, 253
Hypoarousal, 205, 212, 215, 225
Hypoarousal continuum, 225
Hypoglycemia, 109, 165
Hysteria, 16–17, 21, 22–23, 41, 188
conversion, 16, 21, 41
phobic, 16, 21, 41

Ibogaine, 84, 90, 291
Idiot savants, 217
Ilex paraquayensis, 35
Illusory poodle, 202
Illusions, 5, 9, 41, 104, 166, 176, 178, 262, 274,
278, 307
general, 177
idiosyncratic, 177, 178
Imageless thought, 277

Image illustration, 106
Image representation, 148, 163, 168, 170
  activation of, 168
  impairment of, 184, 185–186
Imagery, 2, 15, 82, 96, 105, 106, 108, 110, 111,
    112–149, 165, 171, 175, 176, 184, 198,
    203, 213, 222, 227, 258, 265, 275, 276,
    277
  action in, 113–114, 116
  body, 15, 222
  censorship, 171
  colors of, 113, 127
  complex, 111, 118, 124, 127–128, 139, 141,
    145–148, 258
  constants, 5, 96, 108, 115, 125, 137–139,
    258
    see also Form-Constants
  eidetic, 3
  formation of, 175
    see also Hallucinations, determinants of
  habitual experience, 171–173
  identity designation, 171
  intrusive, 188
  measurement of, 120–121
  memory, 119, 128, 145–148
  mental, 2, 105, 142, 265, 275, 276
  movement of, 113, 127
  object depiction, 171
  representation, 5, 106
    see also Image representation
  in observers:
    trained observers, 119–132
    untrained observers, 112–119
  simple, 258
  wish-fulfillment, 171
Imaginary companions, 3, 14
Imagination, 105, 261, 267
Imagining, 148, 243, 248, 250, 250–253,
    259, 272
Immortality, 33
India, 20, 24, 25, 31, 83
Indians, 27, 31, 34–40
  American, 27, 34–40
Indo-European, 25, 31, 32
Indole Alkaloids, 290–291
Information processing, 6, 147, 163, 184–188,
    290
  reciprocal limitation of, 174–175
Inspiration, 228–229
Intrusive images, 188–191

Jackson, H., 147, 299
Jamaica, 29
James I, King, 25, 26
James, W., 1, 103, 104, 105
Janet, P., 287, 305
Jarvik, M. E., 5, 81, 147, 300
Jesus, 16

Jimson weed, 35, 36
Juhasz, J. B., 6, 241
Jung, C. C., 136, 172

Kaempferia galanga, 24
Kali, 15
Kandinsky, V., 109–110
"Kangaroo" posture, 90
Kant, E., 12
Kava, 25
Kayakangst, 15, 41
Kennedy, R. F., 200
Ketamine, 59, 89, 101, 108, 116, 132, 134,
    224, 292, 293
Kim, K., 21
Kinesthetic hallucinations, 10, 13, 65, 105
Klüver, H., 87, 96, 109, 111, 112, 137
Korea, 21
Kraepelin, E., 22
Kratom, 30
Krishna, Gopi, 202, 226, 228–229
Kubie, L. S., 302
Kundalini experience, 202, 226, 228–229
Kyphosus fuseus, 24

La Barre, W., 3, 9, 111
Larkspur (Delphinium nudicaule), 38
Lavater, L., 232, 242
Leary, T., 106, 120–121, 146, 148, 298
Leuner, H., 147
Lexical thought, 168–169
Lilliputianism, 263
Lilly, J. C., 120, 146
Lindsley, O., 120
Locke, J., 260, 261, 269
Locoweed disease, 85
Lophophora williamsii, 34, 137
  see also Mescaline; Peyote
Love apple, 26
LSD, 12, 33, 54, 57, 58, 59, 61, 62, 63, 66,
    71, 88, 89, 90, 93, 94, 95, 98, 100, 103,
    108, 111, 121, 124, 125, 132, 134, 141,
    142, 143, 147, 175, 190, 198, 199, 200,
    201, 210, 214, 222, 224, 230, 289, 290,
    291, 294–295, 296, 297, 298, 299, 308
LSD therapy, 294–295
Ludlow, F. H., 4, 108
Lycopodium selago fern, 38
Lysergic Acid Diethylamide, see LSD

Macropsia, 13
Malayan mejapi, 15
Malcolm, N., 242
Mallarme, S., 27
Mambog, 31
Mandalas, 221
Mandragora officinarum, 25
Mandrake, 25

Manichaeism, 33
Marihuana, 30, 93, 108, 124
  see also Cannabis; Hashish
Masks, 34
Masserman, J. H., 93
Maté, 35
Maudsley, H., 2, 3
Maury, L F. A., 263
McKellar, P., 109, 110, 115, 119, 130
Mead, 31, 42
Medicine, 34, 38
Medicine-Power, 14, 38
Meditation, 6, 215
Medullary Paralysis, 55
Melton, J., 248
Melzack, R., 2
Memories (memory), 3, 6, 184, 187, 189, 210,
    250, 280
Menomini Indians, 138
Mescal, 39
Mescaline, 12, 58, 62, 67, 71, 82, 84, 89, 95,
    103, 106, 108, 111, 119, 124, 125, 130,
    137, 141, 145, 147, 224, 290, 293, 296,
    308
Mesembranthemum spp., 24
Mesolithic, 14, 31, 39
Methoxyharmalan, 67
Methysticodendron amesianum, 38
Mexico, 29, 38, 138
Mice, 88–90, 101
Michaux, H., 106
Micropsia, 13
Migraine, 110, 144–145
Milton, J., 105, 249
Mimosa hostilis, 38
Minnesota-Perceptual Diagnostic Test (MPDT),
    218
Mitragyna speciosa, 30
Moderate Empiricism, 280
Mongooses, 83, 84
Monkeys, 84, 92–94, 101, 102, 103
Moreau (de Tours), J. J., 3, 4, 106, 107, 146,
    149, 227–228, 287
Morphine, 147
Moslem, 20, 26, 33, 42
Motor Eating, 203, 224
Multiple Personality, 17
Multiple-Unit Activity, 54
Mushrooms, 24, 32–33, 38, 84, 85
Music, 19, 130, 221, 222
Myers-Briggs-Type-Indicator (MBTI), 218, 225
Myoclonic Jerking, 55
Myristica fragrans, 25
Mysteries, 40
Mystical, 6
Myth, 18

Naranjo, C., 137

Narcolepsy, 13, 41
Narcosynthesis, 297
Narcotic Snuff, 13
Negative Hallucinations, 166, 305
Neisser, U., 148, 164, 183
Neoteny, 22
Nerval, G. de, 229
Neuronal Activity, 55, 61
New Guinea, 24
Nicotiana rustica, 34
  see also Tobacco
Nightmares, 188, 269
Night Terrors, 3, 248, 269
Nirvichar samadhi, 205
Nitrous oxide, 59, 62, 108
Noradrenalin, 6
Norepinephrine, 76
N. tabacum, 34
Nutmeg, 25, 106

Odin, 15
Oesterreich, T. K., 21, 22
Olfactory Hallucinations, 10, 13, 65, 130, 307
Ololiuqui, 38
Oneness Experience, 81, 209, 227
Opium, 30, 104, 106, 107, 147
"Oral Syndrome," 87
Osborne, L., 244
Out-Of-The-Body State, 201, 223

Pan, 15
Pancratium trianthum, 24
Papaver somniferum, 30
Paracelsus, 27, 30
Parachlorophenylalanine (PCPA), 92
Paranormal Hallucination, 167
  see also Supernatural
Parica Snuffs, 36
Parish, E., 141
Pascal, B., 209
Penfield, W., 145, 146, 165, 169, 279, 301
Pentobarbital, 89, 96–97
Pentylenetetrazol, 58, 63, 68
Perception-Hallucination Continuum, 205, 214,
    220, 225, 228
  see also Continuum
Perception-Meditation Continuum, 205, 209,
    211, 214, 215, 225
  see also Continuum
Perceptions, 1, 2, 5, 53, 81–82, 98, 100, 183,
    197, 202, 204, 213, 228, 251, 259, 260,
    262, 265, 269, 272, 279, 280–282, 283,
    284, 306
  animals, 94–95
  coherence of, 271–272
  distortion of, 53, 65
  delayed, 281
  events, private, 2, 81

public, 2, 81
nonsensory, 279
past, 281, 283
  see also Memory
veridical, 259, 262, 280, 283
vivacity of, 269
Perceptual Constancies, 206, 251
Perceptual Nidus Theory, 177–180
Perceptual Release Theory, 147, 175–177, 299,
    301–302
Perky, C. W., 174, 267, 270, 272
Peyote, 12, 34, 36, 37, 108, 137–139, 296
Peyotl, 39
"Phantom limb," 2, 303
Phencyclidine, 59, 62, 66, 224, 292
Phenobarbital, 124
Phenothiazine, 53, 77
Phenylethylamines, 293–294
Pictures, 284, 285
  abstract, 284
  novelty of, 284, 285
Pigeons, 85–86, 95–100
Pineal Gland, 68
Piperidine Derivatives, 291–293
Piper methyisticum, 25
Piptadenia peregrina, 36
Pleasure Principle, 18, 187
Plotinus, 27
Poe, E. A., 4
Poetry, 106, 221, 229, 249
Poets, 229, 247
Pontogeniculooccipital Spikes, (PGO), 76
Possession, 3, 10, 21, 22, 40, 41, 228, 229
Possession Trance, 22, 211
Pot, 27, 42
Preconscious Stream, 172
Prince, R., 22, 23
Prognostication, 10
Prophecy, 10
Proust, M., 198
Pseudohallucinations, 104, 167, 175
Psilocybe yungensis, 38
Psilocybin, 12, 58, 94, 100, 108, 111, 124, 205,
    210, 211, 217, 218, 224, 227, 258, 290
Psychedelic, 96, 112, 148, 167, 288
Psychoanalysis, 273, 309
Psychoanalytic Theory, 148, 165
Psychopathology, 228, 304
Psychosis, 64
Psychotomimetic Drugs, 53, 67–68
  see also Hallucinogens
Purkinje, J. E., 105, 106, 110, 169

Qat, 33

Rabbits, 214, 230
Rabelais, 27
Ramakrishna, 209

Ras Tafari Cult, 29
Rationalism, 260
Rats, 86, 92, 100, 101
Reality, 224, 248, 249, 255
Reality Principle, 18, 187
Reality Testing, 1, 5, 66, 72, 74–75, 78, 105,
    175, 188, 203, 204, 224, 231
Rebound, 212
Reciprocal Roles, 241
Red Bean, 37
Red Bean Cult, 37
Reindeer, 85
REM, 4, 214, 215, 224, 302
REM State, 3, 11, 13, 14, 18, 19, 21, 40, 41, 74
  alcohol induced, 5
  rebound, 5
  see also D-Sleep
Representative Experience, 258
Restitutional Hallucinations, 187
Retrieval Theory, 146–148, 281–285, 299
Retrieved Perceptions, 260, 284, 285
Retrospective Hallucinations, 187
Revelation, 10, 22, 40
Reveries, 264
Rhythm, 19
Ritual, 18–20
Role Theory, 241
Rorschach, 19
Ryle, G., 2

Sacred, 41, 42
Sacred and Secular, 17–20, 41
Sacred Culture, 17, 18
Saint Anthony's Fire, 3, 291
Saint Francis, 209
Saint Teresa (of Avila), 208, 226, 231
Samādhi, 205, 207, 208, 211, 212, 224, 226,
    306
San Pedro, 137
Sarbin, T. R., 6, 241
Savage, C. Wade, 6, 257
Savichār, 205, 207
Schematic Images, 171
Schizophrenia, 6, 12, 13, 53, 60, 64, 65, 66–67,
    68, 71, 75, 77, 110, 172, 173, 187, 205,
    206, 219, 244, 308
  drug-induced, 66–67
Schizophrenic Art, 110, 206
Schopenhauer, A., 12
Schultes, R. E., 29, 38, 39
Scotoma, 181
Scythians, 28
Secular, 17–20, 41
Secular Culture, 17
Segal, S. J., 105, 121, 174, 267
Seizures, 55, 58, 68
Self-Administration, 83, 295–296
  of hallucinogens, 82–83, 295–296

Sensations, 105, 213, 265, 274–279
  coherence of, 275
  vivacity of, 275
  voluntariness of, 275–276
Sensory Bombardment, 2, 149
Sensory Deprivation (and attenuation), 2, 11,
    13, 15, 23, 40, 41, 53, 72, 73, 90, 93, 110,
    145, 148, 175, 276
Sensory Isolation, 303
Sensory Pudding, 203, 224–227
Sensory Systems, 60–64
  modulation of, 61, 64
Sensory Thoughts, 279
Sensory-to-Motor Ratio, 203, 205, 224
Serotonin, 6, 12, 205, 227, 290
Shackleton, Sir E., 14
Shamanic Journey, 25
Shamanism, 10, 14, 19, 21, 34, 40
Sidgwick, H., 263–264
Siegel, R. K., 1, 5, 81, 264, 285, 300
Signal Anxiety, 170
  see also Avoidance behavior
Similarity Argument, 266–269, 279
Singing, 19
  double, 19
Sinhalese, 15
Sirhan, S., 200
Skepticism, 266
Sleep, 4, 11–12, 54, 77, 214, 224, 264, 303
  deprivation, 77
  rhombencephalic (paradoxical), 54
  slow-wave, 54
Slocum, J., 14
Slow-Wave Sleep (SWS), 61
Smythies, J. R., 103, 145
Snuffs, 36–37
  parica, 36
  cohoba, 36–37
Social Psychology, 6, 241, 244
Social Roles, 241
Social Role of Hallucinator, 244
Sociopathy, 14, 20
Solipsism, 266
Soma, 31–33, 42
Soul, 10, 18, 221–223
South America, 137
Spirits, 23
Stateboundness, 132, 197–204, 210, 220, 227
State-Dependent Learning, 199, 296
Stereotypy, 91, 101–102, 198, 209
Stramonium, 291
Strauss, J. S., 6
Stress, 188–190
Subconscious, 210
Subcortical Activity, 224
Subcortical Arousal, 198
Subliminal Perception, 279
Sudilovsky, A., 102, 103

Suggestion, 21
Supernatural, 10, 14, 18, 20, 24, 34, 39, 41
Symbols, 2, 3, 198, 220–221
Synesthesia, 10, 82, 166, 222
Syphilis, 110
Szasz, T. S., 244, 245
Szuman, S., 106

Tabernanthe iboga, 24, 84
Tactile Hallucinations, 10, 13, 82, 88, 94, 102
Talking, 22
Teonanacatl, 39
THC (Tetrahydrocannabinol), 92, 95, 100, 112,
    114–115, 124, 125, 142, 294
Thinking, 1, 3, 18, 130, 148, 250, 259
Thompson, F., 4, 27
Thoughts, 260, 274–279
  coherence of, 276
  compelling, 277
  novelty of, 261
  projection of, 173, 277
  unconscious control of, 276
  vivacity of, 276–277
  voluntariness of, 275
Thunderbolts, 25
Thunderstones, 31
Tibet, 19
Tibetan Chöd, 15
Toads, 25, 32, 290
Toadstools, 25, 32, 42
Tobacco, 25, 26, 34
Toby, J., 245
Toloache, 35, 36
Topographic regression, 183
Trance, 3, 10, 16, 21, 22, 23, 40, 210, 211
Transcendental Meditation, 225
Trichocereus Pachanoi, 38, 84, 137
Trophotropic Arousal, 197, 208, 211
Tukano Indians, 137

Uexküll, J. von, 5, 95
Unbidden Images, 188
Unconscious, 22

Veda, 28
Vertigo, 306
Vicarious Retrieval, 147
Vinho de jurema, 38
Visions, 3, 10, 14, 21, 40, 105, 203, 216, 233,
    248, 251, 287
Vision Quest, 5, 14, 34, 39, 41, 253
Visual Evoked Response (VER), 63
Visual System, 63–64
Vivid, 270, 275
  meaning of, 270
Vodūn, 10, 23, 41
Vodūn Quest, 10
Volatile Solvents, 93

Volitional Direction, 172
Voltaire, F., 26
Voluntary Experiences, 264

Waking-Dream, definitions of, 205, 216, 224
    see also Hallucinations, definitions
Walking, 22
Wallace, A. F. C., 136
Wasson, R. G., 31, 32
Weiss, P. A., 7
West, L. J., 6, 147, 176, 264, 287
"Wet Dog Syndrome," 91
Windigo, 15, 41

Winters, W. D., 4, 53, 89, 289
Witchcraft, 25, 30, 42, 245
Witches, 13, 25, 246
    flight in, 13

Yagé, 137
Yantra, 306
Yaupon, 34
Yoga Masters, 209
Yost, R. M., 285

Zazen, 205, 209, 224
Zen Masters, 209